# Revision Symbols

W9-AVC-588

| | | |
|---|---|---|
| ab | Abbreviations | 15.2 |
| adj | Adjective forms | 8.4 |
| adv | Adverb forms | 8.8 |
| agr | Agreement | 17 |
| amb | Ambiguous reference | 18.7 |
| ap | Apostrophe | 13.1 |
| ca | Case | 8.1–2, 18.1–2 |
| cap | Capitals | 15.1 |
| coh | Coherence (paragraph unity) | 5 |
| coord | Coordination | 19.2b |
| cs | Comma splice | 11.6g |
| d | Diction | 28–31 |
| dm | Dangling modifier | 24.5 |
| doc | Documentation | 36–39 |
| emp | Emphasis misplaced | 23.4 |
| exact | Exactness | 29–30 |
| fig | Inappropriate figure of speech | 31 |
| frag | Fragment | 21 |
| fs | Fused (run-on) sentence | 22.1 |
| gl/gr | Glossary of Grammatical Terms | p. 671 |
| gl/u | Glossary of Usage | p. 649 |
| gr | Obvious grammatical error | 8, 17–18, 21–25 |
| hyph | Hyphen | 13.2 |
| inc | Incomplete comparison | 25.4 |
| ital | Italics | 14.3 |
| k (awk) | Awkward sentence | 26 |
| lc | Lower case | 15.1 |
| lev | Inappropriate usage | 28–29 |
| log | Logic | 32–35 |
| mixed | Mixed construction | 23.1 |
| mm | Misplaced modifier | 24.1–4 |
| ms | Manuscript form | 15.4, 38.5 |
| n | Number | 15.3 |
| om | Omitted words | 25.3 |
| p | Obvious punctuation error | 10–14 |

| | | |
|---|---|---|
| pass | Passive voice ineffective | 26.4b |
| pl | Plural needed | 8.1–2 |
| pron | Pronoun | 8.2 |
| ref | Pronoun reference | 18.3–7 |
| rep | Repetition | 27.1 |
| run-on | Run-on (fused) sentence | 22.1 |
| shift | Needless shift | 25.1 |
| sing | Singular needed | 8.1–2 |
| sp | Spelling | 16 |
| st | Sentence structure | 7, 22–27 |
| sub | Subordination | 19.2a, 26.2 |
| t | Tense | 8.5–6, 25.1 |
| trans | Transition | 5.6 |
| var | Variety in sentence structure | 19 |
| vb | Verb form | 8.5–6 |
| w | Wordiness | 26.3, 27 |
| ww | Wrong word | 16.2, p. 649 |
| $\lor$ | Apostrophe | 13.1 |
| $\stackrel{\land}{:}$ | Colon | 12.2 |
| $\stackrel{\land}{,}$ | Comma | 11 |
| $\odot$ | No comma | 11.6 |
| — | Dash | 13.3 |
| ... | Ellipsis | 14.2 |
| ! | Exclamation mark | 10.2c |
| - | Hyphen | 13.2 |
| $\odot$ | Period | 10.2a |
| "/" | Quotation marks | 14.1 |
| $\stackrel{\land}{;}$ | Semicolon | 12.1 |
| [ ] | Brackets | 13.5 |
| ( ) | Parentheses | 13.4–5 |
| ¶ | Paragraph needed | 5–6 |
| No ¶ | No paragraph | |
| // | Parallelism | 20.1, 25.2 |
| x | Obvious mistake | |
| $\land$ | Obvious omission | |
| # | Space needed | |
| $\mathcal{S}$ | Delete | |
| ? | Unclear | |
| ~ | Transpose | |

# The Macmillan
# College Handbook

# The Macmillan College Handbook

## Gerald Levin

UNIVERSITY OF AKRON

Macmillan Publishing Company
NEW YORK

Collier Macmillan Publishers
LONDON

Macmillan Publishing Company
866 Third Avenue, New York, New York 10022

Collier Macmillan Canada, Inc.

Library of Congress Cataloging-in-Publication Data

Levin, Gerald Henry.
The Macmillan college handbook.

Includes index.
1. English Language—Rhetoric—Handbooks, manuals,
etc. 2. English language—Grammar—1950-  —Handbooks, manuals, etc. 3. Report writing—Handbooks,
manuals, etc. I. Title.
PE1408.L4133   1987        808'.042         86-8405
ISBN 0-02-370230-3

Printing:   2 3 4 5 6 7        Year: 7 8 9 0 1 2 3

ACKNOWLEDGMENTS

VIRGINIA ADAMS. "Causes of Crime, Maybe." Copyright © 1977 by The New
York Times Company. Reprinted by permission.
RICHARD MORAN. "Slums Need To Be Improved First, Then Prisons." *Los Angeles
Times,* January 7, 1986. Reprinted by permission of the author.
*Readers' Guide to Periodical Literature.* Copyright © 1985 by The H. W. Wilson
Company. Material reproduced by permission of the publisher.
HOPE RYDEN. *America's Last Wild Horses.* New York: E.P. Dutton, Inc., 1970. Reprinted
by permission of Roberta Pryor, Inc.
CARL SAGAN. "Planetary Exploration." Copyright © 1977 by Newsweek, Inc. All
rights reserved. Reprinted by permission.
DON SHARP. "Under the Hood." Copyright © 1980 by *Harper's* Magazine. All rights
reserved. Reprinted from the June, 1980 issue by special permission.
*Social Sciences Index.* Copyright © 1985 by The H. W. Wilson Company. Material
reproduced by permission of the publisher.
*Webster's New World Dictionary.* Copyright © 1970, 1972, 1974, 1976, 1978, 1980
by Simon & Schuster, Inc. Reprinted by permission of Simon & Schuster,
Inc.
GEORGE F. WILL. "A World of Crushingly Particular Experiences," in *The Pursuit
of Virtue and Other Tory Notions.* Copyright © 1982 by The Washington Post
Company. Reprinted by permission of Simon & Schuster, Inc.

ISBN  0-02-370230-3

# Preface

*The Macmillan College Handbook* has been designed to serve not only as an accessible and comprehensive reference guide but also as an effective teaching text. It may be used as a rhetoric or guide to writing essays, paragraphs, and sentences. The thorough discussion of writing, revising, and editing the whole essay in the early chapters and the discussion of the persuasive and documented essay in the later chapters keep the focus throughout on the writer's chief concern—the essay itself. As a grammar and as a correction guide, the handbook gives a thorough account of the traditional parts of speech, the parts of the sentence and their arrangement, and the rules and current conventions of punctuation in standard written English in the United States. The chapters on the sentence do more than state rules and give examples: they discuss *why* sentences are effective and ineffective and give a full explanation of how to build or correct sentences. For the student who needs a quick reference only, checklists at the end of each chapter review the key points and often repeat examples. These checklists serve as a handbook in miniature.

Another purpose of *The Macmillan College Handbook* is to widen the student's repertory of writing styles and inventive skills. To achieve this, the book teaches by example, illustrating the styles of standard written English through abundant examples of sentences and paragraphs from contemporary writers in various fields. Later chapters contain complete essays by several contemporary writers, including George F. Will and Carl Sagan. The writing of essays is demonstrated at various stages of composition; examples are the multiple drafts of the sample personal essay in Chapters 3–4 and the sample documented essay in Chapter 39. Some of the student writing has been produced in individual and collaborative exercises conducted in the classroom and the library.

## The Plan of the Handbook

*The Macmillan College Handbook* is organized in nine parts and two glossaries. Although chapters may be assigned in any order that the instructor finds useful, they can be assigned and discussed sequentially as well.

Following the introductory discussion of standard English and the levels and varieties distinguished throughout the book, Part I takes up the writing of the whole paper, including ways of finding and analyzing a subject—illustrated through the development of a student's personal essay from the initial choice of subject to the final revision and editing. Part II introduces the elements of the essay and shows how to build paragraphs and sentences. The elements of sentences are in turn discussed in Chapter 8—a systematic description of the traditional parts of speech. In this way, matters of grammar are presented not independently but as knowledge necessary in writing effective sentences and essays.

The book also treats sentence correction as a necessary component of effective writing. Part III opens with thorough chapters on punctuation—the uses of the comma, the semicolon, the colon, the apostrophe, and other punctuation marks. The concluding chapters discuss the mechanics of the paper and the rules of spelling.

By demonstrating ways to vary sentences and give ideas proper emphasis, Part IV prepares for the discussion of incomplete or ineffective and wordy sentences in Part V. Knowing what makes sentences effective helps the student to understand why other sentences are ineffective. These chapters on the sentence stress choices open to the writer as well as the need for revision in the course of writing.

Moving from the whole essay to the words themselves, the handbook treats diction in Part VI—first, the dialects of standard English; then abstract and concrete, general and specific words, slang, and jargon; the uses of the dictionary; and finally the uses of figurative language. Part VII returns to the whole essay. Four chapters are devoted to the forms of argument, the persuasive essay, and the reasoning it employs and should avoid. In Part VIII, four chapters explain in detail research techniques and the documented paper—the finding and interpretation of evidence, and the organization and the documentation of the paper itself, according to both MLA and APA methods. Part IX discusses the special demands of certain professional and academic writing—business letters, resumes, course notes, and examination answers. The concluding glossaries of usage and grammatical terms provide additional help with diction and grammar. The charts inside the front and back covers provide keys to sections or pages of the text and the corresponding correction symbols.

## The Philosophy of the Book

Writing as a continuous act of planning, writing, and revision is today a major concern of composition, and this book reflects that concern. But the book also recognizes that no single "process" of writing exists. The process that each writer follows is the sum of habits developed gradually in various kinds of writing. Few if any writers proceed in the same way in every writing situation: some produce essays that satisfy all readers in a single draft, and some must write several drafts. Some use the traditional topic or sentence outline in preparing to write the essay; others use freewriting or the other techniques of invention described in Chapter 2—sometimes drawing on these in successive drafts of the paper. Some revise extensively and edit in the course of writing the first and later drafts; others revise and edit only after producing a full draft.

This book, then, does not suggest that all successful writers follow identical procedures. But it does assume that writers learn by example. Linguists disagree on how much of our "sentence sense" is learned; this book assumes that we do not learn to write effectively only by experimentation and constant writing. We learn to write as we learn to speak—by hearing and reading sentences—and we discover ways of improving our writing in the same way. Both the unpracticed and the practiced writer need models of effective sentences, paragraphs, and essays.

## Accompanying Materials

A complete package of supplements for instructors and students accompanies the handbook. In the *Instructor's Manual,* I suggest ways to teach the handbook and provide answers to the exercises. *The Macmillan College Workbook* by Alice MacDonald, University of Akron, offers students an opportunity to increase mastery of basic skills through varied and interesting exercises and self-tests. Although the workbook parallels the organization of the handbook and uses its definitions, it is a self-contained text appropriate for use independent of the handbook. An *Answer Key* for instructors accompanies *The Macmillan College Workbook.* The *Test Bank* for the handbook, two parallel sets of diagnostic tests, is available in a printed form and as a *Microtest* software program for Apple and IBM computers.

## Acknowledgments

I wish to acknowledge advice on early drafts and suggested examples given by numerous colleagues at the University of Akron. I owe a particular debt to William Francis, Alan Hart, Bruce Holland, Robert Holland, Martin McKoski, Kenneth Pakenham, Sally Slocum, and Linda Weiner. Alice MacDonald advised me on the chapters on special writing and gave invaluable criticism of the whole manuscript. The University of Akron students whose writing appears in this book include Steven Carroll, Marilyn Holler, Cathleen Jenkins, Paul Kim, Susan Mitchell, Sandra Montevideo, Rick Pflaum, and Robert Streharsky, and I am grateful to them and to other students for their interest and cooperation.

I wish to thank the following reviewers who commented on early drafts: Lucien L. Agosta, Kansas State University; Harry Brent, Baruch College—CUNY; Barbara Carson, University of Georgia; Dick Fulkerson, East Texas State University; Dennis R. Hoilman, Ball State University; George Miller, University of Delaware; Patricia Y. Murray, DePaul University; and Peter T. Zoller, Wichita State University. I owe special thanks to E. Jean Amman, Ball State University, and Raymond A. St. John, Bob Jones University, who added to the book immeasurably through their criticism of successive drafts.

I wish also to thank the following people at Macmillan: Wendy Polhemus, production editor, for her exceptional attention to the details of the book; Andy Zutis, designer, for the readability of the text. To Eben W. Ludlow, executive editor, I owe the greatest debt, not only for suggesting this book but also for getting the early drafts on track and for his advice at all stages of the project. Finally, I could not have written this book without the support and help of my wife, Lillian Levin.

**G. L.**

# Brief Contents

# Detailed Contents

# Introduction
# to the Student

## I.1 The Aims of This Handbook

This handbook describes one form of English used throughout the United States—standard written English. Specifically, it does the following:

- provides a grammar of standard written English for use in writing and revision;
- gives help with punctuation and the mechanics of writing;
- gives advice on making sentences, paragraphs, and various kinds of essays as effective as possible;
- gives the essentials of sound reasoning.

This book also

- describes the process of writing essays—from the original planning and drafting to final revision and editing;
- suggests ways of finding worthwhile and interesting topics;
- describes how to research and write the library paper.

**I.1a Improving Your Writing Skills.**   The main purpose of this book is to sharpen and refine skills you already possess. In beginning a college course in writing, you already possess experience in communication. But, like other communication skills, skill in writing can sharpen through the practice and discussion you get in a composition course.

This book provides a guide to the fundamentals of English grammar and punctuation and gives help with such problems as lack of agreement, misplaced or dangling modifiers, and unneeded or missing commas or apostrophes. It also gives help with unclear or unfocused sentences and paragraphs and with the organization of the essay, and it suggests ways to support

1

**I.2**

the ideas of the essay and develop them logically. Throughout the book you will find detailed discussion of possible choices in sentence structure, organization, and diction—choices that allow you to fit a piece of writing to a particular audience and occasion.

**I.1b Understanding the Process of Writing.**    Another purpose of this book is to describe common procedures in writing essays. The word *process* widely refers to these procedures or series of activities usually performed in writing. These include the beginning acts sometimes referred to as prewriting—searching for a topic, thinking about its implications and ways to develop it, using imagination to discover details, writing trial sentences and paragraphs, and planning the essay through outlines and other methods.

The writing of the essay usually consists of one or more drafts and your revision of these. The drafting and revision of the essay include corrections in spelling, punctuation, grammar, and phrasing of ideas. A final editing concludes the writing of the essay. These are not activities that you always perform step by step. Indeed, during the course of writing, you will do even more searching, thinking, and imagining. You may change the focus and organization as the essay takes shape into a whole. The opening chapters of the book describe this process in detail.

# I.2    Situations and Writing Skills

How you put your skills and knowledge to use depends on the writing situation. Consider some common situations in college and everyday writing.

College writing is often assigned writing. Your composition instructor may ask you to write an impromptu essay on an assigned topic or on a topic of your choice. Essay quizzes and exams are other kinds of assigned writing. These writing situations are similar to many you encounter out of the classroom. For example, as a witness to a traffic accident, you may be asked by the police or a motorist involved to write down what you saw. At work you may be asked to write a memorandum quickly on an urgent matter.

Writing on demand calls for skills people often take for granted. Recording and giving a report of important details in clear sentences is one important skill; doing so concisely is another. The skilled writer pays close attention to the wording to avoid clouding the message with irrelevant information or unnecessary repetition. A related skill is the ability to choose words appropriate to the person receiving the message. A memorandum addressed to a working partner probably will be worded differently from a message to supervisors or employers. Anyone who has tried to reduce a long message to a few words in a telegram or a memorandum knows how difficult it is to give the message a clear focus and organization and at the same time to be concise and include essential information.

Other writing situations give you more time to think and plan. How much thinking, planning, and revising you do varies with the occasion and kind of writing. The many ideas and details contained in a term paper, for example, require a complex organization; those of a telegram or memorandum probably do not. The amount of planning and revising also varies with experience. Practiced writers organize their ideas and make them concise and exact without being highly conscious of what they are doing. Certain acts of writing you perform habitually; others, thoughtfully and cautiously.

Choosing words suitable to the audience and occasion of the essay is one of these acts. So are editing and proofreading the final draft of the essay. Making these choices requires an awareness of the various levels and dialects of English.

# I.3   Standard English

**I.3a   Standard and Nonstandard English.**   **Standard English** is the dialect of people who conduct the affairs of the country—specifically, those who run its schools, conduct its business, operate its courts, make its laws, and govern its political life. The term **nonstandard** means usage unacceptable to one class of English speakers and writers—those who exert influence and shape opinion about language throughout the United States. In some communities, standard English may be the dialect of the majority, whereas in other communities it may be that of the minority.

Standard American English is a cultivated or learned dialect, and a highly flexible one, capable of dealing with concrete experience and abstract ideas. Its large and varied vocabulary is one of its most important features. It is equally powerful and flexible as the language of everyday affairs and the language of business, governmental, and intellectual life and is expressive and beautiful when used with skill. However, these are qualities that characterize other dialects, as Part V of this book shows. Standard English is not "better" or more "correct" or more expressive or more beautiful or more useful than other dialects in all respects.

**I.3**

**I.3b The Advantages of Standard English.** If Standard English is not more expressive or useful in all of its features than other dialects, why study or seek to improve one's mastery of it?

One important reason for its study has already been suggested. In the United States, a person must speak and write the prevailing standard to make a career in politics, teach school, or find a white-collar job. People may, of course, find jobs in communities or occupations where their own special dialect prevails, and they may attain great success in these worlds. However, success in school, business, government, and other areas of American life depends on a mastery of the standard spoken and written throughout the country.

**I.3c Formal, Informal, and General English.** The flexibility of Standard English comes from the wide choices in sentence structure and diction it offers speakers and writers in different personal, social, and business situations. These are usually defined according to levels or varieties of usage—often defined broadly as formal, informal, and general.

**Formal English** tends to be what the word *formal* suggests— speech and writing that are "at attention," each idea stated precisely, in tightly constructed sentences that point up similarities and contrasts. Here is an example:

> Whether we like it or not—and many may disagree with my thesis because painting, or music, or some other art is more important to them—the art of the moving image is the only art truly of our time, whether it is in the form of the film or television. The moving picture is our universal art, which comprises all others, literature and acting, stage design and music, dance and the beauty of nature, and, most of all, the use of light and of color.
> —BRUNO BETTELHEIM, "The Art of Moving Pictures"

**Informal English**, both in speech and writing, assumes familiarity between speaker and listener, writer and reader—a familiarity that permits the writer to be less precise and more conversational or colloquial. In informal English we find everyday words and expressions, and sometimes slang that has been absorbed from another dialect. Here is an example from a magazine review of an "Indiana Jones" movie:

> The whole movie is designed as a shoot-the-chutes, and toward

the end, when the heroic trio, having found the sacred stone and freed the stolen children from the maharajah's mines, are trying to escape in a tiny mine car, and a shift in camera angles places us with them on a literal roller-coaster ride, the audience laughs in recognition that that's what we've been on all along. . . . The movie relates to Americans' love of getting in the car and just taking off—it's a breeze.

—PAULINE KAEL, *The New Yorker*, June 11, 1984

**I.4**

*Formal* and *informal* are best defined as the extreme limits of a wide spectrum of words, phrases, and sentence constructions. Sharing qualities of both formal and informal is **general English**—the speech of radio and television usually, the writing of newsmagazines, journals, and newspapers. It is the prevailing standard of communication in the schools and in business and governmental affairs. General English employs the filled-out structures and the often abstract and technical words of formal English and the looser conversational sentence structure and vocabulary of informal English. Here is a typical specimen:

In any negotiation with an auto dealer, the typical buyer is at a disadvantage. The buyer usually doesn't know what the car cost the dealer. If the buyer is examining several cars on the lot, each is likely to carry a different mix of optional equipment and thus a different sticker price, resulting in confusion as numbers are thrown around. If a trade-in is part of the deal, there are still more numbers—and an opportunity for the dealer to balance a low selling price on the new car against a low trade-in allowance on the old.     —*Consumer Reports*, April 1983

Usage is not always a simple matter. Learning to speak and write a language is learning to make adjustments to new situations and purposes. Despite the labels given to various words and phrases, the borders between formal and informal usage and between standard and nonstandard words, phrases, and grammar are not always exact ones. Their defining features, as we shall see, are inseparable from their use.

This handbook distinguishes formal or informal usage when the writing departs in a marked way from general. It also points out usage considered nonstandard. Where no designation appears, the usage should be considered general.

# I.4  The Plan of This Book

**Organization.** To locate the information you need, you may find it helpful to know how this book is organized.

**I.4**

Briefly, the book moves from the whole essay to its parts, beginning with the process of writing and continuing with discussion of paragraphs and sentences, matters of diction, and sound reasoning. In the final chapters the discussion returns to special kinds of writing important in college and business—the documented paper, examination answers, letters, resumes.

For help in planning and organizing the whole essay, consult Part I (Chapters 1-4). These chapters give an overview of the writing process and an extended example of the planning and writing of an important piece of writing—the personal essay. In these opening chapters, you will also find discussion of other important kinds of writing.

Part II (Chapters 5-9) describes ways of organizing paragraphs, making effective transitions, and analyzing ideas. The methods of paragraph analysis discussed include definition, division and classification, example, comparison and contrast, analogy, process, and causal analysis. This part also discusses ways of building sentences and includes a review of basic terms of sentence grammar.

Part III (Chapters 10-16) on sentence punctuation deals with end punctuation, the comma, the semicolon and colon, and the apostrophe and other punctuation marks. Part III also deals with the mechanics of the paper and with spelling.

Part IV (Chapters 17-20) focuses on sentence grammar and style. You will find here discussion of choices English writers (and speakers) make in different situations. The topics include agreement; pronoun case and reference; parallelism and other kinds of sentence arrangement.

Part V (Chapters 21-27) deals with sentence faults, including fragments and run-on sentences; misplaced words, phrases, and clauses; dangling modifiers, split constructions, shifts and omissions; sentence variety; and wordy sentences.

Part VI (Chapters 28-31) concerns diction—specifically, the spoken and written dialects of English, levels of usage, and technical words and other classifications. This part also describes the uses of the dictionary, gives help on spelling, and discusses figurative language—simile, metaphor, personification—and related uses of language.

Part VII (Chapters 32-35) deals with sound reasoning—first with ways of building sound arguments, then with fallacious arguments and ways of avoiding them.

Part VIII (Chapters 36-39) describes the documented paper—specifically, ways of finding a subject and limiting it and the process of collecting materials, including the uses of reference books and other library sources. Later chapters discuss how to use primary and secondary sources, take notes, quote and paraphrase, document the paper, and prepare the manuscript. The concluding chapter traces the writing of a documented paper, illustrating the process through a first and second draft.

**I.4**

Part IX (Chapters 40-41) discusses special kinds of writing—notes, summaries, letters, resumes, examination answers. The book concludes with glossaries of usage and grammatical terms.

**I.4b Correction and Revision.**   Once you are familiar with the plan of the book, you will develop your own ways of using it. Note that many of the topics discussed in separate chapters are closely related. For example, knowing how to use the comma depends on knowing how to use the semicolon and colon; it will be useful to consult both discussions. And knowing how to place clauses to prevent misreading depends on knowing how to place words and phrases in the most effective order in the sentence. Cross-references direct you to these related discussions. You will find checklists of important topics at the end of the chapters.

In commenting on your papers, your composition instructor may depend on section and subsection numbers, or on the abbreviations given on the inside cover of the book. You may want to make your own checklist of sections to which your instructor refers you.

# Writing the Whole Essay

# Writing Essays

This chapter discusses the occasions for writing, the audience, the purposes of writing, and the methods of achieving them. These methods include narration, description, various kinds of exposition (or explanation), and argument. As we shall see, the use of these methods depends in part on the nature of the essay and in part on the occasion of the essay—the reason for its composition—and its audience.

The remaining chapters of Part I describe the process of writing an essay—from the beginning search for a topic and suitable focus to the writing of one or more drafts and the final stages of revising and editing. The concluding chapter of Part I traces the writing of a particular essay from the first to the final stage.

## 1.1 Occasions and Audiences

The reasons for which you write are different from day to day. Sometimes you make the decision, for example, in writing a letter to a friend or a newspaper or in making a list of chores to be performed. Sometimes others create the writing situation or occasion, for example, when you take down an important telephone message or write an impromptu essay or a quiz in a college course.

Audiences vary as much as occasions. In making a list of chores, you are writing for an audience of one—you. In writing a letter or taking down a telephone message, you are writing for another person. Of course, much of the writing you do is for larger audiences—for your instructor and classmates sometimes, or for the readers of a letter to a newspaper. Audiences are different in size as well as in background and interest.

Considering the audience is essential in planning and writing an essay. Though many writers believe they are writing to be read by other people, they write as if they alone are to be the only readers. In failing to keep their readers in mind, they forget to perform essential acts. In conversing with these same people, they would pause when necessary to explain a word or an idea or to repeat a statement. These acts are essential in writing, too. Of course, many people speak as they write; they are interested only in themselves and not in their audience and therefore show no concern about being understood. Those truly interested in communicating with others do show concern.

Wanting to be understood, these writers give attention to details and to the clarity of their sentences. In your own writing, how much you explain usually depends on the topic or subject of your essay. You probably sense that an unfamiliar or difficult topic requires more detail and explanation than does a familiar one. Your aim or purpose in writing shapes these decisions.

For example, in writing a set of instructions on the use of a power saw, you would explain the process step by step, omitting no essential detail. Writing an essay on conserving forests, you might give only those details on tree cutting needed to illustrate good and bad techniques. The purpose of each piece of writing determines the amount of detail you need to give. The amount of detail also depends on the background and knowledge of the audience—specifically, on whether the audience is a general or a special one. The more special the audience, the fewer details you need to provide on some or all matters in the essay.

## 1.2 Special and General Audiences

**1.2a Writing to Special Audiences.** A general audience vary in their background and knowledge of the subject; they vary most when the subject of the essay is scientific or technical, less when the writing concerns everyday experiences. A special audience, by contrast, shares the same knowledge and background. These at least are the assumptions writers and editors make in deciding how to address their readers. We see this difference in the readership of popular magazines like *Time* and *Newsweek*. Some magazines choose to address a wide audience of varying interests, background, and knowledge. Even magazines that focus on a particular subject or interest—sports and astronomy magazines, for example—may conceive their audience as a general one. Others like *Scientific American* and *The Atlantic Monthly* address a special or restricted audience of rather similar background and knowledge.

**1.2**

**dev**

Magazines with a general readership often assume that since the knowledge and background of the audience vary it is best to use plain, nontechnical, concrete words and abundant details and illustrations. Magazines on specialized subjects often assume their readers are familiar with the technical terms and ideas of the subjects discussed in the magazine and are interested in technical and theoretical discussions and can understand them. Of course, much of the writing in these magazines is also concrete, but it may also be technical and theoretical, using at times highly abstract language.

The following instructions on how to buy a portable stereo—one of the popular Soundabouts or Walkmans—appears in a magazine column directed to a special audience:

> First, narrow your range of choice. If you're like most readers of *Stereo Review*, you would be unlikely to buy a home or auto tape deck without a noise-reduction system (Dolby, dbx, or DNR), and by requiring noise reduction in any portable tape player you are considering, you can eliminate perhaps 80 per cent of the players on the market. As in shopping for any hi-fi equipment, avoid brand names that are totally unfamiliar or that sound suspiciously similar to famous brand names. For example, if you come across a "Xony Walkaway," simply walk away.
> —MYRON BERGER, "Choosing a Personal Portable,"
> *Stereo Review*, September 1983

The author knows his audience well enough to gauge its knowledge about portable stereos and its buying habits. Knowing what kind of information to provide, he names the noise-reduction systems as a reminder of the kind used in home and auto tape decks. But he does not describe or define them. He does describe the kind of equipment that the buyers should not consider. For as much as readers of the magazine know about stereo equipment, they may not know much about fake or unreliable products.

The information may be even more specialized if the audience consists of a single reader who has written to ask a specific question or a small number of readers known to read the column. Or the columnist may give this information in language suited to both the special reader and the reader with somewhat less knowledge of special terms. For example, a reader of the same magazine writes to another columnist asking about stereo recording tape:

> What are the differences among ferric, chrome, and metal tapes, and when should one use each type? Also, is "70-microsecond"

the same thing as "high bias" and "120-microsecond" the same as "normal bias"?

The reader continues with a description of his equipment.

**1.2 dev**

In responding, the columnist gauges how much this and other readers of the column know about recording tape, and he answers accordingly. Here is part of his response:

> The terms ferric, chrome (or ferri-cobalt, or $CrO_2$-equivalent), and metal are used to describe the various magnetic materials with which recording tape is coated. Ferric-oxide tape is the most common type and has been around since 1939. Its required bias—an ultrasonic tone, fed to the tape along with the music, that lowers distortion and noise—is called normal bias. Cassettes using normal bias *also* use 120-microsecond (or $\mu$s) playback equalization (bias is not used during playback). Since two sections of one switch can handle both the recording-bias level and the appropriate playback equalization, a single switch (or detector pin) is sufficient.
>
> —CRAIG STARK, "Tape Talk," *Stereo Review*, July 1983

The columnist responds in technical language suited to the questioner. But the columnist also is careful to explain terms for readers possessing less knowledge than the questioner about recording tape.

**1.2b Writing to General Audiences.** Were the columnists just quoted always addressing a general audience—some knowing much about stereo equipment, some knowing little—they would probably write less technically. They would look for ways to explain technical matters in nontechnical language, possibly through examples or analogies with familiar objects.

For example, an article on ocean sailing in a magazine with a wide readership gives these facts about the Gulf Stream:

> Writers looking for a capsule description of the Stream frequently refer to it as "a river in the ocean." In reality, however, the Gulf Stream is only the most impressive part of a huge system of ocean currents known collectively as the North Atlantic subtropical gyre—a clockwise circulation of water that is driven partly by the prevailing wind patterns and partly by the rotation of the earth.
>
> —TONY GIBBS, "Racing to Bermuda," *The New Yorker*, July 18, 1983

The author follows this explanation with much more detail about the Gulf Stream—details we would expect to find in a geography textbook. But it is also essential information in an explanation of racing in the Atlantic Ocean. The author knows that the readership of the magazine is a general one, including many readers who know much about sailing and many who know little about ocean currents even if they sail boats.

Obviously the line dividing general from special audiences can be a fine one. The reader familiar with some aspects of a subject may be unfamiliar with others. This difference is worth keeping in mind in gauging the audience for the essay, in planning the writing, and then in making a decision on how to begin it.

**1.2c Gauging Your Audience.** Deciding what audience you want to reach is essential in planning an essay. Once you have a specific audience in mind, you can decide what terms or ideas need to be defined. For a general audience, you will need to define all important terms and ideas as simply as you can. And it is wise to do the same for a special audience, giving the meaning of important terms and showing the way they are used. Some readers will need a reminder of these meanings. Unless the essay requires that you present details chronologically or in a conventional order known to the audience, a good procedure is to build to unfamiliar or difficult ideas or details.

How well you know your audience will affect your decisions too. If you know the audience personally, you may decide to write informally, as if you were conversing about the subject. If you do not know the audience well, you may decide to write more formally. You will be most successful if you have a picture of your audience in mind when you begin writing and keep that picture in mind in the course of writing and revision.

**1.2d Generating Interest.** A successful essay holds the audience's attention and interest throughout. One way to hold interest and attention is to capture it in the very first paragraph, perhaps by stating or showing the audience why the subject interests you and should interest them.

The following opening paragraph of a book on recent discoveries in astronomy generates interest by explaining why the black hole is so fascinating an object and allowing the reader to picture it:

> A black hole is one of the most fantastic things ever predicted by modern science. It is a place where gravity is so strong that nothing—not even light—can escape. It is a place where gravity is so strong that a hole has been rent in the very fabric of space and time. Surrounding this yawning chasm is a "horizon" in the geometry of space where time itself stands still.

And inside this hole, beyond this horizon, the directions of space and time are interchanged.

—WILLIAM J. KAUFMANN, III,
*Black Holes and Warped Spacetime*

**1.2 dev**

The author gives the general reader a brief, clear definition of the complex phenomenon the book will discuss; the definition itself awakens interest. In addition, the author tries to capture attention through riddles or paradoxes about black holes. Were he to give more detail on each idea, he would probably distract the reader from the topic of the paragraph and the preface.

The following opening paragraph in another popular book on recent advances in physics begins even more broadly by stating the importance of the subject to the general reader:

Human understanding of the nature of the universe and the laws of creation was advancing in the 1970s with a speed that left the experts breathless. Inhabitants of a small planet were gazing across a vast ocean of space and discerning the beginning of time. They thought they could also make out strange places called black holes, where time seemed to come to an end. Others peered with even greater rewards into the micro-universe—into the realm of particles, much smaller than atoms, from which nature made galaxies and brains. There they found deep connections between cosmic forces and the qualities of matter on which they acted.

—NIGEL CALDER, *The Key to the Universe*

The succeeding paragraph then states the subject directly:

My book describes those advances. In detail, they extended mankind's knowledge of the contents of the material universe but, behind the question "What?", the question "Why?" was becoming more insistent. . . .

The ideas of the paragraph and the book must be important enough to warrant the dramatic presentations illustrated by the opening paragraphs just quoted. The writer risks losing the reader if the subject seems not to warrant so dramatic an introduction. To avoid a pretentious or overly dramatic opening, essayists sometimes appeal directly to the interests of the reader or depend on humor. The writer of the following paragraph does both:

"Size," Julian Huxley once remarked, "has a fascination of its own." We stock our zoos with elephants, hippopotamuses, giraffes, and gorillas; who among you was not rooting for King Kong in his various battles atop tall buildings? This focus on the few creatures larger than ourselves has distorted our con-

**1.2**
**dev**

ception of our own size. Most people think that *Homo sapiens* is a creature of only modest dimensions. In fact, humans are among the largest animals on earth; more than 99 percent of animal species are smaller than we are. Of 190 species in our own order of primate mammals, only the gorilla regularly exceeds us in size. —STEPHEN JAY GOULD, "Sizing Up Human Intelligence"

You can lose the interest of both the general and the special audience if you give unnecessary explanatory detail. Whatever the interests and background of the audience, an account consisting of all detail and no interpretation or commentary may prove as uninteresting or boring as a general statement of ideas presented without detail or illustration. But it is better to err in giving too much detail than in giving too little; even the specialist may need a reminder of basic terms and will be grateful for illustrations of these.

### EXERCISES

1. Be ready to discuss the decisions you need to make in explaining to each of the following audiences how to parallel park:
   **a.** a student driver
   **b.** a person who has not driven for many years
2. Write a paragraph for a general audience explaining an idea or institution that you have come to understand through reading or through a course you are taking—for example, the theory of the Big Bang or the Electoral College as an institution. Assume that your audience possesses some knowledge of the subject or field but no specific knowledge of the idea or institution itself. Rewrite your paragraph for a different audience that possesses no knowledge of the subject or field.
3. The following are opening paragraphs of recent newspaper or magazine columns. Determine from the kind of detail and the amount given in the paragraph the conception the writer has of the audience—namely, how much the audience knows about the subject and what its interests and concerns are. Be ready to discuss how well the paragraphs generate interest in you.

   a. No, those weren't extra packs of marked cards up New York Yankee manager Billy Martin's pinstriped sleeve last week. And it wasn't a dealer's paraffin that adorned the bat of Kansas City Royals' smoothie George Brett; it was dark and sticky pine tar. But the high-noon shoot-out of gamesmanship that made a Brett home run disappear and then suddenly reappear belonged to a saga that is centuries old, reenacted from the riverboats of Mississippi to the roulette wheels of Monte Carlo: the eternal search for the edge

> —PETE AXTHELM, "Psst, Somebody May Be Cheating," *Newsweek*, August 8, 1983

**1.3**
**dev**

b. Can a system of voting be devised that is at the same time rational, decisive and egalitarian? Studies of this question by philosophers, political scientists and economists (including the two of us) suggest that the answer is no. These characteristics of an ideal system are in fact incompatible. A method of voting may avoid arbitrariness, deadlock or inequality of power, but it cannot escape all three. The continuing analysis of this dilemma has led to a deeper understanding of existing voting systems and may lead in time to the discovery of better ones.

> —DOUGLAS H. BLAIR and ROBERT A. POLLAK, "Rational Collective Choice," *Scientific American*, August 1983

c. To hear some network-watchers talk, the logos for the television networks these days should not be a circle, an eye, and a peacock. A dinosaur would serve all three. The networks, according to this metaphor, are failing to adapt to the sudden change made in their environment by the killing wind of new technology. In this Darwinian view, the networks' bigness and bureaucratic rigidity prevent them from responding to the mortal challenge; meanwhile, ingenious and aggressive predators, each with relatively modest territorial aspirations, dart about nibbling at their flanks.

> —ERIC MINK, "Why the Networks Will Survive Cable," *The Atlantic Monthly*, December 1983

## 1.3 Purposes in Writing

Decisions on what to include in an essay and how to organize it depend on more than the character of the audience. They also depend on the purpose of the essay. The essay may have one or more of the following functions:

- giving expression to a personal or social belief or feeling
- exploring one's own experience or some aspect of the world to make discoveries
- giving information
- proving an idea
- persuading others to accept a truth or belief

**1.3**

**dev**

The purpose of your essay may be to express a personal belief or credo, or to express a political credo like the Pledge of Allegiance. Or it may be to explore a problem, as in a newspaper column that explores the difficulties of being a working mother. Or it may be to discover what the world of nature is like, as in an article on travel in a remote part of the country. Your purpose may be to give information, as in an article that gives advice on finding a job. Or it may be to prove that fad diets make people vulnerable to disease or to persuade them to support a change in the law governing advertising.

These purposes are by no means independent of one another. In writing an essay, you may have more than one purpose in mind—for example, to give expression to a personal belief and at the same time explore experiences that seem to support it, or to prove an idea and persuade readers to act on the proof.

**1.3a  Expressing Feelings and Beliefs.**  Many statements merely state or express a feeling or attitude. The exclamation "Wow!" expresses joy or amazement over an unexpected happening. So may a personal essay in which you express pleasure or frustration in starting college or moving into a new neighborhood or learning to repair an automobile. The opening paragraph of an expressive essay may announce this purpose directly or may imply it, as in this opening paragraph from an essay on being in love:

> Love is an illness, and has its own set of obsessive thoughts. Behold the poor wretch afflicted with love: one moment strewn upon a sofa, scarcely breathing save for an occasional sigh up-sucked from the deep well of his despair; the next, pacing *agitato*, his cheek alternately pale and flushed. Is he pricked? What barb, what gnat stings him thus?
>
> —RICHARD SELZER, "Love Sick"

If the essay expresses your personal feelings only, you may decide to give no more than the details that do so. The same consideration guides your choice of words. Selzer's colorful and evocative words convey the feeling of being in love. Your choice of words depends on whether you want to name your feelings or to evoke them for the reader.

You make the same decisions in expressing your personal beliefs or credo. Writing of this kind can be informative or persuasive in intent, but many statements are for the purpose of self-expression only. We find statements of this sort often in diaries and journals:

Perhaps this is the main value of a habit of writing, of keeping a journal—that so we remember our best hours and stimulate ourselves. My thoughts are my company. They have a certain individuality and separate existence, aye, personality. Having by chance recorded a few disconnected thoughts and then brought them into juxtaposition, they suggest a whole new field in which it was possible to labor and to think. Thought begat thought.                     —HENRY DAVID THOREAU, *Journal*

**1.3** **dev**

**1.3b Discovering the World.**   In another essay you might explore the nature of your world in light of your personal beliefs or outlook. This technique suggests one of the original purposes of the essay as writers of the past used it—as a trial effort or attempt to understand something, an attempt that does not have to result in any conclusive discovery. The act of discovery is an ongoing one—an unfinished process at the point the writer decides to bring the essay to an end.

An essay that explores experiences and ideas in this way suggests the ongoing discovery in its tone, as in this passage from a book describing travel experiences:

> Reading my notes of the trip—images, bits of conversations, ideas—I hunted a structure in the events, but randomness was the rule. Outside, sheltered by a live oak, a spider spun a web. Can an orb weaver perceive the design in its work, the pattern of concentric circles lying atop radiating lines? When the mystical young Black Elk went to the summit of Harney Peak to see the shape of things, he looked down on the great unifying hoop of peoples. I looked down and saw fragments. But later that afternoon, a tactic returned to me from night maneuver training in the Navy: to see in deep darkness you don't look directly at an object—you look to the left; you look at something else to see what you really want to see. Skewed vision.            —WILLIAM LEAST HEAT MOON, *Blue Highways*

Compare this statement with Thoreau's statement of purpose in going to live at Walden Pond:

> I went to the woods because I wished to live deliberately, to front only the essential facts of life, and see if I could not learn what it had to teach, and not, when I came to die, discover that I had not lived.            —*Walden*

**1.3c Giving Information.**   A grocery list, an explanation of how to cut down a tree, a census report, an encyclopedia article—all of these give information. None make judgments, express feelings about the object or process, draw lessons, argue

**1.3**

**dev**

a thesis. The report of a scientific experiment, as in the following passage describing the use of a computer to imitate or "model" real things, usually does no more than give an exact account of a process:

> [Art education instructor Marla Schweppe] picks up a gadget called a puck, about the size of a cigarette pack, that's attached by a cord to the foot-by-foot-and-a-half digitizing tablet. Beneath the plastic cover of the tablet is a mesh of electric wire. The puck's position on the wire grid is electronically conveyed to the black-and-white TV and displayed as a tiny cross. To demonstrate, Schweppe slides the puck across the table. A cross appears on the screen and follows her movements. She keeps her eye on the screen, not the puck; it's like mirror drawing. She moves the puck to the left, and the cross skids over to a box in the menu marked "2D"; she presses a button on the puck, and a new menu appears. This time she selects a box labelled "draw." She has signalled the computer that she wants to draw a two-dimensional object. . . .
> —SUSAN WEST, "The New Realism," *Science 84*, July/August

Some kinds of informative writing do make judgments about the worth of the information or interpret the evidence. The author of the article on computer modeling concludes with this judgment:

> Still, many things simply defy the cool touch of an equation— the soft folds of clothing, the asymmetry and expressiveness of a human face, a cascading waterfall. It may be that reality can't be copied by a machine. It could be that the men who make computer graphics are just fooling themselves. "If you think you're going to do realistic pictures," says one scientist, "then you'd better take along a lunch, 'cause it's gonna be a long time."                                    —SUSAN WEST, "The New Realism"

As in other kinds of writing, your purpose in giving information guides the amount of the detail and the vocabulary and sentence structure of the essay. Susan West is giving the general reader information about experimental work with computers. Had she been writing a manual for the special audience of computer workers, she would have provided much more exact instruction. The amount of detail she does provide is enough to meet her purpose.

West does use technical computer language in her exposition, but she defines each word and relates it to the process she describes. Were she writing for an audience familiar with computer "modeling," such explanation would not be necessary. The readership of *Science 84*, the magazine in which her article appeared, is a mixed audience of general readers and specialists. Writers for the magazine therefore usually provide all necessary definitions and their context or use.

**1.3**
**dev**

**1.3d Persuading.** In writing a persuasive essay, you are encouraging your readers to change their thinking or beliefs or take action on the matter at issue. Notice that persuasion means more than only giving reasons; an informative essay or article may give reasons without trying to persuade readers to accept them.

Persuasive statements take various forms. Consider the following statements in letters asking for payment of a bill:

I will appreciate your paying this bill as soon as possible.
Please remit payment on receipt of this bill.
Pay up or else!

The third statement is obviously persuasive, but so are the first two. In fact, both are disguised commands. The writer had the choice of making a strong request or commanding or threatening. The writer might also have given reasons in an effort to be persuasive or have argued why the person receiving the letter had an obligation to pay.

The purpose of persuasive writing is to convince. It is writing directed usually to a special audience that the author identifies at some point in the essay—often in the answer to counterproposals or arguments. For example, in arguing for mandatory universal service for all young Americans, the writer of the following paragraph answers the criticism that mandatory service would infringe on individual liberty:

> In response, I would note that while there obviously have been problems related to the mandatory military draft, the requirement of mandatory education—mandatory, at least, up to a certain age—is widespread in contemporary societies. As in all matters that weigh the rights of the individual against the needs of the whole society, it comes down ultimately to a question of balance and of judgment where reasonable people may draw the line at different places.
> —DAVID S. SAXON, "Mandatory Universal Service,"
> *Chronicle of Higher Education*, April 25, 1984

The paragraph is persuasive in another sense: the author looks for a common ground or understanding with his critic. He is seeking to reconcile their different views on the issue.

As in other kinds of writing discussed, in persuasion purpose and audience guide the many decisions of the writer. One

**1.3**

**dev**

of these decisions concerns the appropriate vocabulary. Commands must be simple and direct in their wording. Requests, explanations, and arguments usually employ more words, in part because they wish to avoid seeming blunt.

EXERCISES

1. Rewrite the following messages as requests, commands, and threats, and be ready to discuss the differences in wording:
   **a.** "Everyone should have the paper in by Monday."
   **b.** "We need volunteers for the cookie sale."
   **c.** "Your club dues are two months overdue."
   **d.** "Papers free of spelling errors will receive special consideration."
2. Decide what is the chief purpose of each of the following statements or paragraphs from various sources. Be ready to discuss what may be subordinate aims or purposes:

   a. [statement on the copyright page of a book] All rights reserved including the right of reproduction in whole or in part in any form.

   b. [magazine advertisement] Total response *is* balanced performance, and it's the very essence of the new Pontiac 6000. In the Pontiac 6000, total response means controlled ride motions *without* harshness, while maintaining minimal lean in hard cornering.

   c. We know only two sets of people: the ones we really know, our families, friends, and other acquaintances; and we know celebrities. These are the only faces we recognize. Everyone else is a stranger. In the checkout line at the supermarket we know the face of Mary Tyler Moore or Mother Teresa on the cover of a magazine, but the person ahead of us, the person who is about to buy the magazine, is a stranger—we don't know that face, we may never see it again. There is a strange intimacy between us and these famous people who don't know us, though we know them, in a shallow way. We recognize their faces, and sometimes know a few facts about them, who they are or were married to, where they are from, their hobbies. Celebrities are different from the people we live with. They are rounded off and complete. They are easier to have clear ideas about, less complicated, and unless they hold political office we can't be hurt by them. They are like dolls for grownups to play with, talk to, and dream about. When I worked for a publishing company I got a letter from a woman who wrote books about the people she saw on television: would

we be interested, she wondered, in publishing a novel about Starsky and Hutch?
—JOHN GARVEY, "Dead or Alive," *Commonweal*, February 27, 1981

d. I have faith that for every piece of information there is someone somewhere who wishes to receive it. In that spirit I am putting down a few notes on the topic, "How to raise a woodchuck." Admittedly this is not a problem on everyone's mind; but if you live in woodchuck country, which in the East is almost anywhere, it is possible you will find yourself holding a baby woodchuck and wondering what to do with it.
—FAITH MCNULTY, "How to Raise a Woodchuck," *Audubon*, March 1977

e. During two decades of work among blacks and Spanish-speaking Americans of the Southwest (in the Rio Grande Valley they often prefer to be called Chicanos, but up in the hills of New Mexico some shun that word in favor of Hispanic-Americans), and among Pueblo and Hopi Indians, as well as some Athabaskan Indians in Alaska, I have tried to gain some sense of how words such as "race," "ethnic heritage," and "class," not to mention "history" itself, become for particular children moments—and longer—of self-observation, reflection, hopeful anticipation, or sheer dread.
—ROBERT COLES, "Minority Dreams, American Dreams," *Daedalus*, Spring 1981

3. Write down the decisions you would have to make in writing two of the following:
   a. a note taped to the refrigerator asking someone not to eat the breakfast plums
   b. a note to a repairman explaining why the refrigerator is not working
   c. a note to a friend giving unasked-for advice
   d. a letter to a department store explaining a bounced check
   e. a letter of complaint to the same store over a defective toaster
   f. a letter to the same store applying for a job
4. Write a note or a letter illustrating these choices.

# 1.4   The Methods of Writing

Description, narration, exposition, and argument—the chief forms of writing—serve the writer in achieving the various purposes discussed. These methods may be used exclusively or may be combined in various ways.

**1.4**
**dev**

**1.4a  Description.**   A **description** gives a picture of a person, an object, a scene. Sometimes the picture is of a broad area, as in the following description of Yosemite Falls in California:

> During the time of the spring floods the best near view of the fall is obtained from Fern Ledge on the east side above the blinding spray at a height of about 400 feet above the base of the fall. A climb of about 1400 feet from the Valley has to be made, and there is no trail, but to any one fond of climbing this will make the ascent all the more delightful. A narrow part of the ledge extends to the side of the fall and back of it, enabling us to approach it as closely as we wish. When the afternoon sunshine is streaming through the throng of comets, ever wasting, ever renewed, the marvelous fineness, firmness and variety of their forms are beautifully revealed.
> —JOHN MUIR, *The Yosemite*

The description may be limited to a smaller area, as in the following picture of a university dormitory:

> Off the lobby were side chambers with Persian rugs, dark wood paneling, leather armchairs, a grand piano, and paintings of nineteenth-century physicians with pork chop whiskers and impressive scowls. I picked up the keys to my room from a security guard behind a desk and went upstairs. After the Versailles of the lobby, the living quarters seemed like barracks— cement staircases, low ceilings, plain white paint, long sets of identical doors. Inside my room there was a desk, dresser, and narrow, hard bed.      —CHARLES LeBARON, *Gentle Vengeance*

Sometimes a description combines a scene of the past with a scene of the present:

> The town I was born and raised in disappeared. The only trace left behind to mark the location of the old clapboard house we lived in is the Long Island Rail Road, which still penetrates and crosses the town through a deep ditch, and somewhere alongside that ditch, behind a cement wall, is the back yard of my family's house. All the rest is gone. The yard is now covered by an immense apartment house. The whole block, and the other blocks around where our neighbors' clapboard houses and backyard gardens were, are covered by apartment houses, all built fixed to each other as though they were a single syncytial structure. The trees, mostly maples and elms, are gone. . . .
> —LEWIS THOMAS, *The Youngest Science*

1.4
dev

Description has various uses. In expressing your feelings about a gadget, you would probably describe it. You would certainly describe the gadget in more detail if you were giving information about how it works. The same would be true of an advertisement that encourages people to buy it.

**1.4b Narration.** **Narration** usually presents a series of events in the order of occurrence. Newspaper stories sometimes take the form of plain narration—a statement of facts without much explanation or description. Here is an example from a report of a power failure in New York City:

> Repair crews worked today to restore power to a 20-block area in midtown Manhattan that was darkened when a fire in an underground electrical substation cut service Wednesday.
> Six hundred police officers were guarding the area, deterring looters with street lights run by 62 mobile generators. No arrests were reported.—*Akron Beacon Journal*, August 11, 1983

Narration is basic to many kinds of writing. Fictional stories contain some narration, and so do historical accounts, reports of experiments, and personal histories as in this account of required military drill at Ohio State University during the First World War:

> One day General Littlefield picked our company out of the whole regiment and tried to get it mixed up by putting it through one movement after another as fast as we could execute them: squads right, squads left, squads on right into line, squads right about, squads left front into line, etc. In about three minutes one hundred and nine men were marching in one direction and I was marching away from them at an angle of forty degrees, all alone. "Company, halt!" shouted General Littlefield, "That man is the only man who has it right!" I was made a corporal for my achievement.
> —JAMES THURBER, *University Days*

**1.4c Exposition.** Informative writing depends on **exposition** or explanation. Explanation uses the following methods:
1. Definition. A **definition** explains what something is by setting it apart from all other objects like it. Dictionary definitions give this information in a formal way:

> *crumb:* A tiny fragment of bread, cake, or the like.
> —*Standard College Dictionary*

Sometimes the definition gives information about the connotations or feelings or ideas often associated with the word:

**1.4**

**dev**

*crumb: U.S. Slang* A contemptible person.
*crummy: U.S. Slang* Inferior; cheap; shabby.
—*Standard College Dictionary*

See 6.1 for additional discussion of definition.

Your own definitions probably will be less formal than those of your desk dictionary. How complete you make the definition depends on how much information you believe your readers need. In an informative article on quoting candid statements of political candidates, a newsmagazine works a series of definitions into an explanation of speaking "off the record":

> In fact, off the record is used more as a device for giving out information than for hiding it, since there is little reason for a public figure to tell a reporter something that will never turn up in print or influence what does turn up. Reporters sometimes go back to their sources to put off-the-record remarks on the record, or else to use them under other traditional rubrics. According to the etiquette, with something said "on background" or "not for attribution," the source may be described though not identified (a top White House official). Some "background" information requires even more vaguely described "sources" and "deep background" means the journalist must state the information solely on his or her own authority— a device resorted to frequently by foreign-policy sources who fear involving their countries in a diplomatic incident.
> —" 'I Don't Want to Be Quoted,' " *Newsweek*, August 27, 1984

Definitions here are woven into the discussion—not set apart or identified as formal dictionary ones. The more the definition is set apart or identified, the more formal the discussion will seem to the reader.

2. Classification and Division. **Classification** puts various objects into a single group or class: for example, classifying robins, orioles, crows, and eagles as birds. Dictionary definitions that single out a thing begin with the class or genus to which the thing belongs:

> *creek: U.S.* A stream intermediate in size between a brook and a river.　　　　　—*Standard College Dictionary*

**Division** begins with a class or genus and names the things that compose it. The class is then divided into its known parts:

> *pneumonia:* Inflammation of the lungs, a disease of bacterial or viral origin occurring in many forms, as *bronchial pneumonia* or *lobar pneumonia*.　　　　　—*Standard College Dictionary*

The division is conducted according to a single principle—here the origin of the disease (pneumonia can originate in the bronchial tubes or in a lobe of the lung). Usually the writer tells us whether the division is complete (the word *as* in the dictionary definition just given tells us that the division is incomplete).

As these definitions show, classification and division are closely related to definition. You will find them integral to explanations of relationships among various objects. Biology and chemistry texts use classification and division in demonstrating relationships of various animals or substances. For additional discussion see 6.2.

3. Example.   An explanation may consist of one or more **examples.** Indeed, you would probably find it difficult or impossible to express certain ideas without examples. Your textbooks depend on examples to explain important principles and ideas. So does almost all discourse concerned with ideas, as in this discussion of the harm created in giving undeserved recommendations to students, friends, and relatives:

> The existing practices also pose many problems for the individuals caught up in them. Take, for instance, a system where all recommendations given to students are customarily exaggerated—where, say, 60 percent of all graduates are classified as belonging to the top 10 percent. If a professor were to make the honest statement to an employer that a student is merely among the top 60 percent, he might severely injure that student's ability to find work, since the statement would not be taken at face value but would be wrongly interpreted to mean that his real standing was very near the bottom.
>
> —SISSELA BOK, *Lying*

In writing of any sort, you are wise to include examples of ideas discussed, for your readers need a context, a sense of the area of experience to which the idea relates. A discussion of general problems you have with your writing would be vague without specific instances such as the one Sissela Bok provides. The reader always needs a context for information, and examples supply this context. For additional discussion see 6.3.

4. Comparison and Contrast.   **Comparison** states the similarities between two or more things; **contrast** states the differences. The word *comparison* sometimes refers to both kinds of analysis.

The things being compared and contrasted usually have equal importance. In explaining the effects of aspirin and codeine as painkillers, you would need to give equal attention to both—citing similarities as well as differences. Some explanations deal with similarities only, others with differences only. Explanation

**1.4**
**dev**

of why aspirin and codeine kill pain requires discussion of the similarities only; explanation of why one drug is not addictive and the other drug is requires discussion of the differences only, though you may want to comment on the similarities. For additional discussion see 6.4.

5. Analogy.   **Analogy** is a special form of comparison used for illustration. The comparison is between two unlike things that share a few important characteristics. For example, you might give a point-by-point comparison of two activities—writing an essay and drawing a picture—to show how similar are the acts performed in each. The analogy is a good one if the differences do not significantly reduce the importance of the similarities. See 6.5 for more discussion of illustrative analogy and 32.2 for discussion of analogy used in argument.

6. Process.   A **process** is a series of connected acts, each leading to the next. Because of this interconnection, processes are repeatable, like a disease process that recurs as each person becomes infected. Some processes are natural ones—for example, swallowing and photosynthesis. Others are the inventions of human beings—for example, the process of writing an essay, riding a bicycle, or baking a cake. A process resembles narration in that the steps are presented chronologically, but narration and process are not the same thing because the events of narration need not be causally related.

Process analysis is particularly important in informative science reports. In maintaining lab notes, you will be keeping records of various processes. See 6.6 for additional discussion of process.

7. Causal Analysis.   You employ **causal analysis** in tracing the causes of an event or its effects or both. You might, for example, discuss the immediate and not-so-immediate events that led to your decision to attend college. Or you might discuss the effects of a book that influenced you in several ways.

Causal analysis is closely related to process analysis when it traces a chain of interconnected events. Not every such series constitutes a process, however. In a process, the events must occur and recur in the same order because of demonstrable causes. The economist who demonstrates that inflation always occurs when demand exceeds supply, and further shows that inflation has occurred repeatedly in this way, is trying to demonstrate a historical process. The biologist or medical researcher is asking the same kind of questions in examining a series of physiological events that seem related. In answering an exam question in an economics or biology class, you may be asked to trace a series of events and discuss whether they are interrelated and illustrate a process. See 6.6 on causal analysis in exposition and 32.3 on causal analysis in argument.

**1.4d Argument.**   Whereas exposition seeks merely to inform us about an event, an **argument** weighs evidence and draws conclusions. Many advertisements give information about a product and in doing so combine explanation with argument to state its benefits and defend the evidence presented for them. You use argument when you weigh the evidence you gathered in laboratory experiments and show how this evidence gives support to a hypothesis or scientific theory. You also use argument in giving reasons for your support of a political candidate or your opposition to a proposal or existing policy.

**1.4**
**dev**

The following paragraph argues that the American West expresses the American view of law and order—"the true source of lawlessness and disorder is not the people's licentiousness":

> The signs of it are always the same. Rude, bullying ruffians stalk the streets as though they owned them, shoot up the town for the fun of it, and make unseemly advances to gentlewomen. The sheriff does nothing; he is a drunkard or a coward or politically paralyzed. The mayor of the town turns a blind eye. We soon find out the cause of all this. The town is in the clutches of a lawless regime. Sometimes it is a cabal headed by the mustachioed owner of the gambling casino. More often, the town boss is the local cattle baron who long ago seized control of the town just as the great landed magnates of medieval Italy seized control of Italy's free communes. To the cattle baron of the Western, as to a medieval Visconti, a free community bordering one's demesne is intolerable and must be brought to heel.
> —WALTER KARP, "What Westerns Are All About,"
> *Horizon*, Summer 1975

The author builds a persuasive argument through facts that give strong support for the thesis concerning law and order. This assemblage of facts is a common form of argument in many kinds of writing. Another common form is systematic inference from beliefs or truths—the process referred to as **deduction.** Chapters 32-35 define and illustrate these important kinds of argument and distinguish good arguments from bad ones.

As we noted at the start of this section, description, narration, exposition, and argument together serve various purposes and in certain kinds of writing are inseparable. For example, an advertisement may describe a car in words or pictures, narrate a particular driver's experience with one of the cars, state the special or distinguishing features, and finally argue that these

**1.4**

**dev**

features are superior to those of another make. And various methods of analysis may develop the exposition of the car's features. Thus the advertisement may compare the two cars in detail, mentioning a few of the similarities but stressing the differences.

These, then, are ways in which occasions, audiences, and purposes invite decisions of various kinds. The following chapter describes the writing process in more detail—in particular, general stages of prewriting, writing, revision, and editing, and the various activities that occur in each of the stages. Chapter 3 traces the writing of an actual essay through these stages.

**EXERCISES**

1. Suggest how description may be used to develop each of the following topics for the purpose of expression, giving information, and persuasion:
   **a.** buying a used car
   **b.** registering for college classes
   **c.** losing a friend
   **d.** getting a traffic ticket
2. How might narration be used to develop each of these topics?
3. What methods of analysis would be appropriate in an exposition used to develop one of the topics?
4. Write a short account of an event you witnessed recently— a sports event or an unusual experience in traffic or at school. Include the following in your account:
   **a.** a narrative of the event
   **b.** a description of important aspects of it
   **c.** an explanation of the event as a whole or an aspect of it
   **d.** an argument defending the evidence presented in your explanation
5. Be ready to discuss the form of writing contained in the following paragraphs and the purpose the form might serve in an essay or book:

> a. The Suwannee is slow and crooked, molded by banks of gray sand in low water, spilling out through miles of eerie, moss-hung forests during flood. Large, pencil-legged heron and egret stand motionless in the shallows, as if waiting for something. Sometimes a bull alligator will bellow in the night, a deep anguished sound that carries for miles. The dark waters of the river come from a place where tall forests and fields of flowers lie awash in what could be the drift of an enchanted sea,

where on certain islands the ground trembles and trees lean if a man passes close to them.

—MICHAEL JENKINSON, *Wild Rivers of North America*

b. To understand television, think of a tall wire standing vertically, reaching from the ground to the sky, and radiating sound and light waves in the electromagnetic spectrum. Think of these waves moving out in all directions from the very top of the tall wire toward the horizon. The sound waves, at the horizon, will bend slightly and follow the earth's curvature for a relatively small distance. The light waves, however, will continue past the horizon in a straight line, tangent to the earth's surface, out into space. The limiting factor of a television signal, then, is the curvature of the earth at the visual horizon. Beyond that, television signals are on their way to another planet, perhaps, but they cannot be received by anyone on earth.

—ROBERT LEWIS SHAYON, *The Crowd-Catchers*

c. Eighteenth-century philosophers, who were fascinated by astronomy, noticed that the beneficent order of the universe is not the result of stars and suns' intending the general good of the universe. And the philosophers came to a similar conclusion about society: A good society is remarkably independent of individuals' willing the social good. A good society is a lumpy stew of individuals and groups, each with its own inherent "principle of motion." This stew stirs itself, and in the fullness of time, out comes a creamy pureé called "the public interest." This is the Cuisinart theory of justice. The endless maelstrom of individuals' pursuing private goods produces, magically, the public good. But of course it is not done by magic at all; it is done by definition.

—GEORGE F. WILL, *Statecraft As Soulcraft: What Government Does*

d. Why are the more massive stars hotter stars? The weight of the outer layers of a massive star causes great pressure at the center. If the star is not to collapse, it must attain a high temperature, since only then can the gas pressure balance this weight. The higher temperature increases the energy production, which maintains the star against its own gravity—which would otherwise cause it to fall in upon itself. If such a star overheats, it expands. The expansion cools the center, and the energy-production rate decreases, again stabilizing the star. Thus a star is a stable, giant, thermonuclear furnace—

a ball of gas held together by gravity and saved from collapse by the internal pressure of gas heated by the nuclear fuel.

—JESSE L. GREENSTEIN, "Natural History of a Star"

## Checklist for Writing Essays

**1.1**   Consider the occasion, audience, and your purpose in organizing and developing your essay.

**1.2a-b**   A general or mixed audience needs more details and examples than does a special audience.

**1.2c**   Gauging the knowledge and background of your audience is essential in deciding how to begin the essay.

**1.2d**   Capture the attention and interest of your readers through details of the subject.

**1.4a-b**   Description and narration can help in developing personal experiences and ideas.

**1.4c**   You can develop your exposition or explanation through one or more of the following—definition, division, classification, illustration, comparison and contrast, analogy, process, and causal analysis.

**1.4d**   Argument—a defense of an action, a policy, or a proposal—is an important way to persuade your readers.

# Finding and Analyzing a Subject

Experienced writers sometimes seem to put words on paper without previous thought or preparation—ideas and details appearing magically and falling into place effortlessly. Actually writers do prepare, and they also do considerable thinking and imagining in the course of writing. The act of writing is often an act of continuous rethinking and revision of the ideas and organization.

Writers prepare to write in a number of ways. They read extensively, browse in newspapers and magazines, keep diaries and journals, make lists and outlines, ask questions of themselves and others. Sometimes they quickly discover a topic or central idea and methods of developing it during the initial planning; at other times they give ideas considerable thought and work them out in trial paragraphs and longer drafts.

Few writers produce finished ideas and sentences that require no revision or editing. Many writers let their ideas and facts take shape slowly or "incubate." In an hour or a day, or with longer essays a week or a month, they return to these ideas and supporting facts and begin shaping them into an essay. They do so in their heads as well as on paper, arranging ideas and details, making lists, outlining, and drafting sentences and introductory or concluding paragraphs.

This chapter discusses various ways of finding a subject and then of analyzing it to discover relationships and common themes and possibly new ideas, impressions, and details.

## 2.1 Ways of Finding a Subject

**2.1a Reading and Discussion.** There is no substitute for reading in discovering new experiences and ways to use them

33

**2.1**

**dev**

in writing. Indeed much writing you do echoes reading you have done, though you may not be aware of this fact. You can return to this same reading for inspiration as you begin to write or in the course of the writing itself. Books, magazines, and the daily newspaper provide a constant source of ideas and impressions that later may suggest a subject or ways of developing an essay once you have a purpose in mind.

Many valuable ideas and details also come out of discussions with friends and, on occasion, interviews you participate in or conduct. In some of your college courses, you will engage in extensive discussion, and you will do so informally with your classmates. These are valuable sources of topics and ideas. Jotting them down in a notebook or recording them in a journal can be of immense help later.

**2.1b  Keeping a Diary or Journal.**   Many writers find that keeping a record of thoughts and impressions in a journal or diary helps generate ideas and serves as an aid to memory. Journals and diaries have different uses—the **journal** containing reflections and musings recorded at various times, the **diary** usually containing a day-to-day account of experiences and impressions. The columnist William Safire suggests that the diary is a valuable means of recovering forgotten ideas and details:

> Diaries remind us of details that would otherwise fade from memory and make less vivid our recollection. Navy Secretary Gideon Welles, whose private journal is an invaluable source for Civil War historians, watched Abraham Lincoln die in a room across the street from Ford's Theater and later jotted down a detail that puts the reader in the room: "The giant sufferer lay extended diagonally across the bed, which was not long enough for him . . ."          —"On Keeping a Diary"

The novelist Virginia Woolf kept a diary throughout most of her career, recording thoughts and impressions that she constantly put to use. In one entry, she discusses the value of writing rapidly and freely:

> I note however that this diary writing does not count as writing, since I have just reread my year's diary and am much struck by the rapid haphazard gallop at which it swings along, sometimes indeed jerking almost intolerably over the cobbles. Still if it were not written rather faster than the fastest typewriting, if I stopped and took thought, it would never be written at all; and the advantage of the method is that it sweeps up accidentally several stray matters which I should exclude if I hesitated, but which are the diamonds of the dustheap.
> —[January 20, 1919]

**2.1**
**dev**

The entry suggests perhaps the best reason for keeping a diary—to sweep up "the diamonds of the dustheap," stray thoughts and perceptions that may serve in looking for a subject. A diary or journal entry may provide the impulse to write an essay—perhaps one in which you use the idea or perception to explore your feelings or discover a truth about the world or about yourself. These ideas and perceptions can be the starting point of your exploration, and you may turn to them in the course of writing to discover other ideas. You may, indeed, want to jot down ideas for other essays at another time.

Diaries and journals of scientists need to be more precise in the recording of facts and ideas than the daily or occasional record of people and ideas. Scientists use journals to keep careful records of their findings, for they cannot risk trusting the details and the results of their research to memory. The notebook in your science course may serve the same purpose. In it you may keep a record of your experiments, giving an orderly account of each and making notes on your findings. You may also make notes on other possible lines of investigation.

In your composition course, you may find it useful to keep a journal of ideas and impressions suggested by your reading and class discussions. Such a journal can help in preparing to write short class papers as well as longer essays.

**2.1c Looking at the World.** The ideas you record may come from reading, reflection, or even daydreaming. Impressions may arise from looking at the world and recording observations of interest. You need not see a "point" in the observation that you record. Impressions you do record are like photographs of a fascinating or beautiful scene or object.

The randomness of these impressions makes them useful in finding a subject. The imagination has an opportunity to explore the world without guidance. In Virginia Woolf's diary a passage describing children at play shows the act of imagination and the sense of discovery that accompanies it:

> In the evening sometimes there's a game of stoolball. I caught them at it, as I stood in the road beneath, pink and blue and red and yellow frocks raised above me, and nothing behind them but the vast Asheham hills—a sight too beautiful for one pair of eyes. Instinctively I want someone to catch my overflow of pleasure. —[August 11, 1921]

Your notebook may do for you what her daily diary did for Virginia Woolf or what the sketchbook does for the artist: the notebook permits you to record the colors, sounds, smells, and shapes of the world. You may decide to record these in words

**2.1**

**dev**

and phrases that later you can form into sentences and paragraphs. However, words and phrases do need a context—a noting of their connection, perhaps a note too on their significance.

**2.1d Brainstorming.** Reading and discussion, notebooks and journals are direct ways to find a subject and generate ideas. But the discovery of impressions and ideas can also be indirect. On occasion you will find it useful to perform other activities that awaken the memory. William Least Heat Moon suggests the value of what he terms "skewed vision"—the technique of learning to see things in the dark by not looking at them directly. Letting your imagination play upon a subject is a way of skewing vision. For in letting imagination play, you are not thinking intently about the subject or its development or about a central point or thesis.

One of these activities is called brainstorming. In brainstorming, you depend on chance associations and discoveries that occur in quickly writing down words and phrases. The technique is similar to the jotting down of things to do—one activity often suggesting another. Brainstorming is especially useful in seeking an unusual point of view or approach to a subject. Scientific teams use brainstorming to discover ideas and new areas of investigation; government officials and business people use it to analyze problems and find solutions.

Brainstorming often starts with a specific topic or a general notion or idea. Assume that you need to find a topic for an essay assigned in your composition course—an essay to be based on personal experience for a purpose and audience of your choosing. One recent experience seems promising—your audition for the college orchestra.

In brainstorming, you quickly write down a few words and phrases suggested by the audition:

getting ready
auditions in high school
psyched up for tests in college skills
reasons for joining the orchestra

These in turn may suggest the following:

practicing
talking to orchestra members
high school orchestra audition
playing in high school orchestra
tryout for the high school tennis team
college entrance exams
doing math

performing for friends and family
playing for pleasure
performing with a group
sight reading
writing under pressure
intonation
breath control
timing
ensemble playing
not letting the mind wander
knowledge of music
talking to orchestra head
self-confidence
overcoming jitters
choosing a career

**2.1**
**dev**

Perhaps one of these words or phrases immediately suggests a limited topic and perspective. For example, *sight reading* may suggest a paper on skills required for a successful audition. The description of these skills may have several purposes, one possibly expressive of your feelings or autobiographical, another expository or explanatory—giving advice to people preparing to audition. Brainstorming is a valuable way of clarifying the purpose of the essay and defining the subject and audience exactly.

**2.1e Linking and Grouping Ideas.** If none of the ideas immediately suggest a topic, you might then analyze and sort the items to discover possible relationships, as in this grouping:

| *1* | *2* |
|---|---|
| performing with a group | talking to orchestra members |
| playing for pleasure | talking to orchestra head |
| choosing a career | practicing |

| *3* | *4* |
|---|---|
| sight reading | having self-confidence |
| ensemble playing | overcoming jitters |
| knowledge of music | not letting the mind wander |
| breath control | |
| intonation | |
| timing | |

*5*
high school orchestra tryout
playing in the high school orchestra
the high school tennis team
college entrance exams
writing under pressure
doing math

Looking to see what the items in each group have in common, you decide to label the five groups as follows:

1. Purpose of audition
2. Preparing for audition
3. Skills to be tested
4. Personal qualities needed for success
5. Previous experience

Very large groupings may suggest additional breakdowns. The fifth grouping, you decide, might be divided into two subgroups:

Previous experience
  Other auditions
  Playing in the high school orchestra

This random grouping may suggest a limited topic that you can write about from experience and observation.

Gabrielle Lusser Rico suggests an alternate method that she calls clustering.[1] Figure 2.1 illustrates the process using words and ideas from the list on p. 36. Figure 2.1(a) shows how the word *skills* leads the writer to the phrases *high school auditions* and *psyching up for tests*, these in turn suggesting *getting ready* and *college*. The phrase *tryout for tennis team* suggests the word *audition*, which in turn suggests the ideas and activities clustered with it.

Figure 2.1(b) illustrates additional clusters developed in the course of planning an essay on auditioning. As the various clusters show, the writer has broadened the original topic in describing the process of choosing a career in music. The original topic (auditions) has led to a new and interesting one.

Success in brainstorming depends on your writing down words and phrases quickly and letting your imagination play upon them. The particular advantage of clustering is in the visualizing of ideas and details and their numerous relationships. Of course, you will make many chance associations that you may decide not to use in writing your paper. None of these methods of discovery binds you to one topic or one approach.

Brainstorming and clustering need not be as extended as the particular search just illustrated. A quick jotting down of ideas and details may be sufficient to find your topic. Planning longer essays may require more, and you will have occasion to do additional brainstorming and clustering during the writing and revision of the essay.

[1]*Writing the Natural Way* (Los Angeles: Tarcher, 1983).

**2.1f Freewriting.** A technique similar to brainstorming calls for continuous, undirected writing—ideas and impressions put on paper without pausing to edit grammar, spelling, or punctuation. As in brainstorming and clustering, the success of freewriting depends on putting words on paper as quickly as possible. This procedure is thus similar to the improvisations of the musician whose fingers wander over the piano keyboard or trumpet keys at random. As new combinations of sound emerge in these improvisations, so do surprising images and ideas emerge in this kind of writing. The imagination has been brought to play upon the subject.

**2.1**
**dev**

Here is an example of freewriting prompted by a car ride into Cleveland from Akron:

```
        Coming in from the south on the interstate, first
a view of Cleveland on a bluff above a wide valley. An-
other interstate crosses the valley from east to west.
Then a sign for Broadview Heights, but already the view
is lost. No sense of height. Just ragged-looking frame
houses and just after you pass into Cleveland the
steelworks, belching smoke, one tall stack that looks
on fire. The car turns toward Terminal Tower past a
huge lot with what seems like hundreds of post office
delivery cars. Enormous lots on the other side of the
interstate, too. The turn of the road suddenly to down-
town and north. If you miss the turn into downtown or
up the Inner Belt to the lake, you pass over the river
that cuts the city in half. It doesn't look like much
of a river but it once caught fire, maybe the only
river in the U.S. that has happened to. What you notice
as you drive is what you expect to see.
```

Here is a revision of the paragraph, the details organized to develop a topic idea drawn from the final sentence:

```
        In driving into an unfamiliar city, you see what
you expect to. Driving into Cleveland from the south on
the interstate, the city comes into view across a wide
valley—on what seems a bluff. Perhaps you notice the
```

**FIGURE 2.1    Clustering**

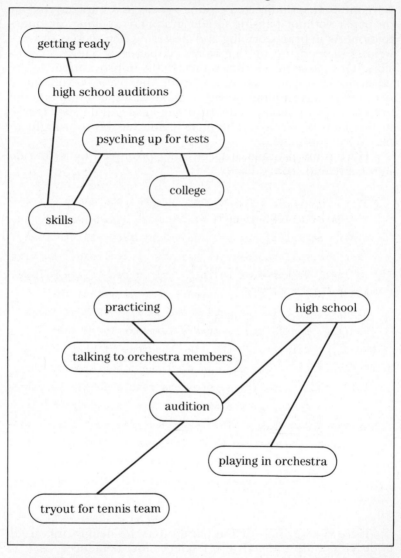

(a)

site, knowing you would pass through Broadview Heights
first. When you reach a sign marking the border of
Broadview Heights, the view has disappeared. You have
lost a sense of height: on each side of the road you

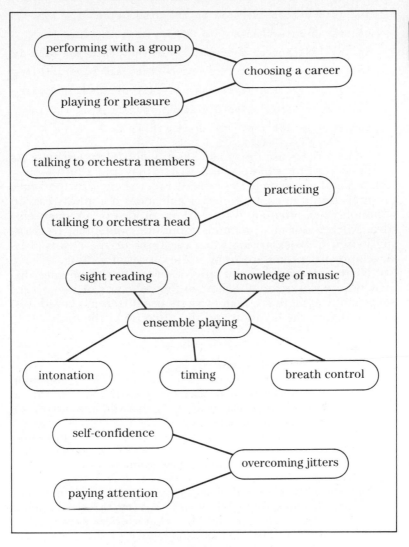

**(b)**

see only ragged frame houses and, shortly, as you pass
into Cleveland steelworks with stacks belching smoke.
One tall stack looks on fire. As the road turns toward
downtown, you pass a huge lot with what seems like

**2.1**

**dev**

hundreds of postal delivery cars. Enormous empty parking lots border the road on the other side. The road
passes an interchange, and if you miss the turn north
to the lake you pass over a river that cuts the city in
half and once caught fire—maybe the only river in the
United States that ever has. But all of these are mistaken impressions. The Cleveland you see from the interstate is not the city as it really is.

Some writers use the journal as a means of freewriting. As
in the preceding example, the writer may put down words,
phrases, and whole sentences rapidly. Freewriting gives the writer
an opportunity to capture images and ideas not always easy to
summon when attention is focused on an idea or a sequence of
ideas worked out in a preliminary outline. Sometimes freewriting loosens a block arising when the topic or the means of its
development are not apparent at the outset of writing.

Neither freewriting nor any other of the techniques discussed here works for all writers in the same way or even works
successfully at all times. Many writers use different procedures,
depending on the occasion and the purpose of the essay.

**EXERCISES**

1.  For a week keep a journal record of observations about your
    friends or fellow students. Record these without concern for
    possible meanings. Any trait or act that you find interesting
    or unusual is worth recording.
2.  Choose one of these observations and brainstorm it, writing
    down as quickly as possible every idea or image that it calls
    to mind. Again, don't look for a point or meaning in the
    idea or image.
3.  Classify the ideas and images you collected by putting them
    into obvious groups. When you complete this classification,
    name the quality or idea that characterizes each class. A
    quality or an idea that falls into none of the groups may
    constitute a class of its own.
4.  Choose one of the groups you arrived at, and write freely
    on any topic suggested by it. You need not have a point or
    central idea in mind as you do so. If a point or idea does
    occur to you, record and mark it for later use. Probably a
    number of such ideas will occur to you in the course of your
    writing.

## 2.2 Analyzing the Subject

**2.2a Lists and Outlines.** Brainstorming and freewriting are valuable ways of searching for a subject. But there are times when a simple list of items or topics will better serve your purpose. In preparing to write a quiz or examination answer, you may have time only to list points or details or to outline the topics if the answer is to take the form of an essay.

Topic outlines can be useful in analyzing the subject to find a limitation or specific focus for the essay. Here is a short topic outline—based on topics derived in 2.1—that may be sufficient for a short autobiographical paper.

```
TOPIC: How I perform at auditions
  I.   Earlier auditions and tryouts
       A.  The high school orchestra
       B.  Tennis team
  II.  Preparing the audition
       A.  Practicing
       B.  Psyching up
  III. Personal qualities and habits
```

Here is a topic outline for a longer paper comparing the experience of auditioning for the college orchestra with similar experiences in high school and college. Such a comparison would give important information to a friend preparing for an audition for the college band or orchestra or a tryout for a team sport.

```
TOPIC: Auditioning for the college orchestra
METHOD OF DEVELOPMENT: Comparison with other auditions
  I.   Getting ready
       A.  Getting information about the orchestra
           1.  Talking to orchestra members
           2.  Talking to orchestra head
       B.  Preparing the audition
           1.  Practicing
           2.  Getting into the right frame of mind
               a.  Developing self-confidence
```

```
        b.  Overcoming jitters
        c.  Concentrating on the audition and
            tryout
   II.  Getting ready for other auditions
        A.  High school experiences
            1.  Auditioning for the high school orchestra
            2.  Trying out for the high school tennis team
        B.  College experiences
            1.  College entrance exams
            2.  Classroom experiences
                a.  Writing under pressure
                b.  Working math problems
```

Assume that in outlining the essay you decide your topic or way of developing it is too broad. You therefore decide to limit your comparisons to high school or college experiences instead of trying to discuss both kinds. The outline is only a preliminary plan of action—one that you will change several times in the course of writing. In the act of writing a long essay, you will probably discover other ways to limit the topic or develop it. The longer the essay, probably the more backtracking and re-writing of the draft you will do.

**2.2b  Asking Questions.**   A useful way to analyze your subject is to ask the same questions that reporters ask:

| | |
|---|---|
| What? | What happened? |
| Who? | Who is responsible? |
| Where? | Where did the action occur? |
| When? | When did it occur? |
| How? | How did it occur? |
| Why? | Why did it occur? |

Newspaper and magazine writers often answer these questions in their opening paragraphs. Here is an example:

*Where*
*What*          Cape Canaveral, Fla.—Discovery, its space debut spoiled for a third time, remained grounded today while engineers checked out a computer
*Why*            program revamped to ensure that the shuttle misses no vital signals during liftoff. NASA rescheduled the launch for Thursday morning—24 hours and one minute later.

*Who*
*How*

With each new delay casting more doubt on the shuttle's dependability, officials nevertheless stopped the countdown clock late Tuesday night, less than 12 hours before today's planned 8:35 a.m. liftoff.

**2.2**
**dev**

*SPECIFIC*
*FOCUS*
*Why*

The postponement gives computer experts time to be absolutely certain they have fixed an electronic malfunction that could have prevented the new ship's booster rockets and fuel tank from peeling away after they exhausted their fuel. If they remained attached, their dead weight would block the shuttle from reaching orbit, and it would have to ditch in the Atlantic.

—*Akron Beacon Journal*, August 29, 1984

Once you have answered these six questions, you can decide which question to focus on in your discussion. The third paragraph of the preceding story focuses on the purpose of the flight's postponement. Here is an essential function of opening paragraphs in stories and essays: to give the reader direction, to give a specific focus.

Not all of these questions may be pertinent to your essay, but asking them at the start of your investigation can help you limit it properly and find a specific focus for the essay. Here is a paragraph that uses the question "why" to focus discussion on the rapid disappearances of rain forests throughout the world:

Why are these forests—the richest, oldest, most complex ecosystems on earth—being cut down at such a rate? Why destroy a forest? To sell its timber, to get at the gold and iron underneath, to get more land for agriculture. There are psychological motives, too: the wish to conquer nature; fear of the unknown; nationalistic and strategic desires to occupy uncontrolled regions. Overpopulation is usually cited as the main cause of deforestation. Rain forests are often used as safety valves by governments to defuse pressure for land reform. The safety-valve theory is misguided. Rain forests are not empty; small groups of people are already living wherever the forest can support human life. Nor is the intact forest idle. It conditions the soil, regulates rainfall, and maintains the water cycle far beyond its own borders. Most attempts to turn rain forest into farmland have failed disastrously, damaging the forest, disrupting the soil and water balance for other farmers, and leaving the settlers even more desperate for land.

—CATHERINE CAUFIELD, "The Rain Forests,"
*The New Yorker*, January 14, 1985

**2.2**

**dev**

This summary paragraph, occurring early in the essay, outlines causes and effects developed in detail later. In doing so, the paragraph serves as a guide for author and reader.

The following opening paragraphs from a talk to librarians do more. The writer informally states how the subject originated, defines the subject and focus, and briefly introduces the thesis:

> This was to be a talk about fantasy. But I have not been feeling very fanciful lately, and could not decide what to say; so I have been going about picking people's brains for ideas. "What about fantasy? Tell me something about fantasy." And one friend of mine said, "All right, I'll tell you something fantastic. Ten years ago, I went to the children's room of the library of such-and-such a city, and asked for *The Hobbit*; and the librarian told me, 'Oh, we keep that only in the adult collection; we don't feel that escapism is good for children.'"
>
> My friend and I had a good laugh and shudder over that, and we agreed that things have changed a great deal in these past ten years. That kind of moralistic censorship of works of fantasy is very uncommon now, in the children's libraries. But the fact that the children's libraries have become oases in the desert doesn't mean that there isn't still a desert. The point of view from which that librarian spoke still exists. She was merely reflecting, in perfect good faith, something that goes very deep in the American character: a moral disapproval of fantasy, a disapproval so intense, and often so aggressive, that I cannot help but see it as arising, fundamentally, from fear.
>
> —URSULA K. LE GUIN, "Why Are Americans Afraid of Dragons?"

**2.2c Particle, Wave, Field.**   In a special form of analysis (called tagmemic analysis), an object is looked at in three different ways:

1. as a **particle** or an **object**—as something existing at one particular moment, without concern for how it behaves or interacts with other objects;
2. as a **wave** or something in the **process** of moving or changing;
3. as something acting or functioning as part of a **field** or system, or as a system in itself—an organization of parts.

Here is an example of these three perspectives from a magazine report on laser lifts, devices that control spacecraft from the ground:

*Object*
*Process*

*Field*

A brilliant beam of laser light lances up from the ground, reflects off a mirror orbiting hundreds of miles away, and reaches toward a small rocket nozzle attached to one of the satellites. The rocket flares to life, propelling the satellite toward its desired final destination—an orbit higher than the shuttle can reach. Within a few minutes, each of the satellites has been sent on its way, propelled by the energy of the laser's beam.
—BEN BOVA, "A Laser Lift,"
*Science 84*, September, 1984

This kind of analysis begins in the foreground, close to the object, and in the course of the discussion moves away from it—far enough away to show the object in relation to other objects in its field. You as writer are viewing the object as a photographer does—from various angles that reveal its many qualities. In the third sentence of the paragraph, the author draws very far back to show the spatial relationship between laser beam and satellite. We know what a laser lift is when we know what it looks like (a laser is a brilliant beam of light), how it behaves (the laser lift reflects off a mirror and reaches toward a rocket nozzle), and how it fits into a system or field (it is responsible for the ignition of the rocket and propulsion of the satellite).

The analysis may give additional information about the object through the following:

1. how it differs from similar objects—for example, how laser lifts differ from other kinds of devices that lift spacecraft;
2. how much variation exists in the class or type—for example, how many designs of laser lifts exist;
3. how laser lifts fit into the general class of rocket fuels or propellants.

The article on laser lifts tells us how the device is different from the chemical rocket:

Unlike a chemical rocket, whose fiery power comes from the release of the fuel's inherent chemical energy, a laser rocket acts more like a huge teakettle. The laser itself never leaves Earth but fires an intense beam of light up into the spacecraft where it heats the propellant to such high temperatures and pressures that it comes spewing out the nozzle with tremendous energy.                        —BEN BOVA, "A Laser Lift"

This kind of analysis is often useful in deciding on a topic or focus for an essay. Assume you want to analyze the composition course you are taking. Your purpose in writing is to give information to a younger brother or sister who is considering college. You can view the composition course in the same three ways:

1. as **object**—the subject matter and aims of the course;
2. as **process**—the day-by-day activities, the process of learning to read and write;
3. as **field**—the place of the composition course in the curriculum or degree program of the college.

You might further develop the analysis through the following:

1. **contrast**—how English composition and beginning French differ in subject matter or day-by-day activity or in function in the curriculum or program of the student;
2. **variation**—how this composition course differs from similar courses at other schools;
3. **distribution**—how the beginning composition course relates to other writing courses offered by the college.

Some of these topics may require research—for example, talking with fellow students or with college officials, or reading college bulletins, journals, and books. This requirement may influence your choice of a topic and specific focus if you wish to write entirely from your own experience. See Chapters 36-38 for discussion of research methods and documentation.

**2.2d "Incubation."** Having found your subject and analyzed it, you may let the ideas, impressions, and details "incubate" in the mind. You have probably had the experience of waking after a night's sleep and discovering a way to organize ideas or solve a problem that puzzled you the day before. Many writers habitually wait a few hours or longer before they begin organizing and writing the essay. Though your first thoughts are often good ones, they may improve if you take the time to test them.

There is probably no single procedure that works well for every writer. Different techniques exist for different writing tasks. You will do different things in writing exams than you do in writing a documented paper. Furthermore, some writers work better through direct thinking and planning, others through the indirect techniques described in this chapter. You will discover the ways best for you by experimenting with these methods and working frequently with those that prove most useful.

**EXERCISES**

**2.2**
**dev**

1. Arrange the following topics into clusters that show their relationships. Then suggest several subjects that these topics might develop:
   a. aerating the soil
   b. clearing brush
   c. seeding
   d. weeding
   e. fertilizing
   f. destroying insects
   g. harvesting
   h. furrowing
   i. propping young plants
   j. pruning young plants
   k. watering
   l. propping mature plants
2. Write a scratch outline, then a formal topic outline for an essay on one of the subjects you discovered through your cluster. Write down methods of development appropriate to the essay.
3. Analyze a newspaper or magazine report of an important event to find out how many of the six questions listed in 2.2b are answered. Be ready to discuss how informative you find the report and why.
4. Show how one of the following can be viewed as an object, a process, or a system or field:
   a. a school team
   b. a fountain pen or ballpoint pen
   c. a tire jack
   d. a chemistry experiment
   What topics for an essay does your analysis suggest?
5. Opening paragraphs often suggest the focus of the essay—on the characteristics of an object, on a process, on the relationship of the object to others like it. In the following paragraphs, what words or phrases establish the focus?

> a. The 17,000 commercial bakeries of the U.S. turn out some 20 million loaves of bread per day, as well as large quantities of cakes, pies and cookies and such specialized items as pizza crust, bagels, croissants and hallah. The sheer volume has forced bakers increasingly toward advanced machinery and automatic processes. Rising demand (the results of marketing efforts) and new methods of distribution such as the in-store bakery (typically in a supermarket) and the franchised cookie shop have abetted the trend. This year the total size of

the market for wholesale, retail and in-store bakers is expected to be $30.1 billion.

—SAMUEL A. MATZ, "Modern Baking Technology," *Scientific American*, November 1984

**2.2 dev**

b. Inventors had begun to think about television more than a century ago, but they didn't call it that, and the very notion met its inevitable skeptics. "Shall we ever see by electricity?" wondered an editorial in *The Electrician*, a technical journal of the day. The answer, of course, is that there are now more than half a billion television sets in use, one for every 10 people on Earth. But without the television camera invented in 1923 by Vladimir K. Zworykin, who had arrived from Russia only a few years before, television would have remained a curiosity, captivating but impractical.

—DONALD G. FINK, "The Tube," *Science 84*, November

c. What is chance? Dictionaries define it as something fortuitous that happens unpredictably without discernible human intention. Chance is unintentional and capricious, but we needn't conclude that chance is immune from human intervention. Indeed, chance plays several distinct roles when humans react creatively with one another and with their environment.

—JAMES H. AUSTIN, "Four Kinds of Chance"

d. In simplest terms, a technology is a way of doing things with objects that are not part of one's own body. Technological change or innovation is the application of a new way of doing things that results in the modifications of the products, services, or processes that support society. These definitions are important because their very breadth emphasizes the pervasive nature of technological change in modern American society, our dependence upon technologies, and the enormous scope both of the opportunities and of the problems associated with them.

—IVAN L. BENNETT, JR., "Technology As a Shaping Force," *Daedalus*, Winter 1977

6. The following words and phrases suggest various connections. Connect them into a single cluster, in the manner shown on pp. 40–41. Then write down several topics suggested by the cluster and list ideas and details.

looking for defects

    tire tread                             oil consumption

           condition of engine

                         warranty

engine wear

       upholstery

                    reputation of dealer

      buying a used car

  buying from a friend

        buying from a dealer

                        financing

   biking

                   newspaper ads

          cheap transportation

       paying for college

   student loan

       commuting

renting an apartment        sharing an apartment

       college dorms

 taking the bus             living at home

# Checklist for Finding and Analyzing a Subject

**2.1a** Reading and discussion are indispensable in finding subjects and generating ideas and details.

**2.1b** Diaries and journals are helpful, too.

**2.1c** Personal experiences and observations of the world are your main sources of ideas and details.

**2.1d** Brainstorming is useful in recalling ideas and images stored in memory.

**2.1e** These ideas and images can be linked and grouped to discover patterns and common themes.

**2.1f** Freewriting is a valuable way to discover ideas and relieve writing blocks.

**2.2a-b** Lists, outlines, and questions will help you analyze a subject.

**2.2c** You can analyze an object in three different ways—as an object, a process, or a system or field.

**2.2d** Let ideas incubate to discover new ideas and ways of developing them.

# Writing a Personal Essay

The previous chapter discusses ways of finding a subject and searching for ideas and details. This chapter traces the writing of a personal essay—from the initial planning to the first draft. The following chapter describes the revision and editing of the same essay.

For the purpose of illustration, assume you do the following in writing a short essay. Having found a subject and searched for ideas and supporting details, you consider a specific focus and organization. You may do so with the help of a topic or sentence outline. In the course of outlining the paper and drafting a trial paragraph, a central idea or thesis may occur to you. So may new ideas and details and possibly a new focus or organization.

Unless the writing is *impromptu*—an essay you are asked to write without warning or preparation—writing the essay at a single sitting is exceptional. You may make several false starts before discovering a voice or tone suited to the subject. And in the course of writing you may also discover an improved focus or organization. "I make use of two or three cameras almost all the time," the Japanese film director Akira Kurosawa has said. "I cut the film freely and splice together the pieces which have caught the action most forcefully, as if flying from one piece to another." The same continuous revision marks all stages of the writing process, including the editing of the final draft. This general process, however, will vary with particular essays.

## 3.1 Purpose and Focus

**3.1a Defining Your Purpose.**   The topic and limitation you choose depend on your purpose. So does the length. Sometimes you decide how long your essay needs to be, and sometimes your audience decides. Newspapers and magazines often prescribe a length for letters and articles.

Consider a letter to a newspaper complaining about various services provided in your city—street repair, emergency health assistance, and garbage pickup. These are all matters of concern to you. You even consider discussing other city services like welfare and recreation. Figure 3.1 shows how many divisions are possible if the purpose of your letter is to encourage general improvements.

**3.1**

**dev**

Probably you have a limited purpose in mind—to give the letter's readers information about a specific problem and get their support in finding a solution. Assume your purpose is to get a pothole on your street repaired. You are generally concerned about inefficient city services, but you are particularly concerned about street repair, and you hope to persuade city officials to deal with this particular nuisance. Perhaps other readers will support your request.

However, you do want to call attention to inefficiency and indifference. In considering your purpose and audience, you

FIGURE 3.1   **Broad and Restricted Focus**

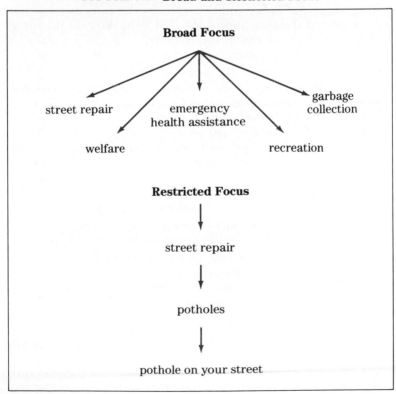

realize that your letter can deal with your general and specific concerns. Perhaps you can do so by making the pothole—your specific concern—your main topic and your general concern with city services your subordinate one.

The narrower the topic, the more specific your details will be. The broader your topic, probably the more general will be your examples—dangerous streets and roads rather than a spe- 'ific street and a particular pothole.

**3.1b  Choosing a Focus.**   You have limited your topic and decided how to present it. You choose next a specific focus—a view of the pothole that shows the seriousness of the problem and brings together your various concerns. A useful focus might be a description of the pothole from the viewpoint of an approaching driver or passenger in the car, or the viewpoint of an observer at curbside. Each of these views has its advantages. The curbside observer can give a broader picture of the dangers presented to the driver, passenger, and pedestrian. Driver and passenger can give details that the curbside observer cannot. In photographing a scene, you try to focus the camera from the best angle and distance and in the best light. You do the same in describing the hazards of the pothole.

### EXERCISES

1. Assume that one of the following statements has inspired you to write an essay. What purpose can the discussion of the idea serve? And to what audience would you write?

   a. In science the credit goes to the man who convinces the world, not to the man to whom the idea first occurs.    —SIR WILLIAM OSLER, *Life of Sir William Osler*

   b. The time to enjoy a European trip is about three weeks after unpacking.
   —GEORGE ADE, *The Hungry Man*

   c. An Idea isn't responsible for the people who believe in it.    —DON MARQUIS, *The Sun Dial*

   d. It's all that the young can do for the old, to shock them and keep them up to date.
   —GEORGE BERNARD SHAW, *Fanny's First Play*

2. What general limitation will help you best to satisfy your purpose in writing and communicate most effectively with your audience?

3. What more specific focus will help you be more detailed and more persuasive?

4. Write an essay on one of the preceding four statements to illustrate your answers to these questions.

# 3.2 Organization and Unity

**3.2a The Meaning of Unity.** After defining the purpose of your letter and deciding on a focus, you are ready to organize your discussion and give it unity. **Unity** means that the essay develops one idea at a time and develops it fully. It also means that where various methods together develop the essay—description, narration, and exposition, for example—the essay does not switch from one to another without warning the reader.

Since the purpose of the letter is to generate support in readers of the newspaper and perhaps awaken concern in city officials, the first consideration is how much description and narration to use and how much explanation to give. The order of your reasons for adopting new procedures needs to be considered. And so does the order or arrangement of the main divisions of the letter—the description of the pothole, your explanation of the hazards, your argument weighing the cost and benefit of repair. The greater the number of parts or divisions, the more attention you need to give the coherence and unity of the letter.

The arrangement and coherence of these parts depend on your purpose in writing. Since your purpose is to get the pothole repaired, your description of it and a narrative of the accident may be more effective if presented before your explanation of why safe streets are a wise investment. Since the idea or the details that come at the end of the letter will seem the most prominent or emphatic, you will be most persuasive in concluding with the points you want readers to remember most.

**3.2b Unity and Audience.** Special audiences suggest special ways of organizing sections and the essay as a whole. For example, how to sail a boat or repair a flat tire can be explained in various ways. The most obvious is to present the steps chronologically. Others are possible if the audience is familiar with sailing or repairing tires. Auto mechanics, for example, probably do not require a full description of how a new tire jack works. And you need not present steps chronologically: you might begin with less familiar or more difficult steps, giving brief attention to familiar and easy ones in the course of your explanation.

**EXERCISE**

Suggest different ways the following topics might be developed in an informative essay addressed to beginning drivers who have received driving instruction but have had little driving

**3.3**

**dev**

experience. Suggest what methods of development—description, narration, exposition, argument—are appropriate to your purpose and audience:
   **a.** parking on a hill
   **b.** backing into a narrow space
   **c.** entering a heavily traveled expressway
   **d.** parallel parking

## 3.3 Thesis

**3.3a  What a Thesis Is.**  The word **thesis** refers to the central idea or the central proposal or point being argued in the persuasive essay. The central idea of expressive and informative essays is sometimes called the thesis. We will use *thesis* to refer to the central point or idea in these kinds of essays, too.

Not all essays contain a thesis. Essays that express personal feelings or develop impressions of people or places may have no central point though the writer organizes the essay through a central feeling or impression. A set of directions usually makes no point about the process to be performed, though an essay comparing two ways of performing the process may argue that one is better than the other.

Note that a thesis is not the same as a statement of intention or a statement of subject. Your letter to the editor might begin with statements like the following:

> My purpose in writing is to discuss a danger to drivers. A large pothole is causing accidents on my street.

These sentences state the purpose and subject of the letter and inform the newspaper readers of why you are writing it. Neither is a substitute for the thesis—the direct statement that you want the pothole repaired:

> To prevent further accidents, the city must repair the pothole immediately.

**3.3b  Placing the Thesis.**  Where should you place the thesis—at the beginning of the essay, at the middle, or at the end? The answer depends on how much trouble the reader will have understanding it. The placement depends also on how controversial the thesis is. In argumentative essays, the thesis is often stated toward the beginning and restated at the end, following a review of the evidence for it. If the thesis will not be understood without explanatory detail, or if it is so controversial that the evidence in its favor is best presented first, you may decide to build up to it. The same considerations apply to other kinds of essays.

Most essayists prefer to state the thesis early to guide the reader through the discussion and details. The same is true of the central impression in expressive essays that merely describe a person or scene or narrate a personal experience. On occasion, you may wish to delay the statement until the end, to let the details make their effect before you interpret them.

**3.3 dev**

**3.3c Thesis as Controlling Idea.** Regardless of where it appears in the letter or essay, the thesis serves as the controlling idea to which other ideas and all details relate. Here is the opening paragraph of a late chapter of a book on the rights of children. The opening sentence states the thesis of the chapter— that children have the right to earn money and keep it for their own uses. The remainder of the paragraph relates the thesis to earlier rights discussed in the book:

> Children, of any age, should have the right to work for money and to own and use, spend or save, the money they earn. This right, like the right to vote or to manage one's own learning, can stand alone. It could be granted to young people even if no other adults rights were granted.

This thesis paragraph guides the reader through a long account of problems arising from the lack of work. An early paragraph traces the rise of urban youth gangs to a lack of work:

> During the 1950s young people in many large cities formed gangs, each defending a turf and fighting other gangs. Gang activity grew less during the late 60s, but it has now flared up again and in many cities is an increasingly serious and even terrifying problem. Today's gangs are bigger, armed with real guns instead of homemade weapons, and are increasingly criminal and violent. No one seems to have the least idea what to do about them. We might for a start try letting them grow up. Many of those who wrote about gangs and gang members in the 1950s asked the question: What (other than being killed or jailed) makes gang members give up the gang life? In most cases the answer was, being able to get a job, to have money, to get away from their families, to make their own homes, and to get married and start their own families. What was even more striking was that when a gang member became old enough to do these things, the younger gang members did not try to keep him in the gang but let him go, as if they knew very well that gang life was kid stuff, to be given up when you had a chance to do something more grown-up and serious.
> —JOHN HOLT, "The Right to Work"

**3.4**

**dev**

The topic sentences of many later paragraphs in Holt's essay develop the thesis in various ways. Here are several:

Work is novel, adventurous, another way of exploring the world.

Work often makes a visible difference in the world.

Any work is good for children in which they can see what they are doing, how much they are doing, and how well they are doing it.

Like the paragraph on youth gangs, the paragraphs introduced by these sentences contain details that also develop the thesis in various ways. Both the opening thesis of the essay and the topic sentences of the paragraphs give these details a clear focus.

The thesis of an essay, then, can express the central idea, control the amount of detail, and establish a focus and dominant tone. All of these help create in the reader expectations of what the essay will try to accomplish.

**EXERCISES**

1. Locate the thesis in the letters to the editor of a newspaper. Be ready to discuss whether each letter would be more effective had the thesis been presented in a different place and in a different way.
2. Rewrite one of these letters, presenting the thesis in a different place. Make any other changes that you believe will improve the letter, and be ready to justify your changes.

# 3.4 Writing a Personal Essay: Choosing a Topic

The rest of this chapter traces the writing of a particular essay, the kind sometimes assigned at the start of composition courses—a personal essay that uses personal experiences to develop a thesis. We will trace the process from the initial choice of topic to later revisions and the final editing. Later chapters will consider other types of essays.

**3.4a  A Note on the Personal Essay.**  Though personal essays are mainly expressive, they can also be informative and even persuasive. Job or college applications often require a personal statement of interests and goals as well as information about previous employment or education. Newspaper and magazine columnists like Russell Baker, Ellen Goodman, William

Raspberry, Roger Rosenblatt, and Andy Rooney often use their personal experiences to argue a point.

Often the personal essay is a short autobiography—an autobiography of the moment that tells us what the author is thinking or feeling in putting words on paper. The word *essay* suggests this kind of momentary flight of mind or exploration—being derived from a Latin word meaning *to weigh*. "I add, but I do not correct," the French essayist Montaigne wrote about his early personal essays, some of which resemble the journal entries discussed in 2.1b. The writing of essays was for Montaigne, as it is for many essayists today, an act of continuing self-discovery. "I desire to be seen in my simple, natural, and everyday dress, without artifice or constraint; for it is myself I portray."

Since personal essays have different purposes, they have different kinds of focus and organization. These differences explain why no two personal essays—or indeed essays of any kind—are written quite in the same way.

You can write personal essays on any topic that captures your imagination and interest. In a popular collection of humorous essays, the television commentator and writer Andy Rooney discusses soap, jeans, warranties, mail, names of streets and banks, watching football on television, Fourth of July statistics, the draft, hair, eyeglasses, and telephones. The newspaper columnist Ellen Goodman writes on a wide range of important issues of the day—crime, the draft, raising children, changes in family life. Tom Wicker and George F. Will write on a wide variety of topics suggested by current political and social events. No two essayists write with the same opinions or attitudes or from the same point of view.

**3.4b Characteristics of the Personal Essay.**   However humorous or serious your essay may be, the topic is one you should make your own. An essay will be your own if you choose a topic with these characteristics:

- The topic is one to which you can bring personal knowledge and experience.
- The topic reveals your personal interests and concerns.
- The topic lets you say something interesting or important about yourself or about the world.
- The topic is restricted enough to explore experiences in depth.

**3.4c Experiences and Thoughts.**   Assume that earlier in the day you were delayed at the bank auto-teller because of a "down" computer and consequently missed a class. This unpleasant experience is one of several recent ones caused by non-working computers.

You have also had some pleasant and interesting experiences with computers. Perhaps the magazine advertisement shown in Figure 3.2 catches your eye and reminds you of other personal experiences. The ad talks about the many uses of home computers including planning the family budget or computing "anything from interest paid to calories consumed." One sentence in particular describes an experience of your own:

> Because just by playing games or drawing colorful graphics, your son or daughter will discover what makes a computer tick—and what it can do. They can take the same word processing program you use to create business reports to write and edit book reports (and learn to type in the process).

It occurs to you in reading the ad that computers very much complicate life today, as your experience at the bank shows. You recall a newspaper story on trouble new government computers have been causing taxpayers. Yet, as the ad suggests, computers do have their good points.

Here may be a topic for a personal essay you have been assigned to write in your composition course. It is to be an essay on a topic of your choosing that says something important and interesting about you or about the world. The topic you consider is the following:

> How computers affect our lives.

**3.4d  The Broad Topic and the Narrow.**  Because you have had various experiences with computers, the topic looks promising. But how broad should the topic and its discussion be?

An essay on so broad a topic as the many effects of computers probably will be extremely general. In the space of a few pages, you will probably state some ideas or give details about computers, perhaps referring to personal experiences. You will not be able to develop your ideas or experiences or connect them.

However, your essay need not be either an abstract discussion of computers or a highly detailed account of your experiences from which you draw no conclusions. Though some essays do consist only of ideas and others consist of an assemblage of facts or details, most essays contain both. The reason is that, in thinking about a topic, you usually range between ideas and the experiences that suggest them. You know, too, that others think the same way. As readers and writers, we are fascinated by events as well as ideas.

## FIGURE 3.2

# "Dad, can I use the IBM computer tonight?"

It's not an unusual phenomenon. It starts when your son asks to borrow a tie. Or when your daughter wants to use your metal racquet. Sometimes you let them. Often you don't. But when they start asking to use your IBM Personal Computer, it's better to say yes.

Because learning about computers is a subject your kids can study and enjoy at home.

It's also a fact that the IBM Personal Computer can be as useful in your home as it is in your office. To help plan the family budget, for instance. Or to compute anything from interest paid to calories consumed. You can even tap directly into the Dow Jones data bank with your telephone and an inexpensive adapter.

But as surely as an IBM Personal Computer can help you, it can also help your children. Because just by playing games or drawing colorful graphics, your son or daughter will discover what makes a computer tick—and what it can do. They can take the same word processing program you use to create business reports to write and edit book reports (and learn how to type in the process).Your kids might even get so "computer smart," they'll start writing their own programs in BASIC or Pascal.

Ultimately, an IBM Personal Computer can be one of the best investments you make in your family's future. And one of the least expensive. Starting at less than $1,600 † there's a system that, with the addition of one simple device, hooks up to your home TV and uses your audio cassette recorder.

To introduce your family to the IBM Personal Computer, visit any ComputerLand® store or Sears Business Systems Center. Or see it all at one of our IBM Product Centers. (The IBM Data Processing Division will serve business customers who want to purchase in quantity.)

And remember. When your kids ask to use your IBM Personal Computer, let them. But just make sure you can get it back. After all, your son's still wearing that tie. **IBM**

### The IBM Personal Computer and me.

†This price applies to IBM Product Centers. Prices may vary at other stores.

For the IBM Personal Computer dealer nearest you, call (800) 447-4700. In Illinois, (800) 322-4400. In Alaska or Hawaii, (800) 447-0890.

Courtesy of International Business Machines Corporation.

**3.5**

**dev**

The more specific and well focused your essay, the more your readers will be able to relate their experiences to yours. In picking a topic, then, you might begin with personal experience, showing how computers have changed your life. You could then show how your experiences resemble those of friends or family. From experiences such as these you can proceed to ideas that readers can test by their own experience.

Here is a narrower statement of the topic:

How computers affect my life.

In its dependence on your personal experience and knowledge, this topic is an improvement over the first. The topic will let you say something about yourself and at the same time say something about other people and their experience.

**EXERCISES**

1. Here are the characteristics of a topic you have made your own:
   - The topic is one to which you bring personal knowledge and experience.
   - The topic reveals your personal interests and concerns.
   - The topic lets you say something interesting and important about yourself or your world.
   - The topic is limited enough for you to explore it in depth.

   Suggest an aspect of the following topics that would meet these four characteristics:
   **a.** outdoor cooking
   **b.** tall people and short
   **c.** fat people and thin
   **d.** city neighborhoods

2. Quickly write down the images and ideas brought to mind by an advertisement. Make a list of topics suggested by these images and ideas. Then single out a few that meet these four characteristics. Be ready to discuss how they do.

## **3.5** Limiting the Topic Further

**3.5a  A Narrower Range of Topics.**   How much can you say about your experience with computers in an essay of 600 to 800 words—the length of the essay assigned?

Writing on all the calculators and computers that affect your life, or only about those that affect you in a single day, you would have space for a few details on each. Here are some you might discuss:

- the computer that runs the automatic teller at the bank you visited
- the pocket calculator you used at the grocery store
- the calculator used for your math homework the night before
- the word processor used to write a high school term paper
- the computerized catalog that gives you information on books at other libraries
- the computer on which you are learning to program in a college course

**3.5b Classifying the Topics.** The calculators and computers mentioned in this list are so various that you need first to sort them out and organize them in some way. There are various ways of classifying them. The general classes you choose depend on the purpose of your analysis and the point you want to make through it.

The computers and calculators might be put into these classes:

1. those you have had experience with in school
2. those you have had experience with outside school

This classification may help you reach some tentative ideas, one of which may serve as a thesis for your essay.

Here are a few ideas that might occur to you in thinking about or possibly brainstorming the subject. Some are suggested by experiences outside school:

- Because computers now do the jobs of people, we have little contact with people in banks and other work places.
- Computers make business transactions impersonal.
- Pocket calculators make it easier to keep track of money.
- Computers make the world a smaller place.

Computers used at school suggest other ideas:

- Computers make it easier to write course papers.
- Computers make it easier to find books in the library.
- Computers save time in solving problems in math.
- I am freer to think when I use a pocket calculator than when I do the figuring in my head.

Sorting ideas in this way sometimes suggests an unusual idea or point of view from which to consider the subject.

Here is an example. Suppose that, during your sophomore year in high school, your parents opposed your using a calculator in a math course. It occurs to you that the reasons they gave were not the real ones; for contrary to their prediction, your work in math improved.

Here is a promising topic suggested by your personal experience. An essay describing it will tell the reader about your interests and concerns, and it may lead to an idea or a thesis worth developing. The topic also relates to other experiences that may be worth exploring—for example, your experience with calculators in college math and other courses. And you recall your experiences writing for the first time with a personal computer that serves as a word processor. Perhaps new ideas and episodes will occur to you in the process of writing about your high school and college experience.

### EXERCISES

1. Topics are often generated by the reading you do—a newspaper account of a computer malfunction at a bank or a power plant, a discussion like the following in a book on the social uses of computers. Though the discussion may not have immediate bearing on your own experience, it may suggest ideas for exploration of comparable situations or needs in your own life. Following a quick reading of the paragraph, write down as many ideas or comparable situations as you can think of:

> The need for complex behavior by machines is quite apparent in many cases. To take one simple example, consider the problems that will face those who will try to explore the surface of Mars. They will want to send machines to do the work, but the machines will inevitably face situations that were not foreseen by the planners back on Earth, and the round trip signalling time from Mars to Earth and back to Mars will run into quite a few minutes, during which disaster may face the exploring equipment. Thus it will be necessary to any sophisticated machine exploration to have a program in the local (on Mars) computer that is directing the equipment, a program which has the ability to make choices and call for actions in situations that have not all been carefully examined beforehand. We will want at least a low level of intelligence for the machines we send to Mars to explore and relay back their measured results.
>
> —RICHARD W. HAMMING, *Computers and Society*

2. Be ready to discuss which of the ideas or topics in 3.5a and 3.5b can best be developed in an essay that lets you do the following:
   a. Use your personal experience and knowledge.
   b. Say something important and interesting about yourself.
   c. Say something important and interesting about other people and their experiences.

**3.** How might each of the following statements be limited to meet the three aims just named:

    a. You might as well fall flat on your face as lean over too far backward.

        —JAMES THURBER, *The Bear Who Let It Alone*

    b. It is easier for a man to be loyal to his club than to his planet; the by-laws are shorter, and he is personally acquainted with the other members.

        —E. B. WHITE, *One Man's Meat*

    c. If you have to keep reminding yourself of a thing, perhaps it isn't so.

        —CHRISTOPHER MORLEY, *Thunder on the Left*

    d. Necessity never made a good bargain.

        —BENJAMIN FRANKLIN, *Poor Richard's Almanac*

# **3.6** Organizing the Paper

**3.6a Outlining.** Your high school experience with calculators looks promising as a topic. So does a comparison of calculators in college math courses and different kinds of computers whose usefulness is perhaps not so obvious. You jot down a few ideas that suggest a plan:

```
High school
    Doing math with a calculator
    Using a personal computer for English papers
College
    Doing math and English
    Using a PC to write a term paper
    Using the computerized catalog at the library
```

This range of topics is so broad that you decide to narrow the comparison to your experiences in high school math and English. Here is a short topic outline that works out the comparison:

```
I.  High school experiences with calculators
    A.  Math courses
    B.  Attitude of teachers
    C.  Attitude of my parents
```

**3.6**

**dev**

II.  High school experiences with a personal computer

    A.  Writing a paper on a word processor

    B.  Attitude of teachers

**3.6b  A Trial Paragraph.**   With the help of this outline, you begin your essay with a freely written trial paragraph introducing your experiences. The purpose of this free, unfocused writing is to find a focus for the essay and test the comparison in your outline. In writing the paragraph, you state your subject and give a brief account of your experience, without concern for a specific central idea:

*Trial Paragraph*

    Like most teenagers my experience with computers began with video games I played as a teenager at the mall near our house in Akron. These video games sparked my interest in computers, and pocket calculators got me interested too. I first used a pocket calculator in a math course in junior high school I was having trouble with. I found right away I was doing better in math, I wasn't making my usual dumb mistakes. But my parents were against them because I would go on making the same mistakes using one. My math teacher in junior high school must have thought so too because he said something one day. But my situation changed in senior high. I was getting better. Dividing with decimals. Dividing fractions. Multiplying. The "new math" was easier for me than the old was for my parents, which they didn't understand. But they changed their minds when my math got better.

**3.6c  A New Outline.**   As you work through your trial paragraph, you discover you have less to say about calculators than about word processors. You decide therefore to focus on your experience with a processor, introducing this main topic through your experience with calculators. Here is a revised topic outline:

I.  My experience with calculators and word processors

    A.  High school math

```
     B.  Experience in college courses
         1.  Math
         2.  English
II.  Attitudes toward calculators and processors
     A.  Parents'
     B.  Teachers'
     C.  My own attitude
```

**3.6**
**dev**

Remember that your outline is merely an inventory of ideas and details, arranged to show the relationship of main and subordinate ideas. You should not think of the outline as a fixed plan, a blueprint for the essay to be followed without change. It is only an aid to your thinking and writing.

**3.6d A Tentative Thesis.** In revising the paragraph, you jotted down these ideas:

```
Calculators ease the work in math courses.
Computers ease the writing of course papers.
People are suspicious of things that make them
feel helpless.
```

Which of these ideas is the most promising? Which one draws most upon personal experience?

The first two ideas can be developed from personal experience: calculators do ease work in math and computers do ease the writing of term papers. But do they ease work in the same way? And if they do, are the reasons important enough to investigate? This topic turns out to be less promising.

What about the suspicion about computers? Is the source of suspicion fear of mechanical devices—like the public's attitude toward the telephone and automobile at the time they came into use? Or are people really afraid of being displaced by machines? Does your personal experience with computers suggest an answer? These questions are so broad and speculative that your essay is likely to be unfocused and vague.

The hostility you notice in your parents and teachers seems the most promising topic. You have direct, personal experience to draw upon. The topic suggests several ideas that might be explored. Your revised trial paragraph joins various ideas into a single focus.

You are ready now to expand the trial paragraph into a draft of your essay. The draft that follows, like most rough drafts, contains careless errors that need correction in the revision and final editing. The next chapter illustrates these final stages of the writing process.

**3.7** The First Draft

WRITING WITH A WORD PROCESSOR

Like most teenagers my experience with computers began with video games I played as a teenager at the mall near our house in Akron. These video games sparked my interest in computers, and pocket calculators got me interested, too. I first used a pocket calculator in a math course in junior high school I was having trouble with. I found right away I was doing better in math, I wasn't making my usual dumb mistakes. But my parents were against them because I would go on making the same mistakes using one. My math teacher must have thought so too because he said something one day. But the situation changed in senior high. I was getting better. Dividing with decimals. Dividing fractions. Multiplying. The "new math" was easier for me than the old was for my parents, which they didn't understand. But they changed their minds when my math got better.

I used a word processor to write my English papers my last year in high school. My parents were suspicious, and so was my English teacher. Their attitude shows why people are sometimes suspicious of computers. The keyboard of a word processor works like a typewriter, but "function keys" do more jobs than typewriter keys. The words you type appear on the "monitor" or screen above the keyboard. You "edit" them on the screen by erasing whole words or lines or moving them around. You need these extra keys to do this. One advantage of word processors is that it's easy to make changes as you write. Another is you don't have to retype pages.

The computer I use has a printer attached to it. By pressing a button, the text on the screen can be transferred to "hard copy"—which is computer jargon for the kind of typed copy the writer produces on the typewriter-like printer. The printer prints directly from the screen, removing any chance of making a typing error if you "edit" the paper right.

I think teachers are suspicious of calculators and processors because they think writing should be work. For example, the processor and printer seem to be doing all the work. But the word processor doesn't write the paper. And the printer just reproduces what you have written on the processor. The real work is writing and editing the words on the screen, and it is work that takes more skill than writing with a typewriter. I think my math teacher didn't like my using a calculator for the same reason, though my friends did have the same problem with their math teachers. But I think the reasons for not liking these devices go deeper.

Teachers are like parents—at least mine in high school were. Growing up, I heard a good deal from my parents about "being your own person." Parents want kids to be independent. But not so independent they make decisions without asking, which is what I did in deciding to switch into electrical engineering last year. Teachers are the same when they talk about "doing your own work." I think they can be worse. My teachers were. I think because they are paid to know all the answers. And they usually do.

## EXERCISES

1. Review the topics you limited in the exercises in 3.4d. Write down ideas these topics suggest to you—ideas that might serve as a thesis in an essay of your own.
2. The following passages present experiences and observations from which a variety of conclusions might be drawn.

Write down some possible conclusions or ideas suggested by one of them:

a. If you were to ask a qualified driver what he had to do to start his car, he would probably list a series of actions which would include turning on the ignition, pressing the clutch, and shifting the stick into first gear. For each of these steps it would be possible to give an answer to the question "How is it performed?" To turn on the ignition, you have to twist the key clockwise; to disengage the clutch you have to press down on the pedal with your right foot. As you push the enquiry backwards, however, there comes a point when the questions no longer make sense. It sounds nonsensical to ask someone what he has to do to twist the ignition key, or to press down with his right foot. He would be able to demonstrate each of these actions simply by doing them, but he would be unable to describe the steps he had to take in order to get them done.

—JONATHAN MILLER, *The Body in Question*

b. Let's examine a typical American conversation. Joan and Sandra meet on the sidewalk. Preliminary greetings over with, Joan begins to talk. She starts by looking right away from Sandra. As she hits her conversational stride, she glances back at her friend from time to time at the end of a phrase or a sentence. She does not look at her during hesitations or pauses but only at natural breaks in the flow of her talk. At the end of what she wants to say, she gives Sandra a rather longer glance. Experiments indicate that if she fails to do this, Sandra, not recognizing that it is her turn to talk, will hesitate or will say nothing at all.

—FLORA DAVIS, "The Language of the Eyes"

3. Write down as quickly as you can as many ideas and facts or experiences suggested by one of the following as possible:
   **a.** pop music          **d.** greeting cards
   **b.** reading the newspaper    **e.** household chores
   **c.** comic strips
   Now look for patterns in these ideas and facts, grouping them in various ways. Select one of these patterns and use it to organize an essay that says something important about yourself and your world.
4. What additional ideas or terms would need to be explained and illustrated further if the essay on writing with a word processor were directed to children? Rewrite one of the paragraphs for such an audience.

5. Here are three different revisions of the first draft. What changes did the revisers make in organizing the whole essay? Do you consider the essay improved by these changes?

**3.7**

**dev**

*Revision 1*

Teachers and parents are alike——they both want you to do the best while being your own person. But they are inconsistent. I experienced this inconsistency using computer aids in the course of my academic career. It was in a difficult junior high school math course that I first used a calculator, and I found I was doing better because of it. My mind was free to do the important work. Later in high school my algebra and trig classes did not require the use of a calculator. Now in college, I am using a calculator frequently in my engineering courses. My parents, however, feel I would be a better student if I learned math the same way they did. My teachers show the same thinking by insisting on working out the problems to demonstrate your understanding. Whether that would make me a better student is hard to say.

My parents and teachers think in the same way about my writing papers for English on a word processor. Both are suspicious of computers because of a lack of understanding. They think writing should be work. For example, the processor and printer seem to be doing the work of the student. But the processor doesn't write the paper, and the printer just reproduces what the student has written on the processor. What they fail to understand is the real work in writing and editing the text on the screen. This is work that requires more skill than working on a typewriter; nevertheless, the two are alike. But the keyboard of a word processor is provided with

**3.7**
**dev**

"function keys" for the other jobs a processor
can do. The words you type appear on the screen
or "monitor" above the keyboard, and you "edit"
them on the screen by erasing whole words or
lines or moving them around. This is one of the
advantages of a processor—it makes it easy to
change what you write.

The personal computer I have been working
with has a printer attached to it. By your pressing a button, the words on the screen can be
transferred to "hard copy"—which is computer jargon for typed copy. The printer is worth mentioning; it prints directly from the screen, removing
any chance of typing error if the words have been
edited correctly.

Parents and teachers want you to do your own
work independently and make your own decisions.
But teachers are worse, at least mine were, because they are paid to know all the right answers, and they look at computers only from their
point of view.

*Revision 2*

Teachers are like parents in that they talk
about "being your own person." Parents want children to be independent but not so independent
that they make decisions without their input
(which is what I did when I decided to become an
engineer). Even more definitely than parents,
teachers frequently talk about "doing your own
work."

Today the word processor and the printer
seem to be doing the work of the student. Perhaps
teachers are suspicious of calculators and processors because they think writing should be

work. But the processor doesn't write the paper, and the printer just reproduces what the student has written on the processor. Perhaps math teachers are suspicious of calculators for the same reason.

Writing papers on a word processor, I became aware of the suspicious attitude toward computers of both my parents and teachers. To first understand the function of the word processor, you must compare it to a typewriter. It does the same jobs through function keys, and it does more. The words you type appear on the monitor screen above the keyboard, and you edit them on the screen by erasing or moving whole words or lines. Extra keys enable you to do this. One of the advantages of writing on a processor is that you can make changes as you write; therefore, you don't have to retype pages.

I have been working with a personal computer that has an attached printer. The text on the screen can be transferred to "hard copy" (computer jargon for typed copy) with the press of a button. The printer prints directly from the screen, removing any chance of typing error if the text has been edited correctly. This process clearly has advantages over typing just as using a calculator has advantages over laborious mental calculations.

I first used a calculator in a junior high math course, and I found I was doing better work than I had done before because my mind was free to work on the main problems. The situation changed in senior high school. I was able to do well in both algebra and trig without using a calculator. Today in engineering courses I find

the calculator makes my work easier. I conclude
that there are appropriate uses for both the calculator and the word processor. I don't know if I
would be better at math if I hadn't learned to
depend on a calculator. I'm sure my parents think
I would be doing better if I had learned to do
math the same as they.

*Revision 3*

My family is like most families. It is
caught up in a generation gap. The main reason
for this gap, I feel, is that I am more accus-
tomed to modern technology. It all started in
school with my calculator.

I first used a calculator in a junior high
math course I was having trouble with, and I soon
found I was doing better work than before. I was
able to concentrate on the main problem. I know
that using a calculator makes this work easier,
but whether I would be better at math if I hadn't
learned to depend on one is hard to say. I'm sure
my parents think I would be doing better if I had
learned to do math the same way they did.

My experience with a personal computer in
writing papers for English makes not only my parents but also my teachers suspicious of word processors. The keyboard of a word processor, however, works exactly like a typewriter. "Function
keys" like that of a typewriter are provided to
make the processor perform more jobs. The words
you type appear on the "monitor," a screen above
the keyboard, and can be "edited" by erasing
whole words or lines. A person can even move the
words around. The editing feature is the main advantage of a word processor over a typewriter.
After I am done editing the words on the screen,

I can print them. This removes any chance of typing error if the text has been edited correctly.
    Perhaps teachers are suspicious of calcula-
tors and processors because they think these machines are doing our work. But a calculator
doesn't find the numbers any more than a processor writes a paper and edits it. My experience
suggests that technology can widen the generation
gap. Teenagers sometimes know more about new
technology than parents or teachers. The older
generation needs to catch up.

# Checklist for Writing a Personal Essay

**3.1a**  The narrower your topic, the more specific your details are likely to be.

**3.1b**  The more focused your essay, the greater the clarity of the details.

**3.2a-b**  The purpose of the essay and its audience determine its organization and unity.

**3.3a-b**  Place your thesis toward the beginning unless you have reason to build to it later in the essay.

**3.3c**  Let your thesis guide the focus, dominant tone, and amount of detail.

**3.4a-c**  Develop your personal essay out of your own experience and knowledge.

**3.4d**  The more restricted the topic, the more interesting your essay will be.

**3.5a**  The shorter your essay, the more restricted your topic needs to be.

**3.5b**  Use classification to restrict your topic.

**3.6a-d**  Outlining and trial paragraphs are useful in testing and organizing ideas and working out a tentative thesis.

# Revision and Editing

In revising the draft of your essay, you add and drop ideas and details, rephrase, recast sentences, reorganize paragraphs—possibly even reorganize the whole essay. In the process of revising, you become one of the readers of your essay and look at it through the eyes of the reader. "Bear in mind," Jacques Barzun says in giving advice about writing, "that the person you address, friend or stranger, is like you in his capacity for being bored by dull writing and irritated by what refuses to make sense."

In editing the final draft, you correct grammatical, punctuation, and spelling errors that you did not correct earlier. This final proofreading is essential, but under pressure to finish the essay you may perform it hastily. Even when you have little time for revision and editing, you need to do this job well. On occasion, you may want to return to a finished paper to make additional changes and corrections.

Whatever advice you receive on a draft from your teachers, classmates, or friends, decisions in writing, revising, and editing the essay are yours. It is your decision alone that the essay is satisfactory in form and content and ready to submit to readers. You must learn, then, to look at your writing critically—recognizing its good qualities but also its faults.

## 4.1  Revising the Draft

**4.1a The First Paragraph.**  As you revise the first paragraph, you will probably make discoveries about the rest of the draft. Here is the paragraph again:

```
Like most teenagers my experience with computers
began with video games I played as a teenager at the
```

mall near our house in Akron. These video games sparked
my interest in computers, and pocket calculators got me
interested, too. I first used a pocket calculator in a
math course in junior high school I was having trouble
with. I found right away I was doing better in math, I
wasn't making my usual dumb mistakes. But my parents
were against them because I would go on making the same
mistakes using one. My math teacher must have thought
so too because he said something one day. But the situation changed in senior high. I was getting better. Dividing with decimals. Dividing fractions. Multiplying.
The "new math" was easier for me than the old was for
my parents, which they didn't understand. But they
changed their minds when my math got better.

**4.1 rev**

How can you improve this crucial paragraph in its phrasing,
sentence structure, focus, and organization?

You notice immediately the *redundancy* or needless repetition in the opening sentence—the first of several in the paragraph. Here are two possible revisions of the first sentence:

Like most teenagers I became interested in computers in
playing video games at the mall near our house in Akron.

My interest in computers began with video games I
played at a local shopping mall.

The opening phrase in the original sentence (*Like most teenagers*) should modify *I* and not *experience*. But assume that you
choose the second revision because it is concise and clearly focuses on the topic of the paragraph—your interest in computers.
You also shorten the sentence that follows, focusing on pocket
calculators—the real subject of the paragraph:

Pocket calculators also sparked my interest.

Some of the remaining sentences are also wordy. Others
need different kinds of revision. The third sentence, for example, has an obvious misplaced modifier:

```
I first used a pocket calculator in a math course in
junior high school I was having trouble with.
```

The following revision corrects the error:

```
I first used a pocket calculator in a math course I was
having trouble with in junior high school.
```

But this new sentence is awkward and wordy. The following revision is an improvement:

```
I first used a pocket calculator in a junior high
school math course I was having trouble with.
```

The middle sentences of the paragraph also need revision, particularly the comma splice in sentence 4. You use the opportunity also to rephrase the opening words:

| *Original* | *Revision* |
| --- | --- |
| I found right away I was | I soon found I was doing |
| doing better in math, I | better in math; I wasn't |
| wasn't making my usual | making my usual mistakes. |
| dumb mistakes. | |

The concluding sentences are probably the most unclear. You begin by joining the detached phrases to their core:

```
I was getting better in math--dividing with decimals,
dividing fractions, multiplying.
```

The second to last sentence contains another misplaced modifier:

```
The "new math" was easier for me than the old was for
my parents, which they didn't understand.
```

But placing the modifier correctly proves harder than before:

```
The "new math," which my parents didn't understand,
made dividing and multiplying easier for me than the
old math made them for my parents.
```

The revision is wordy and awkward, in part because it introduces facts unrelated to calculators. Here is a better one:

> My parents' hostility to calculators increased because
> they did not understand the "new math."

**4.1**
**rev**

Still the revision leaves the paragraph unfocused and disunified.
Perhaps the reference to the "new math" is better dropped
from the paragraph. So, too, are other details—the undeveloped
statement about the math teacher, for example—essential only
if the paragraphs that follow focus on your math experiences.
But they do not.

### EXERCISE

Following are revisions of alternative paragraphs of the essay
on computers. What decisions did each reviser make? How successful do you find the revisions?

~~Like most teenagers~~ My experience with computers began with

video games I played as a teenager at the mall ~~near our house~~ in

Akron. ~~These~~ Video games started my interest in computers,

began using
and pocket calculators get me interested too. I ~~first used~~ a
while
pocket calculator in a math course in junior high

school. ~~I was having trouble with. I found~~ Right away I was
the However
doing better in math. I wasn't making my same mistakes. ~~But~~ my
calculators
parents were against ~~them~~ because I would go on making

mistakes using one. My ~~math~~ teacher ~~in junior high school~~ must
improved
have thought the same. ~~But~~ My situation ~~changed~~ in senior
in and
high. I was getting better, Dividing with decimals,. ~~Dividing~~
and calculation
fractions, Multiplying. The "new math" made ~~it~~ easier for me
than
~~than the one was for me~~ than for my parents, ~~which they didn't~~

~~understand. But they changed their minds when my math got~~

~~better.~~

when writing
I used a word processor ~~to write~~ my English papers my last year
Both my parents and English teacher were quite
in high school. ~~My parents were suspicious, and so was my~~
suspicious of this type computer as reflected by their attitude.
~~English teacher. Their attitude shows why they are~~

**4.1
rev**

~~suspicious of computers~~. The keyboard of a word processor
*that of a typewriter. However*
works like ~~a typewriter~~. "*f*unction keys" are provided ~~to do~~
*to make the job easier.*
~~more jobs than typewriter keys~~ The words you type appear on
*Words or lines are*
the "monitor" or screen above the keyboard. ~~You "edit" them~~
*edited by moving them around on the screen.*
~~on the screen by erasing whole words or lines or moving them~~
*Extra keys are needed to accomplish this.*
~~around. You need these extra keys to do this~~. One advantage of
*the ease with which changes in writing are made.*
word processors is ~~it's easy to make changes in writing with~~

~~one~~ You don't have to retype pages.

**4.1b  Focus.**    The references to high school math in the first paragraph and to college math in the second focus the essay on calculators in math courses. However, the following paragraph turns to word processors. Here are the opening sentences:

> I used a word processor to write my English papers
> my last year in high school. My parents were suspi-
> cious, and so was my English teacher. Their attitude
> shows why people are sometimes suspicious of computers.

This abrupt series of statements blurs the focus of the essay. The following revision improves the focus:

> My interest in computers began with video games I
> played at a local shopping mall. I knew that my parents
> disliked these games, and perhaps this dislike explains
> why they refuse to take computers seriously. Personal
> computers that operate as word processors and do other
> jobs look to them like mechanical games. So do the
> pocket calculators my friends and I use to do math.

**4.1c  Unity.**    In a unified essay, each idea clearly connects to the central idea. The essay will seem disunified if it discusses several ideas in no particular order and with no apparent connection to the topic idea. Consider again the paragraph that introduces word processors in the draft:

> I used a word processor to write my English papers
> my last year in high school. My parents were suspi-

```
cious, and so was my English teacher. Their attitude
shows why people are sometimes suspicious of computers.
The keyboard of a word processor works like a type-
writer, but "function keys" do more jobs than type-
writer keys. The words you type appear on the "monitor"
or screen above the keyboard. You "edit" them on the
screen by erasing whole words or lines or moving them
around. You need these extra keys to do this. One ad-
vantage of word processors is that it's easy to make
changes as you write. Another is you don't have to re-
type pages.
```

The second sentence suggests that the attitude of parents and teachers toward word processors will be the topic. However, the remainder of the paragraph discusses the processor only; nothing more is said about parents or teachers.

The paragraph that follows in the draft continues discussion of the processor:

```
The computer I use has a printer attached to it.
By pressing a button, the text on the screen can be
transferred to "hard copy"—which is computer jargon
for the kind of typed copy the writer produces on the
typewriter-like printer. The printer prints directly
from the screen, removing any chance of typing error
if you "edit" the paper right.
```

The next paragraph abruptly returns to the suspicion of teachers:

```
I think teachers are suspicious of calculators
and processors because they think writing should be
work....
```

Omitting the reference to parents and teachers and opening instead with a general reference to suspicion of computers unify the second paragraph as well as the one following. Notice additional corrections in grammar:

```
My experience with a word processor in writing pa-
pers for English may explain suspicion toward com-
```

puters. The keyboard of a word processor works like
that of a typewriter, but "function keys" do more jobs
than typewriter keys. The words you type appear on the
"monitor" or screen above the keyboard. You "edit" them
on the screen by erasing whole words or lines or by
moving them around. You need these extra keys to do
this. One advantage of word processors is that it's
easy to make changes as you write. Another is that you
don't have to retype pages.

   The computer I use has a printer attached to it.
By your pressing a button, the text on the screen can
be transferred to "hard copy"—which is computer jargon
for the kind of typed copy the writer produces on a
typewriter-like printer. The printer is worth mentioning because it prints directly from the screen, removing any chance of typing error if the text has been
"edited" correctly.

**4.1d Transitions.**   These revisions unify the essay: each
paragraph deals with one idea at a time. The details on word
processing relate to the central idea—the convenience that makes
teachers suspicious of processors.

   Still, the paragraphs seem abrupt. The ideas need better
connection. Here again is the first paragraph, and a further
revision of the second, with added transitions:

My interest in computers began with video games I
played at a local shopping mall. I knew that my parents
disliked these games, and perhaps this dislike explains
why they refuse to take computers seriously. Personal
computers that operate as word processors and do other
jobs look to them like mechanical games. So do the
pocket calculators my friends and I use to do math.

   A word processor I used in my senior year to write
papers for English may explain <u>this</u> suspicion. A word
processor is a small computer programmed to work like a
typewriter. The keyboard is similar to a typewriter's.
The major difference is that in a processor "function

keys" do many more jobs. <u>Specifically</u>, the words you have typed appear on the "monitor" or screen above the keyboard, <u>and</u> <u>since</u> you "edit" them on the screen, you need extra keys to erase words or whole lines or move them around. Another convenience is that pages you correct don't have to be retyped. The processor has a printer you attach. By pressing a button, you transfer the text on the screen to "hard copy"—computer jargon for the kind of copy the writer produces on the type-writer—like printer. <u>Processors</u> <u>thus</u> <u>make</u> <u>the</u> <u>job</u> <u>of</u> <u>writing</u> <u>look</u> <u>easy</u>.

These transitions connect ideas and details:

the transitional opening sentence, "A word processor I used in my senior year . . ."
transitional words, *this*, *specifically*, and *since*
reference to earlier words and ideas, in the concluding sentences:
Another convenience . . .
Processors thus make . . .

# 4.2   Improving Sentences

**4.2a Redundancy.**   Notice the *redundant* or unnecessary or superfluous words in the first draft. The opening sentence contains an obvious redundancy, corrected earlier:

<u>Like</u> <u>most</u> <u>teenagers</u> my experience with computers began with video games I played <u>as</u> <u>a</u> <u>teenager</u> at the mall near our house in Akron.

Another sentence in the draft is also redundant and contains an opening dangling modifier (see 24.4):

By pressing a button, the text on the screen can be transferred to "hard copy"—which is computer jargon for the kind of <u>typed</u> copy the writer produces on the <u>typewriter—like</u> <u>printer</u>.

The revision in 4.1d eliminates the redundancy and corrects the dangling modifier:

> By pressing a button, you transfer the text on the
> screen to "hard copy"—which is computer jargon for
> typed copy produced by the printer.

We can make this sentence concise:

> Pressing a button transfers the text on the screen to
> "hard copy"—computer jargon for typed copy produced by
> the printer.

**4.2b Repetition.**    Here are other sentences from the revised second paragraph in 4.1d:

> A word processor is a small computer programmed to work
> like a typewriter. The keyboard is similar to a type-
> writer's. The major difference is that in a processor
> "function keys" do many more jobs. Specifically, the
> words you have typed appear on the "monitor" or screen
> above the keyboard, and since you "edit" them on the
> screen, you need extra keys to erase words or whole
> lines or move them around.

The frequent repetition of *you* directs attention from the details of the processor—the subject of the paragraph—to the actor. One solution is to reduce the dependent clause *(that) you have typed*:

> The typed words appear on the "monitor" or screen above
> the keyboard, and since you "edit" these on the screen,
> extra keys erase words or whole lines or move them
> around.

**4.2c Active and Passive Verbs.**    Changing a sentence to the passive voice is a common way of avoiding repetition but not always a desirable one. Here is a proposed revision of a sentence in the draft:

> Extra keys are needed to perform these jobs.

The passive voice makes this sentence awkward and wordy. This revision of the sentence is concise:

```
Extra keys perform these jobs.
```

**4.2**
**rev**

Sentences in the active voice are usually direct and concise and less open to misreading. Compare the following:

*Passive Voice*

```
But the paper isn't written by the processor.
```

*Active Voice*

```
But the processor doesn't write the paper.
```

(See 26.4b on misuses of the passive voice.)

**4.2d Exact Reference.** The sentences of the draft deserve a closer look. Here is the concluding paragraph:

```
        Teachers are like parents--at least mine in high
school were. Growing up, I heard a good deal from my
parents about "being your own person." Parents want
kids to be independent. But not so independent they
make decisions without asking, which is what I did in
deciding to switch into electrical engineering last
year. Teachers are the same when they talk about "doing
your own work." I think they can be worse. My teachers
were. I think because they are paid to know all the an-
swers. And they usually do.
```

These sentences have the qualities of spoken sentences—"clipped" for the sake of emphasis or connected loosely, without exact reference. Consider the following:

```
But not so independent they make decisions without ask-
ing, which is what I did in deciding to switch into
electrical engineering last year.
```

In speaking this sentence, you give the word *which* extra stress to show it refers to the whole idea preceding and not to a single word or phrase:

```
...they make decisions without asking, which is what I
```

did in deciding to switch into electrical engineering
last year.

In writing, *which* requires an exact antecedent. The following
revision specifies what the writer "did":

But parents want their children to be independent—but
not so independent they make decisions on their own.
Mine were angry when, without asking their advice, I
made the decision to switch into electrical engineering.

Here is a partial revision of the original paragraph:

Growing up, I heard often about "being your own
person." Parents want their children to be independent-
-but not so independent they make decisions on their
own. Mine were angry when, without asking their advice,
I made the decision to switch to electrical engineering. Teachers send the same message. When they tell you
to "do your own work," they don't mean they want you to
be "your own person." The message they send is "depend
on me."

The concluding sentence of the draft expresses irritation,
even anger, and momentarily shifts attention from the issue of
independence to the general character of teachers. The following revision connects teachers directly to the issue and at the
same time restates the thesis of the essay:

Most of my teachers in high school wanted things
done their way. More so than parents, they don't want
to lose face. They believe they have to know all the
answers. Because they want us to depend on them for
everything, they don't like computers doing their job.
But computers can make jobs like writing easier. I look
to computers to do just that.

# 4.3 Editing the Final Draft

The revision completed, you are ready to edit the draft for grammar, punctuation, and spelling. Actually you have been editing the draft as you spotted mistakes and corrected them. Recall the unattached or dangling modifier and redundant wording in the draft:

| *Original* | *Revised* |
|---|---|
| By pressing a button, the text on the screen can be transferred to "hard copy"—which is computer jargon for the kind of typed copy the writer produces on the type- writer-like printer. | Pressing a button trans- fers the text on the screen to "hard copy"— computer jargon for typed copy produced by the printer. |

Editing calls for a practiced eye. You must be able to rec- ognize a misspelled word, inaccurate punctuation, or lack of agreement. This recognition is difficult if you customarily mis- spell particular words or omit apostrophes or commas.

A dictionary is necessary to catch misspellings; you should keep one close by when writing. There are other useful checks on spelling. In your composition course, you might keep a list of misspelled words identified by your instructor. See the list of commonly misspelled words in section 16.9.

You can also keep a list of grammatical and punctuation errors and the sections in this handbook that discuss them. The checklists at the end of each chapter serve this purpose. The introduction to this chapter suggests the importance of putting yourself in place of the reader as you revise. You can do the same as you edit the final draft. Your ear may discover errors that your eye misses if you read the draft aloud.

# 4.4 Second and Final Draft

The following is a revised and edited final draft of the paper containing additional details and changes for concision and clar- ity.

## WRITING WITH A WORD PROCESSOR

**4.4**
**rev**

My experience with computers began with video games I played at a local shopping mall. I knew that my parents disliked these games, and perhaps this dislike explains why they refuse to take computers seriously. Personal computers that operate as word processors and do other jobs look to them like mechanical games. So do the pocket calculators my friends and I use to do math.

A word processor I used in my senior year to write papers for English may explain this suspicion. A word processor is a small computer programmed to work like a typewriter. The keyboard is similar to a typewriter's. The major difference is that in a processor "function keys" do many more jobs. Specifically, the typed words appear on the "monitor" or screen above the keyboard, and since you "edit" these words on the screen, the processor has extra keys that erase words or whole lines or move them to other places in the paragraph or essay. Another convenience is that corrected pages don't have to be retyped. The processor has an attached printer. Pressing a button transfers the text on the screen to "hard copy"—computer jargon for typed copy produced by the printer.

Processors thus make the job of writing look easy. One of my teachers objected that a paper I wrote on a processor looked like a bank statement; he was object-ing to the broken letters that a cheap "dot-matrix" printer like mine produces. He didn't want to tell me his real objection—that writing a paper should not be easy. He obviously assumed that the processor and printer made the writing easy by doing the work. But the printer doesn't write the paper. It just reproduces what I write with the processor. The real work is in writing the paper and editing the words on the screen. In fact, the ease of making corrections with a processor gives me greater control over my writing. I used to avoid proofreading a paper to avoid having to edit a page or retype it. The processor encourages me to look for mistakes.

My experience suggests that parents and teachers distrust calculators and processors for the same reason—they make work easy. Maybe the distrust has a deeper explanation. Growing up, I heard often about "being your own person." Parents want their children to be independent—but not so independent that they make decisions on their own. Mine were angry when, without asking their advice, I made the decision to switch to electrical engineering. Teachers send the same message. When they tell you to "do your own work," they don't mean be "your own person." The message they are really sending is "depend on me."

Most of my teachers in high school wanted things done their way. More so than parents, they don't want to lose face. They believe they have to know all the answers. Because they want us to depend on them for everything, they don't like computers doing their job. But computers make jobs like writing easier. I myself look to computers to do just that.

# **4.5** Redefining Purpose and Audience

**4.5a New Purposes, New Choices.** A different audience and purpose require new decisions on how to focus and organize the essay. Your readers may need more detail or less, depending on how much they know about the subject. A general audience usually requires more definition of terms and details than a special audience. The amount of explanation and detail depends also on the purpose of the essay.

Though it gives information and develops a thesis, the essay on writing with a word processor is an expressive essay that explores feelings and ideas about home and school through personal experiences. A particular focus and thesis centering on writing experiences emerge in the course of writing the essay.

**4.5b  General and Specific Explanations.**   Assume you are writing an essay on computers for a different purpose but for the same audience—your composition teacher and classmates. Assume that your purpose is informative—to give instructions on use of processors. Though your audience is a small one, it is a general audience whose knowledge of the subject varies. You can assume that your teacher and most of your classmates know how to type. But only a few know what word processors do.

To explain the convenience of processors in the earlier essay, you gave a few details on their operation:

```
The keyboard is similar to a typewriter's. The major
difference is that in a processor "function keys"
do many more jobs.
```

You now consider adding to the paper the information in the following paragraph, identifying the source of the information in the text or in a footnote:

> Although "core" and "word" are used interchangeably when we talk about a memory address, they are in reality not synonyms. In order to form a memory address, or word of memory, many "cores" are considered to "belong together." Some computers put 16 cores together to form a word; others use 32; yet others use 36 or more. So we can visualize a memory word to consist of a number of cores. Each of these cores, referred to as a "bit" (which stands for "binary digit"), can have either one of two "values": "on" or "off." A bit is "on" when an electrical impulse is present and "off" when no such electrical charge exists. When a bit is "on," we represent that as a 1. When a bit is off, we represent that as a 0.
>
> —JOSEPH M. VLES, *Computer Fundamentals for Nonspecialists*

This information from a textbook on computers is obviously too detailed for your personal essay on writing with a processor; you needed a few details only on how computers work. But the amount of detail here is exactly right in a book informing nonspecialists how computers work. Because the author is writing to a general audience with varying knowledge about computers, he carefully defines each term. Here is his characterization of that audience in the introduction to the book:

> I have attempted to address a wide audience. If you know nothing at all about computers right now, you should find that you know much more after reading this book; the businessman who often comes in contact with computers but would like to gain more knowledge about how to take advantage of computer

equipment should also find useful material here. Yet another group of readers for whom this book will be helpful are those who have considered entering the computer field as a vocation, but who are unsure of what is involved.

Because the audience varies in knowledge of the subject, the discussion of some points needs to be technical and detailed. But it must not and cannot be so technical that the general reader loses the thread of the explanation. You face the same decision in including some of these details and omitting others.

Consider your different choices in addressing an audience knowing the fundamentals. You would have no reason to state these unless you wanted to review them. Writing to an audience of computer specialists, you need only refer to the process. The greater the economy in your presentation of details, the better focused will be your essay.

A persuasive essay requires other decisions. Assume you are writing a letter to college administrators asking them to install word processors for student use in the library or computer center. You would not need much, if any, detail about the operation of processors; however, you would need detail on their effectiveness in comparison to that of typewriters. You would also build your argument in the most persuasive way, perhaps saving the matter of cost until the end of the letter. A letter to fellow students would be organized differently, the convenience of processors perhaps your main focus.

**4.5c Choices in Diction.** Choices in language or diction can be more complex. Though his discussion of computer language is a technical one, Vles succeeds in writing in the same voice that we hear in his description of his audience. He writes as if he were conversing, yet with somewhat more formality.

Textbooks written in a highly impersonal style convey an objective sense of the subject. In reading most textbooks, you probably don't have the sense that the writer is addressing you personally. But occasionally a textbook writer will address you as a fellow learner or observer. Still, you probably would be surprised if the textbook author chatted with you about the subject in a highly informal style. The tone of an essay always requires a delicate adjustment—in the essay on computers, an adjustment between the personal nature of the subject and the writing situation.

As a rule, the more you focus on personal experience, the more informal your choice of words is likely to be. The more you focus on facts, processes, and ideas, and not on personal experience, the more formal the essay will probably be in vo-

**4.5**

**rev**

cabulary and sentence structure. Just as you continually make adjustments in the amount of discussion and detail, so do you make adjustments in diction and tone.

There are no fixed rules that fit every writing situation and purpose, as we see in the revisions and adjustments made in the preceding drafts. You will make new choices, perhaps redefining your purpose and focus and the audience for your essay.

### EXERCISES

1. Rewrite the following paragraph, unifying it by combining sentences and adding transitions. Omit any details or ideas that are unrelated to the topic idea, stated in the opening sentence:

   > Teenagers in our town spend more time in their cars than they spend out of them. Most of their cars are early-1970 models. You see a lot of cars of this sort on the street. With unemployment high, few people can afford new cars. Not as many engines are souped up. There used to be more that were. A lot of time is spent on the square sitting in front of the drugstore. Boys meet their girlfriends at the drugstore instead of picking them up at home to get a space before the square fills. The logos and bumper stickers identify the teenager's high school, and some teenagers drive from neighboring towns to spend the evening on the square. Some of the cars are painted in several colors. There is a lot of blue and gold because these are the colors of the high school in town. Cars that don't find a space keep driving around the square. The police in town try to keep cars from stopping, and there's a lot of talking from the moving cars to the parked ones. Few grownups come down after dark. The town square belongs to teenagers.

2. Were you writing an informative essay on teenage life in a small town, how much of this detail would you include? What changes would you make in diction, and why?

3. What might be the uses of this description in an expressive or a persuasive essay?

4. Suggest different audiences and purposes for one of the following topics. Then write two short essays, directing them to two of the audiences you have identified. Make the purpose of each essay different, too.
   a. buying stereo equipment
   b. finding a job
   c. buying a used car
   d. maintaining a car
   e. understanding an instruction manual

# 4.6   The Writing Process Summarized

This chapter and those preceding trace a general process followed by many writers. This process begins with activities sometimes referred to as prewriting—choosing a topic, finding experiences and ideas to write about, limiting the topic, and considering a possible organization and thesis.

The writing of the essay is a continuation of these activities. Throughout the process of writing, you consider your limited focus, organization, and thesis. As you limit your topic further in one or more drafts of the paper, you formulate your central idea or thesis, or refine the thesis if you began writing with a limited focus in mind. The writing of the first and subsequent drafts may lead to even further limitation of the subject. You may even choose a new organization and thesis. You are giving attention, as well, to your choice of words.

Later revisions follow the writing and early revision of the draft. You may ask others to read one or more drafts and give advice. In your composition course you may discuss drafts with other students. You will probably make changes or adjustments throughout the revision and editing of the paper.

As we noted at the start, not all writers follow these steps in the order illustrated. The writing process seldom occurs step by step. Many writers think out the paper as they write; ideas and details occur to them as they proceed. Other writers plan at length, particularly before writing long essays or chapters. The more writing you do, the more you will develop habits of prewriting, writing, revision, and editing that fit you best.

### EXERCISE

The first draft of the following essay was written impromptu, in response to a *Newsweek* essay—Martin Krovetz's "Going My Way." The second draft immediately follows. Compare these drafts, and be ready to discuss whether you would have made the same changes or would make others.

*Draft 1: Going My Way*
    From time to time, each of us takes a moment to stand back and evaluate where we have been and on which path we are headed in life. In doing so, it seems necessary to relate or compare one's accomplishments, failures, adventures, and values to those of other persons and groups. Has life been rewarding and satisfying to me? Does the future hold promise? Or could I have possibly chosen another avenue of approach in my search for happiness and fulfillment?

**4.6**

**rev**

Most of my acquaintances in high school were just that—acquaintances and nothing more. However, there is one individual I consider my best friend who lives close by and keeps in touch on a regular basis. We continually make judgments about each other to justify how we live our lives. Observing this friend and his lifestyle, which is different from mine, gives me a sense of security about my own way of handling life.

My friend is single and I am married. He has his own business; I am employed by another. Traveling is a frequent event in his life; I am lucky to break away for the weekend. He is a social extrovert, and I like to spend most of my free time with my wife. Free time seems to be more abundant in his schedule than in mine. He has diabetes; I am in excellent health. So you see, we are quite different in many respects, with a strong friendship the one thing we hold in common.

So how is it that I derive security from observing and evaluating the way my best friend lives? To begin, I must say that owning and operating your own business sounds very prestigious, but at times it presents an inescapable dilemma. My friend is a photographer and is in constant demand. If he is not running out at nine at night to drive 75 miles to photograph for insurance purposes a lady with a broken leg, then he is tied up all day Sunday with a wedding. When not on the scene shooting pictures, then it is downstairs to his darkroom to develop film. How much free time does he have? This grinding schedule may endure for days, weeks, or months and then suddenly business stops. I rather enjoy the predictability of my forty hour week. Though time off is seldom at best, I have the advantage of planning ahead.

Being single certainly rids an individual of many responsibilities that married people enjoy. No one to report to, a smaller grocer bill—the single life sure keeps things fresh with the dating scene. I have been married a few years and love my wife dearly, but on occasion I envy that novelty that accompanies a date with a different girl every week. On the other hand, my friends seems to envy the security and stability of my relationship with my wife.

Sharing responsibility is a wonderful feeling. Although problems seem to arise more frequently in a marriage, having someone to help work them out is an experience impossible when one is single. I gather this from conversations with my friend. He seems troubled often and appears to need someone to overcome his dismay at life and his apathy. For these reasons and many more, I find marriage a rewarding institution.

*Draft 2: Going My Way*

**4.6**
**rev**

From time to time we take a moment to stand back and look at where we have been in life and where we are going. Comparing oneself with a friend helps in taking this measure. Has life been rewarding and satisfying for me? Does the future hold promise? Or could I have possibly chosen another avenue in my search for happiness and fulfillment?

Most of my acquaintances in high school were just that—acquaintances. However, one person I consider my best friend lives nearby and keeps in touch. We continually make judgments about each other to justify what we do and how we live. Observing this friend and his lifestyle, so opposite to mine, gives me a sense of security about my own handling of life.

My friend is single and I am married. He has his own business; I am employed. Traveling is a frequent event in his life; I am lucky to break away for the weekend. He is a social extrovert; most of my free time is spent with my wife. So you see we are quite different in many respects, with a strong friendship, at times, the only thing we share.

You may wonder why I derive security from observing and judging the way my friend lives. To begin, I must say that owning and operating your own business sounds prestigious but at times it makes life hectic. If my friend is not running out at nine at night to drive seventy-five miles to photograph for insurance purposes a lady with a broken leg, he is tied up Sunday afternoon with a wedding. When not on the scene shooting pictures, he ventures downstairs to the darkroom to develop film. How, you may ask, does he have a free moment? This grinding schedule may endure for days, weeks, or months, and then suddenly a void. I rather enjoy the predictability of my forty-hour week. Though I seldom have time off, at least there is the advantage of being able to plan ahead.

Being single certainly rids an individual of many responsibilities of married life. No one to report to, a smaller grocery bill, and the single status—these keep things fresh with regard to dating. I have been a husband nearly four years and love my wife dearly, but on occasion I miss the novelty that accompanies a date with a different girl each week. By contrast, my friend seems to envy the security and stability of our marriage. I have come to value my marriage, with its strength seeming to increase as the days progress. Considering the unity marriage has given me, I believe life continues to have a good deal of the positive in store for me.

Having two incomes is a benefit, certainly. A few years ago, misfortune struck when I was laid off. My wife went back to work in order to pull us through. Having the support of your wife spiritually and emotionally through troubled times is a strength unfelt by those who are single. For a marriage to be strong there must be love. Love in marriage is unlike that developed in a friendship or between parents and children. It is the most powerful of all feelings and it is that power which gives me gratitude for the past and optimism for the future. Through my friend I realize life has bestowed on me a gift to which there can be attached no price.

# Checklist for Revision and Editing

**4.1a**   In revising the first draft, become one of the readers to whom the essay is directed.

**4.1b**   Focus the main subject or topic idea of the essay in the opening paragraph and throughout the essay.

**4.1c**   Unify the essay by developing one idea at a time.

**4.1d**   Use transitions to mark changes in subject and focus.

**4.2a-b**   Improve the focus of the paragraph by eliminating repetitive words.

**4.2c**   Use the passive voice sparingly in varying sentences and focusing the subject.

**4.2d**   Give the sentences exact reference.

**4.3**   After creating your first draft, edit for spelling, grammar, and punctuation in the course of writing the essay and at the end.

**4.5a-c**   Consider a new organization and new explanatory details and diction if you redefine the purpose and audience of your essay.

# Building Paragraphs and Sentences

# Organizing Paragraphs

## 5.1 Defining the Paragraph

The **paragraph** is the basic unit of the essay—a unit centering sometimes on a single idea and sometimes on several ideas welded into a whole. The paragraph sometimes is organized as a miniature essay containing a beginning, a middle, and an end. In such a paragraph the beginning sentences state the subject or central idea, the "middle" develop this idea through explanatory details and ideas, and the concluding sentences state the central idea fully or restate it.

Not all paragraphs serve as units of thought. Some simply mark changes in tone or point of view or mark transitions to new ideas. In newspaper and magazine articles, paragraphs frequently consist of a single, sharply focused idea or fact, as in the following paragraph from a newspaper article on Japanese workers:

> Among the major industrial countries, no work force is more diligent than the Japanese. On average, the Labor Ministry said, employees work 2,116 hours a year, compared with about 1,800 hours in the United States.

The succeeding paragraph develops the idea through a series of details:

> That means the typical Japanese works more than an extra month a year compared with the average American. And the figures for Japan do not include overtime or after-hours socializing with colleagues, regarded as critical for maintaining workplace cohesiveness. White-collar workers habitually stay on in the office long after the work day is officially over.
> —CLYDE HABERMAN, "5-Day Week: Can Japanese Love It?"
> *The New York Times*, September 4, 1984

In a much different newspaper article on a New York City

subway tollbooth clerk, rapid paragraph breaks mark changes in subject, tone, and point of view:

> In the booth, the world passes by her, and she often comments.
> "Now that one," Mrs. Wills said, pointing out a man she said hello to. "He looks like Rodney Dangerfield. Comes in here all the time."
> "This one worked his brain," she said when a customer gave her $10.70 for three 90-cent tokens.
> "They don't even know where they are," she said, watching a man and a woman engaged in a passionate goodbye kiss at the turnstile.
> While customers complain of rudeness—the Transit Authority has received an average of 75 complaints a month about rudeness for several years—they can be rude themselves.
> Around midmorning, an old man walked up to the booth and pounded his fist on the glass. He pointed at a gate that was closed because it had been freshly painted. "Why are you doing that?" he shouted.
> —SUZANNE DALEY, "The Travails of a New York Token-Booth Clerk," *The New York Times*, August 27, 1984

In formal essays transitional paragraphs may also consist of one or two sentences only. These paragraphs from the beginning of an address to a scientific association state ideas in summary form, state the questions to be explored in the address, and introduce the central idea or thesis:

> Men have sought to enrich life through development of the pictorial arts, literature, music, drama, and the dance. They have created systems of logic and metaphysics and have tried to analyze the nature of knowledge and reality. They have formulated codes of esthetics and morals and have contemplated the purpose and meaning of life.
> In this vast and interrelated range of concerns and activities, where do the successes lie? What things have men really done well?
> Each man is entitled to his own answer, but my own reply would go as follows. Probably the most conspicuous, the most universally recognized, and the most widely applied success lies in the understanding and control of the forces of physical nature. Coupled with this, I would place the progress that has been made—even though it is but a start—in the understanding of organic nature. —WARREN WEAVER, "Science and People"

The paragraphs to be discussed in the remainder of this chapter are those frequently found in formal and informal essays. These organize and develop a central or kernel idea in various ways.

## 5.2 Focusing Through Topic Sentences

How you begin a paragraph depends on the purpose of the essay, your audience, and the ideas to be developed. In an expository paragraph, for example, if the central idea is one readers will find difficult or controversial, the writer may decide to develop it gradually and open the paragraph with a statement of the subject or topic and build to the central idea, usually called the **topic sentence**:

*Topic*
> It is sometimes said that the unifying element in all of biology is the cell, that cells are the basic units of biology in the sense that atoms are the basic units of chemistry. I am dubious about this. Cellular organization, to be sure, is fundamental in visible organisms (plants and animals), but the world of the microbes is something else again. There has been a long argument in biology about whether these should be called "single-celled organisms" or "organisms without cells." This is more than a war of words; it involves a whole attitude. If one looks at an amoeba, for instance, as something corresponding to a white blood cell in man, the amoeba becomes "simple," "primitive" and the like. This, in the long run, has not been a very useful way of looking at amoebae, and nowadays I think most biologists refer to them as "acellular" rather than as "unicellular." The amoeba meets the problems of nutrition, respiration, coordination, reproduction, without resorting to cellular differentiation.

*Central Idea*
> The amoeba, far from being simple, is quite remarkably complex. But if the amoeba is acellular, we have lost cells as our basic biological unit.
>
> —MARSTON BATES, *The Forest and the Sea*

Bates builds his paragraph to the central or topic idea. He might have begun with this idea, dropping the introductory statement of the subject:

> We have lost cells as our basic biological unit. Cellular organization, to be sure, is fundamental in visible organisms. . . .

Bates's controversial view of cells is given an introduction and careful explanation before its statement at the end.

The following paragraph opens with a complete statement of the central idea:

*Central Idea* { When I first began reviewing the history of college sports, what immediately attracted my attention was how quickly American universities became involved in providing sports entertainment for their students and the general public. According to Frederick Rudolph, discussing the rise of college football in the late nineteenth century, "few movements so captured the colleges and universities. . . . At last, the American college and university had discovered something that all sorts of people cared about passionately." So quickly did the general public seize upon college football as a subject of enthusiasm and identification (aided by the proliferation of mass circulation newspapers) that university presidents, operating in a climate not always conducive to intellectual concerns, began consciously to use the sport as a vehicle for attracting financial and political support, whether from alumni, state legislators, or prospective students and contributors.

—MARK NAISON, "Scenario for Scandal," *Commonweal*, September 24, 1982

**5.2**
¶

Though many readers probably will find it controversial, Naison begins his paragraph with the central or thesis idea. Had he chosen to develop the idea gradually, he might have begun with the history and details that develop it:

According to Frederick Rudolph, discussing the rise of college football in the late nineteenth century . . .

Whether it states the subject only or states the central idea, the opening sentence may suggest how the supporting ideas and details will be organized. The following paragraph tells us that the creatures of sea forests rise upward in gradations and then shows us how they do so:

Life in a sea forest rises toward the top in sharp gradations of movement. Brittle stars, purple sea fans, lavender sponges, ostrich-plume hydroids, flowery sea anemones, and lobsterlike crayfish ring the rockbound holdfast. Above this almost immobile layer of life cruise small sand sharks and rays flapping their robelike wings like finny Draculas. Above them schools of shimmering sardines pass like rain showers, and bass, sheepshead, spiny sculpin, and dainty senoritas dart about. On the outskirts of the forest bonita, barracuda, and albacore sprint

like animated steel arrows, and above the surface the seabird
swirls, occasionally lighting on the brown canopy.

—WESLEY MARX, *The Frail Ocean*

An opening question can direct the reader ahead in the
same way:

**5.2**
¶

> What is "shooting a film," then? If I were to ask this ques-
> tion of everybody, I would no doubt obtain quite different re-
> sponses, but perhaps you would all agree on one point: shoot-
> ing a film is doing what is necessary in order to transport the
> contents of the manuscript onto a piece of film. In doing so,
> you would be saying quite a lot and yet not nearly enough. For
> me, shooting a film represents days of inhumanly relentless
> work, stiffness of the joints, eyes full of dust, the odors of make-
> up, sweat and lamps, an indefinite series of tensions and relax-
> ations, an uninterrupted battle between volition and duty, be-
> tween vision and reality, conscience and laziness. I think of
> early risings, of nights without sleep, of a feeling keener than
> life, of a sort of fanaticism centered about a single task, by
> which I myself become, finally, an integral part of the film, a
> ridiculously tiny piece of apparatus whose only fault is requir-
> ing food and drink.
>
> —INGMAR BERGMAN, "What Is 'Film Making'?"

Paragraphs, of course, do not occur alone; they link to form
the whole essay. The topic sentence may therefore appear in
the succeeding paragraph, perhaps, or in the preceding, as in
the following paragraphs. Note the linking of ideas:

> Some of history's great disasters have been caused by mis-
> understood directions. The heroic but futile charge of the Light
> Brigade at Balaclava in the Crimean War is a striking example.
> "Someone had blundered," Tennyson wrote. That was true,
> and the blunder consisted of the confusion over one word,
> which meant one thing to the person speaking but another to
> the persons spoken to.
>
> The brigade was ordered to charge "the guns." The man
> who gave the order was on a hilltop and had in mind a small
> battery which was very plain to him but was concealed from
> the soldiers in the valley by a slight rise. The only guns *they*
> could see were the main Russian batteries at the far end of the
> valley. Therefore they assumed that "the guns" referred to the
> batteries *they* saw. The command seemed utter madness, but it
> was a command and the leader of the brigade, after filing a
> protest, carried it out.
>
> Fortunately, most misunderstandings don't have such dis-
> astrous consequences. But the continual confusion about such
> general terms as *thing, deal, it, fix,* and the like, certainly can be

frustrating. Taken as a whole, the exasperation, humiliation, disappointment and quarreling caused by misunderstandings probably produce a thousand times the misery and suffering that the Light Brigade endured.

—BERGEN EVANS, "The Power of Words"

**EXERCISE**

Write a paragraph that opens with one of the following ideas. Experiment with the placement of the topic sentence:
   a. High school sports give the school a special identity.
   b. Coaches are different in personality and methods.
   c. The identity of a high school depends on more than its academic program and its teachers.
   d. Waiting in line tells you much about people.

# 5.3 Organizing the Paragraph

Paragraphs may be organized in the following ways:

1. opening with the central idea, followed by supporting details and ideas;
2. opening with the central idea and restating it;
3. opening with a statement of the topic, followed by its restriction and illustration;
4. opening with details that build to the central idea;
5. opening with a question or statement of a problem, followed by the answer or solution.

**5.3a Generalization-Details.**    Earlier paragraphs in this chapter illustrate the common method of opening with a generalization and supporting it with details. In longer paragraphs like the following, the author may restate the central or kernel idea through repetition and restatement. The italicized words and phrases refer directly or indirectly to the opening sentence:

What I have most wanted to do throughout the past ten years is to make political writing into an art. My starting point is always a feeling of *partisanship*, a sense of injustice. *When I sit down to write a book*, I do not say to myself, "I am going to produce *a work of art*." *I write* it because there is some lie that I want to expose, some fact to which I want to draw attention, and my initial concern is to get a hearing. But I could not do the work of *writing a book*, or even a long magazine article, if it were not also *an aesthetic experience*. Anyone who cares to examine my work will see that even when it is downright propaganda it contains much that a full-time politician would con-

sider irrelevant. I am not able, and I do not want, completely to abandon the world view that I acquired in childhood. So long as I remain alive and well I shall continue to *feel strongly* about prose style, *to love* the surface of the earth, and to *take a pleasure* in solid objects and scraps of useless information. It is no use trying to suppress that side of myself. The job is to reconcile my ingrained likes and dislikes with the essentially public, non-individual activities that this age forces on all of us.
—GEORGE ORWELL, "Why I Write"

**5.3b Restatement.**   Orwell restates his central idea through the details of the paragraph—his attitudes, pleasures, likes, and dislikes. On occasion the writer develops the paragraph entirely through **restatement** of the central idea—in the following paragraph through explanation and details of the migrant's life.

The migrant is a minority within a minority. The components of the general migrant population belong to racial or ethnic minorities. In addition, each in turn within his own ethnic group occupies a place at the very bottom of the social and economic hierarchy. He meets the most discrimination, does the hardest work, earns the least money; he has the least job security, the least formal schooling, the lowest status. His migrancy separates him from the larger community; his minority status aggravates the separation.
—LOUISA R. SHOTWELL, *The Harvesters: The Story of the Migrant People*

Restating the central idea in this way emphasizes to the reader its importance.

**5.3c Topic-Restriction-Illustration.**   Some paragraphs open with a broad generalization or statement of the **topic, restrict** it to one area of experience or thought, and finally **illustrate** it:

*Topic*              *American humor* rested less on inherent wit or
                     sharp observation of human failings than on rough
*Restriction*  *drolleries* full of exaggeration and strange usage for
*Illustration* its own sake. The speech became noisy and pro-
                     fuse. It imitated sounds of sucking and smacking
                     and cracking and slicing and chopping and sawing
                     and thumping and poking and digging and clap-
                     ping and exclaiming and hushing. It stuck in extra
                     syllables for elegance and comic surprise. It liked
                     to repeat in the same word the sound of dental
                     consonants that gave a jerky, droll effect. It made
                     comedy out of mouth-widening vowel sounds and
                     speech-yodels whose effect depended upon a swal-

lowed *l*—the gobble of the North American tur-
key. It was at times almost abstract sound. Its character stripped of known words and their meaning,
and left only with sound, might still suggest the
meaning intended, along with the hard, simple,
and at times lyrically beautiful life from which it
came.
—PAUL HORGAN, *Sons of Democracy* [italics added]

Horgan begins with a broad statement about American humor,
immediately restricts the topic to humorous sounds, and then
illustrates them.

**5.3d Details-Generalization.**    The following paragraph
builds through a series of details to the topic sentence or idea
of the paragraph:

> In October 1347 a Genoese fleet made its way
> into the Messina harbor in northeast Sicily. Its crew
> had "sickness clinging to their very bones." All were
> dead or dying, afflicted with a disease from the
> Orient. The Messinese harbor masters tried to
> quarantine the fleet, but it was too late. It was not
> men but rats and fleas that brought the sickness,
> and they scurried ashore as the first ropes were
> tied to the docks. Within days, the pestilence spread
> throughout Messina and its rural environs and,
> within six months, half the region's population died
> or fled. *This scene, repeated thousands of times in ports*
> *and fishing villages across Eurasia and North Africa,*
> *heralded the coming of the greatest natural disaster in*
> *European history—the Black Death.*
> —ROBERT S. GOTTFRIED, *The Black Death*
> [italics added]

*Topic Sentence*

This paragraph opens the first chapter of the book; the
dramatic build to the topic sentence is common in the opening
paragraph of articles or books. Coming in the middle of the
chapter or article or at the end, the paragraph will probably
seem even more dramatic—by contrast with the usual build from
topic sentence to supporting details.

**5.3e Problem-Solution.**    The paragraph that begins with a
statement of the problem may recommend a solution, or it may
do no more than explore the problem, as in the following discussion of nuclear waste:

**5.3**
**¶**

*Problem*    The nuclear-waste disposal problem has been termed "unsolved," but all this really means is that a method of disposal has not yet been decided upon. It would be relatively simple and cheap, for instance, to convert the nuclear wastes into glass rods and dump them in the ocean. The technology for *Solution*    conversion to glass is well established, and no one can claim that we do not know how to dump things in the ocean. Since the oceans are already full of radioactivity—principally from potassium, a naturally radioactive element which is an important component of salt—the radiation exposure to aquatic life would not be significantly increased. *Qualifica-*    The principal danger here is that small additional *tion*    amounts of radioactivity would get into fish which are ultimately eaten.

—Bernard L. Cohen, "A Tale of Two Wastes," *Commentary*, November 1978

These methods of organization may be combined. The question that opens a paragraph may state a problem that the remainder of the paragraph answers. The question or problem also may be stated generally and then restricted and worked out in the detail that follows.

Let us review what these examples tell us about organizing the paragraph:

1. Many paragraphs contain a central or topic idea to which details and subordinate ideas connect.
2. This idea sometimes appears toward the beginning of the paragraph, and it may appear later—particularly if it needs preparation for and deserves special emphasis.
3. When the central or topic idea appears later, the opening sentence usually states the subject or topic of the essay or connects the paragraph to the preceding discussion.

**Exercises**

1. Use one of the following sentences in a paragraph of your own. Restrict the idea you choose to a particular area of experience and conclude the paragraph with illustrations:

    a. The borrower is servant to the lender.
    —Proverbs 22:7

    b. There is no new thing under the sun.
    —Ecclesiastes 1:9

    c. All our words from loose using have lost their edge.    —Ernest Hemingway, *Death in the Afternoon*

    d. There is no substitute for talent. Industry and
all the virtues are of no avail.
        —ALDOUS HUXLEY, *Point Counterpoint*

**2.** Rewrite your paragraph as a question and answer.
**3.** Rewrite it finally as a statement of a problem suggested by
the quotation and an answer to it.

## 5.4 Opening and Closing Paragraphs

**5.4a Opening Paragraphs.** The purpose of opening paragraphs in essays is to inform the reader of the subject and generate interest in it. How broad the introduction is depends on
the knowledge and concerns of the audience. Writing in a science magazine, James A. Van Allen (for whom the Van Allen
radiation belts surrounding the earth are named) begins an article on the need for robot space exploration with a personal
address to the reader:

> There is something about the topic of outer space that in-
> duces hyperbolic expectations. With no difficulty at all I can
> think of a billion-dollar space mission before breakfast any day
> of the week and a multibillion-dollar mission on Sunday. Or-
> dinarily I do not inflict such visions on my fellow citizens, but
> I note that proposals of comparable or lesser merit and of much
> greater cost receive public attention, and some are influential
> in high circles of government. I submit that the proposed per-
> manently manned space station is in this category.
>     —"Space Science, Space Technology and the Space Station,"
>                    *Scientific American*, January 1986

Van Allen does the following in his succinct paragraph:

- states his subject (the cost and merit of manned stations);
- appeals to the interest and concern of his general readers
  (noting the expectations that space exploration generates and
  the concern of the American public with the cost of space
  programs);
- states his thesis (manned space stations discourage other kinds
  of important space exploration).

Van Allen refers to his own interests or concerns. Opening
paragraphs may give more details about the subject and make
only a brief reference to the writer's interest in it. The following
opening paragraph in the same issue of *Scientific American* begins
with a general statement of the importance of the subject and

then provides essential background for understanding the discussion to follow—the writers briefly referring to their interest in cometary exploration:

> The years 1985-86 will one day be regarded as a golden age for cometary astronomy. Indeed, if we had been allowed to choose two years in which to be active as cometary scientists, these would have been our clear choices. Two important comets, Giacobini-Zinner and Halley, have approached within range of observation as they orbit around the sun. Giacobini-Zinner has already yielded a bounty of information as a result of being the first comet to be visited by a spacecraft, and astronomers have deployed an unprecedented array of resources to examine Comet Halley. Data are being gathered by observatories on the earth's surface, by spacecraft orbiting the earth, by vehicles in space and in orbit around other planets and by six spacecraft that will fly near or into the comet's atmosphere.
> —JOHN C. BRANDT and MALCOLM B. NIEDNER, JR.,
> "The Structure of Comet Tails," *Scientific American*, January 1986

Van Allen's opening paragraph states the thesis of the essay; this opening paragraph does not. Though many opening paragraphs do state the thesis (newspaper editorials do so usually), many writers prefer to introduce the thesis gradually. How early the thesis appears depends on the knowledge of the audience (a difficult thesis requires more introduction than a simple one) and on how controversial it is (see 3.3).

Both paragraphs seek to generate interest in the subject of the essay. Successful opening paragraphs do so in various ways. Humor can be successful if, as in this introduction to an essay on amateur sports, it is not exaggerated:

> As I write this, a distinguished professor of Victorian literature is conducting his classes with a black eye. The dashing scar that runs above the upper lip of his colleague, an equally distinguished professor (of Renaissance literature), is healing nicely. These hypercivilized men, both in their 50's, received their wounds not in a barroom or during a demonstration against apartheid but on another field of honor, the squash court.
> —GEORGE STADE, "The Spirit of '85," *New York Times Sports Magazine*, September 29, 1985

The same qualification applies to the dramatic opening paragraph:

> The farmhouse on eastern Long Island that I own and go to on weekends was burgled twice last winter. There have been a lot of burglaries out there recently. Everybody says it wasn't always that way—a few years back you could go away for a week

and leave your door open. Anyway, my farmhouse is in the middle of the farm and, I guess, easy pickings.

—CHARLES SIMMONS, "A Shaggy Duck Story,"
*Harper's Magazine*, August 1985

**5.4b Closing Paragraphs.** Closing paragraphs often restate the thesis of the essay. Van Allen restates his thesis through a statement of the competitive need for other than manned space flight:

> In the meantime the European Space Agency, Japan and the U.S.S.R. are forging ahead with important scientific missions. The progressive loss of U.S. leadership in space science can be attributed, I believe, largely to our excessive emphasis on manned space flight and on vaguely perceived, poorly founded goals of a highly speculative nature. Given the current budgetary climate and a roughly constant level of public support for civil space ventures, the development of a space station, if pursued as now projected, will seriously reduce the opportunities for advances in space science and in important applications of space technology in the coming decade.
>
> —JAMES A. VAN ALLEN, "Space Science, Space Technology and the Space Station"

In scientific writing, the concluding paragraph often suggests what other experiments or investigations should be conducted. Brandt and Niedner conclude their essay on comet tails in this way:

> The massive efforts directed toward Halley and Giacobini-Zinner should dramatically advance understanding of cometary physics, but many questions, including those that emerge from the new data, will remain. The direct exploratory missions provide information based on a series of snapshots taken along single trajectory lines. Global data recording cometary changes over time will be needed to deepen understanding of comet tails. NASA's Comet Rendezvous and Asteroid Flyby mission, planned for launching in the early 1990's, should provide this important information. The vehicle is expected to approach Comet Wild II in 1995 and record valuable data as it travels with the comet along its orbital path for approximately two and a half years. If the mission is successful, it will mark the next logical step in attempts to explore and understand the nature of comets.
>
> —JOHN C. BRANDT and MALCOLM B. NIEDNER, JR.,
> "The Structure of Comet Tails"

A successful closing paragraph reaffirms to the reader the importance of the subject and the thesis of the essay. Like the opening paragraph, it may employ humor, and it may conclude with a dramatic appeal to action and for further thought. However the paragraph concludes, it should not allow the reader to finish the essay with a feeling of loose ends.

**5.5**

**coh**   ## 5.5   Unifying the Paragraph

**5.5a  A Disunified Paragraph.**   In a unified paragraph, details and subordinate ideas connect to a central idea. Here is a disunified paragraph:

> College athletics puts a strain on students and
> faculty when it is the chief activity of the school.
> Classroom cheating creates a strain, too. The wide-
> spread belief of the public that a school's worth is to
> be measured by its teams encourages players to win at
> any cost, and teachers sometimes find themselves under
> pressure to give passing grades to players doing poor
> work or not even attending the course. Students and
> teachers thus are victims of a system not of their mak-
> ing. And cheating in the classroom increases the pres-
> sure on everyone—students, teachers, administrators.

It is obvious what has gone wrong. The second sentence introduces a new and unrelated idea. One source of strain on students and faculty is college athletics; another is cheating in the classroom. If the writer wants to focus on both sources, the ideas and details must connect to both. Finally, ideas and details do not connect in the paragraph. The word *too* in the second sentence suggests that the rest of the paragraph will focus on college athletics and cheating. The writer discusses teams instead. The final sentence returns to the mattter of cheating, without reference to college athletics.

**5.5b  Unifying the Paragraph.**   The paragraph can be unified by subordinating the discussion of cheating to the main topic. This subordination can be achieved through an introductory comparison:

```
Like cheating in the classroom, college athletics puts
a strain on students and faculty when it is the chief
activity of the university.
```

The sentences that follow now will be seen to develop the central topic—the pressure of college athletics. The final sentence should be reserved for another paragraph—one that develops this idea fully in its own right or as a development of the point made in the first paragraph.

**5.5**
**coh**

### EXERCISES

1. The following sentences form a paragraph in a *Newsweek* article, published in the spring of 1983. The sentences are printed here out of sequence. Rewrite the paragraph by putting them in the most logical order.

   **a.** Matteo's mail-order bride had picked up an eye infection on the crowded crossing; the doctor who spotted it chalked a large "E" on her coat and waved her onto the losers lines.

   **b.** She had dreamed too long to be denied.

   **c.** Those who passed inspection filed on through the door that said PUSH TO NEW YORK.

   **d.** The door nearly slammed on their future that day.

   **e.** Those who did not were marked with a big chalk letter— "H" for heart trouble, "F" for facial rash, "X" for a psychological problem—and shunted with the other rejects to be reexamined and possibly sent home.

   **f.** Ellis Island was a symbol of hope for most of the newcomers, but for some of them, running the gantlet of doctors in the examination hall, it became the Isola delle Lagrime—the Isle of Tears.

   **g.** She waited until no one was looking, then dusted the chalk off her coat, slipped under a rope and lost herself in the crowd moving off toward the ferries.

2. Do the same with this scrambled paragraph from Douglass H. Morse, "Milkweeds and Their Visitors," *Scientific American*, July 1985.

   **a.** These species are drawn to the sugary nectar secreted by the flowers, but several of the insects also serve the needs of the plant by carrying pollen, often over considerable distances.

   **b.** Activity at the plants reaches a peak in early summer, when the milkweed's flowers attract bees, butterflies, moths and various smaller insects.

   **c.** Later in the summer milkweed bugs attack the seeds.

    **d.** Other visitors to the milkweed feed on the plant itself: aphids suck the sap, for example, and caterpillars of the monarch butterfly eat the leaves.

    **e.** The common milkweed is host to an annual gathering of insects and other animals.

    **f.** The presence of all this animal life brings in turn parasites and predators, including certain wasps and spiders, and scavengers that lay claim to whatever the predators leave behind.

**5.6**
**trans**

## 5.6  Using Transitions

**5.6a  A Paragraph Without Transitions.**   Assume you have written a paragraph with some care and are satisfied that the ideas connect clearly. But will your reader see that they do?

Consider how much misunderstanding can arise in speaking to people: you routinely repeat statements, backtrack to earlier parts of the conversation, point out connections, underscore important words, ask whether you are being understood. In writing, since you cannot see the effect of your words, you must be especially careful to connect your statements clearly. One means of doing so is the transitional word or phrase.

Here is a paragraph from René Dubos, *Man Adapting*, with omission of important transitions and a breakdown of longer into shorter sentences:

> All technological innovations, whether concerned with industrial, agricultural, or medical practices, are bound to upset the balance of nature. To master nature is synonymous with disturbing the natural order. It is desirable in principle to maintain the "balance of nature." It is not easy to define the operational meaning of this idea. Nature is never in a static equilibrium. The interrelationships between its physical and biological components are endlessly changing. Man placed himself apart from the rest of nature when he began to farm the land and even more when he became urbanized. The survival, let alone growth, of his complex societies implies that he will continue to exploit and upset nature. The real problem is not how to maintain the balance of nature. The problem is how to change it in such a manner that the overall result is favorable for the human species.

You probably grasp the thread of ideas in reading the paragraph quickly. But you probably also pause to guess at connections. Here is the original paragraph, with the omitted transitions in italics:

> All technological innovations, whether concerned with industrial, agricultural, or medical practices, are bound to upset the balance of nature. *In fact*, to master nature is synonymous with disturbing the natural order. *While* it is desirable in principle to maintain the "balance of nature," *it* is not easy to define the operational meaning of this idea. Nature is never in a static equilibrium *because* the interrelationships between its physical and biological components are endlessly changing. *Furthermore*, man placed himself apart from the rest of nature when he began to farm the land and even more when he became urbanized. The survival, let alone growth, of his complex societies implies that he will continue to exploit and *therefore* upset nature. The real problem, *therefore*, is not how to maintain the balance of nature, *but rather* how to change it in such a manner that the overall result is favorable for the human species.
>
> —RENÉ DUBOS, *Man Adapting* [italics added]

**5.6b A List of Transitions.**　Transitional words are basic to the meaning of these sentences: they cannot be omitted without blurring what is said. Here are common transitions that highlight connections and give the reader directions:

*Addition* (developing through ideas and details): and, also, too, furthermore, moreover, in addition, then, indeed.

*Time* (stating when): before, earlier, since, afterward, later, now, meanwhile, in the meantime, until, soon.

*Space* (stating where): here, there, elsewhere, above, below, behind, on this side, on the other side, to the right, to the left, to the north, to the south.

*Qualification* (stating exceptions, limiting, modifying): but, however, nevertheless, notwithstanding, nonetheless, while, though.

*Repetition* (restating ideas and details for emphasis and clarity): to repeat, once again, in other words, in short, in particular, in summary.

*Exemplification* (illustrating): for example, for instance, that is, specifically.

*Cause and Effect* (tracing results or consequences): as a result, consequently, accordingly, therefore, then, for this reason.

*Comparison and Contrast* (showing similarities and differences): similarly, by comparison, likewise, in the same way, as, but, despite, by contrast, on the contrary, on the one hand, on the other hand.

*Summary* (digesting, restating chief ideas): in summary, in brief, in short, in conclusion, finally.

**5.6**
**trans**

**EXERCISES**

**1.** Identify the transitions and explain their use in the following passages:

> a.   Meanwhile, the larger and dominant arm of broadcasting—commercial television—has been approaching youth in the altogether simpler, tackier, more easygoing fashion of the marketplace. Here there are few claims to higher purpose, except when absolutely necessary. Here, too, the young are frankly welcome, not merely as somebody's children but on their own. Commercial television doesn't exactly love kids, either, but it's more fun. Of course, it wants to sell them something; it wants a transaction. But at least it wants them.
>
> —MICHAEL J. ARLEN, "Baretta's T-Shirt"

> b.   Mike Fink passed into legend not only because of his early exploits on the rivers but because he was the last of the boatmen—or so he was called—clinging contentiously to his broadhorn long after the steamboats came, when men could not be induced to travel in a low wooden ark. The tales about him became an elegy to wild days that were past or were passing. "What's the use of improvements? Where's the fun, the frolicking, the fighting?" he cried in one of them. "Gone! All gone!" The sad noisy sentiment mounted through twenty years or more. The exploits of Fink were still being celebrated during the '50's by the western almanacs. He even passed into literary discussion: one writer said that if he had lived in early Greece his feats would have rivaled those of Jason, and that among the Scandinavians he would have become a river-god.
>
> —CONSTANCE ROURKE, *American Humor*

**2.** Answer the following questions about the following paragraph:
   **a.** Which is the central or kernel idea of the paragraph?
   **b.** By which of the methods described in this chapter is the paragraph developed?
   **c.** What transitions does the paragraph contain, and what ideas do they express?

> From the very creation of the movies, the directors exploited motion, the novelty that fetched the rubes, in train wrecks, Indian attacks, and the ultimate commotion of the chase. But whenever human emotions were involved, they acted on the error that they were photographing a stage play. "Acting," everybody knew, entailed the broad gesture, the lilting or trenchant cad-

ence, the cameo stance, the human form seen as a cardboard cutout of certain elemental emotions—greed, shame, pride, penitence, humility, ardor—all filmed at the proper remove of the proscenium arch and composed within its frame. The invention of the medium shot and the close-up, far from challenging the actors to quiet down, made them all the more eager to demonstrate their ability to mime in silence the agonies and ecstasies of their trade. So the early producers, without a second thought, hired stage actors, and the biggest salaries went to the biggest stage names. By getting Sarah Bernhardt they thought they were getting the supreme feast of acting. But any year after the invention of sound, film audiences could see her only as a figure of fun, a dumb creature jerking her sawdust heart around in a puppet world.          —ALASTAIR COOKE, *Six Men*

**5.7** coh

# 5.7 Using Key Words and Parallelism

**5.7a Parallelism.** Transitional words and phrases show the connection between ideas and details. Key words and parallelism do the same (see 20.1). Phrases and clauses that have the same grammatical structure (phrases opening with prepositions, a series of clauses opening with *there are* or *it is*) are said to be **parallel**. Here is a paragraph that uses parallelism to highlight similar or parallel ideas:

> The most understandable mood into which many Americans have been plunged by crime is one of frustration and bewilderment. For "crime" is not a single simple phenomenon that can be examined, analyzed and described in one piece. It occurs in every part of the country and in every stratum of society. *Its practitioners and its victims are* people of all ages, incomes and backgrounds. *Its trends are* difficult to ascertain. *Its causes are* legion. *Its cures are* speculative and controversial. An examination of any single kind of crime, let alone of "crime in America," raises a myriad of issues of the utmost complexity.
> —The President's Commission on Law Enforcement, *The Challenge of Crime in a Free Society* [italics added]

**5.7b Key Words.** Key words, like parallel phrases, may be repeated to keep the central idea in focus. Here is a later paragraph from the same 1967 report:

> The most damaging of the effects of violent crime is *fear*, and that *fear* must not be belittled. Suddenly becoming the ob-

ject of a stranger's violent hostility is as *frightening* as any class of experience. A citizen who hears rapid footsteps behind him as he walks down a dark and otherwise deserted street cannot be expected to calculate that the chance of those footsteps having a sinister meaning is only one in a hundred or in a thousand or, if he does make such a calculation, to be calmed by its results. Any chance at all is *frightening*. And, in fact, when Commission interviewers asked a sample of citizens what they would do in just such a situation, the majority replied, "Run as fast as I could or call for help." Commission studies in several cities indicate that just this kind of *fear* has impelled hundreds of thousands of Americans to move their homes or change their habits.

> —The President's Commission on Law Enforcement,
> *The Challenge of Crime in a Free Society* [italics added]

**5.7**
**coh**

### EXERCISES

1. In the following paragraphs identify key words and parallel phrases that connect ideas and details and give focus to the central or topic idea:

a.  The primacy of the profession, particularly its success in resisting corporate domination, contributed to the development of a distinctive division of labor in medical care. In industry, despite the resistance of artisans, the dictates of the market broke up the work of skilled craftsmen into low-skill—and consequently cheaper—labor. In medicine, physicians maintained the integrity of their craft and control of the division of labor. While medicine itself became highly specialized, the division of labor among physicians was negotiated by doctors themselves instead of being hierarchically imposed upon them by owners, managers, or engineers. And professional interests and ideals decisively influenced the increasingly complex division of labor between physicians and the occupations that emerged with the growth of modern hospitals, clinics, and laboratories.

> —PAUL STARR, *The Social Transformation*
> *of American Medicine*

b.  The social group television likes best to feature in the hours allotted to children is the gang. Sometimes it's a gang of animated human or humanoid figures; sometimes it's a gang of animated motor cars. The audience is invited to like these gangs and identify with the children and adolescents in them, or with the anthropomorphic characters in the animations. Whether the gambit is successful or not depends, of course, on the child. Still, one thing is certain. The reiterated showing of this kind of social grouping, and the social support system that glamorizes it, legitimizes the teenage gang as a viable social structure; any child growing up in this country can scarcely miss the signals.

—ROSE K. GOLDSEN, *The Show and Tell Machine*

2. Write a paragraph of your own on a topic relating to television or radio or movies. Use key words and parallel phrases to connect your ideas and details and to focus on the topic idea.

**5.7**
**coh**

## Checklist for Organizing Paragraphs

**5.1**   Organize your paragraphs into clear units of thought.

**5.2**   Some paragraphs open with a statement of the subject or topic and some open with the central idea.

**5.3a**   You may develop your opening statement through a series of details.

**5.3b**   Restate your central idea in the course of the paragraph for special emphasis.

**5.3c**   One effective method of development is to state the topic and then restrict and illustrate it.

**5.3d**   Some paragraphs build supporting details to the central idea.

**5.3e**   Some state a problem and then discuss a solution.

**5.4a**   Opening paragraphs should state the subject of the essay, generate interest in it, and possibly state the thesis.

**5.4b**   Closing paragraphs should reaffirm the importance of the subject and possibly restate the thesis or suggest avenues for further experiment or investigation.

**5.5a-b**   Unify the paragraph by connecting the ideas and details to the central idea.

**5.6a-b**   Use transitional words and phrases to show the connection between ideas and details and to show addition, explanation, exemplification, qualification, and other relationships.

**5.7a**   Highlight similar ideas and details in the paragraph through parallel wording.

**5.7b**   Repeat key words to focus the reader's attention on the topic idea.

# Building Paragraphs

The previous chapter discusses various ways of organizing paragraphs, making transitions, and emphasizing key ideas. This chapter describes ways of developing the paragraph through analysis of its central idea.

You may develop a paragraph by defining the meaning of a word or by classifying it—that is, by showing the categories or classifications to which a thing belongs. You may develop it in other ways: by dividing or subclassifying one of these classes, comparing members of the same class, or giving examples. You may work out an analogy—a point-by-point comparison—as a special kind of example. Or you may analyze a process or trace causes and effects.

These methods of analysis may be combined. For example, a paragraph on the federal budget may define the word *deficit*, give details on present and past deficits, and make comparisons with personal and family budgets. Or the paragraph may trace the process by which government deficits occur and analyze the causes of the present deficit and its effects. The methods employed depend on how simple or complex the idea is.

## 6.1 Definition

**6.1a Denotation.** **Definition** is essential in the many kinds of writing you do in college and later in life. Quizzes and exams usually ask for definitions. In expository and persuasive essays, you explain words unfamiliar to your readers. A common kind is the familiar dictionary definition that denotes or marks the distinguishing qualities of the object.

In defining a word denotatively, you begin with the class or **genus** to which the thing belongs and then give the specific **differences**—those characteristics that set the thing apart from all other members of the class:

Bearings are flat strips of metal, formed into half-circles about as thick as a matchbook match and about an inch wide. The bearing surface itself—the surface that *bears* the crankshaft and that *bears* the load imposed by the fire-induced pressure above the piston—is half as thick. Bearing metal is a drab, gray alloy, the principal component of which is *babbitt*, a low-friction metal porous enough to absorb oil but so soft that it must be alloyed to withstand high pressures. (I like to think that Sinclair Lewis had metallurgy in mind when he named his protagonist George Babbitt.) When the fire goes off above the piston and the pressure is transmitted to the crankshaft via the connecting rod, the babbitt-alloyed bearing pushes downward with a force of about 3,500 pounds per square inch. And it must not give way, must not be peened into foil and driven from its place in fragments.

—DON SHARP, "Under the Hood,"
*Harper's Magazine*, June 1980

The definition of car bearings is denotative: Sharp singles out the object from all other "flat strips of metal"—that is, from all other things like it.

Notice that Sharp might have assigned car bearings to a broader class—*engine parts*—instead of to the limited class *flat strips of metal*. This broader definition would have begun as follows:

A car bearing is an engine part that . . .

The remainder of the definition then would tell us what the car bearing does. The breadth of the class or genus depends on the purpose of the definition and on the audience—on what Sharp assumes his readers know about engines.

The person looking up *car bearing* in a desk dictionary probably will not find a definition under this phrase. However, the dictionary does provide a general definition of *bearing*:

in *mechanics*, any part of a machine in or on which another part revolves, slides, etc.     — *Webster's New World Dictionary*

A technical dictionary directed to mechanics and engineers will give a more specific definition.

**6.1b Connotation and Etymology.**   A **connotative** definition gives the general and special associations made with a word—its auras of meanings. An **etymological** definition gives the derivation of the word—its original meaning. For example, in defining a mustang for readers who know nothing about horses, the writer might give the etymology or give its connotations—

**6.1**
**¶**

the qualities associated generally with mustangs. The writer of the following paragraph on the mustang does both:

> Nor could the horse itself be contained any longer. So many were scattered in the confusion of the perpetual rustling that stray horses sighted by the Spaniards were dubbed "mestenos" (belonging to the *mesta*, a Spanish word referring to stock growers). In time, this word became mustang, the name by which we still call our wild horses.
>
> —HOPE RYDEN, *America's Last Wild Horses*

**6.1c  Theoretical Definition.**  Some words cannot easily be fitted to a class and distinguished from other members. Ideas are difficult to classify, especially when they are controversial— for example, the idea of obscenity.

Writers who use controversial words often argue or give reasons for their definition. Giving reasons is especially important when the definition proposes an explanation or theory of something, usually in opposition to another current theory or belief. Here is a definition of scrambled, bureaucratic language or "gobbledygook" (a coinage by a Texas congressman in the 1930s). The definition proposes an explanation for its use:

> Gobbledygook not only flourishes in government bureaus but grows wild and lush in the law, the universities, and sometimes among the literati. Mr. Micawber was a master of gobbledygook, which he hoped would improve his fortunes. It is almost always found in offices too big for face-to-face talk. Gobbledygook can be defined as squandering words, packing a message with excess baggage and so introducing semantic "noise." Or it can be scrambling words in a message so that meaning does not come through. The directions on cans, bottles, and packages for putting the contents to use are often a good illustration. Gobbledygook must not be confused with double talk, however, for the intentions of the sender are usually honest.
>
> —STUART CHASE, "Gobbledygook"

Some definitions seek to make an existing definition as exact or precise as possible. In contrast to theoretical definitions, this kind of "precising" definition proposes no explanation or original view. For example, a writer on twentieth-century democracies argues first the need of a precise definition of *democracy*:

> In order to discuss democracy intelligently it will be necessary, therefore, to define it, to attach to the word a sufficiently precise meaning to avoid the confusion which is not infrequently the chief result of such discussions.

He then builds to this definition of the word:

> Since the Greeks first used the term, the essential test of democratic government has always been this: the source of political authority must be and remain in the people and not in the ruler. A democratic government has always meant one in which the citizens, or a sufficient number of them to represent more or less effectively the common will, freely act from time to time, and according to established forms, to appoint or recall the magistrates and to enact or revoke the laws by which the community is governed. This I take to be the meaning which history has impressed upon the term democracy as a form of government. —CARL BECKER, *Modern Democracy*

**6.1**
¶

See 1.4c for additional discussion of definition.

**EXERCISES**

1. Assume you are describing an orange to a child who has never seen or tasted one and wants to know what it is. If you begin with the classification or genus *fruit*, how many specific differences must you give in your definition? What if you begin with the genus *citrus fruits*? What class would you pick in defining the word to a child?
2. Compare the dictionary definition of *orange* with your own. What difference do you find? Does the dictionary fit the word to a narrower class than citrus fruit? Does it give more information than you would give the child? To what audience is the dictionary definition directed?
3. Are there associations you can make with the orange to help the child better understand what it is? How many of these are personal to you, and how many do you think are associations of most people?
4. What is the etymology of the word *orange*? What does its etymology tell you about how the word came into English?
5. Examine the dictionary definitions of the following words. How broad is the genus to which the word is fitted? Can you think of a broader genus or a more limited one with which the definition might have begun?
   **a.** football (game)  **b.** football (object)
6. What help does the dictionary give you in trying to discover the denotative and connotative meaning of the phrase "political football"?
7. What light does the etymology of the following words shed on their current meanings?
   **a.** culture       **d.** tenor
   **b.** agriculture   **e.** soccer
   **c.** baritone

8. What connotations do the following words share? Does the dictionary give special meanings for each word? Does the etymology, if known, illuminate these meanings?
   a. rowdy
   b. roughneck
   c. hoodlum
   d. ruffian
   e. gangster

**6.2**
¶

## 6.2 Classification and Division

You classify when you put various objects or ideas into a group or class—for example, in describing oranges, lemons, limes, grapefruit, citrons as citrus fruit. In an article on "nonce words," William Safire classifies various kinds of word construction as *neologisms* or new words or phrases:

> Life-styles (a term coined in 1929 by psychologist Alfred Adler to be snapped up two generations later by journalists) are a petri dish for neologisms. Anne Soukhanov, associate editor of Merriam-Webster (dictionary makers unsurpassed in citation-gathering), points to the *-mania* construction: *Discomania* in nightclubbing and *condomania* in housing. *Skateparks* accommodate the life-style of skateboarders, and the *CB'ers* have a language that's 10-4 with them. The *-happy* suffix, which originated in "slap-happy" and was popularized by "trigger-happy," has been replaced by the *-aholic* suffix, from "alcoholic," now used in *workaholic, chocoholic,* and *bookaholic.*
>
> —WILLIAM SAFIRE, *On Language*

**Classification** places various items into a single class; **division** begins with a single class and subclassifies its members by a single principle. In the same article on nonce words, Safire divides *sports metaphors* on the basis of their source:

> Sports metaphors have not been letting down the side, especially in providing coinages. *Welcome to the N.F.L.* is a phrase used to point to unexpectedly rough treatment; a *full-court press* is a basketball term now taken to mean all-out effort. The skiing term *hang a left* is used generally to mean to take a left turn; jogging has contributed terms like *ball of the foot* and *foot-strike* which have not yet outstripped their special meanings.

The division may be as complete as knowledge permits, or it may be incomplete. Horses, for example, are sometimes divided according to breed—draft horses bred for work, light horses bred for riding and herding. Ponies are sometimes identified with light horses or as a breed separate from the first two.

Each subclassification or division may in turn be divided by another principle. Thus light horses may be divided according to use: saddle horses (American saddle horse), harness racing horses (trotters), racing horses (thoroughbreds), herding horses (the Appaloosa and Pinto). These divisions are not complete; other uses of light horses exist. In formal divisions of this sort, the writer sometimes warns that the division is incomplete.

**6.2**
**¶**

Division is common in informal essays. In a humorous essay, Andy Rooney divides fences on the basis of "personality":

> Every fence has its own personality and some don't have much. There are friendly fences. A friendly fence takes kindly to being leaned on. There are friendly fences around play-grounds. And some playground fences are more fun to play on than anything they surround. There are more mean fences than friendly fences overall, though. Some have their own built-in invitation not to be sat upon. Unfriendly fences get it right back sometimes. You seldom see one that hasn't been hit, bashed, bumped or in some way broken or knocked down.
>
> —ANDY ROONEY, "Fences"

Division and classification are complementary forms of anal-ysis. In a science course you will have occasion to classify and divide evidence. For example, you may sort out various chemical substances into classes such as acids and bases. Having done so, you may divide or subclassify one of these classes—for example, acids—into organic and inorganic acids. In a literature course, you may classify writers as *Romantics* to show their common char-acteristics, then divide this class on the basis of genre—Romantic novelists, Romantic poets, Romantic dramatists.

### EXERCISES

1. Assume that you are writing an encyclopedia account of American sports for a foreign audience. If you decide to divide the class *sports* on the basis of place (for example, sports played on water), how many divisions will you have?
2. Assume that later in your account you divide ball games. How many ways might this class be divided?
3. Assume that one of your subdivisions or subclassifications is baseball. How many ways might this class be divided?
4. Note that fences can be divided in other ways—for example, on the basis of their material:

   wood fences, metal fences, stone fences, reed fences, etc.

Or on the basis of their use:

> prison fences, cattle fences (or pens), median barriers on expressways

The division would be inconsistent if it mixed these types:

> wood fences, cattle fences, stone fences, median barriers

Are the following divisions of the particular class consistent?
a. *Fruit of the vine*: grapes, raspberries, blackberries, blueberries, strawberries
b. *Organic acids*: citric acid, phosphoric acid, carbonic acid, lactic acid, sulfuric acid
c. *Armies*: divisions, regiments, battalions, infantries

# 6.3  Example

Most ideas need illustration, for the range of experience to which they apply may be so wide that the reader will find them vague without examples. The idea of "runaway industrial dynamism" in the following paragraph can refer to so many phenomena that the reader needs the extended example of fluorocarbons to clarify it:

> Consider only one recent, well-publicized example of our runaway industrial dynamism. A number of American, European, and Japanese companies develop the fluorocarbon spray-can dispenser—a commercial novelty of relatively minor economic significance to the corporate interests of these societies. For nearly two decades, the product is blithely mass-produced, advertised, and marketed on a world-wide scale. It is in daily use everywhere before anybody can collect evidence of its environmental effects—or perhaps even thinks of making such an investigation. Then, a few inquisitive scientists, acting on the basis of their own private research, suggest the possibility that the fluorocarbons may be capable of doing cataclysmic damage to the ozone layer. Their research is disputed and a public debate ensues. Meanwhile, the fluorocarbons already released continue to rise skyward beyond retrieval, perhaps to rend the biosphere permanently and globally.
>
> —THEODORE ROSZAK, *Person/Planet*

Giving examples is essential in most writing. In an exam answer, for example, you do best always to illustrate your ideas, making the abstract idea concrete for the reader. The apt illustration shows that you understand the idea.

**EXERCISES**

1. What example can you give to illustrate each of the following statements?
   a. There are different ways to punctuate an English sentence.
   b. There are different ways of reading a book.
   c. The word *friendship* describes various relationships.
   d. People respond to criticism in different ways.
2. What examples would you add to the following paragraph to make the idea concrete?

> Television can generate conflicting emotions in the viewer in the space of an evening or an hour—in newscasts particularly. The sequence of facts, ideas, images is often so rapid that the viewer experiences a welter of emotions. The result is an emotional short-circuit, a diminishing of thought—if thinking occurs at all. Marshall McLuhan must have had this effect in mind in his famous statement "The medium is the message."

## 6.4 Comparison and Contrast

A paragraph of **comparison** illustrates a point or argues a thesis through similarities between two or more things; a paragraph of **contrast**, through the differences. Some paragraphs do both. In comparing or contrasting, you can present the similarities or differences one by one, as in this paragraph contrasting European and American circuses:

> European circuses are more familial in atmosphere than our American brand, and their stars—like the great dapper Russian clown Popov—tend to work from a presumption of good health and good will. Popov depicts a playful, intelligent, well-dressed man at the top of his form, whereas American clowning stresses lunacy, poverty, misery, weirdness. American thrill acts are just that: lean toward the possibility that the man may plunge down before our eyes and die. But in Europe the same performers will use nets or "mechanics" (wires to the roof) because the premium is on dexterity and grace, not simply nerve. Often there is something of a gulf between the European stars brought to this side of the ocean who keep to the friendly, upbeat motif, and the ones who go whole hog instead for our circuses' preference for suffering and the bizarre.
>
> —EDWARD HOAGLAND, "Pathos and Perfection"

Here is an outline of the paragraph:

| Difference 1 | European circuses | clowns |
|---|---|---|
| | American circuses | |
| Difference 2 | European circuses | acts |
| | American circuses | |
| Difference 3 | European circuses | stars |
| | American circuses | |

**6.4**

¶

You can organize the paragraph in blocks or as a contrast of wholes—first stating the features of the European circus, then the contrasting features of the American circus:

| Differences 1 | European circuses | clowns |
|---|---|---|
| 2 | | acts |
| 3 | | stars |
| Differences 1 | American circuses | clowns |
| 2 | | acts |
| 3 | | stars |

A paragraph of comparison and contrast—presenting similarities and differences both—expands these patterns:

| Similarity 1 | European circuses |
|---|---|
| | American circuses |
| Similarity 2 | European circuses |
| | American circuses |
| Difference 1 | European circuses |
| | American circuses |
| Difference 2 | European circuses |
| | American circuses |
| Difference 3 | European circuses |
| | American circuses |

Or it might follow this pattern:

| Similarities 1 | European circuses |
|---|---|
| 2 | |
| Differences 1 | American circuses |
| 2 | |
| 3 | |

Like definition and the other methods of analysis, comparison is indispensable in much writing you do in college and later. At some point in lab reports or quizzes or papers, you will need to make brief comparisons and sometimes extended ones—comparisons of different experiences you have had, writers in the same period or different periods of American or English literature, two presidents or two government policies. In business, comparison is an essential method of analysis in judging the merits of particular products; much advertising today depends on comparison with other products to show the "competitive edge."

**EXERCISES**

1. Make a list of similarities and differences between two of the following:
   a. two of your friends
   b. a high school and a college teacher of the same subject
   c. two cars you have driven or owned
   d. two houses you have lived in

   Write a short paragraph presenting the similarities and the differences point by point. Then use your comparison and contrast to develop an idea.
2. Rewrite the paragraph, presenting as a whole the qualities of the first friend, teacher, car, or house, and then as a whole the qualities of the second.
3. How is the contrast organized in the following paragraph, and what is its purpose?

> The landscape architect and the lumbermen have very different ideas about the way a tree should grow. To be beautiful and merely expand as it grows tall, a tree should be out in the open, with plenty of light from all sides and no strong icy winds from a single direction to deform it. The lumberman disdains such a specimen tree, for it has retained most of its outspread limbs, every one of them represented by a knot in the wood that might be cut into boards. For lumber, a tree should grow straight and slim, shaded on all sides until every one of its horizontal limbs dies as soon as the leaves on them can no longer get enough light through higher branches in the crown. Thereafter, the trunk will enlarge with no knots and, when sent to the sawmill, yield clear boards from its outer layers (beneath the slabs and bark). The center of the tree can be cut into large timbers for beams, in which the knots will be unimportant.
> —LORUS J. MILNE AND MARGERY MILNE, *The Ages of Man*

# 6.5   Analogy

Comparison gives a relative estimate of two things; both are of equal importance. In Hoagland's paragraph on European and American circuses, both are equally important in the comparison. **Analogy** is a point-by-point comparison that explains or illustrates one thing through another thing that resembles it in some ways but not in all ways:

> Amplifier power, usually measured in watts per channel, is rather like horsepower in cars: it's handy in the tight spots. You don't always drive with the gas pedal jammed to the floor, pulling every bit of available power from the engine. Similarly, an amplifier or receiver rarely operates at full output. But there are moments in music—just as there are moments on the road—when ample power helps you over the hurdles. On the road, you may need the extra power to pass a truck. In music, the equivalent of such a critical moment may be an orchestra fortissimo, a pianist's exuberance in striking a sforzando, or the stentorian proclamations of a great pipe organ. If not enough power is available at such moments, the sound grows harsh and the thrill of the climactic moment turns into sonic hash. The point is that—contrary to popular belief—power doesn't equate with loudness but rather with the purity of sound in loud passages.
>
> —HANS FANTEL, "Sound," *The New York Times*, March 13, 1983

**6.5**
¶

Notice that amplifier power is not like horsepower in all respects. Since analogies are always limited in the number of points of similarities, the writer may tell us that there is danger of drawing more conclusions than the analogy warrants.

Analogy is also used as a supporting argument. Fantel may have used the analogy to argue that we need extra amplifier power to get through the sound peaks, just as we need extra horsepower to get us through tight spots on the highway. In argumentative analogies such as this one, the differences must be examined carefully since significant ones can weaken the analogy. See 32.2 for more discussion of good and bad argumentative analogies.

As Fantel's paragraph shows, analogy is an important device of exposition. Science writers depend on analogy to make difficult ideas clear to readers who have little or no knowledge in the field. But analogy must be used with caution, for it depends on similarities, not identities, and the differences are fundamental though not always apparent.

### EXERCISE

First write down the similarities you see between driving a car and riding a bike. Use these similarities to write a paragraph of analogy directed to a person learning to drive. The purpose of the analogy is to clarify some of the steps the driver must perform. At the end of your paragraph, state the limits of the analogy—that is, the points of dissimilarity between driving a car and riding a bike.

# 6.6 Process

**Process analysis** is a common method of exposition. You could not assemble or operate a stereo or other piece of machinery without an instruction book. Much science writing depends, too, on process. Your chemistry lab manual gives a series of processes. So in many ways does the handbook you are reading.

Some paragraphs trace processes—perhaps a natural process like the circulation of the blood or a mechanical process like assembling a bicycle. The account is usually **chronological**, the steps of the process presented in the order of occurrence. If you present any of the steps out of order, possibly to give them special attention, you should also indicate the natural order.

In describing a process, you must make a decision on where to begin. Giving the details of a recipe is not as easy a job as it sounds, for the person given a recipe to follow may not have the skills one takes for granted in the practiced cook. In the following paragraphs, a skilled shoemaker, describing the process of making a shoe by hand, starts with definitions of his tools, then the pieces of leather he uses. He then describes the process itself, noting alternative procedures. Here are the first two paragraphs of this description:

Here's how you put a shoe together. You stitch the vamp and the quarters together first. Then the quarters are sewed together in the back of the shoe with the edges out (or the flaps out), and then a small strip would be added up the back of the shoe to cover that seam where the two pieces are joined.

Then the insole is cut out to fit the last. Actually, you can cut the insole out first, fit it to the last, then sew the two quarters together with your flax thread and then add the vamp. If you use a cap on the toe it goes across next. Then you start shaping the upper over the last. Wet it and stretch it to conform to the shape of the last and the size of the shoe you want. When you get that stretched and shaped over the last, you should have about a half-inch to three-quarters-inch lap on the underside of the last to attach the sole through. On the bottom of the last, the insole piece comes first and is tacked down in place with a couple of tacks (one in the toe and one in the heel). Then the upper is lapped around, and as it is stretched into place, it is tacked down through an insole into the last. The sole goes onto the top of that; and if you want a heel, you add that onto the top of the sole.  —"Shoemaking," *Foxfire 6*

Process combines with description and narration in expressive and other kinds of essays. Here are the opening paragraphs from a student essay describing roller coaster rides:

**6.6**
**¶**

Roller coasters are by far the most exciting rides in amusement parks. Millions of people each year ride "The Beast" at King's Island near Cincinnati. To be lifted to great heights and quickly dropped to great depths is the thrill of these coasters. But the fun involves much more than entering the car and taking the ride.

First consider the steps prior to entering the car. Entering the park, many people are already thinking about the fearsome ride. On reaching the entrance, I myself find a line extending considerably beyond the gate, down the walkway, and around the corner. Here I collect my thoughts and decide whether a three-hour wait for a thirty-second ride is what a sensible person does. Noticing the many others in line, I am mesmerized into waiting and conquering the ride.

The minutes are long as I stare at the second hand rotating slowly around the clock. I finally reach the corner—only to discover that the gate is another fifty yards away. The line seems endless to some, and they drop out of line, but I will stay strong. As I enter the gate, I see rows and rows of lines weaving back and forth. I notice on many faces the weariness of standing so long. The excitement is still to come.

I finally approach the entrance ramp of the ride—feeling suddenly anxious as I see the grins of those just completing the ride and the frowns of those departing. Those of us in line picture the first hill. We feel the wind rushing through our hair and the coaster shooting jolts into our bodies. But once again we are part of the fatigued crowd: another thirty minutes is left before we have our turn.

—PAUL KIM

All riders share similar feelings in waiting their turn on the coaster, as Paul Kim shows in merging his feelings with those of the others in line. At the same time he expresses his own feelings.

### EXERCISES

1. In a paragraph or two, describe to a child how to cook a hamburger. Then describe the same process to a foreigner who has cooked other meats and fish but not hamburger.

2. In a humorous essay, Russell Baker describes the impossible job of opening a "safety cap" of a plastic bottle:

> Approaching the bottled acid, I grip the cap, press down—there's the trick to conquering the "safety cap": pressing down before turning—and unscrew.
>
> —"Openings"

Baker finds that the cap refuses to come off the bottle. Write your own account of how to remove a stubborn safety cap. Assume you are writing to a frustrated person who asks you for help.

3. Paul Kim concludes his essay on roller coasters as follows:

> The minutes pass finally and my long-awaited turn has come. Only two more people before me! My hands shake as fear sets in. I enter the car. The bar that crosses my legs does not seem very stable, but before I have a chance to complain the journey upward slowly begins. The lift to the highest hill in the country has begun. After many treacherous hills and neck-breaking twists, the ride ends. The thrill has concluded—I walk down the ramp.

What does Kim gain in not describing the ride in more detail? What idea or thesis does his description imply?

4. If Kim wished to focus on the ride and not on waiting in line, what changes would he need to make in his opening paragraphs? What details of the ride would you stress if you were writing the essay?

## 6.7 Causal Analysis

**6.7a Cause as Process.** Tracing causes and effects is probably the most complex of the ways to develop paragraphs. One kind of **causal analysis** traces effects—one effect leading to another in a causal chain. Sometimes this chain of effects is a simple one as in this explanation of why car bearings wear out:

> If the oil level falls too low, the oil pump sucks in air. The oil gets as frothy as whipped cream and doesn't flow. In time, oil pressure will fall so low that the "idiot" light on the dashboard will flash, but long before then the bearing may have run "dry" and suffered considerable amounts of its metal to be peened away by those 3,500-pound hammer blows. "Considerable" may mean only .005 inches, or about the thickness of one sheet of 75-percent-cotton, 25-pound-per-ream dissertation bond—not much metal, but enough to allow oil to escape from the bearing even after the defective filter gasket is replaced and the oil supply replenished. From the time of oil starvation onward, the beaten bearing is a little disaster waiting to spoil a vacation or a commute to an important meeting.
>
> —DON SHARP, "Under the Hood"

**6.7b Remote and Proximate Causes.**    The word *cause* has various meanings. One meaning distinguishes **remote** causes—those distant in time—from **proximate** or immediate causes—those close in time. Thus a defect in the manufacturing of a tire may cause a flat at a later time: this cause is a remote one. The proximate cause, closer in time, is a hard bump that flattens the weakened tire. A remote cause of low oil in the crankshaft might be the ignorance or neglect of the car owner.

Sharp points to owner attitude toward car maintenance as a remote but nevertheless decisive cause:

> But for the most part, once the key goes into the ignition, people assign responsibility for the car's smooth running to someone else—to anybody but themselves. If the engine doesn't start, that's not because the driver has abused it, but because the manufacturer was remiss or the mechanic incompetent. (Both suspicions are reasonable, but they do not justify the driver's spineless passivity.) The driver considers himself merely a client of the vehicle. He proudly disclaims, at club and luncheon, any understanding of the dysfunctions of the machine. He must so disclaim, for to admit knowledge or to seek it actively would require an admission of responsibility and fault. To be wrong about inflation or the political aspirations of the Albanians doesn't cost anybody anything, but to claim to know why the car won't start and then to be proved wrong is both embarrassing and costly.

**6.7c The Four Causes.**    In writing paragraphs of cause and effect, you may find it useful to talk about "cause" in other senses than the immediate and remote. The following four causes are sometimes distinguished:

1. the **material** out of which the object is made
2. the **form** or shape given to the object
3. the **maker** of the object
4. the **purpose** or use of the object

For example, a pencil has the following "causes":

**6.7**
¶

1. wood, graphite, metal, and rubber—its materials
2. the mold, form, or shape used in its manufacture—the encasing of a thin rod of graphite in wood, with the eraser attached
3. the manufacturer—the maker of the object
4. the application of pencil to paper—the purpose or use

In a paragraph or an essay you may focus on one cause or on two or more: how many you discuss depends on the purpose of the analysis. Analysis of substances dumped into a lake will focus on their materials if you want to find out whether the substance is toxic. In trying to identify the manufacturer, you focus on the maker. You focus on the purpose in seeking the use of the chemical. And you focus on the form in conducting a laboratory analysis of its chemical structure. The following paragraph focuses on the material and the formal causes in explaining why the longbow is inefficient by comparison with other kinds:

> Although the longbow, a simple curved stick with a string connecting the ends, figured prominently in Britain's Hundred Years' War and sustained generations of American Indians, it is short on efficiency. The Indians' hunting success, in fact, was due more to their stalking expertise than to technology. The bow is huge, typically 72 inches long, so much of the energy expended in drawing the bowstring goes into returning the massive limbs to their original position rather than shooting the arrow.          —LAURA B. ACKERMAN, "The Bow Machine,"
> *Science 85*, July/August

Causal analysis is as important as definition, comparison, and example in the many kinds of writing you do. Reports of chemistry and biology experiments are reports of causes and effects. In writing about cause, you are not writing about one kind of "cause" always. See 32.3 on causal analysis in argument.

### EXERCISES

1. Write a paragraph distinguishing the proximate or immediate from the remote causes of an important event in your

life, perhaps an achievement that took long preparation and the help of many people. In the course of your paragraph, discuss which of these causes contributed most to your success.

2. Distinguish the materials, form, maker, and purpose of one of the following:
   a. the book you are reading
   b. an essay you wrote recently
   c. the vehicle that brought you to school

3. Write a paragraph illustrating the point Sander Vanocur makes about the "continuous loop" of television news. Develop your paragraph in several ways—for example, through definition, comparison, and example:

> More than fifty years ago Walter Lippmann suggested that newspaper reporting was in large part a process of filling out an established "repertory of stereotypes" with current news. In a similar way, network news is involved with illustrating a limited repertory of story lines with appropriate pictures. One NBC commentator, Sander Vanocur, observed that "network news is a continuous loop: there are only a limited number of plots—'Black versus White,' 'War is Hell,' 'America is falling apart,' 'Man against the elements,' 'The Generation Gap,' etc.—which we seem to be constantly redoing with different casts of characters." Many of the correspondents interviewed complained about the need to fit news developments into developed molds or formulas, and to order stories along predetermined lines; at the same time, most accepted it as a practical necessity. Again, the fact that a film story requires the coordinated efforts of a large number of individuals—reporters, cameramen, sound men, writers, producer, editor and commentator—working on the product at different times, makes it necessary that there be a stable set of expectations of what constitutes a proper story. Moreover, producers generally assume that a given audience will have certain preferences in terms of both the form and the content of news stories. "Every program has certain requirements and guidelines for its filmed reports," an ABC executive explained. "Eventually these might harden into formulas and clichéd plots, but when they fail to hold the audiences' attention, the producer or the program is usually changed."
>
> —Edward Jay Epstein, *News from Nowhere*

## **6.8**  Combining Methods of Analysis

The methods of analysis discussed in this chapter often combine in paragraphs. For example, basic terms often must be defined, and tools or ingredients classified, in describing a process. Paragraphs that trace cause and effect often do so through process analysis. Few paragraphs develop ideas without illustrating them. Here is a paragraph that combines causal analysis with example and comparison:

**6.8**
¶

> Why is violence booming at the moment? There are a few non-political explanations besides the old state-of-the-world stuff. We have, for instance, more leisure to enjoy it now—all our pleasures must grow to fill the space. It is also easier to distance ourselves from pain than it used to be, since it is now almost possible to live a whole lifetime without it ourselves; like savages, we are fascinated by this alien experience, this strange dance people do when they are hurt. My guess is that the great consumers of violence are not themselves dealers in it but full-time onlookers in the last of the great American spectator sports. And finally, the art itself has improved so much; screen violence is far prettier than it used to be, a regular ballet; and technology has opened a treasure trove of methods that has to be explored to the bottom.          —WILFRID SHEED, "On Violence"

This paragraph shows again the importance of transitions (*for instance, also, finally*) in organizing a diverse series of ideas and details. In showing where the discussion has come from and where it is going, transitions are essential in letting the reader follow a train of thought.

The more complex the analysis, the more attention you must pay to how ideas and details in the paragraph form into a whole. An incoherent paragraph lacks a central focus—a central idea to which the ideas and details connect. These connections depend, finally, on how the paragraphs fit into the essay. In revising the essay, you have an opportunity to test not only the unity of your paragraphs but also that of the essay itself and the connection of ideas and details throughout.

**EXERCISES**

1. Assume that you are writing a letter to your school newspaper arguing for a change in a school policy or course requirement. Use at least three of the methods of analysis discussed in this chapter to develop your argument.
2. Revise your letter, directing it to a relative or a friend. To fit this new audience, make changes in the methods of anal-

ysis you used to develop your argument. Be ready to justify these changes.

3. Analyze the structure of Edward Jay Epstein's paragraph to show how he uses several methods of analysis in combination to develop his central idea.

4. The following paragraphs use some of the methods of analysis discussed in this chapter. Identify them, and be ready to explain how the author uses each method:

**6.8** ¶

a. The consequences of man's introduction of heat into his environment can usefully be classified as local, regional, and global. On the local level, the principal effects are the disruption of aquatic ecosystems by the heated effluent from power-plant condensers, and climatic effects ranging from ground fogs (associated with evaporative cooling towers at power plants) to the urban "heat-island" phenomenon. The effects associated with power plants have been well publicized, and we will not pursue them here. On the other hand, the heat that man dissipates in his cities is neither as widely appreciated as a problem nor as well understood scientifically in its effects. We know that our cities are, on the average, sometimes warmer, rainier, and foggier than their rural surroundings. We also know that the rate of energy dissipation by man in the Los Angeles Basin, for example, is equal to nearly 6 percent of the solar energy absorbed over the same area. This is undoubtedly a significant perturbation. However, it is difficult to sort its consequences from other man-induced effects that accompany it, including the city's surface and heat-transfer properties and the usual haze of pollutants.
    —Paul R. Ehrlich and John P. Holdren, "The Heat Barrier," *Saturday Review*, April 3, 1971

b. Equilibrium of this statistical kind is usually known as "thermal equilibrium," because a state of equilibrium of this kind is always characterized by a definite temperature which must be uniform throughout the system. Indeed, strictly speaking, it is only in a state of thermal equilibrium that temperature can be precisely defined. The powerful and profound branch of theoretical physics known as "statistical mechanics" provides a mathematical machinery for computing the properties of any system in thermal equilibrium.

The approach to thermal equilibrium works a little like the way the price mechanism is supposed to work in classical economics. If demand exceeds supply, the price of goods will rise, cutting the effective demand and encouraging increased production. If supply exceeds demand, prices will drop, increasing effective demand and discouraging further production. In either case, supply and demand will approach equality. In the same way, if there are too many or too few particles with energies, velocities, and so on, in some particular range, then the rate at which they leave this range will be greater or less than the rate at which they enter, until equilibrium is established.

—STEVEN WEINBERG, *The First Three Minutes*

**6.8**
¶

c. Differences in attitudes toward space—what would be territoriality in lower forms of life—raise a number of other interesting points. U.S. women who go to live in Latin America all complain about the "waste" of space in the houses. On the other hand, U.S. visitors to the Middle East complain about crowding, in the houses and on the streetcars and buses. Everywhere we go space seems to be distorted. When we see a gardener in the mountains of Italy planting a single row on each of six separate terraces, we wonder why he spreads out his crop so that he has to spend half his time climbing up and down. We overlook the complex chain of communication that would be broken if he didn't cultivate alongside his brothers and his cousin and if he didn't pass his neighbors and talk to them as he moves from one terrace to the next.

—EDWARD T. HALL, "The Anthropology of Manners"

d. A remuda was the large herd of cow ponies embracing all the horses belonging to the cowboys of an outfit. Since the nomadic cowboys literally lived in the saddle, moving from place to place with the cattle, they needed a frequent change of mount to prevent any one animal from becoming played out. Consequently, when a man joined a cattle drive, he brought with him a "string" of perhaps a dozen horses. All these "extra" ponies were herded along the trail in a group by a horse wrangler. A roundup of two thousand to four thousand head of cattle might require a *remuda* of anywhere from three hundred to five hundred horses.

—HOPE RYDEN, *America's Last Wild Horses*

e. These Appaloosa horses, named after the Palouse River along which they once grazed, have been facetiously called two-toned, polka-dotted ponies, and the description can hardly be more accurate. There are six color types, but the two most common patterns are

as follows: The front half of the animal is either white
or roanish, meaning that it is a solid color, interspersed
with white hairs, giving that part of the horse an almost
iridescent cast—much like "shot silk"—when the light
hits it in a particular way. If the basic color of the roan
is black, this half of the animal sometimes appears blue;
if the basic color is brown, it reflects shades of red. The
rear half of the Nez Percé horse is either white, spattered with small roan polka dots, or roan with a scatter-
ing of small white polka dots. A third type of Appaloosa
is called the leopard phase, and an animal so marked is
covered with round polka dots over its entire white or
gray body.   —HOPE RYDEN, *America's Last Wild Horses*

**6.8**

¶

## Checklist for Building Paragraphs

**6.1a-b**   Use a denotative definition to give the properties of an
object or idea, a connotative definition to give the ideas and
feelings associated with a word, or an etymological definition to
explain a current meaning.

**6.1c**   Provide your own definition to make the usage of a word
more precise or to present an explanation or theory in the course
of defining a word.

**6.2**   Classify objects or ideas to show their common properties,
or divide a class of objects or ideas to distinguish their separate
ones.

**6.3**   Make your ideas clear through examples.

**6.4**   Compare and contrast to show similarities and differences
in objects or ideas.

**6.5**   Present an analogy for the purpose of illustration.

**6.6**   Trace a natural or mechanical process for the same purpose.

**6.7**   You can trace a process to explain causation, or distinguish
remote from immediate causes, or discuss the materials of a
thing, or its form or shape, or its maker, or its purpose or use—
or all of these.

# The Sentence and
# Its Parts

This chapter defines the parts of the sentence—phrases and clauses and their constituents or parts. The next chapter discusses the traditional parts of speech—nouns, pronouns, articles, adjectives, verbs, adverbs, prepositions, and conjunctions. These are the elements of sentence building, revision, and editing—the topics of the following chapter and later chapters in this handbook. A separate listing of the parts of the sentence and the parts of speech appears in the glossary of grammatical terms at the end of the book.

Analyzing a sentence requires a recognition of the forms that compose it. A basic grammar names these forms and describes their relationship or structure. Though grammatical knowledge alone cannot make you a better writer of sentences, it can help in analyzing the sentences you write. It provides a common vocabulary through which you and your instructor and classmates can discuss ways of improving sentences.

This chapter begins with a definition of the sentence and then defines clauses and phrases—the larger constituents or parts of the sentence.

## 7.1 Defining the Sentence

**7.1a Sentence Sense.** What makes a sentence complete? This question may seem strange, given the fact you speak complete sentences and did so long before you learned to write. Recognizing complete sentences should not be a problem, yet a little reflection on experience in speaking and writing shows that it is. Consider the conversation in which a friend asks you to repeat an unclear statement or to complete an unfinished one.

And consider written sentences you thought were complete until readers asked you to explain them.

A familiar but undependable definition is that the sentence expresses a complete thought or idea. This definition is undependable because it does not fix the meaning of *complete*: the definition depends on what each speaker and writer has in mind as a complete thought or idea at the moment of speaking or writing. We see how hard it is to find out in our ordinary conversations—with their need for continual clarification and repetition. Obviously what is complete in the mind of the speaker is not complete in the mind of the listener who, in mishearing or misunderstanding a statement, asks for clarification.

**7.1**

**gr**

Nevertheless, as speakers and writers of English we fortunately do agree on what makes the great majority of spoken and written sentences complete. That we do easily converse proves how much common agreement between us exists; so does the relative ease with which we read the words of others. We all agree on the following:

> The car is red.
> Is that car red?
> That car is red!

And we probably all agree that the following are not sentences:

> the car
> the car is
> is red
> car is red

When confusion does arise, it is usually with a word group like the following:

> not at all

If you speak these words and someone asks you to clarify them, you may state the full sentence you had in mind:

> I said the car is not red at all.

Why are we able to clear up confusion over words? As speakers and listeners we share a **grammatical** or sentence sense telling us that some words, phrases, and clauses are constituents or parts of larger wholes and that other words, phrases, and clauses are not. This grammatical sense does not depend on our ability to analyze the constituents that form sentences—that is, on knowledge of formal grammar. You were able at an early age to distinguish a meaningful group of words from a meaningless one before learning any of the rudiments of formal grammar. You sensed then and sense now which of the following groups of words is and is not a sentence:

> sentences not all are complete
> not all sentences are complete

But recognition does not depend on the sight of words alone. It depends both on the intonation and pitch of the voice and on the context of the sentence.

**7.1**
**gr**

**7.1b Context and Vocal Markers.**  **Context** refers to the words that surround a statement and suggest the tone or attitude of the speaker, the intent of the statement, and its overall significance in the conversation or essay. The following word groups are complete thoughts or ideas in the minds of those who know their context:

> going home
> to the bank
> my savings book and bounced check

We also understand the phrases in the following brief conversation because we know their context:

> What are you doing after class?
> Going home.
> Where are you going now?
> To the bank.
> What did you ask me to look for?
> My savings book, bounced check, last bank statement, the letter
>   saying I'm overdrawn.

**Intonation** or vocal stresses further identify the tone or attitude of the speaker. Without the context of spoken conversation, you would not know how to interpret the following:

> going home

Here are four possible interpretations:

> Going home!
> Going home?
> Going home.
> going home,

In speaking the first three of these, you signal in different ways that the statement is complete. Consider the first:

> I'm going home!

No matter what stress you give the word *home*, you drop your voice at the end of the sentence. You drop it also in saying

> I am going home.    ( ↘ )

However, the opposite happens when you ask a question:

> Going home?    ( ↗ )

But notice what happens in pronouncing

> Going home,

The voice drops somewhat in pitch.
Hearing these words, you expect information to follow:

> Going home, I took the "A" train—not the bus.

If no pause occurs, the voice remains suspended:

> Going home    ( → )

In this instance you assume that the speaker will add information about going home before reaching a pause or coming to a stop:

> Going home on the "A" train that evening . . .
> Going home on the "A" train that evening, I missed my stop.
> Going home on the "A" train that evening was a mistake.

The pitch of voice, then, gives essential information about the meaning of a group of words. Sentence sense therefore depends on knowing how the words would be pronounced and in what context. Pitch by itself is not an infallible test of a complete sentence, but at times it is a useful test in identifying groups of words we agree are sentences.

### EXERCISES

**1.** Turn the following scrambled words into sentences:
   **a.** laughed the children at the clown
   **b.** to solve the problem hard was
   **c.** I took the hardest subject was calculus
   **d.** I in math that same summer another course took
   **e.** waste to time no is there
   **f.** over spilt milk is there to cry no time
   **g.** can I in this adventure without your help not succeed or your encouragement
   **h.** based on John Le Carré's spy novel on television the series saw I me led the book to read
   **i.** as interesting for non-engineering students it is and for engineers calculus is

**j.** equally to all students interesting can be few subjects with no background especially those

2. Turn the following phrases into declarative sentences, then into questions:
   **a.** drinking water
   **b.** talking to the woman sitting at the desk
   **c.** the tall woman in the blue dress, sitting at the desk near the window
   **d.** the architect of the building
   **e.** to whoever answers the door
   **f.** to rock the boat in the middle of the river
   **g.** wondering when the bank would open for business
   **h.** whoever turned off the radio and pulled the plug
   **i.** no matter who you see
   **j.** laughed at the mistake

3. The following sentences have different meanings depending on how you punctuate them. Punctuate each of the following in two different ways and state the difference in meaning:
   **a.** is he crazy
   **b.** what a robin
   **c.** going to the beach in this weather
   **d.** we are going to the beach
   **e.** nothing doing

# 7.2  Clauses

**7.2a  The Clause Defined.**  Sentences consist of clauses and phrases. A **clause** consists of a subject and something said or predicated about it:

*Subject*      *Predicate*
*The book* / *has a green cover.*

The clause may also consist of an actor and the action performed:

The men / drank.

Each of the following clauses contains a **subject** and a **predicate** or statement about the subject:

The men / *talked.*
The men / *tested the water.*
The men from the Health Department / *tested the water from the tap.*

The men who knocked on the door / *wanted to test the water from the tap.*

The men wearing white jackets / *tested the water from the tap in the hall upstairs.*

The predicate of the clause may consist of a single verb:

The men / *talked.*

**7.2
gr**

Or of a verb and various complements or words that complete the statement about the subject.

These complements are the following:

**Direct object**—something created by the verb or something that receives the action of the verb:

The artist drew *a picture* on the wall.
The golfer hit *the ball* into the water.

**Indirect object**—the receiver of the action, usually preceding the direct object following the verb:

The coach gave *the team* instructions.
The artist gave *me* the picture.

**Subject complement**—an equivalent **(predicate noun)** or description **(predicate adjective)** of the subject that follows a *to be* or linking verb (*is, are, was, were, will be, seems, becomes*):

The tall man in the white jacket is *a chemist* (predicate noun).
She seems *a woman of her word.*
She becomes *president of the company* tomorrow.
She is *intelligent* and *ambitious* (predicate adjectives).

**Object complement**—a term that completes the direct object, describing or giving information about it:

The voters elected the former congresswoman *governor.*
Jim called me *his friend.*
I consider her *somebody important.*

**7.2b Independent and Dependent Clauses.**   Clauses can stand alone as grammatical sentences, or they can serve as parts of other clauses that do so.

**Independent clauses** (or **main clauses**) can stand alone because they make whole statements or assertions:

I am going home.
We drank.
The men in the hall drank water from the tap.

**Dependent clauses** (or **subordinate clauses**) do not make whole statements and therefore cannot stand alone. They are called dependent because they serve as modifiers or as constituents of independent clauses. Here are some of their uses:

Modifying the subject:

The men *who tested the water* are health officers.

Modifying the subject complement:

The tall man is the chemist *who tested the water*.

Modifying the direct object:

The artist sold the picture *that she had just painted*.

Modifying the verb predicate:

They drank the water *even though it had a strange odor*.

Subject of the clause:

*Whoever gets sick* should call the Health Department at once.

Subject complement of the clause:

The winner is *whoever reaches the finish line first*.

Direct object of the clause:

They ate *whatever grew in the fields*.

Modifying clauses are considered **restrictive** if they limit or change the meaning of the sentence by providing essential information:

The men *who tested the water* are health officers.

This sentence discusses particular people—those testing the water. Omitting the clause would change the meaning:

The men are health officers.

A **nonrestrictive** or appositive modifier adds important but not essential information to identify the thing modified—a fact indicated to the reader by the commas that set off the clause:

The men in white jackets, *who tested the tap water*, are officials from the Health Department.

You know that the men being identified as officials are those in white jackets. The additional fact that they tested the water does not change or restrict the meaning of the sentence. If, however, the writer is talking about two groups of men, all wearing white jackets, the information about the water would be essential or restrictive—a fact indicated to the reader by the absent commas:

The men in white jackets who drank the water became ill. The men in white jackets who did not drink the water did not.

**7.2**
**gr**

Dependent clauses are classified as *noun clauses* (or *nominals*), *adjective clauses* (or *adjectivals*), and *adverb clauses* (or *adverbials*) according to their function as nouns or pronouns, adjectives, and adverbs in the sentence. See 8.1c, 8.4c, 8.8d.

**EXERCISE**

1. Decide whether the clause is independent or dependent. If the clause is dependent, attach it to an independent clause:
   a. the books on the shelf are dusty
   b. because the books on the shelf are dusty
   c. whenever you dust the books
   d. he meant to dust the books on the shelf but didn't
   e. which the convention passed unanimously
   f. since the platform committee had been deadlocked over a key plank
   g. she gave the platform her strong endorsement
   h. that so few of the committee members attended the meeting
   i. they argued for a change in the wording of the plank
   j. whoever objects to the plank and proposes a substitute

# 7.3 Phrases

**7.3a The Phrase Defined.**   **Phrases** are word groups or clusters lacking a subject or a predicate or both:

the green cover
are going
with her brother
giving instructions

Phrases are usually classified according to the part of speech that governs them—thus *noun phrases, verb phrases, prepositional phrases, participial phrases.* (Chapter 8 discusses these classifications.)

Like dependent clauses, phrases serve as modifiers or constituents of clauses, as in the following sentences where they function as direct objects, predicates, and other grammatical units:

| *Subject* | | *Indirect object* |
|---|---|---|
| *The Democratic Convention* | gave | *the congresswoman from Queens* |

*Direct object*

*its official endorsement.*

*Predicate*

The convention *is disbanding.*

*Participial modifier*

The platform committee, *failing to reach agreement,* postponed the vote until Wednesday.

*Adverbial modifier*

The car is missing *from the garage.*

**7.3b Sentence Constituents.**   Our grammatical sense as speakers and writers of English tells us what parts come together to form the smaller and larger units of the sentence. The word *constituent* used previously has a special meaning in describing sentences: it refers to any word, phrase, or clause that helps to form a broader construction. We know, for example, that the following groups of words are constituents of larger groups:

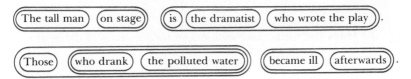

In reading these sentences aloud, speakers usually separate these constituents vocally to clarify them. Some constituents need not be marked to be understood, and markings differ from one speaker to another. But all speakers would introduce a juncture or vocal pause or break to clarify the following sentence:

We hope that good will prevail.

The words *good* and *will* belong to different sentence constituents, as the following marking shows:

We hope that ( good ) ( will prevail ) .

The following sentence would be spoken and marked in a different way:

She is a woman ( of ) ( goodwill ) .

**EXERCISES**

1. Expand the following phrases into clauses:
   **a.** the black Labrador retriever

   **b.** her long-awaited twenty-first birthday celebration
   **c.** is waiting impatiently
   **d.** courageously volunteered to test the water
   **e.** running down the path toward the lake
   **f.** to explain why the plan succeeded
   **g.** the long white trailing scarf
   **h.** someone waiting outside
   **i.** the eagerly awaited qualifying match
   **j.** watching from the sidelines
 2. Attach the following prepositional phrases to a dependent
   or an independent clause:
   **a.** between the acts
   **b.** without a shred of evidence
   **c.** along the high wall
   **d.** in the absence of a written agreement
   **e.** along with his brother
   **f.** aside from the other swimmers
   **g.** with a short furry tail
   **h.** of the hurricane
   **i.** at the side of the road
   **j.** by the end of the performance
 3. Mark the immediate and larger constituents of three of the
   sentences in exercise 2.

# 7.4   Summary of Simple Sentence Patterns

A complete sentence contains at least one main clause. The
subject and predicate may be any one of the following patterns:

Subject + verb:

> Food spoils.
> Fish swim.

Subject + linking verb + complement:

> That animal is a wolf.
> Lemons taste sour.

Subject + verb + direct object:

> The storm struck the coast.
> The voters rejected the amendment.

Subject + verb + direct object + complement

> The newspapers called the statement a lie.
> His opponent called the candidate unqualified.

Subject + verb + indirect object + direct object:

The convention gave the candidate its endorsement.
Her aunt sent Barbara a letter.

Single words, phrases, and dependent clauses modify these simple sentence patterns in various ways. Chapter 8 classifies these words and phrases.

**7.4**

**gr**

## Exercise

1. Complete the following to form sentences:
   **a.** Snow + *verb*
   **b.** The rain-swollen creeks, which empty into the lake + *verb*
   **c.** Snow + *linking verb* + *complement*
   **d.** The ten exchange students in the hall + *linking verb* + *complement*
   **e.** The exchange student + *verb* + *direct object*
   **f.** The chemicals approved for use in orchards + *verb* + *direct object*
   **g.** The chemistry professor + *verb* + *direct object* + *complement*
   **h.** None of the exchange students who signed up for the class + *verb* + *direct object* + *complement*
   **i.** The heavy traffic on the expressway + *verb* + *indirect object* + *direct object*
   **j.** Not everyone who signed up for the class + *verb* + *indirect object* + *direct object*
   **k.** *Subject* + called the dog + *complement*
   **l.** *Subject* + gave her + *direct object*
   **m.** *Subject* + is + *complement*
   **n.** *Subject* + tastes + *complement*
   **o.** *Subject* + considers + *direct object* + *complement*

# Checklist for the Sentence and Its Parts

**7.2a·b** Independent clauses can stand alone as grammatical sentences:

The men in the white jackets are Health Department officials.

Dependent clauses serve as modifiers in independent clauses or as constituents or parts of these clauses:

The men *who tested the water* are Health Department officials.
They drank the water *even though it had a strange odor.*
*Whoever gets sick* should call the Health Department at once.

**7.3a**   Phrases are single words or word clusters that cannot stand alone as grammatical sentences:

in the white jackets
the book with the green cover
giving instructions on how to write the paper
am going to the Health Department with a water sample

# Words and Phrases

This chapter describes the traditional parts of speech, including nouns, pronouns, adjectives, adverbs, prepositions, and conjunctions. These words are defined in part through what they do in the sentence, and for this reason we need additional terms to define words that serve in the usual positions of nouns, adjectives, and adverbs: *nominals, adjectivals, adverbials.* The contrasting *verbals* are verb forms that function as nouns and adjectives.

## 8.1 Nouns

**8.1a Form.** **Nouns** name or point to persons, places, objects, ideas, and acts. The base form of most nouns expresses the singular:

boy, girl, book, foot, child, mouse

To form the plural, most nouns add a special ending or inflection:

boys, girls, books

To form the possessive, nouns add an apostrophe with or without -s:

boy's, boys'

Seven nouns form the plural by changing the base word:

foot, feet
goose, geese
louse, lice
man, men
mouse, mice
tooth, teeth
woman, women

The following form the plural with -*en*:

> brothers, brethren (referring to members of a religious organization)
> child, children
> ox, oxen

**8.1**
**ca**

The possessive of these nouns forms the same way as that of other nouns—through addition of the inflection -'*s*:

> man's hat, men's hats
> child's hat, children's hats

The function word *of* sometimes substitutes for the inflection:

> hat of the man, hats of the men
> hat of the child, hats of the children

Occasionally function word and inflection occur together:

> the stories of Mary (stories about Mary)
> the stories of Mary's (stories told by Mary, not those about her)
> the novels of the Brontë sisters' (the novels by the Brontës, not those about them)

**Noun phrases** are word clusters that function as nouns:

> the red-haired boy
> the girl with the white scarf

**Nominals** are words that function as nouns. A **gerund** is a nominal formed from the verb with -*ing*:

> *Walking* is good exercise.

**8.1b Noun Classes.**   Nouns are traditionally classified in the following ways:

**common nouns** that point to people or objects:

> man, hall, water, tap, wall

**proper nouns** that identify particular persons, places, and things:

> Winston S. Churchill, Eleanor Roosevelt, White House, Lake Erie, Harvard University

**collective nouns** or singular nouns that refer to a group:

> class, crowd, regiment, band, chorus, team

**count nouns** that have singular and plural forms:

> man, men, hall, halls, tap, taps, wall, walls

**mass nouns** that refer to things that cannot be counted and do not have plurals:

health, grease, tennis, wisdom, news

Some words can be both count and mass nouns:

a drink of water          waters of the Niagara
a basket of food          foods of various nations

The following take plurals and therefore are count nouns:

classes, crowds, regiments, bands, choruses, teams

These distinctions are important in determining agreement with subjects and verbs (see 17.1).

**8.1c Noun Functions.**   Nouns perform the following functions:

*Subject*
*Water* is scarce in August (single-word subject).
*The polluted water* ran from the tap (constituent or part of a noun phrase subject).

*Subject Complement*
Those men are *the Health Department officials*.
The water tastes *bitter*.
She became *president*.

**A subject complement** is a noun (or noun phrase) or adjective that follows a linking verb—a form of *to be* (*am, is, was, were*) or a verb of sense (*tastes, smells*) or the verbs *become, appear, seem*—and is the equivalent of the subject.

*Appositive*
The white-haired man, *the landlord of the building*, talked to the officials.

An **appositive** is a noun (or noun phrase) that stands next to another noun and refers to the same person or thing.

*Direct Object*
The officials asked *a question*.

A **direct object** receives the action of the verb.

*Indirect Object*
The officials asked *the landlord* a question.

An **indirect object** is the person or object to whom or for whom the action is done.

**8.1**
**ca**

*Object Complement*
The landlord branded the question *nonsense*.

An **object complement** is the noun (or noun phrase) modifier of a direct object.

*Object of Preposition*
The men are officials of *the Health Department*.
He gave a sarcastic answer to the *question*.

**8.1**

**ca**

An **object of preposition** is a noun that follows a connecting or function word like *in* or *on*. (See 8.9a.)

*Noun Absolute*
*The water being polluted*, the officials shut off the tap.

A **noun absolute** is a phrase consisting of a noun and a participle that modifies the whole sentence.

**8.1d Types of Subject.**    Nouns perform various roles as subject of the clause. A noun may act in the following ways:

as the *agent* or the person performing the action:

*The officials* turned off the tap.

as the *experiencer* of the action:

*The children* enjoyed the performance.

as the *force* or nonhuman thing that acts:

*The wall* of water struck the shore.

as the *instrument* or thing used to perform an action:

*The thermometer* recorded the temperature.

as the *source* of the action:

*The well* in the yard started the epidemic.

as the *location* or where something takes place:

*The box* in the corner contains the books.

as the *patient* or the thing changed by the action:

*The children* were sickened by the water.

Objects of prepositions can also indicate the *path* of an action:

The officials walked through *the yard*.

They also indicate the *goal* or destination:

The officials are walking to *the well.*

Knowledge of these roles or types can help in decisions about when to use active and passive voice (see 8.5c) and in other matters of phrasing.

**EXERCISES**

1. Name the function served by the noun *Jupiter* in the following sentences:
   a. The astronomer explained that the planet Jupiter has several moons.
   b. The largest planet in our solar system, Jupiter, is the size of a small star.
   c. She gave me a large book with pictures of Jupiter.
   d. The largest planet of the solar system is Jupiter.
   e. NASA voted the next planet for exploration Jupiter.
2. Write sentences that use the noun *athlete* (and any necessary modifiers) in the following positions:
   a. subject            e. appositive
   b. direct object      f. object complement
   c. indirect object    g. object of preposition
   d. subject complement
3. Use the following nouns in sentences:
   a. a common noun as subject
   b. a common noun as subject complement
   c. a count noun as subject
   d. a mass noun as direct object
   e. a proper noun as object complement
   f. a proper noun as appositive
4. Write sentences using the following words in the roles or functions indicated:
   a. agent: *dog*          e. path: *yard*
   b. experiencer: *dog*    f. instrument: *pencil*
   c. goal: *campaign*      g. source: *winds*
   d. place: *yard*

# 8.2 Pronouns

**Pronouns** are words that replace nouns and noun phrases. Unlike nouns, they have separate forms to distinguish their use as subjects, objects, and possessives:

I, my, mine, me
we, our, them

They also have separate forms to distinguish gender and number:

he, she, it
I, we
he, she, it, they

**8.2a  Pronoun Classes.   Personal pronouns** identify people or things. Here are their various forms:

*Subjects*

|  Singular | Plural |
|-----------|--------|
| I | we |
| you | you |
| he, she, it | they |

*Objects*

| me | us |
|----|-----|
| you | you |
| him, her, it | them |

*Possessives (used as adjectives)*

| my | our |
|----|-----|
| your | your |
| his, her, its | their |

*Possessives (used as subjects and objects)*

| mine | ours |
|------|------|
| yours | yours |
| his, hers, its | theirs |

The following are additional classes of pronouns.

**Demonstrative pronouns** point to specific things:

| this | these |
|------|-------|
| that | those |

**Indefinite pronouns** do not specify a particular person or object:

another, some, everybody, anybody, nobody, nothing

**Relative pronouns** introduce certain dependent clauses:

who, whom, whose, whoever, whomever
which, whichever
that

**Interrogative pronouns** begin questions:

who, what, which
whoever, whomever, whatever, whichever

*Who* has case forms:

Subject: *Who* is that man?

Object: *Whom* are you calling?
Possessive: *Whose* dog is that?

**Reflexive pronouns** refer to a noun or pronoun:

| | |
|---|---|
| I myself | we ourselves |
| you yourself | you yourselves |
| he himself | they themselves |
| she herself | |
| the dog itself | |

**8.2**
**pron**

**Intensive pronouns** stress the noun or pronoun referred to:

I am going myself (I am going in place of someone else).
The woman herself is going (the woman insists on going).

**Reciprocal pronouns** express mutual relationship:

each other
one another

**8.2b Function of Pronouns.** Pronouns substitute for nouns in the same positions in the sentence:

*Subject*
*He* answered the question sarcastically.

*Subject Complement*
The tenant is *he*, not the woman on the stairs.

*Direct Object*
She answered *him*.

*Indirect Object*
They gave *him* the lab report on the well water.

*Object Complement*
She considered the man *somebody* important.

*Object of Preposition*
She is going to class *with him*.

**EXERCISES**

1. Write sentences that use the pronoun *she* and its object and possessive forms in the following positions:
   a. subject
   b. direct object
   c. indirect object
   d. subject complement
   e. appositive
   f. object complement
   g. object of preposition

2. Write sentences that use the following dependent clauses:
   a. who traveled throughout the western states
   b. whoever travels in Oregon or northern California
   c. which we heard outside the tent
   d. whomever you meet
   e. whose name you are not likely to forget

**8.3**

# **8.3** Articles

Articles fall into two classes—indefinite and definite. The **indefinite articles,** *a* and *an*, identify nouns for the first time. *A* is used before words sounded as consonants:

a book
a horse (the *h* sounded)
a youth
a union (the *u* sounded as a consonant *y*)

*An* is used before words beginning or sounded as vowels:

an apple
an upper floor
an SOS (*S* pronounced as a vowel)

The **definite article** *the* is used with nouns already identified by the speaker or writer:

the book on the shelf
the horse in the stable
the upper floor of the hotel
the SOS sent by the ship

Because they perform the function of adjectives as descriptors of nouns, articles function as adjectives. The special word *adjectival* describes words that behave as adjectives. (See 8.4c.)

# **8.4** Adjectives

**8.4a Definition and Function.** **Adjectives** describe nouns, attribute qualities to them, or modify them in some way. They stand in various positions in the sentence—most commonly next to the noun:

an intelligent woman
my book
these books
the cloth-bound book

or following the noun for emphasis:

the cloth-bound cover, red and gold
an intelligent woman, hardworking and gifted in physics

or as subject complements following linking verbs—the *to be* verbs (*is, was, were, will be,* etc.) and verbs of sense (*tastes, smells, feels, sounds, hears*):

Daisies are *yellow* and *gold.*
That book is *wet.*
The milk smells *sour.*
She felt *tired* after the long ride home.

**8.4**
**adj**

or as objective complements:

She found the water *polluted.*
The president declared the meeting *adjourned.*

**8.4b Inflections and Function Words.** Some adjectives have special forms or take function words to show comparison. The **comparative** suffix *-er* or the function word *more* indicates a degree or quality higher than that expressed by the simple adjective to which inflections and function words attach. The **superlative** suffix *-est* or the function words *less* and *more, least* and *most* combine with the simple adjective to indicate degree:

small, smaller, smallest
small, more small, most small
talkative, more talkative, most talkative

Some adjectives—many consisting of more than two syllables—use function words rather than suffixes to show degree:

furious, more furious, most furious
noticeable, more noticeable, most noticeable

The suffixes that form adjectives include the following:

*-able*: objectionable, remarkable
*-ant*: deviant, radiant
*-ary*: revolutionary, mercenary
*-en*: heathen, woolen
*-ful*: artful, beautiful
*-ible*: terrible, possible
*-ic*: arctic, classic
*-ical*: classical, comical
*-ive*: active, imaginative
*-ory*: illusory, compensatory
*-ous*: generous, devious
*-y*: chilly, sleepy

Some of these words also serve as nouns:

arctic regions, the Arctic
a desert island, a desert
a mercenary soldier, a mercenary
deviant behavior, a social deviant

**8.4**
**adj**

**8.4c Adjectivals.**   **Adjectivals** include articles (*a, an, the*) and other words that function as adjectives. These include the following types of pronouns:

*Indefinite Pronouns*
each book, some books, many books

*Demonstrative Pronouns*
this book, that book, these books, those books

*Possessive Pronouns*
his book, her book, its cover, their covers

*Interrogative Pronouns*
What books are you buying?
Which books do you want to bring?

*Numerical Pronouns*
the first book on the shelf
the second house from the corner

Nouns may also function as adjectives:

the horse show
the word processor

**EXERCISES**

1. Each of the suffixes or word endings listed previously has a particular meaning; for example, *-ory* means "having the nature of." Thus the word *illusory* means having the nature or the qualities of an illusion. Use your dictionary to determine the meaning of the other suffixes, and list one or two adjectives that have the same suffix.
2. The word *classic* can be used as both noun and adjective:

   *David Copperfield* is a classic of English literature.
   Pasta is a classic food of Italy.

   Use the following words as nouns and adjectives in sentences of your own:
   **a.** team          **d.** lawn
   **b.** military      **e.** picnic
   **c.** satellite

3. Use your dictionary to discover the adjective form of the following:
   a. automobile      d. grammar
   b. president      e. family
   c. government

4. Give the simple, comparative, and superlative forms of the following adjectives. Consult your dictionary if you are unsure whether the comparative or superlative can be expressed with *-er* and *-est*:
   a. spare      f. illegible
   b. thin      g. grumpy
   c. revolutionary      h. delicate
   d. careless      i. repulsive
   e. pungent      j. beautiful

5. Use the suffixes in 8.4b to form adjectives from the following words:
   a. mountain      g. photograph
   b. dirt      h. Germany
   c. joy      i. England
   d. evolution      j. Japan
   e. laugh      k. New York
   f. fuss

**8.5**
vb

## 8.5 Simple Verbs

**8.5a What Verbs Do.** Verbs are the heart of the predicate of the sentence. As part of the predicate, they make statements or assertions or predications about nouns or pronouns. These concern actions, states of existence, or present, past, or future circumstances:

> The travelers boarded the plane.
> They are Puerto Rican.
> They live in San Juan.
> They will be visiting relatives in Los Angeles.

Verbs are classified as *main* (or *lexical*), *auxiliary*, and *modal*.

**8.5b Main Verbs.** The **main verb** of a sentence is always a *finite verb* built from the bare *infinitive* or base form (*walk*). This form gives no information about person, tense, and number; it merely names the verb. This absence of limitation explains the descriptive term *infinitive*—meaning without definite limits.

In functioning as a main verb, the base verb or infinitive by its form alone or with inflections or with the subject of its clause gives information on the following:

**8.5**
**vb**

> **person**—whether the verb is making a statement about a subject in the first person (*I*), second person (*you*), or third person (*he, she, it, they*)
>
> **number**—whether the subject is singular (*I, you, he, she, it*) or plural (*we, you, they*)
>
> **tense**—whether the action or state of existence expressed by the verb is present (*lives*) or past (*lived*)

The base verb gives this information with inflections or word endings (*walks, walked*) and without inflection (*walk*). Thus the verb in the following sentence is first-person singular, present tense:

> I walk to school every morning.

The verb in the following sentence is third person plural, past tense:

> They walked to school during the bus strike.

Each verb has two participial forms—a **present participle** and a **past participle.** With the infinitive and the gerund, participles are called **verbals**—words that function as nouns and adjectives (see 8.7). In regular verbs the present participle adds *-ing* to the base form; the past participle adds *-ed*:

> walking
> walked

Simple main verbs may be uninflected or inflected single words (*live, lives, lived*):

> They live in San Juan.
> They lived in Los Angeles.
> She lives in New York.

Complex main verbs are **verb phrases** formed through one or more auxiliaries and base verb or the present or past participle:

> will have lived in New York
> will be living in New York

Section 8.6 describes verb phrases.

**8.5c  Voice.**   **Voice** expresses the relationship between the action and the subject. The voice of the main verb may be active or passive. If the subject performs the act, the verb is in the **active voice:**

> The pilot flew the plane through the storm.

If the subject is acted upon instead of acting, the verb is in the **passive voice:**

> The plane was flown through the storm by the pilot.
> The plane was flown through the storm.

**8.5d  Transitive and Intransitive Verbs.**   Main verbs (simple or complex) are transitive or intransitive depending on whether the verb takes a direct object or can receive action. **Intransitive verbs** do not take a direct object or receive action or an effect:

> She walks often.
> The children sat on the floor.
> They lie on the grass.

**Transitive verbs** do take a direct object and receive action or effect:

> He returned the book to the library.
> The book was returned to the library.
> The book was set on the table.
> He laid the book on the table.

Most transitive verbs can take the passive voice.

**8.5e  Regular Verbs.**   A **regular** simple verb has the same form in the simple past tense (*walked*) and the past participle (*walked*). Simple main verbs give information about tense through subject and base form alone or subject and base form with inflection or word ending—in the third-person singular, the inflection -*s*:

> I walk.                   We walk.
> You walk.                 You walk.
> He (she, it) walks.       They walk.

In the past tense, the regular verb adds the inflection -*ed* in all three persons, singular and plural:

> I walked                  We walked.
> You walked.               You walked.
> He (she, it) walked.      They walked.

**8.5f  Irregular Verbs.**   **Irregular** verbs change in form to show the past tense or past participle or both. The irregular verb *to be* has these forms in past and present:

> *Present*
> I am.            He (she, it) is.       You are.
> You are.         We are.                They are.

**8.5**
**vb**

*Past*

| | |
|---|---|
| I was. | We were. |
| You were. | You are. |
| He (she, it) was. | They were. |

Here are the present, past, and past participle forms of common irregular verbs:

| | |
|---|---|
| arise, arose, arisen | keep, kept, kept |
| bear, bore, borne | know, knew, known |
| begin, began, begun | lay, laid, laid |
| bid, bid, bidden | lead, led, led |
| bite, bit, bitten or bit | lie, lay, lain |
| blow, blew, blown | lose, lost, lost |
| break, broke, broken | pay, paid, paid |
| bring, brought, brought | prove, proved, proved or proven |
| buy, bought, bought | ride, rode, ridden |
| catch, caught, caught | ring, rang, rung |
| choose, chose, chosen | rise, rose, risen |
| come, came, come | run, ran, run |
| dig, dug, dug | say, said, said |
| dive, dove or dived, dived | see, saw, seen |
| do, did, done | shrink, shrank, shrunk |
| drag, dragged, dragged | sing, sang, sung |
| draw, drew, drawn | sink, sank or sunk, sunk |
| drink, drank, drunk | sit, sat, sat |
| eat, ate, eaten | speak, spoke, spoken |
| fall, fell, fallen | spring, sprang, sprung |
| fight, fought, fought | stand, stood, stood |
| find, found, found | steal, stole, stolen |
| flee, fled, fled | swim, swam, swum |
| fly, flew, flown | take, took, taken |
| forget, forgot, forgotten | tear, tore, torn |
| freeze, froze, frozen | tell, told, told |
| get, got, gotten | throw, threw, thrown |
| give, gave, given | wake, woke, woken or waked |
| go, went, gone | wear, wore, worn |
| grow, grew, grown | wring, wrung, wrung |
| hang, hung, hung (objects) | write, wrote, written |
| have, had, had | |

Some irregular verbs do not change the base form for present, past, and past participle:

| | | |
|---|---|---|
| cut, cut, cut | let, let, let | shut, shut, shut |
| hit, hit, hit | put, put, put | |

**8.5g  Linking Verbs.   Linking verbs** connect the subject to a subject complement (or *predicate noun*) or an adjective complement (or *predicate adjective*):

She *is* an excellent student.
She *is* intelligent.

Other linking verbs include *become, look, remain,* and *seem*:

I *become* grouchy around four o'clock.
She *looks* happy in the photograph.
She *remains* happy in her job.
She *seems* happy in the class.

Notice that forms of *be* (*am grouchy, is happy*) can be substituted for these verbs.

Other linking verbs include verbs of sense:

The blanket *feels* soft.
The cherries *taste* sour.
The music *sounds* loud.
The stew *smells* garlicky.

**8.6**
**vb**

# 8.6  Complex Verbs

**8.6a Auxiliary Verbs *Have, Be,* and *Do*.**  The forms of *have, be,* and *do* (meaning *to perform*) serve as main verbs:

I have the flu.
I am sick.
I have been sick.
He did wrong.

They also serve as **auxiliaries** or supplements to main verbs—forms of *have* and *be* combining with the participle forms of the main verb:

I have walked.
He has written.
I am walking.
She is writing.

Forms of *do* also serve as auxiliaries—combining with the bare infinitive or base form of the verb:

*Present*
I do walk, don't walk.
You do walk, don't walk.
He (she, it) does walk, doesn't walk.
We do, don't walk.
You do walk, don't walk.
They do walk, don't walk.

*Past*
I did walk, didn't walk.
You did walk, didn't walk.
He (she, it) did walk, didn't walk.
We did walk, didn't walk.
You did walk, didn't walk.
They did walk, didn't walk.

**8.6**
**vb**

Forms of *do* are obligatory in questions in the absence of the *have* or *be* auxiliary forms:

Do (don't) you walk to school?
Did (didn't) you walk to school?

**8.6b  Modal Auxiliaries.  Modal auxiliaries,** which express the attitude of the speaker or writer toward the action or circumstances, combine with the bare infinitive as follows:

*shall, should*—usually expressing the intent to do something:

I shall walk.

*will, would*—expressing intent, strong intent, and will:

You will walk.

*can, could*—usually expressing capability or possibility:

I can walk.

*may, might*—expressing possibility or giving permission:

I may walk if it does not rain.
They may leave early if they wish.

*must*—expressing obligation or need:

You must leave.

*ought to*—also expressing obligation or need:

You ought to leave.

*dare*—expressing courage or, used with the negative, fear or lack of courage:

I dare not come.

*need*—expressing obligation or, used with the negative, absence of obligation:

I need not come.

**8.6c  Verb Phrases.**   Primary and modal auxiliaries singly or together combine with the base verb or with the present or the past participle of the verb to form a verb phrase. Like the inflected or uninflected main verb (8.5a), the verb phrase expresses person, number, tense, and attitude alone or with the subject of the main clause:

must have walked
should have lived
must be walking
should be walking

**8.6**
**vb**

The base verb or the participle may combine with a **primary auxiliary** (forms of *have*, *be*, and *do*) only:

They do not travel often.
They have lived in San Juan ten years.

Or with a **modal auxiliary:**

They must return this week.

Or with both primary and modal auxiliaries:

They must have returned.

Verb phrases can be modified:

must have walked quickly
should not have walked

Thus future time (defined as *future tense* in traditional grammars) is expressed through the modal *will* joined to a verb or verb phrase:

I will walk.
I will be walking.
I will have walked.

The idea of possible or conditional action is expressed through the modal *would* joined to a verb or a verb phrase:

I would walk.
I would be walking.
I would have walked.

Modals always precede participial phrases they join with to express tense and aspect:

modal auxiliary + *have* auxiliary + participle: would have walked
modal auxiliary + *be* auxiliary + participle: would be walking

**8.6d Aspect.** Verbs in present and past tense in English may be either *progressive* or *perfect* in aspect. **Aspect** refers to the state of the action viewed by the speaker or writer. **Progressive**

**verbs** (verbs in progressive aspect) tell us that the action is continuing or ongoing in the present or was ongoing in the past:

*Present Progressive*
I am walking.

*Past Progressive*
I was walking.

The progressive aspect also stresses the habitual nature or the importance of the event or action:

*Habitual action:* He is always shouting—never talking.
(Compare: He always shouts—never talks in a normal voice.)
*Emphasis:* I am walking as fast as I can.

**Perfect aspect** refers to time—from the point of view or aspect of present, past, or future.

*Present Perfect*
I have walked to school since September.

The **present perfect** shows that an event begun in the past continues into the present.

*Past Perfect*
I had walked to school before the bus strike.

The **past perfect** refers to an event of the past from the perspective of the past. The strike occurred in the past; the speaker is talking about what occurred before and up to the event.

*Future Perfect*
Between the time you leave the house and arrive at school, I
    will have walked downtown and back.

The **future perfect** (one of the traditional future tenses) refers to an event in the future from the perspective of the future.

Perfect and progressive aspects combine in the following way:

I have been walking to school since September.

This sentence implies that an action begun in the past is continuing into the present. It also says that the action has been ongoing, not occasional.

Here are these tenses and aspects for each person, singular and plural:

*Present Progressive*
I am walking.                    We are walking.
You are walking.                 You are walking.
He (she, it) is walking.         They are walking.

*Past Progressive*
I was walking.
You were walking.
He (she, it) was walking.

We were walking.
You were walking.
They were walking.

*Future Progressive*
I (shall, will) be walking.
You will be walking.
He (she, it) will be walking.

We (shall, will) be walking.
You will be walking.
They will be walking.

**8.6**
**vb**

*Present Perfect*
I have walked.
You have walked.
He (she, it) has walked.

We have walked.
You have walked.
They have walked.

*Past Perfect*
I had walked.
You had walked.
He (she, it) had walked.

We had walked.
You had walked.
They had walked.

*Future Perfect*
I (shall, will) have walked.
You will have walked.
He (she, it) will have walked.

We (shall, will) have walked.
You will have walked.
They will have walked.

*Present Perfect Progressive*
I have been walking.
You have been walking.
He (she, it) has been walk-
    ing.

We have been walking.
You have been walking.
They have been walking.

*Past Perfect Progressive*
I had been walking.
You had been walking.
He (she, it) had been walk-
    ing.

We had been walking.
You had been walking.
They had been walking.

*Future Perfect Progressive*
I (shall, will) have been
    walking.
You will have been walking.
He (she, it) will have been
    walking.

We (shall, will) have been
    walking.
You will have been walking.
They will have been walk-
    ing.

**8.6e Mood.** The **mood** of the verb expresses the attitude of the speaker or writer toward the event. A verb in the **indicative mood** shows that the event is a fact—that it has occurred, is occurring, or will definitely occur:

*Indicative*
I walk, have walked, will walk.

I am walking, was walking, will be walking.
I had walked, will have walked.

*Subjunctive*
If I were to walk, I would have to leave an hour earlier.
She demanded that the parade be cancelled.
They requested that everyone walk instead of drive.
Let freedom ring!

**8.6**
**vb**

A verb in the **subjunctive mood** shows that the speaker is only wishing or supposing that the event might occur or recommending that action be taken.

A verb in the **imperative mood** shows that the speaker is issuing a command:

*Imperative*
Walk!
Stop at the light!
Begin!

**EXERCISES**

1. Use the base or infinitive verb *shout* to form finite verbs as follows. Then use the verb in a sentence of your own.
   **a.** present indicative
   **b.** past indicative
   **c.** future indicative
   **d.** imperative
   **e.** present progressive
   **f.** past progressive
   **g.** future progressive

2. Do the same with the following:
   **a.** present perfect
   **b.** past perfect
   **c.** future perfect
   **d.** present perfect progressive
   **e.** past perfect progressive
   **f.** future perfect progressive

3. Change the following sentences from active to passive:
   **a.** The car struck the fence.
   **b.** The coach praised the basketball team for their performance at the state tournament.
   **c.** The storm, which blew in from the west, caused no damage to the town.

4. Write sentences that express the following:
   **a.** an action that took place in the past
   **b.** an action that was ongoing in the past
   **c.** an ongoing action in the past that continues into the present

    **d.** an ongoing action in the previous summer that continued into the fall
    **e.** an action that will occur in the future
    **f.** an ongoing action that will occur in the future
  **4.** Write sentences that combine modals with verbs (and auxiliaries) to express the following:
    **a.** an action that will take place
    **b.** an action that might take place
    **c.** an action that must take place
    **d.** an ongoing action that might have taken place
    **e.** an ongoing action that must have taken place

**8.7**
**vb**

## 8.7 Verbals

Participles, infinitives, and gerunds are sometimes called **verbals.** Derived from verbs, they do not function as verbs though participles and bare infinitives help to form verbs.

The **participle** functions as an adjective:

the walking doll
the walked dog

as a sentence modifier:

*Walking* slowly, she saw an old friend coming toward her.
*Walked* by his owner every day, the dog was well exercised.

and as a constituent of verb phrases:

is walking
has walked

The infinitive phrase or marked infinitive (usually called **infinitive**) functions as a noun:

*To walk* would be sensible.
I like *to walk*.
The best exercise is *to walk*.

as an adjective:

I have no reason *to walk*.

and as an adverb:

She is going *to walk*.

**Gerunds,** formed from verbs, function as nouns:

*Walking* is good exercise.
I enjoy *walking*.

# 8.8 Adverbs

**8.8a Definition and Function.**   The **adverb** is traditionally defined as a word or phrase that modifies or describes verbs, adjectives, other adverbs, and whole clauses:

> He walked *quickly* (modifying the verb).
> He walked *very* quickly (one adverb modifying another).
> She used an *often* repeated phrase (adverb *often* modifying the adjective *repeated*).
> *Fortunately*, the storm caused very little damage (adverb *fortunately* modifying the whole sentence).

In the first three sentences, the adverbs must stand next to the words modified. In the fourth sentence, the adverb modifies the whole sentence and therefore may stand in various positions without altering the meaning:

> Fortunately, the storm caused very little damage.
> The storm, fortunately, caused very little damage.
> The storm caused very little damage, fortunately.

The following adverbs also have this same freedom of movement:

> however, therefore, furthermore, moreover, thus, hence, nevertheless

**8.8b Inflections and Function Words.**   A few adjectives end in *-ly*:

> a likely story, a homely face

Many adjectives add *-ly* to form adverbs:

> softly, loudly, nicely, rapidly

To express the comparative and superlative, these *-ly* adverbs take the function words *more* and *most*:

> more softly, most softly
> more loudly, most loudly
> more rapidly, most rapidly

Some adverbs that have the same form as adjectives can add the inflections *-er* and *-est*:

> *Adjective Forms*
> the *early* showing, the *earlier* showing, the *earliest* showing
>
> *Adverb Forms*
> showed it *early*, showed it *earlier*, showed it *earliest*

The adverb *soon* also inflects for the comparative and superlative:

arrived *soon*, arrived *sooner*, arrived *soonest*

A small group of adverbs form the comparative and superlative with different base words. These adverbs include the following:

laughed *much*, laughed *more*, laughed *most*
cried *little*, cried *less*, cried *least*
spoke *well*, spoke *better*, spoke *best*

**8.8**
**adv**

Some adverbs end with the suffixes *-where* and *-wise*:

going *nowhere*
said *otherwise*

**8.8c Shortened Forms.** Certain adverbs ending in *-ly* shorten the word by omitting the inflection:

| | |
|---|---|
| close | closely |
| quick | quickly |
| tight | tightly |
| wrong | wrongly |

The shortened form is often used before single-syllable or short words:

close-knit family (closely knit family)
quick-acting remedy (quickly acting remedy)

Shortened forms are most common in informal speech and writing:

They gripped the rail tight.
She ran as quick as she could.
They gave the directions wrong.

The *-ly* form is required before the verb:

They tightly gripped the rail.
She quickly ran.
They wrongly gave directions.

**8.8d Adverbials.** Prepositional phrases, noun phrases, and dependent clauses that function as adverbs are called **adverbials**:

He walks *with difficulty* (prepositional phrase).
She is arriving *this month* (noun phrase).
He began walking *when buses stopped running* (adverbial clause).

## 8.9   Connecting Words

Prepositions and conjunctions connect various phrases and clauses.

**8.9a Prepositions.**   **Prepositions** connect nouns, noun phrases, and pronouns to other words in the sentence. They are never inflected:

| | |
|---|---|
| *at* the center | *of* the coach |
| *by* the river | *on* the shelf |
| *before* six o'clock | *throughout* the day |
| *beside* the chair | *to* the team |
| *between* six o'clock and seven | *toward* the library |
| *for* a year | *upon* the field |
| *from* the sidelines | *with* the hammer |

**8.9b Conjunctions.**   **Conjunctions** are a broad class of words defined by their connecting function in sentences. They include the following:

and, but, yet, or, nor, although, since, because, in fact

Some conjunctions connect words to form phrases:

bread *and* butter
to bake bread *and* to churn butter

And some connect clauses:

I like to grow tomatoes *but* don't like eating them.
I grow tomatoes *because* I like eating them.

The **coordinating conjunctions** are the following:

| | | |
|---|---|---|
| and | yet | so |
| but | or | |
| for | nor | |

These words connect phrases and clauses of the same weight or importance:

I grow tomatoes, *but* I don't like eating them.
It may be October, *yet* the leaves have not started falling.

Certain adverbs—called **conjunctive adverbs**—function as conjunctions in coordinating clauses:

It is already October; *however*, the leaves have not started to fall.
It has been raining since Monday; *consequently*, we are postponing our trip.

Here are other adverbs that connect independent clauses in the same way:

| | |
|---|---|
| besides | nevertheless |
| furthermore | still |
| meanwhile | therefore |
| moreover | thus |

**8.9**

**Subordinating conjunctions** join dependent or subordinate clauses to independent or main ones:

*Although* it is October, the leaves have not started to fall.
We are postponing our trip *because* it has been raining since Monday.

Here are a few of the many words that connect clauses in the same way:

| | |
|---|---|
| after | unless |
| as, as if | until |
| before | when, whenever |
| if, if only | where, wherever |
| since | whereas |
| so that | while |

The relative pronouns *who, which,* and *that* also function as subordinators, linking dependent to independent clauses.

Pairs of conjunctions—called **correlatives** because they show mutual or complementary relationships—connect phrases and clauses. Here are a few:

*both-and*:

She is both class secretary and class president.

*either-or*:

She wants to be either secretary or president.

*just as-so*:

Just as runners warm up before a race, so do musicians before a concert.

*neither-nor*:

She is neither secretary nor president of the class.

*not only-but also*:

She is not only the secretary but also the president of the class.

*on the one hand-on the other hand*:

On the one hand, she wants to hold both offices; on the other (hand), she knows that she does not have time to do both jobs.

**EXERCISES**

**8.9**

1. Form simple adverbs from the following adjectives. Then give their comparative and superlative forms:
   a. sure
   b. tame
   c. right
   d. near
   e. loose
   f. general
   g. poor
   h. generous
   i. reasonable
   j. natural

2. Use the following adverbs and adverbials to modify the verb in a single main clause:
   a. furthermore
   b. meanwhile
   c. nevertheless
   d. in fact
   e. for example

3. Use the following correlatives in sentences of your own:
   a. both-and
   b. either-or
   c. just as-so
   d. neither-nor
   e. not only-but also

4. Write sentences containing the following coordinating and subordinating conjunctions:
   a. and
   b. but
   c. while
   d. for
   e. because
   f. yet
   g. when
   h. whenever
   i. so that
   j. or

5. Write sentences containing the following conjunctive adverbs:
   a. however
   b. moreover
   c. meanwhile
   d. nevertheless
   e. thus
   f. furthermore
   g. hence
   h. therefore
   i. still
   j. besides

# Checklist for Words and Phrases

## 8.1  Nouns

*Nouns* name or point to persons, places, objects, ideas, and acts:

boy, boys, boy's, boys'
man's hat, men's hats

*Noun phrases* are word clusters that function as nouns:

the girl with the white scarf

*Nominals* are words that function as nouns:

> *Walking* is good exercise.

*Common nouns* identify people or objects by class:

> man, hall, water, tap, wall

*Proper nouns* identify particular persons, places, and things:

> Winston S. Churchill, Eleanor Roosevelt, White House

*Count nouns* have singular and plural forms:

> man, men, hall, halls, tap, taps, wall, walls

*Mass nouns* refer to things that cannot be counted and do not have plurals:

> health, grease, tennis, wisdom, news

*Collective nouns* or singular nouns refer to a group:

> class, crowd, regiment, band, chorus, team

**8.2** Pronouns

*Pronouns* replace nouns and noun phrases:

> I, my, mine, me, we, our, them
> he, she, it
> I, we, he, she, it, they

*Personal pronouns* identify people or things.

*Demonstrative pronouns* refer to specific things close to the speaker or writer:

> this book, these books, that book, those books

*Indefinite pronouns* do not specify a particular person or object:

> another, some, everybody, anybody, nobody, nothing

*Relative pronouns* introduce certain dependent clauses:

> who, whom, whose, which, of which, that

*Interrogative pronouns* begin questions:

> *Who* is going?
> *Which* is your car?
> *Whose* car is that?

*Reflexive pronouns* refer to the noun or pronoun acting as the subject of a clause:

> You are hurting *yourself* by not going.

*Intensive pronouns* both refer to and stress a noun or pronoun:

I am going *myself.*

*Reciprocal pronouns* express mutual relationship:

They like *each other.*

### 8.3   Articles
The *indefinite articles,* *a* and *an,* identify nouns for the first time.
The *definite article the* is used with nouns already identified by the speaker or writer.

### 8.4   Adjectives
*Adjectives* describe nouns, attribute qualities to them, or modify them in some way:

an intelligent woman

*Adjectivals* are articles (*a, an, the*), pronouns, and other words that function as adjectives.

### 8.5-6   Verbs
*Verbs* make statements or predications about nouns or pronouns:

The travelers *boarded* the plane.

Verbs express:

*Person*—first person (*I*), second person (*you*), or third person (*he, she, it, they*)
*Number*—singular (*I, you, he, she, it*) or plural (*we, you, they*)
*Tense*—present (*lives*) or past (*lived*)
*Aspect*—progressive (*am living*) or perfect (*have lived, had lived, will have lived*)
*Voice*—active (*ate*) or passive (*was eaten*).
*Mood*—indicative (*I go*), subjunctive (*If I were to go*), imperative (*Go!*)

*Intransitive verbs* do not take direct objects:

He *laughed.*

*Transitive verbs* take direct objects and receive action or effect:

He *returned* the book.
The storm *damaged* the coastal towns.

Each verb has a *present participle* (*walking*) and a *past participle* (*walked, written*) that function as adjectives or help form verb phrases.
*Infinitive phrases* (*to* + base verb) function as nouns, adjectives, and adverbs:

The best exercise is *to walk*.
I have no reason *to walk*.
She is going *to walk*.

*Verb phrases* consist of the *have, be,* and *do* auxiliaries and base verbs or participial forms:

I do walk.
I am walking, I have walked.

Verb phrases consisting of *have* and the participle or *be* and the participle join with modal auxiliaries:

I must have walked, I must be walking.

Modal auxiliaries combine with the base verb alone:

I must walk, I can walk.

Modals always precede participial phrases:

modal auxiliary + *have* auxiliary + participle
modal auxiliary + *be* auxiliary + participle

**8.7** Verbals
The participle functions as an adjective:

the walking doll

as a sentence modifier:

*Walking* slowly, she saw an old friend coming toward her.

and as a constituent of verb phrases:

is walking

The infinitive phrase or marked infinitive (usually called *infinitive*) functions as a noun:

*To walk* would be sensible.

as an adjective:

I have no reason *to walk*.

and as an adverb:

She is going *to walk*.

Gerunds, formed from verbs, function as nouns:

*Walking* is good exercise.

**8.8** Adverbs
The adverb is traditionally defined as a word or phrase that

modifies or describes verbs, adjectives, other adverbs, and whole clauses:

> He walked *quickly*.

*Adverbials* are prepositional phrases, noun phrases, and dependent clauses that function as adverbs:

> He walks *with difficulty*.
> She walks *every day*.
> He walks to work *when traffic is heavy*.

**8.9**   Connecting Words
*Prepositions* connect nouns, noun phrases, and pronouns to other words in the sentence and are never inflected:

> to, from, of, upon, toward, on, with

*Coordinating conjunctions* are *and, but, for, so, yet, or, nor.*
*Conjunctive adverbs* include *furthermore, however, nevertheless, still, therefore,* and *thus.*

> *Subordinating conjunctions* include *after, as, if, since, unless.*

> *Correlative conjunctions* include *both-and, either-or, just as-so, neither-nor, not only-but also,* and *on the one hand-on the other hand.*

# Building Sentences

As the previous chapter notes, knowledge of the elements of grammar and writing alone cannot make you an effective writer, any more than knowledge of cars or of a musical instrument makes a good driver or musician. Like driving a car or playing a musical instrument well, writing clear and effective sentences improves with practice. Writing effective sentences also depends on something more.

The habit of reading is essential; you learn to write well through constant exposure to clear and effective sentences. Reading is as indispensable in writing as hearing sentences is indispensable in learning to speak your own language or acquire another. For this reason this chapter and others in this book illustrate effective sentences through examples of excellent writers of the past and present. These examples of building and shaping sentences show only a few of the many possible ways of doing so.

This chapter focuses on various ways of arranging phrases and clauses. Some of the topics are discussed at greater length in Part IV on sentence grammar and style.

## 9.1 Types of Sentences

Written sentences are not necessarily longer or more complex than spoken sentences. In revising sentences that loosely imitate speech, you usually arrange the phrases and clauses with greater care. Knowledge of the various structures or arrangements possible begins with a classification of sentences based on the number and kind of clauses they contain.

**9.1a The Simple Sentence.** The **simple sentence** consists of a single independent clause—a subject and predicate that can

181

stand alone as a self-contained statement. The following passage consists of two very different simple sentences:

> The first case was that of a man called Milliken, an enormous, hulking fellow in his late thirties, swarthy, hairy-chested and with arms and legs on him fit for the strong man in the circus. He ran a milk route at one end of the town.
> —WILLIAM CARLOS WILLIAMS, "Old Doc Rivers"

**9.1**

**gr**

The subject of the sentence may consist of a single noun or pronoun (*he*) and the predicate of a single verb and complement (*ran a milk route*).

In the first sentence, the subject and subject complement of the opening sentence are noun phrases—the second heavily modified:

> *The first case /* was *that of a man called Milliken, an enormous, hulking fellow in his late thirties, swarthy, hairy-chested and with arms and legs on him fit for the strong man in the circus.*

The predicate in the following sentence from the same story consists of compound verbs:

> He *took* one look and *shrugged* his shoulders.

**9.1b The Compound Sentence.** In a **compound sentence** two or more independent clauses and their modifiers join through the coordinating conjunctions *and, but, yet, for, or, nor,* and *so*:

> Rivers was fidgeting / *and* I wasn't in a particularly pleasant mood myself. —"Old Doc Rivers"

> I could feel my face flush / *but* I didn't say anything. —"Old Doc Rivers"

Conjunctive adverbs like *however, furthermore, moreover, therefore, indeed,* and *thus,* and adverbial phrases like *in fact,* also connect independent clauses. Here are alternative sentences that use conjunctive adverbs:

> Rivers was fidgeting; indeed, I wasn't in a particularly pleasant mood myself.
> I could feel my face flush; however, I didn't say anything.

Some compound sentences use a semicolon to join closely related independent clauses:

> But here is a list of some of his undertakings; I copy from the

records: endometritis, salpingitis, contracture of the hand, rup-
tured spleen, hernia, lacerations (some accident, no doubt).
—"Old Doc Rivers"

**9.1c The Complex Sentence.** Through subordinating
conjunctions like *because, since, after, although, when, whenever,* and
*than,* and the relative pronouns *who, which,* and *that* one or more
dependent clauses attach to an independent clause to form a
**complex sentence.** Other dependent clauses may serve as parts
or constituents of independent clauses:

> Rivers made a hobby one time of catching rattlesnakes, *which*
> *abound in the mountains of North Jersey* [adjective clause modifying
> *rattlesnakes*]. —"Old Doc Rivers"

> *As soon as he entered the room* [adverbial clause modifying *could*
> *see*], he could see *that it was all over* [noun clause as direct object].
> She had called in Rivers. He had told her *that he could cure her*
> [noun clause as direct object]. —"Old Doc Rivers"

> The truth is *that during his last years he bought a good-sized lot on*
> *the square before the Municipal Building in the center of town* [noun
> clause as subject complement]. —"Old Doc Rivers"

**9.1d The Compound-Complex Sentence.** In a **compound-complex sentence** one or more dependent clauses attach
to two or more independent clauses:

> He had been in bed in the front of the house and I shall never
> forget my surprise and the shock to my sense of propriety when
> I saw Frankel, whom I knew, coming down the narrow, dark
> corridor of the apartment in his bare feet and an old-fashioned
> nightgown that reached just to his knees. —"Old Doc Rivers"

The sentence opens with two independent clauses:

> He had been in bed in the front of the house / *and* I shall never
> forget my surprise and the shock to my sense of propriety . . .

The second independent clause is modified by the adverbial
clause that completes the sentence:

> when I saw Frankel . . . coming down the narrow, dark corridor
> of the apartment in his bare feet and an old-fashioned night-
> gown . . .

This dependent clause contains additional modifying clauses:

> when I saw Frankel, *whom I knew*
> an old-fashioned nightgown *that reached just to his knees.*

**9.1**

**gr**

**9.1**

**gr**

**EXERCISES**

1. Combine the following sentences into one simple sentence:

   *Example*
   The man with red hair is the swimming coach.

   The man is giving instructions to the team.

   *Combined Sentence*
   The red-haired man giving instructions to the team is the swimming coach.

   The man with red hair, the swimming coach, is giving instructions to the team.

   **a.** Jupiter is the largest planet in our solar system.
   **b.** Jupiter is the fifth planet from the sun.
2. Combine the two sentences into a compound sentence.
3. Combine the two sentences into a complex sentence.
4. Add the following sentence to the compound sentence or the complex sentence to form a compound-complex sentence:
   **c.** Jupiter takes a little more than eleven years to make one complete rotation.
5. Combine the following sentences into a compound-complex sentence:
   **a.** The wolverine reaches a length of three feet.
   **b.** Its name is derived from the word *wolf*.
   **c.** The wolverine is not a wolf.
   **d.** The wolverine is a ferocious animal.
6. Subordinate the italicized clauses to those that follow. Does the revision change the meaning of the sentence?

   *We get noisier and noisier, and Rosalie peels faster and faster,* till her fingers fairly flicker and her hair comes loose in wisps about her forehead.
   —DONALD PEARCE, "Rosalie" [italics added]

7. The following sentences are broken down from longer ones. Combine them into one sentence, omitting unnecessary words, rearranging ideas and details, and adding connectives if necessary:

   *Example*
   The dictionary is outdated.

   The dictionary has a red cover.

   *Combined Sentence*
   The red-covered dictionary is outdated.

**a.** The sky turned green.
A storm was approaching.
**b.** The sky turned green.
A storm was approaching.
The lake began to churn.
Several boats turned on their sides.
**c.** A storm can be terrifying.
It is terrifying when you cannot find shelter.
Driving in a storm is equally terrifying.
**d.** Knowing first-aid techniques is essential in living out of
the city.
Knowledge of them is essential in the city, too.
The emergencies of city and country are the same.
Not having help nearby increases one's responsibility.
**e.** Dogs instinctively recognize friendly people.
Or dogs are thought to do so.
The matter of instinct in animals is controversial.
It is even more controversial in human beings.

**9.2**
**gr**

# 9.2 Building the Sentence

**9.2a Expanding the Subject.**   The subject of the sentence
expands through single-word, phrasal, and clausal modifiers.
The following sentences from a story by Stephen Crane describe
the approach of a lifeboat to the Florida coast, following a ship-
wreck. Phrases and clauses expand the single subject (*mats* and
*captain*) of the following sentences:

> *The brown mats of seaweed that appeared from time to time* / were
> like islands, bits of earth.

> *The captain, rearing cautiously in the bow after the dinghy soared on
> a great swell,* / said that he had seen the lighthouse at Mosquito
> Inlet.                  —"The Open Boat" [italics added]

The compound subject (*squall* and *clouds*) expands in the same
way:

> *A squall, marked by dingy clouds,* and *clouds brick-red, like smoke
> from a burning building,* appeared from the southeast.
>                  —"The Open Boat" [italics added]

**9.2b Expanding the Predicate.**   Like the subject, the predicate expands through single-word, phrasal, and clausal modifiers. You can add many more to the predicate without making
the sentence awkward:

The crest of each of these waves *was a hill, from the top of which the men surveyed, for a moment, a broad tumultuous expanse, shining and wind-riven.*        —"The Open Boat" [italics added]

The monstrous inshore rollers *heaved the boat high until the men were again enabled to see the white sheets of water scudding up the slanted sea.*        —"The Open Boat" [italics added]

**9.2**

**gr**

The third wave *moved forward, huge, furious, implacable.*
—"The Open Boat" [italics added]

To hold together, the details and ideas that form the predicate must be closely related.

**9.2c "End Focus."**    The opening of the sentence usually presents information known to the reader, the end of the sentence information that is new:

> *Given Information          New Information*
> The red book on the table / is my chemistry text.

If you reverse the nouns phrases, the emphasis changes though the new information now appears at the beginning:

> My chemistry text / is the red book on the table.

If the new information appears at the beginning, it receives unusual stress in speech:

> Who wrote the book?
> *Our chemistry teacher* did.

Since it is difficult to show this unusual stress in writing, you have the option of the passive voice:

> It was written *by our chemistry teacher.*

Usually what you put at the end of the sentence gets the attention of the reader, particularly if the words themselves stress the idea:

> The third wave moved forward, *huge, furious, implacable.*
> —"The Open Boat"

Notice how the emphasis of the sentence changes in the following revision:

> Huge, furious, implacable, *the third wave moved forward.*

As important as the opening adjectives are, the emphasis now falls to the forward movement of the wave. This natural emphasis found at the end of the sentence is called end focus.

End focus is useful in building sentences. Because the sentence thrusts forward to new information, the predicate generally can take greater modification than the subject can. Stephen Crane ends the sentence to the left with a series of phrases that, placed at the beginning, would overweigh the sentence:

| *Original* | *Ineffective Revision* |
| --- | --- |
| The correspondent saw an enormous fin speed like a shadow through the water, hurling the crystalline spray and leaving the long glowing trail. —"The Open Boat" | Speeding like a shadow through the water, hurling the crystalline spray and leaving the long glowing tail, an enormous fin was seen by the correspondent. |

**9.2**
**gr**

Notice how, in the revision, sighting of the shark loses importance; the change from the active verb *saw* to the passive verb *was seen* makes the sighting of the shark seem less important than the shark's movement through the water. Yet the sighting is as important in the sentence as the movement of the shark. See 9.3b for additional discussion of end focus.

**9.2d Sentences in Combination.** In speaking and writing, you usually coordinate and subordinate sentences with little if any conscious choice. Dependent clauses are embedded naturally as sentence constituents—subjects, objects, complements, modifiers. But numerous choices are open to you. You can choose how to open and close your sentences and arrange sentence elements or constituents throughout.

You may also choose to vary your sentences. In the course of revision, you may decide to shorten or lengthen them so that important ideas stand out. Too many sentences of the same structure and length create monotony and weaken the emphasis important ideas deserve.

The following paragraph consists entirely of simple sentences, each focusing on a single aspect of the experience:

> Slowly and beautifully the land loomed out of the sea. The wind came again. It had veered from the northeast to the southeast. Finally, a new sound struck the ears of the men in the boat. It was the low thunder of the surf on the shore. "We'll never be able to make the lighthouse now," said the captain. "Swing her head a little more north, Billie."
>
> —STEPHEN CRANE, "The Open Boat"

This sequence of short sentences gives us the rapidly changing perceptions of the narrator.

Consider the variety of sentences in this later paragraph. Crane builds longer compound and compound-complex sentences to a very short climactic simple sentence:

**9.2**

**gr**

Their backbones had become thoroughly used to balancing in the boat, and they now rode this wild colt of a dinghy like circus men [*compound*]. The correspondent thought that he had been drenched to the skin, but happening to feel in the top pocket of his coat, he found therein eight cigars [*compound-complex*]. Four of them were soaked with seawater; four were perfectly scatheless [*compound*]. After a search, somebody produced three dry matches; and thereupon the four waifs rode impudently in their little boat, and with an assurance of an impending rescue shining in their eyes [*compound*], puffed at the big cigars and judged well and ill of all men. Everybody took a drink of water [*simple*].          —"The Open Boat"

In another paragraph Crane does the reverse, building from short sentences to longer ones—each sentence focusing on a separate act or perception:

And the oiler rowed, and then the correspondent rowed [*compound*]. Then the oiler rowed [*simple*]. It was a weary business [*simple*]. The human back can become the seat of more aches and pains than are registered in books for the composite anatomy of a regiment [*complex*]. It is a limited area, but it can become the theater of innumerable muscular conflicts, tangles, wrenches, knots, and other comforts [*compound*].
          —"The Open Boat"

The power of Crane's narrative and description in these paragraphs arises through contrasts in sentence pattern as well as in sentence length.

These sentences and paragraphs occur in a literary work. Exposition also uses contrasts in pattern and length to highlight ideas. The highlighting in the following paragraph is unusually dramatic:

In the language of screen comedians four of the main grades of laugh are the titter, the yowl, the bellylaugh and the boffo. The titter is just a titter. The yowl is a runaway titter. Anyone who has ever had the pleasure knows all about a bellylaugh. The boffo is the laugh that kills. An ideally good gag, perfectly constructed and played, would bring the victim up this ladder of laughs by cruelly controlled degrees to the top rung, and would then proceed to wobble, shake, wave and brandish the ladder until he groaned for mercy. Then, after the shortest possible time out for recuperation, he would feel the first wicked tickling of the comedian's whip once more and start up a new ladder.          —JAMES AGEE, "Comedy's Greatest Era"

Agee's paragraph gives heavy and deserved emphasis to the short sentences of definition. Had Agee made his succeeding

sentences as short as these, the essay would have been monotonous. A series of long, unvaried sentences can have the same
effect.

In a first or second draft of an essay, you probably will not
give full attention to the length or shape of your sentences.
Many may be simple in structure and loosely connected. Revision gives you an opportunity to connect these sentences and
tighten their structures. Very long sentences that you find yourself having to read twice can probably be reduced to their component ideas. A string of very short sentences probably can be
combined effectively.

**9.2**
**gr**

The next section discusses special ways of building sentences
through deletion of unnecessary words and the combining of
short sentences containing related ideas.

### EXERCISES

1. Combine the following short sentences into a single sen-
tence, using the first as the kernel sentence. Avoid over-
loading the beginning of the sentence:
   **a.** Gypsy moths are infesting trees in the Northeast.
   They are brown or white.
   Their larvae eat leaves.
   **b.** Hydrogen is colorless.
   It is inflammable.
   It has no smell.
   It is the lightest of all the elements.
   **c.** The team consisted of boys and girls.
   They were juniors and seniors.
   They attended the same high school.
   They had won several state championships.
   Several members of the team had competed in national
   swimming tournaments.
   **d.** Several senior members of the team were entering col-
   lege on athletic scholarships.
   They were hoping to qualify for the American Olympic
   swimming team.
   Two of them would be attending college on the West
   Coast.
   One of them would attend college in the East.
   **e.** Few athletes are "natural" athletes in the popular sense
   of the word.
   Agility and muscular coordination are the products of
   long training.
   The wish to succeed is certainly crucial to success.
2. Break the following passage from Crane's "The Open Boat"
into simple sentences. Try combining the sentences in other

ways. What differences in focus and effect do you discover between your own combined sentences and Crane's? Does the meaning or merely the emphasis of the paragraph change?

> Their backbones had become thoroughly used to balancing in the boat, and they now rode this wild colt of a dinghy like circus men. The correspondent thought that he had been drenched to the skin, but happening to feel in the top pocket of his coat, he found therein eight cigars. Four of them were soaked with seawater; four were perfectly scatheless.

**9.3**
**gr**

3. Combine the simple sentences of Crane's paragraph on p. 187 into compound, complex, or compound-complex sentences. What is gained or lost in doing so?


# **9.3** Combination and Deletion

Later chapters show ways of improving sentences through combining clauses, reducing clauses to phrases and phrases to single words. This section describes ways of deleting unnecessary words and combining clauses in the course of building sentences.

**9.3a Deletion.**   The more unnecessary words a sentence contains, the fewer details and ideas you can add. So making sentences concise through deletion is a necessary step in building them. The following identical subjects, verbs, and complements can be deleted from the sentence. So can indefinite pronouns implied in the sentence.

*Identical Subjects*

| | |
|---|---|
| The coach is talking excitedly, and the coach is waving his arms. He is talking to the rival coach. | The coach is talking excitedly to the rival coach and waving his arms. |

*Identical Predicates*

| | |
|---|---|
| The coach is talking excitedly, and the rival coach is talking excitedly too. They are talking about the winning field goal. The coach is waving his arms. | The coach is waving his arms and talking excitedly to the rival coach about the winning field goal. |

*Identical Complements*

| | |
|---|---|
| The coach is a native Chicagoan, and the team captain is a native Chicagoan too. They roomed together at college. They are friendly rivals as a result of their long friendship. | Native Chicagoans and college roommates, the two coaches long have been friendly rivals. |

**9.3**
**gr**

*Indefinite Pronouns*

| | |
|---|---|
| Explaining to a child why wars occur is difficult for someone. They lack knowledge of people and life. | Explaining to children why wars occur is difficult because they lack experience of people and life.<br>or:<br>Children lack the experience necessary to understand why wars occur. |

**9.3b Clause Reduction.** Reducing clauses to modifying phrases or embedded phrases—constituent subjects, objects, or complements, for example—is one way of expanding sentences without loss of focus or clarity. Consider the following sentence:

The coach is tall and he is also red-headed, and he is giving instructions to the team of swimmers consisting of boys and girls.

This sentence lacks focus and clarity. It gains both in the following revision through reduction of independent clauses into modifying phrases:

The tall, red-haired coach is giving instructions to the boy-and-girl swimming team.

The same reduction is possible with dependent clauses:

| | |
|---|---|
| As he talked excitedly to the team, he waved his arms. | Talking excitedly to the team, he waved his arms. |

Notice the different emphasis given the ideas of the sentence if the modifying phrase follows the main clause:

He waved his arms, talking excitedly to the team.

Here are examples of reducing clauses to phrases:

| | |
|---|---|
| The box that is on the chair contains books. They are books on the Second World War. | The box on the chair contains books on the Second World War. |

The explanation that the defendant gave failed to convince the jury.

The explanation the defendant gave failed to convince the jury.
or:
The explanation given by the defendant failed to convince the jury.

His rambling but colorful explanation failed to convince the jury, though they were interested but skeptical.

The defendant's rambling but colorful explanation failed to convince the interested but skeptical jury.

The position of sentence elements is crucial in giving them emphasis. Sentence elements coming toward the end—even a modifying phrase—usually seem more emphatic, given the forward momentum or end focus discussed previously (see 9.2c). Compare the following:

She worked at the hospital to pay her tuition, and she increased her hours during the summer months.

Working at the hospital to pay her tuition, she increased her hours during the summer months.
or:
She worked at the hospital to pay her tuition, increasing her hours during the summer months.

You can sometimes reduce independent clauses to a single clause if they contain closely related ideas:

Doctors are increasing rapidly in number, but doctors are not increasing in rural areas of the United States, and they are needed in these areas.

The number of doctors is increasing rapidly in the United States but not in rural areas where they are needed.

The greater the concision, the more you can expand a sentence without loss of focus or clarity:

The number of doctors is increasing rapidly in the United States but not in rural areas—particularly in the Southeast and the West—where they are needed.

Compare the following:

| | |
|---|---|
| It rained last year on the Fourth of July and it rained the previous Fourth of July, but I don't think it will rain this coming Fourth of July. | It rained the last Fourth of July and the previous one, but I don't think it will rain this coming one. |

**9.3**
**gr**

Good summers come in cycles, and bad summers come in cycles. Good winters and bad winters come in cycles too. These cycles occur especially in the Midwest.

Good and bad summers come in cycles, and so do good and bad winters, especially in the Midwest.
or:
Good and bad summers and winters come in cycles, especially in the Midwest.

**9.3c Phrase Reduction.**  Reducing phrases to single-word modifiers is another important means to concision. Compare the following:

The foreman sat in the front row of the box reserved for the jury. He listened intently to the witness.

The foreman, sitting in the front row of the jury box, listened intently to the witness.

The sky filled with clouds put a halt to our picnic in the backyard. We had been planning a long time to have the picnic in the backyard. We moved the picnic into the house.

Because of the cloudy sky we moved our long-planned backyard picnic indoors.

**EXERCISES**

1. Add one or more dependent clauses to one of the following independent clauses:
   **a.** Learning to drive takes time and patience.
   **b.** Storms come up suddenly.
   **c.** Studying for an examination can be a waste of time.
2. Add to this sentence as many phrases as you can—to the limit of clarity and intelligibility.
3. Build a compound-complex sentence from the following kernels:
   **a.** The dam burst.
   **b.** The bell rang.
   **c.** The crowd surged forward.

**4.** Build a sentence using the following phrases:
   **a.** buying a used car
   **b.** to mow a lawn
   **c.** looking up at the sky
   **d.** scaling a fish
   **e.** to run through the park

**9.3**
**gr**

**5.** Combine as many of the following short sentences as possible into one or more longer sentences—turning some of them into phrases, combining clauses, and eliminating unnecessary words:

   **a.** We ordered dishes in the restaurant and ordered them by name.
   We did not know what the names of the dishes meant.
   We found we had ordered dishes that were highly peppered or seasoned.
   One dish consists of raw fish.
   It had been sliced thin.

   **b.** The trees were budding by the middle of May.
   The shrubs that flowered in April were now in full blossom.
   So were the early spring flowers.

   **c.** A good pair of shoes should have these qualities.
   They should have stitches that are even and not visible.
   They should have soles that will last long.
   They should fit well but not be so tight that they pinch.
   The soles should be flexible.

   **d.** A number of bands performed at the concert.
   Some had two members, and some had three or more.
   Some played rock, and some played country and bluegrass music.
   A string quartet would have been out of place at this concert.

   **e.** Not many buildings on campus were built before 1970.
   Those built before 1970 have thicker walls and higher ceilings.
   Classes in these buildings are quieter than those in newer buildings.

   **f.** We discussed *Hamlet.*
   We discussed Hamlet as a character and read various interpretations of his behavior.
   Then we saw a videotape of the play.
   We discussed how closely the performance realized the character of Hamlet.

   **g.** Not many of us had read *Hamlet* before.
   Only a few had seen a performance of it.
   None had seen a performance of *Hamlet* in a theater.

Those who had seen performances of it watched it on television or at the movies.

**h.** Talking about a character is easier than writing about a character.
Writing about Hamlet is an example.
He is so complex a character that I find it impossible to identify a central quality.
Hamlet makes too many statements about himself to do so.

**i.** I read that dogs are "brilliant animals."
Dogs are certainly intelligent.
However, I don't know how to define that intelligence.
My dog, for example, responds to words.
But what he hears and what he understands I cannot say.

**j.** Whatever explanation he intended to give, he changed his mind.
He guessed that we were suspicious about where he had been.
The car looked as if it had been driven long and hard.
The wheels were caked with mud.
The windshield was spattered with mud.
The bumper on the front of the car was badly dented.

**6.** Build the sentences in these opening paragraphs of this first draft of a student paper. Delete unnecessary words and combine clauses where possible:

> There are examples of euphemism everywhere.
> At my high school, students were graded every six
> weeks. Students who were failing a subject in the
> third week of the first grading period were given
> a report by the instructor. This report was to be
> taken home and signed by the parents. These re-
> ports were officially titled "Progress Report."
>
> I had never received one. For the first half
> of my freshman year I didn't know what "Progress
> Reports" were. I certainly didn't think they were
> bad. The title "Progress Report" implies that
> they are a part of the regular report on the stu-
> dent's work. The name in no way suggests that the
> student is having problems and needs help. A par-
> ent receiving his child's "Progress Report" is

9.3
gr

```
likely to look at the title, assume that it's
just another paper from school to sign, and for-
get about it.
```

# 9.3 gr

# Checklist for Building Sentences

**9.1a**  Join a subject, predicate, and modifiers into a single sentence:

> It was acute appendicitis.
> He ran a milk route at one end of the town.

**9.1b**  Join two or more independent clauses (and no dependent clauses) into a compound sentence:

> Rivers was fidgeting and I wasn't in a particularly pleasant mood myself.
> —WILLIAM CARLOS WILLIAMS

**9.1c**  Join one independent clause and one or more dependent clauses into a complex sentence:

> Rivers made a hobby one time of catching rattlesnakes, which abound in the mountains of North Jersey.
> —WILLIAM CARLOS WILLIAMS

**9.1d**  Join two or more independent clauses and one or more dependent clauses into a compound-complex sentence:

> Bears are no longer a common sight, and wolves have vanished because they were hunted fiercely.

**9.2a**  Expand the subject through modifying words, phrases, and clauses:

> The brown mats of seaweed that appeared from time to time were like islands, bits of earth.    —STEPHEN CRANE

**9.2b**  You can add more information to the predicate than to the subject:

> The correspondent saw an enormous fin speed like a shadow through the water, hurling the crystalline spray and leaving the long glowing trail.    —STEPHEN CRANE

**9.2c**  Put new information at the end of the sentence:

> The red book on the table is my chemistry text.

**9.2d**  Too many sentences of the same structure and length can make a paragraph or essay seem monotonous.

**9.3a**  Delete unnecessary words in building your sentences:

| | |
|---|---|
| The coach is talking excitedly, and the coach is waving his arms. | The coach is talking excitedly and waving his arms. |

**9.3b**  Reduce clauses to phrases for this same purpose:

| | |
|---|---|
| The box that is on the chair contains books. They are books on the Second World War. | The box on the chair contains books on the Second World War. |

**9.3c**  Reduce phrases to single words in building sentences:

| | |
|---|---|
| The foreman sat in the front row of the box reserved for the jury. He listened intently to the witness. | The foreman, sitting in the front row on the jury box, listened intently to the witness. |

# Punctuation and Mechanics

# End Punctuation

The following chapters discuss rules and conventions of sentence punctuation and departures from them. Rules govern written communication of a formal and general nature. They also govern informal writing, though writers of the informal or journalistic essay increasingly favor minimum punctuation of the sentence and the paragraph.

Punctuation changes from one age to another. Nineteenth-century writers depended more on the colon and the semicolon than do many writers today. Journalism has influenced this trend—newspapers and popular magazines favoring shorter sentences, with minimum punctuation, and paragraphs of two or three sentences. Some journalists and editors assume that short paragraphs are easier to read and hold the attention.

But short paragraphs are not easy to read when you are forced to jump from one to another. A rapid shift in focus makes it difficult to grasp as a whole an idea or a series of related ideas divided among several paragraphs. Within a single developed paragraph, punctuation shows the relationship between ideas and details and so improves the focus. The discussion of punctuation in the chapters that follow emphasizes these relationships. Notice that, in many instances, you can choose punctuation that best expresses both the relationship of ideas and the nuance of meaning you wish your sentence and paragraph to convey.

This chapter begins with the important connection between vocal inflection and written punctuation.

## 10.1  Punctuation and Meaning

**10.1a  Voice and Meaning.**  When you speak a sentence, you punctuate it with your voice to convey meaning and emotion. Your listener hears the stops and pauses through changes in pitch. This same listener depends on equivalent punctuation in reading the sentence instead of hearing it.

Consider the following unpunctuated words:

The law requires dogs to be leashed

The meaning intended would be clear if you heard these words spoken. The inflection of voice would tell you that the speaker means one of the following:

a statement of fact
exclamation of surprise, shock, or outrage
a question

Here is how you would punctuate the written sentence to express each of these responses:

The law requires dogs to be leashed.
The law requires dogs to be leashed!
The law requires dogs to be leashed?

**10.1**

**p**

Hearing these sentences, you depend on inflection of voice to tell you whether the speaker is feeling surprise, shock, or outrage. However, punctuation cannot entirely express the exact intent or meaning of the statement, though it does indicate whether the sentence is a statement, an exclamation, or a question. For their interpretation you depend on **context**—the occasion and the surrounding statements.

In writing these sentences, you may state your intention if you cannot express it exactly through punctuation:

I am surprised (or shocked or outraged) that the law requires dogs to be leashed.

**10.1b What Punctuation Does.**　In general, punctuation allows you to control meaning in the absence of vocal inflection or pitch. So various are the inflections and tones of the many dialects of English that written punctuation can express only a few of them. Since most speakers of these dialects share a written standard, written punctuation conforms to established conventions of usage—its main purpose being to set off complete sentences and clarify the relationship between phrases and clauses.

Thus we know that, in written English, a dependent clause is restrictive if commas do not set it off:

Most of Morocco is so desolate that no wild animal bigger than a hare can live on it. Huge areas *which were once covered with forest* have turned into a treeless waste where the soil is exactly like broken-up brick.

> One day a poor old creature *who could not have been more than four feet tall* crept past me under a vast load of wood.
>
> —GEORGE ORWELL, "Marrakech" [italics added]

Commas set off the nonrestrictive clause in the following sentence of Orwell:

> She answered with a shrill wail, almost a scream, *which was partly gratitude but mainly surprise.*    —"Marrakech" [italics added]

Speakers distinguish similar parenthetical or explanatory details through pauses marked by inflection or pitch. However, no exact correspondence exists; for these markers vary from dialect to dialect, and in some dialects they are barely distinct.

In fiction, writers occasionally italicize and capitalize to convey the feelings and the tone or attitude of characters, as in these examples from two contemporary short stories:

> "What's going to happen to him now?" I asked again.
> "They'll send him away some place and they'll try to cure him." He shook his head. "Maybe he'll even think he's kicked the habit. Then they'll let him loose"—he gestured, throwing his cigarette into the gutter. "That's all."
> "What do you mean, that's *all*?"
> But I knew what he meant.
> "I *mean*, that's *all*." He turned his head and looked at me, pulling down the corners of his mouth. "Don't you know what I mean?" he asked softly.    —JAMES BALDWIN, "Sonny's Blues"

> As soon as the children saw they could move their arms and legs, they scrambled out of the car, shouting, "We've had an ACCIDENT!"
> —FLANNERY O'CONNOR, "A Good Man Is Hard to Find"

Even when used expressively in fiction, punctuation is still limited in what it can convey. In the first passage, James Baldwin uses italics to convey nuances of meaning, yet he tells us that the final speaker asked the question softly; in the second, Flannery O'Connor capitalizes the final word *accident* to show the force of the exclamation.

Though punctuation is typically used less expressively than in fiction, it still offers wide opportunities to convey attitude and emotion. If, for example, you want to stress a particular idea, you can italicize it—as Baldwin does—or place it between dashes. To show that the idea is an aside or a momentary interruption, you can set it in parentheses. To show that two ideas are parts of a single idea or thought, you can join them with a semicolon. The colon introduces explanatory statements or details or an amplification of an idea.

**10.1**

**p**

**EXERCISES**

1. Describe the various ways the following sentences can be punctuated, and give the corresponding meanings:
   a. The dog bit the mailman
   b. More people watch television than read newspapers
   c. Stop smoking
   d. Please stop smoking
   e. Is that why you turned off the radio
   f. The election ended in a landslide
2. How much does the punctuation of the following statement help to convey the meaning of statements and the tone or attitude of the speaker?

> We had a lady come in about six months ago. She wanted her car in the same spot. I said, "Sorry lady, can't put it in a certain spot." She said, "I want it in *that* spot." She came back and I had it in *that* spot. She said, "Thank you." I said, "Okay, lady." She came back again and we was filled up. She wanted *that* spot again, and I said, "No, I'm filled, lady. I can't give you *that* spot. I can't give you *any* spot."  —STUDS TERKEL, *Working*

# 10.2 End Punctuation

### 10.2a Period. The **period** marks the following:

The *plain statement of fact*:

The cat is sitting on the piano.

The *indirect question*:

She asked why the class had been canceled.

*Compare*
She asked, "Why has the class been canceled?"

The policeman asked who had found the dog.

*Compare*
The policeman asked, "Who found the dog?"

The *unemphatic request or command*:

Ask for a seat on the aisle.
Give the dog the bone.

*Compare*
Don't tease the dog!

**10.2b Question Mark.**    Use the **question mark** after a direct question:

> Why was the order canceled?
> The man at the corner asked, "Is this Market Street?"

Omit the question mark after an indirect question:

> The customer asked why the order had been canceled.

If the question mark ends a quoted statement, omit the comma that normally separates the question from the speaker tag:

> *Incorrect*
> "Why was the order canceled?," the customer asked.
>
> *Correct*
> "Why was the order canceled?" the customer asked.

**10.2**

**p**

Note that the question mark immediately follows the question and not the speaker tag:

> *Incorrect*
> "When does the class meet," the student asked?
>
> *Correct*
> "When does the class meet?" the student asked.

The question mark follows an uncertain date:

> The English dramatist and poet Ben Jonson (1573?-1637) wrote
> both comedies and tragedies.

**10.2c  Exclamation Mark.**    Use the **exclamation mark** after **commands** and **interjections**—sudden statements that express amazement or pleasure or a similar emotion:

> Sit!
> Nothing doing!
> I don't believe it!
> Wow!

Omit the exclamation mark in making requests:

> Turn in your papers by three o'clock.

The exclamation mark is always used alone. The normal comma that separates a quotation from the speaker tag is omitted:

> "Sit!" he commanded the dog.
> "Don't tease the dog!" the old woman shouted from the porch.
>
> *Compare*
> "Please sit down," the woman said.

As in indirect questions, the exclamation mark is omitted in reporting a command.

*Incorrect*
I told the dog to sit!

*Correct*
I told the dog to sit.

Use the exclamation mark sparingly to express surprise or shock. A paragraph or an essay containing a string of exclamation marks loses its force:

*Ineffective*
We saw a falling star just before ten o'clock! It set the sky ablaze! It may not have been a falling star! It may have been an unknown object!

**10.2**

**P**

### EXERCISES

1. Punctuate the following sentences as statements, questions, and exclamations if possible. See the examples on p. 201 of the meanings possible through punctuation:
   **a.** hands over your head
   **b.** please turn off the lights when you leave the room
   **c.** down in front
   **d.** the street flooded minutes after the rain began
   **e.** who says all politicians are crooks
   **f.** I wonder why the traffic took so long to clear
   **g.** I asked why did the traffic take so long to clear
   **h.** what a movie
   **i.** explain yourself
   **j.** you're joking

2. Punctuate the following passage from a story by Nathaniel Hawthorne. The first speaker is a gentleman of the city where the second speaker, a young man named Robin, is searching for his uncle, Major Molineux:

   well my good lad why are you sitting here inquired he can I be of service to you in any way
   I am afraid not sir replied Robin despondingly yet I shall take it kindly if you'll answer me a single question I've been searching half the night for one Major Molineux now sir is there really such a person in these parts or am I dreaming
   Major Molineux the name is not altogether strange to me said the gentleman smiling have you any objection to telling me the nature of your business with him
   then Robin briefly related that his father was a cler-

gyman settled on a small salary at a long distance back in the country and that he and Major Molineux were brothers' children the major having inherited riches and acquired civil and military rank had visited his cousin in great pomp a year or two before had manifested much interest in Robin and an elder brother and being childless himself had thrown out hints respecting the future establishment of one of them in life the elder brother was destined to succeed to the farm which his father cultivated in the interval of sacred duties it was therefore determined that Robin should profit by his kinsman's generous intentions especially as he seemed to be rather the favorite and was thought to possess other necessary endowments

for I have the name of being a shrewd youth observed Robin in this part of his story

I doubt not you deserve it replied his new friend good-naturedly but pray proceed.

—Nathaniel Hawthorne,
"My Kinsman, Major Molineux"

## Checklist for End Punctuation

**10.2a**   Use the period to mark a plain statement of fact, an unemphatic request or command, and an indirect question.

The cat is sitting on the piano.
Ask for a seat on the aisle.
She asked why the class had been canceled.
The policeman asked who had found the dog.

**10.2b**   The question mark appears after a direct question but not after an indirect one:

"Why was the order canceled?" the customer asked.
The customer asked why the order had been canceled.

**10.2c**   Use the exclamation mark with commands and interjections:

Sit!
I don't believe it!

# The Comma

Many of us punctuate written sentences as we do the sentences we speak. Since we pause in speaking to mark an interruption or a parenthesis, we do the same in writing the sentence. Like other punctuation marks, the comma corresponds in its uses to pauses and changes in pitch in speech. But these pauses and pitch changes vary too widely from speaker to speaker to serve as a guide to written sentences.

The conventions that govern the use of the comma in writing reflect the speech habits most of us share. But they do not and cannot reflect our individual speech patterns and dialects. Given this diversity, these conventions serve an important purpose: they aid written communication through a standard of usage. They also mark sentence constituents that are clear in speech but unclear in writing without the assistance of vocal markers. The conventions described in this chapter are the conventions of written English.

## 11.1 Words and Phrases

**11.1a Single Words.**  Use commas to set off words that qualify or change the emphasis of the sentence:

> However, we need facts to make the decision.
> He explained, also, that prices would increase.
> We are going, too.
> There is, consequently, nothing you can do.

Omit the comma when the adverb is essential to the meaning and is not merely an additional or parenthetical comment:

> He *also* explained that prices would probably increase (he said one thing and added something more).
> He explained that prices would probably increase *also* (prices would increase as well as do something else).

**11.1b Introductory Verbal Phrases.**    Always set off introductory verbal phrases:

> Shouting, the old man waved a white cloth at the passing cars (*opening participle*).
> To explain the process clearly, you need a diagram (*opening infinitive phrase*).

**11.1c Modifying Phrases.**    Nonrestrictive phrases add parenthetical, nonessential information to the sentence. Use commas to set them off:

> We need, as a result, more facts to make the decision.
> In fact, the winter was longer than we had expected.

Set off modifying phrases that follow the main clause if they are not nonrestrictive:

> She ate rapidly, worrying that she would miss her train.

Restrictive modifiers limit the meaning of the sentence. Do not set them off:

> The woman *dressed in blue* is the soloist.

Short modifying phrases are usually set off when they open the sentence—even when the phrase is essential to the meaning:

> In addition to electrons and positrons, there were roughly similar numbers of various kinds of neutrinos, ghostly particles with no mass or electric charge whatever. Finally, the universe was filled with light.
> —STEVEN WEINBERG, *The First Three Minutes*

The comma is sometimes omitted when the introductory phrase is short:

> At the end of the first three minutes the contents of the universe were mostly in the form of light, neutrinos, and antineutrinos.    —STEVEN WEINBERG, *The First Three Minutes*

**11.1d Contrast.**    Set off contrasting words and phrases, no matter where they appear in the sentence:

> Scott, not Amundsen, died in the Antarctic.

The exceptions are phrases introduced by *but* meaning "except":

> No one but Mozart could have written that concerto.

Here the phrase *but Mozart* restricts the meaning.

**11.1e Absolute Phrases.** The **absolute phrase** modifies the whole clause or the sentence, not any individual word. Since the phrase connects with no single element grammatically and stands alone, it is always set off by a comma:

> Six boys came over the hill half an hour early that afternoon, running hard, *their heads down, their forearms working, their breath whistling.*   —JOHN STEINBECK, "The Red Pony" [italics added]

> He could see the two other boys down below, *the ball going back and forth between them as if they were bowling on the grass,* and Glennie's crew-cut head looking like a sea urchin.
> —RICHARD WILBUR, "A Game of Catch" [italics added]

**11.1f Appositives.** Don't set off a restrictive or defining **appositive** word or phrase—one that identifies the person or thing:

> The explorer Scott died in the Antarctic.

A nonrestrictive appositive supplying additional but nonessential information is always set off:

> Scott, the rival of Amundsen, died in the Antarctic.

Commas can set off internal appositives as well as final ones:

> The 1970 Superbowl, the final game of the professional football season, drew a larger television audience than either the moonwalk or Tiny Tim's wedding.
> —MURRAY ROSS, "Football Red and Baseball Green"

> I continued to see the *braceros,* those men I resembled in one way and, in another way, didn't resemble at all.
> —RICHARD RODRIGUEZ, *Hunger of Memory*

However, dashes usually set off longer appositives or emphatic short ones, particularly when the sentence contains commas:

> When men split the nucleus of the atom, they unleashed into terrestrial nature a basic energy of the cosmos—the energy latent in mass—which had never before been active in any major way on earth.   —JONATHAN SCHELL, *The Fate of the Earth*

At the end of the sentence, an appositive may be set off with a comma or a dash:

> She read Rachel Carson's book, *Silent Spring.*
> She read Rachel Carson's influential book—*Silent Spring.*

The dash is the usual punctuation. See 13.3.

**11.1**

**,**

**EXERCISES**

1. Add commas where needed:
   **a.** Contrary to what you heard the court will be in session.
   **b.** Saul Bellow's novel *The Victim* was published in 1947.
   **c.** George Plimpton's *Paper Lion* an account of his training with a pro football team was first published in 1966.
   **d.** She found the book interesting her curiosity about the life of the professional player growing from page to page.
   **e.** He insisted finally that no action be taken.
   **f.** We cannot take action no matter what happens.
   **g.** The time having elapsed the teacher collected the exams.
   **h.** Nothing happened except for the scuffle in the street.
   **i.** Joe Louis the heavyweight boxer wrote an autobiography.
   **j.** The heavyweight boxer Joe Louis wrote an autobiography.

2. Capitalize and add periods and commas where needed in the following paragraphs:

> a. It was chill though August and the two men sitting with bowed heads grew stiff with cold and weariness and were forced to rise now and again and walk about to warm their stiffened limbs it did not occur to them probably to contrast their coming home with their going forth or with the coming home of the generals colonels or even captains but to Private Smith at any rate there came a sickness at heart almost deadly as he lay there on his hard bed and went over his situation.
>
> —HAMLIN GARLAND, "The Return of a Private"

> b. Morning dawned at last slowly with a pale yellow dome of light rising silently above the bluffs which stand like some huge storm-devastated castle just east of the city out to the left the great river swept on its massive yet silent way to the south bluejays called across the river from hillside to hillside through the clear beautiful air and hawks began to skim the tops of the hills the older men were astir early but Private Smith had fallen at last into a sleep and they went out without waking him he lay on his knapsack his gaunt face turned toward the ceiling his hands clasped on his breast with a curious pathetic effect of weakness and appeal.
>
> —HAMLIN GARLAND, "The Return of a Private"

# 11.2   Clauses

**11.2a  Adverbial Clauses.**   Here are a few of the subordinating conjunctions that introduce adverbial clauses:

| | | |
|---|---|---|
| after | because | unless |
| although, though | before | until |
| as | if, if only | when |
| as long as | since | whenever |
| as soon as | that | |

Opening adverbial clauses usually are set off by a comma:

> When we came into tunnel country, the flicker and hollow amplification stirred Neil awake.
> —JOHN UPDIKE, "The Happiest I've Been"

However, you can omit the comma if the subject of the adverbial and the subject of the main clause are the same:

> When he came to the highway Neil turned right, toward Olinger, instead of left toward the Turnpike.
> —JOHN UPDIKE, "The Happiest I've Been"

The same applies to brief opening clauses:

> Since Jim left she has talked twice to him.

Don't set off restrictive adverbial clauses that follow the main clause:

> The weekend is the time when you probe to see how much people really like you. During the week they are forced to be with you and be nice to you because their work requires it.
> —MAX GUNTHER, "The Weekend World"

In general and informal writing, a comma sometimes marks a pause before a restrictive modifier:

> We hike on weekends, except when it rains.

**11.2b Adjective Clauses.** The following italicized words introduce adjective clauses:

> The year *that* the Vietnam War ended was 1973.
> Spring is the season *when* the azaleas bloom.
> The family left the state *where* they have lived for ten years.
> I read *Vietnam: A History, which* describes the war. The man *who* wrote the book is Seymour Karnow.

As with adverbial clauses, commas set off nonrestrictive adjective clauses. Compare the following sentences:

| *Restrictive* | *Nonrestrictive* |
|---|---|
| The Elizabeth Taylor who wrote numerous stories and novels is not Elizabeth Taylor the actress. | The British writer Elizabeth Taylor, who wrote numerous stories and novels, is not the actress Elizabeth Taylor. |

Note the commas that mark the nonrestrictive modifier in the sentence to the right. These commas set off nonessential information.

The relative pronoun *that* usually introduces a restrictive clause. The relative pronoun *which* usually introduces a nonrestrictive clause:

> The Dickens novel that I saw dramatized is *Nicholas Nickleby*.
> *The Mystery of Edwin Drood,* which Dickens left unfinished, has also been dramatized.

**11.2**
**,**

**11.2c  Coordinate Clauses.**  The following words introduce independent clauses—those that stand alone as self-contained sentences or join with other independent or dependent clauses—coordinate or equal in importance:

> and, but, for, yet, or, nor, so

The comma usually divides coordinate clauses:

> It is raining today, *and* it will probably rain tomorrow.
> It will not rain today, *but* it surely will rain tomorrow.
> Take the course next semester, *for* it won't be offered again.
> Take the course, *or* go to the dean and ask for an exemption.
> The bear did not move or make any noise, *nor* did I.
> He made good sense about why I should take the course, *yet* I
>     was unconvinced.
> His argument made good sense, *so* I took his advice.

The comma is sometimes omitted when the clauses are short:

> I saw the bear and so did Margaret.
> The bear looked at me and I looked at it.
> It did not move nor did I.

The comma is often omitted when the clauses form a single idea:

> He was now forty-six and his wife was over fifty.
> —PENELOPE MORTIMER, "The Parson"

On occasion writers omit the comma for special emphasis:

> The train rolled up and he sat down spiritlessly under the slow-wheeling fan that stirred the heat.
> —SAUL BELLOW, *The Victim*

**EXERCISE**

First decide whether the italicized words, phrases, and clauses are restrictive or nonrestrictive. Then add commas where needed:

1. I am not however as convinced about going *as I was.*
2. There is no way that I can go *if you don't.*
3. *If you cannot go* I can't either.
4. William Jennings Bryan *popularly known as "The Great Commoner"* ran for president and lost.
5. *"The Great Commoner" William Jennings Bryan* opposed Clarence Darrow in the Scopes Trial.
6. Washington *the first President of the United States* did not live in the present White House.
7. The famous journalist *who wrote a book on the American language* is H. L. Mencken.
8. H. L. Mencken *who wrote the famous book The American Language* was called "the Sage of Baltimore"—a compliment both to Mencken and to the city *where he lived his entire life.*
9. The book *that earned Annie Dillard the Pulitzer Prize* is *Pilgrim at Tinker Creek.*
10. The game *now in the seventeenth inning* had already broken the record.
11. The last king of England *who personally led troops into battle* was George the Second.
12. George the Second *who personally led troops into battle* was the last king of England to do so.
13. *If nobody comes to the door* look for the key under the mat.
14. Look for the key under the mat *if nobody comes to the door.*
15. The election will take place as scheduled *even though one of the candidates withdrew.*
16. *Though I mailed the entry late* I still won the drawing.
17. She will call *when she finds out who won.*
18. The package *which arrived yesterday* contains presents for the children.
19. The explanation *which* I rejected will not surprise you.
20. We accepted the explanation *that she gave.*

# 11.3 Series

**11.3a Words, Phrases, and Clauses.** Use commas to divide words, phrases, and clauses that form a series or listing of names or items:

*Words and Phrases*
    The East River area had such gangs as the Buckaroos, Hookers, Daybreak Boys, and Swamp Angels, while the Chrystie, Forsyth, and Elizabeth street region had the notorious Slaughter House gang.
                                    —ROBERT E. RIEGEL, *Young America*, 1830–1840

[Napoleon Bonaparte] All the qualities of Renaissance Italy appeared in him: artist and warrior, philosopher and despot; unified in instincts and purposes, quick and penetrating in thought, direct and overwhelming in action, but unable to stop. Barring that vital fault, he was the finest master of controlled complexity and coordinated energy in history.
—WILL and ARIEL DURANT, *The Age of Napoleon*

*Clauses*

**11.3**

**,**

To be sure, most women tend to fret more than most men over the small details of life and the rules of behavior, they tend to worry more about how things look, they are more afflicted by the fear of missing trains or losing one glove, they cry more readily [*clauses*]. But on the very big matters, the times requiring exactly the right hunch, the occasions when the survival of human beings is in question, I would trust that X chromosome and worry about the Y. [*phrases*]
—LEWIS THOMAS, *The Youngest Science*

Though many writers omit the final comma of the series, its omission can create ambiguity. Omitting the comma after the phrase "Daybreak Boys" may suggest that the name of the gang is "Daybreak Boys and Swamp Angels."

**11.3b Coordinate Adjectives.**    A special problem arises with adjectives arranged in a series. In the following sentence the adjectives are coordinate—that is, they are of equal importance as modifiers:

He was a man of about fifty, tall, portly, and imposing, with a massive, strongly marked face and a commanding figure.
—SIR ARTHUR CONAN DOYLE, *Adventures of Sherlock Holmes*

You can test whether adjectives are interchangeable by reversing their order or adding *and* between them:

He was a man of about fifty, portly, tall, and imposing . . .
He was tall, portly, a man about fifty, and imposing . . .

This test shows that each adjective modifies the subject of the sentence, *he*.

But note the italicized words in the following:

On the right side was a *small wooden thicket*, which led into a narrow path between *two neat hedges* stretching from the road to the kitchen door, and forming the tradesmen's entrance.
—SIR ARTHUR CONAN DOYLE, *The Adventures of Sherlock Holmes*

Here *small* modifies the phrase *wooden thicket*, and *two* modifies *neat hedges*. The adjectives *small* and *wooden*, *two* and *neat*, cannot be interchanged. When two or more adjectives precede the noun modified and can be reordered, commas separate them.

**EXERCISE**

Add commas where needed:
1. The gray cloudy sky promised rain.
2. She described herself as friendly curious interested in music somewhat ambitious but not excessively so.
3. In the driveway is a battered 1973 coal gray Plymouth.
4. Hand this book to the tall blonde haired girl talking to the boy on the stairs.
5. The dogs barked the cats snarled and the children hooted.
6. The tattered discolored dark green pages made the book impossible to read.
7. The discolored dark green tattered pages made the book impossible to read.
8. The very long dark green spotted carpet showed the true age of the house.
9. To find the source of the noise, she looked first to the north then to the west and finally to the south.
10. She asked that we collect the specimens that we tag them and sort them according to type and finally that we write a brief description of each.

# 11.4 Quotations

The comma separates the speaker tag from a direct quotation:

Patrick Henry said, "Give me liberty or give me death!"

Note that the comma is omitted in the following:

"Give me liberty or give me death!" Patrick Henry said.

Commas also set off a speaker tag that interrupts a quotation:

"But if thought corrupts language," George Orwell wrote, "language can also corrupt thought."

See 10.2b on indirect quotations.

# 11.5 Other Uses of Commas

**11.5a Dates.** A comma divides the day of the month from the year:

May 17, 1930

You need not include it if you give only the month and year:

May 1930

The comma follows the year when the date appears before the end of the sentence:

She was born February 14, 1934, in Boston, Massachusetts.

**11.5b Numbers.**    Commas divide units in numbers:

1,180
10,180
100,180
1,000,000
100,000,000

Omit commas in round numbers up to four figures and in addresses:

1000 books in the room
13527 Fourth Avenue

**11.5c Addresses.**    Commas separate the units of an address but not the ZIP code:

Cuyahoga Falls, Summit County, Ohio 44221

**11.5d Titles, Degrees, and Identifying Phrases.**    Commas separate titles that follow the proper name:

Elizabeth Dole, secretary of transportation
Mary O'Connell, M.D.

**EXERCISE**

Add commas where appropriate:

1. The year 1939 marks the beginning of the Second World War.
2. Germany invaded Poland on September 1 1939 on the pretext that she was protecting German nationals living in the country.
3. He lives at 3255 Westlawn Avenue Akron Ohio a city in the northeastern part of the state.
4. The official census of the ward showed 32550 residents of voting age.
5. The woman on the platform is Elizabeth McClintock Nobel Prize Laureate.
6. The woman on the platform is Nobel Prize Laureate Elizabeth McClintock.
7. "Ask not what your country will do for you" President Ken-

nedy said in his inaugural address of January 20 1961 "ask what you can do for your country."
8. President Kennedy was shot on November 22 1963 in an open automobile in Dealy Plaza in Dallas Texas.
9. Marcus Welby M.D. was a popular television show in the 1960s.
10. Send your letter to Daniel J. Boorstin Librarian Library of Congress Washington D. C. 20540.

# 11.6  Misuses of the Comma

Misuses of the comma often arise in mistaking one sentence constituent for another. You can sometimes discover unnecessary commas by reading a doubtful sentence aloud.

**11.6a Single Comma Between Subject and Verb.**   Don't use a comma to divide the subject from the verb. In the following sentence, the comma mistakenly divides the long noun phrase subject from the predicate:

*Incorrect*
The course scheduled for eight o'clock on three days a week, may have to be rescheduled.

*Correct*
The course scheduled for eight o'clock on three days a week may have to be rescheduled.

The longer the subject noun phrase, the greater the risk of treating it as a modifying phrase.

**11.6b  Comma Between Verb and Direct Object.**   Don't use a comma to divide a verb and its direct object. The obvious error in the following sentences probably arises from carelessness:

She passed, the test.
The judge levied, a heavier fine than usual.

The error in the following sentence is not so obvious:

*Incorrect*
The judge said, that he was levying a heavier fine than usual.

*Correct*
The judge said that he was levying a heavier fine than usual.

The error arises because the writer adds a comma as in punctuating a direct quotation:

The judge said, "I'm suspending the fine for this first offense."

Omit the comma in an indirect quotation:

The judge said he was suspending the fine for this first offense.

**11.6c Comma Between Verb and Subject Complement.**
Don't use the comma to divide the verb from the subject complement:

*Incorrect*
The reason for the hike in food prices is, that the drought reduced the corn harvest.

*Correct*
The reason for the hike in food prices is that the drought reduced the corn harvest.

**11.6**
**,**

The long noun phrase subject again seems to invite a comma. But a comma is incorrect. To decide whether you need a comma, reduce the subject to its core:

The reason is that the drought reduced corn production.

**11.6d Commas with Restrictive Modifiers.**   Restrictive modifiers do not require commas because they provide essential information or identify the noun modified:

*Incorrect*
The book, that helped me the most, is a primer on economics.

*Correct*
The book that helped me the most is a primer on economics.

*Incorrect*
Be sure, that you sign every page at the top.

*Correct*
Be sure that you sign every page at the top.

See 11.1c on restrictive and nonrestrictive modifiers.

**11.6e Comma Between Coordinate Nouns.**   Don't use the comma to divide coordinate nouns, as in the compound subject of the following prepositional phrase:

*Incorrect*
I see no difference between my sentence, and your sentence.

*Correct*
I see no difference between my sentence and your sentence.

To make the sentence easier to read or to emphasize a phrase, writers sometimes use a comma between long coordinate noun phrases like the following:

The depression was closer to home; in New York I used to see apple-sellers on the street corners, and, now and then, a bread line, but I had a very thin awareness of mass poverty.
—MARY McCARTHY, "My Confession"

The optional comma here makes this long sentence easier to read.

**11.6f Comma Between Coordinate Verbs.**  Don't use the comma to divide coordinate verbs:

*Incorrect*
He explained his absence, and promised to be punctual in the future.

*Correct*
He explained his absence and promised to be punctual in the future.

Writers also occasionally divide long coordinate verb phrases:

What with the telephone, radio, movies, television, and the other distractions that modern life has to offer, the reading of the advertising mail fits comfortably into the necessity to be entertained, and will do service for a good deal of the reading of other kinds which might otherwise have been done.
—ASHLEY MONTAGU, "The Annihilation of Privacy"

**11.6g Comma Splice.**  Commas sometimes wrongly "splice" or join unrelated independent clauses:

*Incorrect*
The woman is Jane's mother, she is visiting this week.

*Correct*
The woman is Jane's mother. She is visiting Jane this week.

*Incorrect*
She drove from Connecticut despite the snowstorm, she could not postpone the visit.

*Correct*
She drove from Connecticut despite the snowstorm; she could not postpone the visit.

If the two parts of the sentence are closely related, you can coordinate the independent clauses:

The woman in the blue dress is Jane's mother, and she is visiting Jane this week.
She drove from Connecticut despite the snowstorm, for she could not postpone the visit.

The error is easier to spot when the subject of the second clause is different from the subject of the first:

*Incorrect*
Everyone admires courage, Jane insisted on entering the tournament even though she was still recovering from an accident.

If the two parts of the sentence have different subjects, make each a separate sentence or, if the ideas are closely related, use a colon or semicolon (see 12.1a and 12.2a):

**11.6**
**,**

Everyone admires courage. Jane insisted on entering the tournament even though she was still recovering from an accident.

Everyone admires courage: Jane insisted on entering the tournament even though she was still recovering from an accident.

The comma may also divide complementary clauses that form a single idea, as in this statement about the writer Jonathan Swift:

Not only does he see the value of good manners, good conversation, and even learning of a literary and historical kind, he also sees that agriculture, navigation and architecture need to be studied and could with advantage be improved.
—GEORGE ORWELL, "Politics vs. Literature:
An Examination of *Gulliver's Travels*"

**EXERCISE**
Correct those sentences that contain unnecessary commas:
1. Few sports are played as they used to be, football today is a violent sport, and a popular sport with many because it is violent.
2. A sport like soccer, which has less body contact than American football, sometimes encourages spectator violence.
3. Football, baseball, and tennis, but not ice hockey or soccer, are sports with a wide television audience.
4. Ask for a discount, not for a refund.
5. You have no grounds for complaint, you can write down what happened and what redress you want, but I doubt it will do you any good.
6. Give this envelope to the man at the door, don't give it to the woman at the desk.
7. We came to the fork in the road and paused, we decided to turn back and ask directions.
8. The long hot summer and the lack of rain particularly in August, produced fires throughout the West.

9. We came to the fork in the road and then turned south.
10. We came to the fork in the road, but could not decide whether to drive south to Cincinnati by way of Dayton, or to drive to Columbus first.
11. No one stopped to help, each car slowed down to observe the accident and then drove away.
12. His not very convincing explanation is, that the traffic was too heavy to stop the car.
13. Waste not, want not.
14. The person who told you about Italy has never been there.
15. The beach that his friends had described to him, was on the north shore, close to the tip of the peninsula.

**11.7**
**,**

# 11.7 Comma to Prevent Misreading

Occasionally we need a comma to prevent the misreading of a sentence. In the following sentence the word *before* creates momentary confusion:

> A few weeks before he arrived home with a bad cough and a high fever.

A comma following the introductory phrase makes the sentence immediately clear:

> A few weeks before, he arrived home with a bad cold and a high fever.

The same correction clarifies the following sentence:

*Confusing*
On the team of twenty one or two will qualify for the Olympics.

*Clear*
On the team of twenty, one or two will qualify for the Olympics.

**EXERCISE**

Decide whether the following sentences are punctuated correctly. Add commas or remove them where necessary:
1. More errors result from carelessness, than neglect.
2. Many years after he wrote that he was returning to Idaho, where he had been raised.
3. The tall pine tree, which we planted a few years ago is dying.
4. Few people who knew her or had read her books realized that she was nearly blind.
5. Among the ninety six students held scholarships.
6. At twenty degrees below the car is hard to start.

7. I have more faith in their honesty, than you have.
8. Few who know her, and who have read her books, realize that she is over eighty years of age.
9. He addressed the class that was graduating midyear.
10. He reasoned, that the water would be warmer on the south shore than on the north.
11. He told the class about the strange animal, swimming close to shore.
12. On the ledge above the fire continued to burn out of control.
13. I have never heard a better singer, or heard a worse backup band.
14. The last time we drove to St. Louis overnight we stayed in Indianapolis.
15. At the age of thirty one sometimes discovers a change in feelings and goals.

**11.7**
**,**

# Checklist for Using Commas

**11.1a**   Use commas to set off words that qualify or change the focus of the sentence:

However, we need facts to make the decision.
We are going, also.

**11.1b**   Use commas to set off introductory verbal phrases:

Shouting, the man waved a white cloth at passing cars.
To explain the process clearly, you need a diagram.

**11.1c**   Use commas to set off nonrestrictive modifiers but not restrictive ones—modifiers essential to the meaning:

He also explained that prices would probably increase.
She ate rapidly, worrying that she would miss her train.

**11.1d**   Set off contrasting words and phrases, no matter where they appear in the sentence:

Scott, not Amundsen, died in the Antarctic.

**11.1e**   Always set off absolute phrases:

The motion to adjourn having been made, the meeting ended.

**11.1f**   Set off a nonrestrictive appositive but not a restrictive one:

The explorer Scott died in the Antarctic.
Scott, the rival of Amundsen, died in the Antarctic.

**11.2a** Commas usually set off opening adverbial clauses:

When you reach the highway, you turn right.

Omit the comma when a restrictive adverbial clause follows the main clause:

She is walking to school even though it is raining.

**11.2b** Set off nonrestrictive adjective clauses but not restrictive ones:

John, who still has tickets to sell, will be home later.
He is the person who has tickets to sell.

**11.2c** Separate coordinate clauses unless they are short:

It is raining today, and it will probably rain tomorrow.
She hopes to finish college and he hopes to finish, too.

**11.3a** Divide words, phrases, and clauses that form a series:

Her sisters are a teacher, a lawyer, and a doctor.

**11.3b** Divide coordinate adjectives only if they are interchangeable:

He was short, thin, and bald.

**11.4** Separate the speaker tag from the direct quotation:

Patrick Henry said, "Give me liberty or give me death!"

**11.5a** Divide the month and day from the year:

May 17, 1930

**11.5b** Divide units in numbers:

10,543,230

**11.5c** Separate the units of an address but not the ZIP:

Cuyahoga Falls, Summit County, Ohio 44221

**11.5d** Separate titles that follow the proper name:

Elizabeth Dole, secretary of transportation

**11.6a** Don't divide the subject from the verb:

*Incorrect*
The course scheduled for eight o'clock, may have to be rescheduled.

*Correct*
The course scheduled for eight o'clock may have to be rescheduled.

**11.6b**   Don't divide the verb from the direct object:

*Incorrect*
The judge levied, a heavier fine than usual.

*Correct*
The judge levied a heavier fine than usual.

**11.6c**   Don't divide the verb and subject complement:

*Incorrect*
The reason for the hike in food prices is, that the drought reduced the corn harvest.

*Correct*
The reason for the hike in food prices is that the drought reduced the corn harvest.

**11.6d**   Restrictive modifiers do not require commas:

*Incorrect*
The book, that helped me the most, is this one.

*Correct*
The book that helped me the most is this one.

**11.6e**   Don't use a comma to divide coordinate nouns:

*Incorrect*
He is my friend, and your friend too.

*Correct*
He is my friend and your friend too.

**11.6f**   Don't use a comma to divide coordinate verbs:

*Incorrect*
He is my friend, and wants to be yours.

*Correct*
He is my friend and wants to be yours.

**11.6g**   Don't "splice" two independent clauses with a comma:

*Incorrect*
The woman in the blue dress is Jane's mother, she is visiting her for a week.

*Correct*
The woman in the blue dress is Jane's mother. She is visiting her for a week.
That woman is Jane's mother; she is visiting her for a week.

**11.7**  Use commas to prevent the misreading of a sentence:

*Confusing*
A few weeks before he caught a bad cold.

*Clear*
A few weeks before, he caught a bad cold.

# The Semicolon and Colon

Semicolons and colons are less used in general and informal writing than they used to be, probably because of newspapers and magazines that favor a plain style. However, the idea is mistaken that sentences and paragraphs become easier to read through a minimum of punctuation. Semicolons and colons are an important means to sentence and paragraph unity, for we do not always see the relationship between the ideas and details in a string of simple sentences. In connecting these sentences, semicolons and colons serve as a kind of transition—a signal to the reader that ideas are closely related or that an idea is to be developed or amplified by the clause or the sentence that follows.

This chapter shows how semicolons and colons mark these relationships.

## 12.1 The Semicolon

**12.1a Semicolon with Independent Clauses.** The **semicolon** joins independent clauses in the absence of a period or a coordinating conjunction (*and, but, for, yet, so, or, nor*). The semicolon shows that the two ideas are so closely related that they form a single idea:

> Night fell quickly; at about four o'clock the fog poured down the San Francisco hillsides, covered the bay, and clouded the windows.          —Maxine Hong Kingston, *China Men*

> When I was a child I thought we lived at the end of the world. It was the eternity of the subway ride into the city that first

gave me this idea. It took a long time getting to "New York"; it seemed longer getting back.

—ALFRED KAZIN, "The Open Street"

Note how the semicolon in Kazin's third sentence distinguishes closely related ideas from those in the preceding sentences.

Occasionally the semicolon replaces the comma before a co-ordinating conjunction, usually for greater emphasis:

Yellow fever continued as the great threat to the New World; *but* in Europe cholera and typhoid were the outstanding problems.

—CHARLES-EDWARD AMORY WINSLOW, *The Conquest of Epidemic Disease*

**12.1**

**;**

The parasite is an organism which has become adapted to life in the tissues and cells of some higher form of life; *and* in the process of adaptation (like human beings who have become parasites on society) it has lost the capacity to earn an honest living in the world outside.

—CHARLES-EDWARD AMORY WINSLOW, *The Conquest of Epidemic Disease*

**12.1b Semicolon for Addition and Amplification.** The semicolon may also introduce an amplifying phrase or clause that explains the preceding idea or serves as an afterthought:

Sale of land could never be more than temporary; so when Indians, from Plymouth Rock to Oregon, sold land, they thought of the sale as a temporary arrangement. The moment that the payment ceased to come the land returned to the tribe; *or so they thought* as long as they could.

—MARI SANDOZ, "Some Oddities of the American Indian" [italics added]

Ours is an age of fiendish competition; *and the constant effort*, not so much to get ahead as to keep afloat, is hardly calculated to make us less frantic. Ours is an age of incessant anxiety; *and our vivid awareness* of the fact is scarcely calculated to make us less anxious. Ours, all too graphically, is an age of violence; *and being reminded* of the fact at every turn is hardly calculated to make us less scared.

—LOUIS KRONENBERGER, "Unbrave New World" [italics added]

**12.1c Semicolons in Series.** Semicolons separate a series of coordinate clauses in the absence of coordinating conjunctions:

He wore a flimsy shirt of material that must have been imitation silk; it opened on the chest on the dirty hem of an undershirt; his light cotton shirt was soiled.    —SAUL BELLOW, *The Victim*

The reeds were strands of color passing light like cells in water. They were those yellow and green and brown strands of pond algae I had watched so long in a light-soaked field. My eyes burned; I was watching algae wave in a shrinking drop; they crossed each other and parted wetly.

—ANNIE DILLARD, "Lenses"

**12.1**

**;**

A large raw wound constantly oozes out protein; the body burns up calories trying to heal the wound; bacteria settle on open wounds.

—ELIZABETH MORGAN, *The Making of a Woman Surgeon*

Recall, then, some event that has left a distinct impression on you—how at the corner of the street, perhaps, you passed two people talking. A tree shook; an electric light danced; the tone of the talk was comic, but also tragic; a whole vision, an entire conception, seemed contained in that moment.

—VIRGINIA WOOLF, "How Should One Read a Book?"

Semicolons can hold together a large number of ideas and details—each sentence presenting one idea at a time:

But other sources of vogue words are taking over. Games and sports, for example: *Square one*, a games term, is what we reluctantly go back to; a basketball phrase, *one-to-one*, is used now to describe any direct confrontation, tête-à-tête or match-up; football has contributed *cheap shot* (a tackle after the whistle, or late hit), and *blind-side*, a verb for dealing an unexpected blow. Because an old-time baseball pitcher never knew which way his spitball would break, the verb *to spitball* now means "to speculate."        —WILLIAM SAFIRE, *On Language*

Occasionally semicolons divide a series of phrases to stress the similarity or parallelism in ideas:

Education is about civilization. Lose sight of that and you lose sight of humanity. Then education is divorced from the great virtues: truth, justice, compassion, humility. Special interests dictate their own ends: the individual's concern with looking out for No. 1; economic interests' concern with expanding their earnings at any cost; governments' concern with controlling and directing their citizenry and with extending their hege-mony [*noun phrases*].

—HILARY THIMMESH, "Education Is About Civilization," *Chronicle of Higher Education*, June 20, 1984

Without the Hebrew Scriptures and the New Testament; without Aristotle, Plato, Aquinas, and a host of other thinkers; without Sophocles, Dante, Shakespeare, and a host of other poets; without the political thinkers and the lawgivers, the doctors and the saints and the reformers down to our own day, we would have no terms for oppression and injustice, no norms of right and wrong, no language of the ideal [*prepositional phrases*].
—HILARY THIMMESH, "Education Is About Civilization"

**12.1d Semicolon with Conjunctive Adverbs.** The semicolon, not the comma, is used with conjunctive adverbs (*thus, however, therefore, nevertheless, furthermore, moreover*) and adverbial phrases (*in fact, on the contrary*) that connect independent clauses:

> Inflation rose at a higher rate than in 1980; *thus,* many economists predicted an increase in interest rates.
> Inflation rose over 300% as a result of the war; *therefore,* the government devalued the currency.
> Few people understand growth cycles; *nevertheless,* economists continue to talk as if cycles were understood.
> Economics is hard for me to understand; *in fact,* the English writer Thomas Carlyle called it "the dismal science."
> It was a scene I wanted to forget; *however,* it stuck in the mind.

Notice that the adverb may appear later in the second clause instead of introducing it:

> Inflation rose at a higher rate than in 1980; many economists *thus* predicted an increase in interest rates.
> Inflation rose over 300% as a result of the war; the government *therefore* devalued the currency.
> Few people understand growth cycles; economists *nevertheless* continue to talk as if cycles were understood.
> Economics is hard for me to understand; Carlyle, *in fact,* called it "the dismal science."
> It was a scene I wanted to forget; it stuck in my mind, *however.*

**12.1e Semicolons and Commas in a Series.** Commas separate a simple series:

> We visited Lansing, Springfield, and Columbus on our trip.

When one or more members of the series contain commas, semicolons divide its main parts:

> We visited Lansing, the capital of Michigan; Springfield, the capital of Illinois; and Columbus, the capital of Ohio.

Semicolons are especially important in longer sentences containing such a series:

He looked proud and fatherly as he pointed to his young charge standing at an upright at the far end of the room and working things over with the team of experts: Lou Spencer, a former dancer turned choreographer and nightclub-act creator; Noel Sherman, song and special-material writer; and Joe Zito, song arranger and conductor.    —LILLIAN ROSS, "The Sound"

In the following long sentences, the semicolon highlights parallel ideas as well as antithetical or contrasting ones.

**12.1**

**;**

Men lost faith in the state not because Christianity held them aloof, but because the state defended wealth against poverty, fought to capture slaves, taxed toil to support luxury, and failed to protect its people from famine, pestilence, invasion, and destitution; forgivably they turned from Caesar preaching war to Christ preaching peace, from incredible brutality to unprecedented charity, from a life without hope or dignity to a faith that consoled their poverty and honored their humanity. Rome was not destroyed by Christianity, any more than by barbarian invasion; it was an empty shell when Christianity rose to influence and invasion came.    —WILL DURANT, *Caesar and Christ*

### EXERCISE

Add the necessary commas, semicolons, and other marks:
1. However difficult you find talking with him about your problems be as forthright as you can.
2. You will find him difficult to talk to about your problems however you will gain from being direct and honest.
3. The meeting began with a welcome from the mayor the head of the revenue office outlined the budget for the coming year using charts of city services one of her assistants discussed a tax increase reduction of administrative costs and better coordination with the state budget office.
4. At the county fair we ate hot dogs pizza and corn on the cob rode the Ferris wheel drove Dodge-'Em cars and parachuted and watched the dog trials the baking competition, and the cattle auction.
5. He was so sick that he had to be taken to the hospital and he was not the only person who became sick from overeating.
6. The Algonquin family of Indians included the Chippewas living between Lake Erie and what is today North Dakota the Cheyennes living in what is today Nebraska and the Blackfeet living northeast of the Rocky Mountains.

7. She is unwilling to run for president nevertheless I recommend our nominating her.
8. The blackfish includes the sea bass and tautog the herring includes the pilchard and the sprat the carp includes the minnow the dace and the goldfish.
9. The concerts this summer include an all-Handel program an all-Beethoven program an overture the Fifth Symphony the Third Piano Concerto a Mozart and Mahler program a Mozart concerto and the Mahler Fourth Symphony.
10. The exhibition now on display includes Manet Cézanne and Picasso the exhibition opening in May will present Spanish painters of different periods.

## 12.2  The Colon

**12.2**
**:**

**12.2a  Explanation and Amplification.**  The colon usually shows that an explanation, an amplification, or a restatement of the initial statement follows. The colon most commonly introduces ideas or a series of details that explain the preceding clause:

> The range of cures or terminations of boredom is a wide one: migration, desertion, war, revolution, murder, calculated cruelty to others, suicide, pornography, alcohol, narcotics.
> —ROBERT NISBET, "Boredom"

> So it is with the ascendancy of political parties: the more powerful a party-in-office becomes, the greater the boredom it produces in the public mind.    —ROBERT NISBET, "Boredom"

> Fundamental to the territorial principle are two opposing impulses: there is the urge to intrude on the property of one's neighbor, and the urge to avoid it.
> —ROBERT ARDREY, *The Territorial Imperative*

> Thus the main objection which had previously hampered the acceptance of inoculation with the smallpox itself was removed: and the value of the new method of "vaccination" came swiftly to be recognized in all of Europe.
> —WILLIAM MCNEILL, *Plagues and People*

**12.2b  Misuses of the Colon.**  Use the colon following a complete statement. Don't use the colon to introduce an indirect quotation:

*Incorrect*
Ardrey states: that the territorial principle is dual in impulse.

*Correct*
Ardrey states that the territorial principle is dual in impulse.

The colon does not divide a participial, an infinitive, or any other modifier from the main clause:

*Incorrect*
Ardrey gives numerous examples of the territorial imperative: drawing on Konrad Lorenz and other zoologists.

*Correct*
Ardrey gives numerous examples of the territorial imperative, drawing on Konrad Lorenz and other zoologists.

**12.2**
**:**

*Incorrect*
To give examples of the territorial imperative: Ardrey draws on numerous studies of animal behavior.

*Correct*
To give examples of the territorial imperative, Ardrey draws on numerous studies of animal behavior.

**12.2c  Quotations.**   Phrases and short clauses that introduce quotations take commas or the more formal colon:

He said, "I cannot decide who is the better candidate."

Long introductory clauses usually take the colon:

He said after he had listened to the speeches and thought for a while: "I cannot decide who is the better candidate."

**12.2d  Final Appositive.**   The colon sometimes marks a final appositive:

Most heroes, whatever magazine they came from, looked like members of one of two families: Pat Ryan's or Flash Gordon's.
—JULES FEIFFER, *The Great American Comic Book Heroes*

The use of the colon is formal in this position. The dash is the less formal and more common marker (see 13.3):

Two diseases attacked the colonists—malaria and yellow fever.

**12.2e  Additional Uses.**   The colon is also used as follows:

to show time:

4:30 A.M.

to give biblical citations:

Exodus 4:16

to separate title and subtitle:

Michael Crichton, *Five Patients: The Hospital Explained*

to close salutations in business letters:

Dear Mr. Smith**:**

**EXERCISE**

Punctuate the following sentences:

1. A major source of the world's oxygen is the vast rain forest of northern and central Brazil that rain forest, like those of Africa and Central America, is disappearing.
2. The vast South American rain forest is disappearing it is falling to developers hungry for grazing and farming land.
3. Catherine Caufield, in her book on rain forests, states "Tropical rain forests are being destroyed faster than any other natural community."
4. The movie *The Emerald Forest* shows the effects of the disappearance of rain forests on Indian tribes tribal warfare loss of Indian culture the denuding of the land itself.
5. The son of an American dam builder disappears into the rain forest years later the father enters the forest to search for the boy.
6. The course includes the following writers the novelists Mark Twain Henry James and Kate Chopin the nineteenth-century poets Walt Whitman and Emily Dickinson the twentieth-century poets Robert Frost Hart Crane and Wallace Stevens.
7. Mozart was a late eighteenth-century composer Ravel was a composer of the early twentieth century.
8. She called at 12 15 in the afternoon and later at 5 20 she apologized for missing the session.
9. She gave these reasons for not coming her car was not running smoothly and the distance was too great to drive having had a mechanic look at the engine she didn't want to arrive late.
10. The street was crowded with carts trucks large vans filled with furniture from the building marked for demolition construction workers spectators from the neighborhood children on the way home from school.

**12.2**

**:**

# Checklist for Using Semicolons and Colons

**12.1a**   The semicolon connects independent clauses in the absence of a period or coordinating conjunction:

> Interstate 71 connects Cincinnati and Columbus; Interstate 77 connects Akron and Cleveland.

**12.1b**   The semicolon attaches explanatory or amplifying words and clauses:

Ours is an age of fiendish competition; and the constant effort, not so much to get ahead as to keep afloat, is hardly calculated to make us less frantic.    —LOUIS KRONENBERGER

**12.1c**    Semicolons join a series of coordinate clauses when the coordinating conjunction (*and, but,* etc.) is omitted:

Interstate 71 runs diagonally through the state of Ohio; Interstate 77 runs north and south; Interstate 70 runs east and west.

**12.1d**    The semicolon, not the comma, is used with conjunctive adverbs:

Interstate 77 is the shortest route from Cleveland to Jacksonville; nevertheless, I prefer to drive by way of Richmond.

**12.1e**    Semicolons divide a series when one or more of the members contain commas:

We visited Lansing, the capital of Michigan; Springfield, the capital of Illinois; and Columbus, the capital of Ohio.

**12.2a**    The colon introduces clauses that explain or amplify the preceding sentence:

We visited Lansing and Springfield: these are the capitals of Michigan and Illinois.

**12.2b**    Don't use the colon to introduce an indirect quotation or to divide a modifier from the main clause:

| *Incorrect* | *Correct* |
|---|---|
| He said that: he was coming. | He said that he was coming. |
| He gave numerous examples: drawing on studies of animal behavior. | He gave numerous examples, drawing on studies of animal behavior. |

**12.2c**    Use the colon after lengthy introductions to quotations:

The colonial statesman Patrick Henry, a member of the Virginia House of Burgesses, said: "Give me liberty or give me death!"

**12.2d**    The colon introduces final appositives:

Several of the eastern states have extensive coastlines: Rhode Island, New York, Maryland.

**12.2e**    Colons are used in showing time, in biblical citations, in titles, and in salutations:

4:30 A.M.
Exodus 4:16
Michael Crichton, *Five Patients: The Hospital Explained*
Dear Mr. Smith:

# The Apostrophe and Other Punctuation Marks

This chapter describes the uses of the **apostrophe**—a difficult punctuation mark to master. The chapter also describes the uses of the hyphen, the dash, parentheses and brackets, and the slash mark.

## 13.1 The Apostrophe

The apostrophe has the following uses.

**13.1a Contraction.** Contracted words use the apostrophe to show omission:

| | | |
|---|---|---|
| I'm | you're | we're |
| can't | won't | wouldn't |
| couldn't | he'll | who's |

The apostrophe also shows omissions in pronunciation in reproducing speech:

"good ol' boy"
"S' long, ev'rybody!"

**13.1b Possession.** The apostrophe is used with nouns and certain indefinite pronouns to show **possession:**

| | |
|---|---|
| the student's opinion | Jane's winning of the prize |
| anyone's opinion | [possessive -*s* before gerund] |

The function word preposition *of* can also show possession:

| | |
|---|---|
| Rachel's boyfriend | boyfriend of Rachel |
| the friend's hat | the hat of the friend |
| the friends' hats | hats of the friends |

Note that possession can be shown without use of the apostrophe:

orange rind
paper margin
book cover

Many writers use the function word *of* to show possession:

the rind of the orange
margin of the paper
cover of the book

**13.1**
**'**

The apostrophe and the function word are sometimes both necessary. Compare the following:

She owns a picture of Monet [a likeness of the French painter].
She bought a picture of Monet's [a picture painted by Monet].

If a singular noun ends in -*s*, possession is shown through the apostrophe and -*s*:

Yeats's poems

Omitting the possessive -'*s* is acceptable when the word itself ends in -*s* or the word following begins with -*s* or -*z*:

Aristophanes' plays
Yeats' system of thought

Plurals ending in -*s* merely add the apostrophe:

friends' hats

Those that do not end in -*s* add both apostrophe and -*s*:

the children's toys
the men's coats

In compound phrases the apostrophe is added to the last word only:

his brother-in-law's hat
the secretary of state's address

**13.1c Plurals.**    The apostrophe shows the plural form in the letters of the alphabet, abbreviations, and words discussed as words:

P's, Q's, and U's
Four-H's [Four-H Clubs]
the number of I's in the essay

The apostrophe may be omitted if the plural meaning is clear:

Ps and Qs [but not *Us*]
7s and 8s
the 1960s

**13.1d Apostrophe Misused with Possessive Pronouns.** The words *his, its, yours, theirs,* and *whose* show possession without an apostrophe:

I have a coat of hers [not *hers'* or *her's*].

And note the difference between *it's* and *its*:

*Contraction*
It's raining.

*Possession*
The dog is chasing its tail.

The word *its* is the possessive form of the pronoun *it* and therefore does not require an apostrophe.

**13.1**
'

### EXERCISES

1. Add apostrophes where needed:
   a. The womans coat is on the couch.
   b. We cant come on Saturday because we are going to my sister-in-laws wedding.
   c. The child pulled the three cats tails.
   d. All of the cats scratched after having their tails pulled.
   e. No ones coming to the party.
   f. You have used too many buts in this paper.
   g. The number of PhDs in chemistry is decreasing.
   h. Those whose degree is in biology are decreasing, too.
   i. Shes fortunate to have a job in so crowded a field.
   j. She knows the as, bs, and cs of computer programming.
2. Form the possessive of the following:
   a. the sister of Liz
   b. the cake of the mother-in-law
   c. a play of Plautus
   d. the son of Venus
   e. the skin of the banana
   f. a novel of Dickens
   g. her reunion with her son and daughter-in-law
   h. the library of each of the three presidents
   i. a sonnet of John Keats
   j. the uniform of the Marine

## 13.2 The Hyphen

**13.2a Compound Words.**   The **hyphen** connects compound words that form a single idea:

Italian-American
second-class
double-header
Boston-New York-Washington corridor
composer-conductor

**13.2**

—

These multisyllabic phrases are hyphenated to distinguish the separate words. The following phrases formed from two-syllable words do not require hyphenation to distinguish them:

flimflam
checkbook
cordwood

But hyphenation is not consistent in multisyllabic words. When in doubt, consult the dictionary.

**13.2b Compound Phrases.**   Certain modifying phrases require hyphenation to distinguish them from the word modified:

a short-distance runner [a runner in a short-distance race]
a short distance runner [a runner short in height]

The hyphen in the following is unnecessary because there is no danger of misreading these conventional adverb-adjective phrases:

badly needed rain
happily married couple

Hyphenation is often dropped when the modifying phrase follows the word modified. Compare the following:

last-minute purchase
purchase made at the last minute

**13.2c Compound Numbers, Fractions, Letters.**   The hyphen makes the following compounds easy to read:

763-0111
four hundred sixty-eight thousand dollars
X-cars
forty-four and nine-tenths

Hyphenate numbers from twenty-one to ninety-nine in spelling them out.

**EXERCISE**

Consult your dictionary to find out whether the following are hyphenated:
1. life time guarantee
2. ten light years from earth
3. object lesson
4. over flight
5. present participle
6. ill fated life
7. namby pamby
8. post impressionism
9. Rocky Mountain spotted fever
10. scorched earth policy

# 13.3 The Dash

The **dash** has the following uses.

**13.3a Apposition.** Use a dash to set off a single-word **appositive** coming at the end of a sentence:

There is one cure for boredom—work.

Appositives that open sentences must be set off by a dash:

Piety, honesty, fortitude—these were the virtues of the early Massachusetts colonists.

Note that the summary word *these* follows the dash.

Use a dash or the more formal colon to set off appositives that close sentences (see 12.2):

These were the virtues of the early Massachusetts colonists—piety, honesty, fortitude.

These were the virtues of the early Massachusetts colonists: piety, honesty, fortitude.

Dashes usually set off an appositive occurring in the middle of a sentence, and always set off an appositive that contains commas:

The virtues of the early Massachusetts colonists—piety, honesty, fortitude—helped them survive a harsh world.

**13.3b Explanation and Illustration.** The following sentences of William Manchester's describe Winston Churchill. In each of the sentences, dashes set off explanatory phrases and clauses:

> He was a ferocious enemy of Germany in both world wars, yet after each he begged the British government—in vain—to dispatch emergency shipments of food to its starving people.

> He despised the thump of staplers—the only sound he hated more was whistling—so in fastening pages he used a paper punch and threaded tape through the holes.

> His niche in history—it is a big one—is secure. And so is his place in our affections.

**13.3**
—

> In the House his rhetorical metaphors were those of the battlefield—events marched, political flanks were turned, legislative skirmishes fought, ultimata delivered, and opponents turned to surrender, to strike their colors, to lay down their arms.
> —WILLIAM MANCHESTER, *The Last Lion:*
> *Winston Spencer Churchill*

**13.3c Emphasis.**   If you want to show that an addition to the sentence is an aside, use parentheses instead of dashes:

> The virtues of American Puritans (the ones portrayed in colonial American literature) sustained the Massachusetts colonists in a harsh world.

Though you can use dashes to show that an idea is parenthetical, they tend to stress the addition by setting it off in a striking way.

**13.3d Interruption.**   Use dashes to show an interruption in thought or speech, or to mark a deliberate pause, or to convey shock or surprise, or to express an attitude:

> John Smith—or do I mean Miles Standish?—is a character in a Longfellow poem.

> I hoped—for nothing.

In the following sentence a dash breaks the normal sentence structure for special emphasis:

> He injected—my visitor—into my solitary nightmare common sense, the world, and the hint of blacker things to come.
> — JAMES BALDWIN, *Notes of a Native Son*

The dash also sets off a longer interrupting comment:

> Circling around in her mind like old people, she got back to where she started—which Aunt Ethel never used to do; she never used to get back!        —EUDORA WELTY, "Kin"

He was coming to meet us—that is, making his way down through the field.  —EUDORA WELTY, "Kin"

This second conservatory contained—was, rather, bursting at the seams with—a raging congestion of the most vicious-looking nettles you ever saw in your life.
—JULIA STRACHEY, "Can't You Get Me Out of Here?"

And the dash marks an abrupt break in statement:

"Mother, don't say things like that," he said. "You shouldn't, even when you're—"

"Please!" she said. "The subject is closed. The subject is closed. I will say no more about your father, poor, weak man, and that woman with the dog's name. But you—you. Have you no heart, no bowels, no natural instincts?"
—DOROTHY PARKER, "I Live On Your Visits"

Note that, in typing, two hyphens constitute a dash.

**13.4**
**( )**

## **13.4** Parentheses

**Parentheses** set off explanatory ideas and details. The following conventions govern their use.

If the parenthesis is a question or exclamation, the question or exclamation mark comes inside the closing parenthesis:

There is the admirable line-drawing of the self-possessed old farmer that came out first in the *Dial* with the title *American Peasant* (did Art Young supply that title or the *Dial*?).
—EDMUND WILSON, *The Shores of Light*

This convention applies also when the parenthesis stands apart from other sentences:

The motivating promise of Signal existed already in the product. (It was found, incidentally, by the J. Walter Thompson creative team who invented the product after "brainstorming" on toothpaste generally and finding an obscure chemist who had perfected a method of tube manufacture which could lay a stripe on the toothpaste.)
—DAVID BERNSTEIN, *Creative Advertising*

There were also the pleasures of overeating. I thought of some particularly voluptuous cream buns which could be bought for twopence each at a shop in our town. (This was 1916, and food-rationing had not yet started.)
—GEORGE ORWELL, *Such, Such Were the Joys*

Place punctuation that does not belong to the parenthesis outside, not inside, it:

> Ostensibly we were supposed to admire the Scots because they were "grim" and "dour" ("stern" was perhaps the key word), and irresistible on the field of battle.
> —GEORGE ORWELL, *Such, Such Were the Joys*

**EXERCISE**

**13.5**

**[ ]**

Add dashes and parentheses, depending on the amount of emphasis you think the appositive or interrupting phrase should receive. Add other dashes needed to punctuate the sentence:

1. Three cars in the backlot the blue sedan, the red hatchback, the yellow convertible were sold yesterday.
2. The blue sedan the sedan with the yellow stripe not the one without has a dent on the hood.
3. The rumble seat the folding seat in open cars years ago probably will never come back into style.
4. The rumble seat but I'd better define the term for you before explaining what it was for!
5. Lincoln the large city west of Omaha not the small town in north central Illinois is the site of a state university.
6. The blue sweater the one I wore last night is missing.
7. I am missing my blue sweater not the one you gave me but the one I wore last night.
8. *Tosca* the opera by Puccini not Verdi is a melodrama.
9. Several of Bach's sons Johann Sebastian Bach the great eighteenth-century organist and composer were famous composers in their own day.
10. Not all J. S. Bach's twenty children born from his two marriages survived infancy.

# 13.5  Brackets

**13.5a Explanation.**  Use **brackets** to add an explanation or comment to a quotation. If you use parentheses, the addition will seem that of the author you are quoting:

> Of mass in its slow-moving, relatively unenergetic terrestrial state, Einstein remarked, "It is as though a man who is fabulously rich [i.e., mass] should never spend or give away a cent [i.e., of its energy]; no one could tell how rich he was," and on that ground Einstein excused his nineteenth-century predecessors for failing to notice what he called the "tremendous energy" in mass.    —JONATHAN SCHELL, *The Fate of the Earth*

The Latin word *sic*, meaning "thus" or "as I found it," is added to a questionable word in a quotation to show that the possible error or unusual form is in the text quoted:

> Thomas Jefferson wrote in the first draft of the Declaration about "rights inherent and inalienable [*sic*]," and in the final draft about "certain unalienable rights; that among these are life, liberty, and the pursuit of happiness."

**13.5b Parenthesis Within Parenthesis.**   If a parenthesis itself contains a parenthesis, this second one appears in brackets. The following sentence contains a bracketed citation to a source:

> The reviewer quotes Einstein's own definition (*The Meaning of Relativity* [Princeton: Princeton UP, 1956], p. 24).

**13.6**
*/*

**EXERCISE**

Assume that you are quoting the following statement and wish to define the italicized words. Look up the italicized words in your dictionary, and add your definition to the quotation:

> "Dinosaurs lived during the *Mesozoic era*. Dinotheres lived during the *Miocene epoch,* and like the dinosaurs are now extinct."

# 13.6  Slash

Use the **slash** to mark alternate or contrasting terms:

either/or
credit/noncredit courses
pass/fail option

The slash also marks off lines of poetry quoted without indentation. Indent a quotation of more than three lines of a poem following a line of text:

> Milton's poem "L'Allegro" contains these famous lines:
>     Sport that wrinkled Care derides,
>     And Laughter holding both his sides.
>     Come, and trip it as ye go
>     On the light fantastic toe.

If you quote fewer than three lines without separating and indenting from the sentence, use a slash to mark the line break:

> Milton's poem "L'Allegro" contains the famous lines: "Come, and trip it as ye go / On the light fantastic toe."

Note that a space appears before and after the slash.

# General Exercises on Punctuation

1. Add capitalization and other needed punctuation to the following sentences:
   a. the full title and subtitle of steven weinbergs book is the first three minutes a modern view of the origin of the universe.
   b. the phrase rumble seat has almost disappeared.
   c. steven spielberg who directed jaws also directed close encounters of the third kind and e.t.
   d. the course is being offered on a credit noncredit basis.
   e. the following cities on the southern atlantic coast perrine miami coral gables hollywood fort lauderdale are connected by an interstate highway.
   f. william faulkners novel the town is about the snopes family so is his novel the mansion.
   g. in his autobiographical novel the cancer ward alexander solzhenitsyn describes events during the year of stalins death 1953.
   h. the italian phrase buon giorno is used to greet people in the morning buona sera to greet people in the evening.
   i. the concluding chapter of noam chomskys book language and mind is titled language and philosophy.
   j. the word boost comes from a nautical word meaning to haul.

2. Punctuate the following paragraphs, capitalizing and adding periods, commas, semicolons, and colons where appropriate:

   a. In arriving at a scientific law there are three main stages the first consists in observing the significant facts the second in arriving at a hypothesis which if it is true would account for these facts the third in deducing from this hypothesis consequences which can be tested by observation if the consequences are verified the hypothesis is provisionally accepted as true although it will usually require modification later on as the result of the discovery of further facts.
   —Bertrand Russell, *The Scientific Outlook*
   [2 sentences]

   b. And then before I could open my lips the east spoke to me but it was in a Western voice a torrent of words was poured into the enigmatical the fateful silence outlandish angry words mixed with words and even whole sentences of good English less strange but even more surprising the voice swore and cursed violently it riddled the solemn peace of the bay by a volley of abuse it began by calling me Pig and from that went crescendo into

unmentionable adjectives in English the man up there raged aloud in two languages and with a sincerity in his fury that almost convinced me I had in some way sinned against the harmony of the universe I could hardly see him but began to think he would work himself into a fit.
— JOSEPH CONRAD, "Youth" [6 sentences]

c. I went to the railway as a messenger boy because I despaired of ever becoming anything better and besides though the hours eight to seven were hard the pay a pound a week was excellent and with money like that coming in I could buy a lot of books and get a lot of education it was with real confidence that at last the future had something in store for me that I left the house one morning at half past seven and went down Summerhill and the tunnel steps to go to the Goods Office on the quay upstairs in the long office where the invoice clerks worked under the eye of the Chief Clerk I met the other junior tracers Sheehy Cremin and Clery and the two senior tracers our job was to assist the invoice and claims clerks bringing in dockets from the storage shed and enquiring in the storage shed for missing goods hence our title.
— FRANK O'CONNOR, "Go Where Glory Waits Thee" [4 sentences]

# Checklist for Apostrophes and Other Punctuation Marks

**13.1a** The apostrophe shows omission in contracted words:

isn't      won't
aren't     you're

**13.1b** The *-'s* is used with nouns and certain indefinite pronouns to show possession:

the student's opinion      Jane's winning of the prize.
anyone's opinion

**13.1c** The apostrophe shows the plural form in letters of the alphabet, abbreviations, and words discussed as words:

p's and q's
Four-H's
the number of the I's in the essay

**13.1d** Do not use the apostrophe with possessive pronouns such as *its* and *hers*.

**13.2a**    The hyphen connects compound words:

Italian-Americans
first-class

**13.2b**    Certain modifying phrases require hyphenation to distinguish them from the word modified:

a short-distance runner

**13.2c**    Hyphens ease the reading of compound numbers and phrases:

76-10036
four hundred and forty-four dollars

**13.3a**    Use dashes to set off appositives at the beginning or in the middle of the sentence:

Ohio, Illinois, Michigan—these are large manufacturing states.
The three large manufacturing states of the Middle West—
Ohio, Illinois, Michigan—have had high unemployment.

**13.3b**    Explanatory and illustrative words and phrases may be set off with dashes:

Three large states have suffered chronic unemployment—and these are not the only ones.

**13.3c**    Dashes give special emphasis to parenthetical statements:

The virtues of the early Massachusetts colonists—those portrayed in early Colonial literature—sustained them in a harsh climate.

**13.3d**    Dashes set off interrupting comments:

John Smith—or do I mean Miles Standish?—is a character in a Longfellow poem.

**13.4**    Parentheses set off explanatory comments:

The virtues of the early Massachusetts colonists (those portrayed in early Colonial literature) sustained them in a harsh climate.

**13.5a**    Explanatory comments added to quotations appear in brackets:

The budget director told the congressional committee, "This fiscal year [1984] will bring a higher deficit."

**13.5b**    A parenthesis within a parenthesis appears in brackets:

The reviewer quotes Einstein's own definition (*The Meaning of Relativity* [Princeton, N.J.: Princeton UP, 1956], p. 24).

**13.6**   The slash marks a contrast in terms and sets off lines of poetry:

> either/or      credit/noncredit courses
> "Come, and trip it as ye go / On the light fantastic toe."

# Quotation Marks and Italics

## 14.1 Quotation Marks

**14.1a Quoting Sentences.** Put direct quotations in quotation marks:

> William G. Perry, Jr., states in his essay "Examsmanship and the Liberal Arts": "In a great university the picture of a bright student attempting to outwit his professor while his professor takes pride in not being outwitted is certainly ridiculous."

If the quotation consists of more than four typed lines, indent it and omit the quotation marks:

> William G. Perry, Jr., states:
>> Students who have dared to understand man's real relation to his knowledge have shown themselves to be in a strong position to learn content rapidly and meaningfully, and to retain it. I have learned to be less concerned about the education of a student who has come to understand the nature of man's knowledge, even though he has not yet committed himself to hard work, than I am about the education of the student who, after one or two terms at Harvard, is working desperately hard and still believes that collected "facts"

```
constitute knowledge. The latter, when I try to
explain to him, too often understands me to be
saying that he "doesn't put in enough generali-
ties." Surely he has "put in enough facts."
```

**14.1b Conventional Punctuation.** Note the following conventions in punctuating quotations.

The period that ends the sentence appears before the final quotation mark:

```
Thomas Jefferson wrote to James Madison, "A little re-
bellion now and then is a good thing."
```

Note that the final period of the quotation changes to a comma if the speaker tag follows:

```
"A little rebellion now and then is a good thing,"
Thomas Jefferson wrote to James Madison.
```

Question marks and exclamation points appear in the same place as the period. But in the following sentences they appear outside the final quotation mark:

```
They shouted the name "Napoleon"!
Why did they shout the name "Napoleon"?
```

In these instances the exclamation point and the question mark punctuate the whole sentence and not the single word *Napoleon*.

Semicolons appear after the closing quotation mark when a quotation opens the sentence and a second clause follows:

```
Jefferson wrote to Madison about the worth of "a little
rebellion"; the seventeenth-century John Bradshaw wrote
that "rebellion to tyrants is obedience to God."
```

**14.1c Quoting Words and Phrases.** Quoted words and phrases appear in quotation marks also, as in these sentences from an essay on the Boy Scout *Handbook*:

What used to be known as artificial respiration ("Out goes the bad air, in comes the good") has given way to "rescue breathing."

And throughout there is a striking new lyricism. "Feel the wind blowing through your hair," the scout is adjured, just as he is exhorted to perceive that Being Prepared for life means learning to "live happy" and—equally important—"to die happy."

To its young audience vulnerable to invitations to "trips" and trances and anxious self-absorption, the book calmly says: "Forget yourself."    —PAUL FUSSELL, "The Boy Scout Handbook"

Don't put a slang or inappropriate phrase in quotation marks ("fink," "nerd," "sweet guy") because you are unsure of its appropriateness. Use the expression without quotation marks if it is appropriate or find another. You do use quotation marks or italics in discussing a word or phrase:

**14.1**

" "

The slang expression "nerdy" is always used comically.

**14.1d Quotations Within Quotations.**    A quotation may contain a second quotation. This second appears in single quotation marks:

One historian says the following about Jefferson: "His political temper is best revealed in his statement to Madison, 'A little rebellion now and then is a good thing.' "

**14.1e Divided Quotations.**    If you interrupt a compound sentence with a speaker tag or a personal comment, do not capitalize the beginning word of the second clause:

*Quotation*
"Most people who bother with the matter at all would admit that the English language is in a bad way, but it is generally assumed that we cannot by conscious action do anything about it."
—GEORGE ORWELL, "Politics and the English Language"

*Incorrect*
"Most people who bother with the matter at all would admit that the English language is in a bad way," Orwell states. "But it is generally assumed that we cannot by conscious action do anything about it."

*Correct*
"Most people who bother with the matter at all would admit that the English language is in a bad way," Orwell states, "but it is generally assumed that we cannot by conscious action do anything about it."

Note that a divided quotation requires a semicolon *following* the interrupting phrase if the original sentence is divided by one:

*Quotation*
"The mind, the throat, are clogged; forgiveness, forgetfulness, that have arrived so often, fail."
—JOHN UPDIKE, "The Dogwood Tree"

*Incorrect*
"The mind, the throat, are clogged," Updike writes, "forgiveness, forgetfulness, that have arrived so often, fail."

*Correct*
"The mind, the throat, are clogged," Updike writes; "forgiveness, forgetfulness, that have arrived so often, fail."

**14.2**
• • •

# 14.2   Ellipsis

**14.2a  Ellipsis in Quotations.**   An **ellipsis**, consisting of three periods, shows the omission of words in quotations:

*Original Passage*
Linguistics is the scientific study of language. At first sight this definition—which is one that will be found in most textbooks and general treatments of the subject—is straightforward enough. But what exactly is meant by "language" and "scientific"? And can linguistics, as it is currently practised, be rightly described as a science?
— JOHN LYONS, *Language and Linguistics*

*Quotation of the Opening Sentences with Omission*
Lyons states: "Linguistics is the scientific study of language. At first sight this definition ... is straightforward enough. But what exactly is meant by "language" and "scientific"?

The omission of the dependent clause *as it is currently practised* would change the meaning of the concluding sentence and therefore is incorrect:

And can linguistics be rightly described as a science?

Lyons is discussing current linguistics only, not linguistics past and present.

In the following quotation, the ellipsis indicates that the omission occurs at the end of a sentence:

*Original Passage*
There is a misconception of tragedy with which I have been struck in review after review, and in many conversations with

writers and readers alike. It is the idea that tragedy is of necessity allied to pessimism.

—ARTHUR MILLER, "Tragedy and the Common Man"

*Quotation with Omission*
The playwright Arthur Miller states in an essay: "There is a misconception of tragedy with which I have been struck in review after review. . . . It is the idea that tragedy is of necessity allied to pessimism."

The fourth period is the normal period of the sentence.

Ellipsis is seldom used to show that opening or closing words have been omitted in a quoted passage. See 37.3d for additional discussion of ellipsis in quotation.

**14.2**

**. . .**

**14.2b  Other Uses of Ellipsis.**   Ellipsis marks a pause as the writer seeks the right phrase or seeks to surprise the reader:

In a surgical operation, a risk may flash into reality: the patient dies . . . of *complication*.     —RICHARD SELZER, *Mortal Lessons*

Ellipsis also shows the voice trailing off:

She scrambled out, over the pile of loose earth that had fallen back into one end of the grave, calling to Paul that she had found something, he must guess what . . .

—KATHERINE ANNE PORTER, "The Grave"

There are teachers who know that the way they have to teach is bad and boring. Luckily there are still enough, with a bit of luck, to overthrow what is wrong, even if the students themselves have lost impetus.

Meanwhile there is a country where . . .

—DORIS LESSING, Preface to *The Golden Notebook*

Ellipsis can imply there is more to say on a topic:

It is possible for literary students to spend more time reading criticism and criticism of criticism than they spend reading poetry, novels, biography, stories. A great many people regard this state of affairs as quite normal, and not sad and ridiculous. . . .

—DORIS LESSING, Preface to *The Golden Notebook*

Some uses of ellipsis are more common in fiction than in nonfictional prose. In the following passage, a tenacious ship captain, trying to navigate through a storm, shouts in broken phrases to his first mate:

"Keep on hammering . . . builders . . . good men. . . . And chance it . . . engines. . . . Rout . . . good man."

In another passage the rapid shouts of the first mate are punctuated with dashes:

> "Watch—put—in—wheelhouse—shutters—glass—afraid—blow
> in."                                    —JOSEPH CONRAD, *Typhoon*

# 14.3  Italics

**14.3a  Emphasis.**  Use **italics** (or underlining in typing) to
give emphasis to an important word or phrase, or to suggest the
inflection or stress given a word in speaking the sentence:

> Before the teacher came my father took me aside to ask *why*
> she was coming, what *interest* she could possibly have in our
> house, in a boy like me.
> —JAMES BALDWIN, *Notes of a Native Son*

Use italics sparingly for this purpose. The emphasis diminishes
if too many words are italicized.

**14.3b  Titles.**  Italicize the titles of books, magazines, newspapers, movies, plays, book-length poems, art objects, and other
entities:

> *Time and the River*—a novel by Thomas Wolfe
> *Newsweek*
> *U.S. News and World Report*
> *New York Times*
> *London Times Book Review*
> *The Double Helix: A Personal Account of the Discovery of the Structure
>     of DNA*—a scientific memoir by James Watson
> *In Memoriam*—a poem by Tennyson
> *Mona Lisa*

Note that titles that are integral parts of a work—the titles
of essays, chapters, short poems, articles, editorials—are put in
quotation marks:

> Chapter 2, "Things Are Not Always What They Seem," in Paul
> Davies, *Other Worlds: Space, Superspace, and the Quantum Universe*

> Richard Armour, "Three Teachers Who Changed My Life,"
> *Christian Science Monitor*, December 17, 1979

**14.3c  Foreign Words.**  Foreign words and phrases also appear in italics:

> This did not trouble Rousseau. In the spirit of the French Revo-

**14.3**
**ital**

lution, which leaned upon his ideas, he saw *fraternité* as the fulfillment of humanity.

—HANNAH ARENDT, *Men in Dark Times*

**EXERCISES**

1. In an introductory phrase, identify Abraham Lincoln as the author and identify the source of the statement and its date:

    I claim not to have controlled events, but confess plainly that events have controlled me.

    —Letter to A. G. Hodges, April 4, 1864

**14.3**

**ital**

2. The following passage contains quoted phrases and dialogue that appear in quotation marks in the original. Add the quotation marks:

    In the evening Most stopped writing and gruffly assailed the talkers as toothless old women, cackling geese, and other appellations I had hardly ever before heard in German. He snatched his large felt hat from the rack, called to me to come along, and walked out. I followed him and we went up on the Elevated. I'll take you to Terrace Garden he said we can go into the theater there if you like. They are giving *Der Zigeunerbaron* tonight. Or we can sit in some corner, get food and drink, and talk. I replied that I did not care for light opera, that what I really wanted was to talk to him, or rather have him talk to me. But not so violently as in the office, I added.          —EMMA GOLDMAN, *Living My Life*

3. The italicized words in the following quotation are punctuated as a quotation in the original. Drop the italics and add quotation marks to show that the words are a quotation:

    F. Scott Fitzgerald says in the opening paragraph of one of his stories: "When I hear a man proclaiming himself an *average, honest, open fellow,* I feel pretty sure that he has some definite and perhaps terrible abnormality which he has agreed to conceal—and his protestation of being average and honest and open is his way of reminding himself of his misprision."

4. Add a parenthetical comment to the following sentence or to a sentence of your own:

    Parents and children seldom see a problem in the same light.

5. Attach an appositive to the sentence above, either at the beginning or at the end.

**6.** Punctuate the following lines of poetry without indenting them:

> Matthew Arnold's "Dover Beach" finishes with these lines:
> And we are here as on a darkling plain
> Swept with confused alarms of struggle and flight,
> Where ignorant armies clash by night.

# Checklist for Quotation Marks and Italics

**14.1a**   Put direct quotations in quotation marks:

> William G. Perry, Jr., states in his essay "Examsmanship and the Liberal Arts": "In a great university the picture of a bright student attempting to outwit his professor while his professor takes pride in not being outwitted is certainly ridiculous."

**14.3**
**ital**

If the quotation consists of more than four typed lines, indent it and omit the quotation marks.

**14.1b**   The period that ends a sentence appears before the final quotation mark:

> Thomas Jefferson wrote to James Madison, "A little rebellion now and then is a good thing."

The final period of the quotation changes to a comma if the speaker tag follows:

> "A little rebellion now and then is a good thing," Thomas Jefferson wrote to James Madison.

Quotation marks and exclamation points appear inside the final quotation mark except in the following instances:

> They shouted the name "Napoleon"!
> Why did they shout the name "Napoleon"?

Semicolons appear after the closing quotation mark:

> Jefferson wrote to Madison about the worth of "a little rebellion"; the seventeenth-century John Bradshaw wrote that "rebellion to tyrants is obedience to God."

**14.1c**   Quoted words and phrases appear in quotation marks:

> What used to be known as artificial respiration ("Out goes the bad air, in comes the good") has given way to "rescue breathing."   —PAUL FUSSELL

**14.1d**   An interior quotation appears in single quotation marks:

> One historian says the following about Jefferson: "His po-

litical temper is best revealed in his statement to Madison, 'A little rebellion now and then is a good thing.' "

**14.1e**   If you interrupt a compound sentence with a speaker tag or a personal comment, do not capitalize the beginning word of the second clause:

> "Most people who bother with the matter at all would admit that the English language is in a bad way," George Orwell states, "but it is generally assumed that we cannot by conscious action do anything about it."

A divided quotation requires a semicolon following the interrupting phrase if the original sentence is divided by one:

> "The mind, the throat, are clogged," Updike writes; "forgiveness, forgetfulness, that have arrived so often, fail."
>
> —JOHN UPDIKE

**14.2**   Ellipsis marks the omission of words in quotations:

> The playwright Arthur Miller states in an essay: "There is a misconception of tragedy with which I have been struck in review after review. . . . It is the idea that tragedy is of necessity allied to pessimism."

Ellipsis also marks a pause in the middle of a statement or a trailing or breaking off in the sentence:

> In a surgical operation, a risk may flash into reality: the patient dies . . . of *complication*.          —RICHARD SELZER

> She scrambled out, over the pile of loose earth that had fallen back into one end of the grave, calling to Paul that she had found something, he must guess what . . .
>
> —KATHERINE ANNE PORTER

**14.3a**   Use italics (or underlining in typing) to give special emphasis to an important word and phrase, or to suggest the inflection or stress given a word in speaking the sentence:

> Before the teacher came my father took me aside to ask *why* she was coming, what *interest* she could possibly have in our house, in a boy like me.          —JAMES BALDWIN

**14.3b**   Italicize the titles of books, magazines, newspapers, movies, plays, book-length poems, art objects, and other entities.

**14.3c**   Foreign words and phrases appear in italics.

# Mechanics

## 15.1 Capitalization

**15.1a Sentence Openers.**  The first word of a declarative sentence, a question, and an exclamation is always capitalized. Also capitalize the first word of a question following an introductory statement:

> We have discussed the meaning of symbols generally because, as we said, man's ultimate concern must be expressed symbolically! One may ask: Why can it not be expressed directly and properly? If money, success or the nation is someone's ultimate concern, can this not be said in a direct way without symbolic language? —Paul Tillich, "Symbols of Faith"

Writers occasionally capitalize the first word of a complete sentence following a colon, particularly if the second sentence itself contains a colon:

> This leads to the second characteristic of the symbol: It participates in that to which it points: the flag participates in the power and dignity of the nation for which it stands. —Paul Tillich, "Symbols of Faith"

**15.1b Capitalization in Quotations.**  Capitalize the first word of a quotation:

> A character in Shakespeare's *Julius Caesar* gives the famous warning, "Beware the Ides of March."

> The opening lines of Wordsworth's sonnet are the following: "The world is too much with us; late and soon, / Getting and spending, we lay waste our powers."

See 14.1e on divided quotations.

**15.1c Names, Places, Titles.**  Capitalize names, places, titles, months, days of the week, religions, organizations, historical events, and geographical regions:

President John Smith
His Honor, the Mayor of Cleveland, Ohio
the Rocky Mountains
Thursday, July 4, 1985
the Italian Renaissance
Roman Catholicism
the South

**15.1**

**cap**

Do not capitalize if you are merely identifying a position or job:

Wilson is president of the company.
She was the governor of Kentucky in 1985.

However, the following capitalization is common:

She is now Governor of Kentucky.

Do capitalize if the position is part of a title:

Ronald Reagan became President of the United States in 1981.

**15.1d  Seasons and Objects.**   Do not capitalize the seasons or words designating kinds of objects:

last winter, next summer, this fall, this spring
the early symphonies of Beethoven
the laws of the various states
moonlight, sunlight, starlight
the moons of Jupiter
the rings of Saturn

Do not capitalize the word *earth* except when discussing various planets:

The planet earth has one moon.
The spaceship is now earthbound.

Capitalize *earth* when you mention it with other planets:

Mercury, Venus, Earth, and Mars are the inner planets of the solar system.

# 15.2  Abbreviations

**15.2a  General Conventions.**   Personal names take periods when abbreviated:

President John F. Kennedy
the British novelist C. P. Snow

So do abbreviated words and phrases:

1600 Pennsylvania Ave.
Pittsburgh, Penn. [but no period after PA]
Dept. of State
American Medical Assn.
Columbia Broadcasting Co.
Fig. 1, p. 22, vol. 3
etc.
ch. [chapter]

Many compound abbreviations take periods to avoid confusion:

**15.2**
**ab**

3 A.M. [*not* 3 AM]
e.g. [*not* eg]
i.e. [*not* ie]

However, abbreviations today dispense with periods if the reference is clear:

BA [Bachelor of Arts], PhD [Doctor of Philosophy]
AFL-CIO [American Federation of Labor–Congress of Industrial Organizations]
CBS [Columbia Broadcasting Company]
UN [United Nations]
CT [Connecticut], MA [Massachusetts], ME [Maine], OH [Ohio]

Use numerals, not words, before symbols:

92° F [*not* ninety-two degrees F]
14' or fourteen feet
100 m or one hundred meters
14 g or fourteen grams

**15.2b Dates, Time of Day.** Use numerals to give dates and the time of day:

May 30, 1929
3 P.M. [*not* three PM]
12 A.M.

Spell out the number before the word *o'clock* and in giving fractions:

| | |
|---|---|
| five o'clock | a quarter past eight |
| five in the evening | half past eight |
| twenty to seven | two-thirds |

Writers occasionally give the date in words:

the thirtieth of May, 1929

But not:

the 30th of May, 1929

Do not write out the year except at the beginning of a sentence:

1929 [*not* nineteen hundred twenty-nine]
Nineteen twenty-nine was the year of the market crash.

**15.2**
**ab**

**15.2c Addresses.**   Give an address in numerals:

1226 N. Ridge Rd.

However, writers occasionally spell out a numbered street to avoid confusion:

1226 Twenty-sixth Ave.

Give highway numbers in numerals:

I-77
Ohio 176

**15.2d Place Names.**   Do not abbreviate the name of a state or country in the text of your paper:

*Incorrect*
Plains, Ga., is south of Atlanta.

*Correct*
Plains, Georgia, is south of Atlanta.

The exception is abbreviations like *USA* and *UK*:

He has lived in the USA since 1934.

Here are the abbreviations of the American states, the District of Columbia, and Puerto Rico:

| AK | Alaska | GA | Georgia |
|----|--------|----|---------|
| AL | Alabama | HI | Hawaii |
| AR | Arkansas | IA | Iowa |
| AZ | Arizona | ID | Idaho |
| CA | California | IL | Illinois |
| CO | Colorado | IN | Indiana |
| CT | Connecticut | KS | Kansas |
| DC | District of Columbia | KY | Kentucky |
| DE | Delaware | LA | Louisiana |
| FL | Florida | MA | Massachusetts |

| | | | |
|---|---|---|---|
| MD | Maryland | OK | Oklahoma |
| ME | Maine | OR | Oregon |
| MI | Michigan | PA | Pennsylvania |
| MN | Minnesota | PR | Puerto Rico |
| MO | Missouri | RI | Rhode Island |
| MS | Mississippi | SC | South Carolina |
| MT | Montana | SD | South Dakota |
| NC | North Carolina | TN | Tennessee |
| ND | North Dakota | TX | Texas |
| NE | Nebraska | UT | Utah |
| NH | New Hampshire | VA | Virginia |
| NJ | New Jersey | VT | Vermont |
| NM | New Mexico | WA | Washington |
| NV | Nevada | WI | Wisconsin |
| NY | New York | WV | West Virginia |
| OH | Ohio | WY | Wyoming |

**15.2**
**ab**

Here are abbreviations of certain countries:

| | | | |
|---|---|---|---|
| Aus. | Austria | Jap. | Japan |
| Austral. | Australia | Mex. | Mexico |
| Can. | Canada | Sp. | Spain |
| Eng. | England | UK | United Kingdom |
| Gr. | Greece | USSR | Soviet Union |
| Gt. Brit. | Great Britain | W. Ger. | West Germany |

**15.2e A List of Common Abbreviations.** Here are abbreviations for words commonly used:

| | |
|---|---|
| adj. | adjective |
| adv. | adverb |
| anon. | anonymous |
| assn. | association |
| assoc. | associate |
| ave. | avenue |
| b. | born |
| c., ca. | about [used with dates: c. 1536] |
| (c) | copyright [(c) 1983] |
| cf. | compare [used in notes to refer the reader to another passage] |
| col. | column |
| colloq. | colloquial |
| comp. | compiled by, compiler |
| conj. | conjunction |
| cp. | compare |
| d. | died |
| diss. | dissertation |

| | |
|---|---|
| div. | division |
| ed. | editor, edited by, edition |
| e.g. | for example |
| et al. | and others |
| etc. | and so forth |
| ex. | example |
| fig. | figure |
| govt. | government |
| i.e. | that is |
| illus. | illustrator, illustrated by, illustration |
| inc. | including, incorporated |
| introd. | writer of introduction |
| l., ll. | line, lines |
| ms., mss. | manuscript, manuscripts |
| n. | noun |
| n.d. | no date [used in notes where publishing date is missing in source] |
| no. | number |
| n.p. | no place or no publisher [used in notes where place of publication or publisher is not given in source] |
| obj. | object, objective |
| op. | opus or work [Beethoven Symphony No.5. Op. 67] |
| pl. | plate |
| poss. | possessive |
| pref. | preface, writer of preface |
| prep. | preposition |
| pron. | pronoun |
| pt. | part |
| rev. | revision, review, writer of revision or review |
| ser. | series |
| sing. | singular |
| soc. | society |
| subj. | subject, subjective |
| vb. | verb |

**15.3**
**num**

# 15.3 Numbers

**15.3a Cardinal and Ordinal Numbers.**  Cardinal numbers state quantity:

1, 2, 3, 4, 5, 6, 7, 8, 9, 10, 22, 81
100, 1,000, 10,000, 1,000,000, 1,000,000,000
hundredth, thousandth, millionth, billionth

Ordinal numbers, which give position in a series, are abbreviated as follows:

1st, 2nd, 3rd, 4th, 5th, 6th, 7th, 8th, 9th, 10th, 22th, 81st

**15.3b Conventional Uses.**  Use numerals, not words, in expressing figures when you give a large number:

*Incorrect*
The backyard measures twenty-five by forty-five feet, twenty by thirty-three feet, and the house itself one hundred twenty by one hundred fifty-seven feet.

*Correct*
The backyard measures 25 by 45 feet, the front yard 20 by 33 feet, and the house itself 120 by 157 feet.

**15.3**
**num**

Use not more than two words in writing out numbers:

three apples, thirty-three apples

Use numerals if more than three words would be required:

3,325 applications [*not* three thousand three hundred twenty-five applications]

Always use numerals to express numbers using decimals:

His grade point average is 3.4 [*not* three point four].

Give a small number in words if it opens the sentence:

Forty-three people applied for the job.

Try not to start the sentence with a number requiring more than two or three words:

3,325 applications were filed during 1984.

Reword the sentence:

People filed 3,325 applications during 1984.

**15.3c Roman Numerals.**  Roman numerals have been largely replaced by arabic numerals, but they have special uses. Capitalized roman numerals mark acts and scenes of plays. Capitalized numerals mark individual volumes of multivolume works; lowercase numerals mark the pagination of the front matter or introductory pages to a book:

*King Lear*, I:iii
G. Jean-Aubry, *Joseph Conrad: Life and Letters*, I, xi

The following seven letters form the numerals:

I, i, 1
V, v, 5
X, x, 10
L, l, 50
C, c, 100
D, d, 500
M, m, 1,000

Here are the numerals from one to twenty:

| | | | |
|---|---|---|---|
| I, 1 | VI, 6 | XI, 11 | XVI, 16 |
| II, 2 | VII, 7 | XII, 12 | XVII, 17 |
| III, 3 | VIII, 8 | XIII, 13 | XVIII, 18 |
| IV, 4 | IX, 9 | XIV, 14 | XIX, 19 |
| V, 5 | X, 10 | XV, 15 | XX, 20 |

When a letter of lesser number follows one of equal or greater number, the two are combined:

II, 2
XV, 15
CX, 110

When a letter of greater number follows one of lesser number, the number is decreased:

IV, 4
IX, 9
XL, 40
XC, 90

When a letter stands between two letters both greater in number, subtract the letter numerically from the second and add the remaining number to the first:

XIV, 14  XXIV, 24  CIX, 109

Following these rules, you can combine letters to form larger numbers:

XCII, 92
CXII, 112
CMXLIX, 949

**EXERCISES**

1. Abbreviate where possible:
   a. National Broadcasting Company
   b. Government Printing Office, Washington, District of Columbia

    **c.** Linguistic Society of America
    **d.** Sydney, Australia
    **e.** Association of American University Professors
    **f.** I. M. Copi, *Introduction to Logic*, Sixth Edition
    **g.** Erwin H. Ackerknecht, *A Short History of Medicine*, revised
    edition
    **h.** 777 Seventy-seventh Avenue, North Canton, Ohio
    **i.** Figure seven, page twenty-one, volume forty
    **j.** Plate number eight
**2.** Give the following arabic numbers in roman numerals:
    **a.** 57   **b.** 99   **c.** 115   **d.** 515   **e.** 1,543

## 15.4 Guidelines for Typing Papers

**15.4a Format.** In typing course papers, observe the following guidelines on format unless your instructor specifies different ones (see Figure 15.1 for illustration of the first page of a student paper):

Use good quality twenty-pound white paper, not yellow second sheets or onion skin, or specially prepared erasable paper.

Write on one side of the page only.

Use a new black or blue ribbon, not a worn ribbon or a red or green one.

Put your name at the left margin one inch below the upper border. Below your name give the course title, your instructor's name, and the date. Double-space between these.

Leave ample margins on each side of the page, at the top, and at the bottom. Margins of 1 to 1-1/2 inches are standard. Your instructor may ask you to leave wider ones for comments and corrections.

Center your title two spaces below the date and two to four spaces above the first line of text. Do not italicize or capitalize all letters of your title:

Writing with a Word Processor
How to Buy a Used Car

If you use a cover page for a longer paper, capitalize all letters of the title and center your name two spaces below it. Below your name put the course title, your instructor's name, and date:

ON WAITING IN LINE

by Paul Kim

English 112–1, Mr. Levin

September 30, 1984

FIGURE 15.1   The First Page of a Student's Paper

Paul Kim

English 112-1

Mr. Levin

September 30, 1984

On Waiting in Line

Rollercoasters are by far the most exciting rides in amusement parks. Millions of people each year ride ''The Beast'' at King's Island near Cincinnati. To be lifted to great heights and quickly dropped to great depths is the thrill of these coasters. But the fun involves much more than entering the car and taking the ride.

First consider the steps prior to entering the car. Entering the park, many people are already thinking about the fearsome ride. On reaching the entrance, I myself find a line extending considerably beyond the gate, down the walkway, and around the corner. Here I collect my thoughts and decide whether a sensible person waits three hours for a thirty-second ride. Noticing the many others in line, I am mesmerized into waiting and conquering the ride. The minutes are long as I stare at the second hand rotating slowly around the clock. I finally reach the corner--only to discover that the gate is another fifty yards away. The line seems endless to some, and they drop out of line, but I will stay strong.

As I enter the gate, I see rows and rows of lines weaving back and forth. I notice on many faces the weariness of standing so long. The excitement is still to come.

**15.4**
**ms**

On the first page of the paper, put the title as shown.

Double-space the paper including indented quotations.

Indent the first word of each paragraph five spaces from the left margin. Indent quotations of more than four printed lines ten spaces from the left margin. Incorporate quotations of fewer than four printed lines into the text. (See 14.1a.)

Avoid beginning a page with the concluding word or phrase of a paragraph on the preceding page.

From the second page to the end, number the paper in the upper right-hand corner, half an inch below the upper border. Add your last name before the numeral as follows:

**15.4**

**ms**

```
Wilson 3
```

After typing the paper, make corrections neatly above the line, using a caret to show the addition of a word or phrase:

```
      wary                        e
The ʌ buyer discovers the hiddʌn defects in a used car.
```

Strike a line through words you delete. Use whitening fluid to erase a letter or a word in typing the paper. Don't use it to erase whole words or sentences after completing the typing. If additions are extensive, retype the page.

Handwritten papers and those written on a word processor should follow these same guidelines. Use ink if writing by hand, not pencil. The printer attached to your word processor may have special fonts or permit boldface or shadow printing. Use these special effects only after consulting your instructor. Ask your instructor whether printing with dot matrix is acceptable.

**15.4b Punctuation.**   The following rules governing the typing of papers also apply to handwritten papers and those written on a word processor.

Leave two spaces between a period and the following word:

Proofread your paper carefully. Look up words if in doubt about their spelling.

Leave one space after a semicolon and a colon:

Proofread your paper carefully; check your spelling.
Look for the following: fragments and comma splices.

Space the three periods of an ellipsis evenly. Leave a space between the word preceding and the word following the ellipsis:

I am shocked . . . and unwilling to say anything more.

Two hyphens in typing equal a dash:

We saw one of Eugene O'Neill's late plays--*Hughie.*

Do not leave a space before or after a hyphen or a dash.
Break words at the syllable as shown in your dictionary:

sec-ond
se-cret

Do not carry a single letter to the next line. Though the word *secondary* consists of four syllables (*sec-on-dar-y*) break the word as follows:

**15.4**

**ms**

sec-on-dary

See 38.5 on the mechanics of the documented paper.

**15.4c Proofreading.** Proofread the paper carefully for omitted words and unclear or wordy sentences. In a second reading of the paper, check for spelling, grammatical errors, and faulty diction. Many writers find it useful to check spelling from the last word of the paper to the first. Reading the paper aloud is useful in catching errors.

## Exercise on Mechanics

Correct the mistakes in the following paragraphs as you would in revising typed or handwritten copy:

George F Will in his book Statecraft as
Soulcraft writes Once politics is defined nega-
tively, as an interprise for drawing a protective
circle around the individuals sphere of self-in-
terested action, than public concerns are by definition distinct from, and secondery to, private
concerns". Will warns that people will start
blaming goverment rather than themselves for
things that that go wrong. Because they believe
only the government have responsibility to the
public good, to use Wills phrase.
      I can site no better example of Wills point
then the failure of people of many cities of our
country to take an interest in homeless people

and famileis the number of which is increasing.
People blame the government for doing nothing. Of
course, its problem of government at all levels
including the federal and local levels but people
can do something in giving their time and money
as we did for ethiopian famine releef last Winter.

## Checklist for Mechanics

**15.1a**   The first word of a declarative sentence, a question, and an exclamation is always capitalized. Capitalize the first word of a question following an introductory statement.

**15.1b**   Capitalize the first word of a quotation:

> A character in Shakespeare's *Julius Caesar* gives the famous warning, "Beware the Ides of March."

**15.1c**   Capitalize names, places, titles, months, days of the week, religions, organizations, historical events, and regions. Do not capitalize if you are identifying a position or job:

> Wilson is president of the company.

Capitalize if the position is part of a title:

> Ronald Reagan became President of the United States in 1981.

**15.1d**   Do not capitalize the seasons or words designating kinds of objects:

> last winter, next summer, this fall, this spring
> the early symphonies of Beethoven

Do not capitalize the word *earth* except when discussing various planets:

> The planet earth has one moon.
> Mercury, Venus, Earth, and Mars are the inner planets of the solar system.

**15.2a**   Personal names, words, and phrases take periods when abbreviated:

> the British novelist C. P. Snow
> 1600 Pennsylvania Ave.
> Fig. 1, p. 22, vol. 3

Most compound abbreviations take periods to avoid confusion:

3 A.M. [*not* 3 AM]

You can dispense with periods in abbreviations if the reference is clear:

AFL-CIO
UN

**15.2b**   Use numerals to give dates and the time of day:

May 30, 1929
3 P.M.

Spell out the number before the word *o'clock* and in giving fractions:

five o'clock                          two-thirds
a quarter past eight

**15.2c**   Give an address in numerals:

1226 N. Ridge Rd.

You can spell out a street number to avoid confusion:

1226 Twenty-sixth Ave.

**15.2d**   Except for abbreviations like *USA*, do not abbreviate the name of a state or country in the text of your paper:

*Correct*
Plains, Georgia, is far south of Atlanta.

**15.3b**   Use numerals, not words, in expressing figures when you give a large number:

The backyard measures 25 by 45 feet, the front yard 20 by 33 feet, and the house itself 100 by 150 feet.

Use not more than two words in writing out numbers:

three apples, thirty-three apples
3,325 applications

Use numerals to express numbers using decimals:

His grade point average is 3.4.

Give a small number in words if it opens the sentence:

Forty-three people applied for the job.

# Spelling

The purpose of this chapter is to give help for common spelling problems. Many of these arise from a confusion between words that resemble one another in sight as well as sound and yet are spelled differently. Others arise from apparent as well as real inconsistencies between spelling and pronunciation—the first topic of the chapter. Though the dictionary remains the best resource of the uncertain speller, a knowledge of certain groupings and patterns can help in improving spelling. We can learn much from how English words are formed and from regularities they share.

## 16.1 Spelling and Pronunciation

We learn to spell mainly by analogy with words we know. Because we are used to seeing words like *courageous* and *outrageous*, we attach the *-ous* suffix to other words like them. Sometimes the ear guides us in spelling, and sometimes the eye.

This dependence on eye and ear is a major cause of misspelling. Thus the eye may deceive us in spelling the word *ridiculous*:

ridicule
ridiculeous

The spelling of *courageous* deceives us. The ear will not correct the misspelling because we do not hear the *-e* suffix even if we break the word into syllables in pronouncing it. The ear also deceives us. We may spell the word *apparatus* by analogy with *courageous*:

apparatous

Pronunciation is often an unsafe guide in English spelling,

271

for many words that look alike are not pronounced alike:

enough, dough, through, rough

And many words are pronounced in different ways by Americans and other English-speaking people. Differences in the accent and elision of words create additional problems, H. L. Mencken points out in his study of the American language:

> The chief movement in American, in truth, would seem to be toward throwing the accent upon the first syllable. I recall *mámma, pápa, ínquiry, céntenary, álly, récess, ídea, álloy* and *ádult*; I might add *défect, éxcess, áddress, súrvey, mústache, résearch* and *rómance*. All these words have the same accent on the second syllable in the *Concise Oxford Dictionary*. . . . In American the secondary accent in *necessary*, falling upon *ar*, is clearly marked; in English only the primary accent on *nec* is heard, and so the word becomes *nécess'ry*. . . . The same difference in pronunciation is to be observed in certain words of the *-ative* and *-mony* classes, and in some of those of other classes. In American the secondary accent on *a* in *operative* is always heard, but seldom in English.
> —H. L. MENCKEN, *The American Language*

**16.1**

**sp**

Mencken's statement suggests there is no certain guide to spelling in all situations. But we can learn from some of the important causes of misspelling, beginning with confused words.

## 16.2   Confused Words

**16.2a Homonyms.** **Homonyms** are words pronounced alike but having different meanings and spellings. You will find it helpful to look up those unfamiliar to you.

| | |
|---|---|
| assent, ascent | its, it's |
| bare, bear | lead, led |
| boar, bore | meat, meet |
| board, bored | new, knew |
| born, borne | no, know |
| brake, break | passed, past |
| buy, by | patience, patients |
| cite, sight, site | peace, piece |
| coarse, course | plain, plane |
| discreet, discrete | presence, presents |
| fair, fare | principal, principle |
| forth, fourth | rain, reign, rein |
| hear, here | right, rite, write |
| heard, herd | road, rode |
| hole, whole | scene, seen |

straight, strait
their, there, they're
to, too, two
waist, waste

weak, week
weather, whether
which, witch
who's, whose

**16.2b Words That Sound Alike.** The following words are close in pronunciation and in some dialects are indistinguishable. But they are different in spelling and meaning:

accept, except
aisle, isle
all ready, already
allude, elude
allusion, illusion
capital, capitol
complement, compliment
descent, dissent
desert, dessert
elicit, illicit

formally, formerly
gorilla, guerrilla
lessen, lesson
loose, lose
moral, morale
quiet, quite
raise, raze
stationary, stationery
than, then
your, you're

**16.2**
**sp**

**16.2c Partial Resemblance.** Some words look alike because they share the same roots and affixes yet have different meanings or are closely related. These words are further removed in pronunciation from the homonyms and the words similar in sound listed previously:

beside, besides
censor, censure
conscientious, conscious, conscience
credible, creditable, credulous
assure, ensure, insure
climatic, climactic
continual, continuous
deduce, deduct
detract, distract
eminent, imminent
especially, specially
farther, further
flaunt, flout
incredible, incredulous
irremediable, irreparable
irritate, aggravate
off, of
practicable, practical
precede, proceed
respectful, respective
sensual, sensuous

**16.2d One Word and Two.** Many words that are spelled the same (or almost the same) have different meanings when divided into two words:

already, all ready
altogether, all together
anybody, any body
anymore, any more
anytime, any time
awhile, a while

everybody, every body
everyone, every one
maybe, may be
somebody, some body
someone, some one
sometime, some time

**16.2e Different Forms.** The following noun and verb forms are easily confused:

| Noun | Verb |
|------|------|
| advice | advise |
| argument | argue |
| belief | believe |
| breath | breathe |
| choice | choose |
| descent | descend |
| device | devise |
| effect | affect |
| entrance | enter |
| envelope | envelop |
| expense | expend |
| marriage | marry |
| past | passed |
| prophecy | prophesy |
| receipt | receive |
| speech | speak |

**16.2f Possessives.** Here is a brief review of how possessives form with the apostrophe. Ordinarily we add -'s after singular nouns and certain indefinite pronouns:

> the woman's hat
> somebody's hat and coat

With words ending in -s, you have the option of omitting the -'s:

> Keats' poetry

Except for irregular nouns, plural nouns form the possessive by adding the apostrophe:

> the boys' coats, the women's coats

**16.2**

**sp**

Indefinite pronouns do the same:

anybody's coat

The definite pronouns, however, have possessive forms:

I, my, mine                     it, its
you, your, yours                we, our, ours
he, his                         you, your, yours
she, her, hers                  they, their, theirs

The following phrases incorrectly use the apostrophe to form the possessive:

| *Incorrect* | *Correct* |
| --- | --- |
| that book of your's | that book of yours |
| no friend of her's | no friend of hers |
| it's cover (cover of the book) | its cover |
| a friend of our's (or ours') | a friend of ours |
| no books of yours' (plural) | no books of yours |
| books of their's (or theirs') | books of theirs |

**16.2**
**sp**

**EXERCISES**

**1.** Correct any misspelled words in the following sentences:
   **a.** It's the book he sighted in his speech.
   **b.** Their house is build on the cite of the old city hall, on forth street.
   **c.** The doctor examined seven patients that morning.
   **d.** We waited through several scene changes for there appearance on the stage.
   **e.** He's the senator who's speech they herd in Washington.

**2.** Choose the word that fits the sentence:
   **a.** I (*accept, except*) your apology with thanks.
   **b.** She (*alluded, eluded*) to the apology in her letter.
   **c.** The senator addressed the audience (*formally, formerly*) on the issue of jobs in the 'eighties.
   **d.** He spoke of our (*loosing, losing*) jobs if inflation remained higher (*than, then*) last year.
   **e.** He said, "If inflation remains (*stationary, stationery*) or goes down, (*your, you're*) going to benefit."

**3.** Use the following words in sentences that show the difference in their meaning.

   *Example: of, off*
   She is tired of school. She took the cover off the book.

   **a.** beside, besides
   **b.** credible, creditable
   **c.** climatic, climactic

   **d.** farther, further
   **e.** practical, practicable

4. Choose the word or phrase that best fits the sentence:
   a. It took us (*a while, awhile*) to start the fire.
   b. We are not (*all together, altogether*) at the lake.
   c. The high wind (*may be, maybe*) the reason the lake was so deserted.
   d. We will need (*sometime, some time*) to repair the boat.
   e. We (*preceded, proceeded*) into the auditorium.
5. Write sentences using the past and past participle forms of the following verbs:
   | | | | |
   |---|---|---|---|
   | a. begin | | f. | lie |
   | b. dig | | g. | spring |
   | c. do | | h. | swim |
   | d. go | | i. | throw |
   | e. lay | | j. | write |
6. Write sentences using the following words in sentences that show their meaning:
   | | | | |
   |---|---|---|---|
   | a. affect | | d. | prophesy |
   | b. descent | | e. | receipt |
   | c. devise | | | |
7. Use the possessive form of the personal pronouns (*I, you, he, she, it, we, you, they*) in sentences of your own.

# 16.3   Forming Plurals

Mistakes in spelling occur when we forget the usual ways of forming plurals of nouns. Here is a summary of how plurals form.

**16.3a  Regular Plurals.**   Most nouns add -*s* to the singular form:

books, hats, shoes

If the plural ending adds a syllable to the word, the word takes -*es*:

churches, boxes, bushes

Notice that some words have no separate plural forms:

spacecraft, pliers, Japanese, Iroquois, sheep

**16.3b  Nouns Ending in -y.**   The plurals of words ending in -*y* depend on the following:

1. Nouns with a vowel before the -*y* add -*s* ordinarily:
   boys, monkeys.

2. Nouns with a consonant preceding *-y* change *-y* to *-i*, then add *-es*: cherry, cherries.
3. Names ordinarily add *-s*: Murphys, Cassidys, Marys, Jims.

Some place names change to *-ies*:

Rockies

**16.3c  Nouns Ending in -o.**  Most nouns ending in *-o* add *-s*:

radio, radios

Those ending in a consonant and *-o* add *-es*:

potato, potatoes

Some words ending in *-o* have variant plurals (*mosquitos, mosquitoes*) and some do not (*radio, radios*). Consult your dictionary if unsure about these spellings.

**16.3d  Nouns Ending in -f.**  Most nouns ending in *-f* and *-fe* end with the normal plural *-s*:

roof, roofs

Many change the *-f* to *-ve*:

elf, elves

Some form the plural with *-f* or *-ve*:

hoof, hoofs, hooves

**16.3e  Compounds.**  Compound nouns add the plural *-s* to the final word unless the first word is the more important:

police cars
sisters-in-law
system analysts

**16.3f  Plurals of Foreign Words.**  Words derived from other languages, from Latin and Greek in particular, usually form their plurals by using the suffix of the original language:

| | |
|---|---|
| alumnus, alumni | medium, media |
| alumna, alumnae | memorandum, memoranda |
| antenna, antennae | psychosis, psychoses |
| appendix, appendices | radius, radii |
| crisis, crises | thesis, theses |

Some of these words allow an alternate English plural:

| | |
|---|---|
| antennas | memorandums |
| appendixes | radiuses |

**16.3**

**sp**

Notice the standard plurals of the following:

medium          media
phenomenon      phenomena
criterion       criteria

### EXERCISE

Form the plural of the following words and phrases:
1. heroine
2. lady-in-waiting
3. criterion
4. quiz
5. ratio
6. father-in-law
7. truck rig
8. scarf
9. Kennedy
10. rap session

**16.4**
**sp**

## 16.4  Words with -*ie* and -*ei*

**16.4a  Words with Long *e*.**   Words that sound like *be* and *see* usually take -*ie* except after *c*:

believe, niece, relieve, siege, wield
conceive, deceit, receive

Words in which the *c* is sounded like *sh* in *shush* take -*ie* also:

conscience, sufficient

**16.4b  Words with Long *a*, Long *i*, and Certain Other Vowels.**   Words that sound like *hay*, *might*, and *heir* take -*ei*:

neighbor, reign, vein, Seine
height
heir

The words *friend*, *mischief*, *sieve*, and *view* are exceptions to these rules.

## 16.5  Words with Final -*e*

**16.5a  Before Suffix Beginning with a Vowel.**   Before the suffixes -*able*, -*ary*, -*ing*, and -*ous*, the final -*e* is dropped:

use, usable                 relieve, relieving
imagine, imaginary          fame, famous

Exceptions include words that might be confused (*dying*, *dyeing*).

**16.5b  Before Suffix Beginning with a Consonant.**   Before suffixes *-less*, *-ly*, *-ment*, *-ness*, *-some*, and others beginning with a consonant, the final *-e* is kept:

| | |
|---|---|
| name, nameless, namely | same, sameness |
| state, statement | whole, wholesome |

Exceptions include *awful* and *wholly*.

**16.5c Words Ending in *-ce* and *-ge*.** Words ending in *-ce* and *-ge* retain the *-e* before suffixes beginning with *-a* and *-o* and pronounced like *notice* and *advantage*:

noticeable                          advantageous

**16.6**
**sp**

# 16.6   Additional Rules of Spelling

**16.6a Doubled Consonants.**   In the following words we double the final consonant before a suffix that starts with a vowel.

1. One-syllable words ending with a single vowel and consonant:

| | | |
|---|---|---|
| slip | slipped | slipping |
| trot | trotted | trotting |
| nap | napped | napping |

Note that we do not double the consonant in single-syllable words containing two vowels or two consonants:

| | | |
|---|---|---|
| look | looked | looking |
| lock | locked | locking |

2. Two-syllable words, the second syllable of which ends with an accented single vowel and consonant:

| | | |
|---|---|---|
| occur | occurred | occurring |
| submit | submitted | submitting |

Do not double the consonant in two-syllable words containing two vowels or two consonants in the second (accented) syllable. Words containing *-x* do not double the consonant either:

| | | | |
|---|---|---|---|
| remark | remarked | remarking | remarkable |
| detain | detained | detaining | detainable |
| box | boxed | boxing | boxable |

Do not double the consonant before suffixes beginning with a consonant:

| | |
|---|---|
| star | starless |
| deter | determent |

The consonant is not doubled in two-syllable words when the accent falls on the first syllable or shifts to it:

defer          deference
refer          reference

3. The *-l* ending. Words ending in *-l* may or may not double the ending even though the accent falls on the first syllable:

traveler          traveller

**16.6b  Words Ending in *-ic*.**  Words ending in *-ic* add *-k* before a suffix that starts with *-i*, *-e*, or *-y*:

picnicking, trafficking

**16.6c  The Suffix *-able*.**  The suffix *-able* forms adjectives from verbs:

affordable, readable, notable

The suffix is also used with stems ending in hard *c* or *g*:

amicable, navigable

**16.6d  The Suffix *-ible*.**  The suffix *-ible* is used with stems of adjectives derived from Latin verbs and with stems of nouns ending in *-ion*:

divisible, negligible, permissible

Consult your dictionary when unsure about *-able* and *-ible* words.

**16.6e  The Suffix *-ly*.**  When adding the suffix *-ly* to a word ending in *l*, retain the *l*:

formal, formally
regional, regionally

If the word ends in a double *l*, merely add *y*:

hill, hilly

If the word ends with a consonant and *-le*, drop the *e* before adding *y*:

remarkable, remarkably

**16.6f  The Suffix *-cede*.**  The normal suffix is *-cede*. The following words end in *-ceed*:

exceed, proceed, succeed

Only one word ends in *-sede*:

supersede

# 16.7 Prefixes

Here is a list of common prefixes. Notice that, unlike many suffixes, they do not change the stem of the word:

| Prefix | Word | Meaning |
|---|---|---|
| *ab-* | abduct | from |
| *abs-* | abstract (summarize from) | from |
| *ad-* | adjoin | to, toward |
| *ante-* | anteroom | before |
| *anti-* | antidote | against |
| *be-* | befriend | furnish with |
| | beset | around |
| *bi-* | bilingual | two |
| *bio-* | biology | life |
| *co-, com-* | cooperate, complement | together with |
| *con-* | conformist | with |
| *contra-* | contradict | against |
| *counter-* | countermand | against |
| *de-* | decline | down |
| *dia-* | diagonal | across |
| *dis-* | disjoin | separation |
| | dissatisfy | fail |
| *dys-* | dysfunction | bad |
| *en-* | engrave | in |
| *epi-* | epidemic | all over |
| *ex-* | expell | from, out of |
| *extra-* | extracurricular | outside |
| *for-* | forget | put away |
| *fore-* | foreground | in front |
| *hyper-* | hyperactive | excessive |
| *hypo-* | hypodermic | beneath |
| | hypothermia | lacking in |
| *il-* (before *l*) | illogical | not |
| *im-* | immodest | not |
| | immerse | in |
| *in-* | incorrect | not |
| | inflow | in |
| *inter-* | intervene | between |
| *intra-* | intracity | within |

| *intro-* | introduce | within, into |
| *ir-* (before *r*) | irreligious | not |
| *meta-* | metaphor | beyond |
| *mis-* | mistake | wrong |
| *non-* | nonfunctioning | not |
| *ob-* | obstacle | against |
| | object | to |
| *para-* | parallel | beside |
| *per-* | perfect | entirely |
| | pertain | through |
| *peri-* | perimeter | around |
| *post-* | postgame | after |
| *pre-* | pregame | before |
| *pro-* | prophet | ahead of |
| *pur-* | purpose | for |
| *re-* | regain | again |
| *semi-* | semifinal | half |
| *sub-* | submerge | under |
| *super-* | supercargo | over, above |
| *syl-* (before *-l*) | syllogism | with |
| *sym-* (before *m*, *b*, and *p*) | sympathy, symbol | with |
| *syn-* | synthesis | with |
| *sys-* (before *-s*) | system | with |
| *trans-* | transact | across |
| *tri-* | triple | three |
| *ultra-* | ultramodern | extreme |
| *un-* | untrue | not |
| *under-* | underwear | beneath |
| *uni-* | uniform | one |
| *with-* | withdraw | away |
| | withstand | against |

**16.7**

**sp**

## EXERCISE

Use your dictionary to determine how the prefix and the stem join in meaning in the following words:

1. contravene
2. dysentery
3. disinfectant
4. extrapolate
5. subordinate
6. synergy
7. transliteration
8. universal
9. periscope
10. propagate
11. transfigure
12. synopsis
13. hyperbole
14. irruption
15. intravenous
16. misdirection
17. remission
18. epidermis
19. intervene
20. metamorphosis

# 16.8 Suffixes

Here is a list of common suffixes:

| Suffix | Word | Meaning |
|---|---|---|
| *-able* | peaceable | tending to |
| *-age* | postage | cost of |
| | marriage | act of |
| *-ance* | vigilance | state of |
| *-ant* | accountant | person, thing |
| *-ar* | stellar | like |
| *-ary* | supplementary | connecting to |
| *-ate* | dehydrate | cause of |
| | vaccinate | treat |
| | directorate | function, agent |
| *-cy* | bankruptcy | condition |
| | presidency | office |
| *-ence* | excellence | quality, state |
| *-ery* | bakery | place of |
| | surgery | art, profession |
| | slavery | condition |
| *-ful* | hopeful | full of |
| | helpful | ability, tendency |
| | armful | quantity |
| *-ible* | edible | capable of |
| *-ic* | comic | like |
| *-ical* | comical | like |
| *-ice* | justice | condition |
| *-ise, -ize* | galvanize | make into |
| *-ish* | Irish | belonging to |
| *-ive* | creative | characteristic of |
| *-less* | witless | without |
| *-like* | catlike | resembling |
| *-ly* | motherly | like |
| *-ment* | argument | act of |
| | bewilderment | state of |
| *-mony* | matrimony | state of |
| *-ness* | richness | condition |
| *-ory* | laboratory | place of |
| *-ous* | obvious | characteristic of |
| *-some* | loathsome | tending to |
| | chromosome | body |
| *-ulent* | opulent | full of |
| *-ulous* | ridiculous | full of |
| *-ure* | exposure | act, state |
| *-ward* | westward | direction |

**16.8**

**sp**

| -*ways* | sideways | direction |
| -*wise* | likewise | direction, manner |
| -*y* | dirty | characterized by |
|  | victory | state, condition |

**EXERCISE**

Change the following words, using one of the suffixes just listed. Be ready to state how the suffix changes the meaning of the word:

1. flex
2. harm
3. fool
4. memory
5. left
6. fraud
7. clock
8. jealous
9. envious
10. sense

**16.9** sp

# 16.9 Words Often Misspelled

Following is a reference list of words often misspelled. Some of the words are referred to in previous sections and in the "Glossary of Usage" near the end of the book:

absence
absorbable
academy
acceptable
accessible
accidentally
accommodate
accuracy
accustom
achievement
acquainted
acquitted
acreage
across
address
adolescent
advice
advise
affect
aggravate

aggressive
aisle
all right
allude
analysis
annihilate
annoying
anonymous
apiece
apparent
appreciate
aquatic
assassin
associate
athletics
attendance

bargain
basically
biased

believed
beneficial
breadth
bureaucracy
business

calculator
calendar
camouflage
capital
capitol
carrying
category
ceiling
cemetery
changeable
characteristic
chief
cite
coarse
colossal
column
commercial
committee
complementary
complimentary
conceited
conceive
condemn
conscience
conscientious
consensus
convenient
criticism
criticize
curiosity

deceit
deceive
descendant
desperate
develop
diabetes
dilapidated
disappear
disappoint
discernible

discipline
disease
dissipate
distinct

ecstasy
effect
efficient
eighth
elicit
elude
embarrass
environment
equipped
especially
exaggerate
exceed
exercise
exhaust
exhilarate
existence
exorbitant
experience
explanation
extraordinary

fascinate
fiend
finally
forego
foreign
foresee
foretell
foreword
forfeit
forty
fragmentary
frivolous
futilely

gauge
genealogy
government
grammar
grievance
guarantee
guard

**16.9**

**sp**

**16.9**
**sp**

guerrilla
guidance

hangar
hanger
happened
happily
harass
harmonious
heard
height
heroes
heroines
hindrance
holiday
hoping
humane
humorous
hundred
hurriedly
hypocrisy

idiosyncrasy
illicit
illusion
immediate
immensely
incalculable
incredible
independent
indestructible
inflammable
initiative
innocuous
innuendo
integrate
interference
interrupt
intramural
irrefutable
irrelevant
irreparable
its (possessive of *it*)
it's (it is)

jeopardy

laboratory

legitimate
leisure
length
lessen (decrease)
lesson
liaison
lightning
likelihood
loneliness
loose (not tight)
lose (mislay)
luxurious
lying

magazine
maneuver
material
meanness
mediocre
memento
military
millennium
miniature
mischief
missile
mortgage
muscle
mysterious

necessary
nevertheless
niece
noncommittal
noticeable
nowadays

occasion
occurrence
opportunity

parallel
paralysis
particular
pastime
peaceable
perceive
permissible

phase
physical
physiology
picnicking
playwright
portentous
possess
precede
prejudice
prevalent
prey (victim)
principal (main)
principle (standard)
privilege
procedure
proceed
professor
pronunciation
prophecy (prediction)
prophesy (predict)
psychiatry
psychology
psychosomatic
publicly
pursue

quandary
questionnaire
quiet
quite
quizzes

ransom
receipt
referring
recommend
rehearsal
relief
relieve
religious
reminisce
repentance
resemblance
resources
restaurant
rhetoric
rhythm

ridiculous
rigmarole
roommate

sacrifice
sandwich
satellite
scarcity
schedule
secede
secretary
seize
separate
sergeant
sheriff
shriek
significant
similar
skiing
sophomore
sovereign
specimen
speeches
statistics
stayed
stony
straight
strategy
strength
stubbornness
subtlety
suburban
successful
succession
succumb
sufficient
suffrage
summary
superintendent
supersede
suppress
surprise
susceptible
symmetry
synonym

technical

**16.9**

**sp**

**16.9**

**sp**

technique
temperature
tendency
testament
thorough
threshold
through
tobacco
tragedy
truly
twelfth
tyranny

unanimous
unconscious
undoubtedly
unifying
unimaginable
unnecessary
unshakable
urgent
usage
using

vacillate
vacuum
vegetable
vengeance
victorious
visible

waive
warring
weather
Wednesday
weird
whether
wholly
withhold
worshipped
worshiped
worthwhile
writing

yeoman
yield

zoological

# Checklist for Spelling

**16.2a**   Homonyms are pronounced alike but have different meanings and spellings:

their, there, they're

**16.2b**   Other words close in pronunciation are different in spelling and meaning:

than, then

**16.2c**   Words that share the same roots and affixes may differ in meaning or be close in meaning:

assure, ensure, insure

**16.2d**   Many words with the same spelling have different meanings when divided:

everyone, every one

**16.2e**  The noun and verb forms of many words are easily confused:

advice, advise

**16.2f**  Words possessive in form do not take the apostrophe:

yours, his, hers, its, ours, yours, theirs

**16.3a**  Most nouns add *-s* to form the plural:

books, hats, shoes

**16.3b**  Nouns ending in *-y* form the plural with *-s* or *-ies*:

days, cherries

**16.3c**  Nouns ending in *-o* form the plural with *-s* or *-es*:

radios, potatoes

**16.3d**  Nouns ending in *-f* form the plural with *-s*, and many change *-f* to *-ve*:

roofs, hooves

**16.3e**  Compound nouns add *-s* to the final word unless the first word is the more important word:

police cars, sisters-in-law

**16.3f**  Words derived from other languages form their plurals usually with the suffix of the original language:

medium, media

**16.4a**  Words that sound like *be* and *see* take *-ie* except after *c*:

believe, deceit

**16.4b**  Words sounded with long *a*, long *i*, and certain other vowels take *-ei*:

neighbor, height, heir

**16.5a**  The final *-e* is dropped before the suffixes *-able*, *-ary*, *-ing*, and *-ous*:

usable, imaginary, relieving, famous

**16.5b**  The final *-e* is kept before the suffixes *-less*, *-ly*, *-ment*, *-ness*, *-some*:

nameless, namely, statement, sameness, wholesome

**16.5c**  Words like *notice* and *courage* retain the *-e* before suffixes beginning *-a* and *-ou*:

noticeable, courageous

**16.6a** The final consonant usually doubles before a suffix starting with a vowel:

slipped, occurred

**16.6b** Words ending in *-ic* add *-k* before suffixes starting with *-i*, *-e*, or *-y*:

picnicking, trafficking

**16.6c** The suffix *-able* forms adjectives:

affordable, readable

**16.6d** The suffix *-ible* forms adjectives:

divisible, permissible

**16.6e** When the suffix *-ly* is added to a word ending in *-l*, the *-l* is retained:

formally, regionally

# Effective Sentences

# Agreement

Part IV discusses sentence grammar and sentence style or ways of writing effective sentences. Part V discusses ways of improving ineffective sentences.

This first chapter of Part IV deals with sentence agreement between simple subjects and verbs, compound subjects and verbs, and pronouns and their antecedents. The chapter following deals with pronoun case and reference. These are fundamental matters of grammar that even the most experienced writers need to review from time to time. The final chapters of Part IV discuss sentence style—that is, ways of achieving different kinds of emphasis and variety in sentences.

## 17.1 Subject and Verb

Nouns, pronouns, and verbs sometimes use inflections or special word endings to show number, person, and gender. These inflections match or agree in various ways. Few of these matching forms give us trouble. Those that do give trouble fall into various patterns; knowing them will help you in correcting agreement errors.

In English subjects and verbs agree in number and person:

| | |
|---|---|
| I swim. | We swim. |
| You swim. | You swim. |
| She (he, it) swims. | They swim. |

Usually your ear tells you when forms are mismatched:

I swims.
You swims.
She swim.
All of us swims.
She, her brother, and her friends swims.

292

**17.1a  Indefinite Pronouns.**  Agreement problems arise most with special kinds of pronouns and nouns. Generally, pronouns agree in number with their *antecedents*—the nouns or pronouns that appear earlier in the sentence or in a previous sentence:

> *He* knows *himself* better than *his* parents do.
> *She* knows *herself* better than *her* parents do.
> *We* presented *our* case to the board of governors.
> *They* presented *their* case to the board of governors.

The following indefinite pronouns do not refer to specific people or things and are singular in meaning:

| | |
|---|---|
| each | neither |
| one | everybody |
| either | everyone |

The pronoun *none* takes a singular or a plural verb according to the sense:

> None of these apples is better tasting than a Jonathan.
> None of the singers of the past were better trained than singers today.

**17.1**
**agr**

The first sentence refers to "not one" of the apples, the second sentence to all singers of the past.

**17.1b  Collective Nouns.**  Nouns like *committee, family, jury, group,* and *team* take a singular verb when the group acts as a unit:

> The family *is petitioning* for a reduction in property tax.
> The jury *has reached* its verdict.
> The committee *is filing* a unanimous report.

Collective nouns take the plural when the sentence refers to separate actions of members of the group:

> The family *are coming* to Cleveland from different parts of the state.
> The jury *are* in disagreement over the verdict.
> The committee *are* filing conflicting reports.

If the sentence sounds awkward to you, specify the members:

> The family members are coming . . .
> The jury members are in disagreement . . .
> The committee members are filing . . .

Words derived from Latin and Greek sometimes form their plurals with different affixes. Thus *memorandum* is the singular form of the word, *memoranda* the plural. Similar words—*data* and *media,* for example—sometimes appear with singular verbs though the form and sense of the word are plural:

The data presented *is* probably fake.

Words like these usually follow the agreement rules governing collective nouns. The dictionary will give you the right forms.

Phrases that state a unit of measurement take the singular:

Two-thirds of a pint *is* the amount of milk required by the recipe.

The plural is correct when the subject refers to independent units:

Two pints of milk are in the refrigerator.

**17.1**
**agr**

**EXERCISES**

1. Complete the sentence in both the present and the past tense (*is, are, was, were*):
   a. Anybody who eats green apples
   b. Either of the twins
   c. Some of the hay in the yard
   d. Each of the books on the table
   e. No one with any sense
   f. Everyone in the city or suburbs
   g. One who has the proper training
   h. Few of the jury members
   i. Neither of the Plymouths in the parking lot
   j. Everybody who wants to come
2. Select the word that agrees with the subject:
   a. The committee (*is, are*) assembling from seven states.
   b. The committee (*is, are*) meeting in Washington, D.C.
   c. None of the family (*agrees, agree*) on where to hold the reunion next year.
   d. The print media (*loses, lose*) circulation in prosperous times.
   e. Few of the jury (*is, are*) serving for the second time.
   f. Each of the members (*was, were*) polled by the judge when they delivered the verdict.
   g. Almost all of the team (*is, are*) taking the bus.
   h. Not one of the team (*is, are*) taking the train.
   i. Congress (*is, are*) assembling in January for a special session.
   j. The cabinet (*was, were*) not all in favor of the proposal.
3. Write sentences that use the following:
   a. the word *class* in the singular
   b. the word *class* in the plural
   c. the word *medium* in the singular

**d.** the word *media* in the plural
**e.** the word *committee* in the singular
**f.** the word *committee* in the plural

**17.1c  Mass and Count Nouns.**   Some of the words discussed previously refer to things in the mass—that is, to things
like food or drink that we cannot count. **Mass nouns** always take
the singular:

> The food *is* spoiled.
> Wet grass *is* hard to mow.

But collections or varieties of food or grass take the plural:

> Various foods in the warehouse *are* spoiling.
> The different grasses planted in the spring *are* sprouting.

With mass nouns we are talking about the sum of things—
various foods, various grasses. **Count nouns** refer to groups that
can be singled out and counted:

> Chemicals *are defined* by their molecular structure.
> Politicians *have* different speaking styles.

**17.1**
**agr**

The agreement of pronouns follows the same rules:

*Mass Noun*
The food will be spoiled if it is not refrigerated.

*Count Noun*
The chemicals should not be heated in their bottles.

**17.1d  Titles.**   Titles always take the singular:

*Reds* is almost as long a movie as *Gone with the Wind*.
*The Ambassadors* is one of Henry James's later novels.
"The Sisters" is the opening story of James Joyce's *Dubliners*.

**EXERCISE**

Complete the sentence using a verb in the present tense or the
past tense:

> *Example*
> Food is scarce in rainless countries.
> Food has been scarce in the country because of drought
> and war.

**1.** The water in the pool
**2.** English teachers, unlike teachers of other subjects,
**3.** The movie *Jaws*
**4.** The rain that fell last night

5. Detergents advertised on television
6. Foodstuffs stored without refrigeration
7. The popular novel and later the popular movie *The Color Purple*
8. Contact sports like football
9. The sports equipment stored in the fieldhouse
10. A breed of dog like the beagle or the collie

**17.1e  Delayed Subjects.**   In sentences that begin with the expletive *there*, the subject follows the verb. The verb agrees with this delayed subject, not with *there*:

> *Verb   Subject*
> There *is* an *explanation* for what happened.

**17.1**

**agr**

The expletive *there* is sometimes called the "dummy" subject because it merely fills the opening of the sentence. The sentence has the same meaning as the following:

> An *explanation exists* for what happened.

The error in the following sentence is easier to make:

> There is not and cannot be any excuses for these mistakes.

The verb must agree with the plural subject *excuses*:

> There *are* not and cannot be any *excuses* for these mistakes.

The word *it*, by contrast with *there*, always takes a singular verb when functioning as a simple pronoun. The pronoun *it* and the noun *call* are synonymous in the following sentence:

> *It's* the *call* I've been waiting for.

In the following sentences, the expletive *it* is a dummy word—a word empty of meaning as in the sentences to the right:

| *Kernel Sentence* | *Transformed Sentence* |
|---|---|
| Cooking is fun. | It is fun to cook. |
| Ohio is cooler than Georgia in the summer. | It is cooler in Ohio than in Georgia in the summer. |

The verb following the dummy *it* is always singular, regardless of what follows in the sentence:

> It is Margaret who is coming, not Barbara.
> It is her sisters who are coming, not her college roommates.

**17.1f  Inverted Subjects.**   When the sentence inverts or reverses the subject and verb, agreement is with the subject, not with the noun or pronoun of the opening modifier:

| Kernel Sentence | Transformed Sentence |
|---|---|
| The famous Mrs. Malaprop appears in the play *The Rivals.* | In *The Rivals* appears the famous Mrs. Malaprop. |
| A dozen red cars were parked outside the restaurant. | Outside the restaurant were parked a dozen cars—all red. |

**17.1g Subject and Complement.**   Occasionally the verb mistakenly agrees with the complement instead of with the subject:

*Incorrect*
The *cause* of the epidemic *were* the brown rats.

*Correct*
The *cause* of the epidemic *was* the brown rats.

The mistake probably occurs because the writer is anticipating the subject complement *rats* that names the cause.

**17.1**
**agr**

**17.1h Intervening Words.**   Words that come between subject and verb can be mistaken for the subject of the sentence:

*Incorrect*
The *book,* with other books on the same subject, *are failing* to win a large audience.

*Correct*
The *book,* with other books on the same subject, *is failing* to win a large audience.

*Incorrect*
The nineteenth-century woman *novelist* like George Eliot and the Brontës *were anxious* to be taken seriously.

*Correct*
The nineteenth-century woman *novelist* like George Eliot and the Brontës *was anxious* to be taken seriously.

The subject and verb can agree as follows:

These books, with others on the same subject, *are failing* to win a large audience.

George Eliot, the Brontës, and other nineteenth-century woman novelists *were anxious* to be taken seriously.

Or

Nineteenth-century women novelists like George Eliot and the Brontës were anxious to be taken seriously.

The longer the intervening phrase or clause, the greater the risk of missing agreement with the subject:

*Incorrect*
The nineteenth-century woman *novelist,* who did not publish under a male pseudonym and unlike George Eliot and the Brontë sisters did not gain the respect of the reading public, *are now getting* recognition.

Agreement here is mistakenly with the nearby *George Eliot* and *the Brontë sisters* in the intervening clause. The verb must agree with *novelist*:

The nineteenth-century woman novelist . . . is now getting recognition.

Sometimes agreement depends on the sense of the sentence. Compare the following:

**17.1**
**agr**

The woman from Ohio was *the only one* of the visitors who *was* stricken with food poisoning.

The woman from Ohio was *only one* of the visitors who *were* stricken with food poisoning.

The singular *was* is required in the first sentence because just one person was stricken with food poisoning—the woman from Ohio. The plural *were* is required in the second because a number of the visitors were stricken, not only the woman from Ohio.

**EXERCISE**

Decide whether the verb should be singular or plural, and give your reasons:

1. Each of us (*is, are*) going to the beach.
2. Some of us (*is, are*) not going.
3. The committee (*is, are*) arriving at different times.
4. The team (*was, were*) sent off the field for various infractions.
5. The board of governors (*is, are*) making (*its, their*) decision about the scholarships this afternoon.
6. *Wings* (*was, were*) one of the first sound films.
7. Bacon (*is, are*) high in cholesterol.
8. Bacon bits (*is, are*) sometimes not real bacon.
9. Gravel (*was, were*) shoveled on the driveway.
10. There (*is, are*) not one but several books on the subject.
11. It (*is, are*) the onion that smells.
12. It (*was, were*) the apples that spoiled, not the peaches.
13. It (*is, are*) not the fault of the growers that the canker spread so quickly through the groves.

14. In the northern skies (*appears, appear*) the Aurora Borealis.
15. Throughout the novels of Thomas Hardy (*occurs, occur*) amazing coincidences.
16. One of the novels, which contains fewer unhappy characters, (*is, are*) *The Woodlanders*.
17. Not a single person in the room, not even the people who paid beforehand for their tickets, (*was, were*) told that the flight had been rescheduled.
18. Few of us—and probably none—(*know, knows*) what to do in an emergency during flight.
19. There (*is, are*) seldom opportunities such as this one to learn emergency procedures.
20. Whoever leaves the room last (*is, are*) to turn off the lights.
21. There (*was, were*) not one in the room who (*was, were*) willing to volunteer for the committee.
22. There (*is, are*) several members of the committee who (*is, are*) going to volunteer.
23. The culprit (*turns, turn*) out to be the raccoons coming into the yard from the woods.
24. The last days of the war (*was, were*) a time of hope for the leaders of the country, who (*was, were*) hoping to halt the fighting.
25. It (*is, are*) the World Series that (*occupies, occupy*) the sports fan in the fall, not politics.

**17.2**
**agr**

# 17.2   Compound Subjects

Subjects joined by *and* usually take plural verbs:

Minneapolis and St. Paul are cities in Minnesota.

An exception occurs with compound subjects beginning with *each*:

Each city and each county in the state levies taxes.

Special problems arise with other words that join subjects.

**17.2a *Or* and Other Conjunctions.**   Here are the conventions governing *or* and other conjunctions:
The conjunction *or* takes the singular verb in sentences like the following:

Minneapolis *or* St. Paul *is* the capital of Minnesota.

The verb of this sentence cannot be plural because the sentence states two alternatives, only one of which can be true. If the subjects are different in number, the verb agrees with the nearest one:

> Neither Milwaukee nor the twin cities Minneapolis and St. Paul *are* on the Missouri River.

The verb is also singular in sentences using the following phrases:

> Organic chemistry, *in addition to* calculus and physics, is a requirement for the degree.
> Organic chemistry, *along with* . . .
> Organic chemistry, *together with* . . .
> Organic chemistry, *as well as* . . .
> Organic chemistry, *besides* . . .

**17.2**

**agr**

These nonrestrictive modifiers add important but not essential information to the sentence. The sentence says that organic chemistry is a requirement for the degree, and it adds the important information that calculus and physics are requirements too.

**17.2b Phrases.**   Compound subjects that form a single phrase or idea take the singular verb:

> *Ham and eggs* is a popular dish in England and America.
> *Mutt and Jeff* was a popular cartoon strip in the 1940s.

In the following sentences these foods and cartoon characters are referred to as individual things or people:

> Ham and eggs are popular American foods.
> Mutt and Jeff were popular cartoon characters.

The same is true of stage and film actors and actresses who form a team—for example, Katharine Hepburn and Spencer Tracy:

> As an acting team Hepburn and Tracy are remembered through their many films.

**17.2c Correlatives.**   The correlative conjunctions *either/or*, *neither/nor*, *not only/but also*, and other pairs take singular verbs when the subjects are singular:

> *Either* Minneapolis *or* St. Paul *is* the capital of Minnesota.
> *Neither* St. Cloud *nor* Rochester *is* the capital.
> *Not only* calculus *but also* physics *is* a requirement for the major.

The verb is plural when both subjects are plural:

> Neither Latin and Greek nor logic and advanced composition *are* requirements for the major.

When the correlative subjects are singular and plural, the verb agrees with the nearer subject:

Neither Latin and Greek nor *logic is* a requirement.
Neither logic nor *Latin and Greek are* requirements.

The same rule governs subjects different in person:

Neither *she* nor *I am* invited.

But note the awkwardness of the following:

Neither *I* nor *she is* going.

The following revision is preferable:

I am not going, nor is she.

**EXERCISE**

Complete the sentence, using the appropriate form of the verb:
  1. Either Marge or Barbara
  2. Neither Barbara nor her sisters
  3. The three R's—reading, writing, and arithmetic—
  4. Not only the three sisters but their aunt
  5. The sisters, together with their aunt and uncle,
  6. The sisters together with their friends
  7. Together with the ingredients called for in the recipe, the three tablespoons of sugar
  8. The ingredients called for in the recipe, in addition to
  9. The President and his advisers
  10. The advisers or the President
  11. The whole family, including the cousins from Stamford,
  12. The campaign slogan "Throw the rascals out!"
  13. The campaign manager, as well as the office workers,
  14. The phrase *bread and butter*
  15. Few of the campaign slogans

**17.3**
**agr**

# **17.3** Pronouns and Antecedents

A pronoun agrees in number with its antecedent—the noun or pronoun that appears earlier in the sentence or the paragraph and to which the pronoun refers:

Walking up the stairs is my *wife*, not *her* twin sister.

The considerations governing agreement between subjects and verbs also govern pronouns and their antecedents.

**17.3a Compound Subjects.**  Compound subjects usually take plural pronouns:

Chicago and Evanston have *their* own police departments.

The words *each* and *every* make the antecedent singular:

Each city has *its* own police department.
Every woman in the room has *her* own fascinating story.

A compound phrase that expresses a single idea takes a singular pronoun:

The cartoon strip *Mutt and Jeff* had *its* own special humor.

When the word *or* joins a singular and plural noun or pronoun in a compound subject, the pronoun agrees with the antecedent closer to it:

The city or the suburbs are raising their property taxes.

**17.3**

**agr**

**17.3b Indefinite Pronouns.**  The indefinite pronouns *each, everyone, everybody, no one, nobody, some, someone, something, nothing,* and *everything* usually take a singular pronoun:

Of the gains in productivity, each has *its* benefits and risks.

A special problem arises when the subject refers to human beings. *His* traditionally refers to both men and women:

Each of us is donating *his* salary for the benefit.

To show that the statement also refers to women, many speakers and writers specify both men and women:

Each of us is donating *his or her* salary.

Another solution is to use a plural subject:

All of us are donating our salaries for the week.

**17.3c Collective Nouns and Pronouns.**  The rules of agreement in number between collective nouns and verbs govern pronouns and their collective antecedents. The sentence takes a singular pronoun if the pronoun refers to the group as a whole; a plural verb, if the pronoun refers to the members of the group individually:

The committee has *its* special rules or procedure. *It* governs *itself*, however, through the House code of ethics.

The committee have *their* own separate codes of conduct, though the committee as a whole acts according to the House code. The members govern *themselves*.

**17.3d Agreement with the Nearer Antecedent.** Where two antecedents are different in number, the pronoun agrees with the nearer one:

Not just Barbara but many of her friends are buying *their* tickets.

The plural is, however, appropriate when the sense of the sentence is plural:

Not just her friends but Barbara, too, are buying *their* tickets.

**EXERCISES**

1. Choose the verb and pronoun forms appropriate to the sentence:
   a. Each of the suburbs (*has, have*) (*its, their*) mayor and council.
   b. New York, Washington, Boston, and Chicago (*has, have*) (*its, their*) airports close to heavily populated areas.
   c. Every city and every suburb (*need, needs*) to protect (*its, their*) water supply from chemical pollution.
   d. The team (*is, are*) practicing for (*its, their*) last game.
   e. Either you or your lab partners (*is, are*) to clean (*your, their*) equipment before leaving.
   f. The principal, along with the teachers and counselors, (*is, are*) meeting with (*her, their*) lawyer at three o'clock.
   g. Neither the pilot nor the stewardesses can explain (*his, her, their*) disappearance from the airport.
   h. John or his brothers (*was, were*) in Vietnam during (*his, their*) years in the Army.
   i. Not one of the students and not one of the teachers (*is, are*) attending the meeting.
   j. Few of the students and even fewer of the teachers (*is, are*) attending the meeting.
2. Correct any errors in agreement.
   a. Hydraulics is concerned with the laws of movement in liquids and its application in engines.
   b. Hydraulics and aeronautics are closely related sciences, though each are taught in different departments of the engineering college.
   c. Among the widely read novels of Willa Cather is *My Antonia*.
   d. Among the novelists who have written about Chicago is Saul Bellow and Nelson Algren.
   e. One of the recent novels of Alice Walker is *The Color Purple*.
   f. Each of Saul Bellow's novels and each of Alice Walker's have been published in Great Britain.

**17.3**
**agr**

**g.** The committee on scholarships will announce their decisions in April.

**h.** Elizabeth, in addition to taking organic chemistry and physics, is taking genetics.

**i.** Belgium, along with Holland, Denmark, and Norway, was occupied by Germany during the Second World War.

**j.** No one who has owned a dog want to support so harsh a law.

**k.** Not only the President and his cabinet but the Speaker of the House are attending the ceremony.

## Checklist for Agreement

**17.3 agr**

**17.1**   Make the subject and verb agree in number.

**17.1a**   An indefinite pronoun takes a singular verb if it refers to a single thing, a plural verb if it refers to two or more things:

> Each of the tomatoes is spoiled.
> All of the tomatoes are spoiled.

**17.1b**   A collective noun takes a plural verb when referring to the members of a group individually, a singular verb when referring to the group as a unit:

> The committee have been arriving throughout the week.
> The jury has reached its verdict.

**17.1c**   Mass nouns take a singular verb, count nouns a plural:

> The food is spoiled.
> Various foods in the warehouse are rotting.

**17.1d**   Titles take singular verbs:

> *Reds* is almost as long a movie as *Gone with the Wind*.

**17.1e**   In sentences beginning with the expletive *there*, the verb agrees with the subject:

> There is no explanation for what happened.

The expletive *it* takes a singular verb, no matter what follows in the sentence:

> It is her sisters who are coming.

**17.1f**   Verbs agree with the inverted subject, not with an opening modifier:

> In *The Rivals* appears the famous Mrs. Malaprop.

**17.1g** The verb should agree with the subject and not with the complement.

**17.1h** Verbs agree with their subjects, not with intervening modifiers:

> A group of old books and magazines sits on the table.

**17.2a** When *or* joins singular nouns or pronouns of a compound subject, the verb is singular. When the nouns or pronouns are singular and plural, the verb agrees with the nearer subject:

> Minneapolis or St. Paul is the capital of Minnesota.
> Neither Milwaukee nor Minneapolis and St. Paul are on the Missouri River.

Subjects joined by *in addition to, along with, as well as, together with,* and *besides* take singular verbs:

> Organic chemistry, in addition to calculus and physics, is a requirement for the major.

**17.2b** Compound subjects that form a single phrase take singular verbs:

> Ham and eggs is a popular dish.

**17.2c** Correlatives take singular verbs when the subjects are singular, plural verbs when the subjects are plural:

> Either Minneapolis or St. Paul is the capital of Minnesota.
> Either Minneapolis and St. Paul or Milwaukee and Madison are on the Mississippi.

Where the correlative subjects are singular and plural, the verb agrees with the nearer subject:

> Neither Latin and Greek nor logic is a requirement.

**17.3a** Compound subjects take plural verbs:

> Chicago and Evanston have their own police departments.

**17.3b** The pronouns *each* and *every* make the subject singular:

> Each municipality has its own police department.

Indefinite pronouns take the singular:

> Everyone in the room has met the candidate.

**17.3c** The pronoun is singular if its antecedent is a collective noun; plural, if the antecedent refers to the members of the group individually:

> The committee has its special code of conduct.
> The committee have their own separate codes.

**17.3d**   When two antecedents are different in number, the pronoun agrees with the nearer one:

> Neither Bill nor his sisters are buying their tickets until the day of the concert.

# Pronoun Case and Reference

Putting the right pronoun in the right place in the sentence is something you do naturally. People rarely say "Me is going home" or "Give the book to I," but they do occasionally confuse subject and object positions, using expressions like "between you and I" and asking "Who do you want to speak to?"

These forms are easily confused. One source of confusion is that the pronoun *I* "sounds" more correct than *me* in a phrase like "between you and I." "We girls" and "we guys" sound strange to some people and not strange at all to others. The same is true of "us girls" and "us guys" in the subject position where standard English requires the word *we*.

Another source of confusion is that word order governs English sentences. Since *who* is usual in the subject position at the beginning of the sentence, people naturally say or write:

*Who* are you speaking to?

Few pause to decide that the opening pronoun is the object of the preposition *to* and therefore requires the objective case:

*Whom* are you speaking to?

Some uses of pronoun case and reference are matters of exactness and clarity; others are matters of social correctness and acceptability. All of us know the conventions that govern usage in our circle of friends without being told. However, we do not always know the conventions governing at work or school or in age or social groups different from our own. These matters are the subject of this chapter.

307

# 18.1 Nouns and Pronouns

**18.1a Subject Pronouns.** Most English nouns add *-s* or *-es* or another inflection or word ending to show singular and plural:

> boy, boys
> box, boxes
> child, children

Some nouns change in form:

> woman, women
> tooth, teeth

Pronouns usually change in form to show singular and plural and to show the use of the pronoun as subject, object, and possessive. To use the correct form, you must know how the pronoun is used in the sentence.

**18.1** **ca**

**18.1b Subjects and Subject Complements.** The pronoun subject form occurs in the same subject positions filled by nouns:

> *Correct*
> The coach and I watched the play from the sidelines.
>
> *Incorrect*
> The coach and me . . .
>
> *Incorrect*
> Me and the coach . . .

A noun or pronoun following a *to be* verb—*is, are, was, were, will be*—is called the *subject complement* (or *predicate nominative*). Because it refers to the subject (see 8.1c and 8.2b) the subject complement must be in the same case. Compare the following:

> She is the tennis pro, not her sister.
> The tennis pro is she [*subject complement*], not her sister.

Informal English departs from this standard occasionally:

> The tennis pro is Mary, not her.

The informal expression "It's me" is common in speech and occurs in writing at the general level.

**18.1c Pronoun-Noun Phrases.** When used as appositives, pronouns take the case of the nouns they stand next to:

Those in the front row, my classmates and I, cheered loudly.
The speaker recognized us—my classmates and me.

**18.1d Comparisons with *As* and *Than*.** Elliptical clauses
often cause mistakes in agreement. Parts of these clauses are
deleted on the assumption that the sense is clear:

She is as smart as I [*am smart*].
He gave James more than she [*gave him*].

Here are the clauses:

She is smart        I am smart.
He gave James     she gave him.

In these sentences the subject form of the pronoun is used after
the words *as* and *than* when the verb and object of the elliptical
clause are deleted. The mistake occurs when subject and object
forms are confused:

*Incorrect*
She is as smart as me.

*Incorrect*
She is smarter than me.

Notice the different meanings of the following sentences:

He gave James more than he [*gave him*].
He gave James more than [*he gave*] him.

The first sentence omits the verb and object; the second sentence, the subject and verb.

If in doubt about the pronoun case, complete the construction as shown.

**18.1**
**ca**

**EXERCISE**

Correct the sentences that are unacceptable in general and formal English:
1. The collection plate passed down the row to us at the end.
2. We hikers are a rugged bunch.
3. She thinks John is brighter than me.
4. It is me, Jim, speaking.
5. Don't laugh at me when you hear me stutter.
6. Us neighbors should organize a carpool.
7. Explain the plan to us, not to them people.
8. He gave hisself a boost up the ladder.
9. They gave theirselves a rest.
10. They are not as confident about the outcome as us.

## 18.2   Object Pronouns

**18.2a   Object Pronoun Forms.**   The object form of the pronoun is used in the same object positions filled by nouns:

> We gave the tickets to the usher.
> We gave the tickets to him.

The following mistakes probably occur because the speaker or writer loses sight of the object position in the sentence:

> *Incorrect*
> The lawyer wrote to my husband and I that the claim had been settled.

> *Incorrect*
> She asked her the question, not he.

Here are the correct forms:

> The lawyer wrote to my husband and me . . .
> She asked her the question, not him [indirect object of *asked*].

The tendency to use the subject forms in object positions sometimes arises from the sense that the subject words sound correct there.

**18.2b   Objects of Prepositions.**   Few of us make the mistake of speaking or writing:

> They gave the tickets to I.

On occasion we may say incorrectly:

> They gave the tickets to you and I.
> There's not enough ice cream left for you and I.
> Between you and I he's dumber than he knows.

The word *you*, in serving as the subject and object of the second-person pronoun, probably leads many people to follow *you* with the subject pronoun *I*. The longer the phrase, the easier it is to assume the subject form is the right form. Some people nervously use the subject pronoun out of fear of being incorrect.

### Exercise

Give the correct pronoun form in the following sentences:
  1. There is little difference in personality between the two brothers and (*they, them*).
  2. She is taller than (*he, him*).
  3. The manager gave the tickets to (*she, her*).

**18.2**

**ca**

4. Give them to (*he, him*), not (*she, her*).
5. Few people make mistakes as foolish as (*they, them*).
6. I know (*her, she*) and (*their, they're*) sister.
7. There are few in the class smarter than (*she, her*).
8. Give the book to no one but (*he, him*).
9. The best photo is of (*they, them*), not (*we, us*).
10. The argument is between (*they, them*) and (*we, us*).

# 18.3  Reflexive Pronouns

The reflexive pronoun shows that the actor and the person acted upon are the same:

She injured herself in the accident.
We did not give ourselves enough time.
The directors of the company voted themselves a raise.

On occasion the reflexive pronoun is used intensively to give special emphasis to a statement:

They must do the job themselves.
I myself explained the action we took.

Use the pronoun sparingly in this way.

**18.3 ref**

### EXERCISE

Use the right form of the pronoun if you find an error in the following sentences:

1. They forgot to tell Frank and I that the road was closed to traffic.
2. They told Bill, the students who had been waiting in the hall, and them that the performance had been cancelled.
3. I would rather hear the bad news from you than from her.
4. We could not explain to the bank official or to the policeman or she where we lost the blank checks or when.
5. They gave us campers directions to the lake.
6. We were certainly as experienced as they.
7. Me and my friends would like to reserve a campsite.
8. To me and my friends it seemed the longest way to go.
9. She herself is to blame, not us.
10. She and myself are to blame, not you and him.

# 18.4  Relative Pronouns

The relative pronouns *who, which,* and *that* can be used in different ways. *Who* refers to people:

They are the couple who bought our house.

*That* refers to objects and can refer to people when introducing a restrictive clause:

The people that bought our house are friends of my sister.

*Which* also refers to things. Occasionally it introduces a restrictive clause:

The toolbox which I put in the garage [not the toolbox which I put in the yard] is gone.
That is not the book which I need for the course.

However, *which* is used more often to introduce a nonrestrictive clause:

The toolbox, which I put in the garage, is gone. [The speaker owns one toolbox, not two.]

**18.4**
**ref**

The possessive form *whose* usually refers to people. In referring to things, some writers use *whose* to avoid an awkward use of *which*. Compare:

The toolbox the latch *of which* is broken is in the garage.
The toolbox *whose* latch is broken is in the garage.

**EXERCISE**

Identify the restrictive and nonrestrictive modifiers in the following, and be ready to explain why each is restrictive or nonrestrictive. Add commas to punctuate the nonrestrictive clauses:

1. The one red-covered book that you find on the shelf is the book I need for the course.
2. This red-covered book which I need for the course belongs to my sister.
3. Few of the people who saw her speak knew that she is the sister of the woman who won the gold medal.
4. My sister and I who saw her speak did not know who she was.
5. Spring came early the year that we lived in Missouri.
6. That is the same car which I saw in the lot last week.
7. The car that I saw in the lot last week is a Ford.
8. None of us who had ever seen her dance were surprised that she won the competition.
9. The town was still recovering from the tornado which had struck the year before.
10. The one previous tornado which struck the town at noon on April 4 did more damage than any storm in the history of the town.

# 18.5  *Who* and *Whom*

**Who** and **whom** give trouble because we do not always depend on the inflection -(who)*m* in identifying a word in the object position. The position of many words, not their *inflection* or special form, gives us this information. So important is position in distinguishing subject and object forms that we commonly say:

Who did he give the tickets to?

We use *who* and not the formally correct *whom* (the object of the preposition *to*) because it appears in the subject position. On occasion we hear or say the following—with full stress on *who*:

He gave the tickets to WHO?

Given ordinary stress, the object form always follows the preposition:

To whom did you give the tickets?

A special problem arises when forms of *who* and *whom* introduce dependent clauses:

*Incorrect*
Give the tickets to whomever asks for them.

The correct form is *whoever* as subject of the noun clause:

*Correct*
Give the tickets to *whoever asks for them.*

The mistake in form arises because, at first glance, *whomever* seems to be the object of *to*.

When in doubt about which form to use, isolate the dependent clause and then try to substitute *he, she,* or *they* as follows:

Give the tickets to (*whoever, whomever*) asks for them.
[*dependent clause*: she asks for the tickets]

Give the tickets to whoever asks for them.

He wondered (*who, whom*) had given him the tickets.
[*dependent clause*: she had given the tickets]

He wondered who had given him the tickets.

He wondered (*who, whom*) the tickets belonged to.
[*dependent clause*: the tickets belonged to them]

He wondered whom the tickets belonged to.

**18.5
ref**

**EXERCISE**

Correct those sentences in which *who* and *whom* are misused:
1. Many people on whom we depend in turn depend on us.
2. Give this message to whoever calls.
3. Give the message to the person who calls at six.
4. The actress who I talked with after the play lives in Cincinnati.
5. The people who we saw driving to the lake waved as they drove by.
6. She was willing to explain the problem to whomever asked.
7. Whoever you tell, don't tell everything that happened.
8. I know where I'm going and whom I'm going with.
9. Tell whomever you want to the full details of the accident.
10. Those whom you tell will repeat the story to whoever asks them.

**18.6**
**ref**

## 18.6 Vague Pronouns

In speaking, you sometimes use *this*, *that*, and *you* without specifying their antecedents:

This is easy for anyone to fix.

If your listeners are obviously confused, you may pause to clarify the reference of these pronouns:

I mean a flat tire.

Vague pronouns in writing often arise from carrying habits of speech into writing. Pronouns need greater support in writing because you cannot depend on voice inflection to clarify their reference.

**18.6a Indefinite *You* and *It*.**    The word *you* is indispensable in conversation:

You have no idea the trouble we've had with the new stove.

In the following sentence, the word is used even more loosely, with the reflexive meaning of *me*—the speaker actually referring to himself:

It gives you no end of trouble.

This informal use of the word makes the following sentence awkward and confusing:

You have no idea the fun you can have with sailboats.

Revising the sentence to make the meaning specific is not always easy. Substituting the indefinite pronoun *one* makes the following sentence stilted:

> One has no idea the fun you can have with sailboats.

This sentence shifts awkwardly from third-person *one* to first-person *you*. This second revision is even worse:

> One has no idea of the fun with sailboats.

This sentence is unidiomatic whether spoken or written.

The use of *one* is, however, idiomatic in the following sentence:

> One can have fun with sailboats.

*One* is used properly in general references to people. *You* is appropriate in addressing a person or a particular audience:

> You can have fun with sailboats.

**18.6**
**ref**

The expletive *it* functions as a "dummy" word in the following sentence:

> It probably won't rain until the weekend.

The sentence will be unclear if the word, in the opening position or later in the sentence, seems to refer to a missing word or antecedent:

> *Vague*
> Rain and snow—it has the same effect on traffic.

> *Improved*
> Rain and snow—both have the same effect on traffic.

Here is a complex example:

> Historians disagree on the character and behavior of Franklin Roosevelt. It seems to be not just a concern of historians but of novelists and filmmakers.

We have two possibilities here: *it* may refer to the word *character* or *behavior* in the preceding sentence. Or it may be the expletive or "dummy" *it* without an intended reference. Here are possible revisions:

> His character and behavior seem a major concern not just to historians but to novelists and filmmakers.

> His character [or behavior] seems a major concern not just to historians but to novelists and filmmakers.

> Novelists and filmmakers, not just historians, seem to be concerned with his character [or behavior].

**18.6b** *That* **and** *Which.*    In speaking the following sentence, you probably would give more than usual emphasis to the word *that* at the start of the second sentence:

> Napoleon let ambition guide him in planning military strategy. *That* is why he did not take the advice of his generals in planning the invasion of Russia.

Here the word *that* refers to the whole idea expressed in the first sentence. We need not repeat the whole idea if it is clear in the context of the paragraph or essay. Sometimes a single word or perhaps a phrase clarifies the reference:

> His ambition explains why Napoleon did not take the advice of his generals in planning the invasion of Russia.

The word *which* is often a source of the same kind of vagueness in a sentence like the following:

**18.6**
**ref**

> The historians give various explanations for Napoleon's blunder, which is why the question continues to be debated.

Here the word *which* has two possible antecedents: the fact that historians give various explanations for the blunder—an idea expressed in the whole first clause—or the word *blunder* itself.

Here is a revision that clarifies the reference:

> The historians give various explanations for Napoleon's blunder, and these explanations show why the question continues to be debated.

The sentence can be tightened:

> The various explanations of historians for Napoleon's blunder continue the debate.

Here is an even better revision:

> Historians continue to debate Napoleon's blunder.

The sense of the original sentence is retained because the word *debate* implies that historians give different explanations for Napoleon's blunder.

Another source of confusion is the use of the pronouns *you, it, that,* and *which* to refer to a word or idea implied earlier in the sentence.

Here are other sources of vagueness in sentences.

**18.6c  Reference to an Implied Word.**    In the following sentence no specific antecedent appears for the italicized word:

> In discussing gun control, she stated the number of *them* in private hands.

The reference is to guns—implied by the modifying word *gun*. To revise the sentence, specify the antecedent:

> In discussing gun control, she stated the number of guns in private hands.

**18.6d Reference to a Possessive Noun.** The reference to the possessive noun in the following sentence is awkward:

> In Emily Dickinson's poetry *she* often uses complex metaphors.

Though the subject pronoun *she* does have a clear antecedent in *Emily Dickinson*, the reference is to a noun used as an adjective modifier, a momentary source of confusion for the reader. The revision here is a simple matter:

> In her poetry Emily Dickinson often uses complex metaphors.

**EXERCISE**

Revise the following sentences to clarify the pronoun reference:

1. Fire, flood, famine, plague—that has been a continual source of suffering of people, rich and poor.
2. One needs all the help you can get.
3. Jefferson had foresight and an understanding of the importance the West would have. It explains his decision to make the Louisiana Purchase.
4. The storm buried the city in snow and closed the highways, which is why we cancelled our trip.
5. Courage and willingness to help people in trouble—it is needed as much today as in the past.
6. In Fawn Brodie's biography she presents new facts about Thomas Jefferson.
7. John worked overtime during the week, and he spent the weekend in the office which is why he is taking this week off.
8. Neither of the two sisters guessed she would win the scholarship.
9. We never doubted she would win the scholarship. That goes without saying.
10. It helps one to know that one can do well if one tries.

**18.7** amb

# 18.7 Ambiguous Reference

**18.7a Reference to Antecedents.** A sentence is ambiguous when the antecedent of a pronoun is uncertain:

Neither Wilson nor Hughes doubted he would be elected.

If *he* refers to both men, you can try to clear up the ambiguity by rewording the sentence:

Wilson did not doubt he would be elected, nor did Hughes.

But the ambiguity remains, for the second clause can mean:

. . . nor did Hughes doubt that Wilson would.
. . . nor did Hughes doubt that he himself would.

Specify the antecedent even at the cost of repetition:

Neither Wilson nor Hughes doubted that Wilson would be elected.

The following revision is appropriate in referring to both men:

Neither Wilson nor Hughes doubted that he himself would be elected.

**18.7b Ambiguous Possessive.**   The following sentence has two possible meanings:

Wilson is famous for his indictment.

We do not know whether Wilson was indicted or made the indictment. Here are possible clarifications of the sentence:

Wilson is famous for his indictment of judicial corruption in the county.

Wilson is famous for his indictment by a grand jury on the charge of judicial corruption.

**18.7**
**amb**

### EXERCISES

**1.** Correct the fault in pronoun reference:
   **a.** I find it strange that we cannot name the act or even refer to it.
   **b.** Einstein and Bohr debated his rejection of the quantum theory that he had helped to create.
   **c.** Neither Einstein nor Bohr changed his position in the course of these debates.
   **d.** After her commendation she found new respect from her fellow workers.
   **e.** Inflation increased as wages fell, which was difficult to explain.
   **f.** Gun control remains a controversial issue, particularly in areas where crime is increasing. That is not surprising.
   **g.** You should not take one's eyes off the road.

    **h.** The invasion of Normandy surprised the Germans, which the Allied command hoped would happen.

    **i.** The Marx Brothers and Laurel and Hardy—it's a slapstick comedy that originated in vaudeville.

    **j.** Groucho, Chico, and Harpo made it the most popular in the movies.

  **2.** Correct any fault in each of the following sentences:

    **a.** The speaker on dog obedience explained that they respond to consistent commands.

    **b.** In Dickens' novels he gives us a picture of London criminals in the nineteenth century.

    **c.** The popularity of rock music is shown by the huge crowds that attend their concerts.

    **d.** In the senator's campaign for the presidency reporters discovered his persistence and idealism.

    **e.** Animal ecology is the study of their distribution and breeding habits.

    **f.** Neither Jefferson nor Adams knew that the other was dying.

    **g.** November through March—it is the best time for skiing in the mountains.

    **h.** The circus performers—tumblers, clowns, highwire acrobats—they are as exciting as ever to see.

    **i.** No one knows how much math they will need later in life.

    **j.** Either Smith or Jones will get the job, and he knows it.

**18.7
amb**

# Checklist for Pronoun Case and Reference

**18.1b**   The subject complement must be in the same case as the subject:

> The tennis pro is she [*subject complement*], not her sister.

**18.1c**   When used as appositives, pronouns take the case of the nouns they stand next to:

> Those in the front row, my classmates and I, cheered loudly.
> The speaker recognized us—my classmates and me.

**18.1d**   The subject form of the pronoun is used after the words *as* and *than* when the verb and object of the elliptical clause are deleted:

> She is as smart as I.

**18.2a**   The object form of the pronoun is used in the same object positions filled by nouns:

The lawyer wrote to my husband and me that the claim had been settled.
She asked her the question, not him.

**18.2b**　The object form of the pronoun follows the preposition:

They gave the tickets to you and me.
Between you and me he's dumber than he knows.

**18.3**　In colloquial English the reflexive pronoun sometimes occurs in the subject and object positions:

Frank and myself are going to the concert.

**18.4**　*That* refers to objects, and it can refer to people when introducing a restrictive clause:

The people that bought our house are friends of my sister.

*Which* occasionally introduces a restrictive clause but usually introduces a nonrestrictive one:

*Restrictive*
The toolbox which I put in the garage is gone.

*Nonrestrictive*
The toolbox, which I put in the garage, is gone.

**18.5**　The object form always follows the preposition:

To whom did you give the tickets?

**18.6a**　The words *you* and *it* can make sentences vague and confusing:

*Confusing*
You have no idea the fun you can have with sailboats.

*Improved*
You have no idea what fun sailboats are.
You can have fun with sailboats.

*Vague*
Rain and snow—it has same effect on traffic.

*Improved*
Rain and snow—both have the same effect on traffic.

**18.6b**　The words *that* and *which* sometimes need specific reference:

*Vague*
Napoleon let ambition guide him on questions of military strategy. That is why he did not take the advice of his generals in planning the invasion of Russia.

*Improved*
His ambition explains why Napoleon did not take the advice of his generals in planning the invasion of Russia.

*Vague*
The historians give various explanations for Napoleon's blunder, which is why the question continues to be debated.

*Better*
Historians continue to debate Napoleon's blunder.

**18.6c** Don't make the pronoun refer to an implied word:

*Unclear*
In discussing gun control, she stated the number of them in private hands.

*Improved*
In discussing gun control, she stated the number of guns in private hands.

**18.6d** Don't let a pronoun refer to a possessive noun:

*Awkward*
In Emily Dickinson's poetry *she* often uses complex metaphors.

*Improved*
In her poetry Emily Dickinson often uses complex metaphors.

**18.7a** A sentence seems ambiguous when the antecedent of a pronoun is uncertain:

*Ambiguous*
Neither Wilson nor Hughes doubted he would be elected.

*Clear*
Neither Wilson nor Hughes doubted that Wilson would be elected.

**18.7b** The possessive pronoun can be ambiguous:

*Ambiguous*
Wilson is famous for his indictment.

*Clear*
Wilson is famous for his indictment of judicial corruption in the county.
Wilson is famous for his indictment by a grand jury on the charge of judicial corruption.

# Sentence Variety

In speaking, you form sentences without concern for their emphasis or shape. That kind of attention begins in a conversation when you discover you are not being understood. The situation is different in writing, for here you are addressing an invisible audience and therefore must anticipate the reactions of your readers. This need to gauge their response explains why, in drafting an essay and later in revising it, you need to look at your sentences, paragraphs, and the whole essay from the point of view of the reader.

Audience is one of several important considerations in constructing sentences. Another consideration is the nature of the idea expressed. A short sentence may be the right length for a simple idea not requiring development. A complex idea sometimes requires a longer sentence. Usually these are decisions taken at later stages of revision and editing. In the course of revision, you may decide to lengthen or shorten some of your sentences—adding details or putting them into a separate sentence; for a string of short sentences can be as monotonous and exhausting as a string of loosely connected clauses. The longer the sentence, the greater your concern will be with how well it holds together and presents your ideas clearly without jumping from one to another. Of course, other concerns come into play here. Writing effective sentences requires a continuous adjustment between the form of the sentence and the meaning you want to express.

This chapter discusses various ways of making sentences effective, of choosing one *style* of sentence rather than another. Style involves writing choices open to you—choices in shaping sentences as well as in shaping paragraphs and the whole essay. When we speak of the style of a writer, we are referring to the same phenomenon as in speaking of a golfer's or a batter's style: we are talking about the habitual ways the writer shapes sentences and chooses particular words. We begin with choices in sentence length.

# 19.1 Length

**19.1a Effective Short Sentences.** Short sentences can be effective if used singly or in a short series for contrast with longer sentences:

> A story is not merely an image of life, but of life in motion—specifically, the presentation of individual characters moving through their particular experiences to some end that we may accept as meaningful. And the experience that is characteristically presented in a story is that of facing a problem, a conflict. To put it bluntly: *No conflict, no story.*
> —ROBERT PENN WARREN, "Why Do We Read Fiction?"
> [italics added]

A series of short sentences can be highly dramatic:

> When I was a boy growing up in the city, I was afraid to walk the streets after dark. Then came years in which I was fearless. I was part of the night. It could hide me, change me, free parts of me that didn't come to life while the sun shone. Now, as close to a man as thirty years have teased me, I feel the old fears returning. I listen. I read. I am convinced the night streets are unsafe. Full circle the darkness is inhabited by a bestiary of threatening shapes that daylight only partially dispels. I sleep with a bayonet under my bed.
> —JOHN WIDEMAN, "Fear in the Streets"

**19.1b Ineffective Short Sentences.** Sentences become monotonous when one short idea follows another without connection or transition. Compare the following—the two moderately long sentences of James Thurber to the right and their breakdown to the left into a series of short, disconnected ones:

| | |
|---|---|
| One morning Muggs bit me slightly. He did so more or less in passing. I reached down and grabbed his short stumpy tail. I hoisted him into the air. It was a foolhardy thing to do. I last saw my mother six months ago. She said she didn't know what possessed me. I don't know either. But I was pretty mad. | One morning when Muggs bit me slightly, more or less in passing, I reached down and grabbed his short stumpy tail and hoisted him into the air. It was a foolhardy thing to do and the last time I saw my mother, about six months ago, she said she didn't know what possessed me. I don't know either, except that I was pretty mad.<br>—JAMES THURBER, "The Dog That Bit People" |

**19.1**
**var**

The sequence of short sentences to the left—sometimes described as "primer style"—suggests, in the speech or writing of a grown person, timidity and caution, the fear perhaps of making a mistake in building a longer sentence. In your revising of sentences, primer style can result from breaking a confusing or ineffective long sentence into short component ones, instead of clarifying the long one.

Advertisements use short sentences to catch the attention of the newspaper or magazine reader. An ad for "age-controlling creme" contains these sentences:

> Young skin holds moisture. Young skin is resilient. Young skin renews itself quickly. Young skin looks fresh, feels firm.

A string of sentences of this kind in ordinary prose soon tires the reader. The repetition of the same words is dramatic, but the effect quickly disappears.

**19.1c  Sentence Fragments.**    On occasion the short sentence may take the form of a **fragment**—a phrase or clause detached from a longer sentence for special emphasis. Advertising depends on fragments of this kind, as in an ad for skin lotion:

> A difference you can see. Skin that's been loved by Revenescence. Younger, fresher, more radiant.

As with a string of very short sentences, the dramatic effect achieved through the fragment quickly ends. Writers therefore use fragments sparingly, sometimes in accord with the occasionally fragmented sentences in speech:

> Technology has its own inner dynamic. When it was possible that technology could bring off a moon landing, then it was certain that sooner or later, the landing would be brought off. *However much it cost in human lives, dollars, rubles, social effort.*
> —C. P. Snow, "The Moon Landing" [italics added]

Snow's concluding dependent clause is detached from the preceding sentence that it modifies. By contrast, the following paragraph contains a series of appositives detached from the opening sentence:

> It is the inanimate enemies who have me baffled. *The hundred and one little bits of wood and metal that go to make up the impedimenta of our daily life—the shoes and pins, the picture books and door keys, the bits of fluff and sheets of newspaper—each and every one with just as much vicious ill-will toward me personally as the meanest footpad who roams the streets, each and every one bent on my humiliation and*

**19.1**

**var**

*working together, as on one great team, to bedevil and confuse me and to get me into a neurasthenics' home before I am sixty.* I can't fight these boys. They've got me licked.

—ROBERT BENCHLEY, "The Real Public Enemies"
[italics added]

Benchley could have attached this long appositive to the opening sentence with a colon or dash, but setting the appositive apart heightens the humor. See 21.2 on the weak sentence fragment.

**19.1d Elliptical Sentences.** The following paragraph consists entirely of noun phrases and adjectives—actually shortened or elliptical sentences and not detached phrases or clauses:

> Buff Chandler. A woman before her time. A feminist in pioneer country. Always, above all else, a presence. Fierce, intense, driving. Easily wounded, easily moved to tears, yet resilient, always ready to work the next day. A mover, always driving and pushing. A relentless woman.
>
> —DAVID HALBERSTAM, *The Powers That Be*

**19.1**
**var**

The opening sentences are shortened versions of the following:

> Consider Buff Chandler. She is a woman before her time. She is a feminist in pioneer country. Always, above all else, she is a presence.

Halberstam uses elliptical sentences to produce a dramatic effect and to highlight the qualities of the woman he is describing.

Like fragments and very short sentences, elliptical sentences are rare in formal writing. In informal and general writing, they should be used sparingly if used at all.

**19.1e Long Sentences.** A series of short sentences can be combined to express a complex idea or narrate or describe a connected action. Compare the following:

| *Short Sentences* | *Combined Sentence* |
|---|---|
| Usually, when a lion sees you he skulks away. He bounds off in great, ungainly leaps, in clumsy dodges. He makes a fool of himself because he is frightened. But one may raise his head and look right at you, then turn as this one did. It may walk off without look- | Usually, when a lion sees you, he skulks away or bounds off in great, ungainly leaps, in clumsy dodges, making a fool of himself because he is frightened; but when one raises his head and looks right at you, then turns as this one did, and walks off without |

ing back. You understand at
once why Bushmen believe
the things they do.

even looking back, you understand at once why Bushmen believe the things they
do.
—Elizabeth Marshall Thomas,
*The Harmless People*

The semicolon in the sentence to the right joins the two parts
into a single connected experience or action.

Sometimes a series of related actions may be combined into
a single sentence and contrasted with shorter sentences:

**19.1**
**var**

> One tree in line of fire had 250 bullets in it, another tree
> 110 lead messengers that missed human targets. Farmer Rum-
> mel's cow lane was piled with thirty dead horses. Farmer Rum-
> mel found two cavalrymen who had fought afoot, killed each
> other and fallen with their feet touching, each with a bloody
> saber in his hand. *A Virginian and a 3d Pennsylvania man had*
> *fought on horseback, hacking each other's head and shoulders with*
> *sabers; they clinched and their horses ran out from under them; they*
> *were found with stiff and bloody fingers fastened in each other.* The
> pegleg Confederate General Ewell, struck by a bullet, had chirped
> merrily to General John B. Gordon, "It don't hurt a bit to be
> shot in a wooden leg."
> —Carl Sandburg, "Gettysburg" [italics added]

Modern prose mixes sentences of varying length in this way,
often for contrast. The following is a particularly effective example. The italicized short sentences highlight important ideas
at points of transition:

> Childhood in America 200 years ago began at home; boys
> and girls were born there, most likely delivered by a midwife
> or simply a neighbor woman. *There were virtually no obstetricians.*
> Commonly the infants were delivered in a room specifically set
> aside for the purpose: the "borning room"—much used be-
> cause the children came one after the other and, alas, died far
> more often than is now the case. Historians estimate that year
> in, year out, about a third or more of all children died in in-
> fancy—in typhoid and smallpox epidemics, of diphtheria, dys-
> entery and respiratory ailments. *Measles exacted a frightful toll.*
> *And, of course, parents were helpless to do much except pray and wait.*
> The medical "treatments" of the day were themselves a major
> source of sickness and even death: bloodletting, purging and
> bizarre concoctions.
> —Robert Coles, "Growing Up in America—
> Now and Then" [italics added]

**19.1f  The Question of Length.**  But a question arises: How long can a sentence be? Is there a limit that writers today observe?

The answer is that sentence length varies from one writer and one kind of writing to another. Writers of fiction sometimes produce sentences of extraordinary length, but these are exceptional. The increasing use of short sentences and minimal punctuation—the substitution of periods for semicolons, for example—is influenced by newspapers and magazines and the widespread but mistaken belief that a series of short sentences (like a sequence of short paragraphs) is easier to read.

Yet long sentences have special uses and can be highly effective in describing continuous events or conveying a single unbroken impression:

> If you happen to be in Hoboken at six in the morning, you can stand on a broad wharf made of cobblestone and concrete, part of which is collapsing into the Hudson River, and look across three-quarters of a mile of open water at Manhattan, a blue silhouette against a sickly-pink sky, and see to your right the World Trade Center, then Brooklyn and dimly, the Verrazano Bridge; to your left you can see all the way to the George Washington Bridge.
>
> —"Hoboken Terminal," Talk of the Town, *The New Yorker*, August 22, 1983

**19.1**
**var**

Many sentences build a series of details from a core sentence. This cumulation gives focus to one aspect of an experience or suggests a single moment's viewing, as in this description of caged chimpanzees in a research lab:

> As we approached the nearest cage, its two inmates bared their teeth and with incredible accuracy let fly great sweeping arcs of spittle, fairly drenching the lightweight suit of the facility's director. They then uttered a staccato of short shrieks, which echoed down the corridor to be repeated and amplified by other caged chimps, who had certainly not seen us, until the corridor fairly shook with the screeching and banging and rattling of bars.  —CARL SAGAN, *The Dragons of Eden*

Dividing the sentence into its component ideas would destroy this single focus.

**EXERCISE**

The following groups of sentences are taken from the first drafts of student papers. Suggest ways that each student can improve both the sentences and the unity of the paragraph. Also suggest ways the student might develop or refocus the ideas.

1. The main reason people attend school is to learn. Students come from a variety of different backgrounds. They bring different aptitudes and interests. Some seem to have more intelligence than others. But intelligence is hard to measure. So are aptitude and interest. Standard grading fails to measure any of these and it should.

2. At my high school students take college-level calculus in their senior, or even junior, years. They must earlier have taken algebra, geometry, and precalculus. These courses are available in regular and accelerated courses. Students taking calculus will have different mathematical backgrounds depending on which track they took. Foreign language courses are similar. Some students had the opportunity to learn basic French, Spanish, or Latin in junior high school. These differences in background need to be taken into account in grading.

3. Students work for grades when they see no point to the course itself. The point of the course becomes the grade. A class which many students have to take in high school is algebra. Algebra is a difficult course and requires memorization and practice. These become ends in themselves. The student studies and gets a good grade and immediately forgets the material. Worse than that, the few students who do retain the knowledge can't apply it. They see no use for it. They are given no use for it. It is just a useless class you have to take—that is the attitude of a majority of students. It can be very useful,

but few know that it is. So a contradiction
arises. The student gets the highest grade in the
course he considers the most useless.

4. Some courses like welding and auto repair
are very useful. They teach basic skills that are
easy to measure. There is no studying in an auto
repair class, just hands-on experience and training. The student learns by doing. If the student
cannot master the basic skills, he fails. He is
graded on the quality of his workmanship. Why is
it easier to measure skills in auto repair than
in algebra or Single Living? But then Single Living has nothing to do with skills. Students taking Single Living know why they are there--to get
an "A" or "B."

**19.2** sub

## 19.2 Subordination and Coordination

**19.2a Subordination.** Subordination is essential in giving
ideas and details focus in sentences. Compare the following:

| | |
|---|---|
| We still take it for granted that a choice between the arts and the sciences is inevitable. A young person inevitably reaches the age when he has to choose between them. He often chooses the arts because he feels that here is humanity, freedom, choice. | By the time a young person has reached the age when he has to choose (we still take it for granted that a choice is inevitable) between the arts and the sciences, he often chooses the arts because he feels that here is humanity, freedom, choice. |
| | —DORIS LESSING, Preface to *The Golden Notebook* |

The sentence to the right—Lessing's original sentence—contains
three kinds of subordination.

(1) *An introductory dependent or subordinate clause* reduced from
the second sentence to the left:

| | |
|---|---|
| A young person inevitably reaches the age | By the time a young person has reached the age |

(2) *A parenthesis*—an embedding of the first sentence to the
left:

> We still take it for granted          (we still take it for granted
>     that a choice is inevitable.          that a choice is inevitable)

(3) *A concluding dependent or subordinate clause* that states the key idea of the sentence:

> because he feels that there is humanity, freedom, choice

Lessing's original sentence shows that a subordinate clause need not contain an idea of lesser importance than the idea of the main clause. In completing the main clause, the subordinate clause states why the young person chooses the arts—the key idea of the sentence. Its end position and the emphatic series give the clause unusual weight. Lessing fits the various ideas into a single economical, well-organized sentence. See 26.2 on faulty subordination in sentences.

**19.2**
**sub**

**19.2b Coordination.**    Coordination is one way of giving equal weight to ideas. Compare the following sentence to the right—Doris Lessing's original statement—and the breakdown of the sentence to the left:

> He does not know that he is already moulded by a system. He does not know that the choice itself is the result of a false dichotomy rooted in the heart of our culture.

> He does not know that he is already moulded by a system: he does not know that the choice itself is the result of a false dichotomy rooted in the heart of our culture.
> —DORIS LESSING, Preface to
>     *The Golden Notebook*

The colon in Lessing's sentence tells the reader that the second clause (*he does not know . . .*) is an explanation of the first. The repetition of *he does not know* makes the sentence dramatic.

**19.2c Climax.**    A series of coordinate clauses can build to a climax also, as in the second sentence of the following passage:

> Clambering onward, we have slowly made our way out of a maze of isolated peaks into the level plains of science. Here, one step seems definitely to succeed another, the universe appears to take on an imposed order, and the illusions through which mankind has painfully made its way for many centuries have given place to the enormous vistas of past and future time.
> —LOREN EISELEY, *The Unexpected Universe*

The coordinated dependent clauses in the following sentence do the same:

But it occurred to me one day as I saw barnacles in broad white bands and masses spread across the rocks *that they were not only arrested, fixed creatures of their appropriate zones between the tides,* but *that they were an expression like the waves, spilled and breaking along the shore.*

> —JOHN HAY, "The Sea of Survival" [italics added]

See 19.3b for further discussion of climax.

### EXERCISES

1. Combine the following short sentences into longer sentences, using subordination and coordination to emphasize key ideas. William Faulkner is the author of the sentences from which these shorter ones are drawn:
   a. The cotton-house is of rough logs. The chinking between them has long fallen.
   b. Tull's wagon stands beside the spring. The wagon is hitched to the rail. The reins are wrapped about the seat stanchion.
   c. He is standing in a litter of chips. He is fitting two of the boards together.
   d. He holds the two planks on the trestle. The planks fit along the edges. He has fitted them in a quarter of the finished box.

**19.2**
**sub**

2. Add phrases or clauses or both to expand the following core sentences:

   *Core Sentence*
   They took shelter

   *Expanded Sentence*
   Hearing the warning siren, they took shelter in the basement, where they had stocked food and water for such an emergency.

   a. They waited more than an hour
   b. The wind shook the house
   c. They knew the storm would not only be a violent one
   d. They heard strange noises
   e. The exam proved unexpectedly grueling
   f. She saw a crash coming
   g. Few experiences are as exhilarating as
   h. The road took an unexpected turn
   i. The passengers climbed out of the bus
   j. The view startled them

## 19.3   Loose and Periodic Sentences

Most of the sentences you speak and write carry different points of emphasis or natural stress. The most prominent occur at the beginning and end of the sentence:

*Where* are you going?
You are going *where*?

These spoken stresses occur naturally as you speak. In writing, you can shape your sentences to take advantage of these stresses.

**19.3a Loose Sentences.   Loose sentences** begin with the core idea and add a series of explanatory or amplifying details or afterthoughts. The beginning of the sentence will seem emphatic to the reader if it contains the important idea, with a series of afterthoughts or qualifications trailing at the end:

> At walking speeds even the nearsighted can see trees, shrubbery, leaves and grass, the surfaces of rocks and stones, grains of sand, ants, beetles, caterpillars, even gnats, flies and mosquitoes, *to say nothing of birds and other wildlife.* Not only is near vision blurred by the speed of the automobile but one's relationship to the countryside is vastly altered. I realized this once while riding my horse from Santa Fe, New Mexico, to the Indian reservations in northern Arizona. My route took me north of Mt. Taylor, *which I knew well because I had passed its southern edge fifty times on the highway from Albuquerque to Gallup.*
> —EDWARD HALL, *The Hidden Dimension* [italics added].

The fact that a sentence element is subordinate does not mean it contains a less important idea always. The modifiers may contain ideas as important as the idea of the main clause:

> He was a great thundering paradox of a man, noble and ignoble, inspiring and outrageous, arrogant and shy, the best of men and the worst of men, the most protean, most ridiculous, and most sublime.
> —WILLIAM MANCHESTER, *American Caesar*
> [describing General Douglas MacArthur]

The important idea that opens the sentence (*a great thundering paradox of a man*) and the three important adjective phrases that conclude it (*most protean, most ridiculous, and most sublime*) receive equal emphasis even though these trailing phrases are grammatically subordinate.

The same multiple emphasis occurs in sentences that end with appositives, particularly those occurring in a series:

**19.3**
**var**

For Lardner is above all the historian of frustration—*of courtships that go on the rocks or, what is worse, end in marriage; of honeymoons that fizzle out, of marriages that turn sour; of plays that flop, prize fights that are fixed, games that blow up; of beauty that is skin deep, affection that is phony, talent that is meretricious.*
—HENRY STEELE COMMAGER, *The American Mind* [describing
the American writer Ring Lardner; italics added]

The long, tightly constructed string of appositives builds in importance.

**19.3b Periodic Sentences.** **Periodic sentences** build through modifying phrases or clauses to the main idea. The full sense is not complete until the period:

While I was not about to dispose of my glasses (which were crucial to any slim hope of success I might have had) I did in fact show up for the first junior varsity practice that year.
—ANDREW WARD, "Offsides"

The tragic, the trivial, the violent, the easily grasped and understood—these were and continue to be the staples of broadcasting, as they are in all of the mass media.
—ROBERT LEWIS SHAYON, *The Crowd-Catchers*

Plunging through high seas and what Churchill called "grey storms"—as usual he was ill—the *Dunotter Castle* lurched toward the Canary Islands.   —WILLIAM MANCHESTER, *The Last Lion*

These sentences show that periodic sentences vary in the degree of suspense or climax they generate. The sentence may build slowly to a main clause that contains an idea of unusual importance or weight:

The boy who was beaten at school, who went too much to church, who carried the fear of poverty all his life, but who nevertheless was filled with the memories of country pleasures; the young bank clerk who worked such long hours for so little money, but who danced, sang, played, flirted—this naturally vigorous, sensuous being was killed in 1914, 1915, 1916.
—DORIS LESSING, "My Father"

Notice the progression from boy to clerk to father—all contained in the concluding phrase *this naturally vigorous, sensuous being*. Here is another sentence that repeats the entire opening main clause:

Surely it is not surprising—with all the new anxieties people are subject to; with science's new capacities for annihilation; with the unquietness of the present and the terrors of the fu-

**19.3**
**var**

ture; the aggressions men exhibit and the guilt they conceal—
*surely it is not surprising* that in view of all this, people should so
much desire these courage-givers and fear-relaxers, these rain
makers and sun lamps of the psyche and the ego.
           —LOUIS KRONENBERGER, "Unbrave New World"
                                       [italics added]

In a sentence of this length, with the predicate delayed so long,
we need a reminder of the subject.

Many periodic sentences in ordinary exposition are less dramatic than Lessing's or Kronenberger's:

> If people are to be brought together again, given a chance to
> get acquainted with each other and involved in nature, some
> fundamental solutions must be found to the problems posed
> by the automobile.    —EDWARD HALL, *The Hidden Dimension*

**19.3**
**var**

> When we set about comparing moralities from culture to cul-
> ture, assessing variations and seeking the common core, we may
> begin by considering how to separate the native's moral values
> from his other values.    —W. V. QUINE, *Theories and Things*

The following paragraph contains periodic sentences of
varying construction:

> Men have argued about the *Iliad* for so long and raised so
> many side issues that it is easy for a critic to forget that it is
> formally a tragedy, saturated with a tragic sense of life and
> constructed with the inevitability of the tragedies of Orestes or
> Macbeth. It is a double tragedy—of Achilles and the Greeks,
> and of Hector and the Trojans, each reinforcing the other. To
> modern taste, the heroes are not the Greeks, who are portrayed
> as quarreling members of a warrior band, but the Trojans, men
> of family united in the community of the city-state.
>            —KENNETH REXROTH, "The Iliad"

Sentences like Rexroth's unfold the idea with gradually building
emphasis.

### EXERCISE

Rewrite the loose sentences as periodic sentences, and rewrite
the periodic sentences as loose ones. You may need to reorder
sentence elements in rewriting them:

> 1. Each human being is a superbly constructed,
> astonishingly compact, self-ambulatory computer—ca-
> pable on occasion of independent decision making and
> real control of his or her environment.
>            —CARL SAGAN, *Broca's Brain*

2. In thinking about this next generation of machine intelligence, it is important to distinguish between self-controlled and remotely controlled robots.
—CARL SAGAN, *Broca's Brain*

3. Starting from the greatest city in the world, almost invisible on a fair-sized map of the continent, one must push the wheels for three quarters of a day before reaching the midland seas that are the country's crown.
—JACQUES BARZUN, "Innocents at Home"

4. A change of thirty degrees between sunup and sundown, repeated without warning of season fifty times a year; highs of 90° to 120° in summer, with natural steam provided free; lows of zero and less in winter, with snowfalls and blizzards and ice-storms—none of these can be called temperate except in the sense of tempering.
—JACQUES BARZUN, "Innocents at Home"

**19.3**
**var**

5. In his teens George Burns started the Pee Wee Quartette with three other Jewish boys, singing in back yards and saloons and afterward passing the hat.
—IRVING HOWE, *World of Our Fathers*

6. Granted that work (and especially paperwork) is thus elastic in its demands on time, it is manifest that there need be little or no relationship between the work to be done and the size of the staff to which it may be assigned. —C. NORTHCOTE PARKINSON, *Parkinson's Law*

7. As our century progresses, as our society and the world become more complex, as the pace of social change accelerates, higher education that is not eminently critical will be increasingly useless.
—KENNETH KENISTON, *Youth and Dissent*

8. Of the horse Indians, the Kiowas had the most horses per person and were foremost in possessing the character traits associated with the horse—bravery, predatism, and audacity.
—MILDRED P. MAYHALL, *The Kiowas*

9. Notable also was the specialization in the use of horses—reserving certain fleet and picked horses for war and buffalo-hunting, never using them as burden bearers or draggers of travois.
—MILDRED P. MAYHALL, *The Kiowas*

10. Had the Plains Indians not used the horse, they might have been quietly pacified, perhaps destroyed, by the encroaching white man.
—MILDRED P. MAYHALL, *The Kiowas*

## 19.4   Inversion

You may on occasion **invert** or reverse normal word order for special emphasis:

These facts I know to be true.

Within a few weeks I was classifying all the boys in the place in the inverse order of their diligence and prowess, and that classification, as I have intimated, I adhere to at the present moment.                                                              —H. L. Mencken, *Heathen Days*

*Never before, it may be said, was the "common man" so free of obligation to serve the interests of the privileged.* He gets a larger share than ever before of the wealth which his labors create, and the right to participate in the government of his nation by the casting of a ballot was never before so nearly universal and so real.
—Joseph Wood Krutch, *Human Nature and the Human Condition* [italics added]

**19.4**
**var**

Far less than in many other nations nominally democratic is there any elite which attempts to impose upon him its tastes in art, literature, or entertainment.
—Joseph Wood Krutch, *Human Nature and the Human Condition*

These are typical inversions in ordinary prose. Overused, sentence inversion can produce a sentence like the following:

*Stilted*
Ordered by the judge to approach the bar, their hands in cuffs, their heads bent down, were the men who had been arrested the night before.

*Improved*
Their hands in cuffs, their heads bent down, the men arrested the night before were ordered by the judge to approach the bar.

## 19.5   Varying Sentence Openings

Repeating the same word at the beginning of successive sentences is a valuable way of achieving emphasis and coherence in a paragraph. In the following, Shirley Jackson humorously describes a driving lesson with Eric, an eighteen-year-old driving instructor:

*Laurie and Jannie and my husband holding the baby* stood on the front porch cheering and waving as I rode off with Eric, crushed into a corner of the seat to avoid touching any of the dual controls, and desperately afraid that if I did the car would go out of control and rocket madly off the road, no doubt killing other innocent people and very probably ending my driving lessons. *Laurie and Jannie and my husband holding the baby* were again on the front porch cheering, two hours later, when I came back with Eric, dismayed and bewildered and not prepared to take levelly any childish prattle about how we would drive around when we had a car.

—SHIRLEY JACKSON, *Life Among the Savages* [italics added]

However, excessive repetition can make the paragraph monotonous:

> Few people know how to listen to music. They like to hear music playing in the background as they work. They do not have the patience to listen to music without doing something else. They do not take the time to learn about music. They know only that music is loud or soft, fast or slow.

**19.5**
**var**

One solution is to open some of the sentences with modifying or transitional phrases:

> *In America today*, few people know how to listen to music. *At work* they like to hear music playing in the background. *They do not have the patience* to listen to music without doing something else. *Indeed*, most do not take the time to learn about music. *They know* only that music is loud or soft, fast or slow.

The last two sentences can be combined, giving the paragraph even more variety.

> Knowing only that music is loud or soft, fast or slow, most do not take the time to learn about music.

Following is a list of possible sentence openers:

1. Subject and verb of the main clause:

> *Few people know* how to listen to music.

2. A prepositional phrase:

> *At work* they like to hear music playing in the background.

3. A transitional adverb:

> *Indeed*, most do not take the time to learn about music.

4. A participial phrase:

> *Knowing only that music is loud or soft*, fast or slow . . .

5. A dependent clause:

*Because they know only that music is loud or soft,* fast or slow . . .

6. An infinitive phrase:

*To listen to music well,* people must know something about its characteristics.

7. An absolute phrase:

*To be sure,* listening to music requires concentration.

**EXERCISE**

Rewrite the following paragraphs to vary the openings of the sentences, adding words, phrases, and clauses. Combine sentences to improve concision and focus:

**19.5**
**var**

a. We know little about the physical world around us. We know little about the things that grow near our houses and how they form what scientists call an "ecosystem." We know little about how people can upset this ecosystem. People used to call this ecosystem the "balance of nature." People talk about flooding and other "natural" disasters. They do not realize that flooding and other "natural" disasters often occur when the ecosystem is upset. We know little about the physical world and how to prevent ecological disasters that are caused by people.

b. Writing is a skill that requires practice. Playing a musical instrument comes no more naturally than writing. Practice is essential. Practice is essential, too, in dancing. Writing calls for a much different kind of practice. The words put on paper must have meaning. The words must form a meaningful whole. The sounds produced in practicing a musical instrument need not form a meaningful whole. Dance steps need not either.

## Checklist for Sentence Variety

**19.1a**    Short sentences can effectively contrast with longer ones:

When I was a boy growing up in the city, I was afraid to walk the streets after dark. Then came years in which I was fearless. I was part of the night.    —JOHN WIDEMAN

**19.1b**    A long series of unvaried short sentences can be monotonous.

**19.1c**   Sentence fragments—detached phrases or clauses—should be used sparingly for special emphasis:

> When it was possible that technology could bring off a moon landing, then it was certain that sooner or later, the landing would be brought off. However much it cost in human lives, dollars, rubles, social effort.                    —C. P. SNOW

**19.1d**   Elliptical sentences should also be used sparingly for special emphasis or dramatic effect:

> Buff Chandler. A woman before her time. A feminist in pioneer country. Always, above all else, she is a presence.
> —DAVID HALBERSTAM

**19.1e**   Combine short sentences to express a complex idea or describe a connected action.

**19.2a**   Subordination is essential in giving ideas and details focus:

> By the time a young person has reached the age when he has to choose (we still take it for granted that a choice is inevitable) between the arts and the sciences, he often chooses the arts because he feels that here is humanity, freedom, choice.
> —DORIS LESSING

**19.2b**   Coordination is one way to give equal weight to ideas:

> He does not know that he is already moulded by a system: he does not know that the choice itself is the result of a false dichotomy rooted in the heart of our culture.   —DORIS LESSING

**19.2c**   A series of coordinated phrases or clauses can build to a climax:

> But it occurred to me one day as I saw barnacles in broad white bands and masses spread across the rocks that they were not only arrested, fixed creatures of their appropriate zones between the tides, but that they were an expression like the waves, spilled and breaking along the shore.          —JOHN HAY

**19.3a**   Loose sentences open with the main idea and add details or afterthoughts:

> My route took me north of Mt. Taylor, which I knew well because I had passed its southern edge fifty times on the highway from Albuquerque to Gallup.          —EDWARD HALL

**19.3b**   Periodic sentences build to the main clause or core idea:

> Plunging through high seas and what Churchill called "grey storms"—as usual he was ill—the *Dunotter Castle* lurched toward the Canary Islands.            —WILLIAM MANCHESTER

**19.4**   Invert or reverse normal word order only for special emphasis:

> Never before, it may be said, was the "common man" so free of obligation to serve the interests of the privileged.
>                                      —JOSEPH WOOD KRUTCH

**19.5**   Vary the opening of your sentences to avoid monotony.

# Parallelism, Balance, Antithesis

## 20.1 Parallelism

**20.1a Parallel Words, Phrases, and Clauses.** Words, phrases, and clauses that perform the same function in the sentence can take the same grammatical form:

| | | | |
|---|---|---|---|
| write | to write | writing | while writing |
| revise | to revise | revising | while revising |
| edit | to edit | editing | while editing |

Here are sentences containing these forms:

*Parallel Subjects*
*Writing, revising,* and *editing* are separate activities.

*Parallel Predicates*
I usually *write a first draft, revise it,* and then *edit it.*

*Parallel Complements*
To produce a good paper, I have *to write a first draft, to revise it a day or two later,* and when I am satisfied with the draft *to edit it.*

*Parallel Modifiers*
I continually make changes in content and sentence structure *while writing the first draft, while revising this draft or a later one,* and *while editing the final draft.*

**Parallelism** is a natural process in speaking and writing sentences. Once you introduce a pattern of words, phrases, and clauses having the same function and importance in the sentence, you continue the pattern using the same grammatical forms. You are unlikely to break the pattern in the following ways:

I usually write a first draft, revising it, *and then edit it.*

I usually write a first draft, revise it, *then editing it.*

Writing, revising, and *to edit* are separate activities.

*To write,* revising, and editing are separate activities.

However, the parallelism need not always be exact. Correlative terms often are not exactly parallel.

**20.1b Correlatives.**   The English sentence favors parallelism after **correlative** terms, those terms that occur in pairs. The following words occur in pairs:

| | | |
|---|---|---|
| either/or | not only/but also | not so much/as |
| neither/nor | whether/or | both/and |

For the sentence to be clear or avoid sounding awkward, the words following each correlative usually must be parallel:

We are either *driving to Cleveland* this weekend or *driving to Chicago*—we haven't decided.

Either *we are going to hike in the park* or *we are going to visit the art museum.*

We haven't decided whether *to hike* or *to visit the museum.*

Hiking is not only *good exercise* but also *great fun.*

The following sentence sounds awkward because the grammatical forms—the infinitive and the gerund—are not the same:

We are going either *to hike* or *swimming.*

Notice that the sentence remains parallel even if you shorten one of the parallel elements:

We are going *to hike* or *visit the museum.*

The grammatical forms—the marked infinitives *to hike* and [*to*] *visit*—here are the same.

**20.1c  Uses of Parallelism.**   Parallelism is an important way to make sentences concise and give the same emphasis to ideas and details:

It was when I found out I had to talk *that school became a misery, that the silence became a misery.*
—MAXINE HONG KINGSTON, *The Woman Warrior* [italics added]

There we chanted together, voices rising and falling, loud and soft, *some boys shouting, everybody reading together, reciting together* and not alone with one voice.
—MAXINE HONG KINGSTON, *The Woman Warrior* [italics added]

Most commonly we come to books with blurred and divided minds, asking *of fiction that it shall be true, of poetry that it shall be false, of biography that it shall be flattering, of history that it shall enforce our own prejudices.*
　　—VIRGINIA WOOLF, "How Should One Read a Book?"
　　　　　　　　　　　　　　　　　　　　　　[italics added]

Parallelism is also an important means of building many related ideas into a single sentence. Notice how the writer of the following sentence varies a long series of parallel phrases without losing the parallelism.

Apart from ethnic differences, the very nature of migrancy makes it possible to isolate certain values and social characteristics commonly found among migrants: a spirit of resignation; a sense of being trapped; an astonishing lack of bitterness; a fierce family loyalty; a buoyant, often subtle wit; a tendency to spend money, when they have it, to meet not only immediate needs but immediate desires; a longing to be somebody, manifested sometimes as a blatant groping for status, more often as a craving for recognition as a human being; a longing for a better life for their children; a quick and generous sympathy for neighbors in trouble; a high incidence of stamina and courage. 　　　　　　　—LOUISA R. SHOTWELL, *The Harvesters*

**20.1**

**//**

In building paragraphs, you can emphasize ideas and details of the same importance throughout by making parts of your sentences parallel. Eudora Welty does so in these opening sentences of a paragraph describing a Mississippi town:

Today Rodney's Landing wears the cloak of vegetation which has caught up this whole land *for the third time, or the fourth, or the hundredth. There is something Gothic* about the vines, in their structure in the trees—*there are arches*, flying buttresses, towers of vines, with trumpet flowers swinging in them for bells and staining their walls. *And there is something of a warmer grandeur* in their very abundance—*stairways and terraces and whole hanging gardens* of green and flowering vines, with a Babylonian babel of hundreds of creature voices that make up the silence of Rodney's Landing.
　　—EUDORA WELTY, *The Eye of the Story* [italics added]

See 25.2 on faulty parallelism.

**EXERCISE**

**1.** Complete the sentence by creating a pattern with the italicized words.

*Example*
The dog *raced out of the house*, leaped into the parked car, and jumped into the back seat where the children sat.

a. He was tired of *mowing the lawn*
b. We need to *trim our spending*
c. *Either* we go to the movies
d. We *either* go to the movies
e. We are going *either* to the movies
f. We are *not only* going to the movies
g. *Not only* are we going to the movies
h. *Whether* we go to the movies
i. She is *both* president of the club
j. We *neither* elected him vice-president

## 20.2   Balance and Antithesis

**20.2a Sentence Balance.**   In a **balanced sentence**, strict parallelism extends to phrases and clauses throughout. Here is a highly balanced sentence favored by many writers in the past and favored by some writers today:

> When young people are as free to walk out of a classroom where they are bored by a dull teacher as grown-up people are to walk out of a theater where they are bored by a dull playwright, the schools will be far more crowded than the theaters, and the teachers far more popular than the actors.
> —GEORGE BERNARD SHAW, *Sham Education*

Here is a rearrangement of the sentence to show this strict parallelism of phrases and clauses:

> When young people are as free
> as grown-up people are [as free]

> to walk out of a classroom
> to walk out of a theater

> where they are bored by a dull teacher
> where they are bored by a dull playwright

> the schools will be far more crowded than the theaters
> the teachers [will be] far more popular than the actors.

**20.2b Uses of Sentence Balance.**   Today this kind of balanced sentence is exceptional in general writing; it is used chiefly in formal writing—for example, in legal documents, treatises, and technical discussions addressed to a professional audience.

One of the famous uses of sentence balance occurs in President John F. Kennedy's inaugural address:

> We observe today not a victory of party but a celebration of freedom—symbolizing an end as well as a beginning—signifying renewal as well as change. For I have sworn before you and Almighty God the same solemn oath our forebears prescribed nearly a century and three quarters ago.
>
> The world is very different now. For man holds in his mortal hands the power to abolish all forms of human poverty and all forms of human life. And yet the same revolutionary beliefs for which our forebears fought are still at issue around the globe—the belief that the rights of man come not from the generosity of the state but from the hand of God.
>
> We dare not forget today that we are the heirs of that first revolution. Let the word go forth from this time and place, to friend and foe alike, that the torch has been passed to a new generation of Americans—born in this century, tempered by war, disciplined by a hard and bitter peace, proud of our ancient heritage—and unwilling to witness or permit the slow undoing of those human rights to which this Nation has always been committed, and to which we are committed today at home and around the world.

Balanced sentences like President Kennedy's can convey strong emotion. The balancing also heightens the importance of the ideas of the sentence by giving each component idea the same, unusually heavy stress. This heavy stress is perhaps the reason sentence balance is rare in everyday prose writing.

**20.2c Antithesis.** **Antithesis** is the balancing of *contrasting* phrases and clauses. Like the balance of similar phrases and clauses just discussed, it can be carried through a series of sentences, as in this passage from Martin Luther King, Jr.'s, 1963 letter written from the Birmingham, Alabama, jail and addressed to clergymen of the city:

> How does one determine whether a law is just or unjust? A just law is a man-made code that squares with the moral law or the law of God. An unjust law is a code that is out of harmony with the moral law. To put it in the terms of St. Thomas Aquinas: An unjust law is a human law that is not rooted in eternal law and natural law. Any law that uplifts human personality is just. Any law that degrades human personality is unjust. All segregation statutes are unjust because segregation distorts the soul and damages the personality. It gives the segregator a false sense of superiority and the segregated a false sense of inferiority.

**20.2**
**//**

**20.2d  Uses of Antithesis.**   This exact balance of contrasting or antithetical phrases, carried throughout several sentences or a paragraph, is exceptional, too, in ordinary prose. But we do find a modern use of antithesis in short pointed contrasts like the following:

> Radicalism is a term the meaning of which everybody thinks he knows, and the definition of which nobody can give.
> —HOWARD MUMFORD JONES, *O Strange New World*

> The American's attitude toward culture was at once suspicious and indulgent. Where it interfered with more important activities, he distrusted it; where it was the recreation of his leisure hours or of his womenfolk, he tolerated it. For the most part, he required that culture serve some useful purpose.
> —HENRY STEELE COMMAGER, *The American Mind*
> [describing the nineteenth-century American]

**20.2**

**//**

Where extended antithesis does occur, it tends to be highly dramatic. Like sentence balance, it can be a powerful device if used sparingly.

**EXERCISES**

1. Identify the balance and antithesis used to highlight ideas in the following sentences. Try rewriting a few of the sentences to loosen the balance or antithesis, and be ready to discuss what you gain or lose in your revisions:

   a. Shallow understanding from people of good will is more frustrating than absolute misunderstanding from people of ill will. Lukewarm acceptance is much more bewildering than outright rejection.
   —MARTIN LUTHER KING, JR., *Letter from Birmingham Jail*

   b. Nearly every advance of science has two faces. One smiles on us and lifts the aspirations of man; the other scowls sternly on all future hopes.
   —WALTER ORR ROBERTS, "Science: A Wellspring of Our Discontent"

   c. Everything comes over the rocks to seaward. Wood is riven into splinters; the bones of seamen and of sea lions are pounded equally into white and shining sand.
   —LOREN EISELEY, *One Night's Dying*

   d. All critical public expression—true or untrue, extravagant or relatively restrained—is packed into the same

crate and labeled "Dangerous: Rhetoric. Do Not Open."
—MEG GREENFIELD, "In Defense of Rhetoric,"
*Newsweek*, July 9, 1984

e. Their leaves departed, trees in winter stand naked
to our gaze, their structure laid bare.
—ALLEN LACY, "The Grandeur of Trees in Winter,"
*The Wall Street Journal*, February 12, 1982

f. The young are developing superior powers for
sharing their attention. Many youngsters watch one game
on television while listening to another over the radio
through transistor headphones. Brokers can watch the
ticker while talking over the telephone, most adults can
confer while eating lunch, and mothers learn to mend
while keeping watch on a playground bully.
—CAROLINE BIRD, *The Crowding Syndrome*

g. Naked I came into the world, naked I shall go
out of it! And a very good thing too, for it reminds me
that I am naked under my shirt, whatever its color.
—E. M. FORSTER, "Two Cheers for Democracy"

h. We see him on horseback, a sea of cattle around
him, but he has paused in the life of a hero to roll, with
the skill of a magician, using no more than the hands
God gave him, an immortal cigarette. The Bull Durham
pouch dangles at his chin, the noose between his chapped
lips.
—WRIGHT MORRIS, *A Bill of Rites, A Bill of Wrongs,
A Bill of Goods* [describing the American cowboy]

i. He who has nothing to assert has no style and can
have none: he who has something to assert will go as far
in power of style as its momentousness and his conviction will carry him.
—GEORGE BERNARD SHAW, *Man and Superman*

j. Where necessity ends curiosity begins, and no
sooner are we supplied with everything that nature can
demand, than we sit down to contrive artificial appetites.
—SAMUEL JOHNSON, "On Idle Curiosity"

**2.** Identify the clauses and phrases balanced in the following
passage:

He who lets the world, or his own portion of it, choose
his plan of life for him has no need of any other faculty
than the ape-like one of imitation. He who chooses his
plan for himself employs all his faculties. He must use

**20.2**
*//*

observation to see, reasoning and judgment to foresee, activity to gather materials for decision, discrimination to decide, and when he has decided, firmness and self-control to hold his deliberate decision.

—JOHN STUART MILL, *On Liberty*

**3.** Rewrite this passage in your own words, giving it a conversational tone. Be ready to discuss how your rewriting is different from Mill's.

## Checklist for Parallelism, Balance, Antithesis

**20.1a**   Words, phrases, and clauses that perform the same function in the sentence can take the same grammatical form:

Writing, revising, and editing are separate activities.

**20.2**

**//**

**20.1b**   Parallel words, phrases, and clauses follow correlative terms:

We are either driving to Cleveland this weekend or driving to Chicago.

**20.1c**   Parallelism is one important way to make sentences concise and give equal emphasis to ideas of the same importance:

It was when I found out I had to talk that school became a misery, that the silence became a misery.

—MAXINE HONG KINGSTON

**20.2a**   Sentence balance gives equal emphasis to similar ideas of the same weight in the sentence:

For man holds in his mortal hands the power to abolish all forms of human poverty and all forms of human life.

—PRESIDENT JOHN F. KENNEDY

**20.2c**   Antithesis gives equal emphasis to contrasting ideas of the same weight:

We observe today not a victory of party but a celebration of freedom—symbolizing an end as well as a beginning—signifying renewal as well as change. —PRESIDENT JOHN F. KENNEDY

# Correcting Sentences

# Sentence Fragments

This chapter and those following discuss common faults in writing, beginning with the sentence fragment. Other topics include fused sentences, misplaced and dangling modifiers, split infinitives, shifts in person and tense, and excessive subordination or overloading the sentence with too many modifiers. Since so many sentence faults carry habits of speech into writing, this chapter begins with this important consideration.

## **21.1** Writing and Speech

Fragments, comma splices (see 11.6g), and fused sentences are faults in writing because they impede communication. But they are not always faults in speech.

Here is a statement from an interview with Sam Crawford, a baseball player in the major leagues between 1899 and 1917:

> Yeah, I'm sort of hard to find. Still bounce around a lot, you know. Always on the move. Probably a hangover from all those years in baseball—Boston today, Detroit tomorrow, never long in one place. I do have a house down in Hollywood, but I can't take that town. Too much smog. Too many cars, all fouling up the air. Can hardly breathe down there. Too many people, too. Have to stand in line everywhere you go. Can't even get a loaf of bread without standing in line.
> —LAWRENCE S. RITTER, *The Glory of Their Times*

Crawford's clipping or fragmenting of his sentences to single out or stress each idea is a common feature of informal speech. Sections 19.1c and 19.1d discuss fragmented and elliptical sentences in writing.

The following transcribed statement of a racing jockey illustrates another speech pattern—the splicing of ideas so they follow in rapid succession:

If a jockey's in trouble and he hollers for help, that other rider has to do everything in his power to help—whether it's gonna cost him the race or not. One possibility: there's horses all around him, he's in the middle, he can't control his horse. So he's gonna run into another horse, he' gonna clip the other horse's heels. If he does this, he's gonna fall, and the people behind him are gonna fall over him. That's what happened today.                                        —STUDS TERKEL, *Working*

The jockey's spliced sentences give us a sense of the action on the race course.

The pauses and halting stops—called *junctures*—that punctuate spoken statements are features of both statements. The speech of the baseball player and the jockey is vital, spontaneous, and highly expressive. Their formal speech and writing would be tighter than informal statements such as these.

To be vital and expressive, written sentences must not depart too widely from the rhythms of speech. At the same time, these rhythms and speech habits sometimes create confusion and momentarily interrupt the flow of ideas in written English. Thus, when they occur in written English, we call them *fragments* or *fused sentences* or *comma splices* to call attention to these problems.

**21.2**
**frag**

**EXERCISES**

1. Rewrite the interview statements of Sam Crawford, turning the shortened or clipped sentences and the phrases into complete sentences. Be ready to discuss what is gained or lost in your rewriting.
2. Rewrite the statement of the racing jockey, breaking it into shorter, complete sentences. Again, be ready to discuss what is gained or lost in your rewriting.

# 21.2  Fragments

**21.2a  A Test for Fragments.**   The **sentence fragment** is a detached phrase or clause or some other part of the sentence that ordinarily does not stand alone. Occasionally writers use detached phrases and appositives to give ideas special emphasis (see 19.1c). Detached clauses and absolute phrases, however, seldom stand alone because they usually lack clear and immediate reference. It is important, then, to distinguish the many kinds of fragments and know how to join these to core sentences.

The following sentence contains a core or main sentence, a modifier, and an appositive:

Walking down the street, the man waved at the car—a police cruiser that had turned the corner.

Here is the core or main sentence:

the man waved at the car

Here is the modifier:

walking down the street

And here is the appositive:

a police cruiser that had turned the corner

The appositive is itself modified:

a police cruiser        that had turned the corner

The main sentence makes the assertion that the man waved at a car. By contrast, the appositive

a police cruiser that had turned the corner

makes no assertion: the appositive merely names a thing and the action performed.

If in doubt whether any part of this appositive is a complete sentence, ask yourself questions like the following:

What is the cruiser that makes the turn doing?

Another test of the sentence fragment is to speak the sentence. Speaking the following usually tells you they are incomplete:

walking down the street
a police cruiser
a police cruiser that had turned the corner

You do not lower the pitch of your voice to mark the end of a sentence. Notice that the pitch of your voice drops in speaking the following complete sentence:

The man waved at the car.

But your voice does not drop if you intend to continue the sentence.

With the main sentence, you raise the pitch lightly to signal the subject or the verb, depending on which word you want to stress:

The *man* waved at the car.
The man *waved* at the car.

**21.2**
**frag**

With fragments you frequently stress the first word, as in these examples from the transcribed statement of the baseball player:

> *still* bounce around a lot, you know
> *always* on the move
> *probably* a hangover from all those years in baseball
> *too* much smog

Here, then, is an important test of sentence fragments: they sometimes begin with a word pronounced at a higher than ordinary pitch.

**21.2b  Detached Subjects and Predicates.**  Fragments may take the form of detached subjects or predicates. Here are completions of the sentences spoken by the baseball player quoted in 21.1a:

> Too many cars, all fouling up the air, [are on the street]. [*detached subject*]
> [There are] too many people, too. [*detached subject*]
> [I] can hardly breathe down there. [*detached predicate*]
> [Hollywood has] too much smog. [*detached object*]

Though these detached parts of the sentence may be clear when spoken, they can confuse the reader when written.

**21.2c  The Detached Phrase.**  Many fragments take the form of detached phrases like the following:

> a police cruiser
> walking down the street
> over the bridge
> to explain what happened

These phrases are easily attached to a main sentence:

> Walking down the street, we saw the police cruiser.
> The police cruiser drove slowly over the bridge.
> She refused to explain what happened.

Longer phrases are sometimes harder to detect:

> Walking down the street toward Main Street, where a parade of war veterans, National Guard units, and the high school band would march at six o'clock . . .

This long phrase contains an embedded clause that completes or modifies the main sentence:

> where a parade of war veterans, National Guard units, and the high school band would march at six o'clock . . .

**21.2**
**frag**

The embedded clause perhaps mistakenly suggests to the writer that the sentence is complete.

**21.2d The Detached Clause.** Fragments may take the form of dependent clauses like the following:

> that had turned the corner
> because the car was speeding
> whenever you want
> since you went away

Dependent clauses, too, are easily attached to a word or phrase in the main sentence:

> The car that had turned the corner began to speed.
> I waved at the car that had turned the corner.
> The cruiser turned on its siren because the car was speeding.
> Because the car was speeding, the cruiser forced it to stop.
> Leave whenever you want.
> The neighborhood has changed since you went away.

**21.2**

**frag**

Dependent clauses are easily mistaken for complete sentences. The opening words of these clauses give you help in deciding whether the sentence is a fragment; for each of these attaching words gives a signal, telling you to connect the clause to a word in the main sentence:

> The car *that* . . .
> The cruiser turned on its siren *when* . . .
> The cruiser forced it to stop *because* . . .
> Leave *whenever* . . .

**21.2e Appositives.** Fragments may take the form of appositives. Here again is the main sentence, shortened slightly:

> The man waved at the car—a police cruiser.

*Car* and *police cruiser* mean the same thing in this sentence. The appositive *police cruiser* renames the subject. A pair of dashes or a pair of commas sets off an appositive that occurs in the middle of the sentence:

> The car at the corner—a police cruiser—picked up speed.
> The car at the corner, a police cruiser, picked up speed.

See 11.1f on the punctuation of appositives.

**21.2f Absolute Phrases.** Fragments may take the form of absolute phrases (see 8.1c and 11.1e). An absolute phrase normally attaches to a main sentence without a connecting word or a conjunction:

> The cruiser turned on its siren, the reason being that the car was speeding.

Set apart from the main sentence, the absolute phrase becomes a fragment:

> The reason being that the car was speeding.

### EXERCISE

First decide whether the following words compose a fragment. If they do, turn them into a complete sentence by creating a main sentence and attaching the fragment to the whole sentence or to words or phrases in it:

1. the mower standing near the curb yesterday needs repair
2. running down the street without looking ahead of him
3. except for the answer you forgot to finish
4. giving as much help as the class needs to solve the equation
5. which tells you something about calculus
6. no matter who answers the door
7. give no money to whoever comes to the door even if it is my neighbor
8. after the game ended and the fans started running toward the players
9. nine times out of ten
10. whenever you are ready lock the door and come out to the car
11. that we found in the backyard near the fence
12. explain your reason for not rejoining the club
13. whoever drives the Ford should have the tires checked
14. the mural being completed and ready to be shown
15. his having argued that the policy would bankrupt the school district
16. the first person who entered the classroom
17. wondering when the results of the bar exam would be announced
18. they disagreed that dues should be raised
19. the dues having been raised without the consent of the members
20. however the results of the exam appear to you

**21.2**
**frag**

## Checklist for Fragments

**21.2a**   A spoken fragment often begins at a higher pitch than a complete sentence:

> *still* bounce around a lot, you know
> *always* on the move
> *probably* a hangover from all those years in baseball

**21.2b**  Fragments may be detached subjects or predicates or a part of the predicate:

| | |
|---|---|
| too many cars | Too many cars are on the street. |
| | He owns too many cars. |

**21.2c**  Many fragments are detached phrases:

| | |
|---|---|
| over the bridge | She drove over the bridge. |
| driving in the dark | She missed the crossroad, driving in the dark. |

**21.2d**  Fragments may be detached clauses:

| | |
|---|---|
| that turned the corner | The car that turned the corner began to speed. |
| whenever you want | Leave whenever you want. |
| after you left | The fire started after you left. |

**21.2e**  Fragments may be detached appositives:

| | |
|---|---|
| the blue and white car on the corner | The police cruiser—the blue and white car on the corner—started its siren. |

**21.2f**  Fragments may be detached absolute phrases:

| | |
|---|---|
| the reason being that the car was speeding | It started its siren, the reason being that the car was speeding. |

# Fused and Stringy Sentences

## 22.1 Fused Sentences

A **fused sentence** joins independent clauses into a single sentence without intervening punctuation:

Don't forget to fill the tank you're out of gas.

Management and labor reached agreement yesterday on the contract however they are waiting to announce it.

The negotiations were long and bitter in fact they were almost broken off several times.

You can revise the fused sentence in several ways—
by dividing the sentence into two sentences:

Don't forget to fill the tank. You're out of gas.

by using a comma, colon, or semicolon:

Don't forget to fill the tank: you're out of gas.

Management and labor reached agreement yesterday on the contract; however, they are waiting to announce it.

Management and labor reached agreement yesterday on the contract, but they are waiting to announce it.

The negotiations were long and bitter; in fact, they were almost broken off several times.

If you suspect you have fused two complete sentences, read the sentence aloud, listening for the juncture or break that marks the end of a clause or a sentence in speech.

**EXERCISE**

Correct the following sentences by breaking them into shorter sentences or adding the punctuation:

1. I am taking a course in computer science as a matter of fact I am taking it for the second time.
2. Listening to music requires complete attention you will hear sound but you won't hear the music if you are reading a book or working a puzzle.
3. The report of a fifth physical force called "hypercharge" challenges the current theory of gravity however few scientists accept the evidence as indisputable.
4. Few people know him as well as I do I met him in high school later however we lost touch moving as we did from job to job.
5. I have several reasons for not making a decision now I will notify you when I have made it I won't make it now.
6. People have mistaken ideas about dogs they do have feelings they do understand words and they do think.
7. Dr. Watson met Sherlock Holmes shortly after Watson returned from India he had been wounded there in the second Afghan war.
8. He first saw Holmes in a chemical lab studying blood stains "Why, man, it is the most practical medico-legal discovery for years," Holmes said to him, referring to haemoglobin.
9. Watson and Holmes in this way discovered their common interest in medicine indeed they shared other interests they discovered in the days that followed.
10. Watson discovered strange habits in Holmes his friend would sit for hours silently he walked miles he had immense energy.

**22.1**
**fs**

## **22.2** Stringy Sentences

Long, rambling sentences that string clauses and phrases quickly lose the reader's attention:

Old soldiers never die, the old song says, they just fade away as everyone knows who tries to remember the name of a famous politician whom everyone talked about once but whom nobody now remembers even though his face was in the papers daily, and everyone has had the same experience with long-retired actors and actresses.

What makes a sentence ramble is a matter of judgment. A long, well-knit sentence will not seem to do so if it keeps our attention focused on the core idea and we see the relation of part to part as we read it. A loosely connected sentence will seem stringy if we lose sight of the core idea or fail to see how one part of the sentence connects to the next. We soon lose interest in what the writer is saying.

Like other confusing sentences, the stringy sentence often originates in habits of speech typified by this statement of a telephone operator:

> You know he's lonesome and he wants to talk to somebody, and there you are and you can't talk to him. There's one person who feels badly and you can't do anything.
> —STUDS TERKEL, *Working*

In speech we are used to hearing a series of continuous clauses. The speaker just quoted might have let the two sentences ramble in this way:

> You know he's lonesome and he wants to talk to somebody, and there you are and you can't talk to him, and there's one person who feels badly and you can't do anything.

In spoken and written English, the change of topic ("and there you are," "and there's one person") creates the sense that the sentence rambles.

**22.2**

**st**

In written English, two coordinate clauses often begin with the same word:

> He is lonesome and he wants to talk to somebody.

If a third coordinate clause beginning with the same word is added, the sentence will seem unusually emphatic:

> He is lonesome and he wants to talk to somebody and he cannot find anyone to listen.

Coordinated sentences such as this are exceptional because of the unusual emphasis created through the repetition of the subject term (*he*).

Additional coordinate clauses will also make the sentence ramble:

> He is lonesome and he wants to talk to somebody and he cannot find anyone to listen and he calls me for this reason.

However, a third coordinate clause beginning with a different conjunction is common:

> You know he's lonesome and he wants to talk to somebody, but there is no one he can talk to.

**EXERCISE**

Correct the following stringy sentences by eliminating unnecessary words, breaking them into shorter sentences, or revising the punctuation:

1. Mow the lawn without touching the flowers, and pick up the grass instead of leaving it on the ground, and trim the hedges, but don't cut them too short, and weed where you can, too.
2. The last person I met on my trip to Los Angeles was an agent for a famous television actress, a man who introduced himself, and it was obvious he had no other talk except about her—he talked about nothing else.
3. Few people know as much about the fourteenth century as she does, shown by her book about the fourteenth century which is mainly about the black plague which killed so many people and the social and political consequences of the plague.
4. I would like to answer that question frankly and honestly, but we all realize that caution is a virtue in talking about matters still in the courts, and I am sorry to disappoint you in not being able to say more than I have said already.
5. The train stopped at the viaduct—for what reason none of us in the coach could discover, though we could see people on the track, including several who had been riding in our coach and someone whom we had seen at the station in Denver where we had boarded.

**22.2**
**st**

# Checklist for Fused and Stringy Sentences

**22.1** A fused sentence joins independent clauses into a single sentence:

*Fused*
The negotiations were long and bitter in fact they were broken off several times.

*Revised*
The negotations were long and bitter; in fact, they were broken off several times.

**22.2** Long, rambling sentences lose focus and confuse the reader.

*Stringy*
He is lonesome and he wants to talk to somebody and he cannot find anyone to listen and he calls me often for this reason.

*Revised*
He calls me often because he is lonesome, wants to talk to somebody, and can't find anyone to listen.

# Mixed Constructions
# and Other Faults

## 23.1 Mixed Constructions

**23.1a From Phrase to Predicate.** Mixed constructions begin the sentence with one kind of structure and continue or end with another. The result is confusion as one reads the sentence—a sense that the writer began with one idea in mind and changed to another idea in midsentence.

Consider the following:

On meeting his uncle was a surprise.

The confusion arises because the sentence mixes the following constructions:

an adjective phrase—*on meeting his uncle*—that the reader expects to modify a noun
a predicate—*was a surprise*

The sentence can mean either of the following:

On meeting his uncle he showed his surprise.
Meeting his uncle was a surprise.

If in doubt about how to revise such a sentence, ask what is the subject of *was*—that is, what was the surprise—and revise the sentence to give the answer.

Here are other common mixed constructions. The following sentence begins with an adverbial clause and jumps to the predicate without stating the subject:

If Alice comes should be the time to discuss the matter.

To revise the sentence, ask this question:

If Alice comes, what will happen or who will do what?

361

Then complete the sentence by stating the answer:

If Alice comes, we should be able to discuss the matter.

Here is an alternate revision:

We can discuss the matter if Alice comes.

The following sentence is awkward, too:

Because Alice was late made us angry.

Here is a satisfactory revision:

We were angry because Alice was late.

**23.1b  From Independent Clause to Predicate.**  A sentence will seem confused if an independent clause leads into the predicate:

He protested was the reason for his dismissal.

Independent clauses (*He protested*) do not serve as subjects. To revise, change the independent clause to a dependent one:

*That he protested* was the reason for his dismissal.

Here are alternate revisions:

His protest caused his dismissal.
The cause of his dismissal was his protest.

**23.1c  From Statement to Question.**  The following sentence shifts from a statement to a question:

I asked is she coming home for Thanksgiving?

Here are possible revisions:

I asked, "Are you coming home for Thanksgiving?"

*Formal*
I asked whether she was coming home for Thanksgiving.

*Informal*
I asked if she was coming home for Thanksgiving.

See 10.2b on direct and indirect questions.

**EXERCISE**

Correct the following mixed constructions:
1. After talking to the teacher was when he made the decision.
2. She asked will the exam cover the whole book.
3. Everyone missed the final question shows that there had been no time to cover the final chapter in class.

4. By explaining your absences may persuade him to give you a make up.
5. The exam was easy surprised her.
6. In looking at the car was the mechanic who had looked at it the week before.
7. In all the years we lived in Pittsburgh were the happiest of our lives.
8. The mechanic said I can't find the engine leak.
9. She asked whether you are going to Pittsburgh tomorrow by car?
10. She is going to Pittsburgh by plane is what worries me.

## 23.2 False Equation

The following sentence is confusing:

The one movie I saw was in August.

*Was* suggests that the title of the movie will follow. Here is a satisfactory revision:

The one movie I saw in August was *Star Wars*.

The confusion arises because *to be* verbs (*is, are, was, were*) equate similar ideas or similar things (see 8.1c and 9.1), and they also express time relationships:

*Equivalent Things*
The election will be a much talked-about event.

*Time*
The election will be in November.

When the sentence expresses equivalence, the subject and subject complement should be similar.

The inequivalence creates greater awkwardness in the following sentence because the subject and subject complement are not similar or close in meaning:

The only help I need is how to wire the speakers.

The following revision changes the subject complement to an equivalent term:

The only *help* I need is *being shown* how to wire the speakers.

But the revised sentence is wordy. The following revision is satisfactory:

I need help in wiring the speakers.

Consider another kind of false equation:

**23.2**
**st**

Hunter's stew is where you cook meat with vegetables.

The word *where* refers awkwardly to an activity. The following is a satisfactory revision:

Hunter's stew is meat cooked with vegetables.

The word *where* is often used informally to refer to a place:

A veterinary college is where you learn to care for animals.

General and formal English state the equivalent term:

A veterinary college is a school that teaches the care of animals.

### EXERCISE

Rewrite the following sentences to correct the false equation:
1. College is when you find out how important friends are.
2. The only baseball game I ever played was in junior high.
3. The one composer we truly liked was at the end of the course.
4. The symphony we heard of Beethoven was in New York.
5. Lacrosse is when you play with webbed rackets rather than sticks.
6. The official explanation for the accident was because a control valve failed to open.
7. Air pollutants are a reason to know chemistry.
8. Organic chemistry and biochemistry are where you study complex molecules and enzymes.
9. The overture is when the conductor starts the performance.
10. Chili is where you mix ground beef, tomatoes, and red pepper and other spices.

**23.3**
**st**

## **23.3** Faulty Predication

The following sentence makes an assertion or predication about the subject:

Word processors may soon replace typewriters.

We can ask the following question about the subject of the sentence:

What will word processors soon replace?

The predicate provides the answer: typewriters. But notice what happens in the following sentence:

> The convenience of word processors may soon replace type-writers.

The sentence at first glance predicates something about word processors, but it is actually talking about their convenience:

> The convenience may soon replace typewriters.

The following revision clarifies the sentence:

> Because of their convenience, word processors may soon replace typewriters.

In the following example, the faulty predication arises from a less obvious confusion in meaning:

> Agreement between subject and verb causes many writers problems.

It is not agreement that causes problems but uncertainty over how some subjects and verbs match in sentences:

> Uncertainty over agreement between subject and verb causes many writers problems.

This sentence is also unsatisfactory because the words *uncertainty* and *problem* overlap in meaning. Here is a satisfactory revision:

> Many writers are uncertain about the agreement between subject and verb.

**23.4**
**emp**

**EXERCISE**

Correct the faulty predication in the following sentences:
1. The popularity of country music will soon catch up with rock in other countries.
2. The lack of exercise makes many people take up jogging.
3. The United States has a long way to catch up with China's population.
4. Mountain climbing probably exceeds the hazards of other outdoor sports.
5. Cooperation among the nuclear powers causes worry around the world.

# 23.4 Misplaced Emphasis

When one of the phrases or clauses contains a highly dramatic or exciting action, it is best to put it late in the sentence—preferably in the main clause. Compare the following:

> While the car caught fire we were talking about the weather.
> While we were talking about the weather, the car caught fire.

The first sentence puts the emphasis on the talk about the weather, but weather is probably not the idea the writer wants to emphasize. In the second sentence, the emphasis is properly on the idea stated in the main clause.

Achieving proper emphasis is not always so simple a matter. In simple sentences that begin with the subject and end with the predicate, the end of the sentence is usually an emphatic position. The reason is that the predicate usually expresses the action or goal:

> The car parked at the end of the street caught fire.

This "end force" carries over to dependent or subordinate clauses that conclude the sentence:

> Wilson was a Southerner by birth and breeding, *although he made his career in the North.*
> —Gerald W. Johnson, "The Cream of the Jest" [italics added]

**23.4**
**emp**

The italicized subordinate clause receives approximately the same emphasis as the main clause by virtue of its position at the end of the sentence. If the main clause were placed at the end, it would receive full emphasis:

> Although he made his career in the North, Wilson was a Southerner by birth and breeding.

Word order is crucial. The position of each clause in the sentence depends on which idea the writer wants to emphasize. See 9.2c for additional discussion of end focus.

The emphasis given to phrases can be controlled in the same way. The following sentences have the same meaning, and neither sentence is awkward:

> Looking at pictures requires active participation, and a certain amount of discipline *in the early stages.*

> Looking at pictures requires active participation, and, *in the early stages*, a certain amount of discipline.
> —Kenneth Clark, *Looking at Pictures* [italics added]

The difference is in the idea given emphasis at the end of each sentence.

### EXERCISE

Correct the emphasis in the following sentences if you think it is misplaced:

1. When most people are getting up, farmers have done half a day's work.
2. As the barn burned, they watched from the road.
3. When streets are icy, accidents happen.
4. The snowpack melts as the streams overflow.
5. Fish start dying in the lakes when the rain becomes acid.

## General Exercise

Correct the faults in the following sentences:

1. The one book I read was during spring vacation.
2. The fact he must give a talk is the reason he's nervous.
3. Her reputation was her chocolate cake.
4. The rise in the cost of money requires many people to put off buying new houses.
5. A hurricane is when the winds rise above 73 miles per hour.
6. Close to the top of the ridge, where a hurricane was destroying a stand of trees in a storm no one was expecting, we saw a herd of elk.
7. People watching a crime and not even calling the police is because they think someone else will report it, an article in *Psychology Today* suggests.
8. Discovering that she had read the wrong pages and was unprepared for the exam was when she decided to talk to the instructor about withdrawing from the course, taking it the following term.
9. The last time we drove to Detroit and stopped in Toledo on the way.
10. We wondered if we should stop in Bowling Green on the way home?
11. The only person I knew well was in the army.
12. Calculus is where you find out if you're suited for engineering.
13. Because the bus broke down is the reason I'm late this morning.
14. The bus broke down on the expressway though the driver managed to drive it to a parking area where the passengers could board another bus.
15. An eclipse is where astronomers measure the curving of starlight passing near the sun.
16. The two books by George Orwell we read were at the beginning of the course.
17. The unexpected result of the examination is the reason she is switching from chemistry to physics.
18. Getting into college is when you start making decisions for yourself.

**23.4**
**emp**

**19.** Americans eat more fat than they should explains the increase in coronary disease.

**20.** On arrival at the airport was a long delay at customs.

# Checklist for Mixed Constructions and Other Faults

**23.1a**    Mixed constructions begin with one kind of structure and continue or end the sentence with another:

*Mixed*
On meeting his uncle was a surprise.

*Revised*
On meeting his uncle he showed surprise.

**23.1b**    An independent clause cannot serve as the subject:

*Mixed*
He protested was the reason for his dismissal.

*Revised*
That he protested was the reason for his dismissal.

**23.1c**    Don't mix a declarative statement with a question:

*Mixed*
I asked is she coming for Thanksgiving?

*Revised*
I asked whether she is coming for Thanksgiving.

**23.2**    Make the subject and the subject complement identical:

*Inequivalent*
The one movie I saw was in August.

*Revised*
The one movie I saw in August was *Star Wars*.

**23.3**    Make the predication about the actual subject and not about an aspect of it:

*Faulty Predication*
The convenience of word processors may soon replace typewriters.

*Revised*
Because of their convenience, word processors may soon replace typewriters.

**23.4** A dramatic idea may be misplaced in a subordinate clause:

*Misplaced Emphasis*
While the car caught fire we were talking about the weather.

*Revised*
While we were talking about the weather, the car caught fire.

# Misplaced Words, Dangling Modifiers, Split Constructions

This chapter discusses common faults of word order, beginning with the misplacing of single words and phrases and clauses. The chapter also discusses "squinting" modifiers, dangling modifiers, and split infinitives and similar constructions.

As with certain other sentence faults discussed in earlier chapters, many faults of word order arise from habits of speech; many sentences that are clear when spoken are unclear when written. Often the revisions required to make written sentences clear involve a tightening of spoken patterns. Other faults of word order arise from a breaking of noun phrases and verb phrases common in speech. Sometimes your ear is a reliable guide in correcting errors of this kind, but most of the time you must depend on your eye.

## 24.1 Single-Word Modifiers

In writing, you can avoid awkwardness and ambiguity by putting a modifier as close to the word modified as possible. **Single-word modifiers,** for example, can convey different emphasis and meaning by the various positions they occupy in the sentence. In the following sentences the word *only* modifies different words and phrases and in doing so conveys different ideas.

Modification of the subject—*I*:

In the family *only* I drive a Ford. [No one else in the family drives a Ford.]

Modification of the verb—*own*:

I *only* recommend a Ford. [I don't insist that you buy one.]

Modification of the object—*Ford*:

I recommend *only* a Ford. [I recommend a Ford and no other car.]

Modification of the whole sentence:

I have one car to recommend *only*. [I have no other car to recommend.]

These changes in the position of the single-word modifier can affect the emphasis given the word or phrase and sometimes the meaning of the sentence. Compare the following:

| | |
|---|---|
| One picked one's way among the mines and booby traps of the hospital, hoping *only* to avoid the hemorrhage and perforation of disgrace.<br>—RICHARD SELZER, *Letters to a Young Surgeon* [italics added] | One picked one's way among the mines and booby traps of the hospital, hoping to avoid only the hemorrhage and perforation of disgrace. |

**24.1**

**mm**

Such modifiers sometimes occur in different parts of informal sentences without a change in meaning, as in the following:

I *only* have one thing to say.
I have *only* one thing to say.
I have one thing to say, *only*.

**EXERCISES**

1. State the exact meaning of each sentence:
    a. She is going to class only today.
    b. She is only going to class today.
    c. Only she is going to class today.
    d. She is even going to class.
    e. Even she is going to class.
2. Decide which sentences are awkward or unclear, and be ready to explain why they are:
    a. There is almost no gas left in the tank.
    b. No gas is almost left in the tank.
    c. Almost no gas is left in the tank.
    d. No gas is left in the tank almost.
    e. Only some gas is left in the tank.

## 24.2 Squinting Modifiers

Sometimes a modifier is placed between two words, both of which it seems to modify. This modifier is called a "squinter" because it looks in opposite directions at the same time—at the phrase that precedes it and the phrase that follows:

*Ambiguous*
People who watch television *rarely* read much.

The sentence can mean the following:

People who *rarely* watch television read much.
People who read much watch television *rarely* .

Each of these sentences is a satisfactory revision of the original sentence.

**EXERCISE**

**24.2**

**mm**

Revise the following sentences that contain squinting modifiers:
1. The team that practices often wins.
2. The teacher said after class she would discuss the exam.
3. The surgeon said presently the scar would fade.
4. People who eat green apples once in a while will get bad stomachaches.
5. Not everyone who eats green apples immediately gets sick.
6. She explained during the recess she wanted to talk further about my decision.
7. She urged us strongly to defend our ideas.
8. Runners who fail to warm up slowly lose agility.
9. The tree that grew in the shade quickly lost its leaves.
10. Those who saw her fall suddenly called for help.

## 24.3 Misplaced Phrases

**24.3a Prepositional Phrases.** Prepositional phrases usually precede or follow the words they modify. Phrases that modify verbs can be moved to other parts of the sentence for special emphasis:

She described her mistake, *with a grin.*
She described her mistake, *grinning.*
*With a grin*, she described her mistake.
*Grinning*, she described her mistake.

Take care with the placing of modifiers when you add other modifiers. Consider the following:

He described his mistake *to the man with a grin.*

The following revisions are awkward and unidiomatic:

He described, *with a grin*, his mistake *to the man.*
He described his mistake, *with a grin*, *to the man.*

The solution is to place the phrase next to the word it modifies:

*With a grin*, he described his mistake *to the man.*
*Grinning*, he described his mistake *to the man.*

**24.3b Verbal Phrases.** The same considerations of clarity and idiomatic expression govern verbal phrases. Each of the phrases in the following sentences has a clear reference:

*Clear*
Driving down the highway, we saw the bear.
People in the van, driving down the highway, saw the bear.
To see a grizzly, you must drive into the back country.
You must drive into the back country to see a grizzly.

Misplacing the modifier creates momentary, sometimes comical, ambiguity:

**24.3**
**mm**

*Ambiguous*
We saw the bear driving down the highway.

The ambiguity in the following sentence is not as obvious as in the one just discussed:

*Ambiguous*
Hunting for food, you must drive into the back country where grizzlies roam.

The writer probably means that the grizzly and not the driver is hunting for food. The sentence is not ambiguous if the writer means that the driver is hunting for food.

**EXERCISE**

Correct any of the following sentences that you find unclear or awkward. Be ready to give the reason for your correction:

1. She, with paper and pencil in hand, made a list of the people in the room.
2. She made a list of the people, with pencil and paper in hand, in the room.
3. He explained with some reluctance how the accident had occurred to the policeman.

4. He explained to the policeman how the accident occurred with some reluctance.
5. An accident at the corner was seen, leaning out of the window.
6. Following the directions given on the package, the cake came out a dark brown.
7. To keep alive during the winter, you should water the shrubs heavily in the fall.
8. The children on the swings ignored their mothers, pushing one another gleefully.
9. Not wanting to drive back for the water jar we had left on the porch meant looking for a place to get water on the road.
10. We caught sight of the steamer, coming around the bend near the inlet.

# 24.4 Misplaced Clauses

**24.4a Adjective Clauses.** Noun clauses (see 7.2b) are rather fixed in the position they can assume—as subject, as object, as subject and object complements, and as object of prepositions. Adjective clauses (see 7.2b) are also bound to fixed positions following the words they modify, though they can stand at a distance from them in the sentence if the reference of the clause is clear:

The box arrived which he had left on the bus.

Momentary ambiguity can arise when the adjective clause has two possible antecedents:

The box arrived with the mail that he had left on the bus.

The following revision removes the ambiguity but is awkward:

With the mail arrived the box that he had left on the bus.

The following revisions are not awkward:

The box, *which he had left on the bus*, arrived with the mail [nonrestrictive modifier—only one box is being discussed].
He never saw again the box *that he had left in the station*.
The box *that he had left on the bus* arrived with the mail [restrictive modifier—two boxes are being discussed].

**24.4b Adverb Clauses.** Adverb clauses (7.2b) have greater freedom of position in the sentence:

I like Dickens *because he combines humor with pathos.*
*Because he combines humor with pathos,* I prefer Dickens to other novelists.

Like adjective clauses, adverb clauses should stand as close as possible to the words they modify. Intervening modifiers can create awkwardness and confusion:

I like Dickens, who wrote *David Copperfield,* because he combines humor with pathos.

This revision of the sentence is even more awkward and confusing:

Because he combines humor with pathos, I like Dickens, who wrote *David Copperfield.*

The awkwardness and confusion arise from the prominence given the information about *David Copperfield* by putting it at the end of the sentence. The fact that should be stressed is not that Dickens wrote the novel (this information merely identifies Dickens as the author), but that the person writing the sentence likes the combination of humor with pathos in the novels. The solution is a simple one—a reduction of the adjective clause to a phrase:

**24.4**

**dm**

I like Dickens, the author of *David Copperfield,* because he combines humor with pathos.

### EXERCISE

Rewrite those sentences that contain misplaced clauses:
1. The snow caused the flooding, which melted quickly.
2. Because the streams overflowed, the people near them had to be taken to high ground.
3. The people had to be taken to high ground when the streams overflowed, because they were in danger.
4. Not many people knew that she was the writer's first wife, who did not know him well.
5. Whatever the cost, better have the car repaired, which our insurance should cover.
6. No matter what you are told, read all the chapters assigned, which the exam will cover.
7. Read all the chapters assigned, but not the final unassigned chapter, which the exam will cover.
8. The final chapter of the chemistry text discussed the molecule, the whole of which was assigned for the exam.
9. Not one of the experiments we performed was on the exam, which I assumed would be.

10. She is one of the few people in the course whose aim is to enter medical school.

# 24.5  Dangling Modifiers

Section 24.3b considered the following sentence:

Hunting for food, you must go into the back country where grizzlies roam.

The verbal phrase *hunting for food* is misplaced in the sentence, connecting to the word *you* instead of to the word it modifies— *grizzlies*. This section discusses verbal phrases that hang or "dangle" in the sentence without reference to any specified word or phrase.

**24.5a  Participial Phrases.**  Sentences may be unclear if participial or adjective phrases dangle or hang awkwardly in the sentence, unconnected to a specific word:

*Ambiguous*
*Driving down the highway*, a grizzly was seen.

**24.5**
**mm**

To correct the sentence, name the doer in the main clause:

*Revised*
Driving down the highway, we saw the bear.

Note that absolute phrases do not dangle since they modify the whole sentence and not particular words:

No objection being heard, the meeting adjourned.
The plan having failed, the committee is proposing another.

See 8.1c on absolute phrases.

**24.5b  Gerund Phrases.**  Gerunds or verbal nouns end in *-ing* and can take objects and adverbial modifiers (see 8.7):

*Chopping wood* requires a sharp axe.
*Running slowly* is just as tiring as *running fast*.

Like participial phrases, gerund phrases can dangle in the sentence when the doer is not mentioned or named:

*Ambiguous*
In chopping wood, the axe must have a sturdy handle and a strong blade.

To correct the sentence, name the doer in the main clause:

*Clear*
In chopping wood, a person needs an axe with a sturdy handle and a strong blade.

**24.5c Infinitive Phrases.** Infinitive phrases also require a specific reference in the sentence. In the following sentence the lack of specific reference creates momentary ambiguity:

*Unclear*
To hit a golfball off the tee, a good driver is needed.

*Revised*
To hit a golfball off the tee, the golfer needs a good driver.

Changing the verb of the main clause to the active voice improves sentences of this kind.

The passive verb in the following sentence does not present the same problem:

More work is required to pass the course.

This sentence refers to general conditions of passing the course —conditions that refer to everyone. Therefore the sentence does not have to specify who is required to do the work. The following sentence does need to specify the doer:

**24.5**

**mm**

*Unclear*
To pass the course, more work is needed.

The opening infinitive modifier creates the expectation that the person taking the course will be named. Here is a satisfactory revision:

*Revised*
To pass the course, you need to do more work.

**24.5d Reduced Clauses.** Reduced or shortened clauses can also dangle:

*Unclear*
When presented with the facts, the request to resign was withdrawn.

To correct the sentence, specify who was presented with the facts and who withdrew the request:

*Revised*
When the manager was presented with the facts, he withdrew the request that the employee resign.

*Or*

When the manager was presented with the facts, he withdrew his resignation.

**EXERCISE**

Correct those sentences that contain dangling modifiers:

1. After hammering the nails, the wood should be treated with shellac.
2. The registrar was notified on hearing that the transcript had not been sent.
3. An application will be sent, once the transcript is received.
4. To write well, a good dictionary is essential.
5. Dragging under the car, it was impossible to remove the limb while climbing the steep hill.
6. Forced to climb the stairs, the top floor was hard to reach.
7. Considering how far Los Angeles is from Denver, it's remarkable how short the flight was.
8. On hearing the motion, there was a call for the question.
9. Given the different opinions expressed, it's no wonder the motion lost.
10. Far up the mountain was seen a herd of elk, taking photos.

**24.6**
**mm**

## 24.6 Split Constructions

**24.6a Splitting Subject and Verb.**   Splitting a pronoun subject from its verb creates awkwardness:

*Awkward*
*We*, wondering what had caused the explosion and fire, *whispered* about the accident anxiously.

*Revised*
Wondering what had caused the explosion and fire, we whispered about the accident anxiously.

The split is not awkward when the subject is a noun or a noun phrase:

*The crowd of people*, wondering what had caused the explosion and fire, whispered about the accident anxiously.

**24.6b Splitting Verb Phrases.**   Verb phrases are occasionally split with single words and absolute phrases:

I have *fully* considered the matter.
I have, *to be honest about it*, not yet considered the matter.

But splitting the phrase with a long adjective modifier usually makes the sentence sound awkward:

*Awkward*
I have, *not wanting to make a decision at this time*, not yet considered the matter.

*Revised*
Not wanting to make a decision at this time, I have not yet considered the matter.

**24.6c Split Infinitives.**   Writers occasionally split the infinitive to achieve emphasis or to avoid ambiguity:

> The ability of water to *readily* evaporate and condense in the atmosphere has a profound effect on monsoon circulation.
> —PETER J. WEBSTER, "Monsoons" [italics added]

Placing the adverb *readily* before the words *evaporate* and *condense* shows that it modifies both words, not just one or the other as in the following ambiguous revisions:

> The ability of water *readily* to evaporate and condense in the atmosphere has a profound effect on monsoon circulation.
> The ability of water to evaporate and condense *readily* in the atmosphere has a profound effect on monsoon circulation.

If the infinitive must be split, it is best to restrict the splitting to a single word. In the following sentence, the long interruption makes the sentence unidiomatic:

*Awkward*
We asked them to, knowing there would not be enough room, ride in separate cars.

Here is a satisfactory revision of this sentence:

*Revised*
Knowing there would not be enough room, we asked them to ride in separate cars.

**24.6**
**mm**

### EXERCISE

Correct those sentences that contain awkward split constructions.

1. We decided, having discussed whether we were doing the right thing, the future so uncertain, not to buy the car.
2. We, uncertain what size car we would need, thought it best to wait until spring.
3. The mayor asked the council to, given the extent of the flooding, vote to make money available for relief.

4. They voted to quickly as possible deal with the emergency.
5. Only those people who have had, recently, first aid training should assist.
6. He is willing to as soon as possible transfer the deed.
7. The remaining campers, certain that the weather forecast was mistaken, decided to remain in the park.
8. One, if on the highway for a long trip, should carry sufficient supplies and food for an emergency.
9. We don't intend to foolishly sacrifice our advantage by discussing our moves with reporters.
10. Spring is the best season to, after preparing the soil, transplant flowers and shrubs.

## General Exercise

Correct the sentences that contain misplaced words, phrases, or clauses, dangling modifiers, and split constructions:

1. The manager wants to—after school starts and he knows how many new employees he will need—hire a few boys and girls to work after school.
2. She explained yesterday her car had broken down.
3. He, refusing to consider any solution that meant an increase in taxes, vetoed the bill.
4. After biking twenty miles from the outskirts to the center of town, the sponsors of the race awarded the prizes.
5. We explained the solution to the problem that we had worked out overnight.
6. One book is worth giving, a lesser known novel of Charles Dickens, *Little Dorrit*, to someone interested in ninteenth-century England.
7. I can't think of a reason anymore to go.
8. To find water, the soil must be tested by a hydrologist.
9. A hornet entered the car when opening the window.
10. She was angry enough to rudely and abruptly cancel the meeting.

**24.6**
**mm**

## Checklist for Misplaced Words

**24.1**  To avoid awkwardness and ambiguity, put single-word modifiers as close to the word or phrase modified as possible:

| *Awkward* | *Clear* |
|---|---|
| In the family I bought a Ford only. | In the family only I bought a Ford. |

**24.2**  Avoid squinting modifiers that point to the phrase that precedes and the phrase that follows:

*Ambiguous*
People who watch television rarely read much.

*Clear*
People who rarely watch television read much.

**24.3a**  Prepositional phrases should immediately precede or follow the words they modify:

*Ambiguous*
She described her mistake to the man with a grin.

*Clear*
With a grin, she described her mistake to the man.

**24.3b**  Put verbal phrases close to the words they modify:

*Ambiguous*
We saw the grizzly driving down the highway.

*Clear*
Driving down the highway, we saw the grizzly.

**24.4a**  Put adjective clauses with the words they modify:

*Ambiguous*
The box arrived with the mail which he had left on the bus.

*Clear*
The box that he had left on the bus arrived with the mail.

The box, which he had left on the bus, arrived with the mail.

**24.4b**  Put adverb clauses close to the words they modify:

*Awkward*
I like Dickens, who wrote *David Copperfield*, because he combines humor with pathos.

*Improved*
I like Dickens, the author of *David Copperfield*, because he combines humor with pathos.

**24.5a**  Participial modifiers dangle in the sentence if they do not clearly refer to specified words:

*Ambiguous*
Driving down the highway, a grizzly was seen.

*Clear*
Driving down the highway, we saw a grizzly.

**24.5b-c**  Gerund and infinitive phrases dangle in the sentence when the doer is unmentioned or unnamed:

*Ambiguous*
In chopping wood, the axe must have a sturdy handle and a strong blade.

*Clear*
In chopping wood, a person needs an axe with a sturdy handle and a strong blade.

|  |  |
|---|---|
| To hit a ball off the tee, a good driver is needed. | To hit the ball off the tee, a golfer needs a good driver. |

**24.5d**   Reduced or elliptical clauses can also dangle:

| *Unclear* | *Clear* |
|---|---|
| When faced with the facts, the request to resign was withdrawn. | When the manager was presented with the facts, he withdrew his request that the employee resign. |

**24.6a**   Don't split the subject and predicate with a long modifier:

| *Awkward* | *Improved* |
|---|---|
| We, wondering what had caused the explosion and fire, whispered about the accident anxiously. | Wondering what had caused the explosion and fire, we whispered about the accident anxiously. |

**24.6b**   Don't split a verb phrase with a long adjective modifier:

| *Awkward* | *Revised* |
|---|---|
| I have, *not wanting to make a decision at this time*, not yet considered the matter. | Not wanting to make a decision at this time, I have not yet considered the matter. |

**24.6c**   Don't split infinitives with long modifying phrases:

| *Awkward* | *Improved* |
|---|---|
| We asked them to, knowing there would not be enough room, ride in separate cars. | Knowing there would be enough room, we asked them to ride in separate cars. |

# Shifts and Omissions

## 25.1 Shifts

Shifts in person and number of pronouns (from *I* to *you* or from *I* to *we*) and in tense, mood, and voice (see 8.2) often occur in spoken communication. They occur in written communication, too, as in the following sentences from letters to a newspaper complaining about proposed storage of chemical wastes in a populated area:

1. The politicians who want to bury these wastes close to where people get their drinking water forget you will need their votes in November.
2. When we talked to the people downtown, they say the wastes will be kept out of the water, but we don't believe they will.
3. If we had a say in the matter, these wastes won't be dumped where people get their drinking water.

These sentences are awkward for different reasons.

**25.1a Person.** Shifts in person make sentences awkward. The first writer (1) shifts from the third person *politicians* to the second person *you*. The statement shows that these words refer to the same people. The following revision removes the awkwardness:

The politicians who want to bury these wastes close to where people get their drinking water forget they will need their votes in November.

The following sentence contains a different kind of shift in person:

One hardly knows what to do, particularly when you can't get help from people paid to give it.

The sentence shifts from third person *one* to second person *you*. The shift probably occurs because of the idiomatic use of *one* in the opening phrase (*One hardly knows*). This use of *one* is characteristic of formal English:

> One gets no help from people paid to give it.

Note that the word *one* in a string of clauses and phrases produces a stilted and unclear sentence:

> One should realize that one will lose the confidence of one's voting constituents.

Here are possible revisions:

> One should realize that voters will lose confidence.
> You should realize that you will lose the confidence of voters.

Shifts in person can be troublesome in paragraphs and essays. Compare the following paragraphs:

<table>
<tr><td>*Awkward*</td><td>*Improved*</td></tr>
<tr><td>*We* seldom think of the problems a candidate faces in talking to an audience on television rather than face to face. *You* have to take into consideration the pressure when *you* can't see how they are taking your words. Candidates who are effective speakers before live audiences become dull or tongue-tied when facing a camera.</td><td>We seldom think of the problems a candidate faces in talking to an audience on television rather than face to face. We have to consider the pressure on candidates who cannot see the response of the audience to their words. Candidates who are effective speakers before live audiences become tongue-tied when facing a camera.</td></tr>
</table>

**25.1**
**shift**

The paragraph to the left makes a series of awkward and illogical shifts in person. The paragraph to the right is consistent throughout.

**25.1b Number.**   Shifts often occur when a plural pronoun is part of the antecedent:

> *Incorrect*
> Each of us should write to their councilwoman.

*Their* mistakenly agrees with *us*, not with *each*—the subject of the sentence. This mistake probably occurs because the closest pronoun to *their* is the plural *us* and therefore has the attention of the writer. The opening pronoun *each* focuses on the individual, not on the group. The following sentences are correct:

> Each of us should write to his or her councilwoman.
> All of us should write to our councilwoman.

See 17.1 on number agreement.

### EXERCISE

Correct the shifts in person and number in the following:
1. You can get help in emergencies if one dials 911.
2. If a person parks in a yellow zone without their permit, they may find their car towed away.
3. Nobody should have to pay more than their share.
4. If you can get a mechanic to repair the car on a Sunday, expect to pay them overtime.
5. One can't help giving their opinion on the matter when asked.
6. People should realize that you can't clean up the environment without spending money.
7. You can clean up toxic waste dumps near populated areas if they do care about a clean environment.
8. The property owners in the neighborhood has his drinking water threatened by toxic wastes.
9. The city of Dayton is threatened by toxic wastes leaking into their underground water.
10. Each of us property owner has a view of their own on the issue.

**25.1c Tense.** Needless shifts in tense may give the reader the impression that different people are speaking or that different events are occurring. Here again is sentence (2):

> When we talked to the people downtown, they say the wastes will be kept out of the water, but we don't believe they will.

The writer of the sentence shifts from the past *talked* to the present *say*. The error probably occurs because the writer is using *say* in the sense of "They'll say anything." The tenses are consistent in the following sentence:

> When we talked to the people downtown, they said the wastes will be kept out of the water, but we don't believe they will.

However, the sentence is still unsatisfactory because the word *they* at the end is ambiguous: *they* can refer to both *people* and *wastes* earlier.

**25.1**
**shift**

Here are satisfactory revisions of the original sentence:

When we talked to the people downtown, they said the wastes will be kept out of the water, but we don't believe they will keep them out.

When we talked to the people downtown, they said they will keep wastes from getting into the water, but we don't believe them.

**25.1d Literary Present Tense.**   In a summary of a novel or story, movie or play, the present tense is required because the summary describes what is happening in the time frame created by the author, not in actual time:

In the final scene of *Abe Lincoln in Illinois*, Lincoln says farewell to the townspeople of Springfield at the train station, his wife standing at his side.

Be careful not to shift to the past tense in the course of the summary:

Lincoln finishes his address, and then the train departed.

The same rule applies to statements made in the past:

*Incorrect*
Lincoln said at Gettysburg that the United States was "one nation indivisible."

*Correct*
Lincoln said at Gettysburg that the United States is "one nation indivisible."

**25.1**
**shift**

**EXERCISE**

Correct the fault in tense in the following sentences:
1. *Star Wars* was a western movie disguised as science fiction.
2. When we saw *Star Wars*, we understood now why it was so popular a movie.
3. Before we could ask them to our house for Thanksgiving, they ask us to theirs.
4. The floor had to be swept, then should have been washed with a detergent.
5. Einstein stated in his special theory of relativity that mass was a form of energy.
6. In *Sunrise at Campobello*, Franklin Roosevelt was stricken with polio but makes the decision to continue his career in politics.

7. The press seldom photographed President Roosevelt as he sits in his wheelchair.
8. Not everyone agrees that the press should disclose the full details of presidential illness.
9. Certainly everyone agrees that the fact that the President is ill must be reported and what the outcome was.
10. In John Steinbeck's *The Grapes of Wrath*, victims of the Oklahoma drought in the 1930s sought work in California fields and orchards.

**25.1e Sequence of Tenses.** Tenses must be in proper sequence to show how events are related in time. Here are the past and perfect tenses in English:

*Past:* the act completed

He walked to school.

*Past Progressive:* the act in progress in the past

He was walking to school.

*Present Perfect:* the act begun in the past and continuing into the present

He has walked to school since he was eight.

*Present Perfect Progressive:* the act begun in the past and still in progress in the present

He has been walking to school every morning.

*Past Perfect:* the act completed before another event that occurred in the past

He had walked before he spoke his first word.

*Past Perfect Progressive:* the act begun and occurring in the past before another event

He had been walking the day before he celebrated his first birthday.

When we join two clauses describing two related actions in the past, the proper sequence of tenses shows the exact relation in time:

*Inexact*
The meeting was a success because it has been planned carefully.

*Exact*
The meeting was a success because they had planned it well.
[The plan was made before the meeting occurred.]

**25.1**
**shift**

*Inexact*
She said that the plan has succeeded.

*Exact*
She said that the plan had succeeded.
[The plan must have succeeded before the woman commented
on it.]

If the plan was in operation at the time the woman was
speaking, the exact statement would be the following:

She insisted that the plan was succeeding.

**25.1f Mood.** Here is a review of the three moods of English
sentences:

*Indicative Mood:* states a fact or asks whether an event has occurred.

I walked to school.
Did you walk to school?
Are you walking to school?

*Imperative Mood:* gives a command.

Forward march!
Watch your step!
Halt!

*Subjunctive Mood:* states a wish, demand, or condition contrary
to fact.

I wish the meeting were over.
I ask that the meeting be adjourned.
If I were there, I would ask that the meeting be adjourned.

Compare these statements in the indicative and imperative
moods:

If I go, I will look for you.
Walk out if the meeting is adjourned!

These sentences state alternative actions, one of which *will* occur. Notice that if you try to state the first of the sentences in
the subjunctive, the sentence becomes awkward and illogical:

Were I to go, I will look for you.

The indicative mood today usually substitutes for the subjunctive except in formal demands, or in statements of desire
beginning *I ask* or *I wish*, or in parliamentary or judicial procedure:

**25.1**
**shift**

*If it please the court,* I shall present the case in favor of my client.

Certain kinds of writing—for example, legal briefs— distinguish carefully between indicative and subjunctive to highlight the difference between fact and possibility.

Shifts from indicative to subjunctive or from subjunctive to imperative are rare:

*Inexact*
If they were to adjourn the meeting, the bill will be sent to the committee.

*Exact*
If they were to adjourn the meeting, the bill would be sent to the committee.
If they adjourn the meeting, the bill will be sent to the committee.

*Inexact*
If they were to adjourn the meeting, walk out!

*Exact*
If they refuse to adjourn the meeting, walk out!

**25.1**
**shift**

Sentence (3) quoted at the beginning of the chapter illustrates a shift in mood:

If we had a say in the matter, these wastes won't be dumped where people get their drinking water.

The sentence begins in the subjunctive ("if we had a say in the matter" or "suppose we had a say"), and it changes to the indicative ("these wastes won't be dumped. . . ."). Here are possible revisions in both the subjunctive and indicative:

*Subjunctive*
If we had a say in the matter, these wastes *wouldn't* be dumped where people get their drinking water.

*Indicative*
If we have a say in the matter, these wastes *won't* be dumped where people get their drinking water.

Shifts from the indicative to the imperative mood are far more common:

*Incorrect*
You should proofread, and watch for comma faults!

*Correct*
You should proofread and especially watch for comma faults.

**25.1g Voice.**    Shifts from active to passive voice—or from passive to active voice—can make sentences awkward:

| *Awkward* | *Revised* |
|---|---|
| We finished the discussion but agreement was not reached by us. | We finished the discussion but did not reach agreement. |
| The race was won and the California ski team immediately left for the Olympic trials in Vermont. | The California ski team won the race and immediately left for the Olympic trials in Vermont. |

### EXERCISES

**1.** Correct the faults in the following:
  **a.** If I were king, you will be queen.
  **b.** He smashed the fender and the door was dented.
  **c.** He said he had a suit my size and would I try it on.
  **d.** The beginning writer can learn something from reading for style, but don't imitate apishly.
  **e.** The exam was finished at twelve and then we had lunch.
  **f.** If you were not sick, come to the meeting with us!
  **g.** Though she went to the play against her will, it was much enjoyed.
  **h.** After we had built the fence, we decided to sell the lot.
  **i.** I hammered the door shut and the windows were sealed.
  **j.** Watch for the railroad crossing, and then the road will turn sharply to the right.

**2.** Finish the sentence, using the correct sequence of tenses:
  **a.** She trimmed the bushes while
  **b.** She was trimming the bushes when
  **c.** He had written to the company after
  **d.** We have written to the company even though
  **e.** Were I to write the company
  **f.** He would write the company
  **g.** The contest winners were announced and
  **h.** Be it resolved that
  **i.** If I had driven to Wilmington with you
  **j.** Watch for a blue car with Arizona license plates and

**25.2**
**//**

## 25.2  Faulty Parallelism

**25.2a Missing Parallelism.**    Phrases and clauses that serve the same function in the sentence—for example, compound predicates or modifying phrases and clauses—should be **parallel** in structure (see 20.1). The following sentence lacks parallelism:

She believed her plan would succeed and which would earn her
a promotion.

The first dependent clause *(that) her plan would succeed* is the
direct object of *believed*. The second dependent clause *which would
earn her a promotion* is also a direct object of *believed* and is similar
in idea to the first clause. The two clauses therefore should be
parallel in form:

She believed (that) her plan would succeed and (that it) would
earn her a promotion.

Correlative phrases and clauses should be parallel for the
same reason—to highlight the similarity in ideas:

*Neither* Jim *nor* his wife speaks or writes Italian or French, though
they are planning to work and travel in Italy and France.
Jim and his wife *not only* are learning Italian *but also* are learning
French.
Jim and his wife are *not only* learning Italian *but also* learning
French.

See 8.9b for a list of other correlatives.

**25.2b  Misleading Parallelism.**   Sentences may seem awkward if parallel phrases and clauses do not express parallel ideas:

*Awkward*
He wants to learn chess and to have enough time to do so.

This sentence shifts from what the person wants to do (*to learn
chess*) to what the person needs in order to do it (*to have enough
time to do so*). To revise, add a verb to the second part of the
sentence:

He wants to learn chess and hopes to find enough time to do
so.

Here is a second example of *misleading parallelism*—subject
complements that seem parallel in idea but are not:

She is *anxious about the interview* and *eager to call us* if it goes
well.

The shift in idea is from what the person feels (*is anxious about
the interview*) to what she plans to do (*is eager to call us if it goes
well.*) The simple addition of *is* will correct the sentence:

She is anxious about the interview and is eager to call us if it
goes well.

So will subordinating the first clause to the second:

**25.2**

//

Because she is anxious about the interview, she is eager to call us if it goes well.

Compare the following paragraphs from a student paper. The sentence elements requiring parallelism are underlined in both versions. Notice also the rephrasing of ideas:

**25.2**
**//**

*Original*

The spatial arrangements of my college classrooms which are composed by the students turn out to be the opposite of how my public school teachers made the arrangements. The spatial arrangements of the classroom or where students choose to seat themselves illustrate nonverbal communication. In choosing a particular seat in the classroom students are signaling to the other members of the class what kind of person they are, their relationship to the rest of the class, where in the classroom they feel the most comfortable, and even their intentions as students. Furthermore, students are then able to use nonverbal communication to etch out their own niche in all the classes they attend.

*Revised*

The spatial arrangements of my college classrooms, composed by the students who choose their own seats, are different from the arrangements of my public school classrooms. These arrangements illustrate nonverbal communication. In choosing a particular seat, students are signaling to other members of the class what kind of person they are, what relationship they wish to have with the class, where in the room they feel the most at ease, and what their intentions are as students. In this way, they use nonverbal communication to control their relationships with their teachers and fellow students.

**EXERCISE**

Correct any faulty parallelism in the following sentences:
1. They know that a nice house costs money and which is hard to find unless you have enough for a down payment.
2. Either we look for a new car or spend money fixing our old one.
3. The house needs a coat of paint, new window sashes, and an expensive new roof.
4. She is not only good in math but is in political science and French.
5. You need patience to train a dog, make it sit on command, and not jumping on people.
6. To train a dog, you need both patience and the dog needs to see your firmness.
7. The dog doesn't know whether to sit or do you want it to lie down?
8. She wants not so much to train the dog as it should not jump on people.
9. The committee made the decision to support her candidacy and to notify her of its decision.
10. I am ready whenever you are and when John is.

**25.3** Omitted Words

25.3
∧

We routinely omit words clearly implied in the sentence:

We know (*that*) he walks four miles every morning.

But occasionally omission creates awkwardness.

**25.3a Articles.**   Omitted articles make the following sentences awkward:

She saw an enormous dog and bicyclist on the road.

The word *bicyclist* cannot take the modifier *an*. More seriously, we cannot tell whether *enormous* describes just the dog or the dog and the biker both. Here is the needed revision:

She saw an enormous dog and a bicyclist on the road.

Omitting the article *the* can also make a sentence confusing:

We need advice of the doctor.

This ambiguous sentence can be taken to mean that we need advice *about* the doctor or that we need advice *from* the doctor. If the second is the meaning intended, the sentence may be worded:

We need the advice of the doctor.
We need advice from the doctor.
We need the doctor's advice.

**25.3b Conjunctions.**   The omitted conjunction makes the following sentence momentarily ambiguous:

He expected the child who was wading in the pond would not go out too far.

*Revised*
He expected that the child who was wading in the pond would not go out too far.

**25.3c Verbs.**   The omission of auxiliaries in the following sentence confuses the meaning:

*Confusing*
I am not and never been a smoker.

*Revised*
I am not and have never been a smoker.

We need to repeat a verb if the omission creates misunderstanding. Compare the following:

| A Missouri hog-and-grain farmer isn't any more likely to worry about what people in New York think of, say, Clark County, Missouri, than people in London or Dakar think of Clark County, Missouri. | A Missouri hog-and-grain farmer isn't any more likely to worry about what people in New York think of, say, Clark County, Missouri, than *he is to worry about* what people in London or Dakar think of Clark County, Missouri. |

—CALVIN TRILLIN, "American Royal," *The New Yorker*, September 26, 1983

The awkward sentence to the left seems to talk about what Missouri farmers worry about and what Londoners and citizens of Dakar, Senegal, think about. The repetition of the verb phrase *(he) is to worry* tells us the sentence is talking about the Missouri farmer only.

**25.3d Adverbs.**   You must sometimes repeat an adverb to clarify your meaning. Consider the following sentences:

Jim never loses his temper and blames others if they do the same.

If the sentence means that Jim never loses his temper and never blames others, repeat the adverb:

Jim never loses his temper and *never* blames others if they do.

You need not repeat the adverb if the sentence is worded as follows:

Jim never loses his temper or blames others if they do.

**25.3e Prepositions.**   The omission of a preposition can create awkwardness or confusion. Compare the following:

| | |
|---|---|
| She is curious and looking forward to visiting French Canada. | She is curious *about* and looking forward to visiting French Canada. |
| He is as fascinated and deeply involved in city politics as his wife is. | He is as fascinated *by* and deeply involved in city politics as his wife is. |

## 25.4   Incomplete Comparisons

Once introduced, a comparison should be completed. If someone says to you

There's nothing more tiring.

you may ask

More tiring than what?

The person then completes the comparison:

There's nothing more tiring than standing in line for an hour.

Sometimes the comparison misleads by omitting essential words:

I like Mary more than Jane.

The following revisions clarify the meaning:

I like Mary more than I like Jane.
I like Mary more than Jane does.

Compare the following:

| *Incomplete* | *Complete* |
|---|---|
| Pizza is as popular with grown-ups as teenagers. | Pizza is as popular with grown-ups as (it is) with teenagers. |

| Pizza in this restaurant is as good if not better than at home. | Pizza in this restaurant is as good as, if not better than, the kind my father makes at home. |

## EXERCISE

Correct the omissions if necessary. Rephrase the sentence if necessary:

1. Her reputation was her chocolate cake, not to mention her apple pie.
2. We always have and always will like country music.
3. He is tired and angry with the constant bickering in committee meetings.
4. He likes eating more than Jane.
5. They want help of their parents.
6. He has no knowledge or interest in scuba diving.
7. She has knowledge and will continue on the life of early settlers in Minnesota.
8. Her book is as good if not the best on the subject.
9. They watched the fire with concern and not knowing what to do.
10. I am worried as you and will more until this crisis is over.
11. She seldom asked for favors and offered to do favors for others.
12. In the waiting room of the office sat an old man and young woman.
13. It never rains on Memorial Day and also rains on Labor Day.
14. Country music is as popular with Northerners as Southerners.
15. Dogs are as smart and different to live with than cats.

**25.4**
**inc**

# General Exercise

Correct any faults in the following sentences:

1. My sister dislikes ice cream more than him.
2. She also dislikes ice cream with chocolate sauce and a paper dish.
3. Yogurt is not only delicious but it is lower in fat than whole milk.
4. If you were in my position, you will make the same decisions.
5. All hand in his exam when the bell rings!
6. In his book *Plagues and People*, William McNeill described how bubonic plague and other diseases influenced European history.

7. A chronic and acute disease like malaria and bubonic plague have different social effects on populations.
8. Bubonic plague succeeded in wiping out more than a third of the people in many countries in the thirteenth century.
9. The shark was not aware and curious about the swimmer.
10. The woman in charge explained that the museum has closed for the rest of the week.
11. Since they wanted to see the outcome of the trial, the week's adjournment was resented.
12. Anyone who has seen a rugby match will see a resemblance to American football, but notice the difference in scoring.
13. I am interested and curious about the history and present programs of the college.
14. I enjoy tennis more.
15. Raising tomatoes is hard as lettuce.

# Checklist for Shifts and Omissions

**25.1a**   Shifts in person make sentences awkward and confusing:

*Incorrect*
Politicians forget you will need support from people like us in November.

*Revised*
Politicians forget they will need support from people like us in November.

**25.1b**   Shifts from singular to plural in pronouns and their antecedents can be confusing:

Each of us should write to their councilwoman.

All of us should write to our councilwoman.

**25.1c**   Don't shift tenses needlessly:

When we talked to the people downtown, they say the wastes will be kept out of the water.

When we talked to the people downtown, they said the wastes will be kept out of the water.

**25.1d**   Summaries of novels and plays, books and essays, should be in the present tense, not the past tense.

**25.1e**   Tenses must be in proper sequence to show how events are related in time.

The meeting *was* a success because it *had been planned* carefully.

**25.1f**   Don't shift the mood of the sentence needlessly:

Were I to go, I will look for you.

Were I to go, I would look for you.

**25.1g**  Shifts in voice can also make sentences confusing:

| | |
|---|---|
| We finished the discussion but agreement was not reached by us. | We finished the discussion but did not reach agreement. |

**25.2a**  Make compound predicates parallel in structure:

| | |
|---|---|
| She believed her plan would succeed and which would earn her a promotion. | She believed her plan would succeed and would earn her a promotion. |

**25.2b**  Make parallel phrases and clauses express parallel ideas:

| | |
|---|---|
| He wants to learn chess and have enough time to do so. | He wants to learn chess and hopes to have enough time to do so. |

**25.3a**  Omitted articles can create awkwardness:

| | |
|---|---|
| She saw an enormous dog and bicyclist on the road. | She saw an enormous dog and a bicyclist on the road. |

**25.3b**  Omitted conjunctions can create ambiguity:

| | |
|---|---|
| He expected the child who was wading in the pond would not go in too far. | He expected that the child who was wading in the pond would not go in too far. |

**25.3c**  Omission of auxiliary verbs can make sentences awkward and confusing:

| | |
|---|---|
| I am not and never been a smoker. | I am not and have never been a smoker. |

**25.3d-e**  Adverbs and prepositions must be repeated sometimes to clarify meaning:

| | |
|---|---|
| Jim never loses his temper and blames others if they do. | Jim never loses his temper and never blames others if they do. |

**25.4**  A sentence that introduces a comparison should complete it:

| | |
|---|---|
| There's nothing more tiring. | There's nothing more tiring than standing in line. |

# Awkward Sentences

Previous chapters discuss various ways of making sentences clear and effective. But some of these ways weaken sentences or make them awkward if overused. For example, subordination is an important means to giving ideas proper focus, but excessive subordination can create an awkward sentence. Sentences also need to repeat words and give specific details to make ideas clear; however, excessive repetition and excessive detail can overload and unbalance sentences. This chapter discusses disunified, overloaded, and unbalanced sentences. The following chapter discusses repetitive and wordy ones.

## 26.1 Sentence Unity

A unified sentence deals with one idea at a time and connects related details. Disunified sentences join unrelated ideas and details that deserve separate sentences and separate focus. Sometimes these details are attached to the sentence as trailing modifiers:

> The tall, red-haired man in the white jacket is the swimming coach—a hot-tempered but understanding man, competitive but not ruthless, a tournament swimmer himself for many years, having trained in high school for state meets, and later in college, from which he graduated with honors in American history and political science.

The details about the coach's high school and college swimming and academic career shift the focus from the idea that opens the sentence—the fact that the man is the new swimming coach. They create a new subject as the sentence progresses to the end. Here is a satisfactory revision that unifies the details and omits those irrelevant to the topic idea:

The tall, red-haired man in the white jacket is the swimming coach. A hot-tempered but understanding man, he is competitive but not ruthless, having been a tournament swimmer himself for many years. He trained in high school for state meets and trained later in college.

The reason for combining clauses, instead of presenting ideas in separate sentences, is to keep closely related ideas together. Here is a heavily coordinated sentence that succeeds in combining related ideas without loss of focus:

> But I remember the smell of the big schoolroom, a smell of ink and dust and boots, and the stone in the yard that had been a mounting block and was used for sharpening knives on, and the little baker's shop opposite where they sold a kind of Chelsea bun, twice the size of the Chelsea buns you get nowadays, which were called Lardy Busters and cost a half-penny.
>
> —GEORGE ORWELL, *Coming Up for Air*

**26.1**
**awk**

Orwell's sentence is tightly constructed. The various details connect as things Orwell remembers. Compare the following highly informal, humorous sentences—the first of them containing a series of trailing modifiers, the second joining two loosely related ideas that develop the topic idea of the paragraph. The writer is discussing his wife's belief that he knows how to recognize "real" Americans:

> My credentials for the position consisted partly, I assume, of the simple fact that I was born and raised in Kansas City, Missouri, which used to be called the Heart of America, for the very good reason that it is smack in the middle of the country, if you don't count Hawaii and Alaska—which I never have and don't intend to. Also, I was then in the midst of what turned out to be fifteen years of travelling around the country as a reporter, and some of the people I knew in New York had begun to consider me an authority on such matters as how the Best Western Motel in some Iowa city stacked up against its Holiday Inn.
>
> —CALVIN TRILLIN, "American Royal,"
> *The New Yorker*, September 26, 1983

As long as these sentences are, they do not seem wordy; for they are appropriate to the humor and ideas they convey, and the details in both clearly relate to the topic idea.

Even when the details center on the same idea, the sentence may seem too long. How many ideas and details you present in a single sentence sometimes depends on your judgment of how much information the reader can grasp in reading it. The decision depends, too, on how formal or informal the essay is. You may tire quickly in reading highly formal, compressed writing that never wastes a word and seldom depends on a familiar phrase or colloquial structure. You can tire also from the lean, tense informal style of many journalists—perhaps a necessity of the limited space available in newspapers and effective in a short column, but ineffective in a long essay or book.

### EXERCISE

The following essay is the second draft of a student paper, written in response to the following statement of Edward T. Hall and Mildred Reed Hall in their essay "The Sounds of Silence": "We know from research that everyone has around him an invisible bubble of space that contracts and expands depending on several factors: his emotional state, the activity he's performing at the time and his cultural background." Review the discussion of paragraph unity (5.5) and unity in the whole essay (3.2b). What revisions would you make of the sentences, the paragraphs, and the whole essay?

**26.1**
**awk**

At this university, the classrooms are spacious enough to allow me to spread my books, purse, and writing implements about me without invading the space of another. Walks and driveways are wide enough so I can pass another person on foot or in the car without physical contact. Eating facilities are large and varied enough so I can find a place to eat without standing in line for long or being jostled. I can usually spend but a few minutes in line before getting into the Xerox room at the library. Study carrels are large enough to accommodate all my personal needs while studying. Lines for registration are well controlled so I need not step on anyone's feet or be stepped upon. All of these activities are provided for well at this university, but there is one that seems to be unsolvable.

There is an exception to all this smoothness of operation, and it occurs daily both coming and

going to classes in the university. I can't take
my car to class, but there seems to be no place
to safely leave it. I spend more time than I'd
like trying to zip into a parking place before
another student, younger, with quicker reflexes,
does. However, I don't begrudge the student taking my parking place or the space I thought was
mine. It is "survival of the fittest" out there
in the parking lot, and they win the battle as
fairly as someone can when there are no rules.

I do feel angry that I've put myself in circumstances where I cannot rid myself of my car.
It seems so foolish to ride around and around
searching, finding and then losing a space for my
car. What is even more foolish is repeating this
two or three times each morning. Perhaps this
scenario is a reminder or a symbol of the fool-
ishness I display daily in the classroom. I recognize and admire the quickness and resourceful-
ness of students younger than myself. I wonder
how I could be so foolish to think I could keep
up with them inside or outside the classroom. And
it is this reminder that angers me.

Nevertheless, I keep coming back to fill a
space at study carrels, lunch rooms, the Xerox
room, the sidewalk, and registration lines. The
students are great. I'm the one who has to live
with my image of myself, struggling for an advantage when there is none—except to learn as best
I can, and to park wherever I can.

**26.2**
**sub**

# 26.2  Excessive Subordination

**26.2a  Opening Modifiers.**  A string of loosely related modifiers at the beginning of a sentence can divert attention from
the subject:

> Piloting his own plane, which he had learned to fly in the air force, which he joined in 1951 at the start of the Korean War, Ferguson won the cross-country race.

The modifiers of this awkward sentence are distracting because they have nothing to do with the central idea—that Ferguson won the cross-country race. If the information about when and where Ferguson learned to fly is important, the sentence should state it in a separate sentence:

> Piloting his own plane, Ferguson won the cross-country race. He had learned to fly in the air force, which he joined at the start of the Korean War.

**26.2b Concluding Modifiers.** We saw previously that a trailing string of modifiers can be distracting if they introduce new ideas:

> Ferguson won the cross-country race, which he entered at the last moment, persuaded by his wife that he might win, having almost succeeded on three previous tries, in 1972, 1975, and 1980—the year he retired as a cargo pilot.

Again, the information provided in the modifiers is not closely related to the idea that Ferguson won the race. When trailing ideas and details closely relate to the core idea, the sentence will not seem overloaded. The author of the following sentence arranges the modifiers climactically:

> The first penguin was merely like the speck of beginning life in the yolk of a new-laid egg, its movements equally slight and equally irresistible because it was driven, dancing and rolling, shimmering and vibrant down the horizon of the ice with all the will to live of a whole world behind it.
> —GRAHAM BILLING, *Forbush and the Penguin*

**26.2c Unbalanced Sentences.** Beginning and ending a sentence with subordinate clauses can create awkwardness. In the following sentence the core is squeezed between two clauses of the same type:

> *Since crime makes people feel unsafe,* gun sales increase *since people believe guns are their only protection.*

The two dependent clauses should stand together because they are parallel in meaning (see 20.1 and 25.2). The following revision avoids needless repetition:

> Since crime makes people feel unsafe and they believe guns are their only protection, gun sales increase.

**26.2**
**sub**

Reducing a clause to a phrase may correct the problem:

Gun sales increase because people, *feeling unsafe*, believe guns are their only protection.

**EXERCISE**

Revise the following sentences to correct excessive subordination or imbalance:

1. Driving to Seattle to ride the monorail, which had been constructed during the World's Fair, held when she was a child, she stopped to visit an old friend.
2. She could not find the house, which she thought was on the main street which was a mile from the interstate, which cut north to Seattle.
3. After driving from one end of the street to the other, she stopped to call her friend, after making sure she was in the right town.
4. The person who answered was not her friend, who had driven to Portland that morning.
5. Because he is a poor speaker, Hanson was not elected because he failed to persuade the audience.
6. At the end of the street, where the fire was out of control, the warehouse had burned to the ground, the neighboring drugstore now in flames.
7. The man with the injured foot finished second in the race, in the face of competition from some of the fastest runners in the state, including San Francisco and Los Angeles, which produced the winners of the last marathon.
8. Knowing that the qualifying exam would test knowledge of genetics, I reviewed my notes, believing they would be more helpful than the text.
9. As soon as I read the exam questions, I began to write as soon as I had decided which ones to answer first.
10. Writing with increasing confidence, I remembered facts and ideas I thought I had forgotten, writing an answer to the first question.

**26.3**
**w**

# **26.3**  Too Many Nouns

**26.3a  Nominalization.**   When nouns do the work of other parts of speech, sentences become formal and sometimes hard to read. This transformation of nouns is called **nominalization**. Here are examples:

| | |
|---|---|
| his statement that | he says |
| their fighting | they fight |

| | |
|---|---|
| my painting of | I paint |
| her correction of | she corrects |
| the correcting of | to correct |
| the pain of the cut | the painful cut |
| the foolishness of the remark | the foolish remark |
| the naming of the boat | they named the boat |
| her explanation of the mistake | she explained the mistake |

The following sentences illustrate the process:

It took me a whole month *to paint* the house.
I *painted* the house in a month.
The *painting* of the house took me the whole of a month.

The infinitive *to paint* and the verb *painted* in the first and second sentences are transformed, in the third sentence, into the nominal *painting*.

Yet nominalization has important uses. In the third sentence the nominalization of the subject lets the writer discuss the house painting as an activity. Nominalization also give the act weight and emphasis. These are the effects of nominalization in formal writing like the following:

**26.3**
**w**

A further refinement of servo control is possible through the addition of a *phase-locked loop* (PLL), perhaps in conjunction with a quartz-crystal oscillator.
—Alan Lofft, "Choosing a Turntable,"
*Stereo Review*, May 1983

The author might have written:

Manufacturers can refine servo control through the addition of a phase-locked loop . . .

But the desired emphasis would be lost. The focus of the discussion is on the refinement of servo control, not on the manufacturers.

Nominalization is thus a valuable resource—as the following sentences illustrate:

The *Fifth Symphony* is an expression of Beethoven's faith in life.
The *Fifth Symphony* expresses Beethoven's faith in life.

The first sentence focuses on the act of expression, the second sentence on the *Fifth Symphony* itself.

But heavily nominalized sentences may create a formal effect unsuited to the context. The more nouns the sentence contains, the more formal it will sound. Nevertheless, a formal, highly impersonal tone may be what the writer wants:

Nonpayment of this bill will necessitate our taking legal action.

This statement is deliberately threatening, and threats gain force when they seem impersonal. The full weight of the law presumably stands behind the writer—as if "legal action" were a force set in motion automatically when bills are unpaid.

In short, the more nominalized the sentence, the more objective and the less personal or human it may sound. Compare the following:

| | |
|---|---|
| He made the statement that he is coming. | He said he is coming. |
| Their fighting is a frequent occurrence. | They fight often. |
| Her correction of the mistake occurred yesterday. | She corrected the mistake yesterday. |
| She wanted to make the correction without delay. | She wanted to correct it right away. |

**26.3**

**w**

Nominalization also may change the meaning of the sentence:

The nurse treated the painful cut.
The nurse treated the pain of the cut.

**26.3b Revising Nominalized Sentences.**   Following are three ways to improve overnominalized sentences:
   1. Focus on the action rather than on the act.

| *Pretentious and Wordy* | *Plain and Concise* |
|---|---|
| The idealization of America by immigrants from Eastern Europe occurred in different ways. | Immigrants from Eastern Europe idealized America in different ways. |
| The not unexpected decision to join the navy was not a surprise to us. | We were not surprised that he decided to join the navy. |

   2. Reduce prepositional phrases to adjectives.

| | |
|---|---|
| It was a day of sunshine. | It was a sunny day. |
| | *Or:* The day was sunny. |
| He bought a car at great expense. | He bought an expensive car. |

3. Change nouns to verbs or adjectives.

Their donation of money to the Cancer Society is an annual occurrence.

They donate money to the Cancer Society annually.

The loudness of the bark awakened the sentry.

The loud bark awakened the sentry.

Nonpayment of this bill will necessitate legal action.

We will sue if you don't pay this bill.

### EXERCISES

1. Reduce the number of nouns in the following sentences.
    **a.** Correction of this paper requires a number of steps.
    **b.** She has experience with music and dance.
    **c.** The falsification of the evidence was a disturbance to the judge.
    **d.** The fact of significance is that no person has received a citation under the new law.
    **e.** The supply of the required electric power source and fittings to operate the equipment is the responsibility of the customer.
2. Rewrite in plain English the following university regulations governing student conduct.

    **a.** The disciplinary power of the University is inherent in its responsibility to protect its educational purposes and processes through the setting of standards of conduct and scholarship for its students and through the regulation of the use of its facilities. The established standards of conduct apply to a student whenever he is on property owned, leased, or operated by the University or in housing occupied or used by recognized University student groups.

    **b.** Reports of alleged misconduct may originate from University faculty or staff, University students, University security officers, area residents, or off-campus government law enforcement agencies.

    **c.** The University prefers to develop responsible student conduct through counseling, guidance, admonition, and example, and it prefers, therefore, to proceed carefully but informally whenever possible. However, if the student so desires, he may bring an advisor or an attorney with him to any discussion or investigation which may follow the first fact-finding session in which the student

**26.3**

**w**

is informed of the charge of alleged misconduct. Conferences with the student (and, if he chooses, with his counsel) are designed to develop in depth all facts pertinent to the alleged misconduct.

# 26.4  Active and Passive Verbs

**26.4a  Uses of the Passive Voice.**  Use the passive voice to emphasize the receiver of the action and not the actor or agent:

| *Active Voice* | *Passive Voice* |
|---|---|
| The hunter shot the wolf. | The wolf was shot by the hunter. |

These sentences say the same thing but with a different emphasis. The passive voice is appropriate when the actor is unknown or when the sentence focuses on action performed:

> The house was destroyed by the fire, which raged through the neighborhood.
> The package was delivered on Friday.

The passive voice also helps to avoid a long and awkward opening subject:

*Awkward*
> That the storm could have struck without a public warning by the weather bureau disturbed many people.

The following revision is idiomatic:

*Improved*
> Many people were disturbed that the storm could have struck without a public warning by the weather bureau.

**26.4b  Misuses of the Passive Voice.**  Don't use the passive voice if the actor of the sentence is important and needs identification:

*Awkward*
> The fender was dented by the accident.

The writer of the sentence disguises the cause by attributing the dented fender to the accident. The following revision mentions the actor but plays down his importance:

*Awkward*
> The fender was dented by me in the accident.

26.4
pass

*Revision*
I dented the fender in the accident.


**26.4c Seeking Objectivity.** The passive voice gives the impression of objectivity: it can create the impression that subjective or personal feelings play no role in the activity and play none in the reporting of it. Papers in learned journals routinely contain statements like the following:

> It will be demonstrated in this paper that . . .
> The molecular structure of heavy water will be discussed in this paper . . .
> The conclusion to be drawn from this study is that . . .
> It is to be hoped that these findings will . . .
> Objections may be raised to examining Shakespeare's sonnets from the point of view of . . .

Creating an objective tone is possible without depending heavily on the passive voice. The opening paragraph of the following scientific article shows that writers can discuss the subject without constant use of the passive voice:

> Many machines imitate nature; a familiar example is the imitation of a soaring bird by the airplane. One form of animal locomotion that has resisted imitation is walking. Can it be that modern computers and feedback control systems make it possible to build machines that walk? We have been exploring the question with computer models and with actual hardware.
> —Marc H. Raibert and Ivan E. Sutherland, "Machines That Walk," *Scientific American*, January 1983

The active voice and occasional use of the personal pronoun can enliven the writing, as in this excerpt from another scientific article:

> Allow me to show you the rest of my laboratory. Although my work is concerned almost entirely with the properties of matter under enormous pressure, most of the laboratory space is now given over to instruments that play ancillary roles in the investigation: the laser, the microscope, the spectroscope and the automatic equipment that can record the spectroscopic data. Indeed, it would be easy to miss the novel device that makes the rest of the work possible, because it can be held readily in the palm of one hand.
> —A. Jayaraman, "The Diamond-Anvil High-Pressure Cell," *Scientific American*, April 1984

**26.4**
**pass**

This paragraph shows the accepted use of the passive voice when the actor is unimportant:

my work is concerned almost entirely with . . .
most of the laboratory space is now given over . . .
it can be held. . .

The personal references at the beginning of the passage reduce the formal effect considerably.


**EXERCISES**

1. Revise the following passages to make the verbs active and to reduce wordiness. Retain the passive only if emphasis should fall on the action and not on the actor:
   **a.** That is the car that was hit by me.
   **b.** The car that was struck on the right by the truck had just been stolen.
   **c.** The dance attended by my sister and her boyfriend was sponsored by the senior class.
   **d.** American foreign policy is not made overnight or guided by one person or group of advisers.
   **e.** A fine will be levied by this magistrate upon drivers convicted by this court.
   **f.** The paper was not written by the student in time to meet the deadline.
2. Rewrite the following statements in the active voice. Be ready to discuss whether your revision improves the clarity or emphasis of the original sentence:

   a. When the hazards of dangerous play are not fully understood by children, protective measures similar to those controlling accessibility to dangerous poisons should be followed.
   —American Red Cross, *Standard First Aid and Personal Safety*

   b. If rust damage does occur, the car must be inspected by a company representative. The contact may be made directly to the dealer, and arrangements made through him. An appointment will be made at the dealership for an inspection to determine the extent of X's liability.          —A clause in a warranty contract

   c. Receipts covering the performance of regular maintenance should be retained in the event questions

**26.4**

**pass**

arise concerning maintenance. These receipts should be transferred to each subsequent owner of this car.

—Automobile warranty

# Checklist for Awkward Sentences

**26.1**   Disunified sentences join ideas and details that deserve their own sentences and separate focus:

*Awkward*

The tall, red-haired man in the white jacket is the swimming coach—a hot-tempered but understanding man, competitive but not ruthless, a tournament swimmer himself for many years, having trained in high school for state meets and later in college, from which he graduated with honors in American history and political science.

*Revised*

The tall, red-haired man in the white jacket is the swimming coach. A hot-tempered but understanding man, he is competitive but not ruthless, having been a tournament swimmer himself for many years. He trained in high school for state meets, and later trained in college.

**26.4**
**pass**

**26.2a**   A string of loosely related modifiers at the beginning of a sentence diverts attention from the subject:

Piloting his own plane, which he had learned to fly in the air force, which he joined in 1951, at the start of the Korean War, Ferguson won the cross-country race.

Piloting his own plane, Ferguson won the cross-country race. He had learned to fly in the air force, which he joined at the start of the Korean War.

**26.2b**   Trailing modifiers will distract the reader if they are loosely related to the central idea:

Ferguson won the cross-country race, which he entered at the last moment, persuaded by his wife that he might win, having almost succeeded on three previous tries, in 1972, 1975, and 1980—the year he retired as a cargo pilot.

Persuaded by his wife that he might win, Ferguson entered the cross-country race at the last minute and won. He almost succeeded on three previous tries, in 1972, 1975, and 1980—the year he retired as a cargo pilot.

**26.2c**  An unbalanced sentence may begin and end with sub-ordinate clauses that express similar or parallel ideas:

| | |
|---|---|
| Since crime makes people feel unsafe, gun sales increase since people believe guns are their only protection. | Since crime makes people feel unsafe and they believe guns are their only protection, gun sales increase. |

**26.3a**  When nouns do the work of other parts of speech, sentences become excessively formal and hard to read:

| | |
|---|---|
| He made the statement that he was coming. | He said he was coming. |

**26.3b**  Simplify overnominalized sentences by focusing on the actor, by reducing prepositional phrases to adjectives, or by changing nouns to verbs or adjectives:

| | |
|---|---|
| His not unexpected decision to join the navy was not a surprise to us. | We were not surprised that he decided to join the navy. |
| It was a day of sunshine. | The day was sunny. |
| The loudness of the bark awakened the sentry. | The loud bark awakened the sentry. |

**26.4a**  The passive voice is appropriate when focusing on the action performed and not the actor or cause of the action:

The car was overturned by the storm and caught fire.

**26.4b**  The passive voice can create ambiguity in disguising the actor:

| | |
|---|---|
| The fender was dented by the accident. | I dented the fender in the accident. |

# Wordy Sentences

## 27.1 Repetitive Sentences

Advertising depends on emphatic repetition of words and phrases, as in this magazine advertisement for a utility company:

> We won't keep quiet about Cleveland. We never have. We believe strongly in the future of Cleveland-Northeast Ohio, and we're talking it up every day. Our Area Development Department is staffed with a team of experts whose job is to help sell Cleveland-Northeast Ohio to business and industry, both in and outside of the area.

Such emphatic repetition favored by advertisers is inappropriate in ordinary writing unless the ideas deserve special emphasis. Continuous repetition of the same words and phrases throughout a paragraph or essay will soon tire readers and blur the focus.

**27.1a Unnecessary Repetition.** A sentence will be ambiguous or confusing if you fail to specify one of several antecedents or omit essential words. (See 18.6 and 18.7 on pronoun reference and 25.3 on omitted words.) At the same time, you can make the sentence wordy in needlessly repeating a name:

> Johnson explained the budget proposal; then Johnson turned the meeting over to his assistant.

Johnson's name is repeated needlessly at the start of the second clause. We usually delete the name in the following clause and substitute a pronoun:

> Johnson explained the budget proposal; then he turned the meeting over to his assistant.

**27.1b Necessary Repetition.** Repetition is sometimes necessary to avoid ambiguity:

| *Ambiguous* | *Clear* |
|---|---|
| Johnson explained the budget proposal, then turned the meeting over to his assistant, who said *he* would comment on other features of the budget later. | Johnson explained the budget proposal, then turned the meeting over to his assistant, who said that *Johnson* would comment on other features of the budget later. |
| Give the proposal to Johnson, not to Wilson, unless *he* protests. | Give the proposal to Johnson, not to Wilson, unless *Johnson* protests. |

Where the sentence implies a word, it may be deleted to make the sentence concise. The relative pronoun *that* is commonly deleted in sentences like the following:

> We know (*that*) John isn't coming.

But stating the pronoun at times helps to avoid momentary confusion in reading the sentence:

> We just found the book assigned is out of print.
> We just found *that* the book assigned is out of print.

With the omission of the pronoun the reader may stumble over the words that open the sentence:

> We just found the book assigned . . .
> We just found that the book assigned . . .

**27.1c Redundancy.** A redundant statement repeats an idea needlessly in different words:

> This morning we will now search for the missing cash.
> The result of the investigation was the consequent dismissal of the cashier and his resulting arrest.

Your ear probably alerted you to the redundancy of the first statement but perhaps not to that of the second. In the first, the words *this morning* and *now* say the same thing. In the second, the words *result, consequent*, and *resulting* mean the same thing.
Here are satisfactory revisions of these sentences:

> This morning we will search for the missing cash.
> The result of the investigation was the dismissal of the cashier and his subsequent arrest.

Redundancy is harder to spot in a sentence like the following:

> His failure as secretary of state is partly to blame for his ineffective conduct of foreign policy.

The sentence repeats in the predicate what it says in the subject: the secretary's failure is the same thing as his ineffectiveness. Here is a satisfactory revision:

> As secretary of state he failed to conduct foreign policy effectively.

**27.1d Same Words, Different Meanings.** Using the same word with different meanings makes a sentence awkward:

| *Awkward* | *Revised* |
|---|---|
| He will present the report to the committee presently. | He will present the report to the committee shortly. |

Sometimes the repeated words have approximately the same meaning, but their occurrence in different phrases in the sentence may be awkward:

> *In point of fact,* we have *the facts* to prove the case.

The opening phrase can be changed to *indeed* without loss.

**27.1**

**rep**

### Exercises

**1.** Be ready to discuss how effective the following sentences are in their phrasing and construction, and how they might be improved in conciseness, clarity, and focus:

> a. It will be in place, by way of illustration, to show in some detail how the economic principles so far set forth apply to everyday facts in some one direction of the life process.
> —THORSTEIN VEBLEN, *Theory of the Leisure Class*

> b. It is circumstances that determine the contents of the mind, and therefore the principal differences in the minds of men are due to circumstances.
> —LESTER WARD, *Applied Sociology*

> c. Regimentation of material and mechanical forces is the only way by which the mass of individuals can be released from regimentation and consequent suppression of their cultural possibilities.
> —JOHN DEWEY, *Liberalism and Social Action*

d. One-half to his mother, if living, if not to his father, and one-half to his mother-in-law, if living, if not to his mother, if living, if not to his father. Thereafter payment is to be made in a single sum to his brothers. On the one-half payable to his mother, if living, if not to his father, he does not bring in his mother-in-law as the next payee to receive, although on the one-half to his mother-in-law, he does bring in the mother or father.
—From an insurance policy; quoted by
STUART CHASE, *The Power of Words*

2. Eliminate as much needless repetition as you can from these paragraphs from a student essay on ads for golf equipment:

> Being a fan of golf, I find I am sometimes the typical golfer in golf advertisements and sometimes not. In an ad for a leading golf shoe producer, I discovered that if I were a true golfer, I would be in Scotland playing one of those old courses and in order to play these courses in comfort I needed their shoes.
>
> In another ad, this time for golf gloves, the golfer is portrayed as a "preppy." The fashionable gloves are supposed to give more style to your golf game. It's bad enough the guy pictured in the ad is cleanly groomed with every hair in place. Even the most ignorant of people should realize that it is impossible to golf with a pink sweater draped over your shoulders with its sleeves balled together in front.
>
> The third and most discouraging image of a golfer is that of the six-foot, blonde-haired, blue-eyed golfer. This golfer is as strong as an ox, can hit the ball three hundred yards, and to top it off doesn't have an ounce of fat on his body. This perfectly describes the men I ran across in an ad for golf clubs. In reality most golfers are older and drive golf carts around the course because they want to give their flabby

```
bodies a rest. I couldn't even discover what slim
young golfers had to do with this company's
clubs.
```

## **27.2** Needlessly Specific Sentences

Details in the following sentences are unrelated to the central idea:

He admired President Franklin Roosevelt, the architect of the "New Deal," for overcoming his physical handicap.

John Fitzgerald Kennedy, the thirty-fifth President of the United States, and Lyndon Baines Johnson, the thirty-sixth President, had very different childhoods.

Sometimes the full names of presidents and other important people are given for dramatic effect or special emphasis, but their inclusion is distracting and even pretentious in ordinary references. We do require the first names of Presidents Roosevelt and Johnson, but to understand the points made about them we do not require the information that President Roosevelt designed the "New Deal" or the middle names of President Kennedy or President Johnson. Nor do we need to know what number their presidencies were. The following revisions give the minimum information necessary:

He admired President Franklin Roosevelt for overcoming his physical handicap.

President Kennedy and President Lyndon Johnson had very different childhoods.

In descriptive writing, additional details are not distracting if they make a scene or experience vivid. But these details must be selected and organized carefully. Needless details blur the picture instead of enhancing it.

## **27.3** Overqualification

We are used to qualifying our statements in speaking to people, and qualification is normal in writing, too:

With change, *it seemed*, prosperity was coming. Many of the new buildings of Dublin might be unlovely, but *at least* they were earnests of success.     —JAN MORRIS, *Travels* [italics added]

> *For like it or not, whatever your opinions*, the drums of tragedy
> sound still in Dublin, muffled but unavoidable, as they sound
> nowhere else on earth.    —JAN MORRIS, *Travels* [italics added]

These are normal qualifications, occurring as a single phrase in
the first example and as a pair in the second. They do not clutter
the sentence. The main idea emerges clearly and immediately.

But be careful not to overqualify your sentences. The main
idea will diminish in importance if you do so:

> It takes no great intelligence, *I should add*, and no great amount
> of knowledge of the subject, *it seems to me*, to realize how im-
> possible a thing a flying saucer is.

The italicized phrases delay the completion of the core idea.
Carried throughout a paragraph, needless qualification can bury
the main idea. The following revision loses nothing in omitting
the qualifying phrases:

> It takes no great intelligence and no great amount of knowl-
> edge of the subject to realize how impossible a flying saucer is.

**27.3**
**w**

**EXERCISE**

The following answer to an examination question on George
Bernard Shaw's attitude toward vivisection, in the preface to
*The Doctor's Dilemma*, is needlessly repetitive. Revise the answer
to make it concise yet informative:

```
      Shaw used vivisection to expose the false
logic that scientists in his time used to justify
every kind of experiment. He believed that vivi-
section is one of the great horrors of mankind.
He believed that vivisection is an expression of
cruelty and dishonor. I should add that "cruelty"
and "dishonor" are his words. He states that
honorable men do not act dishonorably to dogs.
Shaw believed that vivisection was not only cruel
but also useless, stating that no medical break-
through had ever come about due to the efforts of
a vivisectionist. Shaw attacks the vivisectionist
logic, which states that vivisecting is worth-
while since it might be of help to medicine. Shaw
```

refutes this logic by noting that one would, he
points out, never be permitted by society to put
his mother in an oven in order to discover how
long someone can survive at 500° Fahrenheit, even
if the experiment produced knowledge of benefit
to people. And certainly no one would let someone
vivisect his own dog. The essence of Shaw's argument is that the claimed "right to knowledge" is
not an absolute right, nor is the right to live
if we deny others this right.

# 27.4 Phrase and Clause Reduction

**27.4a Clause Reduction.** You can sometimes shorten your
sentences effectively by reducing clauses to phrases or to single
words. The dependent clauses in the sentence to the left are
reduced to participial and prepositional phrases in the one to
the right.

**27.4**

**w**

| *Original* | *Revised* |
| --- | --- |
| Beethoven, who was becoming increasingly deaf, wrote a famous letter to his brothers that concerned his affliction. | Beethoven, becoming increasingly deaf, wrote a famous letter to his brothers concerning his affliction. |

In the following, the clause in the sentence to the left is reduced
to a single word in the sentence to the right.

| | |
| --- | --- |
| The symphony that is his fifth is an expression of his faith in life. | The *Fifth Symphony* expresses his faith in life. |

**27.4b Phrase Reduction.** Many phrases can be reduced
to single words or shorter phrases.

| | |
| --- | --- |
| Stating the matter as bluntly as I know how, I believe the play cannot succeed even if it is revised. | To be blunt, the play cannot succeed even if revised. |
| To be as frank as possible, the play is a failure. | Frankly, the play is a failure. |

These sentences have the same meaning. But phrase reduction can also change the emphasis or focus of the sentence. Compare the following:

| | |
|---|---|
| In his loneliness Beethoven found solace in nature. | The lonely Beethoven found solace in nature. |

The sentence to the right changes the emphasis from Beethoven's loneliness to the solace Beethoven found in nature. In the following, the sentence to the right gives greater emphasis to Beethoven's deafness—the cause of his new strength of spirit.

| | |
|---|---|
| Beethoven as a deaf man was stronger in spirit than Beethoven as a man in possession of his hearing. | Beethoven deaf was stronger in spirit than Beethoven possessed of hearing. |

**EXERCISE**

Reduce the following sentences to the fewest words possible without changing the meaning:

1. Haydn, who was Beethoven's teacher, found him to be a difficult student.
2. Though we seldom know the exact reasons why wars occur, we usually know the general reasons why.
3. The book that is second from the left on the first shelf contains the essay that is assigned for Monday.
4. The astronaut whose name is Scott is not the same man as the explorer of the Antarctic whose name is Scott, too.
5. The play that concerns the life of Winston Churchill gives a picture of his life that is tragic.
6. The book on the table, which is titled *War and Peace*, is the longest novel that I have ever read.
7. The house that is the third from the corner on the north side of the street is where I live.
8. Snow that falls rapidly and is wet is hard to shovel.
9. Sores that are red and swollen and painful and hot are infected sores.
10. The last person who is in the room should shut the doors and the windows that are open.
11. The part of Italy that is on the border with Switzerland is one of the parts of the country that is the most beautiful.
12. The north of Italy that is in the wide region that includes Milan and Turin is the region of Italy that is industrial.
13. The recent biography published in 1984 by Michael Scammel of Alexander Solzhenitsyn, the famous writer and winner of the 1970 Nobel Prize, is a book of more than eight hundred pages.

27.4
w

14. The most famous novels of Solzhenitsyn, which were published before the Soviet Union sent him into exile, include *The Cancer Ward* and *The First Circle*—novels that Solzhenitsyn based on his experiences as a political prisoner in the Soviet Union.
15. *The Gulag Archipelago*, by Alexander Solzhenitsyn, is a history of Soviet political prisons during the dictatorship of the Soviet leader Joseph Stalin, the general secretary of the Communist Party who was the head of the state.

# 27.5 Circumlocution

**27.5a Circumlocution Defined.** Circumlocution means taking the long way around in speaking or writing:

> There is a not unlikable actor in the cast who has attracted the interest of all those delighting in the thespian arts.

The reviewer means that a likable actor is on stage. He chooses the long way around ("a not unlikable actor in the cast," "the interest of all those delighting in") probably to generate suspense. In a long review or essay, our attention begins to flag as we wait in vain for a specific reference.

The phrase *thespian arts* is also a circumlocution—a flowery way of saying *theater* or *the movies*. Trying to avoid the commonplace statement, the writer says something pretentious.

Circumlocution and inflated phrases keep sentences from coming to the point. The following sentence illustrates circumlocution and other faults discussed in this chapter:

> The quasi-peaceable gentleman of leisure, then, not only consumes of the staff of life beyond the minimum required for subsistence and physical efficiency, but his consumption also undergoes a specialization as regards the quality of the goods consumed.
>
> —THORSTEIN VEBLEN, *The Theory of the Leisure Class*

Note the needless substitution of *staff of life* for the simple word *bread*, the needless repetition of *consume, consumption*, and *consumed*, and the substitution of the phrase *as regards the* for the simple word *of*. The nominalized phrase *gentleman of leisure*, joined with other noun phrases, weighs down the sentence. Veblen is saying that rich people eat more than they need to and are fussy about what they eat. Probably few will understand the sentence even after a second reading.

**27.5**

**w**

**27.5b A List of Circumlocutions.** Here are familiar expressions that take the long way round:

a factor in the cause of
all things considered
as far as can be determined
as to the outcome of
at this point in time
by means of
due to the fact that
for the purpose of
for the reason that
in connection with
in spite of the fact that
in terms of

in the event of
in the nature of
in the process of
in this day and age
more or less
no matter what may be said
notwithstanding
on account of
with regards to
with respect to
without regard for

Some of these are pat phrases, used without knowledge of their meaning or concern for precision. We need many of them to smooth our everyday conversation. The harm arises when they substitute for thinking and bury sentences in words.

**27.5**

**w**

**EXERCISES**

1. Eliminate the circumlocutions in the following sentences. Be as direct as you can:
   a. In the not unlikely event that the storm blankets the area, we will not venture out.
   b. I want to discuss your policy with regards to work that is presented to you late.
   c. We are in the process of deciding whether to close the office in the event of the impending national celebration.
   d. He explained the change in personnel in terms of the rapid fall in productivity.
   e. There is a not inconsiderable amount of money that exists for the purpose of guaranteeing the election of the candidate.
2. Identify circumlocutions in letters to a newspaper or magazine. Be ready to discuss their effect.

## General Exercises

1. Rewrite the following statements from U.S. government documents to make them less wordy and formal. Be ready to discuss the reasons for your changes:

   a. The purpose of the following guidelines is to state the minimum standards of educational fair use under

Section 107 of H.R. 2223. The parties agree that the conditions determining the extent of permissible copying for educational purposes may change in the future; that certain types of copying permitted under these guidelines may not be permissible in the future; and conversely that in the future other types of copying not permitted under these guidelines may be permissible under revised guidelines.         —Public Law 94-553

b. A number of comments assumed that the proposed regulation would deal with the "notice" to be used in connection with unsupervised reproducing equipment (e.g., coin-operated machines) under section 108 (f) (1) of the Act. However, that section specifically refers to a "notice that the making of a copy may be subject to the copyright law" and does not require our further regulatory determination of the contents of the notice. Accordingly, the proposed regulation deals only with the warnings of copyright prescribed by sections 108 (d) and (e).

—Announcement from the Copyright Office,
Library of Congress, August 17, 1977

**2.** The following are opening paragraphs of drafts of essays on George Orwell's novel *Nineteen Eighty-Four*. What advice would you give to the writers on improving their sentences and on stating the purpose and the topic of the essay?

a. In <u>Nineteen Eighty-Four</u>, George Orwell suggests that totalitarianism is the realization of trends evident in our world today—for example, "doublethink," which is a concept or idea that enables people to hold contradictory beliefs or contradictory thoughts and feelings. Doublethink may be the realization of trends in public language, advertising, and even education. Our educational system is supposed to provide its students with the opportunity to develop their intellectual abilities; however, this may not be the case.

But in order for one to understand how this idea of doublethink fits into our society today,

we must first understand Orwell's idea of doublethink. He says that Doublethink means the power
of holding two opposite beliefs in one's mind si-
multaneously, and accepting both of them. As one
can see, the individual who uses doublethink is
playing tricks with reality, but at the same time
he feels that "reality" has not been violated. In
essence, doublethink is the ability to tell deliberate lies while genuinely believing in them.
It is the ability to say "black is white" and to
know that black is white, forgetting that one had
ever thought otherwise. Now, after defining
doublethink, I would like to show how it is prevalent in our educational system.

b. On the basis of the situations I personally experienced throughout my high school years,
I would have to make the claim that the mental
processes inherent in Orwell's "doublethink" are
alive and well there. Although the principal of
my high school stated to our class that high
school was a place to mature and take up responsibility and independence, I found the exact opposite was true. We were told in high school that
"now" was the time to begin branching out and
formulating one's personality and philosophy. Yet
I myself and many of my friends encountered incredible opposition on the part of the school
administration when attempting to do so. In this
essay I will relate experiences of discrimination, threatened expulsion, and authoritative
repression because of various eccentricities and
views which were deemed incorrect while truly
being socially acceptable outside the confines of
the school.

# Checklist for Wordy Sentences

**27.1a**   Needless repetition can make a sentence wordy:

| | |
|---|---|
| Johnson explained the budget proposal; then Johnson turned the meeting over to his assistant. | Johnson explained the budget proposal; then he turned the meeting over to his assistant. |

**27.1b**   Repeat a name when a pronoun has two possible antecedents:

Johnson explained the budget proposal, then turned the meeting over to his assistant, who said that Johnson would comment on other features of the budget later.

**27.1c**   A redundant statement repeats an idea needlessly in different words:

| | |
|---|---|
| The result of the investigation was the consequent dismissal of the cashier and his resulting arrest. | The result of the investigation was the dismissal of the cashier and his subsequent arrest. |

**27.1d**   Using the same word twice in the sentence, with different meanings, can create awkwardness:

| | |
|---|---|
| He will present the report to the committee presently. | He will present the report to the committee shortly. |

**27.2**   Sentences may be needlessly specific in giving details unrelated to the central idea:

| | |
|---|---|
| He admired President Roosevelt, the architect of the "New Deal," for overcoming his physical handicap. | He admired President Roosevelt for overcoming his physical handicap. |

**27.3**   Do not overqualify your sentences:

| | |
|---|---|
| It takes no great intelligence, I should add, and no great amount of knowledge of the subject, it seems to me, to realize how impossible a thing a flying saucer is. | It takes no great intelligence and no great amount of knowledge of the subject to realize how impossible a flying saucer is. |

**27.4a**   Shorten sentences effectively by reducing clauses to phrases or to single words:

| | |
|---|---|
| Beethoven, who was becoming increasingly deaf, wrote a famous letter to his brothers that concerned his affliction. | Beethoven, becoming increasingly deaf, wrote a famous letter to his brothers concerning his affliction. |

**27.4b**   Reduce wordy phrases to single words or shorter phrases:

| | |
|---|---|
| In his loneliness Beethoven found solace in nature. | The lonely Beethoven found solace in nature. |

**27.5a**   Avoid circumlocution or taking the long way around in making a statement:

| | |
|---|---|
| There is a not unlikable actor in the cast who has attracted the interest of those delighting in the thespian arts. | A likable actor is in the cast. |

**27.5b**   Circumlocutions are often pat phrases, used without knowledge of their meaning or concern for precision:

a factor in the cause of
in the nature of

# Diction

# Words and Occasions

We do not use the same words for all occasions. All of us have a formal and informal language that we adjust easily to particular social, business, and work situations. These different languages, or speaking and writing styles, derive from the general social dialect that we share with family, friends, and people at work. They also derive from special dialects—sometimes a slang dialect we share with a special circle of friends or a technical dialect we talk with other sports or music fans, hobbyists, or fellow workers. Since what is appropriate language in one social or business situation may not be appropriate in another, we need to know the social conventions that govern various dialects at various levels of formal and informal usage.

This chapter discusses general matters of usage and defines the three levels of American English. The following chapter addresses the appropriateness of special vocabularies to various audiences; it also discusses slang, jargon, and the uses and misuses of technical words. Later chapters in Part VI discuss various uses of the dictionary and the uses of figurative language—for example, metaphor, simile, and personification—in various kinds of writing.

## 28.1 Dialects and Standard English

All of us grow up speaking and writing more than one variety of English, probably without our being aware of this fact. The Standard English learned in school—the variety of English described in this book—is only one of many kinds spoken and written in America.

Though we commonly talk about speaking and writing "English," as if English were a single language, considerable variations exist in the United States. The differences may be ones of region, class, age, or occupation. People of New England, the Midwest, the South, and the West may speak with very different pronunciations and "accents." Variations exist also in states within a region and cities within the state. Many Chicagoans speak with a pronunciation and accent different from from those of people living in southern Illinois. In some regions of the United States, grammar and vocabulary are also markedly different.

In some communities several languages may prevail—as in Amish communities of Pennsylvania where people speak and write a dialect, "native Pennsylvania German," and in addition speak and write German and English. One observer of the Amish gives this account of their language practices:

> The Amish speak three distinctive tongues, with some elements of each occurring in all. They can read, write, and speak English without any interference from either of their other languages, although on informal occasions such interference may obtain. Their native Pennsylvania German dialect is primarily an oral language. A passive knowledge of High German is demonstrated in reading the Bible aloud or quoting it with their own distinctive pronunciation. Roles and functions tend to organize around each language. When speaking English the Amishman adapts to the English-speaking person.
> —John A. Hostetler, *Amish Society*

Hostetler is making the point that the spoken and written forms of English the Amish child learns in school serve the purposes of communication with non-Amish visitors. Spoken dialects serve the same purposes in Amish family and social groups:

**28.1**
**d**

> An Amish person may shift his conversation from the dialect to English, or from English to the dialect, whichever he finds most appropriate for the situation.

Like the Amish, you may come from a family that speaks English and a second language. Even in families where English is the single language, differences exist. Though grandparents, parents, and the younger members speak and write the same language, each age group has its own special vocabularies, idioms, and even sentence phrasing. And each member old and young probably shares a separate dialect with friends and groups outside the family.

Variations also exist within every age group, though its members share a common language. Los Angeles teenagers share a special language probably not spoken or even understood completely by their parents or teachers, who speak their own.

Subgroups of these teenagers—Chicanos, blacks, the "Valley girls" identified in a popular song in the early 1980s—may have their own special languages. Each teenager probably speaks several dialects, each appropriate to a different group or activity.

**28.1a Dialects.    Dialect** is the term we use to describe variations based on vocabulary, grammar, or pronunciation. Following is an example of nonstandard Southern white speech:

> I *ain't* gonna sit in *no* chair and let *no* crazy lawyer tell me *no* lies about *no* law that *no* judge has in *no* law books that *no* smart politician wrote or *nothin'* like that, *nohow.*
> —Cited from WILLIAM LABOV by ELIZABETH CLOSS TRAUGOTT,
> *The History of English Syntax*

Here for contrast is an example of the Los Angeles "Valley girl" dialect popularized in songs and movies:

> Grody old grownups may have missed it, like TOTALLY, but a bitchen new single from southern California has been riding the airwaves *to the max* this summer.
> —*Newsweek*, August 2, 1982

The sentence rhythm probably characterizes other dialects this group shares with other Los Angeles teenagers. It is the slang words that mark this special dialect.

A dialect may be occupational and, unlike the dialect of Los Angeles teenagers, not limited to one region or age group or class. The following technical discussion of stereo equipment appeared in a magazine with a national circulation:

> To achieve a smooth, "seamless," and inaudible transition from one driver to another, it is important for both the phase and amplitude of the driver signals to be controlled at and near the crossover frequency. Even the directivity patterns of the two drivers need to be matched in the crossover region, and, while it is unlikely that they will be inherently optimal, a certain degree of control over the speaker's overall directionality characteristics is possible by appropriate design of the crossover network.
> —JULIAN D. HIRSCH, "Technical Talk,"
> *Stereo Review*, February 1984

Different as these dialects are, they share a basic structure as well as other features with standard written English. This structure or arrangement of sentence parts is basic to all dialects of English. Regardless of color and region, we understand the statement of the Southern speaker quoted previously even if the

**28.1 d**

structure of the sentence is not in essential features the same for all speakers and writers of English. Vocabulary ranges more widely; the talk of Valley girls and the technical talk of the writer on stereo require translation for those outside the group.

Some of these dialects depart widely from the grammatical usages of Standard English, and those who speak and write the standard dialect often condemn elements of the dialect as nonstandard. The term *nonstandard* refers to usage unacceptable to a special class of English speakers and writers—those who influence opinion about language throughout the United States.

**28.1b  Standard English as a Dialect.**  Standard English is the dialect used by those who conduct the affairs of the country. We noted previously (I.3a) that in some communities Standard English is the dialect of the majority; in other communities, it may be that of the minority. Those who do not speak or write Standard English often still respect it as the "prestige" dialect indispensable to social and economic success in certain areas of life.

Though it is the prestige dialect throughout the United States—the English taught in the schools and used to conduct the affairs of business and government—Standard English is one of the many expressive dialects spoken and written by Americans, as we noted in the introduction to this book. The statement of the Southern white quoted previously is highly expressive by any definition of the word.

Few who master a dialect not their own give up their own. Mastering Standard English thus does not require the sacrifice of other dialects. It is one important resource of the writer, but other dialects may prove useful in different speaking and writing situations. In the words of James Sledd, "the writer should know and be able to use the full range of resources which are made available to him by the several varieties of the language at his command."

**28.2**
**d**

# 28.2  General and Special Audiences

The level at which you write depends on your audience as well as on the subject and the occasion. Formal writing and informal writing are often directed to special audiences, general writing to a general audience. Technical subjects usually call for the special vocabularies that make the writing formal. Letters of congratulation or condolence are usually formal; informal occasions make an informal style in letters or memos appropriate.

At times you want to write impersonally and formally: a personal tone will not do. Letters of application present such an occasion. But formal writing need not be stuffy or impersonal. Writing a formal letter, you can address your reader seriously and naturally, but in more carefully constructed sentences than you ordinarily speak. Your informal speech and informal writing are likely to be more personal.

Your writing indeed always has a "voice," though you are probably not aware of this fact. On occasion, you may become aware of voice in sensing that you have taken the wrong approach to your reader. In a letter of application, for example, you may sense that the letter is too chatty or, conversely, is stiff and even unfriendly. You may make several new starts to find a proper voice or style.

**28.2a  Special Audiences.**  The less familiar you are with your audience, the less shared knowledge you can depend upon. Giving directions to a stranger, you may point and gesture carefully and also choose your words with care. In giving directions to a friend, you probably nod or talk less precisely—referring to "the house over there," rather than to the "white house with the picket fence, on the southwest corner of Main and Sixth Street."

**28.2**

**d**

Members of each group share special background and information. This shared knowledge indirectly determines how each person speaks and writes. For example, you may not finish a sentence if you are certain your listeners know what you mean. You may choose a less exact word for the same reason. Of course, you can be too elaborate or precise in choosing words, just as you can be too restricted or vague. You ordinarily make adjustments of this sort in writing, just as you do in speaking. Most of your conversations with strangers or friends probably show a continuous interplay between speaker and listener, as in the return by the speaker to something said earlier—repeating or explaining words and ideas.

**28.2b  General Audiences.**  An important decision in writing depends, then, on how general or special your audience is (see 1.2). A general audience consists of people who vary in interest and knowledge of the subject, and vary also in background. In writing to a general audience, you usually must define and explain more of your terms and ideas to be sure you reach each of its members.

A newspaper addresses a wide general audience in its news columns, but columns on sports, music, automobiles, gardening, and business address special audiences. These audiences are familiar with the subject and its special terms. The editor of the paper takes account of these differences in adding or striking out words and sentences. The more technical the discussion, the more formal the vocabulary is likely to be. Even a technical article on viruses, written to people who know much about science, may begin at a fairly general level and continue in a highly formal style:

> For an animal or a plant the cell is the fundamental unit of structure and function. For a virus the cell is merely a means of making new virus particles. A virus particle consists of one or more strands of nucleic acid (DNA or RNA) enclosed in a protein shell called a capsid.
> —KAI SIMONS, HENRIK GAROFF, and ARI HELENIUS, "How an Animal Virus Gets Into and Out of Its Host Cell," *Scientific American*, February 1982

**EXERCISES**

1. Assume you are writing instructions for different groups of people on how to find a particular street or neighborhood. Be ready to discuss what decisions you would make about language or diction in writing to each of the following:
   **a.** friends who live in a neighboring town or city
   **b.** children
   **c.** teenagers
   **d.** English-speaking visitors from another country
2. Be ready to discuss whether the following paragraphs address a general or a special audience, and how you know:

> a. Few episodes in the history of reform movements are more surprising than the one in 1848 in which a few women in upstate New York organized a convention and issued a "declaration of rights" that might have come from a group of current women's liberationists. The declaration charged that man had sought by "injuries and usurpations" to establish "an absolute tyranny" over woman, deprive her of legal rights, profitable employment, educational opportunities and the "unalienable right" to vote. The force behind that convention was a 32-year-old mother of four, Elizabeth Cady Stanton. It began a career that established her, side by side with Susan B. Anthony, as the most forceful, stimulating and original-minded figure in the women's movement in the next half century.
> —MILTON RUGOFF, opening paragraph of a review of a biography, *The New York Times Book Review*, October 21, 1984

**28.2**
**d**

b. It was apparent from her first manual of etiquette, "Miss Manners' Guide to Excruciatingly Correct Behavior," that Miss Manners took a dim view of the notion that children are born naturally good, creative and wise. "If children are born naturally good," she inquired in that book, "why do they teach themselves to walk by holding on to the edge of the dining room table cloth? If they are naturally creative, why do they all draw alike?"

—ERICA ABEEL, opening paragraph of a review of a book on raising children, *The New York Times Book Review*, October 21, 1984

c. The exasperating tendency of a poured liquid to cling to the outside of the container is known as the teapot effect. What causes it? One immediately thinks of surface tension, but it turns out that another factor is more important: the pressure is higher at the outer surface of the fluid than it is at the inner surface, so that the liquid is pushed against the container.

At times, such as when one is pouring acid, one needs to forestall the effect so that the liquid will not run down the side of the container and onto the counter. The technique is to put a glass stirring rod across the top of the container. The liquid then runs along the rod and arrives unspilled in the container one is trying to fill.

—JEARL WALKER, "The Amateur Scientist," *Scientific American*, October 1984

**28.3**
**d**

# 28.3 Levels of Usage

**28.3a Formal.** Formal English is appropriate in writing to general audiences about business matters, public affairs, and ideas. Official or public communications usually are in formal English—particularly those calling for an objective statement of facts. The public statements of government officials, prose in college catalogs, letters from corporations, newspaper editorials, textbooks—these usually are in formal English (see I.3). Its characteristics are the following:

- an abstract vocabulary, with many of the words derived from Latin and Greek;
- completed constructions in preference to contracted ones (*is not* in preference to *isn't*);
- complex and occasionally balanced sentences.

The following is an example from a magazine essay on the influence of social groups on our beliefs and actions:

> When I think of what makes me a dedicated member of a social group I realize that burdens and crises are more effective than benefits. Perceived threats to the common good stir us to work and sacrifice to a degree that appeals to self-interest never can. This behavior in turn reinforces our sense that the "tribe" we sacrifice for is *our* tribe.
> —ANDREW OLDENQUIST, "On Belonging to Tribes,"
> *Newsweek*, April 5, 1982

Latin and Greek words like *dedicated* and *crises* and abstract words like *social group, burdens, benefits* and *perceived threats* mark the statement as formal. And so do the complex, periodic sentence construction (19.3) and balancing of phrases and clauses (20.2), as in this sentence from the same essay:

> I don't think I am unusual in sensing that if, and only if, I perceive a thing as *mine*, will I be proud when it prospers, ashamed when it deteriorates and indignant when it is threatened.          —ANDREW OLDENQUIST, "On Belonging to Tribes"

But formal writing need not and does not avoid personal reference. The writer refers to himself in this sentence, at the same time depending on sentence balance for special emphasis. Formal speech and writing need not be stiff or impersonal.

**28.3**
**d**

**28.3b Informal.**   Informal or colloquial English is appropriate in writing about personal matters and everyday experiences addressed to general and special audiences. All of us have both formal and informal ways of talking, and the same is true of our writing, though we may not always be aware of the difference.

Informal English is marked by the following:

- concrete words and fewer Latinate words (*think about* rather than *contemplate* or *reflect*);
- contractions;
- many simple and compound sentences;
- more loose than periodic sentences.

Here is an example of informal English—a humorous description of American restaurants:

> Some restaurants are easy to avoid. You know better than to enter an eatery shaped like a doughnut or bowler, right? Well, the same rule applies to ethnic architecture—Chinese pa-

godas, Dutch windmills, mini-Mount Vernons, mock Elizabe-
thans and too-tall A-frames.

—CURTISS ANDERSON, "Dinner at the Make-Sick
Restaurant," *Newsweek,* June 13, 1983

In depending on colloquial patterns and familiar phrases,
the author writes as if he were conversing. Most of his sentences
are loose, but when they build to the subject as in periodic sentences, they may do so with inclusion of the pauses or interruptions that mark colloquial speech:

If the menu is printed on breadboards, meat cleavers, Ping-
Pong paddles, barbecue bottles, cowhide—on anything, in fact,
except paper—call an ambulance, not a cab.

—CURTISS ANDERSON, "Dinner at the Make-Sick Restaurant"

**28.3c General.**    General English blends qualities of formal
and informal and is appropriate in writing to general and special
audiences (see I.3). It is the English spoken and written by people in their business or public affairs as well as in their everyday
communications. Sentences at this level are sometimes periodic
and balanced, and loose sentences are common. The subject
matter may be concrete or abstract—concerned with experiences or with ideas, as in the following discussion of inflated
language:

**28.3**
**d**

I long ago stopped wondering why major thunderstorm
activity is preferred to major thunderstorms. It is because of
the national affection for unnecessary word activity. Once upon
a time, weathermen spoke of showers. (I heard one of them
say, "We may have a scattered shower.") Showers were succeeded by shower activity. More recently, the shower area has
taken over. All this has happened because we love to pump air
into the language and make it soft and gaseous. Newsmen borrow the style from those they consider authoritative, such as
the airforce general who talked one day about the nuclear deterrent and how well it deterred. It deterred so well, the general
said, that the Russians were not in a position to attack us with
any confidence factor. The general did not say the Russians
lacked confidence. They lacked a confidence factor.

—EDWIN NEWMAN, *Strictly Speaking*

Academic or philosophical writing in textbooks, treatises,
and the like need not be formal though the subject matter may
invite a formal style. The following philosophical discussion of
metaphor is written in a general style:

The molecular theory of gases emerged as an ingenious
metaphor: likening a gas to a vast swarm of absurdly small

bodies. So pat was the metaphor that it was declared literally
true, thus becoming straightway a dead metaphor; the fancied
miniatures of bodies were declared real, and the term "body"
was extended to cover them. In later years the molecules have
even been observed through electron microscopy; but I speak
of origins.            —W. V. QUINE, *Theories and Things*

Though the ideas of the passage are highly abstract, familiar
phrases give us the sense of a philosopher conversing with us
about the role of metaphor in science. The general style in no
way diminishes the seriousness or depth of what he has to say.


**EXERCISES**

1. Identify the level of usage in the following passages on the
   basis of subject matter, vocabulary, and sentence construction. Identify the audience for each of the passages.

   a. A moment's reflection should suffice to establish
   the simple proposition that every historian, willy-nilly,
   must begin his research with a question. Questions are
   the engines of intellect, the cerebral machines which
   convert energy to motion, and curiosity to controlled
   inquiry. There can be no thinking without questioning—
   no purposeful study of the past, nor any serious planning for the future. Moreover, there can be no questioning in a sophisticated sense without hypothesizing,
   and no systematic testing of hypotheses without the construction of hypothetical models which can be put to the
   test.      —DAVID HACKETT FISCHER, *Historians' Fallacies*

   **28.3**
   **d**

   b. Having heard less about the awful consequences
   of study, the Middle Atlantic Colonies seem to have been
   more willing to gamble, and the Dutch who settled New
   York tolerated girls in their primary schools from the
   very beginning. These were church sponsored, and strict
   and total segregation was the rule. Smaller towns with
   one building at their disposal specified that "Boys and
   Girls should be separated as much as possible from each
   other." Girls again got the drafty back rows and the chilly
   corners. The good burghers of New Amsterdam took
   particular pains to guarantee that their thrifty mixing
   of the sexes did not encourage social evils.
   —ELAINE KENDALL, "Beyond Mother's Knee,"
   *American Heritage*, June 1973

   c. The dynamic that operated in the post-Civil War
   decades to create new and exclusive positions for women
   emerges with special clarity in white-collar occupations.

An expanding and modernizing economy did increase the number of clerical and office jobs, particularly for typists and stenographers—and it was women who filled them. In the 1870s, men typically worked as stenographers and scriveners; women composed less than 5 percent of this group. By 1900, the women held fully three-quarters of these jobs.

—SHEILA M. ROTHMAN, *Woman's Proper Place*

d. Atlas sits on a concrete slab in the middle of the basement and, in the manner of his namesake, appears to hold up the house. A single fat cylinder leads heat upstairs and is surrounded by a wider cylinder of sheet metal which leads cool air from upstairs back down for recycling. If you can imagine all the warmth from all the radiators in a four-bedroom house shimmering up from a single heating grate, you will have some idea of Atlas' formidable powers. Almost all winter we have a full-time sauna/mitten-drying/bread-rising room.

—MARK KRAMER, "Wood Heat"

e. It used to be that home was a place to stay in and enjoy. The house had been built by a carpenter who did it from a plan in his head. There are rooms in those houses that weren't designed for anything special. There were usually four or five bedrooms, a living room, a parlor, a big kitchen, but then there were spare rooms. The builder didn't have any idea what you were going to do with your spare room. It wasn't his business. You could make up what the room was for as you went along living. There was always one floor above the top floor, too, the attic.     —ANDY ROONEY, "On the House"

**2.** Rewrite the following formal statements in an informal style. Be ready to discuss the changes in vocabulary and sentence structure needed to make the statements informal:

a. No person, either before or after he is subpoenaed or sworn as a witness, shall knowingly solicit or accept any valuable thing or valuable benefit to corrupt or influence him with respect to his testimony in an official proceeding.     —Ohio Ethics Law

b. No person, without privilege to do so and with purpose to prevent, obstruct, or delay the performance by a public official of any authorized act within his official capacity, shall do any act which hampers or impedes a public official in the performance of his lawful duties.

—Ohio Ethics Law

**28.3**

**d**

# Checklist for Words and Occasions

**28.2a** In writing to a special audience, define terms and explain ideas outside the knowledge and vocabulary you share.

**28.2b** In writing to a general audience, define your terms and explain your ideas fully for each of its members.

**28.3a** Formal English is appropriate in writing to general audiences about business matters, public affairs, and ideas of a general nature.

**28.3b** Informal English is appropriate in writing to general and special audiences about personal matters and everyday concerns and experiences.

**28.3c** General English, which blends features of formal and informal English, is appropriate in writing about business and everyday concerns.

# Audience and Usage

The kinds of words we use depend not only on the subject of the essay but on the audience for that essay. The audience for an article on a technical subject will determine how technical the vocabulary is. For general readers technical words indispensable to the discussion may require translation into plain terms. In other kinds of writing, the more general the audience, the more concrete the vocabulary probably will be. With philosophical subjects abstract words are possible with a special audience that routinely uses them. This chapter begins with the difference between abstract and concrete words.

## 29.1 Abstract and Concrete Words

A statement of ideas uses **abstract words** that do not refer to specific things. But you can illustrate these ideas through **concrete words** that do refer to objects or particular people that embody these ideas. Compare the following:

| *Abstract* | *Concrete* |
|---|---|
| Historical novels often contain symbolic characters. | Ivan Denisovich, in Solzhenitsyn's novel about Soviet prisons, represents millions victimized by Stalin and his police state. |
| The media influence aggressive public behavior. | Televised fights between baseball and other sports players encourage spectators to fight in the stands and on the field. |
| Scientific achievement often has a price. | Many pesticides that increase crop production at the same time pollute water and air. |

Certain writers depend on abstract words in whole passages. The following excerpt defining a word that the writer will use in discussing the Industrial Revolution is entirely abstract:

> The first important word is *industry,* and the period in which its use changes is the period which we now call the Industrial Revolution. *Industry,* before this period, was a name for a particular human attribute, which could be paraphrased as "skill, assiduity, perseverance, diligence." This use of *industry* of course survives. But, in the last decades of the eighteenth century, *industry* came also to mean something else; it became a collective word for our manufacturing and productive institutions, and for their general activities.
> —RAYMOND WILLIAMS, *Culture and Society*

By contrast, the following passage on an Iranian nomadic people names objects in describing nomad life:

> It is not possible in the nomad life to make things that will not be needed for several weeks. They could not be carried. And in fact the Bakhtiari do not know how to make them. If they need metal pots, they barter them from settled peoples or from a caste of gipsy workers who specialize in metals. A nail, a stirrup, a toy, or a child's bell is something that is traded from outside the tribe. The Bakhtiari life is too narrow to have time or skill for specialization. There is no room for innovation, because there is not time, on the move, between evening and morning, coming and going all their lives, to develop a new device or a new thought—not even a new tune. The only habits that survive are the old habits. The only ambition of the son is to be like the father.
> —J. BRONOWSKI, *The Ascent of Man*

**29.1**
**d**

Most writing combines the abstract and the concrete, moving from ideas to concrete details and examples, or, as in the paragraph just quoted, from examples to ideas. Writing that moves from one abstract statement to another, without reference to concrete experiences or objects, can exhaust the reader.

## 29.2  General and Specific Words

How general or specific you need to be in choosing words depends, as with abstract and concrete words, on how important it is to name the class to which an object belongs or to name the thing itself. **General words** name this class; **specific words** name the thing. The following words and phrases refer to the same thing:

    implement
    tool
    hammer
    claw hammer
    small-headed claw hammer
    small iron-headed claw hammer

This statement is vague and jars the ear:

    I pounded the nail with an implement.

The following holds back the name as if to create suspense about it:

    I pounded the nail with a tool.

The following does the opposite, naming specific qualities of the tool:

    I pounded the nail with a small iron-headed claw hammer.

This sentence gives the impression that the special qualities of the hammer are important.

You do not need the adjectives if you want merely to name the tool used:

    I pounded the nail with a hammer.

**29.2**
**d**

But you do need to be more specific in pointing to one hammer among several:

    I pounded the nail with a small-headed claw hammer.

The addition of the adjective *iron* is superfluous unless you want to stress the metal.

How specific you are depends, then, on your purpose in writing. If you wish to express your feelings about a scene or object, you need to give an exact description. If, however, your purpose is to give information, you need to be much more exact. In an essay that is both informative and persuasive, George Orwell moves from general words (*measurements, units*) to specific equivalents:

> Obviously you have got to have the metric system for certain purposes. For scientific work it has long been in use, and it is also needed for tools and machinery, especially if you want to export them. But there is a strong case for keeping on the old measurements for use in everyday life. One reason is that the metric system does not possess, or has not succeeded in establishing, a large number of units that can be visualized. There is, for instance, effectively no unit between the meter,

which is more than a yard, and the centimeter, which is less than half an inch. In English you can describe someone as being five feet three inches high, or five feet nine inches, or six feet one inch, and your hearer will know fairly accurately what you mean. —GEORGE ORWELL, *As I Please*

## EXERCISES

1. Make the following sentences as specific as you can without adding superfluous words.
   **a.** Several phenomena of nature are killing the forest.
   **b.** The fish he caught was inedible.
   **c.** She put several objects for painting the house on the porch.
   **d.** The shelf was full of different reading materials.
   **e.** He failed the driving test because he made several mistakes.
   **f.** She took a variety of courses that show she had not made up her mind about a major.
   **g.** She used an implement to collect the things on the ground and in the bushes.
   **h.** She prepared the chicken in a special way to make it less fattening.
   **i.** The weather turned nasty.
   **j.** We had engine trouble on the trip to Cincinnati.
2. Rewrite the following abstract passages in concrete language:

> a. Learning to read effectively also demands sensitivity to choices, but of a different nature. The skillful reader learns to observe and judge the choices that the writer has made—though no reader ever succeeds in becoming attuned to all of them. It is possible, of course, to "over-read" a book, to imagine options that the writer never confronted.
>
> —Commission on English,
> *Freedom and Discipline in English*
>
> b. To find deeper meaning, one must become able to transcend the narrow confines of a self-centered existence and believe that one will make a significant contribution to life—if not right now, then at some future time. This feeling is necessary if a person is to be satisfied with himself and with what he is doing. In order not to be at the mercy of the vagaries of life, one must develop one's inner resources, so that one's emotions, imagination, and intellect mutually support and enrich one another. Our positive feelings give us the strength

**29.2**
**d**

> to develop our rationality; only hope for the future can
> sustain us in the adversities we unavoidably encounter.
> —Bruno Bettelheim, *The Uses of Enchantment*

## 29.3  Slang

**Slang** is found often in informal writing and less often in general and formal writing. When writers do use slang in general writing they use it sparingly, as in the following statement about New Yorkers, for slang can tire even the reader familiar with it:

> Arrogance, a rank weakness for glitz, sleaze, and sin, and a willingness to put up with environmental conditions that would drive more rational sorts to opt for a swift change of venue are among the character defects that many out-of-towners associate with residents of this city that allegedly never sleeps.
> —Andy Logan, "Around City Hall,"
> *The New Yorker*, January 28, 1985

The origin of the word *slang*—probably from the Norwegian word for nickname—gives us an understanding of the use of slang today. Slang offers a shortcut in speaking—a way to express ideas through images. "We all knew each other," a politician is quoted by *Newsweek*. "There was a lot of talk about who might be available—a lot of massaging. . . . There were a few elbows bent and a few stories told. But in St. Louis, everybody was hot to trot."

As in the colorful talk of this speaker, slang depends on clipped phrases (*a lot of massaging*) and flashy metaphors (*hot to trot*)—a way of speaking and writing that depends on a confidential relationship with the listener or reader, for slang is used by a particular group. Like the cant or secret language of thieves, it can serve the group as a protection from outsiders.

Here perhaps is one reason slang is short-lived: it loses its confidentiality as it spreads to people outside the group. Another reason is that colorful metaphors soon fade in interest, making the colorful slang of a television talk-show host stale quickly. An interesting suggestion is that slang is a game of words that can quickly lose its interest when the words become overfamiliar.

Some slang becomes part of the language; the word *shortcut* is an example. The word *addict* (*television addict*) is another. *Glitz* and *sleaze* are gaining acceptance. The reason for its occasional adoption is that slang can express ideas and feelings through

**29.3
d**

the vivid pictures metaphors bring to mind. Once slang is absorbed into the language, the word *colloquialism* (meaning a term of conversation) describes such a word or expression.

### EXERCISES

1. Write down slang words and phrases that you associate with a particular group—for example, rock musicians, football fans, people interested in fast cars. Be ready to discuss how widely used or restricted in use you believe these words are.

2. The columnist Dan Carlinsky gives these examples of "hash-house Greek" in a humorous essay. How many of the expressions do you recognize or use? What kinds of food or ways of preparing food do the words refer to?

| | |
|---|---|
| Adam and Eve on a raft | on the hoof |
| bowl of red | on wheels |
| bucket of mud | radio |
| draw one | spot |
| hail | stretch |
| ninety-five | wreck 'em |

3. What images and feelings do the following words convey to you?
   **a.** glitzy   **b.** sleazy   **c.** smarmy   **d.** nerdy   **e.** wimpy

# 29.4  Jargon

**29.4
d**

**29.4a  Uses of Technical Words.**   **Jargon** is the name for special, technical vocabulary of a profession or craft: auto mechanics talk a special jargon (or *argot*), and so do astronauts, football players, English teachers, and thieves.

Like slang, jargon can be confusing to readers, particularly if used out of its field. Sports talk is probably familiar enough not to cause confusion, but the jargon of special fields and activities like computer programming—the source of the widely used jargon word *input*—is not familiar to all members of general audiences and therefore can create confusion.

But jargon does have important uses in general and technical writing, as the following passage from an article on "micromechanical devices" shows. The article appeared in a magazine directed to scientists as well as to general readers:

> The etch rate of a doping-dependent etchant (a category that overlaps the categories of isotropic and anisotropic etchants) depends on the type of dopant atoms and their concentration. The isotropic etchant HNA is doping-dependent in some

mixture ratios; it etches heavily doped silicon much faster than it etches lightly doped silicon. On the other hand, the anisotropic etchants potassium hydroxide and EDP etch silicon that has been heavily doped with boron much more slowly than they etch silicon lightly doped with boron.
—JAMES B. ANGELL, STEPHEN C. TERRY, and PHILLIP W. BARTH, "Silicon Micromechanical Devices," *Scientific American*, April 1983

In the paragraphs that follow this excerpt, the writers carefully define special terms; in the passage they further discuss "doping-dependent etchants." Once defined, the words form a special language—a sequence of technical terms with their own grammatical forms (*dope, doping, doped*). Technical writing of this sort comes to resemble a shorthand whose concision and concreteness are virtues in scientific and other kinds of specialized writing.

**29.4b  Misuses of Technical Words.**  Could the technical ideas just discussed be stated in plain English, without the use of special terms?

This is the question you face in choosing to write in a technical style. Certainly you will need many more words in a nontechnical explanation of such processes and ideas in presenting them to a general audience unable to grasp the following definition from the essay on micromechanical devices:

> Silicon is a semiconductor, one of the elements that lie between the metals and the nonmetals in the periodic table of the elements.

The general reader must know what a semiconductor is to understand this definition. To special readers who know the meaning of terms in chemistry and physics, the definition is clear.

But writing becomes jargon in another sense of the word— clumsy and unintelligible language, the words vague in their use, the string of words twisted and incoherent. The general reader and the special reader both struggle with the meaning of the sentence, the paragraph, and the whole essay. Much technical writing becomes jargon in this sense. When you discover that you have used jargon of this kind, you will do best to restate the ideas in the simplest language possible, using technical words only where no simple English equivalents of them exist. Usually such words do exist.

An equally serious problem is the confusion technical jargon creates in the discussion of serious issues. The jargon word may

29.4
d

disguise the facts and confuse the issue. One critic of jargon cites these deceptive uses of the word *environment*:

> In the jargon of the traffic planning industry, what an *environmental* area really means is a device for channeling motor traffic out of your street into someone else's, if possible three or four blocks away. There are man-made *environments*, or buildings, and, in the advertisements, engineering *environments*, or factories. To make their job sound exciting advertisers write, "The *environment* is fast-moving and structured," and succeed in making it sound alarming.    —PHILLIP HOWARD, *Weasel Words*

### EXERCISES

1. The authors of the following paragraph identify the jargon of a school of psychology in the 1960s and 1970s, the Human Potential Movement. What are these jargon words, and how do the authors explain them to the general reader? How many of the words do you recognize in current pop psychology?

> Because it was concerned with the "expansion of human potential," the new psychology was for everyone. "If there is one statement true of every living person it must be this: he hasn't achieved his full potential." HPM methods were not about "making sick people well"— they were about "making well people better." In fact, the new techniques worked best on people who were "healthy" and "open." . . . The point of achieving one's full potential, according to HPM ideologues, was not to be able to get more work done, or make a greater contribution to society, or any other old-fashioned "inner-directed" goal—but simply to have more fun.
> —BARBARA EHRENREICH and DEIRDRE ENGLISH,
> *For Her Own Good*

**29.4**
**d**

2. A British sociologist gives us this account of the special jargon of British criminals:

> *Blagging* is the term for robbery, for which one might be *tooled up* (armed). A *blag job* might be to get money, or it may be in pursuit of *tomfoolery* (jewelry). For the less brave, the same objective might be attained by *flying a kite* (passing a dud check). The police, an experienced criminal might claim, only obtained his conviction because they *verballed* him (attributed incriminating statements to him). Despite the protestations of his *brief* (counsel), the jury convicted and the *beak* (judge) gave him a *lagging* (three years imprisonment).
> —SEAN MCCONVILLE, "Prison Language"

Consult the *Dictionary of American Underworld Lingo, Dictionary of Americanisms, Dictionary of American English,* and other reference books to find out whether any of these British terms have ever been in use in the United States. What equivalent American terms do you find for the exclusively British terms?

3. Examine special dictionaries in the reference section of your library to find out how many of the special or technical terms in the following passage they define. Use these dictionaries to write a paraphrase of the passage—a rendering of the content in your own words—for a reader unfamiliar with football:

> Techniques known as "butt-blocking" and "butt-tackling" got wide circulation, along with their wicked antecedents: "spearing," "spiking," and "sticking." Players rammed head-first into pileups, into defenders, into hapless quarterbacks, and into immobile running backs to put the finishing touch on tackles. The helmet became the game's principal article of intimidation.
> —JOHN UNDERWOOD, *The Death of an American Game*

## Checklist for Audience and Usage

**29.4**

**d**

**29.1**  Make your writing concrete by naming things:

Scientific achievement often has a price.

Many pesticides that increase crop production at the same time pollute water and air.

**29.2**  Be as specific as your discussion requires:

*General*
I pounded the nail with a hammer.

*Specific*
I pounded the nail with a small-headed claw hammer.

**29.3**  Slang, appropriate only to special audiences, can confuse and tire the general reader.

**29.4a**  Technical jargon, appropriate in writing on technical matters to special audiences, creates confusion in discussions out of its field.

**29.4b**  The word *jargon* is also the term for clumsy and unintelligible language, vague words, and twisted and incoherent sentences.

# Uses of the Dictionary

The dictionary is an indispensable tool in writing and reading. The ordinary desk dictionary gives the current meanings of words in alphabetized order, and it gives other information on the origin and pronunciation of words; on current, rare, and obsolete meanings; and on synonyms and antonyms—words similar and opposite in meaning.

Having a desk dictionary at hand is essential in writing your papers. In the course of editing, you will need the dictionary to check spelling and verify the meaning of words. In typing your paper, you will find information in the dictionary about syllable breaks. You will also find listings of special symbols and abbreviations. Since desk dictionaries give this information in different ways—some present it in the alphabetized listing, some present it in various tables—you should examine your own dictionary carefully before using it.

This chapter describes how to find this information. It also discusses historical dictionaries that trace the meanings of a word past and present and special dictionaries that give information about the past and the contemporary world. Chapter 36 on the documented paper discusses technical dictionaries for use in writing documented papers.

## 30.1 Abridged and Unabridged Dictionaries

Contemporary desk and college dictionaries give information about words currently in use. These dictionaries include the following:

*American College Dictionary*
*American Heritage Dictionary of the English Language*
*Random House College Dictionary*
*Funk and Wagnall's Standard College Dictionary*
*Webster's New Collegiate Dictionary*
*Webster's New World Dictionary*

449

These abridged dictionaries omit obsolete words not in common use. For complete information on these, you need to consult an unabridged dictionary like *Webster's Third New International Dictionary*, with its valuable citations of word use, or *The Random House Dictionary of the English Language*.

Historical dictionaries give detailed information on current and past meanings of current and obsolete words. The most important is the *Oxford English Dictionary* (OED), which is universal in its coverage of English words. Essential dictionaries on American usage are the *Dictionary of American English* and *Dictionary of Americanisms*. Historical dictionaries are particularly valuable in investigating the meaning of unfamiliar words in older books containing words with archaic or obsolete meanings.

**EXERCISE**

Use your college dictionary and an unabridged dictionary to compare the definitions of one of the following words. What additional information or meanings do you find in the unabridged dictionary?

| | |
|---|---|
| **a.** blood | **f.** leer (verb) |
| **b.** crow (noun) | **g.** naughty |
| **c.** deck | **h.** sonata |
| **d.** diet | **i.** virus |
| **e.** humor (noun) | **j.** windmill |

**30.2**
**d**

# 30.2  Old Words, New Meanings

In the course of speaking and writing, you need to verify the meanings of your words, particularly special meanings you suspect are controversial. Verification is especially important with words having a wide range of meanings.

Words change in meaning from one period to another. The following passage from a 1983 article on disabled Americans contains words in use fifty or a hundred years ago. But many of these have new meanings or nuances created in political and social discourse in the 1970s and early 1980s.

The disability legislation of the past 15 years is based on familiar civil-rights principles such as equal opportunity, nondiscrimination, integration, free choice and self-help, to name a few. The thread linking all these principles is the concept of access—access to education, to employment, to public facilities and services, to transportation, to housing and to other resources needed by disabled people to more fully realize their rights as citizens. Architectural barriers compromise access. They are seen in this context as obstacles that limit opportunity, promote discrimination, prevent integration, restrict choice and frustrate self-help.

—GERBEN DEJONG and RAYMOND LIFCHEZ, "Physical Disability and Public Policy," *Scientific American*, June 1983

Consider the word *integration*. This controversial word has a general meaning for most people today: it refers to the granting of full civil rights to black Americans, American Indians, Hispanic Americans, and Chicanos. But the word has additional and quite separate meanings for supporters and opponents of integration. To some people *integration* refers to the knitting of blacks and other minority people into the whole social, cultural, and economic fabric of American life; to others, it refers to the granting of equal opportunities in schooling and work—but not in housing or other areas.

Obviously those who use the word with these different meanings misunderstand one another, and they may not be aware of this fact. They are probably unaware, too, that these meanings change rapidly in the course of social and political debate. Though dictionaries do account for some of these meanings, change in the usage of words is so rapid that no dictionary is totally up-to-date; new meanings as well as new words come into existence rapidly.

**30.2**
**d**

### EXERCISES

1. How much help does your dictionary give you in understanding the meaning of the following words in the passage just quoted?
   **a.** access
   **b.** disability
   **c.** discrimination
   **d.** nondiscrimination
   **e.** resource
2. Which of the italicized words and phrases in the following passages do you think were either not in use in 1900 or were used with different meanings? And what are your reasons? Check the words you choose in the OED. If you can't find them, they weren't used.

   a. Neither the technology nor the environmental impact of *nuclear energy* ends with the generation of electricity at the *reactor*. The nuclear fuel must eventually be removed from the *reactor core*—not so much because the fissile component would be used up but because the ac-

cumulating *fission* products "poison" the *chain reaction* by
absorbing *neutrons*.
—PAUL H. EHRLICH, ANNE H. EHRLICH, and
JOHN P. HOLDREN, *Ecoscience: Population,
Resources, Environment* [italics added]

b. A *pulsar* is thought to be a spinning *neutron star*
that emits a narrow beam of *electromagnetic radiation*. As
the beam sweeps through the sky like the light from a
lighthouse it intermittently points toward the earth, where
it is observed as a series of pulses. In the case of some
pulsars the interval between pulses is so regular that the
stars are in effect celestial clocks.
—"Science and the Citizen," *Scientific American*,
September 1985 [italics added]

# 30.3   Denotative and Connotative Definitions

Dictionaries give information on two essential kinds of
meaning in words—**denotative** and **connotative** meaning. The
dictionary gives both the *denotations*—the characteristics to which
the word refers—and some or all of its familiar *connotations*—
auras of meaning people associate with it. Some dictionaries tell
us that the word *yellow* generally connotes cowardice, the word
*red* connotes anger, and the word *blue* sadness or melancholy.
The dictionary may omit connotations limited to a class or region.

Consider the word *ghetto*. The word today denotes a section
of a town or city in which any minority population is confined
through racial, religious, or economic discrimination. *Ghetto* still
denotes sections to which Jews have been confined. This denotative definition points to or names all districts of cities that
people call ghettos.

The word *ghetto* also connotes attitudes and qualities—some
of these identified with ghettos by almost everyone and some
identified with them by some people only. Thus *ghetto* generally
connotes discrimination, poverty, misery, injustice. By contrast
with this general connotation, special connotations of *ghetto* differ widely. Hearing the word, many people think only of the
Jewish ghettos of Europe in earlier centuries or the Warsaw
ghetto of the early 1940s where an enormous number of Polish
Jews were imprisoned and starved and where they resisted their
Nazi captors. Other people think of the black neighborhoods of
large American cities or impoverished Puerto Rican or Chicano
neighborhoods or American Indian reservations.

**30.3**
**d**

One dictionary of current usage gives us this definition of *ghetto*:

> *1.* in certain European cities, a section to which Jews are, or were, restricted: the word is also applied, often in an unfriendly sense, to any section (of a city) in which many Jews live; hence, *2.* any section of a city in which many members of some national or racial group live, or to which they are restricted.
> —*Webster's New World Dictionary of the American Language*

This definition gives both the denotation and the most general connotation of the word. But notice that it does not give the connotations evident in the following description of the "Harlem ghetto" in New York City.

> All of Harlem is pervaded by a sense of congestion, rather like the insistent, maddening, claustrophobic pounding in the skull that comes from trying to breathe in a very small room with all the windows shut. Yet the white man walking through Harlem is not at all likely to find it sinister or more wretched than any other slum.—JAMES BALDWIN, "The Harlem Ghetto"

**EXERCISES**

**1.** What are the chief denotative meanings of the following words? Does your dictionary illustrate any of these meanings in familiar phrases or use contrasting words as part of the definition? What do these words connote to you? Do you find these connotations listed in your dictionary?
  **a.** mortal          **d.** slick
  **b.** malignant     **e.** stool pigeon
  **c.** jackpot

**2.** What is the meaning of *ghetto* in the following passage from a report of a 1968 national commission on disorder in American cities? What help does the dictionary give in understanding the use of the word?

> The rising concentration of impoverished Negroes and other minorities within the urban ghettos will constantly expand public expenditures for welfare, law enforcement, unemployment and other existing programs without reversing the tendency of older city neighborhoods toward decay and the breeding of frustration and discontent. But the most significant item on the balance of accounts will remain largely invisible and incalculable— the toll in human values taken by continued poverty, segregation and inequality of opportunity.
> —*Report of the National Advisory Commission on Civil Disorders*

**30.3**
**d**

## 30.4 Etymology

**30.4a Definition of Etymology.**  The **etymology** or origin of a word is sometimes a help in understanding the current meaning. The dictionary gives the etymology in parentheses or brackets toward the beginning or at the end of the definition. Figure 30.1 shows *Webster's New World Dictionary*'s definition of the word *integrate*. Appearing in brackets toward the beginning of the definition, the etymology tells us that the word derives from the past participle form of the Latin verb *integrare*. The original meaning of *integrate* is "to make whole, renew."

**30.4b Changing Meanings.**  Like *integrate*, the original meaning of a word may be the same as the current meaning, or it may not be, for words change with use. The etymology of the word *ghetto* is the Italian word *borghetto*, the diminutive form of *borgo* or *borough*, according to *The Oxford Universal Dictionary*. Another dictionary identifies the Italian word for foundry (*ghetto*) as the source: the district in which the city of Venice confined or "ghettoed" its Jewish inhabitants from the fifteenth to the middle of the nineteenth century was the site of a foundry. The word *ghetto* does not today carry the meaning of foundry for English speakers.

Indeed, we will misread a passage or mislead readers in assuming that the etymological or original meaning of a word like *ghetto* is its one correct or "right" meaning. For example, the word *giddy* originally meant "possessed by a god." The word

**30.4**
**d**

### FIGURE 30.1  Sample Definition

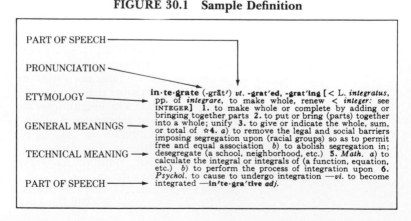

PART OF SPEECH

PRONUNCIATION

ETYMOLOGY

GENERAL MEANINGS

TECHNICAL MEANING

PART OF SPEECH

**in·te·grate** (-grāt′) *vt.* -grat′ed, -grat′ing [ < L. *integratus*, pp. of *integrare*, to make whole, renew < *integer*: see INTEGER]  **1.** to make whole or complete by adding or bringing together parts  **2.** to put or bring (parts) together into a whole; unify  **3.** to give or indicate the whole, sum, or total of  ☆**4.** *a*) to remove the legal and social barriers imposing segregation upon (racial groups) so as to permit free and equal association  *b*) to abolish segregation in; desegregate (a school, neighborhood, etc.)  **5.** *Math. a*) to calculate the integral or integrals of (a function, equation, etc.)  *b*) to perform the process of integration upon  **6.** *Psychol.* to cause to undergo integration —*vi.* to become integrated —**in′te·gra′tive** *adj.*

now means "light-headed." A poem by the eighteenth-century writer Oliver Goldsmith contains the line "She said twenty giddy things that looked like joy." The twenty things, Goldsmith is saying, are frivolous statements, not inspired ones, though we might think so if we gave the word *giddy* its etymological meaning.

If the original meaning of a word is not the same as the current one, it may nevertheless shed light on its present connotations. The etymology is especially useful in understanding present connotations unmentioned in the main definition. The original meaning of *daisy* embedded in the word—day's eye— helps us to understand the slang meaning of the term—according to the *New World Dictionary* "something outstanding or notable." For the flower, with its rays extending from the yellow center, suggested the sun to the Anglo-Saxons—the Germanic people who invaded England in the fifth century A.D. and spoke and wrote the earliest form of English.

### EXERCISES

1. What information if any does your dictionary give on the origin of the following words? Is this information of help in understanding a current use of the word?
    a. grudge
    b. stooge
    c. stool pigeon
    d. superficial
    e. ventriloquist

**30.4**
**d**

2. Use your desk dictionary to discover the etymology of *sloth, shirk, goof, idling,* and *proletariat* in the following passage. Be ready to discuss what help etymology gives in understanding the passage:

> One of the good old long-lost Anglo-Saxon words that carried a real punch is "sloth." Inactivity and unresponsiveness in those upon whose cooperative efforts we depend always *feels* to us like sinful negligence. The persistence of this taboo over the centuries of social cooperation testifies to the universality of the temptation to shirk or "goof off." It is described as "laziness," avoidance of exertion, idling, a propensity for "taking it easy." It was the privilege of the master, not of the slave, of the wealthy, not of the proletariat. But inactivity and idleness may (also) be an expression of fear, self-distrust, or self-misunderstanding.
> —KARL MENNINGER, "The Sin of Sloth"

# 30.5   Other Information in the Definition

In addition to giving the current meanings and the origin of words, the dictionary gives information on the following, sometimes in this order:

the part of speech;

pronunciation of the word (using the phonetic alphabet);

the syllabication of the word, important in hyphenating it in typing a paper;

the current meanings, beginning with the most recent and finishing with the least recent;

technical senses of the word—the meaning of *integral* in mathematics;

field labels if the word has meanings in different fields of science, social science, medicine and other professions or areas of research or study (the *New World Dictionary* definition of *integration* gives the meaning of this word in psychoanalysis, "the organization of various traits or tendencies into one harmonious personality");

derived forms like *integral*;

obsolete or discarded meanings;

archaic or seldom-used meanings;

information on usage—on preferred meanings, idioms, and forms of the word;

slang or unconventional colloquial expressions;

dialectal meanings, or meanings peculiar to a neighborhood or region of the country or a social or occupational group;

synonyms and antonyms if any.

**30.5**
**d**

## EXERCISES

1. Use the dictionary definition of *integrate* to answer the following:
   **a.** Is the verb transitive or intransitive? Or is it both?
   **b.** What syllable is given primary stress? What syllable receives secondary stress?
   **c.** What is the most common meaning of the word?
   **d.** What help does the etymology give in understanding the meaning pertaining to racial groups?
   **e.** What are the different uses of the word in mathematics?
2. Use the dictionary definition of *nice* to answer the following:
   **a.** From what language did English speakers adopt the word? From what language is *nice* ultimately derived?
   **b.** Is the original meaning of the word the same as any of its current meanings? Does the dictionary give you information on meanings no longer current?

   **c.** Does the dictionary give you the general or broad connotation of the word or merely denotations?

**3.** Use the dictionary definition of *nigh* to answer the following:

   **a.** Is *nigh* a native English word, or is it a borrowing from another language?

   **b.** What is its current meaning?

   **c.** Does it have meanings now rarely used?

   **d.** Does it have special meanings in any dialects?

   **e.** What help does the etymology give you in understanding its various meanings?

**4.** What help does your dictionary give you in pronouncing the following words?

   **a.** present (noun)       **f.** notoriety

   **b.** present (verb)       **g.** Worcester (Massachusetts)

   **c.** Aristophanes       **h.** wholly

   **d.** immunity           **i.** analysis

   **e.** ravioli

# 30.6   Synonyms and Antonyms

Synonyms are words that share approximately the same meaning; few words in English have exact synonyms. Antonyms are words opposite in meaning. The information that dictionaries give about these words varies. Some dictionaries include synonym listings at the end of the definition; some give no listings.

**30.6**

**d**

**30.6a Synonym Listings.** The synonym listing for *discriminate* following the definition of *distinguish* gives help with related meanings or synonyms of the word. Such listings are invaluable, for if the dictionary fails to provide the meaning needed, you may find that meaning in one of its synonyms. The more you consult these listings (in your desk dictionary, if it contains a listing, or in a special dictionary like *Webster's Dictionary of Synonyms*), the sharper your sense of the nuances and precise denotative meanings of words will become.

The synonym listing appears either at the end of the whole definition or at the end of the definition of another synonym. For example, in *Webster's New World Dictionary*, a synonym listing occurs at the end of the definition of *distinguish* (see Figure 30.2).

The synonym listing at the end of the definition of *distinguish* gives the cross-reference to *discern* because it is also a synonym of *distinguish* but in the sense of seeing something clearly. The synonym listing under *discern* marks the difference between *discern, perceive, distinguish, observe,* and *notice.*

## FIGURE 30.2   Sample Synonym Listing

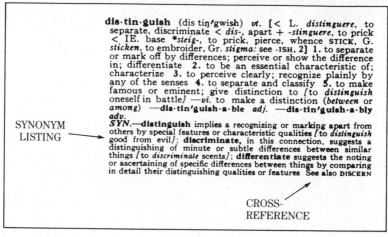

SYNONYM
LISTING

CROSS-
REFERENCE

**30.6b Antonyms.**   Dictionaries give antonyms—words opposite in meaning—less often than they give synonyms. *Webster's New World Dictionary* gives the antonym *sad* at the end of the synonym listing for *happy*. And it lists *precede* as an antonym for *follow*.

**30.6**
**d**

Special dictionaries like *Webster's Dictionary of Synonyms* give additional information. This dictionary lists the synonyms of *distinguished* as follows:

> eminent, illustrious, renowned, noted, celebrated, famous, famed, notorious

These words are discussed and compared in a long article on the word *famous*.

The dictionary also lists these analogous or similar words:

> outstanding, prominent, remarkable, conspicuous

These dictionaries are different from **thesauruses**, which only list the various synonyms of words in various arrangements. See the list in 30.9a of special dictionaries of etymology, slang, and other kinds of words.

### EXERCISES

1. Where do the synonyms of the word *convoke* appear in your dictionary?
2. What are the differences in meaning between the synonyms *dogma*, *tenet*, and *precept*? Does your dictionary compare these words?

3. What synonym of *hateful* would you use to describe something disgusting or offensive in a hateful thing?
4. Under what circumstances would you refer to something as an *enigma* rather than as a *mystery*?
5. What are the antonyms of the words *firm* and *impel*?

## 30.7   Historical Dictionaries

For information about the history of a word from its earliest use to its current ones, consult a historical dictionary like the *Oxford English Dictionary* (or *New English Dictionary*) for words used in England and America. For distinctively American meanings, consult the *Dictionary of American English* or the *Dictionary of Americanisms*.

Historical dictionaries can help you in reading a work containing obsolete or special words. *Oliver Twist*, Dickens' novel about early nineteenth-century London crime, contains references to "cribs" (hideouts), "beaks" (police magistrates), and "lagging" (the sentence of transport to a penal colony). Some of these words occur in dictionaries of current usage. The now obsolete word *fogle* does not, and to understand what "fogle hunters" were, you need to consult the *Oxford English Dictionary*, or its convenient abridgement, the *Oxford Universal Dictionary*. *Fogle*, we discover, was the slang word for silk handkerchief. So a "fogle hunter"—the term Dickens uses to describe juvenile thieves who combed the streets of London—was a thief who stole valuable handkerchiefs.

**30.7 d**

Historical dictionaries are particularly useful in tracing changing meanings. In nineteenth-century literature *virus* refers to a poisonous substance—not to the specific agent of measles and smallpox and other viral diseases identified in the twentieth century.

### EXERCISE

Find the answers to the following questions in the *Oxford English Dictionary*, the *Oxford Universal Dictionary*, the *Dictionary of American English*, or the *Dictionary of Americanisms*:
1. What is the origin of the word *handicap*? Do we still use the word in its original sense?
2. What is the origin of the word *guy*—used to describe an effigy? What additional meaning did it acquire in England in the nineteenth century? Approximately when did the American slang expression *guy* come into existence?
3. What is an obsolete use of the word *hog*? Is the word ever used to describe animals other than swine?

4. In what sports is the word *slog* a special term?
5. What meanings of the word *suffrage* are now rare or obsolete?
6. What is the origin of the word *vermin*? Is the word still used in its original sense? Does it have special meanings in English-speaking countries other than Great Britain?
7. What is the earliest recorded use of gelatin, and to what extent has the meaning changed?
8. What is the origin of the word *barbecue*? How various are its meanings?
9. What is the origin of the word *Eskimo*? Does it describe North American inhabitants only?
10. What possible meanings does the word *nipper* have in this statement from an English publication of 1892—"The mind of the East End 'nipper' is equal to most emergencies"?

## 30.8 Usage

**30.8**<br>**d**

Often we want to know what meanings are appropriate and inappropriate in various situations. Can a word we use informally also be used in formal writing? The amount of discussion of words like *ain't* and of usage generally varies from dictionary to dictionary. The *American Heritage Dictionary* contains short articles, based on the opinions of "usage panels"—writers, editors, and other assumed experts in the use of English. Other dictionaries like *Webster's New World Dictionary* include information on usage as part of the definition.

The dictionary sometimes gives the background or exact range of meanings of certain words. *Webster's New World Dictionary* states that in physics the word *oscillate* means to "vary between maximum and minimum values." You know from this definition not only how to use the word in a discussion on physics but also what the word means in a particular passage or context in a chapter or essay.

Some words are used in various contexts. *Horizon* has special meanings in astronomy and geology. Dictionaries usually distinguish these meanings by field entries. Thus the *New World Dictionary* defines the word *horizon* as "the line where the sky seems to meet the earth." This is the *visible* or *apparent horizon*. Then under the field entry *astronomy* it gives the additional definition *sensible horizon* to distinguish this technical use of the word from its general use:

> the plane extending at right angles to the direction of gravity from the eye of the observer to the celestial sphere

The dictionary indicates what function words or prepositions belong to certain verbs. A lawyer is *admitted to* the bar; we
are *admitted to* a place. The occasional idiom *admit of* is used to
mean "warrant," as in the following sentence:

Her statements will not admit of any other interpretation.

**EXERCISES**

1. What information does your desk dictionary give on the use
   of the following in Standard English:
   **a.** hip (adjective)
   **b.** irregardless
   **c.** lush (noun)
   **d.** nohow
   **e.** that (relative pronoun)
2. Under what field entries do you find an explanation of the
   following?
   **a.** the symbol "F" for function
   **b.** *vessel* as a canal for the conducting of water
   **c.** *bar* as a part of a horse's hoof
   **d.** *bar* as a horizontal line on a shield
   **e.** *close* as a characteristic of vowels

# **30.9** Other Special Dictionaries

**30.9** **d**

**30.9a Dialect, Jargon, Technical Language.** Some dictionaries give you the special jargon or technical language of a
profession or art or craft. Special dictionaries give the special
terms of chemical engineers, doctors, lawyers, musicians, and
sportsmen:

*Black's Law Dictionary*, 5th ed.
Bennett, Harry, ed., *Concise Chemical and Technical Dictionary*,
    3rd ed., 1974
Dorian, A. F., *Dictionary of Science and Technology*, 2nd rev. ed.,
    1982
Brander, Michael, *Dictionary of Sporting Terms*, 1968
*Dorland's Illustrated Medical Dictionary*, 26th ed., 1981
Apel, Willi, ed., *Harvard Dictionary of Music*, 2nd ed., 1969

Some dictionaries supply the terms of a dialect or regional
or social language. In reading a novel of I. B. Singer or Saul
Bellow, you may need a translation of a Yiddish word—and,
more than the translation, its associations and nuances. You will
find this information in Leo Rosten's *The Joys of Yiddish*, a com-
pendium in dictionary form of Yiddish terms and the occasions
of their use, with illustrations from Jewish humor and literature.

Assume you need to know the meaning of the word *k'nocker*. First, Rosten tells you the word is pronounced *"not* 'nocker,' but *K'*NOCK-*er*, with the *k* a separate sound, as in 'Canute,'" then that the word comes from the German *knacken*: "A *knacker* meant someone who cracked a whip, was a doer, a big shot." A derisive term in Yiddish, it means a big shot or show-off, someone "who works crossword puzzles with—a pen (especially if someone is watching)." Rosten finishes his article with examples of the *k'nocker* in Yiddish humor.

A book similar to Rosten's is H. L. Mencken's *The American Language*. This book provides valuable information on usage in America and in Great Britain, as in this account of divided American and British usage of certain prepositions:

> An Englishman never lives *on* a street, but always *in* it, though he may live on an avenue or road. He never lives in a *block* of houses, but in a *row* of them or in a *block of flats* (not *apartments*); an *apartment*, to him, is a room.

**30.9b General Usage.**    There are numerous excellent dictionaries of English and American usage. The most influential of these is H. W. Fowler's *Dictionary of Modern English Usage*—the basis of Margaret Nicholson's *Dictionary of American-English Usage*. An influential and entertaining book is Bergen Evans and Cornelia Evans' *A Dictionary of Contemporary American Usage*.

Following is a short list of other valuable dictionaries and reference books dealing with usage and vocabulary:

Barzun, Jacques, *Simple and Direct*, 1976.
Bernstein, Theodore, *Bernstein's Reverse Dictionary*, 1975.
Craigie, Sir William, and James R. Hulbert, eds., *Dictionary of American English*, 1936-1944.
Crowley, Ellen T., and Robert C. Thomas, *Acronyms and Initialisms*, 1973.
Mathews, Mitford M., ed., *A Dictionary of Americanisms*, 1951.
Morris, William, and Mary Morris, eds., *Dictionary of Word and Phrase Origins*, 1971.
Lewis, Norman, ed., *The New Roget's Thesaurus of the English Language in Dictionary Form*, 1964.
*Oxford Dictionary of English Etymology*, 1966.
Partridge, Eric, *Dictionary of Slang and Unconventional English*, 1970.
———, *Origins: A Short Etymological Dictionary of Modern English*, 1966.
———, *Usage and Abusage*, 1957.
Wentworth, Harold, and Stuart Berg Flexner, *Dictionary of American Slang*, 1975.

**30.9**
**d**

# General Exercises

1. Decide whether your desk dictionary distinguishes denotative from connotative meanings in the definitions of the following:
   - **a.** admonish
   - **b.** giddy
   - **c.** faction
   - **d.** landlubber
   - **e.** liberal (noun)
   - **f.** scintillate

2. What light does the etymology of these words shed on their current meanings?

3. From what languages did the following words come, and what meanings do these carry from them?
   - **a.** expect
   - **b.** italics
   - **c.** maroon
   - **d.** schmaltz
   - **e.** schnauzer
   - **f.** torpedo

4. What does the dictionary tell you about the usage of the following words and phrases today? Are they archaic or obsolete, slang or colloquial?
   - **a.** crummy
   - **b.** come a cropper
   - **c.** fetching (adjective)
   - **d.** tope
   - **e.** binge

5. What information does the dictionary give you about the following?
   - **a.** the verb taken by the noun *wages* (*wages of sin*)
   - **b.** *me* as the complement of *it* or *that* (*That's me!*)
   - **c.** the word *mine* in the phrase *mine honor*

6. What do the following expressions mean? Does the dictionary specify their level of usage?
   - **a.** come at
   - **b.** come in for
   - **c.** come around
   - **d.** rave about
   - **e.** from hand to hand
   - **f.** from hand to mouth
   - **g.** hand down
   - **h.** shove off

7. What is the exact difference in meaning between the following?
   - **a.** faker, imposter
   - **b.** supercilious, overbearing
   - **c.** peculiar, strange
   - **d.** standard, archetype
   - **e.** example, pattern
   - **f.** reflective, contemplative
   - **g.** lavish, extravagant
   - **h.** insurrection, revolution

8. According to the *Oxford English Dictionary* or the *Oxford Universal Dictionary*, what meanings of the following words are obsolete or are limited to England or the British Isles generally?
   - **a.** heifer
   - **b.** hedge
   - **c.** journey
   - **d.** kindle
   - **e.** manifest (noun)
   - **f.** sordid

**9.** The following passages contain colloquialisms and technical terms used by social and professional groups—skiers, Spanish bullfighters, and musicians. What help do special dictionaries—for example, *Dictionary of Sporting Terms* and the *Harvard Dictionary of Music*—in the reference section of your library give the reader seeking an explanation of the special terms and the passage as a whole? If the dictionaries do not explain the word, can the reader depend on context for an understanding of it?

a. Some bumps may be big enough so you'll want to break up your diagonal striding routine with one or two double-poles off the top, thus carrying more speed off the downhill. An experienced skier makes sure to double-pole off the downside of the bump, using gravity to the greatest advantage.

—NED GILLETTE, *Cross-Country Skiing*

b. The mules came through the gate in a rush, the whips snapping, bells jangling and the young bull ploughing a furrow of sand.

They formed up for the paseo as soon as the bull had gone through.

Manuel and Hernandez stood in front. The youths of the cuadrillas were behind, their heavy capes furled over their arms. In back, the four picadors, mounted, holding their steel-tipped push-poles erect in the half-dark of the corral.

—ERNEST HEMINGWAY, "The Undefeated"

c. A damp September evening. I am playing the second-violin part of a Verdi aria for approximately the 500th time. My vibrato is slowing down to a limp tremor, and those redundant legato eighth-notes cross the G and D strings so often that my right wrist is wobbling like a tired penguin's flipper.

—LESLIE DREYER, "The Pit and the Pendulum," *Opera News*, March 14, 1981

# Checklist for Uses of the Dictionary

**30.1–2**  Explain special meanings given a word in speaking or writing.

**30.3**  Distinguish denotative from connotative meanings of a word.

**30.4**  The etymology or original meaning of a word sometimes helps to explain the current meaning.

**30.6**   Use the synonym listings in your dictionary to determine which of several synonyms or antonyms fits your sentence.

**30.7**   Use a historical dictionary to find the meaning of an obsolete or archaic word.

**30.8**   The dictionary explains how a word is used in various fields and how to use idiomatic phrases correctly.

**30.9a**   The dictionary gives information on dialectal words, jargon, and technical words.

**30.9b**   Consult special dictionaries on particular kinds of usage.

# Figurative Language

The subject of this chapter is **figurative language**—words and phrases that depart from the literal meaning of words in unusual ways. The word *cosmetic* has the literal meaning of a product that improves the look of the skin. But we use the word figuratively when we refer to "cosmetic statements" designed to make a policy or explanation seem better than it is.

**Metaphor** talks about one thing as if it were something else. Related to metaphor are other figures considered in this chapter, which discusses both effective and ineffective uses of these figures.

## 31.1  Effective and Ineffective Metaphor

**31.1a Simile, Metaphor, Personification.**   Similes, metaphors, and other figures are valuable in making ideas vivid and concrete. They do so by calling comparisons to mind. Familiar expressions use metaphor that names both the thing talked about and the vehicle that provides the comparison:

> dead of night
> the family of nations
> the dogs of war

Other kinds of metaphor do not name or specify the vehicle:

> He began to walk back along the tracks, for less than a mile away, he knew, where the stream boiled over the lip of a dam, there was a bridge.    —THOMAS WOLFE, *The Web and the Rock*

Thomas Wolfe is making an implicit comparison between a fast-moving stream and a liquid boiling in a container: he names the first and implies the second—the vehicle of the metaphor.

In some metaphors we must guess the thing being described as well as the thing or vehicle used to describe it:

Clambering onward, we have slowly made our way out of a
maze of isolated peaks into the level plains of science.
—LOREN EISELEY, *The Unexpected Universe*

Eiseley is comparing scientific research to a journey—the vehicle
of the metaphor. Neither element of the metaphor is explicitly
named. But notice the explicit metaphor in the embedded metaphor *maze of isolated peaks.*

Metaphor develops from analogy—like the explicit analogy
worked out in the following passage:

The litigating lawyer is a mercenary, one of the few remaining examples of the hired combatant. His premise is hostility. There are rules within which he must ply his trade, but
assuming the court is honest, they are not difficult to enforce,
and therefore not difficult to abide by. The rules observed, the
hostility is socially approved, indeed demanded.
—CHARLES REMBAR, *The End of Obscenity*

The writer may then use these and other terms of the analogy
metaphorically, as Charles Rembar does:

Almost all our occupations are competitive, of course, but in
most callings the battle is waged darkly and with guilt.

A **simile** is a form of metaphor that shows likeness between
two things and announces the likeness through the words *like*
or *as*:

The covers once prized apart would never close; those books
once open stayed open and lay on their backs helplessly flut-
tering their leaves like a turned-over June bug. They were as
light as a matchbox. —EUDORA WELTY, "A Sweet Devouring"

**31.1**

**d**

**Personification,** a form of metaphor, gives human or personal qualities to inanimate things so that they seem to possess
life:

A small sailing craft is not only beautiful, it is seductive and full
of strange promise and the hint of trouble.
—E. B. WHITE, "The Sea and the Wind That Blows"

North Richmond Street, being blind, was a quiet street except at the hour when the Christian Brothers' School set the
boys free. An uninhabited house of two storeys stood at the
blind end, detached from its neighbors in a square ground.
The other houses of the street, conscious of decent lives within
them, gazed at one another with brown imperturbable faces.
—JAMES JOYCE, "Araby"

Metaphor, simile, and personification are important in descriptive writing because of their power to evoke feeling through comparison. Dylan Thomas combines metaphor with personification in the following passage to achieve this effect:

> The town was not yet awake. Birds sang in eaves, bushes, trees, on telegraph wires, rails, fences, spars and wet masts, not for love or joy, but to keep other birds away. The landlords in feathers disputed the right of even the flying light to descend and perch.          —DYLAN THOMAS, *Quite Early One Morning*

Metaphor performs the same service in exposition:

> Focus a little experience, give some scope and depth to your feeling, and it grows imaginative; give it more scope and more depth, focus all experience within it, make it a philosopher's vision of the world, and it will grow imaginative in a superlative degree, and be supremely poetical.
> —GEORGE SANTAYANA, *Three Philosophical Poets*

**31.1b  The Uses of Metaphor.**    Metaphor can intensify a statement or passage:

> *Thunder* is good, *thunder* is impressive; but it is *lightning* that does the work.
> —MARK TWAIN, *Letter to an Unidentified Person* [italics added]

> He had rid himself of the *red sickness* of battle. The sultry *nightmare* was in the past. He had been an *animal blistered and sweating* in the heat and pain of war.
> —STEPHEN CRANE, *The Red Badge of Courage* [italics added]

In the second of these examples, Crane is describing a soldier's feelings about the war just fought. The phrase *red sickness* refers to the blood of battle. The more conventional nightmare metaphor intensifies the impression. The concluding image of the hot, blistered animal conveys the soldier's feelings through a sharp and unforgettable image.

Metaphors may be more complex than these, as in this statement of Crane's—an allusion to the biblical passage "And out of his mouth goeth a sharp sword":

> It had been necessary for him to swallow swords that he might have a better throat for grapes.
> —STEPHEN CRANE, *The Red Badge of Courage*

If the metaphor is farfetched or exaggerated, it can obscure the central idea, as in this confusing statement of a political candidate:

**31.1**
**d**

A beachhead of opportunity and growth lies ahead for Americans who seize the future with their own heart, spirit, and open hands.

The word *beachhead* refers to a piece of shore taken and defended in a war by an invading army. The metaphor is farfetched if the speaker did not mean to introduce images of war. The word *seize* creates more ambiguity; the words *heart* and *spirit* mean the same thing. The concluding metaphor *open hands* makes the statement even more confusing because it conflicts with the image suggested in the earlier hackneyed phrase *seize the future*.

Much scientific and technical writing, aiming at exact definition, seeks to be plain in style and as free as possible of figurative language. In contrast to more technical discourse, scientific exposition for a general audience often depends on metaphor and other figures to make difficult ideas concrete and vivid. On occasion metaphors can be dramatic, like the ones that conclude this highly metaphorical discussion of atoms:

> Under a microscope the material of the rock is revealed to be a tangle of interlocking crystals. An electron microscope can uncover the individual atoms, spaced out in a regular array with large gaps in between. Probing into the atoms themselves, we find that they are almost entirely empty space. The tiny nucleus occupies a mere trillionth ($10^{-12}$) of the atom's volume. The rest is populated by a *cloud* of neither-here-nor-there *ephemeral* electrons, *pinpricks* of solidity *whirling* about in *oceans* of *void*. Even the nucleus, on closer inspection, turns out to be a *pulsating package* of *evanescent* particles. The apparently concrete matter of experience *dissolves away* into vibrating patterns of quantum energy.   —PAUL DAVIES, *Superforce* [italics added]

**31.1**
**d**

**31.1c Submerged and Stale Metaphors.** When metaphors are absorbed into the language, we sometimes no longer respond to them as metaphor. In the passage just quoted, you probably did not read the words and phrases *tangle, interlocking, spaced out, gaps,* and *probing* metaphorically. We refer to these as **dead** or **submerged metaphors.** The following statements contain metaphors most readers probably do not recognize as such:

> The use of the English language as an *instrument* for analysis and exposition is one inheritance from England that we cannot afford to *scrap*.
> —EDMUND WILSON, *A Piece of My Mind* [italics added]

> Life in the United States is much subject to disruptions and frustrations, *catastrophic collapses* and gradual *peterings-out*.
> —EDMUND WILSON, *A Piece of My Mind* [italics added]

New Hampshire is a difficult state to campaign in: Its voters have come to take it for granted that they will be *wooed* on a virtual one-to-one basis by the candidates and tend to be diffident; they hold back on their commitments, producing a large, and *nerve-racking*, undecided vote until very late in the *game*.
—ELIZABETH DREW, "A Political Journal" [italics added]

Dead metaphors form a large group of the familiar phrases we depend on in speaking and writing. Only the most self-conscious speaker or writer tries to or can avoid them, and they are avoided at the cost of an easy style that moves from idea to idea without strain. By contrast with the dead or submerged metaphors in the examples just given, **stale metaphors** considerably weaken writing. These are metaphors we have heard or seen in print so often that they have lost their flavor and originality. At worst, stale metaphors suggest thoughtlessness or insincerity. Here are a few:

| | |
|---|---|
| breezy style of talk | down-to-earth personality |
| air of confidence | apple pie order |
| redhot temper | last-ditch stand |
| swollen ego | killing glance |
| sidesplitting joke | hot potato |

Stale metaphors of this sort occur because the writer does not look for the exact details that will help the reader see the subject or imagine the situation.

**31.1**

**d**

**31.1d Mixed Metaphor.    Mixed metaphors** present conflicting images that blur the idea and usually seem ludicrous:

The critic dug his own grave with his acid tongue.

This sentence becomes ludicrous when you try to imagine or visualize what the critic is doing. Try to visualize the metaphors contained in the following statements:

This city has a barrel of problems and nobody to tackle them honestly.
People squawk about how bad the streets are but sit on their hands when the time comes to fix them.
For those who seek truth in a jungle of madness, life is one big slap in the face.

The overcolorful language of some news reporting and press releases depends on a rapid succession of metaphors that sometimes create the same effect as mixed metaphor:

She is the rural neophyte waiting in a subway, a free spirit drinking Greek wine in the moonlight, an organic Earth Mother

dispensing fresh bread and herb tea, and the reticent feminist who by trial and error has charted the male as well as the female ego.
—Quoted from *Time,* by NORA EPHRON, "How to Write a Newsmagazine Cover Story"

For many readers the statement holds the attention for a while but gradually becomes hard to follow. Writing that calls attention to itself from phrase to phrase and from sentence to sentence has this effect. The reader looks for relief in plain statements and simple images.

**31.1e Hyperbole and Other Figurative Language.**   Metaphor, simile, and personification are the most common figures of speech. Expressive, referential, persuasive, and literary discourse use many others to convey emotional attitudes and make ideas vivid. Here are a few that you may have occasion to use:

1. **Hyperbole.**   Hyperbole is deliberate exaggeration, used in the following sentence to describe a long-held belief about women:

> For a long time I believed that the first pangs of connubial bliss brought with them a new wisdom, a kind of mystic knowledge that slipped with the wedding ring over all the fingers of the bride, so that at last and suddenly and completely she knew how to boil water.   —M. F. K. FISHER, "How to Boil Water"

The exaggeration of the first part of the sentence ("the first pangs of connubial bliss") prepares us for the humorous anticlimax—the surprising "mystic knowledge" that the bride acquires with a wedding ring.

2. **Understatement**.   The opposite of hyperbole is the understatement evident in this humorous cable of Mark Twain to the Associated Press:

> The reports of my death are greatly exaggerated.

Understatement is effective in forcing the reader to consider what has been left unsaid and, in serious discussions, to consider consequences that the discussion merely hints at.

3. **Irony**.   An ironic statement usually implies the opposite of what the words actually say, as in this "notice" that opens Mark Twain's *Adventures of Huckleberry Finn*:

> Persons attempting to find a motive in this narrative will be prosecuted; persons attempting to find a moral in it will be banished; persons attempting to find a plot in it will be shot.

**31.1**
**d**

**Sarcasm** is a bitter or mocking form of irony:

> We are waiting for the long-promised invasion. So are the fishes.
> —WINSTON S. CHURCHILL [on the threat of German
> invasion of the British Isles in World War II]

It is often used for ridicule, as in the following satirical description of a public health director:

> Now Almus Pickerbaugh had published scientific papers—often. He had published them in the *Midwest Medical Quarterly*, of which he was one of fourteen editors. He had discovered the germ of epilepsy and the germ of cancer—two entirely different germs of cancer. Usually it took him a fortnight to make the discovery, write the report, and have it accepted. Martin lacked this admirable facility.    —SINCLAIR LEWIS, *Arrowsmith*

The tone of a statement reflects the attitude of the speaker or writer. Usually inflection of voice makes your tone clear in speaking. In your writing, details or statements must show your attitude clearly. If they do not, your readers may be in doubt whether you intend to be ironic or sarcastic.

4. **Synecdoche.**   Synecdoche is the use of a member of a class to represent the whole class, as in the expression "meat and potatoes" in referring to food. Here is an expression identified as synecdoche by the writer:

**31.1**
**d**

> The star system undoubtedly is the most original invention of the movies—in a synecdochal sense, it contains and *is* the movies.
> —MILTON KLONSKY, "Along the Midway of Mass Culture"

Many synecdoches like "meat and potatoes" are hidden or submerged metaphors, but many others, like that in Klonsky's statement, sharpen ideas.

5. **Metonymy.**   Metonymy is closely related to synecdoche in naming something through a quality or thing associated with it:

> The White House announced a new report dealing with unemployment in textiles and steel.

The terms *White House, textiles,* and *steel* stand for the presidential administration and the textile and steel industries. These metonymies are abbreviated ways of speaking and writing—a valuable saving of words in discourse.

**EXERCISES**

1. What metaphors are mixed in the following statement from the Congressional Record?

With at least $313 billion already obligated to be spent by Congress over the next 40 years on public housing, we have dug a deep trench by obviously biting off more than we could chew.

2. Add a simile, metaphor, personification, or other figure of speech to the following sentence to make the idea vivid for the reader:
    a. The plane had trouble rising from the ground.
    b. Failure needs our help.
    c. Friendships take time to develop.
    d. The skier moved clumsily down the slope.
    e. Listening to rock is different from listening to country music.
3. Russell Baker uses metaphors humorously in the following passage. Identify and interpret them:

Americans don't like plain talk anymore. Nowadays they like fat talk. Show them a lean, plain word that cuts to the bone and watch them lard it with thick greasy syllables front and back until it wheezes and gasps for breath as it comes lumbering down upon some poor threadbare sentence like a sack of iron on a swayback horse. —"American Fat"

# 31.2 Clichés

A cliché is a trite, overused expression that blurs the image or idea the writer wants to express. Many clichés are familiar expressions that call attention to themselves. Stale metaphors are clichés, but not all clichés contain metaphor.

Familiar expressions and phrases become clichés when we sense they substitute for thought. In other words, the cliché gives us the impression of insincerity or of facility—expressing ideas or feelings with the ease of a valentine verse or a birthday message. The following are familiar clichés:

| | |
|---|---|
| right as rain | luck of the Irish |
| chip off the old block | nutty as a fruit cake |
| staff of life | Numero Uno |
| mean as a junkyard dog | Mr. Nice Guy |
| cool as a cucumber | Miss Personality |
| hot as blazes | cheap as dirt |
| apple of her eye | lull after the storm |
| American as apple pie | clean as a whistle |

Here are old sayings or famous quotations that have lost their surprise and originality through constant repetition:

All's well that ends well.
It's the effort that counts.
He snatched victory out of the jaws of defeat.
Not if I were the last person on earth!

People often use phrases of this sort in the mistaken idea that they make writing colorful and exciting. The cure for clichés, stale metaphors, and the like was suggested by Dr. Samuel Johnson in the eighteenth century:

> An old tutor of a college said to one of his pupils: Read over your compositions, and wherever you meet with a passage which you think is particularly fine, strike it out.
> —JAMES BOSWELL, *Life of Dr. Johnson*

### EXERCISES

1. Examine advertisements for a particular product—automobiles, laundry detergent, lipstick, for example—to determine the extent to which these depend on clichés or pat phrases. Be ready to discuss the effectiveness of advertising language.
2. Martin Plissner gives these examples of clichés in politics:

> "Momentum" and "perceptions" were the supreme clichés of 1976, and they were still very much in vogue as 1980 began. But unlike Jimmy Carter, momentum's child four years ago, George Bush and then John Anderson got only so far with it. To deal with their own discomfort about the uncertainties of momentum, reporters found a new concept and a word to go with it, "volatility."

And he gives these additional examples:

> The underdogs were uniformly "dogged" or "undaunted" in their endeavors, taking their "uphill campaigns" from one "last ditch stand" to another, struggling to "get a foothold" before their contributions "dried up," "grasping at straws" as they faced the prospect of being "written off."
> —MARTIN PLISSNER, "The Power of Babble"

How common are these clichés in political campaigns today? What are the current clichés?

## 31.3  Euphemism

**Euphemism** is an inoffensive or a pleasing substitute for some act or condition that we prefer not to name directly. The following is a list of familiar euphemisms:

| | |
|---|---|
| passed away | died |
| the deceased individual | dead man |
| disadvantaged neighborhood | slum |
| senior citizen, golden ager | old person |
| reformatory | prison |
| delinquent | criminal |
| short wait | two hours |
| waste | kill |
| pacify | kill |
| happy | drunk |
| exceptional in quality | poor, rotten |
| low achiever | poor student |
| lacks self control | steals, talks in class, cheats, smokes in the toilet |
| high achiever | does none of the above |

The motive for euphemism is often admirable—to avoid giving pain. Thus the euphemisms for dying soften the harshness of words in consoling people mourning someone who has died. But euphemism can also be used to disguise a harsh reality that needs to be faced. Euphemism may be used to equivocate or mislead someone through ambiguous terms. When a friend asks you to judge a picture or a piece of writing and, disliking the work, you tell him that you find it "exceptional," he probably will think you are giving praise. You have equivocated to avoid telling your friend the truth and to avoid risking the loss of his friendship—an understandable human response.

But euphemism can be vicious, as in the wartime use of the word *pacify* to avoid the word *kill* ("we pacified the village"). The euphemism *waste* also disguises the act. In his famous essay "Politics and the English Language," George Orwell cites the use of the phrase *justifiable severity* to avoid the word *torture*.

Euphemism is vicious when its purpose is to lie or deceive. As the word *waste* shows, euphemism is also dangerous because it is easily misunderstood.

**31.4** d

# 31.4   Rhymed Words

Rhymed words are familiar in poetry and in some descriptive writing. The following descriptive passage uses rhyme words and heavily rhythmic sentences to convey the intense emotion felt by the character or speaker and generated by the action or scene:

The circus train had stopped in the heart of the country, for what reason he did not know. He could hear the languid and intermittent breathing of the engine, the strangeness of men's voices in the dark, the casual stamp of the horses in their cars, and all around him the attentive and vital silence of the earth.

—THOMAS WOLFE, *The Web and the Rock*

Sometimes the vowels of words close to each other rhyme:

vital, silence

And sometimes consonants echo in adjacent words:

engines, strangeness

In ordinary exposition, a string of rhyming vowels or **alliterated words** (words opening with the same consonant sounds) can be distracting or annoying:

I see no *mean* bet*ween* the extr*eme* viewpoints presented.

*R*eally *r*eliable *r*eading tests assist the *r*eading teacher at all grade levels.

To revise annoying sentences of this kind, find substitute words for those that rhyme:

Reliable tests of reading ability help teachers at all grade levels.

**31.4 d**

**EXERCISE**

Revise the following sentences to eliminate the mixed metaphors, clichés, euphemisms, and rhyme words:

1. The sanitary engineer was emptying the receptacle full of discarded food and paper.
2. His response was off target and missed my point.
3. The thunder of her words sank upon the audience.
4. My high-flying kite seemed bright in the sunlight.
5. The speaker then hammered home his point, taking a dig at his opponent as he did so.
6. She is Mr. Right for the job.
7. Exam week almost put me in the booby hatch, but now everything is hunky-dory.
8. The trailer truck is stuck in the mud.
9. His performance of the role of Hamlet was greeted by the audience with a not altogether approving sound.
10. Deaf to the shouts from the gallery, the actor pretended not to hear the names he was being called.
11. We wrestled with what to do about inflation, then punched at each other's solutions.
12. The play is not exactly a barrel of laughs.

13. The candidate's lack of sympathy with the proposal was apparent in the not too favorable comments he made to the press.
14. Nobody knows, I suppose, how many oppose the school's closing.
15. Living on the fast track, he was flying high and fast.

## Checklist for Figurative Language

**31.1a** Use simile, metaphor, and personification to make ideas vivid and concrete.

**31.1b** Farfetched metaphor creates confusion and ambiguity:

> A beachhead of opportunity and growth lies ahead for Americans who seize the future with heart, spirit, and open hands.

**31.1c** Stale metaphors suggest thoughtlessness or insincerity:

> Though he walks with an air of confidence, he has a down-to-earth personality.

**31.1d** Mixed metaphors can be ludicrous and confusing:

> The critic dug his own grave with his acid tongue.

**31.1e** Use hyperbole, irony, and other figures where appropriate.

**31.2** Clichés or trite, overused expressions blur the image or idea:

**31.2** Clichés or trite, overused expressions blur the image or idea:

> I feel right as rain and cool as a cucumber.

**31.3** Euphemisms or inoffensive, pleasing statements can be used to equivocate or disguise the facts:

> Many golden agers live in disadvantaged neighborhoods.

**31.4** In ordinary exposition avoid rhymed syllables that distract the reader:

> Really reliable reading tests assist the reading teacher at all grade levels.

> *Improved*
> Reliable tests of reading ability help teachers at all grade levels.

**31.4 d**

# Sound Reasoning

# Inductive Reasoning

**Exposition** uses evidence to explain and illustrate a process or idea. **Argument** uses evidence to prove a thesis. In your college papers, you use evidence from historical documents or from laboratory experiments to prove a thesis. In a letter to a newspaper you cite facts, use analogy, analyze causes, or make inferences from well-established truths to make a point or defend a position or idea.

Much argumentative writing is persuasive in purpose. Making a case for or against an idea or proposal, debating a public issue, defending a policy or a decision—all of these depend upon persuasive argument. Magazines and newspapers contain persuasive arguments on almost every page. In a newsmagazine a public official defends a particular environmental policy; a later issue contains letters from readers in rebuttal. A newspaper editorial argues for distribution of government surplus food to the poor; a letter to the editor argues that the state drinking age should be raised to twenty-one; a columnist argues that a recent Supreme Court decision erodes the power of the states to administer criminal justice. Argument takes many forms and has many purposes.

This chapter discusses *inductive arguments*—those arguments that draw on personal experience, observation, experiment, and other empirical evidence. *Deductive arguments*, those that make inferences from assumptions and well-established beliefs, are the subject of the following chapter. The later chapters of Part VII discuss persuasive arguments and common logical fallacies.

## 32.1 The Nature of Inductive Reasoning

**32.1a Everyday Inductive Arguments.**   An **inductive argument** is essentially an argument from experience. You are reasoning inductively when, on the basis of a series of bad driving experiences, you predict that you will probably have another unpleasant experience and decide not to use the expressway during rush hour. You are also doing so when you give yourself reasons based on your own analysis of the causes and on a statistical report on rush-hour accidents you heard on the evening news.

An inductive argument generalizes from a variety of sources —personal experience, observation, experiments, statistics, and historical research. Evidence of this kind relies chiefly on the senses—on what you see, experience, experiment with, and discover that other people have experienced, observed, measured, and counted. To be reliable, such arguments must meet certain tests. A good inductive argument generalizes from typical evidence, not from exceptional experiences or circumstances. It also draws limited inferences and makes limited predictions from this evidence alone.

Here is an inductive argument that presents a series of facts and observations, then draws a limited inference from them.

> I hear that computers are indispensable household management tools. I must run a very simple household, because all my important documents, checks and receipts of the past five years are filed in three-quarters of a shoe box. At that rate, I should need about five shoe boxes in my lifetime. Five shoe boxes take up less space than the average computer. Shoe boxes also cost less and don't use electricity. In case of fire, flood or theft, either system is useless, so, all things considered, I don't see the advantages of having a computer when it comes to organizing receipts, warranties and records of payment.
> —KATHERINE GALE DaCOSTA, "Anticomputerism," *The New York Times*, August 27, 1984

**32.1
log**

The writer draws the limited conclusion from her personal experience that a computer will be of no advantage to her in the future, though she recognizes that computers are of use to the phone company and the department store. A later statement in the essay shows that her conclusion is a limited one:

> I've no doubt that computers simplify matters for my local telephone operating company and Macy's. And I like being able to make a payment on my Visa account in one bank and have the transaction recorded immediately in another bank clear across town.   —KATHERINE GALE DaCOSTA, "Anticomputerism"

The inference of an inductive argument is drawn from the specific facts and experiences and from these only and not unspecified ones. The inference also cannot be broader than these facts and experiences allow. Were the opening sentence of the paragraph worded as follows, the inference would be broader than the evidence permits:

> Computers are not indispensable household management tools.

**32.1b  Typical Evidence.**   Most inductive arguments make predictions or inferences from a limited sample of people or events:

> *If the teenagers in my high school are typical,* teenage drivers are as good on the road as anyone.

As the opening clause shows, the writer recognizes that the teenagers in the sample must be typical of all teenagers. If challenged, the writer would have to show that these teenagers as a group represent all American teenagers in background, education, driving experience, and other qualities pertinent to the conclusion.

The word *pertinent* is the important word. If most of the teenagers in the sample were redheads, that fact would not be pertinent to the conclusion. It would be pertinent if most of them drove as much during the week as the majority of American teenagers who have access to cars. What is pertinent evidence is often a matter of dispute in debating a generalization based on observation and statistics.

**32.1**
**log**

**32.1c  The Degree of Probability.**   No matter how strong the evidence you present, the conclusion of your argument can be more or less probable and never certain. You cannot claim certainty because you cannot guarantee you know all circumstances that affect your sample, including all the facts about the teenagers you are surveying. In inductive reasoning, you can never guarantee you possess all pertinent facts. The decision to make the "inductive leap"—to make the jump from facts to generalization or conclusion—is a decision you must make carefully.

The conclusions of inductive arguments always go beyond the evidence: the crucial question is how far they go beyond it with the support of the evidence. You can make predictions about teenagers on the basis of the sample described, but the sample does not allow you to make a prediction about the driving ability of any *single* American teenager. An inductive argument makes a prediction only about the group as a whole.

**EXERCISES**

1. What information do you need to decide whether the students in your high school class were and are still typical of American teenagers as a whole?

2. Assume you can prove the students in the class are typical of American teenagers, and you can prove also that these students on the average have no more traffic accidents a year than their parents. Can you make the following inferences about American teenagers on the basis of these students?

   **a.** American teenagers probably will not have more accidents than their parents in coming years.

   **b.** American teenagers probably did not have more accidents than their parents in past years.

   **c.** American teenagers are as diverse as their parents in training and experience as drivers.

3. How many kinds of evidence does the writer present in the following paragraphs from an article on theories of crime?

   > A more recent biological theory linked violent criminality with the so-called XYY defect in men. Normally, men's cells have two chromosomes, a female X and a male Y; XYY men are born with an extra Y. Some studies of imprisoned criminals have found numerous males with the XYY pattern. But Dr. Fred Sergovich, a geneticist, observes that "if you look only at abnormal populations, you will find only abnormal XYY's." He estimates that the XYY pattern occurs once in 1,000 or so male births and suggests that if the general population could be surveyed, many law-abiding XYY's would probably be discovered.

   > The latest XYY study, reported last year, was done in Denmark by Dr. Herman Witkin, a senior research psychologist at the Educational Testing Service in Princeton, N. J., and his colleagues. Screening a broad population, they found a higher rate of convicted criminals among XYY's than among chromosomally normal males. However, the misdeeds of the convicted men were not notable for their sophistication, and the researchers believe that the elevated XYY rate they observed "may reflect a higher detection rate than a higher rate of commission."

   > In any event, the XYY men in the study were minor offenders, and the investigators found "no evidence that XYY men are more likely to commit crimes of violence than men without the extra Y chromosome."

**32.1**
**log**

Psychologically minded theorists often think of crime as a symptom of mental illness—or as an alternative to it. The psychiatrist Seymour Halleck believes that a person who feels utterly helpless to control his fate may unconsciously choose crime rather than mental collapse because breaking the law can give a liberating sense of power. "During the planning and execution of a criminal act," Dr. Halleck said, "the offender is a free man. He is immune from the oppressive dictates of others since he has temporarily broken out of their control."

—Virginia Adams, "Causes of Crime, Maybe,"
*The New York Times*, December 18, 1977

**4.** How strong do you find the evidence in the following student paragraphs for the conclusions presented? What additional evidence would you add to strengthen these conclusions? Would you qualify the conclusions or draw different ones from the evidence?

Society has always stressed one particular social rule—women are permitted to show emotions while men are not. The question of sensitivity has always plagued men and women. Should men be looked upon as weak and feminine if they show signs of sensitivity? In the past it was believed that in order for men to show their strength and masculinity, most forms of emotion, especially crying, should be suppressed. Crying was looked upon as a weakness that showed a lack of courage and strength. Women were always portrayed as sensitive, fragile creatures excessively affected by emotional traumas.

Today, after the so-called sexual revolution, great changes have taken place. Or have they? Women have taken on the new role of the strong-minded career woman, eager for new challenges and responsibilities. Their concept of the male role has changed also. No longer do they look for the domineering male who takes on all responsibilities. Today women appreciate sensitive men and search for men who display their

**32.1
log**

emotions. With the rise of these modern-day career women, men have begun to question their own feelings and have slowly begun to unmask their true emotions. They have been made aware of many physical and psychological problems that could arise if they continue to hold emotions inside.

Yet, why are many men still criticized if they cry or display an excess of emotion? This criticism is seen in everyday situations. Consider a man who loses his job, walks into a bar, and begins sobbing. The other men in the bar will probably look at this man and think he is a "weakling" or a "sissy." Most men wouldn't approach the crying man and congratulate him for showing his emotions, embrace him, or sit and talk with him. Worse are the reactions of women who expressed this desire for male sensitivity. Seeing this crying man, these women would probably not approach him, congratulate him for displaying his true emotions, and tell him how much they appreciate a sensitive man. Though this example is somewhat exaggerated, it is true of society today. Most women still look for that domineering characteristic in a man. They have not yet learned how to react to evidence of male sensitivity. Society tells men not to be afraid of showing emotion, yet the sensitive man is seldom accepted. He may indeed be considered abnormal.

**32.2** log

## 32.2 Analogy

**32.2a The Nature of Analogy.** Arguments from analogy are inductive in nature because they draw conclusions from observations and experience. Argumentative analogy is like the illustrative analogy common in exposition—a point-by-point comparison between different things that share important similarities (see 6.5). Following is an illustrative analogy used to explain the manufacture of phonograph records.

> The principle that makes it possible to mass-produce thousands and even millions of records of the same performance is essentially that of the waffle-iron: Pour in the batter and close the lid. Except that in this case, the batter is a dollop of vinyl and, instead of the square grid of the breakfast waffle, the press molds into the disk the spiral groove whose undulations represent the sound of music.
>
> —HANS FANTEL, "Sound," *The New York Times*, August 7, 1983

Analogy in argument proves a point. In using analogy as proof, you must do what Fantel does in noting the difference between the batter and the dollop of vinyl—define the limits of the analogy, that is, the extent to which it gives support for the limited conclusion you are drawing from it:

> Since teenagers in my high school get as much driving training as adults, drive under the same conditions, and have no greater number of traffic accidents, they probably are as trustworthy as their parents as drivers.

In developing your own analogics, ask whether the differences between the things analogized weaken the conclusion. These differences may be controversial. In the argument just cited, parents and children may disagree strongly on the definition of "experience." Another difference unmentioned in the argument is age. One parent might argue that the parents cited are older and therefore are wiser and more experienced. The teenager defending the argument insists that age is an insignificant difference when driving is at issue but adds that, if age were significant, the young driver would probably be more agile.

Even more controversial will be the predictions made on the basis of the analogy. In a good argument by analogy, the similarities are pertinent and the differences do not weaken the conclusion. Is the analogy strong evidence for the conclusion that American teenagers are therefore as trustworthy as adult drivers?

**32.2b The Limits of Analogy.**   Like all inductive arguments, those based on analogy can be more or less probable and never certain. The degree of probability depends on how significant the differences are. It also depends on judgments or assumptions that guide the analogy—assumptions sometimes explicit in the argument and sometimes implied, as in the following:

**32.2**
**log**

As the natural food of primates becomes riper and more suitable for consumption, it usually becomes sweeter, and monkeys and apes have a strong reaction to anything that is strongly endowed with this taste. Like other primates, we find it hard to resist "sweets." —DESMOND MORRIS, *The Naked Ape*

This argument from analogy depends on the fact that the human being is a primate. On the basis of this fact Morris argues that the human being, like other primates, likes sweets.

Such an argument can be no stronger than the underlying assumptions and facts. The strength of the argument depends on showing that differences between human beings and other primates are insignificant. Thus we take note of this qualification in the introduction to the book:

> Because of the size of the task, it will be necessary to oversimplify in some manner. The way I shall do this is largely to ignore the detailed ramifications of technology and verbalization, and concentrate instead on those aspects of our lives that have obvious counterparts in other species: such activities as feeding, grooming, sleeping, fighting, mating and care of the young. —DESMOND MORRIS, *The Naked Ape*

As a writer of analogies, you need to test your own carefully in the same way you test those of other writers. One way is to appeal to your own experience. Note that Morris considers "verbalization" an insignificant difference. Do words influence your own preference for sweets? What influence does advertising have on this preference and on what foods you like and dislike? And is there any contrary evidence? What about people who don't eat sweets?

Since analogy seldom provides enough evidence for a strong inference, you need to give other supporting evidence from your experience and observation. Morris does not depend on analogy alone. In his discussion, he notes that human beings have "sweet shops" but not "sour shops," and they end the meal with something sweet. Like Morris, you make your inductive argument more probable the more evidence for the conclusion you present.

**32.2
log**

### EXERCISES

1. Do you believe that the age of adults and their usually greater experience as drivers weakens the argument from analogy discussed previously?
2. How strong do you find the following analogies in support of "nonsmokers' rights"?

> [I]f the person at the desk next to me ate so much pizza that he needed half of my chair as well as his own, the company would make a rule against overeating. Because my co-worker merely poisons the air I breathe eight hours a day, his rights come before mine. It is an accepted principle that one person's right to extend his arm ends before he reaches another person's jaw. I hope that someday the law will recognize that a smoker's rights end where the air I breathe begins.
> —ELIZABETH McGAFFEY, *Newsweek*, June 20, 1983

**3.** What arguments by analogy does the writer of the following paragraphs on the taking of American citizens as hostages reject, and why? What analogy does she use in arguing this rejection?

> I am always struck by a couple of particularly bad formulations that are used in these episodes. One holds that the hostages are "being treated well," so long as they get some food and soap and are not being physically beaten. It reminds me of that old standby about how the woman had been raped "but not harmed" by her assailant. The absence of a bash to the face in neither case constitutes absence of harm or good treatment. By the very act of their capture our hostages are being brutally mistreated.
>
> The other especially unfortunate formulation is that which holds that we are in a "war" with terrorism. But war, with its rules and its purposes and its causes, for all its irrationality and evil, is exactly what we are not in. And to say we are is to do several things. It is to elevate these grubby criminal acts to a status they don't deserve; it is to cast, at least indirectly, all Americans as enemy civilians or belligerents and thus fair game; and it is to misdescribe the nature of the assault itself. Soldiers may behave thuggishly, but there is a difference between soldiers and thugs. And there is a difference too between being a prisoner of war and being a hostage hauled off a plane.
> —MEG GREENFIELD, "Accepting the Unacceptable,"
> *Newsweek*, July 1, 1985

**32.3**
log

# 32.3  Causal Analysis

In looking for causes and effects, you do the same as in arguing from analogy—you seek to make predictions. If you observe the cause of an event in the present, you expect to find the same cause in the future and you may argue that a similar event in the past had the same cause.

### 32.3a  Arguing from Causes.

The word *cause* has different meanings. Assume you recently witnessed a traffic accident "caused" by a drunk driver. Is the driver the "cause" or is the state of intoxication—or more specifically, an amount of alcohol in the blood sufficient to produce intoxication? Or is the "cause" a celebration or a frustrating experience or personal catastrophe that led the driver to drink heavily? Obviously the cause may be any one of these and perhaps may be several.

In looking for causes, you are looking for the following first:

- the *immediate causes*—intoxication and the decision to drive while intoxicated;
- the *remote causes*—the social and psychological conditions or circumstances that encourage drunk driving.

Debate may center on immediate causes or remote causes or both. Considering the immediate cause of the high number of traffic fatalities involving drunk drivers, you argue that measures must be taken to get drunk drivers off the street. Considering the remote causes, you argue that prior circumstances that encourage drunk driving should be the main concern. Fining or jailing drunk drivers is not dealing with the "real cause."

The word *cause* also refers to the following:

- the *necessary conditions*, or conditions that must be present when an event occurs;
- the *sufficient conditions*, or conditions in whose presence the event must occur.

**32.3**
**log**

These conditions are often the subject of investigation in tracing the immediate cause. Thus to prove that a person is intoxicated, you must find alcohol in the blood. Alcohol is a necessary condition of intoxication. But alcohol does not produce intoxication in all quantities. Evidence of a minimum amount in the blood may be sufficient to prove that a driver is criminally liable.

Like all inductive arguments, causal arguments are more or less probable and never certain. Later investigation may prove that alcohol alone cannot produce intoxication. Age, personality, blood type, or other factors may eventually be shown to join with alcohol as necessary conditions of intoxication. The sum of these **necessary** conditions may be cited as the condition **sufficient** to make a person drunk.

In developing your own causal argument, you probably will

not make distinctions as technical as these. But you do need to clarify the kind of cause you are identifying. And you need also to limit your conclusion properly, without claiming certainty for what can at best be a probable one. For example, you can point to a necessary condition of good driving—proper driver training —without claiming that everyone who takes a driving course must be a good driver.

**32.3b  Arguing from Effects.**    An argument may also be developed through effects that point to a cause. In a book published in 1972, Vance Packard argues the following thesis:

> Where technology is in a runaway stage, as in the United States, both mobility and general uprootedness tend to run highest.

Packard gives evidence for this thesis throughout the book, but in the paragraph following this statement he argues through effects:

> About 40 million Americans change their home addresses at least once *each year*. And more than a third of these people move across a county or state line. In this twentieth century there has been a 25 percent increase in people living in a state other than the one in which they were born. That is only mildly suggestive of the amount of total movement that has actually been occurring. The massive leap in mobility that started with World War II can be seen by comparing the proportion of migrants moving across county lines in two five-year periods twenty years apart: 1935-40 and 1955-60. . . . During the twenty-year period from the 1940 Census to the 1960 Census there was a leap of 50 percent in such internal migration.
> —Vance Packard, *A Nation of Strangers*

**32.3**
**log**

Arguments from effects usually combine with arguments from causes or with statistical arguments, as in Packard's book. As in all inductive arguments, the more varied the evidence presented for the conclusion, the stronger the proof.

**Exercises**

1. Distinguish the immediate and remote causes of one of the following:
   a. an exam you recently passed
   b. an argument you engaged in recently
2. What are the necessary conditions of successful performance in a sport or in a similar activity? Do these comprise the sufficient condition?
3. Is the writer of the following passage identifying necessary or sufficient conditions?

The common factor characterizing these "changed" kids who kill, torture, and rape seems to be a form of emotional detachment that allows them to commit unspeakable crimes with a complete absence of normal feelings such as guilt or remorse. It is as if they were dealing with inanimate objects, not with human beings at all. "It's almost as though they looked at the person who got killed as a window they were going to jimmie, as an obstacle, something that got in their way," says Charles King, director in charge of rehabilitation of New York State's Division for Youth.

—Marie Winn, *The Plug-in Drug*

What use might you make of this analysis in an argument of your own?

4. In the following paragraph Vance Packard states a cause, then illustrates its effects. What is the cause, what are the effects, and what are the general implications of the analysis?

The millions of Archie Bunkers and other working people in the land who move suffer more losses in relation to income than do the organization men or women of corporations and government. They don't have a protecting organization to share some of their costs and headaches. Usually they have to hire or borrow trucks or rent haul-type trailers instead of using moving vans. They do their own loading and unloading and they may have to take several trips. Usually, too, the move is more upsetting because they are less used to moving and are likely to be more uneasy in strange surroundings.

—*A Nation of Strangers*

**32.4**

**log**

What use could you make of this analysis in an argument of your own?

## 32.4 Sampling

All generalizations depend on a **representative sample**—that is, on a small group typical of a broader group about which a prediction is made. In his paragraph on mobility and uprootedness in the United States (p. 490), Vance Packard gives statistical information on several groups, including people migrating to different parts of the state and country between 1935 and 1940 and between 1955 and 1960. Deriving a representative sample depends on accurate statistical methods, and we cannot in this short discussion give an account of these. But you can guard against inaccurate or unfair sampling in your own writing by keeping a few simple points in mind.

1. Your sample must be broad enough to be significant. That is, it must canvass enough people to guarantee it represents all of the people your generalization covers. Thus the generalization that most old people are bad drivers would be worth considering if the sample includes old people living in different parts of the country and driving under different conditions—in large cities as well as rural areas. The broader the sample, the greater the probability that differences are accounted for. A sample based on a limited group, even one selected randomly—for example, old people driving cars on a Sunday afternoon on a lightly traveled street—is of little worth. On the same principle, it is important to know the total number that statements about "1 out of 2" drivers or smokers or toothpaste users cited in statistical arguments are referring to. Only two people need be interviewed to create a statistic.

2. Your sample must not be based on special circumstances that would make it unrepresentative or untypical. Basing the sample on the driving of old people observed on icy streets in January is unfair if the generalization refers to their driving in all kinds of weather at all times of the year.

3. Your generalization cannot be broader than the evidence warrants. Your evidence may support the generalization that old people do not drive well on icy streets, but it does not show that old people are worse drivers than younger people in the same circumstances or that they are usually bad drivers.

4. Your sample must be clear in its wording. Unless the terms are exact, your reader will not know what group of people the sample includes and what broader group of people it represents. The phrase *old people* is vague. The sample may refer to people fifty years of age or older or to people in their seventies or eighties, and the generalization it supports may refer to an equally vague group. Terms like *yuppie* and *senior citizen* are often based on social attitudes that bias the sample.

5. The sample or statistical evidence must make a prediction about people in similar circumstances. It is dangerous to make predictions on how Americans will judge future wars on the basis of surveys of American opinion on the Vietnam War. Circumstances that govern social and political attitudes change from year to year and decade to decade.

6. In presenting statistical evidence or generalizing from samples, consider all the facts relevant to their interpretation. Comparing the traffic fatalities in 1974 and 1984, you notice a

**32.4**
**log**

decline for drivers under twenty-one in your state—a fact you might attribute to a hike in the state drinking age in the previous year. The statistical correlation might be significant if the decline occurred only in that age group. It would be less significant if the decline occurred in all groups, though the statistical correlation does provide *some* evidence for the generalization that drinking contributes to traffic fatalities among teenaged drivers. Other evidence is needed to make this argument. And you would have to state other facts that might account for the decline—for example, the change in the speed limit in the intervening years.

### EXERCISES

1. What statistical evidence would you need to prove that people who drive on the right-hand side of the highway (as drivers do in the United States) are better drivers than those who drive on the left-hand side (as drivers do in Great Britain)?

2. What evidence might people present to prove that their pets "understand" English—that is, understand what their owners are saying to them? What would you accept as sound evidence that the pets do understand?

3. Since there is no physical evidence that UFOs have visited earth, can we accept as probable to any degree that they have done so on the basis of UFO "sightings" by some people?

4. What do you believe a judge means in instructing a jury to convict a defendant only if the evidence warrants the verdict "beyond a reasonable doubt"? How certain must the jury be to reach a verdict on this basis?

5. An advertisement for a "nutritive sweetener" includes the following statement:

> An amount equal in sweetness to one teaspoon of sugar contains just 1/10 of one calorie. So it can reduce the number of empty calories in some foods as much as 95%.

**32.4**
**log**

Is the advertisement saying that the 95% reduction is related to one teaspoon of sugar? And what is the meaning of the word *reduce*? Does it mean that the sweetener removes anything from the food? Exactly what does the sweetener do?

## Checklist for Inductive Reasoning

**32.1a** A good inductive argument generalizes from typical evidence, not from exceptional experiences and circumstances.

**32.1b**   Make the evidence in inductive arguments pertinent to the conclusion.

**32.1c**   Don't assume that a prediction about the group as a whole necessarily applies to each individual.

**32.2a**   When you use analogy as proof, be sure that differences between the things analogized don't weaken the argument.

**32.2b**   State the limits of the analogy.

**32.3a**   Distinguish the meaning of the word *cause*—as immediate or remote cause, as necessary or sufficient condition—in developing a causal argument.

**32.3b**   Arguments from effects usually combine with arguments from cause and with other inductive arguments.

**32.4**   In developing a statistical argument, define the sample carefully, make it representative of the class discussed and broad enough to be significant, and do not base it on special circumstances.

# Deductive Reasoning

## 33.1 The Nature of Deductive Reasoning

**33.1a Deductive and Inductive Reasoning.** Deductive reasoning is the counterpart of inductive reasoning. To make a **deduction** is to draw inferences from statements held to be true or certain. These truths may be held on faith or assumed to be "self-evident" truths. Many are truths established through long experience and observation—that is, through the inductive processes described in the previous chapter. A popular example is the statement that all humans are mortal. What is true of all humans, we reason from this material truth, must be true of Socrates and every other human being. If the statement is true, it necessarily follows that Socrates is mortal. In deductive reasoning we make necessary inferences of this kind.

In inductive reasoning, particulars of experience provide the evidence for probable conclusions. In deductive reasoning statements or propositions themselves *(All men are mortal; Socrates is a man)* provide the evidence. If these statements or propositions that form the evidence are true, then the conclusion inferred from them *(Socrates is mortal)* is certain in the sense of being a necessary inference. Many writers who develop deductive arguments assume that the truths presented are sufficient to establish the truth of the conclusion. No other evidence is required, and they rest the argument on the mere statement of the premises. Other writers defend their premises, explaining where they come from and what evidence supports them.

**33.1b Drawing Necessary Conclusions.** This assumption is evident in the following deductive argument of William Raspberry on capital punishment. After discussing the finding of a Maryland jury that "mitigating circumstances" justified not putting a man to death for the kidnap, rape, torture, and murder of a young woman, Raspberry concludes:

> I am no big fan of capital punishment. It too often involves such factors as the wealth, social status and race of both murderer and victim, and whether the crime is a sufficiently "famous" one—matters that have nothing to do with the nature of the offense.
>
> Still, it strikes me that it is possible for a criminal to commit acts so heinous as to place himself outside the category of human, to render him subject to extermination as one might exterminate a mad dog, without consideration of how the animal came to contract rabies in the first place.
>
> —WILLIAM RASPBERRY, "What Is the Death Penalty For?"
> *Cleveland Plain Dealer*, October 22, 1982

Raspberry states as a given truth that particular heinous acts place those who commit them "outside the category of human." This statement is his evidence for the conclusion that particularly heinous acts justify the death penalty. Believing that the statement is an obvious truth, Raspberry presents no other evidence, although he does illustrate his belief in narrating the events of the crime and the jury trial. Inductive evidence joins with deductive argument here as in most persuasive writing; for in explaining his belief, the writer seeks to persuade a sceptical audience, and an appeal to experience is one way of defending the truths of the argument. The argument is still a deductive one, for the inference is made directly from the truth or belief.

In another argument in favor of capital punishment, H. L. Mencken draws on beliefs that in his opinion guarantee his conclusion that a murderer, Russell Whittemore, deserved his execution in Baltimore in 1926:

**33.1**
**log**

> To argue that society, confronted by such a rogue, has no right to take his life is to argue that it has no rights at all—that it cannot even levy a tax or command a service without committing a crime. There are, to be sure, men who so argue, and some of their arguments are very ingenious. But they have not converted any considerable body of reflective men and women. The overwhelming majority of people believe that, when a man adopts murder as his trade, society is justified in putting him to death. They have believed it in all ages and under all forms of government, and I am convinced that they still believe it today. The execution of Whittemore was almost unanimously approved in Maryland. If he had escaped the gallows there would have been an uproar, and it would have been justified.
>
> —H. L. MENCKEN, "On Hanging a Man"

Mencken introduces inductive evidence—his reading of the history of capital punishment and the opinions of Maryland citizens on the issue of Whittemore's execution—in explanation of his basic deductive argument. He also draws on particulars of experience in using exposition, description, and narrative to give a short history of capital punishment, to describe methods of execution, and to narrate Whittemore's death briefly. But his argument is essentially deductive, despite his use of supporting inductive evidence. For Mencken would hold to the self-evident right of society to execute Whittemore even if all Maryland citizens opposed his execution.

We daily draw conclusions from beliefs like Mencken's or from ideas established by long experience or observation. It is this experience and observation that we often appeal to in the course of explaining or defending our argument. Few persuasive arguments depend solely on a bare statement of beliefs or truths. The writer instead shows why these beliefs and truths are capable of proving the thesis.

# 33.2 Formal Deductive Arguments

**33.2a The Process of Inference.** The process of deductive inference is complex, and we can do no more than consider a few essentials in writing deductive arguments. Consider this often heard argument:

> Old people are unsteady drivers because they are infirm.

Here is the argument stated completely:

> If infirm people make unsteady drivers, and old people are physically infirm, then old people are unsteady drivers—a hazard to others on the road.

The argument has a formal structure called a *syllogism*:

> [*Major premise*]   Infirm people are unsteady drivers.
> [*Minor premise*]   Old people are infirm people.
> [*Conclusion*]   Old people are unsteady drivers.

Here is the formula of the argument:

> A = B
> C = A
> C = B

This unqualified or categorical argument is **valid** in its reasoning. The word *valid* means that the process of reasoning from the premises to the conclusion is correct. The process begins with the **major premise**—a proposition that the writer holds

**33.2**
**log**

to be true. To this statement or proposition is fitted the **minor premise**, a second proposition and a more limited generalization than the first. The writer then makes an **inference**: what is true of infirm people must be true of the whole class of old people said to belong to it:

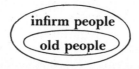

To test the validity of an argument, you place one class into another and look to see whether the conclusion follows directly and necessarily from this placement. Testing the preceding argument demonstrates that the conclusion follows logically. What is true of infirm people must be true of all members of that class—in this instance, old people. But something nevertheless seems wrong with the argument. The reasoning is obviously correct, yet the conclusion will seem to many false.

**33.2b  Sound Reasoning.**  Is it true that infirm people are unsteady drivers? And is it true that all old people are physically infirm? If both of these statements are true and the process of reasoning is correct, the argument is a sound one. But if one or both of the premises are false, the argument is unsound even if the process of reasoning is correct.

To many people the word *valid* means true ("a valid point"). But validity and truth are not the same thing. A logical argument is a valid argument, but a "logical" argument is not necessarily a true one. The premises of the argument may be false, yet the reasoning from these premises may be correct. An argument may be valid in its reasoning and yet be unsound because one or both of its premises are false.

**33.2**
**log**

Thus the preceding argument is valid in its reasoning, but most of us probably will judge it unsound in assuming that *all* old people are physically unsteady or infirm. Of course many old people are infirm, but the minor premise generalizes falsely, and it draws a far-reaching and controversial conclusion from this presumed fact.

Here is an argument that most of us would consider sound— true in its premises and valid in its reasoning:

Unsteady people are bad drivers.
Intoxicated people are unsteady people.
Intoxicated people are bad drivers.

Here is its formula:

A = B
C = A
C = B

By contrast with our first argument, few will argue with these premises. And the process of reasoning shown in the formula is correct.

### 33.2c Undistributed Middle Term.

Many processes of reasoning make an argument invalid. One kind of invalid argument contains what is called an undistributed middle term. The middle term of the argument is the term that appears in both premises (*unsteady people*) but not in the conclusion. In the following argument the middle term is *unsteady drivers*:

Indecisive people are unsteady drivers.
Infirm people are unsteady drivers.
Therefore, infirm people are indecisive people.

This argument is invalid. Here is its formula:

A = B
C = B
C = A

A little reflection tells you that the argument is faulty even if the technical fault is not immediately obvious. It may be true that indecisive people are unsteady drivers. And it may be true that infirm people are unsteady drivers, too. But the conclusion seems wrong: infirm people are not necessarily indecisive. Some infirm people are indecisive and some are not. People can share some characteristics without sharing all—a truth that would help to curb prejudice and stereotyping if understood.

Closer inspection shows something else: the conclusion that all infirm people are indecisive asserts more than the premises do. The conclusion is, in fact, not a necessary inference from the premises at all.

How did this mistake in reasoning happen?

The fault lies with the middle term *unsteady drivers*. The premises may assert that both indecisive people and infirm people are unsteady drivers. But the premises do not assert that *all* unsteady drivers are indecisive or infirm. The middle term is undistributed; that is, it does not refer to all members of the class *unsteady drivers* in one of the premises.

Let us do this and then test the soundness of the argument:

**33.2**
**log**

Unsteady drivers are indecisive people.
Infirm people are unsteady drivers.
Therefore, infirm people are indecisive people.

The argument is now a valid one. The major premise asserts a connection between *all* unsteady drivers and indecisive people. And if all infirm people are unsteady drivers, then they must be indecisive. But is the major premise true? Most of us would probably agree it is not or would at least question its basis. Obviously a person can be an unsteady driver and not be indecisive. Many will also challenge the minor premise—in particular, the meaning of *unsteady*. All terms of the argument must have an exact meaning.

**33.2d  Other Features of Invalid Arguments.**   The following features also make arguments invalid.

1. The meaning of the terms must be the same in both premises or conclusion. Consider the following argument:

Unsteady people are bad drivers.
Unemployed people are unsteady people.
Unemployed people are bad drivers.

The argument is invalid because the word *unsteady* has one meaning in the major premise (intoxicated) and another in the minor premise (without a livelihood). The groups of people cited in the premises belong to different classes—the class of the infirm and the class of the unemployed. No inference therefore can be drawn from the premises.

2. If one premise is negative, the conclusion must be negative too:

No unalert people are good drivers. Drunks are unalert people.
No drunks are good drivers.

3. If both premises are negative, no conclusion is possible. The following argument is invalid for this reason:

No alert people are careless drivers.
No drunks are alert people.
Drunks are careless drivers.

The premises of this argument as well as the conclusion of this argument may seem to you true, but the two negative premises can themselves provide no evidence for the conclusion. You would be judging premises and conclusion true on separate grounds.

Categorical arguments like those just discussed are not the only kind. Some arguments are hypothetical, stating possibilities

**33.2**
**log**

in one or both of the premises. Following is one of several kinds of valid hypothetical argument:

> If a driver is drunk, then he is unalert.
> If he is unalert, then he is a danger to other drivers.
> If a driver is drunk, then he is a danger to other drivers.

**33.2e Enthymemic Argument.** Actually few deductive arguments are stated so formally. Many arguments imply one of the premises or the conclusions:

> Drunks are bad drivers because they are unalert.

We recognize here the formal argument discussed earlier. The major premise (*Unalert people are bad drivers*) is implied in the statement. The author of the argument assumes that this premise is so obvious that it need not be stated explicitly. The person may also state both of the premises but imply the conclusion:

> People get lucky at some time in their lives, and you and I are people.

We call arguments of this kind *enthymemes*. They are the chief form of argument in debates and in persuasive writing. Here is an enthymemic argument on education:

> The teacher's job is to know his subject, inside out, backward, forward and every which way. Nothing unnerves a student more than to have a teacher who doesn't know his or her stuff. Incompetence they cannot abide. Neither can I.
> —SUZANNE BRITT JORDAN, "I Want to Go to the Prose"

The unstated premise here is that students want to learn: they would not be unnerved by an incompetent teacher if they didn't.

At the end of her essay, Jordan implies another truth about students:

> The young people are interested, I think, in taking their knocks, just as adults must take theirs. Students deserve a fair chance, and, failing to take advantage of that chance, a straightforward dismissal.

The unstated idea here is that students should be treated as adults, not as children. The idea is implied in the statement that they want to be treated as adults and want to take the consequences of failure. To emphasize this idea, the writer may state it explicitly. But many conclusions can be left to the inference of the reader.

In the course of a debate, your partner may ask you to defend unstated ideas or premises of this sort. To you the idea

**33.2**
**log**

seems too obvious to require statement or defense. To your partner the idea is not obvious at all. The situation is more complex in persuasive writing since you do not have the reader present to challenge premises, stated or implied, or the conclusions drawn from them. The next chapter discusses these decisions in persuasive writing.

**33.2f Analysis of a Deductive Argument.** Richard Moran's deductive argument in the accompanying essay illustrates the deductive argument that not only draws an inference from a basic assumption or idea but also defends the assumption.

The idea is that of "less eligibility"—stated by George Bernard Shaw in 1926. Prison must be wretched, Shaw states, because "if the prison does not underbid the slum in human misery, the slum will empty and the prison will fill." Richard Moran

---

## Slums Need to be Improved First, then Prisons

### By Richard Moran

Last week, watching news from the prison takeover in West Virginia, our attention again was drawn to the problems that breed violence in our nation's prisons. Overcrowding, idleness and despair are contributing factors, but the crisis cannot be understood adequately without knowledge of the place of prisons in society. And for this we need a historical perspective.

In attempting to explain the deplorable conditions in English prisons, George Bernard Shaw wrote in 1926 that the living conditions of the poor were "so wretched that it would be impossible to conduct a prison humanely without making the lot of the criminal more eligible (desirable) than that of many free citizens. If the prison does not underbid the slum in human misery, the slum will empty and the prison will fill."

Shaw was merely restating the principle of "less eligibility," which was first formulated in the 17th century. In its basic form, the principle maintains that the conditions in prison must always be worse than the standard of living of the poorest members of society. Otherwise people would commit crimes in order to get into prison.

This principle of "less eligibility" still guides our thinking about punishment and our approach to the conditions of confinement. As such, it can help us understand the recent riot at the Oklahoma State Prison, where inmates allege that prison administrators have evidenced a deliberate indifference to the physical and psychological needs of inmates: that inmates are forced to wear degrading striped uniforms, eat rancid food and remain idle all day. The lack of jobs

**33.2**
**log**

draws the conclusion that the indignities suffered in American prisons today arise from this assumption:

> This principle of "less eligibility" still guides our thinking about punishment and our approach to the conditions of confinement. —RICHARD MORAN, "Slums Need to Be Improved First, Then Prisons," *Los Angeles Times*, January 7, 1986

No other assumption will explain these conditions, and Moran does not suggest another, though he states that "to much of the public the conditions at these and other prisons must be shocking and unacceptable." The conclusion he reaches is an immediate inference from this assumption: "The only way to improve conditions in prison is to improve conditions in the slums."

The fact that so many people are shocked by prison conditions is evidence for Moran of the principle. If it were not for the idea of "less eligibility," the prison system and society as a

---

at the prison has left most inmates with no way of earning spending money or "good time" credit. These conditions, it is charged, violate a prisoner's constitutional right to protection against cruel and unusual punishment.

In West Virginia, the rioting inmates complained that their cells were unheated in winter and suffocatingly hot in summer, that they seldom had hot meals and were denied the "right" to wear a beard or mustache.

To those who believe that life in prison must always be worse than life on the outside, these conditions seem just about right. But to much of the public the conditions at these and other prisons must be shocking and unacceptable.

Nevertheless, prison administrators are really not to blame, for they are in a no-win situation. If prisons provide a modest but comfortable standard of living — with adequate food, shelter and health care — if they provide adequate recreational and educational facilities as well as vocational training — things that most of the poor do not have — they will be accused of coddling criminals. And if they do not have a credible deterrent to misbehavior in the prison, such as solitary confinement or short-term withdrawal of food, how can they hope to manage the inmate population?

All of this is not an excuse for conditions at our prisons; there are no excuses — but there are explanations. And the principle of "less eligibility" is an explanation. It helps us understand why efforts to reform the punishment of criminals are limited by the living conditions of the lowest social class. It explains why reform efforts, however humanitarian and well-meaning, can never go beyond this restriction.

The only way to improve conditions in prison is to improve conditions in the slums. There is no other way.

**33.2
log**

whole would have no reason to subject prisoners to the indignities existing in Oklahoma and West Virginia. "To those who believe that life in prison must always be worse than life on the outside, these conditions seem just about right," Moran states. In this way he explains his assumption and defends it.

### EXERCISES

1. The major premise of William Raspberry's supporting argument on capital punishment (p. 496) is the following:

   > Morally rabid people should be treated like rabid animals.

   What is the minor premise of the argument? What is the conclusion? Would Mencken agree with Raspberry's major premise?

2. What beliefs or truths are the basis of the following statement in opposition to capital punishment? Are these stated directly in the editorial, or are they implied?

   > Most supporters of capital punishment concede that it can be justified only as a last resort. But given the lack of any empirical proof that the death penalty works as a deterrent, the religious, philosophical and practical arguments against capital punishment become overwhelming. When the state deliberately executes one of its members in cold blood and as an act of sovereign justice, the state acts with an insupportable claim of total lordship and with irreversible finality. Moreover, no one has yet devised a "humane" method of capital punishment, and the very grisliness of an execution dramatizes its inherent inhumanity.
   >
   > —Editorial, *America*, December 11, 1976

**33.2 log**

3. What inductive evidence supports this argument against capital punishment? What shows that the editors of *America* consider this evidence supporting evidence only?

4. With which arguments concerning capital punishment do you agree—Raspberry's, Mencken's, or *America*'s—and why? What is the origin or basis of your own ideas on the issue?

5. Does the principle of "less eligibility" convince you as an explanation of the deplorable conditions Moran discusses? If you do agree with Moran, why do you? If you don't agree, what other explanation can you suggest? Do you believe that people who want prison to be harsh want to be cruel?

6. What is wrong with the following arguments?
   a. Beauty queens make good wives. So do fashion models and Hollywood starlets. These women must once have been beauty queens.

**b.** Stock brokers don't make good husbands. None of the men I work with are stock brokers. So they must be good husbands.

**c.** Sick people gossip about their neighbors. People with bad colds are sick people and incurable gossips.

## Checklist for Deductive Reasoning

**33.2a** A valid argument reasons correctly from premises to conclusion.

**33.2b** A sound argument is valid in its reasoning and true in its premises:

> If all reptiles are cold-blooded, and snakes are reptiles, then all snakes must be cold-blooded.

**33.2c** The middle term of a valid argument must be distributed in one of the premises:

| *Invalid* | *Valid* |
|---|---|
| All mammals are verte- brates. | All mammals are verte- brates. |
| Whales are vertebrates. | Whales are mammals. |
| Whales are mammals. | Whales are vertebrates. |

**33.2d** An argument is invalid if a term has different meanings in the premises, contains a negative premise and a positive conclusion, or draws a conclusion from two negative premises.

**33.2e** Enthymemes imply one of the premises or the conclusion:

> Drunks are bad drivers because they are unalert.
> People get lucky at some time in their lives, and you and I are people.

**33.2**
**log**

# The Persuasive Essay

## 34.1 The Uses of Argument

Arguments have many purposes in persuasive and other kinds of writing. One common purpose is to challenge mistaken assumptions or premises of another argument. William Raspberry does so in the following statement:

> In one sense, what I am talking about is the importance of developing positive ethnic traditions. Maybe Jews have an innate talent for communication; maybe the Chinese are born with a gift for mathematical reasoning; maybe blacks are naturally blessed with athletic grace. I doubt it. What is at work, I suspect, is the assumption, inculcated early in their lives, that this is a thing our people do well.
> — WILLIAM RASPBERRY, "Black—By Definition"

In persuasive writing, you can use inductive and deductive arguments both to challenge assumptions. An inductive argument would marshal evidence to show that experience and observation contradict the assumption; a deductive argument might present a contrary assumption and explore its implications. You can also use argument to defend a course of action or urge the acceptance of a policy or adoption of a proposal. You might do so through a deductive argument on the inherent worth of the policy or proposal or an inductive argument on its beneficial consequences. Your purpose and audience will determine the kind of argument you choose to develop.

## 34.2 Argument and Audience

**34.2a Assessing the Audience.** Your purpose usually will become clear or better focused as you assess your audience and decide on a persuasive strategy—a way to make your ideas convincing to as many in your audience as possible. Your strategy and focus will depend in large part on whether your audience is a general or a special one (see 1.2).

In writing arguments for a general audience, you probably don't know the range of personal opinions or beliefs, though you probably can guess about the chief concerns and knowledge of the subject of its members. Since many in your audience probably will not accept your premises as given truths, you will be most persuasive if you defend them in the course of presenting your basic argument. Writing to a special audience, you probably do know their opinions and how much they know about the subject, and you can direct your defense to their special concerns.

The *America* editorial opposing capital punishment (see p. 504) is addressed to a general audience. Here again is the paragraph discussed:

> Most supporters of capital punishment concede that it can be justified only as a last resort. But given the lack of any empirical proof that the death penalty works as a deterrent, the religious, philosophical and practical arguments against capital punishment become overwhelming. When the state deliberately executes one of its members in cold blood and as an act of sovereign justice, the state acts with an insupportable claim of total lordship and with irreversible finality. Moreover, no one has yet devised a "humane" method of capital punishment, and the very grisliness of an execution dramatizes its inherent inhumanity.          —Editorial, *America*, December 11, 1976

The editors here direct the argument to those who consider deterrence decisive to the issue. In developing their argument in the whole editorial, they review some of the evidence for and against capital punishment but focus on concerns of the audience.

**34.2**
**log**

The situation in written argument is different from a debate. Here the give and take of ideas forces each participant to state and defend beliefs and opinions fully—this defense occurring even when the debaters are in partial agreement over premises. Thus two debaters may share the premise that the military draft should be restored but disagree over why it should—the first arguing that universal military service is a basic obligation of citizenship, the second arguing that universal military service is a necessity in face of a current military threat. The first debater may argue that both men and women should be eligible because both are citizens; the second may argue in rebuttal that only men can relieve the emergency—a proposition that members of the audience may wish to challenge.

The first job in writing an argument, then, is to assess the beliefs of the audience. The second is to focus the argument through a limitation of the subject.

**34.2b Focusing the Argument.**    In paired essays on the issue of smoking in public places, two writers focus the argument in different ways. The first introduces his discussion through a recent ban on smoking in the company he heads:

> The corporation I head took a deep breath of clean air last week and went cold turkey. Smoking on the job in the home office was absolutely forbidden. Since 1982 it had been restricted to work areas and cafeterias; the hard line stiffened last February when employees were permitted to smoke only at their desks.
> —IAN M. ROLLAND, "A Burning Issue on the Job and Off,"
> *Newsweek*, January 13, 1986

In a later paragraph Rolland focuses on the point at issue for him—the cost of smoking to health of employees and to the country as a whole:

> Anything that kills 350,000 Americans each year deserves decisive action, and all the brawny cowpokes and tawny-haired sirens cannot blow enough advertising smoke to obscure the fact that one out of every seven deaths in this country is linked to smoking. . . .

In the conclusion to his argument, Rolland emphasizes the cost, noting that smoking costs the economy $65 billion each year in "increased medical bills, premature death and time lost from work." Throughout his essay he focuses on the practical consequences of smoking that justify the ban.

In his essay on the same issue, the assistant dean of a law school begins with a brief statement of the facts on the smoking ban in many companies and then focuses on the point at issue for him—that of discrimination against the smoker:

> While no sane person would suggest that discrimination against smokers rises to the moral obscenity of discrimination based on race, sex or religion, the trend is still pernicious. One might have hoped that one of the lessons we learned in the struggle to outlaw job discrimination is that the use of non-job-related criteria to control the distribution of jobs is perverse, counter-productive and dumb.
> —BERNARD J. DUSHMAN, "A Burning Issue on the Job and Off," *Newsweek*, January 13, 1986

**34.2**
**log**

Like the first writer, Dushman focuses on a single issue. In his conclusion he makes discrimination the focus of his thesis:

> But employers ought not to be able to impose their concepts of morality, or health, on employees on pain of loss of a job or ·on denial of the opportunity to compete.

Focusing the argument carefully, as Rolland and Dushman do, keeps the attention of your reader focused on the central argument. The sharper the focus, the more persuasive the argument will be.

# 34.3   Organizing the Argument

**34.3a Deductive Arguments.**   The deductive argument tests the assumptions and reasoning of particular arguments and presents contrary assumptions and reasoning. The argument can be organized in different ways—perhaps building from premises to inferences, or beginning with the inferences or conclusion and then presenting the premises. Here is a deductive argument that begins with certain truths and makes deductions or inferences from them:

> I would remind you of the impossibility of learning to understand and judge many of the important things in youth. The judgment and understanding of practical affairs can amount to little in the absence of experience with practical affairs [*given truths*]. Subjects that cannot be understood without experience should not be taught to those who are without experience [*deduction*]. Or, if these subjects are taught to those who are without experience, it should be clear that these subjects can be taught only by way of introduction and that their value to the student depends on his continuing to study them as he acquires experience. The tragedy in America is that economics, ethics, politics, history, and literature are studied in youth, and seldom studied again [*restatement of given truth combined with statement of fact*]. Therefore the graduates of American universities seldom understand them [*further deduction*].
> —ROBERT M. HUTCHINS, "The Basis of Education"
> [italics added]

**34.3**
**log**

Instead of stating his truths or premises first, Hutchins might have begun with his deductions or inferences and then stated premises. Here is a revision of Hutchins's paragraph that does this:

The tragedy of America is that economics, ethics, politics, history, and literature are studied in youth, and seldom studied again. Therefore the graduates of American universities seldom understand them. Subjects that cannot be understood without experience should not be taught to those who are without experience. Or, if these subjects are taught to those who are without experience, it should be clear that these subjects can be taught only by way of introduction and that their value to the student depends on his continuing to study them as he acquires experience [*inferences*]. [For] I would remind you of the impossibility of learning to understand and judge many of the most important things in youth. The judgment and understanding of practical affairs can amount to little in the absence of experience with practical affairs [*given truths*].

The advantage of this alternative organization is that the paragraph begins with specific facts known to the general audience. Hutchins explains in the paragraphs that follow why the situation is a tragedy.

**34.3b Inductive Arguments.**   The inductive argument uses particulars of experience, observation, experimentation, analogy, statistical evidence, or causal analysis to develop a thesis. It may also test a deductive argument empirically through this inductive evidence. The inductive essay can also be organized in different ways for different persuasive aims. It may build from particulars of experience or other inductive evidence to a conclusion best saved for the end of the essay. Or it may begin with the conclusion and build to controversial evidence.

**34.3**
**log**

The following inductive argument makes a direct appeal to the experience of the reader in support of an inductive generalization: "The virtue of American civilization is that it is unmaterialistic."

This statement may strike a critic as whimsical or perverse. Everybody knows, it will be said, that America has the most materialistic civilization in the world, that Americans care only about money, they have no time or talent for living; look at radio, look at advertising, look at life insurance, look at the tired business man, at the Frigidaires and the Fords. In answer, the reader is invited first to look instead into his own heart and inquire whether he personally feels himself to be represented by these things, or whether he does not, on the contrary, feel them to be irrelevant to him, a necessary evil, part of the conditions of life. Other people, he will assume, care about them very much: the man down the street, the entire population of Detroit or Scarsdale, the back-country farmer, the urban poor or the rich. But he himself accepts these objects as imposed on him by a collective "otherness" of desire, an otherness he has not met directly but whose existence he infers from the number of automobiles, Frigidaires, or television sets he sees around him. Stepping into his new Buick convertible, he knows that he would gladly do without it, but imagines that to his neighbor, who is just backing *his* out of the driveway, this car is the motor of life. More often, however, the otherness is projected farther afield, onto a different class or social group, remote and alien. Thus the rich, who would like nothing better, they think, than for life to be a perpetual fishing trip with the trout grilled by a native guide, look patronizingly upon the whole apparatus of American civilization as a cheap Christmas present to the poor, and city people see the radio and the washing machine as the farm-wife's solace.

—MARY MCCARTHY, "America the Beautiful"

Where you place the series of inductive generalizations and supporting details depends on your judgment about the experience and beliefs of the audience. Mary McCarthy arranges her generalizations and details to win assent from readers who form the broadest class discussed in the paragraph—those neither very poor nor very rich, those who own Frigidaires, Fords, and Buicks. So she makes her appeal to this audience first and refers the audience to the rich, discussed at the end of the long paragraph. Writing to a different audience, she might have organized the paragraph in a different way.

**34.3c Mixed Arguments.**   Mixed arguments combine deductive and inductive arguments. The writer considers both kinds of evidence decisive in developing the thesis. The inductive evidence is not merely explanation of the deductive argument: it has equal status in the essay.

For example, the writer of a persuasive essay may present inductive evidence in favor of space exploration, citing the benefits of such an enterprise by comparison with those arising from other scientific enterprises. Arguing deductively, the writer cites truths or beliefs that support the need for space exploration. The essay by Carl Sagan analyzed in the next section illustrates the mixed argument. So does the accompanying persuasive essay of George F. Will.

Like purely deductive or inductive essays the organization of the mixed essay depends on its purpose and audience. Will joins inductive proof that people are capable of imagining the suffering of others and doing something about that suffering

**34.3**
**log**

## A World of Crushingly Particular Experiences

### by George F. Will

*1*   Odd, isn't it, how the mind works? Or doesn't work, which is much the same thing. One morning recently my thoughts bounced from a tube of toothpaste to Mother Teresa to Paul Volcker.

*2*   Volcker is chairman of the Federal Reserve Board. Mother Teresa has received a Nobel Peace Prize for her service to the poor and dying of Calcutta. My tube of toothpaste is empty.

   To deal with first things first, consider a dawn that breaks on a day without toothpaste. The horror, the horror. As I stood there, enveloped by Chevy Chase and self-pity, a thought struck me with awful force. In Calcutta, people must frequently run out of toothpaste.

*3*   When the Will mind is in high gear, it hippity-hops from one such sunburst to another. In ten weeks I shall have been in Washington ten years, and on a recent morning I came to a conclusion I could have come to anywhere but could hardly have avoided coming to in Washington. It is as follows:

*4*   The world's most serious shortage is, we are told, energy. Or protein. Or democracy. Or something. Most nominees for the title of Most Serious Shortage are arguable, but my nominee is better. It is imagination. I mean imagination of a particular kind: the kind that produces social sympathy—the ability to comprehend, however dimly, how other people live. I don't mean just people in other cultures or neighborhoods, but also neighbors who have sick children and other private worries.

*5*   The other day Paul Volcker said that Americans may have to lower their standard of living. Imagine how that sounded to those Americans (especially the poor, and especially the elderly who are being impoverished by inflation) who have been lowering their standard of living for a while now, and who will do so again if they fill (or if they do not fill) their heating-oil tanks.

*6*   I don't want to make too much of this. Volcker is a very good citizen; and we all say things which, were they put under a moral microscope, would cause us to faint from embarrassment. When Volcker used the category "Americans," we knew whom he meant: the comfortable middle class.

**34.3**
**log**

---

with a deductive argument on the intrinsic worth of all human beings. The two kinds of argument combine in the following paragraph:

   Washington, where big battalions clash over big abstrac-

7    When John Locke wrote that government should rest on the consent of "the people," he meant the consent of a small slice of propertied English males. America's Founding Fathers said that "all men are created equal" and the Father of His Country went on selling slaves until 1798. This wasn't hypocrisy; it was just that "the people" and "all men" were abstractions, categories that took their meanings from peculiar contexts. All categories do; all contexts are peculiar.

8    The city named after the Father of His Country is, of course, an especially peculiar place, full of people marked by one characteristic of government: abstractness. Washington is a city that thinks in large categories, big blocs getting big bloc grants: the farmers, the consumers, the poor, the elderly, the middle class, the people.

9    Washington, where big battalions clash over big abstractions, is even farther mentally than geographically from the world of Mother Teresa. Hers is a world of crushingly particular experiences with crushed people, one at a time. How, then, do you explain her, whose life with the tangible suffering—the sufferers—of Calcutta is a triumph over the natural human tendency toward abstractness?

10    You cannot really explain her life of action by citing her faith. "Faith," wrote Cardinal Newman, "is illuminative, not operative; it does not force obedience, though it increases responsibility; it heightens guilt, it does not prevent sin."

11    Besides, you can't (or so I am increasingly convinced) "explain" anybody by citing anything. You can't really explain anyone, period.

12    I know perhaps six adults really well; I am endlessly surprised at their depths, mysteries and courage. And surely there comes a moment when every parent rocks back on his or her heels, figuratively speaking, and exclaims,"What a complicated creature a four-year-old is!" It is extraordinary how extraordinary the ordinary person is.

13    What distinguishes those, like Mother Teresa, whose extraordinariness is the sort we call saintliness is this: they understand, really understand, and so act as though they understand, what Franz Kafka (fine writer, no saint) meant when he said that "judgment day" is not a "day," it is a court in perpetual session.

**34.3**
**log**

---

tions, is even farther mentally than geographically from the world of Mother Teresa. Hers is a world of crushingly particular experiences with crushed people, one at a time. How, then, do you explain her, whose life with the tangible suffering—the sufferers—of Calcutta is a triumph over the natural human tendency toward abstractness?

—GEORGE F. WILL, "A World of Crushingly Particular Experiences"

**34.3d  Placing the Thesis.**    Though you have a general organization in planning the essay, new possibilities will occur to you during revision. In writing a persuasive essay, you will probably start with a thesis in mind, and you may decide to revise it as the essay takes shape.

Place the thesis where you think it will be most effective. In inductive arguments the thesis frequently appears toward the end. In oral debates the thesis is almost always stated at the start. The same is true of written arguments that argue the pros and cons of an issue. Traditionally, the thesis of persuasive essays follows the introduction and narration or presentation of the background or facts. The arguments confirming the thesis and the refutation of opposing arguments follow. The conclusion of the essay may restate the thesis in light of these confirming arguments and the refutation of opposing views that traditionally follows.

Will introduces his thesis in a paragraph that concludes his long narration of attitudes toward poverty (paragraphs 2-12). In his short discussion of John Locke and his idea that government should have the consent of "the people," Will points out that Locke was thinking in abstractions, not in particulars. Locke had forgotten that "people" include slaves, women, and the unpropertied. Will then introduces his main or confirming argument—that people can do something about human suffering—through the following thesis statement:

> This wasn't hypocrisy; it was just that "the people" and "all men" were abstractions, categories that took their meanings from peculiar contexts. All categories do; all contexts are peculiar.

Will restates his thesis toward the end through the particular worth of each human being:

> It is extraordinary how extraordinary the ordinary person is.

Will's essay shows the advantage of building to the thesis statement through a narration of the facts. Such a narration appeals to the emotions and in this way prepares the reader to give the thesis serious attention. Emotional appeals alone do not make an argument that endures in the mind. Such an argument must be supported by facts, as in Will's essay. But no essay on an issue about which you care deeply can be without emotion.

**34.3**
**log**

Occasionally persuasive essays begin with a statement of the thesis. Newspaper and magazine editorials often begin in this way, influenced by the journalistic practice of putting important facts and ideas at the start of a story or article. But opening with the thesis can seem abrupt in the ordinary essay. Placing the thesis later in the essay has the advantage of preparing an indifferent or a hostile audience for a controversial idea.

### EXERCISES

1. Write a short argument that opens with one of the following statements by Robert M. Hutchins that you agree with or with a truth or belief of your own. Draw inferences from the statement or truth as Hutchins does in the paragraph quoted. Assume that you are addressing the same audience that Hutchins is—those with experience in American education:

   a. It seems clearer to say that the purpose of education is to improve men. Any system that tries to make them bad is not education, but something else.

   b. Society is to be improved, not by forcing a program of social reform down its throat, through the schools or otherwise, but by the improvement of the individuals who compose it.

   c. Man is by nature free, and he is by nature social.

   d. To develop fully as a social, political animal man needs participation in his own government.

2. Reorganize your argument for a different audience. Be ready to explain why your reorganization will be more effective or persuasive.

**34.4**
**log**

## 34.4 A Model Essay

**34.4a A Traditional Organization.** A common type of persuasive essay makes a case for or against a policy or proposal and answers or refutes opponents. How much defense and explanation the argument contains depends on the nature of the audience and on its attitude toward the issue. Organizing an essay for a friendly audience is different from organizing an essay for a hostile one.

Persuasive arguments often follow a pattern or form associated with the legal indictment and defense of the courtroom. Here is the pattern of the argument summarized in the previous section:

1. Introduction to the issue.
2. Statement of the background (called the *narration*).
3. Statement of the thesis—the position to be taken on the issue.
4. Arguments supporting the thesis (called the *confirmation*).
5. Answer to objections (called the *refutation*).
6. Conclusion—a review of the confirming arguments and appeal to the reader's good sense and judgment.

These parts of the argumentative essay may be combined or may be presented in a different order. For example, the background might be presented as part of the confirming arguments. The refutation might precede or be combined with the confirmation. Some essays like George F. Will's (pp. 512–513) depend on confirming arguments only and do not answer objections.

In the essay on pp. 518–520 is a description of these parts, illustrated by Carl Sagan's argument in favor of planetary exploration.

**34.4b Introduction.**   The **introduction** will be most effective if it states the issue as concisely as possible. The essay will not be persuasive unless the reader understands why the issue is worth arguing. Where the issue is long-standing and complex, the introduction may require more than a few sentences or a paragraph to state.

*Paragraphs 1–3.* Sagan opens with a contrast between exploration in the past and exploration in the present. Though he discusses the relative cost of these explorations, his focus is on the similarity of their goals—the "seeking out of new lands and new worlds and, if we are lucky, new life."

The writer may use the introduction to make a direct appeal to the interests or idealism of the reader. Sagan does so in his second paragraph, suggesting that planetary exploration is a need of people today: "The zest for exploration runs deep in the human species." And he notes that "public attention can be riveted to the exploration of other planets even if no humans are aboard." Emotional appeals of this sort are a common feature of persuasive essays.

**34.4c Narration and Thesis Statement.**   The audience must know the background of the case if the writer is to win its assent. Sometimes the background is extensive, as in the legal indictment that states the facts on which the defendant is charged. Both prosecutor and defense lawyer will state these facts fully, for each will have a different version. Where the issue is familiar to the audience, the background serves as a reminder of the

**34.4**
**log**

chief facts. Though the **narration** may be presented as a unit, the writer may also supply pertinent facts throughout the essay—in the introduction as well as in the confirmation and refutation.

The **thesis statement** may appear at the end of an inductive argument that builds through a series of facts. As we noted in the previous section, oral debates usually state the thesis at the beginning. In written arguments that argue the pros and cons of an issue, the thesis usually follows the introduction or the narration. Wherever it appears, the thesis must be prominent. Placed early in the essay, it directs the reader through the argument.

*Paragraphs 1–3.* Sagan combines his narration with his introductory statement of the issue in paragraph 1, giving details of expenditures for planetary exploration today. He gives additional background in paragraph 3, following his statement of the thesis, and he gives additional details as part of his confirmation and refutation.

Sagan states his thesis fully in paragraph 2:

> Were we to turn our great energies and high technologies entirely inward we would, I think, be turning our backs on our future and on our humanity, and denying the 4 billion-year evolution that has brought us—a thinking, feeling, constructive, curious and exploratory species—to real if precarious dominance of the planet earth.

**34.4d Confirming Arguments.**   **Confirming arguments** support the thesis. They may consist of inductive and deductive evidence both: particulars of experiences, analogy, causal analysis, statistics, or assumptions or given truths. **Mixed arguments** present both kinds of evidence. The writer must distinguish each kind and organize it carefully. And the writer must consider what order of evidence will be most convincing. Writers often present their evidence from the less to more convincing so the confirmation does not end anticlimactically.

**34.4
log**

*Paragraphs 4–10.* Sagan begins with those findings of planetary exploration that satisfy our curiosity but also have practical benefits—"the promise of securing answers to some of the deepest questions ever asked . . . " (paragraphs 4-5). He turns then to the retarding effect on scientific investigation if planetary exploration is delayed (paragraphs 7-8) and cites the support of the Carter administration and NASA for the program (paragraphs 9-10). He presents a subordinate argument briefly in paragraph 7: planetary exploration is a spur to technological development.

## Planetary Exploration

### by Carl Sagan

*1*   Almost without noticing, humanity has passed into an age of exploration, discovery and high scientific adventure unmatched since the sixteenth through eighteenth centuries, when plucky European caravels uncovered the nature and extent of our planet. Those vessels were manned, the voyages were risky and the cost was high—about 1 per cent of the gross national products of Spain, England or Holland. Today's vessels are still small, the voyages still lengthy; the ships are unmanned and the effort costs less than 0.1 per cent of the gross national product of the U.S. or the U.S.S.R. (or about 0.3 per cent of their defense budgets). But the ventures are similar: we are engaged in exploration, in the seeking out of new lands and new worlds and, if we are lucky, new life.

*2*   The zest for exploration runs deep in the human species. Were we to turn our great energies and high technologies entirely inward we would, I think, be turning our backs on our future and on our humanity, and denying the 4 billion-year evolution that has brought us—a thinking, feeling, constructive, curious and exploratory species—to real if precarious dominance of the planet earth.

*3*   We recognize the glimmerings of intelligence in the delicate, brilliantly constructed machinery of our new exploratory vessels. The Viking missions to Mars—which have found stunning landscapes and either microbes or an exotic chemistry which simulates microbial metabolism astonishingly well—have shown that public attention can be riveted to the exploration of other planets even if no humans are aboard.

**34.4**
**log**

*4*   The advantages of such voyages go far beyond a resonance with our exploratory instincts, spirit and traditions. We have found planets very different from the earth, worlds in some sense gone awry, places where one or another factor that has made the earth the way it is was a little altered—producing an environment profoundly different from our own. By studying these other worlds we can better understand and utilize the earth, providing an extremely practical rationale for planetary exploration. I believe that its relatively tiny cost will be recovered many times over in the practical insights in comparative planetology that are to be achieved in the earth, atmospheric and life sciences.

*5*   These missions also hold the promise of securing answers to some of the deepest questions ever asked, questions on the origins and destinies of worlds, the nature of our small planet, the possibility of life elsewhere, and the connection of the earth and its inhabitants with the vast, intricate and subtle universe of which we are one extremely small part. The greatest civilizations have traditionally been known not only for how they provide sustenance for the body but also for how they provide sustenance for the mind and spirit.

6        Will the future think kindly of us if we had within our power to continue our exploratory tradition, to provide an extraterrestrial perspective for our planet, to approach these deepest of questions and—when face to face with the decision—we turned back from the cosmos?

7        There is a very real possibility that, without fully understanding the consequences, we may be taking irreversible steps away from the other planets. These missions are complex. They require great planning and an application of the very highest technology available. (Indeed, the spurring of high technology is yet another justification for planetary exploration.) It is usually five to ten years between their conception and their execution. This means that in the working lifetime of a typical planetary scientist or spacecraft engineer there are only a handful of missions.

8        A continuity of effort and commitment is required to maintain the critical mass of skilled personnel. The great planetary missions of recent years, which have for the first time opened our eyes to the true nature of the planets from Mercury to Jupiter, were approved and initially funded in the 1960s. Because of the long lead times, we are just now beginning to feel the serious negative impact of our recent inaction, including a dramatic decline in interest in nonmilitary space activities by the major aerospace corporations, and a severe strain on the extremely competent and innovative NASA centers involved in planetary exploration, particularly the Jet Propulsion Laboratory in Pasadena, Calif., which is without peer on the planet Earth.

**34.4 log**

9        An encouraging sign was provided by the Carter Administration when $10 million—a small amount, but provided constructively early—was added to the proposed NASA budget for studies on the future exploration of Mars, possibly to include a roving vehicle.

10       There is also in the present NASA budget the first major new start in planetary exploration in many years, called Jupiter Orbiter with probe (JOp). JOp is a historically significant mission, the first long-term observational satellite of a planet of the Jupiter family (and its thirteen exotic moons), and the first direct investigation of the atmosphere of such a planet. Organic molecules are almost certainly being produced today in the Ju-

piter atmosphere, whose study therefore may cast significant light not only on the origin and evolution of the planets but also on the origin of life.

11    Apart from its immense scientific importance, JOp would provide the additional funds desperately needed to continue the brilliant American effort in planetary exploration. Citing other priorities, the House Appropriations Committee has recommended deleting JOp from the NASA budget. It is possible, but by no means guaranteed, that Senator Proxmire's Appropriations Committee will recommend JOp and that the House-Senate conference committee will restore it. Even postponement of the mission will do serious damage: the drought in new starts in the decade of the 1970s has been so severe that a commitment to other missions in the next two years is essential if American exploration of the solar system is not to founder.

12    Considering the profound benefits that it is likely to provide for mankind, unmanned planetary exploration is a deeply human enterprise and an extraordinary bargain. It is within our power to ensure its continuance.

---

**34.4e  Refutation.**   The **refutation** often follows the confirmation. The advantage of placing the refutation late in the essay is that these answers are in the readers' minds at the end. But many writers prefer to introduce and answer objections early and end with the confirming arguments to gain the same advantage. The order of ideas in the refutation is important, too. The writer may choose to begin with the less significant objection and end with the most important.

*Paragraph 11.* Throughout the essay Sagan indirectly answers the objection that planetary exploratory is useless, wasteful, and not urgent. He shows that all three objections are mistaken in stressing the human and practical benefits. In paragraph 11, he argues against cuts in the NASA budget, stressing the damage that will arise from postponement of the Jupiter mission. It is the practical consequences of postponement that Sagan wishes to stress in the refutation because the NASA budget was at issue at the time he was writing.

**34.4f  Conclusion.**   The **conclusion** may be used to restate the thesis, review the confirming arguments and the refutation, and make a final appeal to the reader. The length of the conclusion depends on how many ideas the writer wants to review in it.

*Paragraph 12.* Sagan's two-sentence conclusion restates the thesis, stressing both the human and practical benefits of planetary exploration: "Considering the profound benefits that it is likely to provide for mankind, unmanned planetary exploration is a deeply human enterprise and an extraordinary bargain." The final sentence makes a brief final appeal to the reader: it is in the power of the reader "to ensure its continuance."

#### EXERCISES

1. Make notes on the discussion of a current issue in recent newspaper and magazine columns, editorials, and letters. After classifying the evidence you find (for example, as particulars of experience, analogy, causal analysis, sampling, given truths), write an essay that summarizes what you consider important arguments for and against a policy or proposal. Conclude by stating your own position and discussing the evidence you agree with most and least.

2. Write an argumentative essay on an issue of concern to you. Follow the outline given in 34.3a. Rearrange the parts of the argument in a way that will be most persuasive to the audience you have in mind.

3. First analyze the following argument to discover what kind of evidence the author presents for the conclusion. Then write an essay stating the extent of your agreement or disagreement with Menninger. Be careful to clarify the kind of evidence you present for your conclusion:

> Although most of us *say* we deplore cruelty and destructiveness, we are partially deceiving ourselves. We disown violence, ascribing the love of it to other people. But the facts speak for themselves. We do love violence, all of us, and we all feel secretly guilty for it, which is another clue to public resistance to crime-control reform.—KARL MENNINGER, "The Crime of Punishment"

4. Write a persuasive argument of your own on the question of space exploration, if you disagree with Carl Sagan in whole or in part, or on another issue of concern to you. Clarify the nature of your evidence for your reader.

**34.4 log**

## Checklist for the Persuasive Essay

**34.2a** Consider the nature of your audience in choosing a focus and a strategy for your persuasive essay.

**34.2b**   Focus the argument on an issue or an assumption you can explore fully.

**34.3a**   Build your deductive essay from premises to conclusion, or present the conclusion and then the premises and supporting evidence.

**34.3b**   Build your inductive essay from particulars of experience and other inductive evidence to a conclusion, or start with the conclusion and then present the evidence.

**34.3c**   If your argument is mixed, join deductive and inductive arguments in a way best suited to the purpose of the essay and the audience.

**34.3d**   Place the thesis where it will be most effective.

**34.4b**   An effective introduction states the issue concisely.

**34.4c**   Give the background of the issue and a clear statement of the thesis or proposition toward the beginning of the essay unless you have reason to build to it.

**34.4d**   Organize your confirming arguments carefully, distinguishing the kinds of evidence used.

**34.4e**   In your refutation answer objections to your argument.

**34.4f**   In the conclusion you may restate the thesis, review the confirming arguments and refutation, and make a final appeal to the reader.

# Fallacies in Reasoning

In the course of arguing, people sometimes make persuasive appeals and arguments that nonetheless fail in logic. These appeals and arguments fail either in their faulty reasoning—in their circularity or ambiguity, for example—or in their appeal to emotion. Arguments that appeal only to emotion ask the audience to ignore reason altogether.

Fewer arguments appeal to reason than many people believe. Many who appear to be arguing are in fact merely voicing opinions without concern for evidence—the "argument" expressing nothing more than strong emotions. But reason and emotion are not independent faculties. Arguments that appeal to reason also appeal to the emotions; the ideas we argue about are ones we care about strongly.

Few people argue in the dispassionate way often recommended; their aim is to win the argument, not come to mutual agreement with opponents. Clearly, many who engage in Presidential and other political campaigns and in debates over capital punishment, abortion, and nuclear disarmament regard their opponents as enemies. The phrase "war of words" best describes these bitter arguments. We ask who "won" the debate.

Since persuasive writing is seldom unemotional, it is realistic to ask how best we can control emotional appeals rather than eliminate them and how best we can make reason exert its own force. This chapter discusses ways of doing so.

## 35.1  Faults in Reasoning

**35.1a  Circular Definition.**  A definition is *circular* if it uses the term it is seeking to define:

> *Militarism* is the idealizing of the *military* caste and the belief that this caste should rule the country.

523

*"There's so much in what you say that I wonder if I might have thirty minutes or so to digest it."*

Drawing by Geo. Price; copyright © 1983 by The New Yorker Magazine, Inc.

**35.1**
**log**

The word *military* makes the definition circular because it is the word being defined. It thus adds nothing to the definition. The phrase *military caste* is also ambiguous. We do not know whether *caste* refers to members of the armed forces only or to those who favor military rule.

**Circular definition** sometimes occurs because the speaker or writer wants to disguise a belief or avoid coming to the point. Note that the term *militarism* may refer to military dictatorship or to military discipline as the ideal of conduct for citizens of a country. It can also refer to the policy that war is the best means to settle disputes between nations. So broad a term can disguise the real meaning and intention of the writer.

**35.1b Circular Reasoning.**   Like circular definition, a **circular argument** gives evidence for a proposition by restating it in different words:

> *Militarism* is a failed "ism" because the military has failed as a political policy in the twentieth century.

The second part of this sentence is a restatement of the first part. Circular arguments are harder to spot when metaphor substitutes for literal restatement of the proposition:

> Militarism is a failed "ism" because the "man on horseback" is a failed idea.

The phrase *man on horseback*, a metaphor for military dictator, is identical with the word *militarism*. We need to know why the idea of the "man on horseback" failed. The words *ism* and *idea* also mean the same.

### 35.1c Begging the Question.

You **beg the question** in assuming as true the idea you are trying to prove:

> Isn't that movie obviously pornographic?

The word *obviously* shows that the speaker believes the movie is pornographic. The question is also begged if the question is worded as follows:

> Aren't dirty movies pornographic?

An important qualification needs to be made here. The question is not begged if those arguing have previously agreed on what is pornographic and are judging a particular movie by this definition. The question is begged only if the question or point at issue in the debate is the definition of pornography itself.

Recognizing this fault in reasoning is not difficult when a political candidate refers in a speech to his "jackass opponent." Begging the question is difficult to recognize when the adjective is less prominent in the statement. Many arguments that pretend to argue the question actually beg it through loaded words and statements.

**35.1**
**log**

### 35.1d Complex Question.

A **complex question** forces a person to answer an implied question in the course of answering another. Assume you are asked the following question in the course of a debate on building nuclear power plants close to a large city:

> Are you in favor of building these plants and thereby promoting industry and putting people to work?

If you answer no to this question, you are forced into saying falsely that you oppose industry and the jobs the plants will create. The fair way is to ask one question at a time:

Are you in favor of building nuclear power plants?

The question of industry and jobs probably belongs to another argument.

**35.1e Hasty Generalization.    Hasty generalization**, an error discussed in 32.1, is drawing conclusions on the basis of untypical or exceptional evidence. If you base the statement that old people are unsteady drivers on seeing them drive on icy streets, you have "leaped" to a conclusion too quickly. Before making the generalization, you must observe old people driving under all weather conditions. The same faulty reasoning is the basis of the following hasty statements:

Redheads have hot tempers.
Woman reporters are rude and aggressive.
Great Danes have human qualities.

Stereotypes arise from hasty generalizations of this kind. The person making the generalization is probably confirming a prejudice. Once the stereotype is fixed in the mind, it is always possible to find someone who fits the image. Instead of presenting evidence, the person is illustrating a belief or an assumed truth. See 32.1 on adequate generalization.

**35.1f Fallacy of the Single Case.**    Many arguments generalize on the basis of a **single case**. In this fallacy—an instance of hasty generalization—the sample is so small that it cannot be representative of the class described. Usually one unhappy experience with a teacher tells you nothing about teachers as a class. And you cannot make judgments about drivers in a particular age group on the basis of a single observation or encounter. The single case provides the confirmation of a stereotype.

**35.1g Fallacy of the Important Exception.**    A generalization is unproved if an **important exception** cannot be explained. A person may theorize that people of a certain race or ethnic background excel in literature or politics or some other endeavor. The person making the generalization ignores the numerous exceptions or explains them through special circumstances ("they must not have been 100% true American"—or Swedish or Italian or German).

Nor can the theory be supported through the argument that

**35.1**
**log**

"the exception proves the rule." This statement means that the *apparent* exception is the test of the rule—the difficult case that tells us whether the rule indeed applies to all of the particulars it describes.

A weak "maybe" or "perhaps" or "possibly" does not help the problem. If the rule cannot explain an important exception, it is not a rule. The theory or generalization must be reformulated and retested. True, scientists do formulate theories and stipulate definitions on the basis of incomplete or uncertain evidence. But they reformulate a theory if decisive evidence contradicts it. Scientists may, however, disagree on whether the evidence constitutes an important exception.

**35.1h  False Analogy.**    An earlier chapter discussed the legitimate use of analogy in argument (see 32.2). The similarities cited between the things analogized must be pertinent to the conclusion; the conclusion must be drawn from the similarities alone; the differences must not weaken the conclusion.

Many analogies in argument fail to meet these requirements. Consider the following analogy:

> Recruits become soldiers only through constant drill and obedience to superiors. Wars could not be fought and won otherwise. So do children become soldiers in the war against ignorance through drill and obedience to their teachers.

In weighing this analogy, you need to ask whether the differences in age between children and recruits as well as in the kinds of education weaken the conclusion. The phrase *obedience to superiors* is crucial, also. An appeal to experience is indispensable in judging analogies. Is education in fact learning to take orders? Or does one best learn by playing an active role by questioning and challenging authority?

Analogies are not always so obvious, particularly when they depend on metaphor. The following statement appears in a letter to a newspaper following an incident of school vandalism:

> This situation will go on as long as *Pollyanna* teachers insist on *coddling* the savages tearing up our schools.

The word *Pollyanna* implies comparison with a sentimental and overly optimistic little girl; the word *coddling* implies that children are infants. The newspaper reader is probably unaware of the analogy implied by each word though the intent of these words is clear. Metaphors can be insidious in argument in shaping emotional attitudes.

**35.1**
**log**

**35.1i Equivocation.**    To **equivocate** means to use deliberately ambiguous words to deceive. Thus the word *exceptional* can mean both excellent in quality and poor in quality. The statement that a performance is "exceptionally interesting" means either the performance was excellent or it was poor—we cannot tell which. The word *unsteady* means physically infirm; it can also mean intoxicated and indecisive. So the campaign statement that a candidate will not give "steady" leadership equivocates in not stating the disqualifications.

These are obvious examples. Equivocation is hard to avoid when we try to soften statements through euphemism (see 31.3) or when we disguise our feelings or opinions. The language of diplomacy easily falls into equivocation. Politicians resort to it often in promising to give an issue "the attention it deserves"— meaning that the issue will be given no attention at all. When diplomats fail to reach agreement or exchange angry words, they report their meeting as "serious and useful." Language that equivocates also begs the question.

At times loosely defined or indefinite terms create unintentional **ambiguity**. The person making the argument does not see the ambiguity until an opponent calls attention to the term. Sometimes this ambiguity exists without either opponent's recognizing it. This situation occurs with popular terms so wide and loose that they serve everyone in the debate. The term *irresponsible* is an example. A person recommending an increase in welfare is an "irresponsible spender" to one segment of the audience; a person recommending an increase in weapons spending is "irresponsible" to another segment. But both segments agree on the need for "responsible government." Such broad agreement may relieve conflict, but it does not conciliate. Indeed, conciliation is clearly not the intention of the writer.

**35.1**
**log**

**35.1j Either-Or Arguments.**    An **either-or argument**, or **false dilemma**, presents two alternatives as solutions to a problem and ignores other alternatives or solutions. Forced into a dilemma, the reader chooses what seems the only reasonable or sensible proposal or solution:

> Either we drill for oil wherever necessary—even in national forests—or we run out of energy by the end of the century.

A third alternative ignored by the argument is solar energy. Other energy sources are worth considering, too.

In developing a fair argument, you need to identify these alternatives even if in your view they are not feasible. This identification is the job of refutation in pro and con arguments (see 34.4e). In identifying nonfeasible alternatives, you gain an advantage in anticipating objections that people might make to your own argument. Strong arguments identify all serious possibilities and weigh them.

**35.1k Irrelevant Conclusion.** An argument contains an irrelevant conclusion when it does not address the specific issue and instead supports another conclusion. What is irrelevant depends, again, on the point at issue in the debate.

Assume the argument is about whether college parking lots should be equally open to students and faculty. One of the debaters states that fining students who park in faculty lots is unjust. This argument may be worth debating in its own right, but it is irrelevant to the specific issue. So is the counterargument that faculty ought not to be subject to parking fines.

To state an irrelevant conclusion in this way is to win assent not for the particular argument but rather for a general truth that the writer knows is not controversial. Such diversions explain sudden shifts in subject or point of view.

**35.1l Argument from Ignorance.** An **argument from ignorance** reasons incorrectly that a proposition is true because it has not been disproved. Those who insist that earth is being visited by UFOs often argue that no proof *against* UFOs exists. Such reasoning is basic to theories that the government is concealing proof to prevent national panic or to gain a military advantage.

As with the other fallacies discussed, it is easy in writing to commit this fallacy in the desire to prove something for which no evidence exists. Argument from ignorance is a fallacy difficult to combat in debate when one party to the argument is accused of hiding the truth or of being party to a conspiracy. Because conspiracies depend on secrecy, the person accused cannot always provide evidence of innocence.

**35.2** log

## 35.2 Fallacies of Causation

**Fallacies of causation** wrongly identify or simplify causes and effects. These fallacies are among the most common in argument. Following are the two most important ones.

**35.2a *Post Hoc* Fallacy.** The common *post hoc* fallacy assumes that one event is the cause of another on the sole basis that it happens before the second. The name of the fallacy is short for the Latin *post hoc, ergo propter hoc*: "after this, therefore because of this." The sky darkens before a rainstorm; therefore the darkened sky must cause the rain. Pressing a button produces a picture on the television screen; therefore the button is the cause of the picture.

A good causal analysis shows more than temporal relationship: we must trace the process by which one thing leads to another. Investigating the workings of the television set, we discover intricate connections that reveal the "sufficient condition"—those connections of wire and tubes that produce the picture. The condition is sufficient if the effect always occurs in their presence. See 32.3 on cause defined as necessary and sufficient condition.

Stereotypes and prejudices can arise from this kind of reasoning. Large numbers of immigrants enter a city. When the crime rate rises, some point to the immigrants as the cause of the rise, ignoring other possible causes or conditions—for example, the general increase in population or changing economic conditions. Notice that a decrease in the crime rate probably won't be credited to these same immigrants.

**35.2b  Fallacy of Reduction.**   The **fallacy of reduction** singles out one cause without considering other possible ones. The example just given illustrates this kind of thinking. So does blaming a complex event on the decision of a single person or event. A variety of causes produces a disaster like the Iranian hostage crisis or the bombing of an embassy or the rise or fall in the rate of inflation. But it is advantageous in political debates to reduce these events to a single cause—perhaps the act of a single person.

In writing your own arguments, you may wish to single out a cause of an event or an effect, but it is important in doing so to tell your audience what you are doing. Qualify your argument by noting that other necessary conditions probably exist, some of which you can identify, some of which you cannot.

When you do cite a series of contributing causes or necessary conditions, you can make the opposite mistake of discussing them as if they were equal. Your decision to attend college was undoubtedly shaped by a number of causes, not all of them of the same importance. In discussing them, weigh them and suggest their relative importance.

**35.2**
**log**

# 35.3 Appeals to Emotion

### 35.3a *Argumentum ad Hominem.* *Argumentum ad hominem*—in Latin the "argument to the man"—attacks the proposer of an idea or policy to avoid dealing with the idea or policy itself:

> What kind of Neanderthal would want to open federal lands to oil exploration? No one except a dummy blind to the consequences.

The person making the attack "poisons the well" with such a statement, for discussion of the issue becomes impossible once character is attacked. The purpose of the statement obviously is to make the character of the proposer the issue. Of course, the character of a candidate may be the legitimate issue in a political campaign. It is not the issue in a debate over oil leases.

We would not be discussing this fallacy if name-calling were not effective in debate. It is effective because it confirms the beliefs of people who agree with the attacker, and it disposes bystanders to the argument to join the winning side. Clearly the attack is on reason itself. The gain to the name-caller may be shortlived, however, once the emotion of the attack is forgotten and the audience gradually recognizes that the issue remains to be solved.

### 35.3b *Argumentum ad Populum.* *Argumentum ad populum*—in Latin an "argument to the people"—is an appeal to popular feeling or social, racial, sexist, or religious prejudice. In stating qualifications for political office, a candidate may refer to his birth at the place he is campaigning or praise a widely admired local citizen or politician. Negative appeals are possible, too. The candidate may hint at family connections that dispose the audience against the opposing candidate, perhaps referring to his opponent's enormous wealth or a father who made a "fortune in oil."

Appeals to patriotic feeling often divert attention from the point at issue. No public address is without appeal to the interests and loyalties of the audience, but these appeals must not substitute for serious discussion of the issue or introduce irrelevant evidence.

### 35.3c Appeal to Force. An **appeal to force** is a threat—both open and veiled. Open threats are often designed to make

**35.3**
**log**

rational discussion impossible, as in Hitler's statement to the Austrian chancellor in 1938:

> Listen, you don't really think you can move a single stone in Austria without my hearing about it the next day, do you? . . . I have only to give an order, and in one single night all your ridiculous defense mechanisms will be blown to bits. You don't seriously believe that you can stop me for half an hour, do you? . . . I would very much like to save Austria from such a fate, because such an action would mean blood. After the Army, my S.A. and Austrian Legion would move in, and nobody can stop their just revenge—not even I.
> —WILLIAM L. SHIRER, *The Rise and Fall of the Third Reich*

Veiled threats are more subtle, particularly those that appeal to self-interest. Those who are not with us are against us, the speaker or writer implies in suggesting that our supporting a candidate would be a patriotic act. Once threat enters a debate, the issue is seldom decided on reason.

**35.3d Linking.** You **link** when you connect a revered man or woman like Thomas Jefferson, Abraham Lincoln, Eleanor Roosevelt, Dwight Eisenhower, John F. Kennedy, or Helen Keller with an issue, without stating why the person would approve or disapprove of it. We find this appeal frequently in advertising and of course in politics.

If the opinion of a Jefferson or a Lincoln is pertinent to the issue, referring to the person is legitimate. The opinions of former Presidents and other officials are pertinent in a discussion of American involvement in Central America or Southeast Asia. Such appeals or references are weak, however, if they constitute the chief evidence or the only evidence in the argument.

**35.3e Appeal to Authority.** A related appeal asks us to agree with a position merely because the proposer cites an **authority**—a respected historian or "elder statesman" whose opinion we are to accept on the basis of superior knowledge. Such an appeal is fallacious when it constitutes the sole evidence.

It is common in literary discussions to refer to literary "authorities" on William Shakespeare or T. S. Eliot or Emily Dickinson—that is, to scholars and critics who have written extensively about these writers. These scholars and critics may provide us with reliable facts needed to interpret plays and poems without mistaking the meaning of words or allusions. But their opinions cannot be taken as the sole evidence for the "meaning" of the play or poem, at least not without presenting their evidence and explaining why it is worth citing. In writing essays for a

**35.3**
**log**

course in literature, you may cite a writer on the subject in *support* of your interpretation. But the citation should not be your sole evidence. The interpretation must be your own.

The same applies for essays written in other courses. You will need to cite the facts provided by historians and political and social scientists. But their interpretations of these facts cannot and should not substitute for your own analysis and discussion. See 37.1 on the use of primary and secondary evidence in documented papers.

### EXERCISES

1. Identify one or more fallacies contained in the following statements. Then suggest what would be a fair statement of the argument or proposal.
   a. Teddy Roosevelt, a great outdoorsman and conservationist, would have supported my proposal to drill for oil in Yellowstone.
   b. We must drill for oil on federal lands because people are not conserving enough gas.
   c. Do you support the idea that America can go on squandering natural resources without paying a higher price for fuel later?
   d. New sources must be found because we need new supplies of fuel.
   e. We need to oppose the landgrabbers and special interests supporting this bill to drill on federal lands.
   f. Are you in favor of guaranteeing the future of your children by supporting research into solar energy?
   g. Either we find new energy sources, or we all start walking to work.
   h. Why do we need to drill on federal lands? Because we need to find new sources of energy. And abundant sources exist on federal lands.
   i. Exploitation means letting people exploit natural resources for their personal gain without regard to the public interest.
   j. The unanimous vote on the bill in the recent session of Congress shows that the American people—man, woman, child—support this stand.

2. Identify the metaphors and implied analogies in the following statements and evaluate their worth:

   a. If schools continue to harbor vandals and delinquents, they should be run as zoos are—to the benefit of society and to the school themselves.

   b. The diplomatic corps is good training for the advertising agency.

**35.3**
**log**

c. Theology teaches that the sun has been created in order to illuminate the earth. But one moves the torch in order to illuminate the house, and not the house in order to be illuminated by the torch. Hence it is the sun which revolves around the earth, and not the earth which revolves around the sun.

—A doctor of the Sorbonne in Paris, 1671;
quoted in Cohen and Nagel, *Introduction to Logic and Scientific Method*

3. The following paragraphs occur in an essay on the many causes of alienation in the college student. How convincing do you find evidence cited for the concluding statement?

If the future alienated student begins to experience uneasiness as to the meaningfulness of his life, he finds ample reinforcement of his doubts in his day-to-day life in the university community. Students at large universities are almost completely separated from adults. Whether they live in dormitories or apartments, they primarily interact with people who are their own age. Even their house fellows are only a few years older than themselves.

Classes in the first few years at a large university are taught primarily by teaching assistants who again are only a few years older than the students. In effect our campuses can be viewed as affluent ghettoes in which people of similar age and similar interests live almost exclusively with one another. A student can spend months on a large campus without having a conversation with a person over 30.

Isolation from the adult world reinforces deviant trends which develop within the student group. The student who begins to feel that life is meaningless finds other students who feel that life is meaningless. Subcultures dedicated to a rejection of the values of the adult world become powerful influences in the student world. The future alienated student is a prime candidate to become a member of such a subculture. He finds that other members of the alienated group understand his frustration and will help him to escape from the subtle oppressions his parents have imposed upon him. When he experiences failure in school work or social life, the alienation adaptation is readily available and provides him with sustaining group comforts as well as a well-codified series of rationalizations for his inadequacies.

—SEYMOUR L. HALLECK, "Psychiatric Treatment of the Alienated College Student"

**35.3**
**log**

# Checklist for Fallacies in Reasoning

**35.1a**  Don't make your definition circular by using the term you are defining:

> Militarism is the idealizing of the military caste and the belief that this caste should rule the country.

**35.1b**  A circular argument gives evidence for a proposition by restating it in different words:

> Militarism is a failed "ism" because the military has failed as a political policy in the twentieth century.

**35.1c**  Don't beg the question by assuming as true the idea you are proving:

> Isn't that movie obviously pornographic?

**35.1d**  A complex question forces a person to answer an implied question in answering the question asked:

> Do you favor building nuclear plants that put people to work?

**35.1e**  A hasty generalization reasons on the basis of untypical or exceptional evidence:

> Redheads have hot tempers.

**35.1f**  Don't generalize from a single case.

**35.1g**  A generalization is unproved if an important exception cannot be explained.

**35.1h**  In a false analogy, the similarities between the things analogized are not pertinent to the conclusion, and the differences weaken the conclusion.

**35.1i**  Equivocation is deception through deliberately ambiguous words:

> The performance is exceptionally interesting.

**35.1j**  An either-or argument, or "false dilemma," presents two alternatives as solutions to a problem and ignores other alternatives or solutions:

> Either we drill for oil in national forests, or we run out of energy by the end of the century.

**35.1k**  Your argument is irrelevant if it does not address the specific issue and supports another conclusion instead.

**35.1l**    An argument from ignorance reasons incorrectly that an idea is true because it has not been disproved:

UFOs have visited earth because no one has shown they haven't.

**35.2a**    The *post hoc* fallacy assumes that one event is the cause of another merely because the first happens before the second:

The sky darkens before a storm; therefore the darkened sky must cause the rain.

**35.2b**    The fallacy of reduction singles out one cause without looking at possible other causes.

**35.3a**    Don't attack your opponent through an *ad hominem* argument to avoid dealing with the idea or policy itself:

What kind of Neanderthal would open federal lands to oil exploration?

**35.3b**    Don't appeal to popular feeling or prejudice to win your argument.

**35.3c**    Appeals to force are open or veiled threats designed to make reasoned argument impossible.

**35.3d**    To "link" is to connect a revered person with an issue without saying why the person would approve or disapprove it:

Thomas Jefferson would have supported oil exploration on federal lands.

**35.3e**    Don't ask your reader to agree with a view or position merely by referring to or quoting an "authority."

# The Documented Paper

# 36

# Finding a Subject

## 36.1 Occasions and Purposes

An important kind of writing in college and later is the research or documented paper. The college research paper usually has the purpose of acquainting oneself with important sources of facts in a particular field. The legal brief, another kind of research paper, traces court rulings on a specific issue. The policy paper in support of a legislative proposal contains reports on research. Chemists, engineers, historians, literary scholars, and political scientists write reports of their research for use by others.

The usual purpose of the research paper is to shed light on an event, a person, or a current issue through published sources and sometimes unpublished ones. Researchers look at new evidence and ask new questions; they review these earlier findings and report how their own research provides new understanding of the subject.

Your own documented papers will have different purposes and use different approaches:

A term paper for a psychology course may investigate the use of a tranquillizing drug in treating a mental disorder. To compare the action of the drug with another therapy in this paper, you might draw on published research of psychologists, biochemists, and others who deal with mental disorders.

A paper for a sociology course might investigate the social effects of this same drug as well as other tranquillizers. In this paper, you might compare published reports of caseworkers and psychotherapists.

A paper for a chemistry course might investigate recent advances in tranquillizing drugs and describe promising areas for research. Reports of chemical experiments probably will be your chief evidence.

538

Each of these papers asks different questions and uses different methods of research, but each is still a documented paper.

This chapter describes various ways to find a subject for research and to discover source materials for the investigation. The chapters that follow trace the writing of a particular research paper and discuss how to evaluate source materials and use them in writing the paper.

## 36.2 Choosing a Subject

The choice of a topic depends on your purpose in writing. You may begin with a question suggested by a current debate or your classwork. Following are several topics you might investigate.

1. *The assassination of President John Kennedy.* In 1979, a House of Representatives Select Committee issued a controversial report on the killing of President Kennedy in 1963 in Dallas, Texas, and the killing in 1968 of Martin Luther King, Jr. One of the committee's widely discussed conclusions deals with a long-disputed second gunman, who some allege fired at President Kennedy from a knoll overlooking the killing site.

In a *New York Times* article published shortly after the committee report, David W. Belin disagrees with this conclusion. Belin's views are of particular interest because, as counsel to the Warren Commission that investigated the killing in 1964 and concluded Lee Harvey Oswald was the single gunman in Dallas, he is well acquainted with the evidence presented.

Here in part is Belin's discussion of the evidence considered by the Warren Commission:

> In the first place, all of the physical evidence points to a single gunman. Only one gunman was seen at the time of the assassination, and witnesses saw him fire from the sixth-floor window of the Texas School Book Depository. Three cartridge cases were found by that window; a nearly whole bullet was found at Parkland Memorial Hospital on Governor Connolly's stretcher; and two ballistically identifiable portions of the bullet that struck President Kennedy's head were found inside the Presidential limousine.
>
> —DAVID W. BELIN, "The Case Against a Conspiracy," *New York Times Magazine*, July 15, 1979

**36.2**
**doc**

Belin reviews additional evidence, then raises questions about the acoustical evidence presented to the 1979 Select Committee:

In contrast, the acoustical evidence rests on a number of implausible assumptions. For instance, if the Dallas police tape is a genuine tape of the assassination, why did it not pick up the sound of motorcycle engines revving up as the motorcade sped toward Parkland Hospital? Why are police sirens not immediately heard? Why does one hear the faint sound of chimes, although no chimes were found to be in use at or near the scene of the assassination?

Belin's statements might encourage you to explore one of many topics, each of which can be investigated through primary or firsthand sources. The Warren Commission and the 1979 Select Committee findings are available in almost all college libraries. Newspaper and magazine reports on these findings contain additional background and information.

Probably few researchers possess enough background or knowledge of legal procedure to understand all of this evidence or judge its worth. Selecting evidence from the enormous number of documents available requires time and special knowledge. Secondary sources—books by later investigators and commentators—present special problems. For example, many secondary sources reflect conspiracy theories that flourished in the years following the assassination. The qualifications of the writers of these books must be evaluated carefully. These difficulties suggest the importance of choosing a topic within your knowledge and judgment.

This "conspiracy" evidence suggests a promising subject. The Select Committee considered evidence that earlier investigators dismissed or ignored. Given the various opinions on the worth of the evidence, you might investigate the more limited question of how several writers on the killing interpret a single piece of evidence—for example, the acoustical evidence to which Belin refers. Your purpose might be to discover how assumptions shaped the selection of evidence and its interpretation.

**36.2**

**doc**

A large number of articles and books discuss the acoustical evidence. In investigating the background, you might begin with one of the first important accounts of the killing—William Manchester's *The Death of a President*. Your investigation might continue with books like Edward Jay Epstein's *Inquest* that review the evidence at issue. To collect materials, you might begin with general accounts of the assassination in *The New York Times* or another newspaper of record and with newsmagazines like *Time* and *Newsweek*. Sylvia Meagher and Gary Owens' *Index to the JFK Assassination Investigations* will direct you to other evidence.

Almost all of the books on the Kennedy killing are controversial. A comparison of how they interpret a single piece of evidence may suggest a tentative thesis—for example, the thesis that political allegiances or particular assumptions of the researchers color their interpretation of the same evidence.

2. *Three-Mile Island.* The accident at Three-Mile Island, near Harrisburg, Pennsylvania, in April of 1979, heightened public concern about nuclear power plants. The movie *The China Syndrome*, concerning a nuclear power plant in California, was playing in American theaters at the time of the accident. Both the film and the accident were discussed in the press in the months that followed. The Chernobyl nuclear accident in May of 1986, in the Soviet Union, raised new concerns.

Like an investigation of the Kennedy killing, an investigation of nuclear power plants calls for a technical knowledge of physics and engineering beyond the capabilities of many researchers. So if you decide to explore this topic, first assess your ability to handle these materials and find out what sources are available to you.

The nature and risks of nuclear technology might be the subject of your paper, or some of this information might serve as the background for a paper on the public response to the Three-Mile Island or Chernobyl accidents or a paper on media reporting of one of these events. One source of background on nuclear power is Paul H. Ehrlich, Anne H. Ehrlich, and John P. Holdren's *Ecoscience: Population, Resources, Environment.* Nontechnical discussions have appeared in *Scientific American* and other scientific magazines and journals. The contrasting views of columnists like George F. Will (in *Newsweek*) and John Garvey (in *Commonweal*) will tell you much about public concerns. A promising topic and a tentative thesis often come out of reading and comparing sources such as these.

3. *Charles Dickens and Warren's Blacking Factory.* In *David Copperfield*, the semiautobiographical novel of Charles Dickens, young David is sent by Mr. Murdstone, his sadistic stepfather, to London to work at a riverside blacking factory. Few readers of the novel forget David's description of the factory or his feelings:

**36.2**
**doc**

> Its panelled rooms, discolored with the dirt and smoke of a hundred years, I dare say; its decaying floors and staircase; the squeaking and scuffling of the old grey rats down in the cellars; and the dirt and rottenness of the place; are things, not of many years ago, in my mind, but of the present instant.
> —CHARLES DICKENS, *David Copperfield*, Chapter 11

Dickens drew David's experience from his own childhood experience at a blacking factory at the same location, at the time his father was imprisoned for debt. This fact may interest you enough to investigate how Dickens used his childhood experience in *David Copperfield* or in another novel.

For this investigation you will need the help of books on Dickens and reference sources that can direct you to primary materials. You will discover that Dickens, in an autobiographical fragment published by his friend John Forster in the first biography of Dickens, gives the facts of his childhood poverty and experience at the factory. A study of the factory episode or the modeling of the characters Mr. and Mrs. Micawber on Dickens's own parents or the picture of an early nineteenth-century debtor's prison in another novel, *Pickwick Papers*, can show how the materials of life can become the materials of fiction.

You can conduct this kind of investigation with other novels that reflect the social and political conditions of their time. Here is a short list of novels that describe an aspect of American life in the nineteenth and the twentieth century:

Willa Cather, *My Antonia*—Nebraska pioneer life
Kate Chopin, *The Awakening*—the life of women in the late nineteenth century
Stephen Crane, *The Red Badge of Courage*—Civil War America
Ralph Ellison, *Invisible Man*—black urban life
F. Scott Fitzgerald, *The Great Gatsby*—the world of the rich in the 1920s
Henry James, *The Bostonians*—the nineteenth-century suffragette movement
Sinclair Lewis, *Arrowsmith*—medical practice in the early twentieth century
———, *Main Street*—early twentieth-century small town life
Upton Sinclair, *The Jungle*—Chicago and the meat-packing industry in the 1900s
John Steinbeck, *The Grapes of Wrath*—the Middle West dustbowl of the 1930s
Mark Twain, *Huckleberry Finn*—slavery in the early nineteenth century

**36.2**
**doc**

### EXERCISE

Suggest several purposes that the investigation of one of the following topics might serve:
1. the origins of country music
2. gas warfare in World War I
3. the rise of fast-food chains in the 1960s
4. female voters in the 1984 presidential election
5. the Soviet invasion of Afghanistan
6. the origin of the assembly line

7. the origin of the animated cartoon
8. the Senate career of Gerald Ford
9. the Iranian hostage crisis
10. Mark Twain's career as a river boatman

# 36.3  Limiting the Subject

**36.3a  Limitation and Purpose.**  The next step is to limit your subject in light of a specific purpose—the use to which you will put your investigation. With a limited subject and a specific purpose in mind, you are ready to consider particular avenues of investigation and ways to search for materials. Of course, both your purpose and limitation of subject may change as you do more reading and compare the materials you gather. You will probably need to read widely in the literature on nuclear power to discover a worthwhile topic and approach.

How broad or narrow should your initial limitation be?

You will find advantages in beginning with a broad subject and narrowing it gradually. A broad investigation will acquaint you with the background and suggest numerous possibilities for investigation—some more promising than those you had in mind at the start. Investigating the Three-Mile-Island accident, we noted, requires extensive reading on the mechanics of nuclear power; you must understand ideas like meltdown to interpret the controversy. If you find that materials on the topic do not exist, your reading may suggest another.

In limiting your topic, keep the following in mind:

1. The availability, variety, and worth of the materials.
2. The importance of the topic in relation to the purpose of your investigation.
3. A limitation of subject adequate to your purpose.

**36.3b  Availability of Materials.**  Begin with the card catalog and other reference sources in your college library to discover what materials are available. This initial search may be difficult and require time, for the materials will be listed in the library catalog and in reference books under various categories and headings. Background studies may be in their own categories.

In seeking materials on Three-Mile-Island, you probably will have to consult books on physics and engineering to discover the facts about nuclear power plants. The accident itself may be discussed in books on different subjects—for example, those dealing with national energy policy, public attitudes and social

**36.3**
**doc**

action, science and society. In the indexes and reference books discussed in the next section, you will find articles on Three-Mile-Island listed under various headings.

**36.3c  Judging Relevance.**    The documented paper is always informative in nature. It may also be persuasive if you want to change the thinking of your readers on the issue you have investigated. The importance or worth of the materials you choose for the paper depends on the purpose you have in mind.

Assume that in writing about nuclear power plants you have a double purpose—to inform your readers about the advantages and risks of nuclear power, and to persuade them to support building nuclear power plants or oppose them. You may also have in mind a separate topic—national policy on nuclear energy. If you are unsure whether your concern is with power plants or with national policy, you will be unsure what materials to collect and how to judge their importance. Failure to define the purpose of the investigation probably accounts for much of the wasted effort in collecting materials.

Some of the materials you collect will prove interesting in their own right but will have no direct bearing on nuclear power or national policy. Other materials will contain information important to an understanding of the subject and will be persuasive enough to change the minds of your readers. Of course, you may decide to redefine your purpose in the course of collecting and evaluating your materials. But it is essential to have a purpose in mind as you proceed from stage to stage, even if you later redefine it or change the focus of your investigation.

**36.3d  Adequacy of Materials.**    The adequacy of your materials depends on the scope of your investigation. A broad investigation for the purpose of informing readers about national nuclear policy will require a large number of materials usually of wide scope. A narrower investigation into Three-Mile-Island itself, for the purpose of informing readers about the risks, will require a large number of materials, too, but narrower in scope.

If you define your topic too narrowly, however, you may not find enough materials. You may find few materials in your library on the immediate public response to the accident—newspaper and magazine reports perhaps, but no interviews with people living close to the site and no studies on these responses by writers on the accident.

Limiting the topic is not as simple a matter as it may seem at first. You will probably broaden the topic or limit it further as you discover new materials and a new focus.

**36.3**
**doc**

**36.3e Formulating a Thesis.** You will often have a thesis in mind at the start of your investigation. This thesis is at one with the purpose you have in mind—the use that your documented paper will serve. These possible theses relate to nuclear power and national policy:

> Health risks outweigh the economic advantages of nuclear power.
> The economic advantages of nuclear power outweigh the health risks.
> National policy on nuclear power ignores the health risks.
> Scientists (or public utilities) exert too much influence on national policy on nuclear power.

In the course of planning and writing your paper, you may discover another or a more limited thesis emerging. The materials themselves may surprise you and suggest a thesis you could not have formulated at the start of research. For example, you might discover a source of information about health risks or national policy neglected in the materials you have collected. This source of information might become the focus of a new thesis more limited than those suggested previously, but a thesis of even greater importance and interest.

You will find it useful to state this thesis first as a hypothesis—a working idea that your evidence may support. Be ready to change this thesis or qualify it if your evidence does not finally support it completely.

### EXERCISES

1. Assume you wish to study the influence of television on American political life. What two or three purposes might such a study serve?
2. Suggest several possible ways to limit one of the following topics in light of the purposes you have in mind:
   a. television news
   b. the reporting of national elections
   c. the influence of political commentators
   d. television news and newspaper and magazine reporting
   e. the image of politicians on television and in movies
3. List several topics for investigation suggested by a novel or play you have recently read. Be ready to discuss possible uses to which this investigation might be put and how you would proceed with the investigation in the beginning stages.
4. Investigate materials available for a paper on the Chernobyl accident. What primary materials do you find listed in indexes? What secondary materials? How would you determine the reliability of these materials?

**36.3**
**doc**

# 36.4   Collecting Materials

This section discusses some important reference works you will find useful.

**36.4a  Guides to Reference Books.**   A few years ago the number of major reference books was limited enough to list in a small book. Today the number is so great that reference guides are often needed to find those in a special field like English poetry, American history, or medicine. The following are particularly useful in locating these guides:

> *Ayer Directory of Newspapers and Periodicals.*
> Mary N. Barton and Marion V. Bell, *Reference Books: A Brief Guide for Students and Other Users of the Library*, 7th ed.
> *Bibliographic Index* [1937-present].
> Eugene P. Sheehy, *Guide to Reference Books*, 9th ed.
> Louis Shores, *Basic Reference Sources: An Introduction to Materials and Methods.*
> Arthur J. Walford, ed., *Guide to Reference Material*, 3rd ed.
> *World Bibliography of Bibliographies*, 4th ed.

These guides list reference books in various fields. They are particularly useful in locating special bibliographies—many of them included in books on various subjects. *Bibliographic Index*, for example, lists special bibliographies contained in books like Jonathan Miller's *The Body in Question*. In this study of physiology, Miller gives the reader an up-to-date listing of books on the history and philosophy of science, physiology, perception, and the "sociology of healing"—a valuable list if you are seeking background on medical science and sociology.

**36.4b  Indexes.**   An **index** is a descriptive catalog of books and articles. The following are widely used by researchers in various fields. Most have listings under author and subject:

> *Applied Science and Technology Index* [1913–present].
> *Art Index* [1929–present].
> *Biography Index* [1946–present].
> *Book Review Digest* [1905–present]. Includes extracts from the reviews. Invaluable for judging the reliability of books.
> *Dramatic Index* [1909–1949]. Index to articles on authors, plays, and performances in the inclusive dates.
> *Education Index* [1929–present].
> *Essay and General Literature Index* [1900–present]. Essays and articles in essay collections, mainly in the humanities and so-

cial sciences. The first volume covers 1900 to 1934. Indispensable in locating materials not listed in the card catalog or general indexes.

*Granger's Index to Poetry.* First published in 1904. Lists poems in more than 500 anthologies.

*Humanities Index* [1974–present]. Supersedes the *Social Sciences and Humanities Index* (see listing). Author and subject index to specialized periodicals in English and other modern languages, classics, philosophy, and linguistics.

*Index to the [London] Times* [1906–present]. Author and subject index to the British newspaper of record. *Palmer's Index to the Times* covers earlier years.

*Index Medicus.* Author and subject index in medicine and related fields including pertinent articles and books in the humanities and social sciences. Available for computer search through Medline, National Library of Medicine. See Figure 39.2, p. 594.

*International Index to Periodicals* [1907–1965]. Index to specialized periodicals in special fields. Superseded by *Social Sciences and Humanities Index.* Companion to *Reader's Guide to Periodical Literature* (see listing).

*Magazine Index.* Subject index to periodicals; on film.

*Music Index* [1949–present].

*New York Times Index.* Author and subject index to the newspaper of record in the United States. Indispensable to the study of past and current events in the United States and the world.

*Poole's Index to Periodical Literature* [1802–1907]. Subject index to British and American periodicals. The chief source of articles published in the nineteenth century.

*Psychological Abstracts* [1894–present].

*Reader's Guide to Periodical Literature* [1900–present]. The major index to more than 150 periodicals of general interest like *Atlantic Monthly* and *Harper's Magazine.*

*Social Sciences and Humanities Index* [1965–1974]. Supersedes the *International Index to Periodicals.* Since 1974 published as *Social Sciences Index* and *Humanities Index.* See Figure 39.1, p. 593.

**36.4**
**doc**

*Ulrich's International Periodical Directory.* Subject classification of periodicals.

*Vertical File Index* [1935–present]. Index to pamphlets.

**36.4c Encyclopedias and Special Dictionaries.** The following useful encyclopedias and special dictionaries provide detailed information for the general reader and the specialist. Your library may also hold valuable earlier editions of these reference works:

*Bartlett's Familiar Quotations*
*Cambridge Ancient History*
*Cambridge Medieval History*
*Cambridge Modern History*
*Chambers's Encyclopaedia*, 4th ed.
*Collier's Encyclopedia*
*Dictionary of American Biography*
*Dictionary of National Biography* [British]
*Dictionary of Scientific Biography*
*Encyclopaedia of Black America*
*Encyclopaedia Britannica*, 15th ed.
*Encyclopaedia of Religion and Ethics*
*Encyclopedia Americana*
*Encyclopedia Judaica*
*Encyclopedia of Catholicism*
*Encyclopedia of Philosophy*
*Encyclopedia of American History*
*Encyclopedia of World History*, 5th ed.
*Harvard Dictionary of Music*, 2nd rev. ed.
*Hastings' Dictionary of the Bible*
*International Cyclopedia of Music and Musicians*, 10th ed.
*International Encyclopedia of the Social Sciences*
*The Jewish Encyclopedia*
*New Catholic Encyclopedia*
*New Columbia Encyclopedia*, 4th ed.
*New Grove Dictionary of Music and Musicians*
*Oxford Companion to American Literature*, 5th ed.
*Oxford Companion to English Literature*, 5th ed.
*Oxford Dictionary of Quotations*
*The Reader's Adviser: A Layman's Guide to Literature*
*Reader's Encyclopedia of Shakespeare*, ed. Oscar J. Campbell and
    Edward G. Quinn

**36.4d Yearbooks, Almanacs, Bibliographical Guides.**    The following are valuable sources of current facts. Since most of these books appear yearly, the most recent editions should be consulted:

**36.4**
**doc**

*Americana Annual* [1923–present]
*Britannica Book of the Year* [1938–present]
*Collier's Yearbook* [1939–present]
*Facts on File* [1940–present]
*Information Please Almanac* [1947–present]
*International Who's Who* [1935–present]
*[London] Times Atlas of the World*
*New York Times Atlas of the World*
*Selective Bibliography for the Study of English and American Literature*, 6th ed., Richard D. Altick and Andrew Wright, eds.

*Statistical Abstract of the United States* [1878–present]
*United States Government Manual* [1935–present]
*Webster's Biographical Dictionary*
*Who's Who* [1849–present] [British]
*Who's Who in America* [1899–present]
*World Almanac and Book of Facts* [1868–present]
*Year Book of World Affairs* [1947–present]

# 36.5   The Card Catalog

**36.5a Using the Card Catalog.**   In compiling a bibliography of articles and books, you need to consult the card catalog in your library—the combined subject and author and title catalog, or separate author and title catalogs if your library divides them. A computerized subject catalog may also be available.

You will find books listed in the subject index according to headings like the following:

*American Slang:*
American language—Slang—Dictionaries

*Farming in the Middle West:*
Agriculture—United States

*Shakespeare's* Hamlet:
Shakespeare, William, 1564–1616—Tragedies

*Novels about Colonial America:*
United States—History—Colonial period, ca. 1600–1775—Fiction

Most college libraries use the Library of Congress headings—listed in *Library of Congress Subject Headings,* usually available in the reference section of the library. In using the subject catalog, you should consult several classifications to find books pertinent to your topic. The subject catalog lists books under more than one category.

Consult the author and title catalog if you want books by a particular author or if you know the title or want to see what books the library contains by an author who possibly has written on the topic. If you know that Norman Mailer wrote an article on capital punishment for a weekly magazine, the author and title catalog may show other books by the writer on the subject (the catalog probably contains a card for *The Executioner's Song,* Mailer's book on Gary Gilmore, executed in Utah in 1978).

Make a thorough search of the catalog, writing down complete information about the books you find. Don't rely on your memory.

**36.5**
**doc**

**36.5b  Reading a Catalog Card.**    Figure 36.1 illustrates three kinds of catalog card:

Card A for Robert John Morris's *Cholera, 1832* gives the following information about the book:

1. Name of author as main entry.
2. Title, subtitle, and edition of the book.
3. Complete listing of authors up to three names.
4. City, publisher, date (in brackets if the book is in process of publication), and notes about the book.
5. Tracings or other headings under which the title appears in the card catalog.
6. Library of Congress and Dewey call numbers.

The library call number usually appears at the top left of the card.

Card B for Margaret Pelling's *Cholera, Fever and English Medicine, 1825-1865* gives additional information about the series in which the book is published and the book itself. From the tracings we learn about the contents. Card C for *Man and Beast: Comparative Social Behavior* gives information on the origin of the papers contained in the book. The card catalog may list the contents of an anthology or collection.

You can learn much about a book from the catalog card—perhaps that, despite its title, the book is not on the topic you are investigating. Vine DeLoria's *Custer Died for Our Sins* is not a study of General Custer or the battle of Little Big Horn, as the title might suggest, but a collection of essays on Indian rights. Carl Sagan's *Broca's Brain* does contain an essay on the nineteenth-century French surgeon, but the book is actually a collection of essays on modern science and pseudo-science.

**36.5c  The Dewey Decimal Classification.**    Knowing the classification system of your library will help in using it to the best advantage. Dewey Decimal classifies books as follows:

**36.5**
**doc**

| | |
|---|---|
| 000 | General Works |
| 100 | Philosophy |
| 200 | Religion |
| 300 | Social Sciences |
| 400 | Language |
| 500 | Pure Sciences [Chemistry, Physics, Biology, etc.] |
| 600 | Technology |
| 700 | Arts |
| 800 | Literature |
| 900 | History |

The Dewey system classifies books by subject and genre or

**FIGURE 36.1   Sample Library Cards**

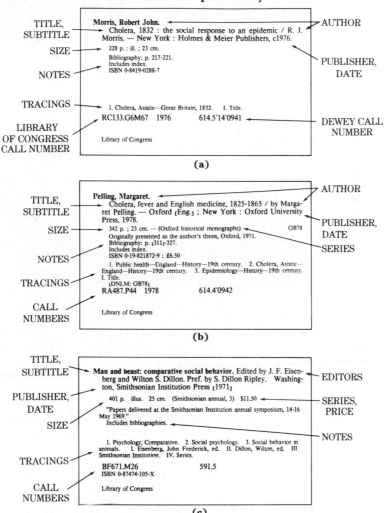

(a)

(b)

(c)

literary type (poetry, drama, novel, biography). This classification is of advantage in browsing. If you are looking for humorous essays, you will find them shelved under the same general number. In other classifications you will find books in the same subject area arranged according to specific topic—for example, books on the history of astronomy and capital punishment. You will need to consult the card catalog to find books by the same author.

**36.5d  Library of Congress Classification.**  The Library of Congress system classifies works by subject, period, and author. In this classification the call number begins with a letter (or multiple letter) instead of a three digit number:

A       General Works
B       Philosophy, Religion
C       Auxiliary Sciences of History
D       History and Topography (except America)
E-F     American History
G       Geography, Anthropology
H       Social Sciences
J       Political Science
K       Law
L       Education
M       Music
N       Fine Arts
P       Language and Literature
Q       Science
R       Medicine
S       Agriculture, Plant and Animal Industry
T       Technology
U       Military Science
V       Naval Science
Z       Bibliography and Library Science

Where useful, the general class is divided according to period. For example, books on English literature and American literature appear under the PR and PS classifications. The PS classification begins with books on colonial American literature and proceeds to modern American literature. In each subclassification, the books are arranged by author: works by the author, followed by critical works. Library of Congress also classifies by genre. Thus works of fiction are classified separately by period and author; in recent years, literary works of an author, including works of fiction, nonfiction, letters, biographical and autobiographical writings, have been classified together. You may find novels of Virginia Woolf shelved with other novels under the PZ classification or with the letters, diaries, essays, and biographical and critical studies of Woolf under the PR classification.

**36.5**
**doc**

### EXERCISES

1. What information does your card catalog give you about the contents of one of the following books:
   **a.** John Updike, *Hugging the Shore*
   **b.** John Gardner, *Grendel*

    **c.** Annie Dillard, *Pilgrim at Tinker Creek*
    **d.** Aleksandr Solzhenitsyn, *The Gulag Archipelago*
    **e.** James Watson, *The Double Helix*
**2.** What does the call number suggest about the nature of the book?
**3.** What information do you find about the contents in one of the reference books listed in 36.4b?
**4.** What articles on the life or philosophy of the writer are listed in one of the same reference books?

## 36.6   Other Uses of the Library

**36.6a Computer Searches and Other Services.**   The library provides other reference services, including computer searching through Lockheed and other data banks. These searches provide special bibliographies on various subjects for a fee. College libraries also depend on computerized catalogs that locate books at nearby libraries and others in the state and country. Your library may have a provision for borrowing books and other materials through interlibrary loan.

Some of the materials you will be seeking are stored on microfilm and microfiche. The library will have special machines available for reading materials in these forms and making photocopies. Most libraries have copying machines available and will inform you on copyright restrictions in making copies.

The library may have a separate audiovisual section containing sound recordings and videocassettes and possibly machines for listening and viewing. Course materials including lectures and practice tapes in language studies are often available on sound recording and videotape. You will probably find a special catalog listing these materials in this section of the library.

**36.6**
**doc**

**36.6b Government Documents.**   The vast number of publications of the United States government are shelved usually in one section of the library under the Library of Congress classifications. These documents include *Congressional Record* as well as reports and bulletins of numerous government departments and agencies like the Department of Education and the Department of Agriculture. You will also find documents published by state governments in this section. Your library may have a special catalog for these publications.

Following is a list of useful guides to U.S. government documents:

*Bibliographic Guide to Government Publications, United States: 1975.*
Anne Morris Boyd, *United States Government Publications*, 3rd ed.
*Government Publications and Their Use.*
*Monthly Catalog of United States Government Publications* [1895–present].
*A Popular Guide to Government Publications*, 4th ed., W. Phillip Leidy, compiler.
*Public Affairs Information Service Bulletin* [1915–present]. Subject index to government publications, including books and periodicals.
Ellen Jackson, *Subject Guide to Major United States Government Publications.*

The following are useful guides to foreign documents:

*Bibliographic Guide to Government Publications: Foreign: 1975.*
*United Nations Documents Index* [1950-present].

### EXERCISES

1. How is Sheehy's *Guide to Reference Books* organized? What information is given about each entry? Of what general value is this information in doing research?
2. What reference books are available in Sheehy for research into the following?
   a. federal regulation of television
   b. U.S. House of Representatives
   c. Battle of Gettysburg
   d. F. Scott Fitzgerald's novels
3. What uses does the *Ayer Directory of Newspapers and Periodicals* have in research on the 1984 presidential election?
4. What indexes and special dictionaries would you use to find articles or information on the following?
   a. articles published before 1960 on Emily Dickinson's poems
   b. drug treatment for schizophrenia
   c. changes in small-town life in America
   d. the origins of the spiritual
   e. the birth of Solidarity Union in Poland
   f. the fiction of Eudora Welty
   g. Supreme Court decisions on capital punishment in the l970s
   h. the Falklands War
   i. laser technology
   j. William Faulkner's education
5. What yearbooks, almanacs, and biographical dictionaries give information on the following? What is that information?

**36.6**
**doc**

**a.** Pulitzer Prize for Fiction in 1980
**b.** the early career of Carl Sandburg
**c.** Junior Senator from Connecticut in 1973
**d.** population of New York City in 1980
**e.** Nobel Prize for Literature in 1964
**f.** the writings of Helen Keller
**g.** the political career of Franklin Delano Roosevelt
**h.** members of the Supreme Court in 1953
**6.** What information does the card catalog give about the nature or subject matter of the following books?
**a.** Frederick Lewis Allen, *Only Yesterday*
**b.** Samuel Butler, *Erewhon*
**c.** Rachel Carson, *Silent Spring*
**d.** Joan Didion, *Salvador*
**e.** Edward Jay Epstein, *Inquest*
**f.** Ernest Hemingway, *A Moveable Feast*
**g.** H. L. Mencken, *Happy Days*
**h.** W. V. Quine, *Word and Object*
**i.** Mario Pei, *The Families of Words*
**j.** James Watson, *The Double Helix*
**7.** With what books are these classified in your library?

# General Exercise

Use the full resources of your library reference section to find answers to the following questions. To locate particular books, consult Eugene P. Sheehy's *Guide to Reference Books* and other guides to reference books listed on pp. 546–547.

**1.** What reference works contain a biography of former Texas Congresswoman Barbara Jordan?
**2.** What is the title of Barbara Jordan's autobiography and the year of publication? What magazines reviewed the book?
**3.** Where can you find the complete text of the Supreme Court *Miranda* decision? What justice of the court wrote the decision? Was the decision unanimous?
**4.** What two or three legal journals published articles on the *Miranda* decision between 1982 and 1985?
**5.** What two books contain discussions of the *Miranda* decision?
**6.** Who is Miranda and why was his conviction appealed to the Supreme Court?
**7.** What is the meaning of the phrase *ad astra per aspera*?
**8.** What people were called *lightning rods* in nineteenth-century America?
**9.** What meanings of the word *flap* are not likely to have occurred in American fiction before 1900?

**36.6**
**doc**

10. Who wrote under the name "David Grayson"? On what American President did he write a biography under his own name?
11. Who was Sojourner Truth, and in what American city did she deliver a famous speech?
12. What is the origin of the town Amana, Iowa?
13. What is the source of the title *Far From the Madding Crowd*— a novel by Thomas Hardy? What is the name of its heroine?
14. What is KOH an abbreviation for?
15. In what novel does the character Simon Legree appear, and what dramatizations of the novel have occurred?
16. What reference book lists lines of poetry by subject?
17. Who was "good King Wencelaus"?
18. Which is the oldest of the New Testament gospels?
19. Who are the joint discoverers of the DNA molecule structures, and in what year did they receive the Nobel Prize?
20. Who won the Nobel Prize for Literature in 1970? How many of his writings had been published in his native country prior to 1970? How many have been published there since 1970?
21. What is the origin of the name *Legionnaire's disease*? Is the disease bacterial or viral?
22. What is a "disease vector"? Do malaria and yellow fever have the same vector? Are these diseases caused by the same microorganism?
23. How does the word *malaria* reflect theories of its origin before the twentieth century?
24. How is a Romanesque arch different from a Gothic arch?
25. What is a "flying buttress," and when was it invented?
26. How is a concerto grosso different from a symphony?
27. How many children did the composer Johann Sebastian Bach have, and how many of them also became composers?
28. What is the present population of the United States?
29. What government department administers the Coast Guard?
30. Does the state of Connecticut have an income tax?

## Checklist for Finding a Subject

**36.1**  The documented paper uses published and unpublished sources to shed light on an event, a person, or a current issue.

**36.2**  Use the question that leads to research to define your subject and find materials to develop it.

**36.3a**  You may want to limit your subject further as your purpose narrows.

**36.3b**   Use the card catalog to find materials.

**36.3c**   A topic is worth developing if it sheds important light on a current issue or changes the reader's view of the past or the contemporary world.

**36.3d**   The adequacy of the materials depends on the purpose and scope of the investigation.

**36.3e**   Let the materials and your analysis of them define your thesis.

**36.4a**   Special guides will direct you to special reference books.

**36.4b**   Special indexes list books and articles on various topics.

**36.4c**   Special encyclopedias and dictionaries provide essential information for the general reader and the specialist.

**36.4d**   So do yearbooks, almanacs, and biographical guides.

**36.5a**   Use the card catalog to compile your bibliography.

**36.5b**   The card often gives important information about the contents of the book.

**36.5c**   The Dewey Decimal system classifies books by subject and genre.

**36.5d**   The Library of Congress classifies books by subject, period, and author.

**36.6a**   The library provides other reference services, including computer searching.

**36.6b**   Special guides will help you locate government documents.

# Sources and Notes

## 37.1 Primary and Secondary Sources

In doing research on a topic, you will use two kinds of evidence if available in your library—primary and secondary evidence. **Primary evidence** is eyewitness evidence, writings of participants, and other first-hand documents. **Secondary evidence** is interpretation of this primary evidence by researchers and commentators. Both kinds of evidence are essential, for primary sources are not always reliable, and secondary sources may be prejudiced or based on incomplete evidence. The numerous articles and books on the Kennedy assassination present a challenge to the researcher on this subject (see 36.2). Though secondary sources are essential in verifying primary ones, they in turn need verification by experienced researchers.

**37.1a Primary Sources.**   You will find an important primary source in the account of events by people who participated in them. Florence Nightingale's *Notes on Nursing* (1859), which describes the working conditions of nineteenth-century doctors and nurses, is a primary source because the author worked as a nurse and directly experienced the conditions she describes.

In providing direct evidence of life and attitudes, primary sources are important in challenging or verifying other evidence. Assume that one of your sources states that sanitation did not become important until the triumph of the germ theory later in the nineteenth century. Florence Nightingale gives direct testimony that this statement is false.

> Oh, mothers of families! You who say this, do you know that one in every seven infants in this civilized land of England perishes before it is one year old? That, in London, two in every five die before they are five years old? And in the other great cities of England, nearly one out of two? "The life duration of

558

tender babies" (as some Saturn, turned analytical chemist, says) "is the most delicate test" of sanitary conditions. Is all this premature suffering and death necessary? Or did Nature intend mothers to be always accompanied by doctors? Or is it better to learn the pianoforte than to learn the laws which subserve the preservation of offspring?

—FLORENCE NIGHTINGALE, *Notes on Nursing*

Primary sources include letters, diaries, autobiographical writings, essays, and even works of poetry and fiction that reflect the conditions of the age. Primary sources include reports of experimental work in the sciences and the social sciences. Numerous accounts by British and American doctors appear in the medical journals of the nineteenth century—*Lancet* and *Medical Record*, for example. An 1856 article in *Harper's Monthly Magazine*—"Why We Get Sick" by Robert Tomes—gives an eyewitness account of the American doctor by a layman. Other primary sources from the same period include Charles Dickens's description of people afflicted with smallpox, in his 1851 novel *Bleak House*, and Alfred Lord Tennyson's description of a nineteenth-century hospital ward, in his poem "In the Children's Hospital."

**37.1b Secondary Sources.** Secondary sources include articles, books, theses, dissertations, and other writings that interpret and evaluate eyewitness and and other primary evidence. Charles-Edward Winslow's book *The Conquest of Epidemic Disease* interprets the statements of Florence Nightingale in light of social conditions and the popular view of sanitation and disease. A secondary source like Winslow's gives the backgrounds and contexts uninformed readers need to interpret primary sources.

Few primary sources can be interpreted by the nonspecialist without the help of works like Winslow's. These suggest what weight to give primary sources as evidence. Many secondary sources examine the assumptions and reasoning of primary sources in order to weigh their value in research. Lester S. King, a medical historian, pathologist, and former editor of the *Journal of the American Medical Association* (important qualifications for a writer on medicine), in his book *Medical Thinking* evaluates two primary sources for the study of nineteenth-century medicine— an 1826 book on pathology by a French doctor, Louis Martinet, and an 1841 book on the philosophy of medicine by an American writer, Elisha Bartlett. After an extensive analysis of medical thought in these books, King summarizes their limitations:

> For the medical writers of the early 19th century, facts took
> the form of generalizations that applied broadly. Physicians were

**37.1**
**doc**

*"And just which of your remarks did I take out of context?"*

Drawing by Joe Mirachi; copyright © 1985 by The New Yorker Magazine, Inc.

concerned with the way that a disease would manifest itself—
not in any single or unique case but in all cases. Such is the
essence of science—concern with the generalization and the
class, not with the unique individual.

There are some disturbing difficulties in Bartlett's account.
Are facts and events synonymous? Are facts and relationships
equally a matter of observation? Does "fact" refer to the phe-
nomenon or to the relationship or to the law or to all three?
The basic question, "What is a fact?" is one to which neither
Martinet nor Bartlett gave a clear answer.

—LESTER S. KING, *Medical Thinking: A Historical Preface*

These comments do more than tell the researcher the worth
of Martinet and Bartlett as sources on nineteenth-century medical thought. They tell the researcher how to interpret particular
statements and interpretations of evidence; they provide the
**context** of ideas that surround statements and facts in source
materials of any period. The researcher must examine state-

**37.1**
**doc**

ments and facts in their many contexts. Secondary sources are essential in discovering these.

**EXERCISES**

1. What primary and secondary sources does your college library contain on one of the following?
   **a.** the legislative career of Abraham Lincoln
   **b.** Winston S. Churchill's leadership of Great Britain during World War II
   **c.** Thomas Jefferson's views on slavery
   **d.** Teapot Dome
   **e.** the Senate career of Gerald Ford
2. What kind of secondary sources would you seek to authenticate the following documents—to show that they are genuine and not fake?
   **a.** a letter of Thomas Jefferson stating his opposition to slavery
   **b.** a letter of Abraham Lincoln that describes the writing of the Gettysburg Address
   **c.** an eyewitness report of the Battle of Gettysburg

# 37.2 Compiling a Bibliography

Following your initial reading, definition of purpose, and working out of a tentative thesis, you need to compile a bibliography of articles and books pertinent to your subject. Your best sources are the card catalog and the reference books discussed in 36.4.

In compiling a bibliography, record complete information on author, title, source, place of publication, and date. If your source is an article, be careful to record the volume of the magazine or journal and the page numbers. Here are sample bibliographic entries for articles and books on uses of metaphor. The form of the entry follows the *MLA Handbook for Writers of Research Papers*, second edition:

**37.2**
**doc**

Barzun, Jacques. <u>Simple and Direct: A Rhetoric for</u>
    <u>Writers</u>. New York: Harper, 1976.

Carnes, Valerie. "The Language of Nowspeak." <u>The New</u>
    <u>Humanities: Culture, Crisis, Change</u>. Ed. Ralph L.
    Carnes and Valerie Carnes. New York: Holt, 1972:
    219–44.

Kintgen, Eugene R., and Norman N. Holland. "Carlos
    Reads a Poem." <u>College English</u> 46 (1984): 478–492.
Lakoff, George, and Mark Johnson. <u>Metaphors We Live By</u>.
    Chicago: U of Chicago P, 1980.

Divide these entries into articles and books if you find this arrangement more useful. Also record call numbers and other information of help in locating materials quickly. In compiling this information, you need to take down enough details to save your returning to the card catalog and reference books.

# 37.3  Taking Notes

**37.3a  Purpose of Notecards.**   A notecard fails to do its job if you must return to the source to check details and the accuracy of your quotations and paraphrase.

Good notes record information from sources in a form useful a week, a month, or even years later. Useful notes do not consist of only words, phrases, or even sentences. In reading an article or book, you absorb that context—the build of ideas and details, their relationship and integration, the point of view of the author, nuances and special accents of words and phrases. Outside this context, words and phrases quoted from the source and interpretive statements of your own often become meaningless. For this reason, you need to reproduce the context of statements concisely but informatively.

**37.3b  Paraphrase, Summary, Quotation.**   In recording information on the notecard, you have a choice between direct quotation, paraphrase, and summary. A **direct quotation** gives the exact words of the author. A **paraphrase** gives the sense of a passage in the researcher's own words. A **summary** of the passage gives the gist or main points:

**37.3**
**doc**

*Direct Quotation*
The attitude that produces the pseudo-technical tone is made up of a desire to dignify the subject and the writer, coupled with the belief that important matters require a special vocabulary.
—Jacques Barzun, *Simple and Direct: A Rhetoric for Writers*
(New York: Harper, 1976), p. 90

*Paraphrase*
The writer adopts a pretentious tone that uses profes-

```
sional jargon to dress up the subject——in the mistaken
belief that significant ideas need special words.
```

*Summary*
```
The mistaken belief that important ideas need dressing
up and the wish to sound important lead the writer to
adopt a pretentious tone and special words.
```

Direct quotation, paraphrase, and summary should not be random or aimless. Use paraphrase or summary to record ideas that lose nothing in translation. Quote only when you cannot put a statement into your own words without a substantial loss of meaning. Sometimes only a direct quotation will convey the nuance or special emphasis carried in the passage. The following passage from George Orwell's essay on language, "Politics and the English Language," loses its special accent and eloquent force in paraphrase:

> In our time it is broadly true that political writing is bad writing. Where it is not true, it will generally be found that the writer is some kind of rebel, expressing his private opinions and not a "party line." Orthodoxy, of whatever color, seems to demand a lifeless, imitative style.
> —GEORGE ORWELL, "Politics and the English Language"

If you wish to convey the essential idea and not the epigrammatic force of the passage, paraphrase is satisfactory. However, the final phrase—"a lifeless, imitative style"—demands quotation.

If you quote too much, the words you quote will seem less important than a few important quoted phrases. The solution is to combine paraphrase with quotation.

```
Orwell says that political writing today is "bad writ-
ing," the product of those who parrot official govern-
ment language. The political conformist favors "a life
less, imitative style." The plain writer by contrast
expresses his own opinions.
```

**37.3**
**doc**

Although this paraphrase loses the force of the original, it captures essential ideas and key phrases.

**37.3c Writing a Notecard.**   A notecard on the passage quoted above from Jacques Barzun's book on modern prose style is shown in Figure 37.1.

## FIGURE 37.1    Ineffective Notecard

> *pseudo-technical tone    "to dignify the*
> *subject and writer"*
> *come and go with fashion*
> *scientist says "sorry not to be able to accept*
> *the experience of more intensive interaction"*
> *Barzun calls him Micawber    criticizes the*
> *words    90*
> *says the writer doesn't want to talk plainly*
> *Simple and Direct, Harper & Row, 1976*

This card will be of limited use to the researcher for the following reasons:

1. Barzun's phrases are quoted out of context.
2. The note does not distinguish Barzun's words from paraphrase.
3. The information is inaccurate—"Micawber" is the name Barzun gives the prose, not the scientist quoted.
4. The quotation is incomplete.
5. The city of publication is missing in the citation.

Here is the original paragraph that the note describes:

**37.3**
**doc**

> The attitude that produces the pseudo-technical tone is made up of a desire to dignify the subject and the writer, coupled with the belief that important matters require a special vocabulary. Since most matters neither have nor need one, the vocabulary is made up of nouns and verbs used metaphorically. They come and go with fashion inside professional and business circles, then spread outside by chance imitation. Here is a scientist declining membership on a committee: "I am sorry not to be able to accept the experience of more intensive interaction with your group and its constituency." This is what I have called Micawber, modern style. *Experience, intensive interaction, constituency* are the pseudo-technical words, brought forth by the attitude of a writer who is unwilling to say plainly: "I am sorry I cannot join the committee; I should have enjoyed working with its members."
>
> —JACQUES BARZUN, *Simple and Direct: A Rhetoric for Writers*

In Figure 37.2, notecard A gives accurate information about this same passage. Notecard B shows a fully punctuated card that later will prove of more use.

**FIGURE 37.2 Effective Notecards**

Barzun defines "the pseudo-technical tone" as the wish to dress up the subject and use a "special vocabulary" since most subjects don't need a special vocabulary, writers create one by turning nouns and verbs into metaphors
Barzun's example of "Micawber" or "modern style": scientist refusing an invitation: "I am sorry not to be able to accept the experience of more intensive interaction with your group and its constituency."
Barzun's translation: "I am sorry I cannot join the committee; I should have enjoyed working with its members."
*Simple and Direct: A Rhetoric for Writers* New York, Harper, 1976, pp. 90-91

(a)

Barzun defines "the pseudo-technical tone" as the wish to dress up the subject and use a "special vocabulary." Since most subjects don't need a special vocabulary, writers create one by turning nouns and verbs into metaphors. In Barzun's example of "Micawber" or "modern style," a scientist refuses an invitation: "I am sorry not to be able to accept the experience of more intensive interaction with your group and its constituency." Barzun's translation: "I am sorry I cannot join the committee; I should have enjoyed working with its members."
*Simple and Direct: A Rhetoric for Writers* New York, Harper, 1976, pp. 90-91

(b)

**37.3 doc**

Each card might have omitted the example. But to omit it would be a mistake. The example makes the definition concrete, and it may prove valuable when the original context is forgotten.

**37.3d  Ellipsis and Other Conventions.**    Ellipsis is a succession of three spaced periods that substitute for omitted words (see 14.2). The omission of these nonessential or nonrestrictive words does not change the meaning of the original passage:

*Original*
I said earlier that the decadence of our language is probably curable. Those who deny this would argue, if they produced an argument at all, that language merely reflects existing social conditions, and that we cannot influence its development by any direct tinkering with words and constructions.
          —GEORGE ORWELL, "Politics and the English Language"

*With Omissions*
. . . the decadence of our language is probably curable. Those who deny this would argue . . . that language merely reflects existing social conditions, and that we cannot influence its development by any direct tinkering with words and constructions.

The following note omits two sentence elements:

*Original*
But if thought corrupts language, language can also corrupt thought. A bad usage can spread by tradition and imitation, even among people who should and do know better. The debased language that I have been discussing is in some ways very convenient.
          —GEORGE ORWELL, "Politics and the English Language"

*With Omissions*
But if thought corrupts language, language can also corrupt thought. A bad usage can spread by tradition and imitation. . . . The debased language . . . is in some ways very convenient.

**37.3**
**doc**

Is the omission in the second sentence justified?

The qualifying phrase *even among people who should and do know better* is essential to the meaning: Orwell is saying that no one is free of corrupting thought and language. The restrictive modifier *that I have been discussing* identifies the debased language and therefore cannot be omitted either. Both omissions are unjustified. Note that the fourth period in the second ellipsis is the normal period of the second sentence.

The omission of a whole sentence or several is shown by the ellipsis following the sentence preceding:

But if thought corrupts language, language can also corrupt thought. . . . The debased language that I have been discussing is in some ways very convenient.

The first period is the normal period of the sentence.

Note the following additional matters of quotation.

1. An ellipsis marks the omission of the opening words of a sentence. But ellipsis at the start is unnecessary unless you wish to warn the reader that the quotation is not a complete sentence. Notice that the lower case of *language* in the following example shows that the quotation is not the complete sentence:

Orwell warns that "language can also corrupt thought."

If *language* opens the sentence, put the first letter of the word in brackets:

Orwell warns: "[L]anguage can also corrupt thought."

2. If a passage you are quoting contains a quotation, punctuate this quotation with single quotation marks:

In discussing "meaningless words" in his essay "Politics and the English Language," George Orwell states: "When one critic writes, 'The outstanding feature of Mr. X's work is its living quality,' while another writes, 'The immediately striking thing about Mr. X's work is its peculiar deadness,' the reader accepts this as a simple difference of opinion."

If you indent this passage in your paper, you omit the opening and closing quotation marks and retain the original punctuation:

George Orwell states in his essay "Politics and the English Language":

When one critic writes, "The outstanding feature of Mr. X's work is its living quality," while another writes, "The immediately striking thing about Mr. X's work is its peculiar deadness," the reader accepts this as a simple difference of opinion.

**37.3**
**doc**

**37.3e  Additions to Quoted Material.**   You will occasionally come upon a probable error in a source—a misspelling or mistaken choice of word. However, the misspelling may be the deliberate choice of the author and not a printer's error; the author may also have chosen the word in question. In these circumstances, add the word *sic* in brackets to show that the error is not your own. *Sic* means "just as I found it."

Smith states, "The two are alien [*sic*] in their thinking."

The writer probably meant *alike*, but *alien* does fit the context and it may be the author's word.

Explanatory information can be added in brackets:

Smith states, "They parted as friends and colleagues on September 6 [1982]."

In quoting a case history from the nineteenth century, a medical historian adds a defining phrase in brackets:

He has been treated at various intervals by different medical men. For about a week he has seemed in the same imminent danger as to-day. A laryngoscopic examination at once reveals the source of the dyspnoea [shortness of breath].
    —STANLEY JOEL REISER, *Medicine and the Reign of Technology*

If you italicize words in a quoted passage for emphasis, state this fact in a parenthesis following the quotation:

Orwell's choice of words and similes is significant: "The inflated style is itself a kind of *euphemism*. A mass of Latin words falls upon the facts like *soft snow*, blurring the outlines and covering up all the details" (italics added).

See 13.5 and 14.3 on other uses of brackets and italics.

**37.3f Plagiarism.**   Plagiarism is the appropriation of another writer's words and ideas as one's own without acknowledgment of the borrowing. Intentional plagiarism is an act of dishonesty. Copyright law protects authors from plagiarism. Colleges usually penalize students who intentionally plagiarize. Though plagiarism in college papers seems a minor offense to many students, it is a serious matter.

Some plagiarism is unintentional, arising from carelessness in note taking. In paraphrasing a passage from a source, the researcher may carry clauses and whole sentences into the rendering without using quotation marks:

**37.3**
**doc**

*Source*
Sylvester Graham was right, of course. His fear that commercially baked, and adulterated, white bread portended a sweeping displacement of natural foods by artificial products has been realized to a disturbing degree in the twentieth century.
—JAMES C. WHORTON, *Crusaders for Fitness: The History of American Health Reformers* (Princeton, N.J.: Princeton UP, 1982)

*Passage in Course Paper*

```
American health reformers were right in fearing that
commercially baked, and adulterated, white bread por-
tended a sweeping displacement of natural foods by ar-
tificial products. One of these reformers was Sylvester
Graham, inventor of the Graham cracker.
```

The plagiarism here is especially glaring since almost the whole passage from the source is reproduced without quotation marks. A common and unintentional form of plagiarism occurs when a short but significant phrase is appropriated from the source:

*Passage in Course Paper*

```
The adulteration of food happened to a disturbing de-
gree in the twentieth century.
```

The words *to a disturbing degree in the twentieth century* are Whorton's, not the researcher's.

The researcher also may incorporate ideas from a source, forgetting their origin. Whorton's statement that health reformers like Graham predicted the adulteration of food should be acknowledged even if Whorton is not quoted.

You can avoid this kind of plagiarism through a careful proofreading of your notes at the time you write them. A final check is essential when you complete your writing of the paper. The best check is to take care in distinguishing direct quotation from paraphrase.

#### EXERCISES

1. Write a notecard that records the essential facts and quotes at least one important phrase from the following paragraph:

> Language is, of course, basically a medium of com-
> munication. To be an adequate medium, language must
> be flexible. But to be flexible is one thing; to be entirely
> elastic and malleable is another. These other two char-
> acteristics, extreme elasticity and malleability, are re-
> quired from the language which is set to infiltrate peo-
> ple's minds and contaminate their mental habits. It is in
> this latter capacity that admen want to employ language.
> And consequently, they do everything conceivable, and
> sometimes inconceivable, to make language infinitely
> flexible and as malleable as plasticene.
>
> —HENRYK SKOLIMOWSKI, "The Semantic
> Environment in the Age of Advertising"

**37.3**

**doc**

2. Write a paraphrase of the paragraph, retaining only the
   essential ideas. Then write a brief summary.
3. Copy the paragraph, omitting all nonessential or nonrestrictive words, phrases, or clauses. Be ready to justify your omissions.

# 37.4 Writing and Revision

**37.4a Outline and First Draft.**    Once you have made notes
on your sources, plan your essay. You may find a scratch outline
sufficient, or you may want to work out the ideas in a topic or
sentence outline.

An outline provides an opportunity to consider the relative
weight of your ideas and details—to decide, in other words, what
ideas to stress and what ideas and details to subordinate. As with
outlines for other kinds of papers, consider the outline for your
documented paper as a tentative plan—a working out of ideas
that does not bind you to one way of writing the paper. In the
course of writing, you may decide to change the order of ideas
or their relative weight. You will also discover alternative ways
to use evidence recorded in your notes; a quotation or idea in
paraphrase may give better support to one point you wish to
make than to another. Keep in mind these various alternatives.

You probably jotted down in your notebook or on the notecards possible uses to which your evidence could be put as you
took notes on your reading; these notes can be of immense use
in recalling the context of the note. Before writing the draft,
read through your notes and jottings to become familiar with
the ideas and details. The more familiar you are with these
materials, the more ideas and details will fall into place as you
write.

Here is an opportunity to consider your thesis. Your evidence will have suggested many ideas. Jotting these down in
your notes or on the reverse side of your notecards, as they
occur to you, will prove valuable later. One of these ideas may
help you to guide your further research and thought.

Like your outline, the first draft is a trying out of your
ideas—a thinking through of the evidence and ideas of the paper. The act of writing can be an act of discovery. Though you
have given considerable thought to the evidence, the act of stating these ideas probably will suggest connections and possibilities that did not occur to you at the start of your investigation.
Changes in focus, emphasis, and subject often occur through
the stages of prewriting, writing, and later revision.

**37.4**
**rev**

**37.4b Strategies of Revision.** As new possibilities arise, you may need to do further reading and note taking. Problems in interpretation often appear for the first time when you try to use a passage to support an idea of the paper. You may discover that interpretation of the passage depends on a missing context—on facts that you had no reason to investigate in paraphrasing or quoting the passage. The missing context may have to do with special meanings that require a historical dictionary. You may need facts that explain a procedure that seemed clear to you when you wrote the note but is not clear when you try to explain the passage in the paper.

In reading your first draft, you will discover points that need development through additional details and facts. You will also discover points that you have overdeveloped. Indeed, you will probably find in the draft more ideas that need cutting than ideas that need expansion. The reason is that you will collect more material in your research than you need to develop your final thesis. Of course, you will not know how much of this material you do need until you have in mind a final thesis and organization of ideas. Few writers like to cut ideas and details from a paper—particularly ideas and details gathered painstakingly. But your paper will be greatly strengthened if you aim for economy of explanation and illustration.

## Checklist for Sources and Notes

**37.1a** Use primary sources—accounts of events by people who participated in them—to verify other sources.

**37.1b** Use secondary sources, which discuss eyewitness and other primary evidence, to authenticate and interpret your primary sources.

**37.2** The following are standard bibliography entries:

> Carnes, Valerie. "The Language of Nowspeak." *The New Humanities: Culture, Crisis, Change*. Ed. Ralph L. Carnes and Valerie Carnes. New York: Holt, 1972: 219–44.
> Kintgen, Eugene R., and Norman N. Holland. "Carlos Reads a Poem." *College English* 46 (1984): 478-492.

**37.3a** In your notes record details and their context in a form useful to you later.

**37.3b** Quote accurately and don't confuse quotation with paraphrase.

37.4
rev

**37.3c**   Use paraphrase or summary to record the sense of the original, and use direct quotation when the wording is highly significant or its nuance or special accent cannot be paraphrased.

**37.3d**   Use ellipsis—a series of three spaced periods—to mark the omission of nonessential words, phrases, and clauses:

> . . . the decadence of our language is probably curable. Those who deny this would argue . . . that language merely reflects existing social conditions, and that we cannot influence its development by any direct tinkering with words and constructions.

**37.3e**   Put your own explanatory information and comments and quotations within brackets:

> Smith states, "The two are alien [*sic*] in their thinking."

**37.3f**   Don't appropriate the words or ideas of another writer without acknowledgment. Proofread your notes to avoid unintentional plagiarism.

**37.4a**   Use your outline and draft to try out the ideas of the paper and test the relative weight of these ideas and details.

**37.4b**   In revising the draft, expand ideas with necessary background and details. Cut ideas and details that don't develop your final thesis.

# Documenting the Paper

This chapter describes traditional methods of documentation through footnotes and endnotes. It also describes the documentation recommended by the Modern Language Association and the American Psychological Association. The purpose of documentation is to identify the source materials completely and accurately. To help the reader verify the information of the essay or article, the writer provides specific information about editions, revisions, and reprints, and other details necessary to locate the sources used.

## 38.1 Footnotes and Endnotes

**38.1a What to Document.** Document all quotations, paraphrases, and ideas that you take from a source. These include the interpretation of evidence of a writer you consulted. Do not document common facts—for example, that cholera is a bacterial disease—familiar quotations (Patrick Henry's "Give me liberty or give me death!"), or familiar proverbs. Do document theoretical definitions of the author on the origin and development of the disease.

**38.1b Note Form and Logic.** The traditional method of documentation gives the sources of all direct quotations and extensive paraphrases in notes at the foot of the page or at the end of the paper. If your instructor asks you to use this method, number the citations consecutively throughout. Your notes may also contain parenthetical comments and ideas suggested by the material but not strictly relevant to the discussion. You should use notes of this sort sparingly. If the addition is important enough to develop at length in the note, it probably belongs in the paper.

Following is the basic note form used for books:

[1]Jacques Barzun, <u>Simple and Direct: A Rhetoric for
Writers</u> (New York: Harper, 1976) 55.

The note for a book follows these conventions:
1. The footnote begins with a raised number.
2. The first line is indented five spaces.
3. The name of the author is given exactly as it appears on the title page. If the initial letter of the first name is given and you must give the whole first name to avoid confusion with another author, the omitted letters appear in brackets:

J[acob] Bronowski

4. The title and subtitle are capitalized and underlined in typing. A colon separates the subtitle from the title.
5. The edition and the series, if any, are given exactly as they appear on the title or the copyright page.
6. If the title page lists more than one place of publication, the first city or place is given, not all. If two publishers are listed, both are given.
7. The name of the publisher may be abbreviated; for example, *MLA*, though *Modern Language Association* appears on the title page of the *MLA Handbook for Writers of Research Papers*. *Harper* is sufficient in identifying *Harper & Row*. Cite university presses as follows:

Princeton UP
U of Michigan P

8. Give volume numbers in arabic numerals. See the following on the placing of the number for a single volume in a multivolumed work, published in different years.
9. The abbreviation *Vol.* is included but *p.* and *pp.* to indicate pages are omitted (see the following).
10. Abbreviations are used as follows:

anon. [anonymous author]
app. [appendix]
c. ["c. 1546": *circa* or about 1546]
comp. [compiler]
diss. [dissertation]
ed. [edition, editor, edited by]
et al. [Latin *et alii*: and others]
fig. [figure]
illus. [illustrator, illustration]

**38.1**
**doc**

inc. [including]
introd. [introduction]
ms., mss. [manuscript, manuscripts]
n.d. [no date of publication given]
n.p. [no place of publication given, no publisher]
no. [number]
n. pag. [no pagination]
p., pp. [page, pages]
pseud. [pseudonym]
rept. [reprint]
rev. [revised, revised by]
sec., secs. [section, sections]
trans. [translator]
U [university]
UP [university press]
vol., vols. [volume, volumes]

The following illustrates the basic note form used for articles:

> ¹Robert Allan Phillips, "Asiatic Cholera," <u>Annual Review of Medicine</u> 19 (1968): 70.

1. The footnote begins with a raised number.
2. The first line is indented five spaces.
3. The name of the author is given exactly as it appears on the first page of the article. The stipulations about first names of book authors govern articles.
4. The title of the article appears in quotation marks. The title of the journal is underlined in typing.
5. Volume numbers of journals are given in arabic numerals immediately following the title as shown.
6. Page numbers follow the year of publication (given in parentheses) and a colon as shown above. The abbreviations *p.* and *pp.* to indicate pages are omitted (see the following).

**38.1**
**doc**

**38.1c Sample Notes.** Following are sample notes and comments on the documentation.

**Multivolume Work Published in the Same Year**
Put the volume number in arabic numerals following city, publisher, and date:

> ¹Edgar Johnson, <u>Charles Dickens: His Tragedy and Triumph</u>, 2 vols. (New York: Simon, 1952) 1: 457–58.

### Multivolume Work Published in Different Years
Put the volume number before the city, publisher, and date:

> ¹Will Durant, <u>The Renaissance</u> vol. 5 of <u>The Story</u>
> <u>of Civilization</u> (New York: Simon, 1953) 42.
> ¹Will Durant and Ariel Durant, <u>The Age of Napo-</u>
> <u>leon</u> vol. 11 of <u>The Story of Civilization</u>. (New York:
> Simon, 1975) 135–36.

Information on the publishing history of *The Story of Civilization*
appears in the bibliography. See 38.2.

### Translation
> ¹Aleksandr I. Solzhenitsyn, <u>The Gulag Archipelago</u>
> <u>1918–1956: An Experiment in Literary Investigation,</u>
> <u>I–II</u>, trans. Thomas P. Whitney (New York: Harper, 1973)
> 99–100.

Note that the given name *Aleksandr* appears on the title page.
Some books of Solzhenitsyn spell the name *Alexander*.

### Multiple Authors or Editors up to Three
> ¹John E. Gedo and Arnold Goldberg, <u>Models of the</u>
> <u>Mind: A Psychoanalytic Theory</u> (Chicago: U of Chicago P,
> 1973) 86.
> ¹Robert P. Stockwell, Paul Schachter, and Barbara
> Hall Partee, <u>The Major Syntactic Structures of English</u>
> (New York: Holt, 1973) 106.

**38.1**
**doc**

### More Than Three Multiple Authors or Editors
Only the first given on the title page is named:

> ¹Arthur M. Eastman, et al., eds., <u>The Norton</u>
> <u>Reader: An Anthology of Expository Prose</u>, 5th ed. (New
> York: Norton, 1980) 310.

### Editor
The name of the editor usually follows author and title:

> ¹Sigmund Freud, <u>Psychopathology of Everyday Life</u>,
> vol. 5 of <u>The Standard Edition of the Complete Psycho-</u>

logical Works, ed. James Strachey (London: Hogarth, 1960) 78–79.

### Multiple Publishers

[1]S. Schoenbaum, Shakespeare's Lives (Oxford: Clarendon Press; New York: Oxford UP, 1970) 226–27.

### Corporate Author

[1]Internal Revenue Service, Your Federal Income Tax, rev. Oct. 83 (Washington: Dept. of the Treasury, 1983) 77.

The title is sufficient if it includes the corporate author:

[1]Freedom and Discipline in English: Report of the Commission on Education (New York: College Entrance Examination Board, 1965) 26.

### Republished Book

The date of a republished book follows the title:

[1]James Baldwin, Notes of a Native Son (1955; New York: Bantam, 1968) 128.

### Book Published Before 1900

A book published before 1900 does not require the publisher:

[1]A. Brigham, A Treatise on Epidemic Cholera (Hartford, 1832) 14.

**38.1**
**doc**

### Play, Poem, Story, or Essay in a Collection by Same Writer

[1]Bernard Shaw, The Doctor's Dilemma, Complete Plays with Prefaces, 6 vols. (New York: Dodd, 1963) 1: 87.

### Play, Poem, Story, or Essay in Anthology or Collection

[1]Erwin H. Ackerknecht, "Paleopathology," Culture, Disease, and Healing: Studies in Medical Anthropology, ed. David Landy (New York: Macmillan, 1977) 75.

### Preface, Introduction, Foreword, Afterword, Intervening Note, or Comment

[1]Mark Schorer, afterword, <u>Main Street</u>, by Sinclair Lewis (New York: Signet-NAL, 1961) 435.

### Journal Article

[1]John H. Knowles, "The Responsibility of the Individual," <u>Daedalus</u> 106 (1977): 58.

### Newspaper or Magazine Article

[1]Calvin Trillin, "Harvard Law," <u>The New Yorker</u> 26 March 1984: 59. [weekly magazine]

[1]Susan West, "The Salt Shake-Up," <u>Science 84</u> Sept. 1984: 16. [monthly magazine]

[1]James Reston, "Amid Riches, Too Much Poverty," <u>Akron Beacon Journal</u> 22 Nov. 1984, Sec. A: 7. [signed newspaper article]

[1]"Helping Kids Survive," editorial, <u>Akron Beacon Journal</u> 22 Nov. 1984, Sec. A: 6. [editorial]

### Letters

[1]Virginia Woolf, "To Quentin Bell," 17 Feb. 1930, letter 2145 of <u>The Letters of Virginia Woolf</u>, ed. Nigel Nicolson and Joanne Trautmann, 5 vols. (New York: Harcourt, 1979) 4: 141.

### Musical Compositions, Recordings, Works of Art

[1]Hector Berlioz, Fantastic Symphony, op. 14.

[1]Robert Schumann, Symphony no. 3 in E flat, "Rhenish," op. 97, cond. Daniel Barenboim, Chicago Symphony Orchestra, Deutsche Grammophon, 2543504.

[1]William Turner, <u>The Shipwreck</u>, Tate Gallery, London.

### Interview

[1]President John Smith, personal interview, Washington College, 18 May 1984.

**38.1**
**doc**

*Encyclopedia and Reference Articles*

[1]Paul Bernays, "David Hilbert," <u>The Encyclopedia of Philosophy</u> 3: 500.

[1]"Plato," <u>Encyclopaedia Britannica</u>, 1974 ed.

[1]"Slavery," <u>Encyclopedia of Black America</u>, 1981.

**38.1d Successive References.** Successive references in footnotes or endnotes no longer require Latin abbreviations (*ibid.*, for the work cited in the preceding note; *op. cit.* for the work cited in an earlier note; *loc. cit.* for the place cited). The name of the author and the work are given in the shortest form possible. Here is the first reference to a book on the 1832 cholera epidemic in England:

[1]Robert John Morris, <u>Cholera 1832: The Social Response to an Epidemic</u> (New York: Holmes, 1976) 84.

The succeeding note refers to the book by author and page:

[2]Morris 86.

If different writers with the same last name (Richard Morris and Robert John Morris) are cited in the text, the succeeding note refers to the book by the author's full name and the page:

[3]Richard Morris, <u>Dismantling tho Universe: The Nature of Scientific Discovery</u> (New York: Simon, 1983) 114.

[4]Robert John Morris 86.

[5]Richard Morris 178.

If you cite different works by the same author, give the author's last name and a short title in succeeding references:

[6]Lewis Thomas, <u>The Medusa and the Snail: More Notes of a Biology Watcher</u> (New York: Viking, 1979) 40.

[7]Lewis Thomas, <u>The Youngest Science: Notes of a Medicine-Watcher</u> (New York: Viking, 1983) 134–35.

[8]Thomas, <u>Medusa</u> 42.

[9]Thomas, <u>Youngest Science</u> 136.

**38.1**
doc

Notice that you repeat the full name of Lewis Thomas in the first citation.

## 38.2  Bibliography

In a paper using footnotes or endnotes, a separate and complete bibliography appears at the end. As with the following Durant entry, it may give additional information. Bibliography entries differ from note entries in the following ways:

1. The first line begins with the author's first and last names at the far left margin. Subsequent lines are indented five spaces.
2. The title of a selection (essay, journal article) is separated from the complete work with a period.
3. The title is set off with a period from what follows.
4. Information on the editor or translator is set off with a period from what follows.
5. The information on city, publisher, and date does not appear in parentheses.
6. Three hyphens and a period substitute for the name of the author in subsequent references (see the following entries on Selzer, Solzhenitsyn, and Thomas).

Following is a sample bibliography:

Ackerknecht, Erwin H. "Paleopathology." <u>Culture, Disease, and Healing: Studies in Medical Anthropology</u>. Ed. David Landy. New York: Macmillan, 1977. 72-77.

Baldwin, James. <u>Notes of a Native Son</u>. 1955. New York: Bantam, 1968.

Durant, Will, and Ariel Durant. <u>The Story of Civilization</u>. 11 vols. New York: Simon, 1935-75.

<u>Freedom and Discipline in English: Report of the Commission on English</u>. New York: College Entrance Examination Board, 1965.

Gedo, John E., and Arnold Goldberg. <u>Models of the Mind: A Psychoanalytic Theory</u>. Chicago: U of Chicago P, 1973.

Johnson, E. D. H. <u>The Alien Vision of Victorian Poetry: Sources of the Poetic Imagination in Tennyson, Browning, and Arnold</u>. Princeton Studies in English 34. Princeton: Princeton UP, 1952.

**38.2**
**doc**

Johnson, Edgar. <u>Charles Dickens: His Tragedy and</u>
<u>Triumph</u>. 2 vols. New York: Simon, 1952.

Knowles, John H. "The Responsibility of the Individual." <u>Daedalus</u> 106 (1977): 57–80.

Selzer, Richard. <u>Mortal Lessons: Notes on the Art of</u>
<u>Surgery</u>. New York: Simon, 1976.

- - -. <u>Rituals of Surgery</u>. New York: Simon, 1974.

Shaw, Bernard. <u>The Doctor's Dilemma</u>. In Vol. 1 of <u>Com-</u>
<u>plete Plays with Prefaces</u>. 6 vols. New York: Dodd,
1963.

Solzhenitsyn, Aleksandr I. <u>The Gulag Archipelago 1918–</u>
<u>1956: An Experiment in Literary Investigation, I–</u>
<u>II</u>. Trans. Thomas P. Whitney. New York: Harper,
1973.

- - -. <u>The Oak and the Calf: A Memoir</u>. Trans. Harry
Willetts. New York: Harper, 1981.

Stockwell, Robert P. <u>Foundations of Syntactic Theory</u>.
Englewood Cliffs, N.J.: Prentice, 1977.

Stockwell, Robert P., Paul Schachter, and Barbara Hall
Partee, <u>The Major Syntactic Structures of English</u>.
New York: Holt, 1973.

[Stockwell's name is repeated because he is not the only author.]

Thomas, Lewis. <u>The Medusa and the Snail: More Notes of</u>
<u>a Biology Watcher</u>. New York: Viking, 1979.

- - -. <u>The Youngest Science: Notes of a Medicine-</u>
<u>Watcher</u>. New York: Viking, 1983.

Trillin, Calvin. "A Reporter at Large: Kansas City,
Mo." <u>The New Yorker</u> 26 Sept. 1983: 57+.

**38.2**
**doc**

[The paging of the Knowles article in *Daedalus* is continuous; the paging of the Trillin *New Yorker* report is discontinuous.]

This bibliography mixes books, journal articles, and reference articles. If your bibliography contains a large number of titles, you can divide articles and books into separate groups. Some bibliographies divide entries according to a topic or period. See the *MLA Handbook for Writers of Research Papers*, 2nd edition, for other rules and sample entries for footnotes and bibliography.

**EXERCISE**

Write a series of footnotes citing the works in the bibliography on pages 580–581. Use the footnote form described in 38.1c.
1. Reference to p. 47 of Shaw's *The Doctor's Dilemma*.
2. Reference to p. 72 of the same work.
3. Reference to p. 14 of *Mortal Lessons*.
4. Reference to p. 16 of the same work.
5. Reference to p. 11 of *Rituals of Surgery*.
6. Reference to p. 12 of the same work.
7. Reference to p. 100 of *Mortal Lessons*.
8. Reference to p. 97 of Trillin's report.
9. Reference to p. 58 of Knowles's article.
10. Reference to p. 99 of *The Doctor's Dilemma*.

# **38.3**   Citations in the Text

The following method of documenting the paper is the one recommended in the *MLA Handbook for Writers of Research Papers*, 2nd ed. (New York: Modern Language Association, 1984). This alternate method dispenses with footnotes or endnotes for citations and instead includes citations in the text to the bibliography (38.1c). Citations to these sources appear in the text in as concise a form as possible. Footnotes or endnotes contain additional facts or parenthetical comments of the author.

Assume that your bibliography contains the following entries to works by Lewis Thomas:

Thomas, Lewis. The Medusa and the Snail: More Notes of
    a Biology Watcher. New York: Viking, 1979.
- - -. The Youngest Science: Notes of a Medicine-
    Watcher. New York: Viking, 1983.

**38.3**

**doc**

References to statements in an essay in *Medusa* and in *The Youngest Science* can be cited in two ways in the text:

In his essay "Medical Lessons from History," Lewis
Thomas states that the nineteenth-century doctor "could
be depended on to explain things, to relieve anxieties,
and to be on hand" (Medusa 135). Thomas's father was
such a doctor, he shows in The Youngest Science (1-11).

```
Thomas states that the nineteenth-century doctor "could
be depended on to explain things, to relieve anxieties,
and to be on hand" ("Medical Lessons from History," Me-
dusa 135). Thomas's father was such a doctor: "[T]here
were so many people needing help," his father told him,
"and so little that he could do for any of them"
(Youngest Science 13).
```

Since the reader will find the full citations in the bibliography, no other information need be included in the note.

If only one work of Thomas is cited, the note may refer to his name rather than to *The Medusa and the Snail*:

```
Fifty years of intense research led to the discovery of
antibiotics and other important drugs (Thomas 135).
```

If an article in a reference book is cited—encyclopedia article, for example—only the author or the title of the article need be given:

```
David Hilbert asked questions that created modern math-
ematics (Bernays).
```

The documented essay in Chapter 39 (pp. 619–622) illustrates this method of documentation.

## 38.4 APA Documentation

The publication manual of the American Psychological Association uses the following method of documentation.

The bibliography of the documented paper in psychology (and other fields using APA documentation) contains the following entries:

**38.4**
**doc**

```
Fenichel, O. (1945). The psychoanalytic theory of neu-
rosis. New York: Norton.
Gedo, J. E., & Goldberg, A. (1973). Models of the mind:
a psychoanalytic theory. Chicago: University of
Chicago Press.
```

Edgerton, R. B. (1966). A traditional African psychiatrist. <u>Southwestern Journal of Anthropology</u>, <u>27</u>,
259–278.

Citations to these sources appear in the text as follows:

Gedo and Goldberg (1973) state that "each of the existing models of the mind is relevant to a different set
of clinical situations...." (p. 172).

The standard psychoanalytic discussion of the Freudian
superego focuses on the phenomenon of projection—the
patient's belief that outside forces are trying to control or criticize him (Fenichel, 1945, p. 430).

**EXERCISES**

Use APA documentation to give information in the bibliography and in the text about the following book. The first quotation appears on p. 3, the second quotation on p. 4.

Author: Paul Starr
Title of book: *The Social Transformation of American Medicine*
Publisher, city, date: Basic Books, New York, 1982
Text:
Paul Starr begins his book on American medicine
with a general characterization: "Modern medicine is one
of those extraordinary works of reason: an elaborate
system of specialized knowledge, technical procedures,
and rules of behavior." For this reason, "The medical
profession has had an especially persuasive claim to authority."

**38.5**
**ms**

# 38.5  Mechanics of the Paper

Before typing your documented paper, ask your instructor
for instructions on its preparation. In your English courses, you
probably will be asked to follow the *MLA Handbook for Writers of
Research Papers*, 2nd edition (1984) or *The Chicago Manual of
Style*. The following recommendations are mainly those of the
*MLA Handbook*, 2nd edition for documented papers. They dupli-
cate in many details the recommendations for course papers
summarized in 15.4.

**38.5a  Paper and Typing Materials.**  Use twenty-pound bond paper, 8½ by 11 inches. Sixteen-pound paper does not take erasures well. Do not use "erasable" paper because it cannot be corrected in ink. Type on one side of the page only, and use a new ribbon.

If you write your paper by hand, use regularly lined paper without holes in the left-hand margin; narrowly lined paper is difficult to read and correct. Don't use "erasable" paper or sheets torn from a spiral notebook. Write in ink, not pencil.

If you use a word processor, use the same paper as in typing. Though dot matrix printers often approach typed pages in the quality of printing, many print indistinctly. A letter-quality printer is the better printer usually for college and business papers.

**38.5b  Line Spacing.**  Double-space the text of a typed paper, indented quotations, and indented lines of poetry. If you are writing the paper by hand, ask your instructor about the spacing.

**38.5c  Margins and Titles.**  Leave margins of 1 inch at the left and at the right of the page, and at the top and bottom. Word processors permit you to "justify" the right-hand margin (that is, align it evenly). This justification is undesirable if it makes the spacing between letters and words uneven. Some word processors allow proportional spacing.

The title should be centered 1½ inches from the top of the page. Skip an extra line between the title and the first line of the text. The title is not followed by a period, is not put in quotation marks, and is not printed in capitals or italicized. In the upper left-hand corner of the first page of an essay or report, put your name, the title of the course, the date, and the name of your instructor. Your instructor may specify a separate title page for your paper. See p. 266 for a sample.

Indent your paragraphs five spaces from the left-hand margin. Block quotations are indented ten spaces as follows:

**38.5**

**ms**

> The biographer of George III, John Brooke, states his purpose in writing and describes his audience in these words:
>
> > I have written this book for the average man not for the scholar, for those who take their ideas of history from illustrated magazines and television programs rather than from the English

<u>Historical Review</u>. I believe it is both possible
and desirable to write history as Gibbon and Ma-
caulay wrote it: so that the average man will understand it and the learned man will not despise
it. This is what I have tried to do. Notes and
references which are of interest only to the
scholar are reserved for appendices. I have followed my invariable practice of going to original
sources as much as possible, but like all scholars I am indebted to the work of my predecessors.
I hope I have made proper acknowledgments to both
the living and the dead. (<u>King George III</u> 20)

If the block quotation contains several paragraphs, indent each
new paragraph of the quotation five spaces.

**38.5d Numbering of Pages.**   Place the page number in the
upper right-hand corner of each page except the first, a half
inch above the first line, and aligned with the right-hand margin
as accurately as possible. You may also put your last name before
the number of each page.

**38.5e Word Spacing and Word Breaks.**   Space once after
commas, colons, and semicolons, and space twice after periods,
question marks, and exclamation points.

Distinguish between the hyphen and the dash, using two
hyphens to make the dash. If your typewriter does not print
brackets, leave space to enter these and other symbols with ink.

Divide words at the syllable break. Use your dictionary to
check the syllabification if in doubt. Do not break a one-syllable
word or break a single letter or the last two letters from the rest
of the word. Break hyphenated words at the syllable only. The
following breaks are incorrect:

| a-bout | happen-ed |
| deal-t | step-fath-er |

Try not to break the last word on the page, and never begin
a line with a final bracket, final parenthesis mark, comma, semicolon, or any other punctuation mark.

**38.5**

**ms**

**38.5f Corrections.** Make corrections neatly above the line, using a caret if you are making an addition:

*Faulkner*
I have a book by on the shelf.
   ∧

Short phrases may be added, but retype or rewrite the page if the addition is extensive.

See 15.1 on capitalization, 14.3 on italics, and 15.3 on abbreviations in the text.

**38.5g Proofreading.** The earlier advice given on proofreading course papers (see 15.5) is applicable to documented papers. Proofread carefully for mistakes in content and mechanics—misstatements, misspellings, sentence fragments, run-on sentences, misused commas and semicolons, and the like.

Probably no advice is more needed and is more ignored, for the prospect of rewriting or retyping a page is not a happy one. It is nevertheless a job that you must do with care. Though all of us quickly spot errors and misprints in the writing of others, we often have trouble spotting our own. In proofreading, try to look at the words as words but don't lose track of the content.

# Checklist for Documenting the Paper

**38.1a**  Document all direct quotations and paraphrases in footnotes or endnotes.

**38.1b-c**  The following are standard note forms:

[1]Jacques Barzun, <u>Simple and Direct: A Rhetoric for Writers</u> (New York: Harper, 1976) 55.

[1]Will Durant, <u>The Renaissance</u> vol. 5 of <u>The Story of Civilization</u> (New York: Simon, 1953) 166.

[1]Robert Allan Phillips, "Asiatic Cholera," <u>Annual Review of Medicine</u> 19 (1968): 70.

**38.5**
**ms**

Use footnotes or endnotes also for additional facts and parenthetical comments of your own.

**38.1d**  In successive references give the name of the author and the title of the work in the shortest form possible:

Barzun 55.

If you are citing different works of the same writer, give the author's last name and the title in shortened form:

```
Barzun, Simple and Direct 55.
```

**38.2**  The following entries appear in a separate and complete bibliography in papers that use footnotes or endnotes:

```
Barzun, Jacques. Simple and Direct: A Rhetoric for
    Writers. New York: Harper, 1976.
Durant, Will. The Renaissance. Vol. 5 of The Story of
    Civilization. New York: Simon, 1953.
Phillips, Robert Allan. "Asiatic Cholera." Annual Re-
    view of Medicine 19 (1968): 69–80.
```

**38.3**  Citations can be included in the text in place of footnotes and endnotes:

```
Fifty years of intense research led to the discovery of
antibiotics and other important drugs (Thomas 135).
```

The sources appear in a bibliography at the end of the paper:

```
Thomas, Lewis. The Medusa and the Snail: More Notes of
    a Biology Watcher. New York: Viking, 1979.
```

**38.4**  APA style includes citations in the text and uses the following bibliographic entry:

```
Gedo, J. E., & Goldberg, A. (1973) Models of the mind:
    a psychoanalytic theory. Chicago: University of
    Chicago Press.
```

*Text*
```
Gedo and Goldberg (1973) present a revised theory of mind.
```

# Writing a
# Documented Paper

This chapter traces the writing of a documented paper from prewriting to the final draft. In doing so, it illustrates the process described in the previous chapters. The chapter concludes with paragraphs from the early drafts and then the completed paper, including the footnotes and bibliography.

## 39.1  Prewriting

**39.1a  Topics Suggested by Reading.**   In his play *The Doctor's Dilemma* (1904), and in the long preface he wrote in 1911, George Bernard Shaw gives an unflattering picture of English doctors as a class. He shows us a profession respectful of science yet ignorant of it, a profession protective of its incompetent members. For example, the doctors in Shaw's play charge large fees for removing nonexistent organs, misapply the discoveries of medical science, and protect one another from public exposure.

Shaw tells us in the preface that there are a "few intelligent doctors who point out rightly that all treatments are experiments on the patient." Most doctors are not men of science, and most "have no honor and no conscience: what they commonly mistake for these is sentimentality and an intense dread of doing anything that everybody else does not do, or omitting to do anything that everybody else does."

A reading of Shaw's play and preface and later class discussion suggest the following questions:

> How true a picture of the nineteenth- and the early twentieth-century doctor does Shaw give?

How much of the picture is descriptive, drawing on Shaw's own experience with doctors and his attitudes and beliefs—for example his belief that doctoring "is an art, not a science"?

How much did doctors in the nineteenth century know about medical science and the causes of disease?

Shaw says in the preface that doctoring "is not even the art of keeping people in health. . . ." It is "the art of curing illnesses." How did doctors try to cure illnesses? Were they unconcerned about preventing illness?

**39.1b  The Purpose of the Investigation.**    Assume that a student decides to make Shaw's play the basis of a documented paper. Investigating the medical backgrounds would help to define Shaw's intention in the play. Did Shaw write *The Doctor's Dilemma* to entertain us with a humorous picture of doctors his audience knew was exaggerated? Or did he write as a satirist, eager to reform medicine through a humorous but truthful picture of doctors in his time?

A broader investigation might focus on nineteenth-century medicine—perhaps through one of Shaw's controversial statements in the preface. Such an investigation might focus more narrowly on ideas about disease and its treatment. One of the benefits of such a study could be insight into some aspect of medicine today.

The more exactly the student defines her purpose, the easier it is to select a subject. Listing questions and possible subjects proves indispensable; so do the ideas jotted down in the course of reading the play.

The student decides to focus her study on nineteenth-century medicine—specifically, on what knowledge of disease doctors used in treating patients. Perhaps knowing the facts of medical practice in the nineteenth century will help to test the popular belief that doctors before the advent of medical science were more caring of patients, even those they could not cure, and depended on knowledge of illness gained from day-to-day experience. Shaw suggests in the play that the best doctors in his time relied on practical experience rather than on instruments and questionable scientific theory. Here is a possible lead to a limiting of the subject.

**39.1**

**dev**

**39.1c  Limiting the Subject.**    The subject proposed is clearly too broad. How limited should the investigation be? The limitation depends both on the length of the paper assigned and on the availability of materials for study.

A broad investigation of nineteenth-century medical practice requires information on a wide range of topics. Getting adequate materials will obviously be difficult. Perhaps investigation of a single nineteenth-century doctor, if documents for such a study exist, would reveal the extent to which one doctor depended on knowledge acquired from daily experience, scientific theory, and instrumentation in diagnosing and treating illness. If no materials for this study are available, perhaps a study of how various doctors treated a specific disease would be possible. It might also support a broader generalization. But the student will need a representative sample of medical accounts describing the treatment of a specific disease.

To discover what materials are available, she examines the subject catalog in the college library and searches the periodicals file. In doing so, she finds that the college library contains a few general reference works on nineteenth-century medicine but no specific books on nineteenth-century medical practice or the treatment of disease, and no current medical periodicals. However, a nearby medical library does contain materials that will be of use.

**39.1d Choosing a Focus.**   The broad topic the student chooses is the history of cholera in England: its first appearance in England in 1832 and its spread to the United States, later epidemics during the nineteenth century, the medical response to a disease unknown to many doctors, prevailing theories and growing scientific knowledge about cholera.

So broad a focus needs to be narrowed—possibly to the treatment of cholera in England and the United States chiefly in 1832 and in later epidemic years. The focus can be narrowed further—to theories of cholera in light of scientific knowledge at the time. Information on the cholera epidemics is essential— a basis for understanding the medical treatment.

This limited topic is a good choice for these reasons:

**39.1**
**dev**

Source materials on cholera and its treatment are available— specifically, reputable studies of the history of cholera in England and first-hand accounts by scientists and medical doctors.

These source materials do not demand special medical knowledge for their interpretation.

Reliable secondary sources exist to help in interpreting this primary evidence—the writings of doctors and observers in 1832 and 1848.

A study of medical views of cholera in these epidemic years is broad enough to support a generalization about nineteenth-century medical practice.

In choosing her topic, the student knows that her findings cannot be conclusive. At best she can reach a limited understanding of the thinking of the nineteenth-century doctor, and she can try to make a limited judgment on Shaw's view of the doctor, though Shaw has now become a subordinate concern. A study reaching broader conclusions and judgments requires more source material than is available, and requires greater competence in the interpretation of medical evidence.

**39.1e Compiling a Bibliography.**    To compile a bibliography, the student first searches reference books for contemporary articles on what medical science knows today about cholera. Figure 39.1 shows typical listings in two of the indexes consulted—*Reader's Guide to Periodical Literature* and *Social Sciences Index*. Figure 39.2 shows the listing of articles on cholera in the specialized *Index Medicus*.

The reference section of the college library includes several general books describing cholera—the most important of these, Wyngaarden and Smith, *Textbook of Medicine*, 17th edition. The subject catalog of the medical library contains these titles:

> Robert John Morris. *Cholera 1832: The Social Response to an Epidemic*. New York: Holmes and Meier, 1976.
> Margaret Pelling. *Cholera, Fever and English Medicine: 1825-1865*. London: Oxford University Press, 1978.
> R. Pollitzer. *Cholera*. Geneva: World Health Organization, 1959.

Studies of cholera usually contain valuable bibliographies of primary and other secondary sources. Through these books and the subject catalog of the medical library, the student locates first-hand accounts of cholera—several of them published in 1832. Here are two:

> A. Brigham, *A Treatise on Epidemic Cholera*. Hartford, 1832.
> John Lizars, *Substance of the Investigations Regarding Cholera Asphyxia in 1832*, 2nd edition. Edinburgh, 1848.

**39.1**

**dev**

The subject catalog of the college library contains a source book of medical history. One of the primary sources included in the book is the major scientific work on cholera in the nineteenth century, John Snow's *On the Mode of Communication of Cholera*. This work, published in 1854, seems indispensable to the investigation.

Finding articles in nineteenth-century periodicals proves more difficult. The student finds a listing of articles in *Poole's Index to Periodical Literature, 1801–1907* and in *Palmer's Index to the [London] Times*. The indexes to *Lancet*, a leading medical journal of

## FIGURE 39.1

**READERS' GUIDE TO PERIODICAL LITERATURE**
December 25, 1985

**Drug abuse**
    *See also*
      Alcoholics and alcoholism
      Cocaine
      Drugs and sports
      Drugs and youth
      Marijuana
This is what you thought: 47% say spend more to fight
  drug abuse [results of survey] *Glamour* 83:43 O '85
         **Conferences**
30 first ladies discuss countries' drug problems. il por
  *Jet* 69:8 N 11 '85
**Drug addicts** *See* Drug abuse
**Drug control** *See* Narcotics laws and regulations
**Drug delivery systems in the body** *See* Drugs—Dosage
  forms
**Drug industry**
    *See also*
      Plough, Inc.
**Drug laws and regulations**
    *See also*
      Narcotics laws and regulations
      United States. Food and Drug Administration
**Drug plants** *See* Botany, Medical
**Drug research** *See* Pharmaceutical research
**Drug stores** *See* Drugstores
**Drugs**
    *See also*
      Botany, Medical
      United States. Food and Drug Administration
    *See also* names of drugs
101 prescription drugs—and how to buy them for less
  [excerpt from The people's pharmacy] J. Graedon. il
  *Good Housekeep* 201:138-9 O '85
        **Dosage forms**
    *See also*
      Ointments
Patchwork medicine [transdermal patches] L. Gourse.
  il *Sci 85* 6:79+ O '85
        **Research**
    *See* Pharmaceutical research
        **Testing**
    *See* Pharmaceutical research
**Drugs and children** *See* Drugs and youth

**SOCIAL SCIENCES INDEX**
December 1985

**Money**
    *See also*
      Bank deposits
      Banks and banking
      Barter
      Capital
      Coinage
      Counterfeits and counterfeiting
      Credit
      Demand for money
      Exchange
      Gold
      Inflation (Finance)
      Interest
      Interest rate
      Laundering of money
      Monetary policy
      Money market
      Money supply
      Prices
      Purchasing power
      Wealth
Hamlet without the Prince: Cambridge macroeconomics
  without money. J. A. Kregel. bibl *Am Econ Rev* 75:133-9
  My '85
Money, prices, and the current account in a dual exchange
  rate regime G. W. Gardner. bibl *J Int Econ* 18:321-38
  My '85
        **Devaluation**
    *See also*
      Money—Australia—Devaluation
      Money—Thailand—Devaluation
Adjustment to monetary policy and devaluation under
  two-tier and fixed exchange rate regimes. J. Aizenman
  *J Dev Econ* 18:153-69 My/Je '85
Anticipated devaluations, currency flight, and direct trade
  controls in a monetary economy. R. C. Feenstra. bibl
  *Am Econ Rev* 75:386-401 Je '85
        **International aspects**
    *See also*
      Balance of payments
      Banks and banking, International
      Foreign exchange
      International liquidity
      International Monetary Fund
      International reserves
      Special drawing rights
      World Bank

**39.1**
**dev**

**FIGURE 39.2**

## INDEX MEDICUS

**CHOLERA**

**HISTORY**
[Some facts concerning the cholera epidemic in Moldavia in 1848] Sibechi G. **Rev Med Chir Soc Med Nat Iasi** 1983 Jul–Sep;87(3):406, 458, 470 **(Rum)**

**MICROBIOLOGY**
Non–01 Vibrio cholerae gastroenteritis in northern California. Kumar S, et al. **West J Med** 1984 May; 140(5):783–4
[An Aeromonas hydrophila choleriform syndrome. Apropos of a case from the Ivory Coast] Dosso M, et al. **Bull Soc Pathol Exot Filiales** 1984 Jan–Feb;77(1):28–31 (Eng. Abstr.) **(Fre)**

**OCCURRENCE**
The epidemiology of cholera in south-west Tanzania. Webber RH, et al. **East Afr Med J** 1983 Dec;60(12):848–56
The diffusion of cholera outside Ibadan City, Nigeria, 1971. Adesina HO. **Soc Sci Med** 1984;18(5):421–8
Identification of the cholera diffusion process in Ibadan, 1971. Adesina HO. **Soc Sci Med** 1984;18(5):429–40

[Why cholera pandemics?] Dodin A. **Bull Soc Pathol Exot Filiales** 1984 Mar–Apr;77(2):127–34 **(Fre)**

**PREVENTION & CONTROL**
A randomized, controlled trial of the toxin–blocking effects of B subunit in family members of patients with cholera. Glass RI, et al. **J Infect Dis** 1984 Apr;149(4):495–500

the nineteenth century and the twentieth, produces first-hand accounts of the 1832 epidemic by doctors and surgeons.

The search proves that a substantial variety of source materials are available for investigation.

**39.1f Taking Notes.**   The student begins her reading with John Snow's *On the Mode of Communication,* for she finds repeated reference to this work in the secondary sources she glances through. Figure 39.3 reprints the passage that she found important.

Suppose the student records the notes in Figure 39.4. Only the person who has read the whole passage will understand these fragments. Without an indication of their context they will be meaningless to the researcher. Even more seriously, they are inaccurate notes, for the writer does not distinguish her own words from those of Snow ("contamination of the water of the much-frequented street-pump"). The notes are also imprecise: the pump whose water was contaminated was a street pump, and this fact needs to be recorded.

The specification is important because Snow is pointing to a neighborhood water supply. The researcher quotes several key

**39.1**
**dev**

**FIGURE 39.3**

There were a few cases of cholera in the neighbourhood of Broad Street, Golden Square, in the latter part of August; and the so-called outbreak, which commenced in the night between the 31st August and the 1st September, was, as in all similar instances only a violent increase of the malady. As soon as I became acquainted with the situation and extent of this irruption of cholera, I suspected some contamination of the water of the much-frequented street-pump in Broad Street, near the end of evening of the 3rd September, I found so little impurity in it of an organic nature, that I hesitated to come to a conclusion. Further inquiry, however, showed me that there was no other circumstance or agent common to the circumscribed locality in which this sudden increase of cholera occurred, and not extending beyond it, except the water of the above mentioned pump. I found, moreover, that the water varied, during the next two days, in the amount of organic impurity, visible to the naked eye, on close inspection, in the form of small white, flocculent particles; and I concluded that, at the commencement of the outbreak, it might possibly have been still more impure. I requested permission, therefore, to take a list, at the General Register Office, of the deaths from cholera, registered during the week ending 2nd September, in the sub-districts of Golden Square, Berwick Street, and St. Ann's, Soho, which was kindly granted. Eighty-nine deaths from cholera were registered, during the week, in the three sub-districts. Of these, only six occurred in the four first days of the week; four occurred on Thursday, the 31st August; and the remaining seventy-nine on Friday and Saturday. I considered, therefore, that the outbreak commenced on the Thursday; and I made inquiry, in detail, respecting the eighty-three deaths registered as having taken place during the last three days of the week.

**39.1**
**dev**

words—"no other circumstance or agent"—instead of the full statement that gives us the needed context.

The bibliography card and notecard that the student writes are presented in Figures 39.5 and 39.6.

The phrases on the new card provide enough information to understand what Snow is saying about the outbreak. We know where and on what days it occurred. The student also quotes the important phrases. To be certain nothing important in the original sentence is lost in the reduction, she might have quoted the entire sentence concerning the common agent. However,

**FIGURE 39.4   Ineffective Notecard**

> Snow
> outbreak in August
> contamination of the water from pump
> impurity in it    organic
> could see
> "no other circumstance or agent"
> Snow was from Yorkshire

only key details and statements need be recorded, though the researcher may require other details and statements later.

Below these details she notes the significance of the phrasing. Facts do not become evidence until they are interpreted. A cross-reference might be made on the card to a supporting secondary source.

The bibliography card tells us that Clendening's book is a reprint of the first edition. This information is recorded in the footnote citing Clendening and in the bibliography of the paper.

**FIGURE 39.5   Bibliography Card**

**39.1**
**dev**

> John Snow, *On the Mode of Communication of Cholera*, 1854.
> In *Source Book of Medical History*, ed.
> Logan Clendening, 468-73
> New York: Dover, 1960
> Originally published 1942
> New York: Henry Schuman

**FIGURE 39.6  Effective Notecard**

Snow, *Communication*                    *Source Book*, 469
studied outbreak of cholera Aug. 31-Sept. 1854 in Soho, London
Snow refers to "irruption of cholera"
"I suspected some contamination of the water of the much-
frequented street-pump in Broad Street..."
says he found "so little impurity in it of an organic
nature, that I hesitated to come to a conclusion."
so Snow knew the disease was cholera.
important phrase "no other circumstance or agent"
he is isolating the cause    looking for the one thing
present in the outbreak.
"there was no other circumstance or agent common to
the circumscribed locality"
Note "organic nature"-important, but what does Snow mean?

The notecard gives the author and title of the work cited in
shortened form.

**39.1g  Quotation and Paraphrase.**    Following is a key statement in Snow.

> Further inquiry, however, showed me that there was no other
> circumstance or agent common to the circumscribed locality in
> which this sudden increase of cholera occurred, and not ex-
> tending beyond it, except the water of the above mentioned
> pump.        —JOHN SNOW, *On the Mode of Transmission of Cholera*

Here is an accurate paraphrase of the statement:

> Snow found no conditions or "agent" shared by those who had
> cholera except the water from the street pump.

**39.1**
**dev**

The writer quotes the word *agent* because she does not know
the exact meaning Snow has in mind. The word *circumstance* is
safely paraphrased as "conditions."

Quoting the phrase "no other circumstance or agent common to the circumscribed locality" shows the exact language of
the nineteenth-century scientist in tracing causes. Snow looks
for the conditions of the outbreak—the time period, the place,
the source of neighborhood water—in addition to looking for a

carrier. All are important: the cause of the outbreak, his analysis shows, is not a simple one.

**39.1h  Ellipsis.**    The writer uses ellipsis in the following ways:

*Omission of Nonessential Clause and Phrase*

| | |
|---|---|
| The keeper of a coffee-shop in the neighbourhood, which was frequented by mechanics, and where the pump-water was supplied at dinner-time, informed me (on 6th September) that she was already aware of nine of her customers who were dead. | The keeper of a coffee-shop in the neighbourhood . . . where the pump-water was supplied at dinner-time, informed me . . . that she was already aware of nine of her customers who were dead. |
| On proceeding to the spot, I found that nearly all the deaths had taken place within a short distance of the pump. | . . . I found that nearly all the deaths had taken place within a short distance of the pump. |

*Omission of Nonessential Concluding Phrase*

| | |
|---|---|
| The pump was frequented much more than is usual, even for a London pump in a populous neighborhood. | The pump was frequented much more than is usual. . . . |

Compare the following sentence in which neither the opening phrase nor the closing phrase can be omitted:

> *With regard to the deaths occurring in the locality belonging to the pump*, there were sixty-one instances in which I was informed that the deceased persons used to drink the pump-water from Broad Street, *either constantly or occasionally*.

**39.1**
**dev**

The opening phrase specifies where the deaths occurred; the closing phrase notes that all of the victims had drunk the water. The fact some had drunk the water "occasionally" suggests that the polluted water was deadly.

**39.1i  Generating a Thesis.**    Having collected these materials, the student needs to sort them and look for possible connections and related ideas. In grouping the cards, she forms several clusters, including the following:

| Chadwick | diet | definitions |
|---|---|---|
| Budd | terror | miasmas |
| Snow | debauchery | polluted water and food |
| | drunkenness | *vibrio cholerae* |

A number of possible ideas and hypotheses occur to her in the course of sorting her details and thinking about their implications. She notes these as she proceeds. Several might serve as the thesis of her paper.

One particular fact catches her attention—that women in England and America were identified as carriers in nineteenth-century cholera epidemics. After considering its possible implications, she decides to add the idea to the second cluster though she is uncertain about the connection.

One question particularly interests her: Why were women in particular identified as carriers of the disease? This idea leads her to stress this attitude toward women in the outline that follows. But the idea will be finally subordinate to a broader conclusion she will reach about Shaw and nineteenth-century medicine—a conclusion she will choose as her thesis.

These considerations lead to a scratch outline of the main topics of the paper and then to the topic outline that follows. Afterward the student writes an introductory paragraph and a concluding paragraph to test the focus chosen.

## 39.2  Outline and First Draft

**39.2a Topic Outline.**   Following is the tentative topic outline for the student's paper on the medical treatment of cholera.

TOPIC OUTLINE

Introduction: Shaw's view of doctors

I. History and nature of cholera

    A. Definition of cholera

        1. Early nineteenth-century definition

        2. The definition today

    B. Theories of cholera up to 1860

        1. Localist theory

        2. Contagionist theory

    C. Early nineteenth-century theorists

        1. Edwin Chadwick

        2. William Budd

        3. John Snow

**39.2**

**dev**

```
II.  Nineteenth-century social attitudes and medical
     theories
     A.  Social attitudes
         1.  General public
         2.  Doctors and surgeons
     B.  Medical theories
         1.  Diet
         2.  Terror
         3.  Drunkenness and debauchery
         4.  Women as carriers
```

Thesis: The treatment of cholera suggests that Shaw's
picture of doctors is not entirely imagined.

**39.2b The First Draft.**    The first draft is a trying out of
ideas—a thinking through of what the evidence suggested, a
discovery of new connections and possibilities. Figure 39.7 on
pp. 601–602 shows the opening paragraphs of the draft.

As the marginal comments suggest, the transition from the
discussion of Shaw to the description of cholera is abrupt—divided awkwardly by the statement of purpose. The description
of cholera is diffuse and overlong. The writer tries in her second
revision to improve these transitions and the focus in each of
the paragraphs.

**39.2c Revisions.**    Figure 39.8 on pp. 603–605 shows a revision of the opening paragraphs just discussed.

This revision corrects the abrupt transitions of the opening
paragraphs of the first draft. The details of Shaw's play and the
details of the disease are also better focused. From the revisions
of these paragraphs and the remainder of the second draft the
student proceeds to the third and final draft of the paper. In
doing so, she writes down various conclusions suggested by her
investigation. One of these conclusions she chooses to present
as her thesis, stated toward the end of the paper:

> The evidence also gives support to Shaw's belief that
> many doctors did not reason as scientists.

Her thesis draws together the various concerns with which her
investigation began.

In preparing the final draft for submission, she edits it carefully for spelling, grammar, and punctuation.

**39.2**

**dev**

**FIGURE 39.7** **Opening Paragraphs of the First Draft**

Shaw attacks the medical profession in his

*Good direct intro to Shaw and build to subject*

play <u>The Doctor's Dilemma</u>, written in 1906. His

attack is blamed sometimes on his eccentric ideas

on medicine and health. Shaw was a vegetarian all

his life, and he was against mass vaccination and

*encouraged?*

other measures that doctors (were for) in his time. A

*gl*

point he makes (through) the preface is ∧ the doctor is

not a scientist and has the same prejudices as

other people. "The smattering of science that

all--even doctors--pick up from the ordinary news-

papers nowadays only makes the doctor more danger-

ous than he used to be," he (states) in the preface.

*rep*

He (states) that the "doctor draws disastrous

conclusions from his clinical experience because

he has no conception of scientific method...."

*You seem to drop Shaw. Abrupt intro of statement of purpose and intro to Pollitzer.*

Medical reports and books on cholera,

written in England and the United States in the

nineteenth century, (show) that social attitudes

and social morality did influence doctors. To (show)

how they did, I shall trace important theories of

cholera, then (show) how social and moral attitudes

influenced them.

*ital*

*that*

Pollitzer suggests ∧ that the word <u>cholera</u>

derives from the Greek word for bile. The word

originally referred to bilious diarrhea. In Greek

**39.2**
**dev**

**FIGURE 39.7** *(continued)*

times cholera was thought the same as other serious
infections of the intestines. In the nineteenth
century so-called premonitory diarrhea was
thought the first stage of cholera. The "rice-
water" discharges of the disease influenced how
English doctors and Englishmen generally looked
at cholera. English doctors saw cholera in India
*Which?* and treated it, but (doctors) did not agree about its
origin and how it is transmitted. Before the
nineteenth century, the general term cholera, or
the more specific "British" or "European
cholera" or "summer diarrhea," described a
*The general* milder enteric disease. (This disease) is marked by
*or the*
*British form?* violent diarrhea and vomiting but the patient
usually recovers in several days.

Asiatic cholera struck England in 1832. This *form*
localizes in the small intestinal tract and causes
violent diarrhea and sometimes vomiting, followed
*rep* by a ~~water~~ diarrhea that looks like rice-water and
later extreme dehydration and loss of
electrolyte, and shriveling and discoloration of
*Trans* the skin. Death is rapid. Cholera is caused by a
*Info about* bacteria, Vibrio cholerae, which the German
*Pasteur* doctor Robert Koch--the rival of Louis Pasteur--
*necessary?* found in 1883.

**FIGURE 39.8 Revision of the First Draft**

In his 1906 play <u>The Doctor's Dilemma</u> and his

preface written in 1911, George Bernard Shaw

attacks doctors of his time and ~~doctors~~ *those* of the

previous century. His main criticism is that the

doctor is not a scientist. The doctor often "draws

disastrous conclusions from his clinical

experience because he has no conception of

scientific method," Shaw states. Another

criticism is that the doctor is a conformist--

subject to the same prejudices as other people of

the age:

> most of them have no honor and no conscience:
>
> what they commonly mistake for these is
>
> sentimentality and an intense dread of
>
> doing anything that everybody else does not
>
> do, or omitting to do anything that everybody
>
> else does.

The reader of the play and preface today asks

*Overcrowded*    if these views were personal to Shaw, (perhaps based

*sentence*    on unhappy experiences Shaw may have had with

*See 26.2*    doctors, or based on his ideas on medicine and

health.) Shaw believed good diet and sanitation,

not scientific remedies like vaccination, were

*Other doctors?*   the best guarantee of good health. Did (others) in

*People*    his time agree with Shaw, and do his play and

*generally?*

**39.2**
**dev**

**FIGURE 39.8** *(continued)*

preface give an accurate picture of medical

practice in the nineteenth century?

One way to answer these questions is to find

out how nineteenth ~century~ doctors (treated) their

*Improved*    patients and reasoned about disease--

particularly a disease they had not (treated)

before. An example is cholera, which some British

*rep*    doctors (treated) in India. Cholera first appeared

in England and the United States in 1832. A reading

of medical reports of the epidemic and reports of

later epidemics shows how doctors reasoned about

cholera. So do the books on cholera written by

doctors in England and America during this period.

These reports and books suggest that social

*Improved -*    attitudes and popular beliefs about the cause of
*you keep*
*Shaw in*    cholera influenced the thinking of doctors and
*view.*
their treatment of patients. However, these do not

tell us how many doctors were influenced by

discoveries made about cholera during these years

and acted upon them. In short, the evidence gives

some support to Shaw's views but not complete

proof.

**39.2**
**dev**

*Good trans*    To understand this evidence, we first must

understand what scientists and doctors today know

about cholera, and what scientists and doctors in

**FIGURE 39.8** *(continued)*

the early nineteenth century knew. The etymology
of the word tells much about earlier theories of
the disease. The word derives from the Greek for
bile—the Greek doctor referring to a form of
diarrhea. In ancient times cholera was identified
with other serious gastrointestinal infections
including ptomaine poisoning. In the nineteenth
century many doctors thought so-called
premonitory diarrhea was the first stage of the
disease, probably because it looked like the
"rice-water" discharges of its later stages.
Cholera was also the name for a milder disease
called "British cholera" or "European" cholera
or "summer diarrhea."

**39.2**
**dev**

## 39.3 The Final Draft

Following is the final draft, with endnotes and bibliography. The documentation follows that described in 38.1c and 38.2. Following the draft in Section 39.4 are several of its paragraphs that illustrate the alternate method of documentation described in 38.3—the citation of sources in the text.

The Medical View of Cholera: 1832-1860

In his 1906 play <u>The Doctor's Dilemma</u> and his later preface, George Bernard Shaw attacks medicine in his time as a "murderous absurdity." "[T]he tragedy of illness at present," he states in the preface, "is that it delivers you help-lessly into the hands of a profession which you deeply mistrust."[1] Many doctors are cruel, lack honor and conscience, and pander to the desires of their patients: "[W]hat they commonly mistake for these is sentimentality and an intense dread of doing anything that everybody else does not do, or omitting to do anything that everybody else does."[2]

Shaw attacks most vigorously their ignorance and misuse of science. The doctor, he states, often "draws disastrous conclusions from his clinical experience because he has no conception of scientific method."[3] But Shaw is not here mak-ing a case for scientific medicine, for he be-lieved in good diet, sanitation, and other means of preventing disease, not in the new therapies of medical science like vaccination. "Doctoring

is an art, not a science," he states. "Doctoring
is not even the art of keeping people in health
. . . it is the art of curing illnesses."[4]

   These statements raise important questions
for readers of the preface and the play. One
question is whether Shaw's views of the medical
profession are subjective and biased views, based
on unhappy experiences with doctors rather than
on his ideas on health and disease. Do the play
and the preface accurately reflect medical practice in the nineteenth century—the period to
which he refers in the preface? And were doctors
influenced more by social attitudes than by medical science? Shaw could well have invented the
doctors he portrays and discusses in the preface.
The world of the play and the preface may be
imaginary.

   A partial answer can be given through how
English and American doctors in the nineteenth
century reasoned about and treated disease—in
particular, a disease new to most of them. Cholera first appeared in Great Britain in 1832 following outbreaks in other European countries; the
epidemic spread quickly to the United States. Numerous medical reports and books describe the
medical response. Many English doctors had observed and treated this disease in Asiatic countries, particularly in India, but most doctors in
England and America were treating the disease for
the first time.

   Cholera is a good test of Shaw's ideas because scientific understanding of the disease in-

**39.3**
**dev**

creased in the nineteenth century; doctors and
scientists discovered first its means of trans-
mission, then its bacterial origin. Cholera is a
particularly good test because social attitudes
stand out in discussions of the disease: Englishmen and Americans identified cholera with the
Asiatic poor and apparently believed that white
people seldom contracted it. In 1832, however,
many white people did contract cholera—a fact
that required a social explanation. For this reason doctors theorized about the disease in numerous articles and books published in England and
the United States in 1832 and later years. These
publications clearly support Shaw's view that
doctors were influenced by social attitudes in
their theory of disease and reports on patients.

The etymology of the word <u>cholera</u> tells much
about nineteenth-century theories and social attitudes toward the disease. The word derives from
the Greek for bile—the ancient Greek term for
the disease referring to bilious diarrhea. In ancient times cholera was also identified with
other serious gastrointestinal infections including ptomaine poisoning.[5] Cholera was also the
name for a milder disease called "British" or
"European" cholera or "summer diarrhea." Today,
the word describes virulent Asiatic cholera,
caused by bacteria identified by Robert Koch in
1883; it was Asiatic cholera that struck England
in 1832.[6]

Localizing in the small intestines, cholera
starts with violent diarrhea and sometimes vomit-

**39.3**
**dev**

ing. The so-called rice-water diarrhea that follows is watery and contains mucus. The final stages of the disease show severe dehydration and shrivelling and discoloration of the skin, loss of potassium and electrolyte, and weak pulse and rapid heartbeat.[7] Medical scientists in the later nineteenth century divided sharply on the effects of the disease on the intestinal lining.[8] Scientists today have isolated most of the conditions that produce cholera.[9]

Because it originated in Asia and struck the poor hardest, cholera came in England to be called "the poor man's disease."[10] Ironically, this opinion seems to be correct, for many well-nourished people survive the cholera bacterium or vibrio without showing symptoms; malnourished people are more susceptible.[11] Thus many Europeans survived cholera epidemics in the East--as did Asiatics. It is not surprising, then, that in the early nineteenth century many doctors thought of cholera as a racial or ethnic disease and, as in ancient times, defined the disease through its symptoms and chiefly through its discharges. For example, many doctors at the time of the first epidemic in England and the United States identified so-called premonitory diarrhea as the first stage of the disease, probably because this diarrhea looked like the "rice-water" discharges of the later stages.[12]

The popular "localist" theory of cholera in nineteenth-century England connected the disease with gases and miasmas rising from filth in poor

**39.3**
**dev**

districts. In 1832 the <u>London Times</u> reported complaints of stench coming from privies and butcher
markets in East London, people referring to the
stench as "pestilential vapour."[13] In her study
of cholera in England, Margaret Pelling states
that many Englishmen believed "all smell is disease."[14] "Localists" like the social reformer Sir
Edwin Chadwick recommended sanitation as a preventive of epidemics though he was ignorant of
the real cause.[15]

The rival "contagionist" theory was that
cholera is water-borne as well as air-borne. In
1849 a Bristol doctor, William Budd, concluded
from rice-water discharges examined under the microscope that cholera is transmitted by "fungoid"
microscopic animals.[16] Budd credited the water-
borne theory to John Snow, who in the same year
argued that cholera spreads through "morbid matter" passing from a patient through discharges.
These pollute food and water and pass in this way
to other patients.[17] In 1854 Snow published his
proof that a cholera outbreak in the Soho section
of London could be traced to a much-used street
pump. Hearing of the outbreak, he suspected that
the water was contaminated: "near the end of evening of the 3rd September, I found so little impurity in it of an organic nature, that I hesitated to come to a conclusion." Snow drew the
conclusion that cholera had to be water-borne:

> Further inquiry, however, showed me that
> there was no other circumstance or agent

**39.3**
**dev**

common to the circumscribed locality in which this sudden increase of cholera occurred, and not extending beyond it, except the water of the above mentioned pump.[18]

Localists responded that the water had been contaminated by air-borne poisons: the agent that could change organic matter into poison in the air could do so in the water.[19] Opinion on the matter was divided for many years afterward.

Scientific reasoning and new theories of causation were replacing old ways of thinking about the disease, Budd and Snow show. Still, medical reports published in the years 1832 to 1866 show that social prejudice influenced many doctors and observers as they searched for evidence in the living conditions of the poor. Diet might be one cause of cholera, they proposed. The London Times reprinted this statement from the Medical Gazette:

> In all the countries which cholera has visited, the most fatal irruptions have been among those whose diet is at once impoverished and stimulated; nor is it possible to conceive anything possessed of these characteristics more strongly than salads, or other raw vegetables, and half-ripe fruits, qualified with copious libations of adulterated gin. Of how many among our poorer brethren do these constitute a part at least, and often a very large part, of their daily subsistence.[20]

**39.3**
**dev**

Ironically, the cleanliness of the food (and water) is not mentioned in this statement. The word <u>raw</u> refers to uncooked vegetables.

Another much-cited cause is the character of the poor. Fear makes the poor susceptible to cholera, several writers note. An 1832 treatise on cholera states: "Both fear and the cholera drive the blood from the exterior upon the heart, arrest or derange the secretions, hinder assimilation, and of course produce indigestion, and disorder of the stomach and bowels."[21] An 1866 treatise makes the same point.[22]

The <u>Times</u> article shows that another cause associated with the poor is drunkenness. The <u>Medical Gazette</u> refers to "copious libations of adulterated gin." An American writer quotes from the Special Medical Council of New York City: "In regard to intemperance, it is now universally known, that Cholera has a most peculiar affinity for the system of a drunkard; so much so, that it is a very rare thing for the intemperate to escape--generally speaking, it is almost as rare for the temperate and uniformly prudent to be attacked."[23] It is one step from this kind of reasoning to the identification of a class of people most disposed to the disease:

As a class of people, the low Irish [in New York City] suffered most, being exceedingly dirty in their habits, much addicted to intemperance, and crowded together in the worst portions of the city, both as regards

**39.3**
**dev**

the kind of houses and the quarter in which
they resided.[24]

Other classes are also susceptible, some
doctors thought, because they are disposed to
sexual debauchery. In his sketch of cholera in
New York City in 1832, another writer states:
"Venereal excesses, and debauchery in general,
exposed in many cases to very sudden and fatal
attacks. In truth there is perhaps no more common
cause of a sudden and rapidly fatal attack, especially if preceded by a neglected diarrhoea, than
a midnight debauch."[25] Asiatics were thought to
be particularly susceptible. John Chapman, writing in 1866, suggests that "solar heat" creates a
"special aptitude" for cholera, refers to debauchery as a "predisposing cause," and draws
this conclusion about the Asiatic origin of the
disease: "As Asiatic races are peculiarly prone
to sexual intemperance, it is not unlikely that
this is one of the causes of the frightful de-
structiveness of the disease amongst them, and
especially in India."[26] The explanation is obviously racial.

Medical reports and theoretical books on
cholera further show that some doctors assumed
women were not only susceptible but were possibly
carriers. Prostitutes are the obvious target of
suspicion in a book published in 1832: "The comparative exemption enjoyed by females, has been
entirely lost to them by a dissolute mode of
life. Women of this class have been among the

**39.3**
**dev**

foremost sufferers from Cholera."[27] This belief probably explains why in 1832 the Oxford Board of Health recommended the reformation of prostitutes as a preventive measure:

> It appears to this Board of great importance . . . that it would be conducive to public health and safety under the present calamity of cholerous sickness to effect some amelioration in the habits of the common prostitute—their homes and homesteads, the localities of their residences, their destitute as well as their debased condition, and generally in their natural and statistical as well as their spiritual and eternal relations.[28]

The statement of the Oxford Board implies that their surroundings and their "destitute as well as their debased condition" made prostitutes contagious. This assumption is also plain in the words natural and spiritual in the final sentence.

The poor, Asiatics, women—these classes are the most susceptible to the disease, in the stated views of medical authorities and observers. Clearly, moral views influenced public attitudes; the suffering of the poor, many believed, was the will of God—a just punishment for their sins.[29] Moral views, too, influenced medical theory. Cholera could not be a contagious disease wrote John Lizars in his 1832 treatise on cholera:

**39.3**
**dev**

The medical man who <u>conscientiously</u> believes in the contagious nature of this appalling disease cannot perform his duty zealously or effectually. He is only mortal, and, in this enlightened age, he knows that no spell or charm can guarantee him from the demon contagion which his terrified imagination has conjured up.[30]

These opinions existed in face of mounting evidence that cholera had a much different physical cause. As we have seen, some doctors and scientists like William Budd and John Snow were looking for evidence that proved a direct link between contaminated water and the outbreak of cholera, though they probably did not dismiss diet, alcohol, or environment as contributing causes.

The medical statements and theories quoted do not prove conclusively that Shaw is correct that doctors in his time had no more honor or conscience than other people, nor that they had "an intense dread of doing anything that everybody else does not do, or omitting to do anything that everybody else does." But the statements do show that Shaw had a basis for stating that doctors were not different from ordinary people in their social attitudes. The evidence shows that social attitudes strongly influenced medical theory.

The evidence also gives support to Shaw's belief that many doctors did not reason as scien-

**39.3**
**dev**

tists. Morris confirms this idea in his study of the literature on cholera:

> The men who wrote the cholera literature of 1832 did not talk in terms of a scientific community, indeed they preferred the more gentlemanly term natural philosopher to that of scientist.[31]

In summary, the treatises on cholera in 1832 clearly reflect social attitudes of the time. Social attitudes more than scientific theory provide the explanation for the causes of the disease and the susceptibility of certain classes of people. The picture of doctors in <u>The Doctor's Dilemma</u>, then, is not entirely imagined. Many doctors were as ignorant of science as we see in the play.

**39.3**
dev

NOTES


¹Bernard Shaw, <u>Complete Plays with Prefaces</u>. 4 vols. (New York: Dodd, 1963) 1: 2.

²Shaw 3.

³Shaw 18.

⁴Shaw 18.

⁵R. Pollitzer, <u>Cholera</u> (Geneva: World Health Organization, 1959) 14–15.

⁶Dhiman Barua and William Burrows, eds., <u>Cholera</u> (Philadelphia: Saunders, 1974) 10.

⁷Nathaniel F. Pierce, "Cholera," <u>Textbook of Medicine</u>, ed. James B. Wyngaarden and Lloyd H. Smith, Jr., 17th ed. (Philadelphia: Saunders, 1985) 1598–1600.

⁸Robert Allan Phillips, "Asiatic Cholera," <u>Annual Review of Medicine</u> 19 (1968): 69–70. Phillips states: "The disease appears to cause virtually no organ or system damage which cannot be explained by the water and electrolyte imbalance resulting from the severe dehydration" (70).

⁹Pierce 1598.

¹⁰Robert John Morris, <u>Cholera 1832: The Social Response to an Epidemic</u> (New York: Holmes, 1976) 85.

¹¹Morris 15.

¹²Morris 15–16.

¹³<u>The [London] Times</u>, July 23, 1832.

¹⁴<u>Cholera, Fever and English Medicine: 1825–1865</u> (London: Oxford UP), 59. Pelling quotes a surgeon of the time: "I have not the slightest

doubt that in <u>certain constitutions</u> of the atmosphere there is nothing so likely to produce disease" (59–60).

[15]Edwin Chadwick, <u>The Health of Nations</u>
(1867; London: Dawsons, 1965) 2: 229–39.

[16]Pelling 170.

[17]Pelling 160, 204.

[18]John Snow, <u>On the Mode of Communication of
Cholera</u>. 1854. <u>Source Book of Medical History</u>,
ed. Logan Clendening (New York: Dover, 1960; rpt.
New York: Schuman, 1942) 469.

[19]Pelling 222.

[20]<u>The [London] Times</u> July 14, 1832.

[21]A. Brigham, <u>A Treatise on Epidemic Cholera</u>
(Hartford, 1832) 352.

[22]John Chapman, <u>Diarrhoea and Cholera</u>, 2nd
ed. (London, 1866) 172.

[23]Dudley Atkins, ed., <u>Reports of Hospital
Physicians and Other Documents in Relation to the
Epidemic of Cholera of 1832</u> (New York, 1832) 66.

[24]Atkins 15.

[25]Atkins 18.

[26]Chapman 170.

[27]John Bell and D. Francis Condie, <u>Epidemic
Cholera</u> (Philadelphia, 1832) 49.

[28]Quoted by Morris 199.

[29]Morris 133–39.

[30]John Lizars, <u>Substance of the Investigations Regarding Cholera Asphyxia in 1832</u>, 2nd ed.
(Edinburgh, 1848) 65–66.

[31]Morris 178.

**39.3**
**dev**

# 39.4 Citations in the Text

Section 38.3 shows how to include citations in the text instead of in footnotes or endnotes. Here are several of the paragraphs of the paper documented in this way. The citations are to the bibliography that follows:

The etymology of the word cholera tells much about
nineteenth-century theories and social attitudes toward
the disease. The word derives from the Greek for bile--
the ancient Greek term for the disease referring to
bilious diarrhea. In ancient times cholera was also
identified with other serious gastrointestinal infections including ptomaine poisoning (Pollitzer 14-15).
Cholera was also the name for a milder disease called
"British" or "European" cholera or "summer diarrhea."
Today, the word describes virulent Asiatic cholera,
caused by bacteria identified by Robert Koch in 1883;
it was Asiatic cholera that struck England in 1832
(Barau 10).

Localizing in the small intestines, cholera starts
with violent diarrhea and sometimes vomiting. The so-
called rice-water diarrhea that follows is watery and
contains mucus. The final stages of the disease show
severe dehydration and shrivelling and discoloration of
the skin, loss of potassium and electrolyte, and weak
pulse and rapid heartbeat (Pierce 1598-1600). Medical
scientists in the later nineteenth century divided
sharply on the effects of the disease on the intestinal
lining (Phillips 69-70). Scientists today have isolated
most of the conditions that produce cholera (Pierce
1598).

Because it originated in Asia and struck the poor
hardest, cholera came in England to be called "the poor
man's disease" (Morris 85). Ironically, this opinion

**39.4**
**doc**

seems to be correct, for many well—nourished people survive the cholera bacterium or vibrio without showing symptoms; malnourished people are more susceptible (Morris 15). Thus many Europeans survived cholera epidemics in the East——as did Asiatics. It is not surprising, then, that in the early nineteenth century many doctors thought of cholera as a racial or ethnic disease and, as in ancient times, defined the disease through its symptoms and chiefly through its discharges. For example, many doctors at the time of the first epidemic in England and the United States identified so—called premonitory diarrhea as the first stage of the disease, probably because this diarrhea looked like the "rice—water" discharges of the later stages (Morris 15—16).

The popular "localist" theory of cholera in nineteenth—century England connected the disease with gases and miasmas rising from filth in poor districts. In 1832 the London Times reported complaints of stench coming from privies and butcher markets in East London, people referring to the stench as "pestilential vapour." In her study of cholera in England, Margaret Pelling states that many Englishmen believed "all smell is disease" (59). "Localists" like the social reformer Sir Edwin Chadwick recommended sanitation as a preventive of epidemics though he was ignorant of the real cause (Chadwick 229—39).

The rival "contagionist" theory was that cholera is water—borne as well as air—borne. In 1849 a Bristol doctor, William Budd, concluded from rice—water discharges examined under the microscope that cholera is transmitted by "fungoid" microscopic animals (Pelling 170). Budd credited the water—borne theory to John Snow, who in the same year argued that cholera spreads through "morbid matter" passing from a patient through

**39.4**
**doc**

discharges. These pollute food and water and pass in this way to other patients (Pelling 160, 204). In 1854 Snow published his proof that a cholera outbreak in the Soho section of London could be traced to a much-used street pump. Hearing of the outbreak, he suspected that the water was contaminated: "near the end of evening of the 3rd September, I found so little impurity in it of an organic nature, that I hesitated to come to a conclusion." Snow drew the conclusion that cholera had to be water-borne:

> Further inquiry, however, showed me that there was no other circumstance or agent common to the circumscribed locality in which this sudden increase of cholera occurred, and not extending beyond it, except the water of the above mentioned pump. (Snow 469)

WORKS CITED

Atkins, Dudley, ed. Reports of Hospital Physicians and Other Documents in Relation to the Epidemic of Cholera of 1832. New York, 1832.

Barau, Dhiman, and William Burrows, eds. Cholera. Philadelphia: Saunders, 1974.

Bell, John, and D. Francis Condie. Epidemic Cholera. Philadelphia, 1832.

Brigham, A. A Treatise on Epidemic Cholera. Hartford, 1832.

Chadwick, Edwin. The Health of Nations. 1867. 2 vols. London: Dawsons, 1965.

Chapman, John. Diarrhoea and Cholera. 2nd ed. London, 1866.

Lizars, John. Substance of the Investigations Regarding Cholera Asphyxia in 1832. Edinburgh, 1848.

**39.4**
**doc**

[London] Times 14 July 1832.

– – – 23 July 1832.

Morris, Robert John. Cholera 1832: The Social Response
    to an Epidemic. New York: Holmes and Meier, 1976.

Pelling, Margaret. Cholera, Fever and English Medicine:
    1825–1865. London: Oxford UP, 1978.

Phillips, Robert Allan. "Asiatic Cholera." Annual Re-
    view of Medicine 19 (1968): 69–80.

Pierce, Nathaniel F. "Cholera." Textbook of Medicine.
    17th ed. Ed. James E. Wyngaarden and Lloyd H.
    Smith, Jr. Philadelphia: Saunders, 1985. 1598–
    1600.

Pollitzer, R. Cholera. Geneva: World Health Organiza-
    tion, 1959.

Shaw, Bernard. The Doctor's Dilemma. Vol 1 of Complete
    Plays with Prefaces. 6 vols. New York: Dodd, Mead,
    1963.

Snow, John. On the Mode of Communication of Cholera.
    1854. Source Book of Medical History. Ed. Logan
    Clendening. New York: Dover, 1960; rpt. New York:
    Schuman, 1942. 468–73.

# Checklist for Writing a Documented Paper

**39.1a**   Your reading may suggest interesting topics for research.

**39.1b**   Decide on a purpose for your investigation.

**39.1c**   Consider the length of the paper and the availability of
materials in limiting your subject.

**39.1d**   In limiting your focus, consider the importance of the
conclusions you might reach.

**39.1e**   Use the standard indexes to compile a bibliography of
primary and secondary sources.

**39.1f**   Record your notes accurately and in a useful form.

**39.1g**  Distinguish between direct quotation and paraphrase.

**39.1h**  Use ellipsis to omit nonessential words, phrases, and clauses.

**39.1i**  Cluster your details and topics to discover related ideas.

**39.2a**  Outline your essay and write trial paragraphs to test your focus and generate a thesis.

**39.2c**  Work from revisions of your trial paragraphs and first draft to your final paper. Edit the final draft carefully.

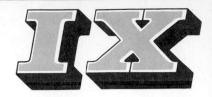

# Special Writing

# Business Writing

This chapter discusses another kind of writing you will be doing in college and later in your working career. It describes how to write a business letter, a job application, and a resume. The chapter focuses on important conventions that govern these kinds of writing.

## 40.1 Letters

**40.1a Effective Business Letters.** When you begin your full-time career, a first task will be to write a letter applying for a job. Once you are on the job, one of your responsibilities will be to write business letters. Letters of application and business letters are successful when they do the following:

1. State the purpose of the letter concisely and directly in the first paragraph.
2. Give the pertinent facts without needless detail in the middle paragraphs.
3. Stress positive qualifications or points without concealing important information.
4. Provide a willingness to cooperate and to keep the communication going in the last paragraph.
5. Emphasize the reader as much as the writer, especially in the opening and closing paragraphs.

The following are some rules on mechanics that will help you keep track of these points, write well-organized paragraphs, and maintain balance among the paragraphs:

1. Single-space the letter, and double-space between your paragraphs with or without indentation. If you use full block or modified block formats (see Figures 40.1 and 40.2), keep the left margins of your home address and/or date flush with the left margins of the complimentary close and signature.

**FIGURE 40.1    Modified Block Format (no letterhead)**

Letter of Job Application

1421 Rider Road
Akron, OH 44380
March 1, 1985

Mr. Robert Smith
Personnel Manager
Tristate Scientific Equipment Company
Public Square
Cleveland, OH 44113

Dear Mr. Smith:

Please consider me for the industrial designer position you advertised in last Sunday's Akron Beacon Journal. My work experience, educational background, and interests meet the qualifications listed in your advertisement. Furthermore, Tristate's fine reputation makes me interested in becoming one of your employees.

At present, I am employed as an associate designer at Computer Design, Inc., in Stow, Ohio. I am seeking new employment because the company is moving its office to San Diego in July, and I would like to continue working in Ohio if possible.

I graduated cum laude from the University of Akron in 1981, with a B.S. in Mechanical Engineering. My overall grade point average is 3.5; my average in my major is 3.7. Following graduation I began work full-time at Computer Design, where I worked part-time during my last two years of college.

In addition to my employment and engineering degree, a special interest also makes me a good candidate for the job. That's my active participation for the last five years in a computer club. I particularly enjoy writing software programs.

You'll find more details on the enclosed resume. The University of Akron Placement Office will send my credentials upon request. Of course, I will be happy to come to Cleveland for an interview at your convenience. In the meantime, I look forward to hearing from you and to discussing employment with Tristate.

Sincerely,

James Walker

ENC

40.1

**FIGURE 40.2  Full Block Format**

Letter of Response

---

**Tristate Equipment Company**
Public Square
Cleveland, Ohio 44113


March 10, 1985

Mr. James Walker
1421 Rider Road
Akron, Ohio 44380

Dear Mr. Walker:

Your credentials arrived today, and we will be happy to discuss the position in industrial design at an interview next week. Will you please call my office to arrange a day and time?

Enclosed is a brochure describing our company and the various jobs it performs in Cleveland and Youngstown, where we have a branch office of more than ten full-time designers and engineers.

I look forward to meeting you and discussing your qualifications. Thank you for writing.


Sincerely,


Robert Smith
Personnel Officer


RS:jk
ENC

**40.1**

2. Keep the first paragraph to no more than seven or eight typewritten lines.
3. Keep the middle paragraphs to no more than 10 typewritten lines each.
4. Keep the last paragraph to no more than six or seven typewritten lines.

Figure 40.1 illustrates one of two basic formats for letters without letterhead—*modified block*. Notice the following features:

1. The address, date, complimentary close, and signature are indented.
2. The paragraphs are unindented.

The response letter on letterhead is in the second basic format—*full block* (see Figure 40.2). Notice these features:

1. The date, complimentary close, and signature are aligned with the inside address and salutation.
2. The paragraphs are unindented.

The letter of request illustrates *indented form* (see Figure 40.3):

1. The address, date, complimentary close, and signature are indented.
2. The paragraphs are indented.

**40.1b Ineffective Business Letters.** Keep in mind the following points in writing letters of application and business letters:

1. Don't crowd several pieces of information or several requests into a single paragraph. For example, when writing a letter of application, devote one paragraph to your academic background if you are giving full details. Devote another to your work experience. Devote a third paragraph to any interests or activities relevant to the job you're seeking.

2. The more direct the letter is, the more effective it will be. The writers of the following sentences avoid making direct statements out of fear of seeming rude or angry. The result is that they weaken the requests:

**40.1**

If I am not intruding on your time, I wonder if I may apply for the position you advertised . . .
Knowing how busy you are at this time of year, I apologize for bothering you about a matter as small as . . .
Please write me whenever you find the time . . .

## FIGURE 40.3    Indented Form

### Letter of Request

1421 Rider Road
Akron, OH 44380
April 15, 1984

Mr. Arthur Riley
President
Akron Car Sales
1740 North Market Street
Akron, OH 44380

Dear Mr. Riley:

    Akron Car Sales has a reputation for standing behind its automobiles. For that reason I'm certain you will want to help me with the car I purchased from you in March 1982. Though my new-car warranty expired one week before the engine and transmission failed, I request that Akron Car Sales replace the engine and repair the transmission at its own expense.

    The enclosed copies of receipts show that your service department worked on the engine and the transmission twelve times during the warranty period. The failure of engine and transmission suggests they were defective at the time I bought the car. The Cleveland office of the FTC informs me that other customers have filed complaints about the same trouble.

    Your service manager, Lou Johnson, told me he cannot make repairs at the expense of Akron Car Sales without your authorization. He has the full service record of the car during the warranty period.

    Please let me hear from you within a few days. Should you prefer to call, my work number is 501-6688. I am at home after 5:00 P.M. The number is 501-0018.

Sincerely,

Joan Walker

ENC

**40.1**

3. On the other hand, letters that issue commands or threats are likely to be ineffective:

> Let me know immediately whether I meet your qualifications for the job . . .
>
> I am writing you before I hire a lawyer to file suit against Akron Motor Sales . . .
>
> I demand an answer by return mail . . .

4. Wordy sentences guarantee that your letter will be ignored or will not be taken seriously:

> If I may have a few moments of your time, I should like to review my qualifications for the position that you advertised in the issue of the *Akron Beacon Journal* dated . . .
>
> Having now reviewed my academic background, I turn to my work experience which I trust meets your qualifications for the position you advertised . . .
>
> With respect to the matter of the warranty which expired the week before the trouble I described commenced . . .

5. Avoid flowery and pretentious salutations and complimentary closes:

> My dear Mr. Roberts
> Mr. Roberts, sir
> Humbly yours
> With all due respect
> Most gratefully
> I remain yours very truly
> Hoping to hear from you at your earliest convenience

6. Avoid irrelevant personal references or details:

> I will be available for an interview, except for the last week in March, at which time my family and I will be taking a long awaited vacation in the "Big Apple" . . .
>
> Patsy Murphy, who worked in your company several years ago, is a good friend of mine and sends her regards . . .

**40.1**

7. Don't sign the letter with your first name only or with a nickname:

> "Butch" Abernathy
> Jane

## EXERCISES

1. Write a letter to the loan officer of a college or a bank asking for a scholarship or an educational loan. Include the following information in the letter:
   a. You lost your scholarship because you had to drop out of school for a semester.
   b. You dropped out of school because of illness.
   c. You have no means of support other than a part-time job.
   d. You will complete your college work within a year.
2. Write a letter to a department store asking for cancellation of a charge for a damaged article you previously returned. Include information on the following:
   a. the date of purchase
   b. the date you returned the damaged article
   c. details of the mistaken charge
3. Rewrite the following letter. Assume that the writer is seeking to negotiate the terms of the offer, not to refuse the job.

1421 Rider Road
Akron, OH 44380
April 1, 1984

Mr. Bob Smith
Personnel Manager
Tristate Scientific Equipment Company
Cleveland, OH 44113

Dear Bob:

It was great having lunch with you and the guys upstairs and receiving your letter of offer. Our mutual friend, Bud Wilkins, was right in suggesting I
write you!

**40.1**

Attractive as the salary and pension plan are, I'm
frankly looking for a few more perks than we discussed. Since I will have to commute to Cleveland,
I was hoping for a travel allowance as well as a
chance to work at home in bad weather. You know
what winters are like in northeast Ohio! Also, Bob,
I wouldn't enjoy sharing an office with what's his

name, the little guy who just joined your firm. To
be honest, I do my best work in an office of my
own. Which is why I'm suggesting a special arrangement with Tristate.

I have an interview next week with another company
that is much impressed with my credentials. If you
can meet my requirements, I'd like to hear from you
and come aboard if possible. But it must be before
the end of the week.

Thanks again, Bob, and I hope you can give my ideas
a hearing.

                              Sincerest regards,


                              Jim


# 40.2 The Resume

The resume or vita states your personal history in a clear
and concise form. It omits unessential facts though you will want
to give personal details that add to your qualifications for a
scholarship or job. Details about your personal interests and
activities—for example, volunteer work and hobbies—should be
as brief as possible.

Since the reader must be able to find essential facts quickly,
use prominent headings (in capitals or italics) to divide the resume in the manner shown. Give the recent facts first under
each heading.

Figure 40.4 on p. 634 presents a model resume.


### EXERCISES

1. Write a bad letter of application for a job in a field of interest
   to you. Then write a good letter of application for the same
   job.
2. Write an ineffective letter of complaint to a local company.
   Then write an effective letter to the same company.
3. Write a resume, following the model on p. 634.

**40.2**

**FIGURE 40.4   Resume**

James Walker
1421 Rider Road
Akron, Ohio 44380
Phone (216) 501-0018

EDUCATIONAL EXPERIENCE:

B.S. cum laude, Mechanical engineering,
University of Akron, June, 1981. Minor fields:
Mathematics, Computer Programming
Buchtel High School, Akron, OH, 1974-78.

WORK EXPERIENCE:

1981-present: Associate designer, Computer
        Designs, Inc., Industrial Plaza, Stow,
        OH 44224
1979-81: Office worker and apprentice designer,
        Computer Designs

HONORS:

Member of Engineering Honor Society
Engineering scholarship, University of Akron

ACTIVITIES AND INTERESTS:

I am an amateur astronomer, belong to an Akron area
computer club, and write software programs. I have
traveled in England and in France, where I lived
for one year. I speak French.

REFERENCES:

My credentials will be sent on request by the
Placement Office, University of Akron, OH 44325.

ADDITIONAL REFERENCES:

Mr. William Stone
President, Computer Designs, Inc.
Industrial Park
Stow, OH 44224

**40.2**

# Checklist for Business Writing

**40.1a**  Effective business letters state the purpose concisely and directly, give pertinent facts only, stress positive qualifications, do not conceal important information, and emphasize the reader as much as the writer.

**40.1b**  Ineffective business letters crowd several pieces of information into a paragraph, avoid direct statements, are wordy, or issue commands or threats.

**40.2**  The resume or vita gives a personal history clearly and concisely and omits nonessential details.

# Course Notes and Examination Answers

This chapter considers important kinds of college writing, some briefly discussed in earlier chapters. These include note taking and examination answers. The chapter also discusses reading notes that will be of permanent use to you.

## 41.1 Course Notes

**41.1a Effective Notes.**   Chapter 37 explains the relationship between taking notes and writing the documented paper. The success of that relationship depends, first of all, upon *accurate* notes, whatever their source. But certain sources create more difficulty with accuracy than others. For example, taking accurate notes on a lecture is a harder to do than taking accurate notes while reading.

The reason is that in taking lecture notes you depend mainly on the spoken word, though your instructor probably writes important words and phrases on the board. In recording ideas and details as the lecture progresses, you can easily lose the thread of the discussion or fail to hear and record a phrase correctly. The "Houghton Mifflin edition" referred to in a lecture becomes "hot muffins" (with a large question mark) in one's notes. Mistakes of this sort are easy to make.

Taking notes on an article or a book, you proceed at your own pace, pausing to digest a difficult idea or example or returning to important passages to correct a note. Correcting notes in these ways is not usually possible in the lecture hall.

Writing accurate, useful lecture notes comes only with practice. However, you will write better notes if you keep the following points in mind.

1. Write your notes in complete phrases or sentences, not in single words. What is clear at the time you write down a single word probably will not be clear a week later and perhaps not even on the same day or a few hours later. If the rapidity of the lecture prevents you from making notes in complete sentences, make your phrases as complete as possible and rewrite them as complete sentences as soon after the lecture as possible.

2. Include connecting words, phrases, and sentences (*thus, therefore, as a result, these form a process*) that show the relationship between ideas and details. Your notes should have the continuity of a well-organized exposition or argument.

3. If in doubt about a proper name, a term, a detail, or an idea, put a question mark in the margin and check your textbook or a reference book for proper spelling or for identifying or explanatory details. Ask your instructor for clarification if necessary.

4. Write brief marginal notes on the significance of what you have recorded. If possible, record the pertinent pages of your textbook or other sources assigned on the topic, and record your thoughts as soon as possible. You are likely to forget them as the lecture progresses and other ideas occur to you.

**41.1b  Ineffective Notes.**   Consider this page of notes taken on an introductory lecture on viruses in a biology course:

Types of infectious agents
Viruses
    acellular in structure, chemical composition or replication
    DNA or RNA core two types of viruses
      old definition and new
    protein coat called capsomere
    some viruses have envelope of protein
    (additional coat sometimes from host tissue)
      enclosing capsomere
    viruses also classified by symmetry (see *Burnet*)
    capsomere has specific configuration (?) determines
    ability to enter host cell
    (determines host specificity)
    and host mounts immune response by recognizing specificity
    and stores memory of first encounter ("memory")

**41.1**

These notes mix words, phrases, and sentences with connecting or explanatory comments, probably those given in the lecture. The writer omits most of these comments and also her own, probably because she wishes to capture the main details and ideas. *Configuration, symmetry*, and *compatible* are the words of the lecturer: the writer put down the words she heard without putting them into her own words, probably because she was uncertain about the meaning. She also uses indentation to show the relationship between ideas—a common practice with notes that consist largely of words and phrases.

How useful will these notes be at the time of a quiz or an exam? They won't be very useful. The notes give the gist of the lecture, but they will be confusing once the writer has forgotten the connections made by the lecturer. She will do better on the quiz or a later exam if she rewrites these notes in her own words and in complete sentences, without depending on indentation. The notation on "Burnet" (mentioned by the lecturer) suggests that her textbook contains additional information and clarification of terms and details.

Here is the pertinent paragraph in the textbook:

> The new approaches have changed the whole outlook on viruses. Even the definition of a virus nowadays is quite different from the old one, which stated that a virus was a microorganism capable of multiplying only within living cells. The present approach is to define a virus as a structure composed of a protein coat surrounding a nucleic acid molecule, either RNA or DNA, which is capable of replication only within living cells. A virus is not an organism; it has no metabolism and is wholly dependent for its reproduction on mechanisms provided by its host cell.
>
> —Sir Macfarlane Burnet and David O. White,
> *Natural History of Infectious Disease*, 4th ed.

This passage clarifies some of the details in the notes by showing the connection between various bits of information including the old definition of virus and the new. The old definition is not given in the notes though the writer refers to it: perhaps the lecturer referred to it without giving the definition or explaining it. The indentation in the notes suggests that the reference was a passing one.

**41.1**

**Exercises**

1. Rewrite the notes on viruses in complete sentences, adding to them explanatory details on RNA and DNA from an unabridged dictionary or a desk encyclopedia or other reference work.

2. Write a summary of this section without looking at it. Then check the summary with the section to see how accurate your memory and your note taking are.

# 41.2  Reading Notes

**41.2a  Ineffective Notes.**  Besides the relationship between taking notes and writing the documented paper, you also found in Chapter 37 various methods of note taking, including summary and paraphrase. In school and on the job, you will use these essential kinds of writing. In preparing for an exam, you will summarize and paraphrase text material. At work, you will use many printed sources in preparation for conferences, meetings, and reports.

The points made about course notes in 41.1 apply to reading notes. Accuracy and full documentation are essential if the notes are to be useful later. A series of words and short, disconnected phrases will be difficult to understand outside their context.

Here are notes taken on a later passage in Burnet and White's discussion of viruses:

> modern classification of viruses
> physical and chemical characteristics
> particles or virions
> infection carried from cell to cell
> DNA and RNA single and double strands and number
>     of genes the criterion

Following is the passage that these reading notes summarize:

> The modern classification of viruses is based on the physical and chemical characteristics of the virus particles, the "virions," by which infection is transferred from one cell to the next. The basic criterion is the nature of the nucleic acid, DNA or RNA, single- or double-stranded, and the number of genes it contains. Also important is the way in which the protein molecules are arranged around the nucleic acid.
>
> —SIR MACFARLANE BURNET and DAVID O. WHITE,
> *Natural History of Infectious Disease*

Again, how accurate are these reading notes, and how useful will they be at a later time?

First, the notes combine exact quotations and paraphrase without distinguishing them. Were the quoted phrases included in a paper or a report, they would mistakenly appear without quotation marks if the writer of the notes forgets that the wording is that of the source. Carelessness in note taking is a common cause of unintended plagiarism—using the words of another writer as your own (see 37.3f).

**41.2**

Second, the phrases will be meaningful only if the writer recalls the original context and their connection to it. The notes don't make clear that the particles or virions are virus particles and that these particles carry the infection. Finally, the omission of the final statement that the classification is also based on the arrangement of the protein molecules makes the notes inaccurate.

**41.2b Effective Notes.**   To make sure your notes are accurate and will be useful later, write them as paraphrase—quoting only those phrases or sentences that cannot be paraphrased without loss of special nuance or emphasis. Here is a paraphrase that captures the essential ideas of the Burnet and White passage:

```
        Viruses are classified today on the basis of the
    physical and chemical properties of virus particles or
    virions. These carry infection from cell to cell. The
    nucleic acid of the virus is single-strand or double-
    strand, DNA or RNA, and contains a varying number of
    genes. This composition is the basic criterion. The ar-
    rangement of the protein molecules surrounding the nu-
    cleic acid is also a criterion.
```

You can also present this information in an outline that shows the connection between ideas:

```
Classification of physical and chemical properties of
virus particles
        1.  kind of nucleic acid and number of genes in
            each
            a.  single-strand or double-strand
            b.  DNA or RNA
        2.  arrangement of protein molecules surrounding
            nucleic acid
```

**41.2**

With a technical passage, be as specific as you can even at the risk of wordiness. The more familiar you are with the subject, the more condensation of ideas will be possible. The outline has the advantage of greater concision, but notice again the danger of haphazard arrangement of words and phrases.

Finally, record full information about the source—author, full title, publisher, and date of publication.

### EXERCISES

1. Write notes on the following discussion of languages and dialects, recording essential definitions and details. Your notes should give enough of the context of these definitions and details so they will be clear to you at a later time:

> Very often in everyday usage of the terms "dialect" and "language," the distinction between them is based very largely upon political or cultural considerations. For example, Mandarin and Cantonese are called dialects of Chinese, but they are more distinct from one another than, say, Danish and Norwegian or, even more strikingly, Dutch, Flemish and Afrikaans, which are frequently described as different languages. It might be thought that the criterion of intercomprehensibility would suffice to draw a politically and culturally neutral line of demarcation between languages. This is indeed the major criterion that a practising linguist would apply in establishing the limits of a language-community. But there are problems. It very often happens that dialect variation is gradual, and more or less continuous, over a wide area. Thus, speakers from two widely separated regions might be unable to understand one another, but there might be no point between any two adjacent dialects at which intercomprehensibility breaks down. Then there is the further, more troublesome problem that comprehensibility is not always symmetrical; nor is it a matter of all or nothing. It is quite possible, and indeed quite common, for X to understand most of what Y says and for Y to understand little or nothing of what X says, when each speaks to the other in his own dialect. For various reasons, then, it is often very difficult to draw a sharp distinction between distinct languages and different dialects of the same language.
>
> —JOHN LYONS, *Language and Linguistics*

**41.2**

2. Compare the following passage and the notes made on it. How accurate are these notes, and how useful will they be at a later time?

> *Passage*
> The fear of death carries over, quite understandably in view of the widespread confusion of symbols with

things symbolized, into fear of the *words* having to do with death. Many people, therefore, instead of saying "died," substitute such expressions as "passed away," "went to his reward," "departed," and "went west." In Japanese, the word for death, *shi*, happens to have the same pronunciation as the word for the number four. This coincidence results in many linguistically awkward situations, since people avoid "shi" in the discussion of numbers and prices, and use "yon," a word of different origin, instead.

—S. I. HAYAKAWA, *Language in Thought and Action*

*Notes*
illustration of common confusion of symbols and what they symbolize
"fear of words having to do with death"
    shi meaning death   pronounced same as four Japanese use "yon" for four for numbers   prices
    word having nothing to do with death
this coincidence results in many linguistically awkward situations

# 41.3  Examination Answers

**41.3a  Effective Answers.**  Though you need exact knowledge of the subject to write a successful examination answer, knowing the facts is no guarantee of success. You will need to organize your details carefully, directing them to the question asked and omitting details not pertinent to it.

Keep in mind the following points in organizing and developing your answer.

1. Know exactly how much time you have to write the answer, and stay within this time limit. An excellent answer to one question will have less weight if you have no time to answer other questions on the exam.

2. Read the question carefully to be certain you understand it. You will lose valuable time if you discover in the course of writing that you misunderstood the question and must rewrite the answer.

3. Organize the answer carefully. Begin with your central idea and develop it with exact details, or build to the idea slowly through an accumulation of detail. Avoid a haphazard assembly of facts and ideas. The structure of your answer should be obvious to your instructor.

**41.3**

4. State the essential details, and state them exactly even though they are familiar ones. The purpose of the exam is to test the exactness of your knowledge.

5. Don't assume that details speak for themselves. Having stated the facts, you need to interpret them. Show how the facts connect and what they imply. A mere assemblage of facts and details tells your instructor nothing.

6. Don't state an idea or an opinion without supporting facts, and don't state your ideas in general terms. Even with the support of details, your answer will be vague if you do not connect ideas to supporting facts.

7. Save time to proofread for sentence structure and spelling. And check the accuracy of your facts: it is easy to confuse names and details when writing under pressure.

**41.3b Focus and Organization.**   Consider the following exam question and answers:

*Question*
How would you distinguish by sight a first-degree burn from a second-degree burn?

*Answer 1*
A first-degree burn is red or discolored, slightly swollen, and painful. A second-degree burn is also red, sometimes spotted or blotched, usually blistered and more swollen, and wet in appearance. It also has penetrated deeper into the surface and takes longer to heal than first-degree burns.

*Answer 2*
First-degree burns are superficial burns caused by staying out in the sun too long or touching hot things. They have the usual characteristics of a bad sunburn. Second-degree burns may hurt more than third-degree burns in which the nerves in the skin are damaged or killed. Hot cooking oil can cause second-degree burns, too. Second-degree burns take longer to heal.

Which is the better answer?
The question asks about visual signs of first-degree and second-degree burns. Answer 1 distinguishes carefully between the signs shared by the two kinds of burn (redness and swelling) and the differences between these signs (in second-degree burns the spotting and blotching of the skin that accompanies the redness and the greater swelling). Answer 1 also pinpoints the additional signs in second-degree burns (blistering and greater penetration of the skin). The difference in healing is stated at the end of the answer—an appropriate place since this sign would be noticed last.

**41.3**

In referring to bad sunburns and cooking oil burns, Answer 2 alludes to the characteristics of first- and second-degree burns instead of naming them. The writer probably assumes the instructor knows the facts about the two kinds of burns. But the question is asking about these facts: the writer should assume that the reader does not know the facts.

Answer 1 is the stronger answer. But Answer 2 does contain one important fact omitted in Answer 1: second-degree burns may be more painful because the nerve ends in the skin are damaged or destroyed in deeper burns. In answering a question of this sort, do not leave essential facts to inference.

Both answers address the question directly. The following answer does not:

*Answer 3*

First-degree burns sometimes seem as serious as second-degree ones because they can hurt as much. Sunburns are a good example. Both can be soaked in cold water, then dressed. The blisters in second-degree burns should not be broken. A doctor or nurse can tell the difference right away and will know how to treat the burn. Third-degree burns are the most serious; the burn area looks white or ashy. Most of the skin has been destroyed. Unlike first-degree and second-degree burns, third-degree ones should not be soaked in cold water because this will cause shock.

Answer 3 does not address the question, and it has no central point or focus. The details are presented haphazardly, in the order they occur to the writer. Probably the writer remembered the differences between third-degree and second-degree burns but not those between second-degree and first-degree burns. Lacking a central point, the answer is diffuse—spreading in all directions. In a well-focused and well-organized answer, the details support a central point. Transitional words give the answer coherence. And a unified answer takes up one characteristic at a time instead of jumping from one to another.

**41.3**

**41.3c Interpretation and Judgment.**    Many exam questions ask for an interpretation of facts:

What does Hamlet's soliloquy beginning "To be, or not to be" show about his state of mind and the revenge he is pursuing against Claudius, the murderer of Hamlet's father?

Consider this answer to this question:

In his soliloquy Hamlet asks if it is better to live or die. He wonders if it is better to suffer the "slings and arrows of outrageous fortune" (one of Shakespeare's most famous lines), or do something to end them. He says life is so painful that many people would kill themselves if they weren't afraid of what would happen to them after committing suicide. Hamlet realizes that "conscience does make cowards of us all" (another famous line in the play). These thoughts show what is on Hamlet's mind just before the players perform "The Murder of Gonzago." Hamlet expects to unmask Claudius through this "play within a play." So we know Hamlet is pursuing the revenge in arranging the play, but the soliloquy tells us what his feelings are about its success.

The writer here assumes that a summary of the speech—a detailed account of Hamlet's thoughts on suicide—defines his state of mind and shows how actively he is pursuing the revenge. The concluding sentences do state that Hamlet is pursuing the revenge, but a mere summary of facts says nothing unless the writer connects them to Hamlet's actions. Facts must be interpreted to have meaning. A mere recitation of the events in the play also says nothing about Hamlet as a person, about the meaning of his actions, or about the attitude or feelings Shakespeare wishes the audience to hold about Hamlet.

In answering a question that calls for interpretation or judgment, place the facts in a context—here the context of the soliloquy at this point in the play. To understand the feelings and thoughts Hamlet is expressing, the reader must know what events led to the soliloquy and how typical these feelings and thoughts are of those Hamlet expresses in earlier scenes.

### EXERCISES

1. On August 14, 1941, President Franklin Roosevelt and British Prime Minister Winston Churchill stated the aims of their allied countries in the Second World War. This statement of aim, the Atlantic Charter, contains the following:

> Britain and the United States seek no aggrandizement, territorial or otherwise.
>
> There should be no territorial changes that do not accord with the freely expressed wishes of the peoples concerned.
>
> The right of all peoples to choose the form of government under which they will live should be respected.
>
> All states, great or small, victor or vanquished, should enjoy access, on equal terms, to the trade and raw materials of the world.

**41.3**

Collaboration should be fostered among all nations with the object of securing, for all, improved labor standards, economic advancement, and social security.

The peace to be established should afford to all nations the means of dwelling in safety within their own borders, and should afford assurance to all men that they may live out their lives in freedom from fear and want.

The peace should enable all men to traverse the high seas without hindrance.

Pending the establishment of a permanent system of general security, all nations which threaten or may threaten aggression should be disarmed.

—EDWARD MCNALL BURNS, *Western Civilizations*

A college exam in world history contained the following question on the Atlantic Charter:

What does the Atlantic Charter imply are the causes of war?

How successful is the following answer to the question?

The Charter says that the U.S. and Britain did not want to seize territory or gain more power through war. They wanted people to live without hunger or fear of their neighbors safely in their own countries, to be able to choose their own government without other countries interfering, to have access to raw materials, and to enjoy free trade. If territory did change hands, people living there would have to agree to the change. These goals cannot be achieved without nations working together to improve living and working conditions. The oceans of the world had to be safe for travel by all nations. The goals of the Atlantic Charter show what the U.S. and Britain believed were the causes of war. Also, the Charter influenced the United Nations Declaration, signed by 26 nations in 1942, and later by others. One purpose of the UN is to prevent war. The Charter recognizes armament as a cause of war. So the Charter does imply many causes of war in the world.

**41.3**

2. Write a practice answer of your own to the following questions:
   a. Given the statements of the Atlantic Charter, how concerned were the United States and Great Britain with the power that large, well-armed nations would exert over small, poorly armed nations when the Second World War ended?

**b.** What does the Charter say or imply about the responsibilities of the big powers following the war?

## Checklist for Course Notes and Examination Answers

**41.1a** Write course notes in phrases or complete sentences.

**41.1b** Ineffective notes mix words, phrases, and sentences haphazardly, without showing their relationship.

**41.2a** Accuracy and full documentation are essential.

**41.2b** Effective notes distinguish between paraphrase and direct quotation and fully document the source.

**41.3a** Effective examination answers address the question directly and state the details exactly.

**41.3b** Ineffective answers substitute summary for interpretation.

**41.3**

# Glossary of Usage

This glossary lists common errors in writing and in words and phrases appropriate to one level of writing but inappropriate to another. The following abbreviations identify the part of speech: verb (v.), adjective (adj.), adverb (adv.), preposition (prep.), conjunction (conj.), noun (n.). The label *colloquial*, which refers to conversational or spoken English, does not mean that the usage is illiterate; it means that an expression may be inappropriate in general and formal writing (see 28.3). The word *jargon* refers to clumsy or repetitive words and phrases that make sentences hard to read (see 29.4).

**A, An.** *A* is used before consonants, *an* before words that are written or sounded with a vowel (a horror film, an hour ago).

**Accept, Except.** *Accept* (v.) means "receive" or "approve of something." *Except* (prep.) means "other than." *Except* (v.) means "to leave out" or "exclude something":

> I accepted his explanation.
> I excepted the tip from the bill.

**Adapt, Adopt.** *Adapt* means "to change something" or "to serve a new use":

> She adapted the play for children.

*Adopt* is "to make one's own" or "to take control":

> We adopted a stray dog.

**Advice, Advise.** *Advice* is the noun:

> She gave me advice.

*Advise* is the verb:

> I advised her to take the course.

**Affect, Effect.**   To *affect* (v.) is "to influence":

Hot weather affects his mood.

To *effect* (v.) is the formal way of saying "to cause" or "to bring about":

The new policy effected a change in attitude.

*Improved*
The new policy changed attitudes.

The noun *affect* refers to an influence or controlling state; the noun *effect* refers to a resulting state:

The experiment measures the affect of nervous impulses.
She is testing the effect of barbiturates on sleep.

**Aggravate, Irritate.**   To *aggravate* is to make worse something already unpleasant:

The shooting aggravated the tension.

The word is used colloquially to mean "to irritate" or "to bother":

*Colloquial*
The sarcastic remark aggravated me.

**Agree to, Agree with.**   *Agree to* means "to consent":

I agree to meet with her.

*Agree with* means "to be in harmony with":

I agree with your thinking on the matter.

**Ain't.**   Nonstandard for *am not, is not, has not, have not.*

**All ready, Already.**   All ready (adj.) means "fully prepared":

I am all ready to go.

*Already* (adv.) means "previously" or "by now":

The plane has already landed. He should have already departed.

**All right.**   The one correct spelling.

**All Together, Altogether.**   *All together* (adj.) means to "be as one":

The family is all together.

*Altogether* (adv.) means "entirely":

I am altogether in agreement.

**Allusion, Illusion.** An allusion is an indirect reference:

> She made an allusion to the accident, afraid to speak of it directly.

An illusion is a deceptive appearance:

> He gives the illusion of being smart.

**Almost, Most.** *Almost* (adv.) means "nearly":

> He almost succeeded.

*Most* (n.) means "the greater part":

> Most who enroll do succeed.

*Most* is used in speech to mean "almost":

> *Colloquial*
> I see her most every night.

*Almost* is the correct word in writing:

> I see her almost every night.

**Among, Between.** In formal English *among* refers to more than two:

> What is a little disagreement among friends?

*Between* is used with two things, including one thing and a group:

> There is no disagreement between John and his friends.

*Between* is used informally as a substitute for *among*:

> a disagreement between friends.

**Amount, Number.** *Amount* is used with noncountable things:

> an amount of sand on the shore.

*Number* is used with countable things:

> a number of rocks on the shore.

**And which, But which.** *And* and *but* should not be used with a relative clause:

> *Incorrect*
> *Jane Eyre* is my favorite novel, and which I read every year.
> *Correct*
> *Jane Eyre* is my favorite novel, which I read every year.
> *Incorrect*
> She ate the broccoli, but which she dislikes.
> *Correct*
> She ate the broccoli, which she dislikes.

gl/u

**Any one, Anyone.**    *Any one* is used to single out one person or thing out of several:

> Choose any one book but don't take them all.

*Anyone* refers to one person or thing without specifying it:

> Anyone can run a computer who makes the effort.

**Anyways, Anywheres.**    Use *anyway, anywhere.*

**Apt, Liable, Likely.**    *Apt* means *tends*:

> He is apt to complain if he gets the chance.

*Liable* means to "be legally obligated." Another meaning is to "be at risk":

> He is liable to the rental agency for the damage to the car.
> He is liable to get pneumonia if his cold persists.

*Apt* is used informally to mean "liable" with the meaning of "likely."

*Likely*, sometimes used as a synonym of *liable*, better expresses the idea of probability:

> *Ambiguous*
> She is liable to get a promotion if she stays with the company.

> *Clear*
> She is likely to receive a promotion if she stays with the company.

**As.**    A confusing substitute for *because* and *while*:

> *Confusing*
> As we are going, we need to lock the windows.

> *Improved*
> Because we are going, we need to lock the windows.

Also a nonstandard substitute for *who* and *whether*:

> *Nonstandard*
> She is the woman as told me the address.

> *Standard*
> She is the woman who told me the address.

**As, Like.**    Both function as prepositions—*as* expressing exact resemblance, *like* expressing similarity:

> He served as a Marine.
> He looks like a Marine.

**gl/u**

(conj.) introduces full clauses:

> As the guide said, the water was too polluted to drink.

*Like* is acceptable in sentences like the following:

> He looks like his father (he looks like his father looks).

**As, Than.** In comparison, pronouns that follow *as* and *than* take the subject or object case form depending on whether they are the subject or object of the governing verb:

> She is as young as I (am young).
> She is older than I (am).
> She praises him as much as (she praises) me.
> She praises him more than (she praises) me.

**As to.** *As to* is a frequent substitute for the formal *in respect to*:

> As to your going, I think you should.

*As to* is a weak substitute for "about" or "concerning":

> I asked as to his grades.

> *Improved*
> I asked about his grades.

**Awhile, A while.** *Awhile*, meaning "for a certain time," is used adverbally:

> Sit awhile!

*A while* singles out the time:

> She won't be back for a while.

**Bad, Badly.** Verbs of sense (*feel, smell, taste*) like *to be* verbs take adjectives as complements:

> I feel so bad.

In general and formal English, *badly* means "imperfectly" or "in a bad way":

> He drives badly.

*Badly* is colloquial for feeling sick or being sorry:

> We feel badly.

**Being that.** The following is colloquial:

> Being that you're sick, we'll stay home.

The standard form is the following:

> We'll stay home because you're sick.

**gl/u**

**Beside, Besides.**   *Beside* means "next to":

> the chair beside the bed

*Besides* means "also" and "moreover":

> Who's coming besides you?

**Between, Among.**   See *among, between.*

**Bring, Take.**   I bring something toward a person or place, and I take something away:

> I brought the cake to the party.
> I took the cake out of the oven.

**But that.**   A jargon phrase that adds deadwood to the sentence:

> *Wordy*
> I don't question but that you're right.

> *Improved*
> I don't question that you're right.

See also *can't help but.*

**Can, May.**   *May* is formal in asking permission:

> May I leave?

*Can* is informal:

> Can I leave?

In formal English the sentence means:

> Am I able to leave?

The context tells us what the speaker or writer means.

**Can't help but.**   A jargon phrase. Compare the following:

> *Wordy*
> I can't help but cry that he left.

> *Improved*
> I can't help crying that he left.

**Center around.**   Redundant. The preferred expression is *center on*:

> The course centers on foreign policy in the 1970s.

**Complement, Compliment.**   To *complement* is "to complete" or "to form part of" or "to add":

> The crew complemented the ship.

To *compliment* is "to praise":

The captain complimented the crew.

**Contact.** Colloquial for "talk to" or "write."

*Informal*
He contacted the police about the accident.

*General*
He wrote the police about the accident.

**Continual, Continuous.** Continual means "intermittent" or "recurrent":

There were continual interruptions from the spectators.

*Continuous* means "ongoing," "without interruption":

There was continuous noise in the room.

**Could of, Should of, Would of.** Confusions with *could have, should have, would have*. Probably confused with the colloquial *could've, should've, would've*:

*Incorrect*
She should of come to the review session.

*Correct*
She should have come to the review session.

**Data.** *Data* is commonly used for the singular and plural.

**Different from.** Use *different from* with a noun phrase to note a difference:

New York is different from Los Angeles.

*Different than* is a colloquial substitute:

New York is different than Los Angeles.

It is used idiomatically in comparisons:

New York was more different than I expected.

**Disinterested, Uninterested.** A *disinterested* observer of an event is impartial or has no wish to gain from the outcome:

He showed he was disinterested when he refused to take sides in the debate.

An *uninterested* observer is indifferent or unconcerned:

He showed he was uninterested when he left the hall and did not return.

gl/u

**Don't.**   *Don't* is a contraction of *do not*, not *does not* (doesn't).

**Due to.**   Idiomatic after the verb *is*:

> The rise in prices is due to the drought.

The phrase is awkward when used with other verbs:

> The rise in prices happened due to the drought.

It is wordy in the following sentence:

> The rise in prices is due to the fact that we are having a drought.
>
> *Improved*
> The drought caused a rise in prices.

**Effect, Affect.**   See *affect, effect.*

**Either, Each.**   These words are not synonyms. Compare the following:

> *Inexact*
> Hydrants are on either side of the street.
>
> *Improved*
> Hydrants are on each side of the street.

**Enthused.**   Colloquial for "be enthusiastic"—the general and formal term:

> She was enthusiastic about going.

**Etc.**   *Etc.* means "and the rest," and "so forth." *And etc.* is redundant.

**Ever.**   The word is redundant in the following sentence:

> There is never a breeze ever.

The word *never* has the meaning of *ever*:

> *Improved*
> There is never a breeze.

**Except, Accept.**   See *accept, except.*

**Explicit, Implicit.**   *Explicit* means "outright," "direct":

> His instructions were explicit.

*Implicit* means "suggested," "indirect":

> His warning was implicit.

**Farther, Further.**   *Farther* refers to addition and also to distance:

> How much farther is Chicago?

*Further* is used in these senses, but is the preferred word in referring to time:

>We need further time to finish the job.

*Further* is also used with abstractions like the following:

>She gave us further knowledge about the city.

**Feasible, Probable.**   *Feasible* means "can be done," not "probable."

*Inexact*
It is feasible he will come.

*Exact*
Spanning the river is feasible.

**Fewer, Less.**   *Fewer* is used with count nouns:

>fewer pages, fewer pencils, fewer glasses

*Less* is used with noncount or mass nouns:

>less water, less grass.

**First, Firstly.**   *First* is the common form.

**Formally, Formerly.**   *Formally* refers to structure or to conventional behavior. *Formerly* refers to action in the past:

>Your essay is formally correct though the ideas need illustration.
>She was formerly vice president of the company.

**Former, Latter.**   *Former* refers to the first of two things mentioned; *latter* refers to the second:

>I do well in chemistry and biology, but I like the former and hate the latter.

With a series of three or more, use first and last.

**Get.**   A colloquial word with a wide range of meanings. In the following sentence it has the meaning of "become":

*Informal*
Driving to school soon gets to be a nuisance.

*General*
Driving to school soon becomes a nuisance.

**Good, Well.**   *Good* is the adjective, *well* the adverb:

*Correct*
The cake tastes good.

*Incorrect*
The cake tastes well.

gl/u

The statement "I feel good" means "I am feeling in good health" or "I am in good spirits."

**Hang, Hung.**    Objects are *hung*, people are *hanged*. The phrase *hung jury* uses the word to mean "deadlocked."

**Hardly.**    *Hardly* is redundant when used with other negative words:

> *Incorrect*
> She has not hardly spoken a word.

> *Correct*
> She has hardly spoken a word.

**Hisself.**    Nonstandard for *himself*.

**Hopefully.**    Colloquial for *I hope*:

> *General*
> I hope the plan will succeed.

*Hopefully* makes the following sentence awkward because it seems to modify the word *war*:

> *Awkward*
> The war hopefully will end.

> *Exact*
> We hope the war will end.

**If, Whether.**    *If* is colloquial for *whether* in the following:

> I will ask if the report is ready.

Use *whether* in general and formal English:

> I will ask whether the report is ready.

**Illusion.**    See *allusion, illusion*.

**Imply, Infer.**    *Imply* means "to hint" or "to suggest something":

> I implied by my sarcasm that he was acting foolish.

*Infer* means "to draw a conclusion from a statement":

> I inferred from his sarcasm that he thought the same of me.

**In, Into.**    *In* refers to the general place or location of something:

> The office is in the building.

*Into* specifies the act of motion:

> She met him going into the building.

**gl/u**

**Individual, Person.**   Though widely used for *person, individual* is best used to single out a person from a group. It can be ambiguous:

>He is not the individual I thought he was.

The sentence can mean either of the following:

>I mistook him for someone else.
>He is a conformist.

**Infer.**   See *imply, infer.*

**Inside of.**   See *outside of.*

**Irregardless.**   Redundant for *regardless.*

**Irritate.**   See *aggravate, irritate.*

**Is when, Is where, Is because.**   These expressions may introduce inexact predicates:

>*Incorrect*
>The picnic is when you eat outdoors.
>
>*Correct*
>You eat outdoors on picnics.
>
>*Incorrect*
>A concerto is where one or more solo instruments play with an orchestra.
>
>*Correct*
>A concerto is a musical composition for one or more solo instruments and orchestra.
>
>*Incorrect*
>The quarantine is because of citrus canker.
>
>*Correct*
>The orchard has been quarantined because of citrus canker.

See *faulty predication* (23.3) and *mixed constructions* (23.1).

**Item.**   *Item* refers to each single article in a list:

>We identified each item on the list.

The word also has the colloquial meaning of "thing" or "matter":

>The committee has another item to consider.
>
>*Improved*
>The committee has another problem (or proposal) to consider.

gl/u

**Its, It's.**   *Its* is the possessive of *it*:

> the tail of the dog, its tail

*It's* is the contraction of *it is*:

> It's snowing.

**Kind of, Sort of.**   Singular with *this* and *that*:

> this kind of food, that sort of fish

Plural with *these* and *those*:

> these kinds of vegetables, those sorts of cars

**Lay, Lie.**   *Lay* means "to put" or "to place something." In the active voice this transitive verb always takes an object that receives the action. In the passive voice, this receiver becomes the subject:

| *Active Voice* | *Passive Voice* |
| --- | --- |
| I lay the book on the table. | The book is laid on the table. |
| I laid the book on the table. | The book was laid on the table. |
| I have laid the book on the table in the past. | The book had been laid on the table. |

*Lie* means to be situated or to recline horizontally and does not take an object:

> Akron lies south of Cleveland.
> I lie down to sleep.
> I lay down to nap.
> I have lain awake since these headaches began.

**Leave, Let.**   *Leave* means "to go away," *let* means "to permit":

> Leave the room!
> Let him explain!

**Liable.**   See *apt, liable, likely*.

**Like.**   See *as, like*.

**Loose, Lose.**   These words are easily confused. *Loose* (adj.) means "free," "unconfined":

> The dog is running loose.
> The bolt is loose.

*Loose* (v.) expresses the same meanings:

> He loosed the dog in the field.

*Lose* (v.) means "to mislay" or "to give up control":

> I lose my way every time I drive to Cleveland.

**May.** See *can, may.*

**May be, Maybe.** *Maybe* (adv.) means *perhaps. May be* is the verb phrase:

> We may be going.

**Most.** See *almost, most*

**Myself, Himself, Herself, Yourself.** These words are used reflexively to call attention to the subject as the actor:

> She fixed the wiring herself.

Compare with the following:

> She insisted that she herself fixed it, not the repairman.

These words substitute colloquially for *me, him, her, your*:

> No one can repair it but myself.

Using the word *me* (or equivalent pronouns) instead of *myself* prevents the sentence from being misread:

> No one can repair it but me.

**Never.** The colloquial use of the word *never* can be ambiguous:

> *Ambiguous*
> He never knew it could be so warm in January.

> *Improved*
> He did not know it could be so warm.

**Nohow, Nowheres.** The standard forms are *in no way* and *nowhere.*

**Not unlikely.** An intensifier that can be overused. *Likely* is sufficient in most sentences:

> It is likely he will come.

**Number.** See *amount, number.*

**Of, Have.** These words are sometimes confused in writing because they sound alike:

> *Incorrect*
> I should of asked permission to leave work early.

> *Correct*
> I should have asked permission to leave work early.

**Of which, Whose.** *Whose* usually refers to people and animate things. It also substitutes for *of which:*

gl/u

That's the book whose cover I tore.

*Improved*
I tore the cover of that book.

**Off, Of.**   These words are easily confused. Compare:

I tore the cover off.
I tore the cover of the book.

**Off of.**   *Of* is redundant:

*Redundant*
He tore the address label off of the cover.

*Improved*
He tore the address label off the cover.

**On account of.**   A jargon phrase that makes sentences wordy:

*Wordy*
I am going on account of what happened.

*Improved*
I am going because of what happened.

**Onto, On to.**   *Onto* means "to put on top of something." *On to* joins an adverb (attached to a verb like *turned*) to a preposition (introducing a phrase like *to the highway*):

The sculptor put the statue onto the pedestal.
The car turned on to the highway from the side street.

**Outside of, Inside of.**   *Of* is redundant:

*Informal*
The car is parked outside of the house.

*General and formal*
The car is parked outside the house.

**Party, Person.**   *Party* is a pretentious substitute for *person*:

*Pretentious*
She is the party I described to you.

*Improved*
She is the person I described to you.

**Person.**   See *individual, person*.

**Phenomena.**   This word is sometimes mistakenly used to describe a singular occurrence. The singular form is *phenomenon*:

*Incorrect*
Political apathy is a phenomena today.

*Correct*
Political apathy is a phenomenon today.

**Plenty.** Standard for "quite enough" or "more than enough":

We have plenty of food.

Colloquial for *very*:

We are plenty tired.

*General*
We are very tired.

**Principal, Principle.** *Principal* (adj.) means "main" or "leading":

The drought is the principal cause of the rise in prices.

The noun form has the same meaning:

She is a school principal.

*Principle* (n.) means "rule" or "maxim":

The first principle of good driving is common sense.

The word is not used as an adjective:

*Incorrect*
Drought is a principle cause of famine.

*Correct*
Drought is a principal cause of famine.

**Previous to.** A jargon phrase that makes sentences wordy:

*Wordy*
He went to the park previous to her.

*Improved*
He went to the park before she did.

**Proceed.** This word means "to advance" or "to continue after a momentary stop." The word is not a synonym of *went*:

*Pretentious*
He proceeded to the park.

*Improved*
He went to the park.

gl/u

**Raise, Rise.**    *Raise* means "to lift something" and in the active voice takes a direct object that receives the action:

> I raised the window.

*Rise* means "to go up" or "to get up" and does not take an object:

> I rise at six every morning.

**Real, Really.**    Though *real* is colloquial for *really* (a real fine movie), *really* is the preferred form in writing:

> a really fine book

**Reason is because.**    A colloquial expression that makes written sentences wordy and awkward:

> The reason for inflation is because interest rates dropped.
>
> *Improved*
> The reason for the inflation is that interest rates dropped.
>
> *Better*
> The drop in interest rates caused inflation.

**Refer, Allude.**    *Refer* means to call attention to directly; *allude* means to do so indirectly.

**Regarding.**    Phrases like *regarding, in regard to, in respect to* have simple equivalents:

> *Wordy*
> In regard to your request for an extension of time, you can have it.
>
> *Improved*
> You can have the extension for the time you requested.
>
> *Wordy*
> I am writing in respect to the matter stated in your letter.
>
> *Improved*
> I am writing in answer to your letter.

**Rise.**    See *raise, rise.*

**Set, Sit.**    In the active voice *set* takes an object that receives the action:

> I set the book on the table.

In the passive voice this receiver becomes the subject:

> *Standard*
> The book was set on the table.
>
> *Nonstandard*
> The book was sat on the table.

*Sit* does not take an object in the active voice.

*Standard*
I sit down. I am sitting on the chair.

*Nonstandard*
I set on the chair.

**Shall, Will.** *Will* is now standard in all three persons, with *shall* reserved for particularly emphatic statements:

We shall conquer!

*Shall* is required in questions asking for consent or agreement:

Shall we begin?

**Similar . . . as.** The correct phrase is *similar . . . to*:

*Incorrect*
She is similar in belief as her sister.

*Correct*
She is similar in belief to her sister.

**Supposed to.** The suffix *-d* is required: *supposed to*, not *suppose to*.

**Sure, Surely.** *Sure* is the colloquial form:

*Colloquial*
That is sure not what he said.

*General*
That is surely not what I said.

**Sure and, Sure of.** These colloquial expressions are inappropriate in writing:

*Colloquial*
Be sure and finish by noon.

*General*
Be sure to finish by noon.

*Sure of* can make a statement ambiguous:

*Ambiguous*
She is sure of coming.

*Clear*
We are sure that she is coming.
She is sure she will come.

**Than, As.** See *as, than*.

gl/u

**Than, Then.**    *Than*, the conjunction used in comparisons, should not be confused with the adverb *then*:

*Incorrect*
This summer is hotter then last [summer].

*Correct*
This summer is hotter than last.

**Than what.**    Wordy for *than*. Compare the following:

*Wordy*
It is simpler than what you think.

*Improved*
It is simpler than you think.

**Their, There, They're.**    *Their* is the possessive form of *they*:

They sold their books.

*There* is an adverb and expletive—a word without meaning that completes a sentence:

*Adverb*
Put the book there.

*Expletive*
There are three books on the table.

*They're* is the contracted form of *they are*.

**Theirselves.**    Nonstandard for *themselves*.

**Thusly.**    Nonstandard for *thus*.

**This here, This there.**    Intensive forms in certain dialects but nonstandard in written English:

*Nonstandard*
This here man is my friend.

*Standard*
This man is my friend.

**Through, Throughout.**    *Through* means "by way of." *Throughout* means "in every part of":

*Confusing*
He discusses the causes of the war through the book.

*Clear*
He discusses the causes of the war throughout the book.

**To, Too.**   *To* is the preposition:

> I am going to the store.

*Too* is the adverb:

> Are you coming, too?

**Type of.**   The phrase *type of* can make a sentence wordy:

> *Wordy*
> Science fiction is the type of fiction I like.

> *Improved*
> I like science fiction.

**Used to.**   The correct form is *used to*, not *use to*.

**Want to.**   Colloquial for *should*:

> *Informal*
> You want to talk to her before the exam.

> *General*
> You should talk to her before the exam.

**Was.**   Nonstandard in the second-person singular:

> you was going

The word is nonstandard in the first-, second-, and third-person plural also:

> we was going, you was going, we was going

*Were* is the standard form.

**Well.**   See *good, well*.

**Where, That.**   The following colloquial use of *where* is inappropriate in writing:

> *Incorrect*
> I read where Alice won the race.

> *Correct*
> I read that Alice won the race.

**Where at.**   *At* is redundant:

> *Redundant*
> Do you know where Des Moines is at?

> *Improved*
> Do you know where Des Moines is?

**gl/u**

**Which, That.**    *Which* refers to things except in biblical and archaic sentences:

> Our Lord which art in heaven.

*That* refers to things and less commonly to people:

> The crew that landed yesterday will remain in port a week.

*Which* introduces nonrestrictive modifiers:

> The ship, which docked yesterday, will be in port a week.

The *which* clause gives additional information about the crew; the *that* clause identifies the crew. (See 11.2b.)

**Who, Whom.**    In general and formal usage *who* (and its derivatives) is used in subject positions, *whom* (and its derivatives) in object positions:

> He is the person who called.
> Give the book to whoever calls.
> He is the person whom you called.
> Give the book to whomever you want.

In colloquial English *who* sometimes replaces *whom* when the object function is not obvious:

> Who did you give the book to?

*Whom* is required immediately after a preposition except when *who* or *whoever* is subject in a clause:

> To whom am I speaking?
> Give the book to whoever answers the door.

## General Exercise

Correct the following sentences if they contain an error in usage:

1. She is doing well in algebra and is doing even better in chemistry.
2. She is doing good in helping deaf children learn sign language.
3. There is much more she can do, and which will help them.
4. An argument occurred among the neighbors and the woman living in the corner house.
5. He refused to except the award on account of he did not agree with the goals of the organization.
6. That's the car of which the hubcaps were stolen.
7. My principle reason for quitting is that I am looking for more interesting work.

8. He entered the room previous to the others.
9. We are altogether in our support for the proposal.
10. She proceeded to explain why she could not support it wholly.
11. The rest of the committee gave there reasons for supporting it.
12. One of the sisters looks more similar to her mother than the other.
13. You soon get use to walking long distances when you live in the country.
14. If you want to change his mind, you want to talk to him before he leaves for New York.
15. The officers of the company voted theirselves a raise in salary.
16. Take names and addresses from whoever comes into the room.
17. Give the package to whoever is at the desk, but ask for identification and ask the person to sign a receipt.
18. That man looks like he needs a good meal worst then anyone I have ever seen.
19. *David Copperfield* is where Dickens describes the London he knew as a boy.
20. We refused to except the decision of the board that the street assessment be increased.
21. I certainly do not agree to their decision on the matter.
22. We arc already to file a protest with the commission.
23. There is nothing farther to say on the matter.
24. We are filing the protest irregardless of what the commission threatens to do.
25. There were continuous outbursts from the spectators at the hearing.

gl/u

# Glossary of Grammatical Terms

**Absolute Construction.**   See *Noun absolute*.

**Active Voice.**   See *Voice*.

**Adjectival.**   A word, phrase, or clause that serves as an adjective. See 8.4c.

**Adjective.**   Traditionally a word that describes or modifies a noun, pronoun, or other nominal. See 8.4.

**Adjective Complement.**   An adjective that follows a linking verb and describes the subject of the clause. See *Linking verb*, *Predicate adjective*.

**Adverb.**   Traditionally a word or phrase that modifies or describes verbs (ran *quickly*), adjectives (*intensely* hot), other adverbs (*very* quickly), and whole clauses (*Fortunately* the storm caused little damage). See 8.8.

**Adverbial.**   A word, phrase, or clause that serves as an adverb in clauses. See 8.8d.

**Antecedent.**   A preceding word or phrase referred to by a pronoun:

> She described the *accident* and how *it* happened.

**Antithesis.**   The balancing of contrasting phrases or clauses in a sentence:

> Radicalism is a term the meaning of which everybody thinks he knows, and the definition of which nobody can give.
> —HOWARD MUMFORD JONES

See 20.2.

671

**Appositive.**   A word or phrase that explains or defines a word or phrase it immediately follows:

> The man in the yard, an official of the Health Department, declared the water safe for drinking.

**Article.**   The words *a, an* (*indefinite articles*), and *the* (*definite article*). Articles function as adjectivals. See 8.3.

**Aspect.**   The feature of the verb that expresses the speaker's view of what is happening. *Progressive verbs* (*I am laughing, I was laughing*) express the event as ongoing in the present, past, or future. *Perfect verbs* show the event or action as beginning in the past and continuing into the present (present perfect: *I have laughed*), as beginning and ending in the past (past perfect: *I had laughed*), or as beginning and ending in the future (future perfect: *I will have laughed*). Compare *Tense.* See 8.6d.

**Auxiliary.**   Auxiliary verbs (*have, be, do*) combine with the present or past participle to form complex verbs (*is writing, has written*). The modal auxiliaries (*shall, should, will, would, can, could, may, might, must, ought,* etc.) combine with the simple base or infinitive verb (*must write*) to express intent, will, possibility, obligation, need, and other ideas. See 8.6a, 8.6b.

**Balance.**   The use of strict parallelism in phrases and clauses throughout a sentence (20.2):

> We observe today not a victory of party but a celebration of freedom—symbolizing an end as well as a beginning—signifying renewal as well as change.
>
> —President John F. Kennedy

**Case.**   The form of a noun or pronoun that shows its grammatical function. English has three cases—*nominative* or *subjective, possessive,* and *objective*. Nouns have the same form in the nominative and objective cases. Nouns form the possessive by adding -'*s* or -*s*'. Pronouns have different forms in all three cases. See 8.1a.

**Clause.**   A clause consists of a subject and a predicate. It may stand alone or may help to form a sentence or to modify a sentence element. See *Independent clause, Dependent clause.* See 7.2.

**Comma Splice.**   The misuse of the comma to join independent clauses without a coordinating conjunction:

> I grow tomatoes, because they upset me I never eat them.

See 11.6g.

**Complement.**   A word or phrase that completes the predicate. A *subject complement* (This book is a *dictionary*) forms the predicate with *to be* verbs; verbs of sense, *become, seem, appear, remain*; and is the equivalent of the subject. An *object complement* identifies the direct object (They appointed Jane *president*). See 7.2a.

**Complex Sentence.**   One independent clause and one or more dependent clauses:

> I grow tomatoes although I never eat them.
> Although I never eat them, I grow tomatoes that are sometimes as big as oranges.

See 9.1c.

**Compound Sentence.**   Two or more independent clauses and their word or phrasal modifiers, joined with coordinating conjunctions:

> The book with the torn cover is an English dictionary, and the book with the red cover is a dictionary.

See 9.1b.

**Compound-Complex Sentence.**   Two or more independent clauses joined with two or more dependent clauses:

> I grow tomatoes although I never eat them, but I do eat all the lettuce and radishes that I also grow.

See 9.1d.

**Conjunction.**   A broad class of words that connect words, phrases (bread and butter), or clauses. *Coordinating conjunctions* (*and, but, yet, for, so, or, nor*) connect clauses of the same weight and importance (I grow tomatoes but I can't eat them); *subordinating conjunctions* (*since, when, although, while,* etc.) connect dependent or subordinate clauses to independent or main ones (Although I grow tomatoes, I don't pick them myself). See 8.9.

**Conjunctive Adverb.**   An adverb that joins independent clauses:

> I grow tomatoes; however, I never eat them.

See 8.9, 12.1d.

**Coordinating Conjunction.**   See *Conjunction.*

**Correlative Conjunctions.**   Conjunctions (*both-and, either-or, neither-or, not only-but also, on the one hand-on the other hand*) that join complementary ideas. See 8.9b, 9.1.

gl/gr

**Dangling Modifier.**  A modifier that has no explicit word in the sentence to modify:

Driving down the highway, a bear was seen.

Without the word *I*, the bear seems to be driving. See 24.5.

**Dependent Clause.**  A *dependent clause* attaches to an independent clause or to a sentence element (see 7.2b):

*Since the water passed the test*, it was declared safe for drinking.
The men *who tested the water* are from the Health Department.

**Direct Object.**  Something that completes a transitive verb by naming the action performed (see 7.2a):

The coach gave *instructions*.

**Double Negative.**  The redundant use of a second negative in a sentence:

You haven't no reason to go.

**Elliptical Clause.**  A clause shortened to a phrase:

She is a better driver than I [am a driver].

**Elliptical Sentence.**  A sentence shortened to a phrase or a sentence with understood omissions (see 19.1d):

[She is] a woman before her time.

**Fragment.**  A detached phrase, clause, or appositive that makes an incomplete statement (see 21.2):

who was driving down the highway
without a reason for failing

**Function Word.**  A word that substitutes for inflections in expressing grammatical meaning (*of* substitutes for *-'s* in possessives (*the man's hat, the hat of the man*).

**Fused Sentence.**  Independent clauses run together without punctuation to form a single sentence (see 22.1):

Don't forget to fill the tank you don't have enough gas to reach Cleveland.

**Future Tense.**  See *Tense*.

**Gerund.**  A verb form ending in *-ing* (*running, laughing*) that serves as a nominal. See 8.7.

gl/gr

**Imperative Mood.**   See *Mood*.

**Independent Clause.**   An *independent clause* can stand alone as a complete sentence:

> The men from the Health Department tested the water.

See 7.2b.

**Indicative Mood.**   See *Mood*.

**Indirect Object.**   In a sentence containing a transitive verb, the first of two objects receiving the action:

> The coach gave *the team* instructions.

See 7.2a.

**Infinitive.**   The base form of the verb without indication of tense, number, or person. In its verbal form (*to walk, to play*), the infinitive can serve as a nominal (I want to *walk*, not ride), an adjectival (I have reason *to walk*), or an adverbial (I am going downtown *to shop*). See 8.5b, 8.7.

**Inflection.**   Change in the form of a word or an affix to show its grammatical meaning (*man, men, man's, men's*).

**Intransitive Verb.**   See *Transitive verb*.

**Linking Verb.**   Any form of the *to be* verb, verbs of sight, smell, taste, sound, or touch, and the verbs *become, seem, appear,* and *remain* and others. These verbs take subject or adjective complements that express equivalence:

> I am a healthy person [subject complement].
> I am healthy [adjective complement].
> I feel better [adjective complement].
> The food tastes good [adjective complement].

See 8.5g.

**Loose Sentence.**   A sentence that begins with the core idea and adds explanatory or amplifying details or afterthoughts:

> The storm broke suddenly, sending people scurrying for cover.

See 19.3a.

**Main Clause.**   See *Independent clause*.

**Modal Auxiliary.**   See *Auxiliary*.

**Mood.**   The feature of the verb that shows the intent of the speaker. Verbs in *indicative mood* state facts (I am going); verbs

gl/gr

in *subjunctive mood* express wish or possibility (If I were going); verbs in *imperative mood* give commands (Go!). See 8.6e.

**Nominal.**    Words, phrases, and clauses that serve as nouns in sentences. See 8.1a.

**Nonrestrictive Modifier.**    A phrase or clause that gives non-essential information and therefore may be omitted without a change in the meaning of the sentence:

> The Health Department officials, *who tested the water*, declared it unsafe for drinking. [adjectival clause]
> *Speaking to the audience from the stage*, the official declared the water unsafe for drinking. [adjectival phrase]
> *When he rose to speak*, the second official explained why the water was unsafe. [adverbial clause].

See 7.2b, 11.6d.

**Noun.**    Nouns name or point to persons, places, or objects, and change in form to show singular, plural, and possessive:

> girl, girls, girl's, girls'

*Common nouns* point to classes of people or objects (girls, mountains). *Proper nouns* point to specific people or objects (Elizabeth, Mount Hood). *Collective nouns* are singular nouns that refer to a group (class, crowd, regiment). *Count nouns* have singular and plural forms (girl, girls). *Mass nouns* refer to things that cannot be counted and do not have plurals (health, grease, tennis). See 8.1b.

**Noun Absolute.**    A phrase modifying the whole sentence and consisting of a noun and a present or past participle:

> The water being polluted, the officials sealed the well.

Also called *absolute construction, absolute phrase.* See 8.1c, 11.1e.

**Noun Phrase.**    A simple noun (men) or a noun and its modifiers (the men from the Health Department) that form the subject, object, or complement in a clause. See 8.1a.

**Object Complement.**    The complement or a word or phrase that forms the predicate with the direct object. See *Complement.*

**Parallelism.**    Words, phrases, or clauses similar in form that perform the same function in the sentence:

> On my vacation I am going *to hike, to swim,* and *to climb.*

**gl/gr**

See 20.1.

**Participle.**   The base verb combined with *-ing* (*present participle*) or *-ed* and other endings (*past participle*) to form adjectivals (the flooding river, the river flooding) or to form a verb phrase (was flooding). See 8.7.

**Passive Voice.**   See *Voice*.

**Past Tense.**   See *Tense*.

**Perfect Tenses.**   See *Aspect* and *Tense*.

**Periodic Sentence.**   A sentence that builds to the core idea through modifying phrases or clauses:

> Of all the imprudences dared by man in his brazen reach for ascendancy, the most arrogant was his decision to stand up, to eschew his all-fours, and, piling his vertebrae one atop the other, to thrust himself erect.          —RICHARD SELZER

See 19.3b.

**Phrase.**   A combination of words lacking subject and predicate that functions as a single unit in the sentence—as a modifier or as a subject or a predicate. See *Noun phrase*, *Prepositional phrase*, *Verb phrase*. See also 7.3.

**Predicate.**   That part of the sentence that makes a declaration or statement about the subject or topic. See 7.2a.

**Predicate Adjective.**   An adjective that follows one of the forms of the infinitive *to be* or another linking verb like *become*, *taste*, and *smell*:

> The water is muddy.
> After a storm the water becomes calm.
> The water smells foul.

**Predicate Nominative.**   See *Subject complement*.

**Preposition.**   A function word, usually followed by a noun or pronoun (*of* the book, *to* the top, *beyond* the ridge) that joins nouns or pronouns to other parts of the clause. See 8.9.

**Prepositional Phrase.**   A preposition and its object (to the west, of the boat, beyond the horizon). See 7.3a.

**Present Tense.**   See *Tense*.

**Progressive Tenses.**   See *Tense* and *Aspect*.

**Pronoun.**   Words that replace nouns and have separate forms to distinguish their use as subject, object, and possessive ( *I*, *my*, *mine*, *me*, *we*, *our*, *them*) and to distinguish gender (*he*, *she*, *it*) and

gl/gr

number (*he, she, it, they*). *Personal pronouns* identify people or things. *Relative pronouns* (*who, whoever, which, whichever, that*) introduce certain dependent clauses. *Interrogative pronouns* (*who, what, which*) begin questions. *Indefinite pronouns* (*some, everybody*) do not specify particular persons or objects. *Reflexive pronouns* refer to the noun or pronoun acting as the subject (*I myself*) or show that the subject and object of the clause are the same (I washed *myself*). The *reciprocal pronouns each other* and *one another* express mutual relationship. See 8.2.

**Restrictive Modifier.**    In a sentence, a phrase or clause that gives essential information:

> The men *who drank the water* are from the Health Department. [adjectival clause]
> *Drinking the water*, they noticed a slightly bitter taste. [participial phrase]
> *When they tested the water downstream*, they found increased pollution. [adverbial clause]

See 7.2b, 11.6d.

**Sentence.**    A statement, a question, a command, a request, or an exclamation containing a subject and a predicate and assumed by the speaker or writer to make a complete statement or express an idea or feeling. See 9.1.

**Simple Sentence.**    A single independent clause and its word or phrasal modifiers:

> The green book has a torn cover.

See 9.1a.

**"Squinting Modifier."**    A modifier placed between two words, both of which it seems to modify:

> People who watch television *rarely* read much.

See 24.2.

**Stem.**    An unchanging word form to which affixes can be attached: *child*(ish), (in)*cred*(ible).

**Subject.**    The topic of the sentence about which something is usually predicated or declared. The subject may act as agent, force, instrument, source, location, patient, path, or goal. See 7.2a, 8.1c.

**Subject Complement.**    The equivalent of the subject (or *predicate nominative*) following a "to be" verb. See *Complement*.

gl/gr

**Subjunctive Mood.** See *Mood*.

**Subordinate Clause.** See *Dependent clause*.

**Subordinating Conjunctions.** See *Conjunction*.

**Tense.** The feature of the verb that shows the time and length or duration of the action. Verbs in the *present tense, past tense,* and what is traditionally called the *future tense* show that the action is occurring at the time of the statement or at a time before or at a time to come. Compare *aspect*. See 8.5b.

**Transitive Verb.** In the active voice *transitive verbs* (The dog bit the man) take direct objects that receive the action. In the passive voice this object becomes the subject of the sentence (The man was bitten by the dog). *Intransitive verbs* (I *laughed*) do not require objects but may take complements (She *seemed* happy). See 8.5d.

**Verb.** Words that make statements or predications about nouns or pronouns. Main or finite verbs (*walk, see, eat, go*) usually show tense by adding an inflection or word ending (*walks, walked*) to the base or infinitive form (*walk*). Tense is also shown without inflection (*I walk*). *Regular verbs* add -d or -ed to form the past tense. *Irregular verbs* change the base word or finite verb to show present tense, past tense, present participle, past participle (*lie, lay, lying, lain*). See 8.5, 8.6. See also *Linking verb, Transitive verb*.

**Verb Phrase.** Primary auxiliaries (forms of *have* and *be*) and modal auxiliaries (*must, should, will,* etc.) combine with the present or past participle to create complex verbs (*have run, must have run, must have been running, will have been running*). Modal auxiliaries combine with the base or infinitive form (*must run, should run, will run*). See 8.6.

**Voice.** The feature of the verb that shows its relation to the subject. The subject performs the action of a verb in *active voice* (The ball struck the net). The subject is the receiver of a verb in *passive voice* (The net was struck by the ball). See 8.5c.

gl/gr

# Index

**Index**

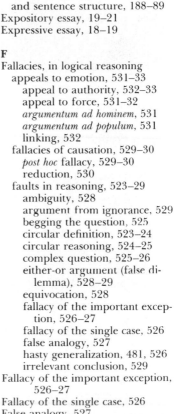

Index

**Index**